Mirages of the Selfe

Anonymous (Anastaise?). Marcia painting her own portrait (*ca.* 1402). Photo: Bibliothèque Nationale de France, ms. fr. 12420: Boccaccio, *De mulieribus claris.*

Mirages of the Selfe

*Patterns of Personhood in Ancient and
Early Modern Europe*

Timothy J. Reiss

STANFORD UNIVERSITY PRESS

STANFORD, CALIFORNIA

2003

Stanford University Press
Stanford, California

Some chapters of this book have been published in earlier versions.

Chapter 16. "Montaigne and the Subject of Polity," in *Literary Theory / Renaissance Texts*, edited by Patricia Parker and David Quint (1986). Reprinted by permission of The Johns Hopkins University Press.

Chapter 17. "Revising Descartes: On Subject and Community," in *Representations of the Self from the Renaissance to Romanticism*, edited by Patrick Coleman, Jayne Lewis and Jill Kowalik (2000). Reprinted by permission of Cambridge University Press.

Chapter 18. "Descartes, the Palatinate, and the Thirty Years War: Political Theory and Political Practice," in *Baroque Topographies: Literature / History / Topography*, edited by Timothy Hampton, Yale French Studies 80 (1991). Reprinted by permission of Yale University Press.

Printed in the United States of America

Library of Congress Cataloging-in-Publication Data
Reiss, Timothy J., 1942–
    Mirages of the selfe : patterns of personhood in ancient and early
modern Europe / Timothy J. Reiss.
        p.   cm.
    Includes bibliographical references and index.
    ISBN 0-8047-4565-X (alk. paper)
    1. Self (Philosophy)—Europe—History—To 1800.   2. Philosophical anthropology—Europe—History—To 1800.   I. Title.
BD438.5 .R4   2003
126'.09—dc21   2002014997

This book is printed on acid-free, archival-quality paper.

Original printing 2003

The last figure below indicates the year of this printing:
12   11   10   09   08   07   06   05   04   03

Designed and typeset at Stanford University Press in 10/12 Sabon.

For
Jean-Pierre Vernant,
whose grace, conversation
and work have transformed
two western generations' understanding
of ancient Greece,

and

for
Daniel Javitch,
without whose urging this book
would not have been undertaken,
and without whose
arguments it might not have been
completed

The condition of the world and of nations, their customs and sects, does not persist in the same form or in a constant manner. There are differences according to days and periods, and changes from one condition to another. This is the case with individuals, times, and cities, and, in the same manner, it happens in connection with regions and districts, periods and dynasties.

—Ibn Khaldūn, *Muqaddimah* 1.57

The human soul is by no means everywhere the same. ... The least glance at the world is there to prove otherwise. The curiosity, the love that has pushed me toward vanished religions and peoples has, it seems to me, something fundamentally moral and sympathetically involved.

—Gustave Flaubert, letter to Saint-Beuve, *Oeuvres complètes*, 2.449

Contents

Illustrations

Acknowledgments

In writing this book interlocutors have been, as always, many. Daniel Javitch is special. Without his request for an "easy" lecture (he smiled) on early moderns the book would not exist. But for that request, I would not have gathered matter now spread over Chapters 1, 13 and 14. Thinking about this matter made me look at the different societies, histories and cultures without whose consideration early modern European experience and understanding would be incomprehensible. This stimulus was not the end of Daniel's role. Without his conversation, reminders and unearthing of essays, chapters and books, this work would have led me to very different arguments. He was reader, listener and critic of various of its hesitant beginnings and finally inspiriting reader of the whole. My dedication recognizes a little of the debt. It implies nothing as to his views on what I have used it for. I also thank Nancy Regalado, who joined in requesting the early lecture, and the audience of New York University's Maison Française and Renaissance and Medieval Studies Program, who provided rich debate, especially over the matter now in Chapter 13. Since then the same audience has several times welcomed and discussed further bits and pieces of what follows. My gratitude is lasting.

As the work expanded back through the European middle ages into antiquity, I incurred other debts to many other interlocutors. One of them goes far back and is, I find, ever more central. Years ago, in Montreal, I was fortunate to have the opportunity of a semester's conversation with Jean-Pierre Vernant. This was just before and during his election to the Collège de France, honoring his then already many years' work on Greek antiquity. For more than sixty years, he has been arguing and demonstrating that to sense the ancient Greeks requires great effort of sympathetic attention to a culture quite different from that of the modern West. This work has been furthered by that of the group that gathered about him, much of whose work my references recognize. Many years ago, I acknowledged how much my *Tragedy and Truth* had benefited from his attention. It did so largely because our conversations occurred while I was writing it. Part 1 of the present book has benefited differently and more distantly, but without him and his work I doubt its chapters would have been written. They would surely not have adopted the cast of argument they have, striving to be attentive to cultural and historical particularities as well as to let these affect and change understanding of one's own culture. With his permission, I rejoice to add his name to my dedication of this book.

Early, Peter Haidu examined Part 1 and my medieval excursus with sometimes frightening but always intellectually generous and friendly care. Later, Philip Mitsis aided me by his own interest in the ancient experiences at issue and proposed several paths. One was what he calls a wild goose chase after early glass anatomies. No such mythical monsters emerged, but the chase was useful fun. Another was Christopher Gill's book on ancient personality, addressed directly in my Introduction, indirectly later. Others were Michael Frede's 1997 Sather lectures on ancient ideas of free will and Anthony Long's projected work on ancient selfhood. Frede generously sent a copy of the lectures and fielded questions. Long was forbearing in letter and conversation. Miles Burnyeat was kind in reply to queries from left field, as Paul Boghossian has been in talk and gift of essays. Froma Zeitlin's benevolent dispatch over the years of essays on gender and Greek writing has counted much in this book. John Chioles' talk and texts have mattered more than he knows. He also patiently answered queries about Greek and read with accuracy and tact an antepenultimate version of Part 1, as did Harold Donohue and Bernhard Kendler. For these *officia* I give thanks and hope for occasions to return the favors. I also thank three anonymous readers of long ago, discomfiting as one was, whose detailed remarks guided me to a stronger case.

As inquiry returned to the European fourteenth to seventeenth centuries, other debts accrued. I first did Chapter 16 in French for *Montaigne*, ed. Steven F. Rendall, Jr. (Paris: J.-M. Place; Tübingen: Günter Narr, 1984). I thank Steve Rendall for pushing. Enlarged, this is in *Literary Theory / Renaissance Texts*, ed. Patricia A. Parker and David Quint (Baltimore: Johns Hopkins University Press, 1986). I thank the Press for consent to reuse its matter, but especially Tim Hampton, who translated the French and bore endless changes I made for English publication, and the editors for their care. For years, Pat Parker has given encouragement, material support and, in her own work, cause for thought. Chapter 17 was first a talk invited by Patrick Coleman at UCLA and the Clark Library in 1994. It became a public seminar at New York University in 1998 invited by Bradley Rubidge and Henriette Goldwyn. I thank conveners and audiences of both occasions for heady debate. Bradley's far too early death leaves a hole of humor, erudition and amity. A version is in *Representations of the Self from the Renaissance to Romanticism*, ed. Patrick Coleman, Jayne Lewis, and Jill Kowalik (Cambridge: Cambridge University Press, 2000). I thank Pat Coleman and Ellen Wilson for editorial patience, Michael Macrakis for urging me to a vital clarification. A version of Chapter 18 was given long ago at Penn State University, invited by David Lachterman. His untimely death also cut short important work and friendship. Tim Hampton printed this version in Yale French Studies 80: *Baroque Topographies: Literature/History/Philosophy* (New Haven and London: Yale University Press, 1991). I thank R. J. W. Evans for his liberal remarks. Its matter, with his revisions, stays similar, but interpreted very differently. Parts of Chapter 15 have been lectures at the University of California, Irvine, New York University and the University of Connecticut. I thank Robert Folkenflik, Margot Norris, Francine Goldenhaar, Thomas Bishop, Osvaldo Pardo and Norma Bouchard for their invitations; them and Vivian Folkenflik, Jane Newman, Gabriele Schwab, Barbara Wright, Rosa Helena Chinchilla, Hassan Melehy, Franco Masciandaro and others in vivacious audiences for their feedback.

I was lucky to debate much of this in graduate seminars at the University of California, Berkeley, in fall 1996, New York University in Fall 1997–Spring 1998, the University of Oregon in Fall 1999–Spring 2000, New York University in Fall 2000–Spring 2001, Stanford University in Fall 2001 and associated material over years in classes at New York University. In the last and over time, Isabel Balseiro, David Barton, Pascale-Anne Brault, Alice Craven, Robert Dimit, Karen Duys, Toral Gajarawala, Ann Gardiner, Belkis Gonzales, Mary Lou Gramm, Shari Huhndorf, Mindy Hung, Catherine Labio, Mary Helen McMurran, Pamela Nichols, Susan Patterson, Claire Pickard, Janusz Solarz, Zeynep Tenger, Jennifer Thomas and David Wondrich were collocutors whose strong inquiry and scholarship recomposed questions and made me rethink fast and facile arguments. The same was so in the first, of Elisabeth Camp, Mika Court, Gao Feng-Feng, Rolando Montecalvo, Kristen Örjasaeter and Dana Shelley; in the second, of Anthony Abiragi, Nuar Alsadir, Daniel Aulbach, Michael Cuesta, Patrick Feeney, Debbie Francis, Scott Herndon, Suzanne Oshinksy, Tyler Rollins, Nicholas Sileno, Cristobal Silva, Kimberly Suchon and Stephanie Unangst; and in the third, fourth and fifth, of Derrick Allums, Sabine Arnaud, Lisa Marie Blasch, Sara Díaz, Erica Dillon, Sarah Doetschman, Sabrina Ferri, Sarah Fessenden, Nancy Hart, Do-Ock Hwang, Suk Kim, Alessandra Monta, Robin Pappas, Hervé Picherit, Christy Pichichero, Roxana Pop, Alexa Schriempf, Sudeshna Sen, Samuel Skippon, Amanda Walling, Benjamin Wooster and Lisa Yount. I thank them. They spur teaching and research. I apologize to those whose part I forget. On specific points, I recall talks with Albert Ascoli, Marcia Brown, Erica Dillon, Robert Dimit, Ana Dopico, Ned Duval, Sabrina Ferri, Joe Fracchia, Peter Haidu, Chris Johnson, Theresa Lamy, Kristen Örjasaeter, Nick Paige, Peter Sahlins and Domna Stanton. Tim Hampton is a generous and sardonic interlocutor, giving leads and finding mislaid or misrecalled citations with unnerving infallibility. His work and our exchanges over years have mattered. Michel Beaujour has repeatedly provoked rethinking. Stephen Orgel from the start and David Halperin, later, were heartening. Near the end, Margreta deGrazia resolved a nagging doubt, as, independently, Jeffrey Schnapp, Michel Serres, and, a bit later, Rachael Delue, Michael Gaudio, Debbie Hawhee and David O'Brien did another. Jenine Abboushi put me onto my epigraph from Gustave Flaubert (in her "French Cultural Imperialism"). Kenneth Krabbenhoft and Albert Rabil have lent and given essential material. All have my gratitude.

Thinking about the "self" not just in the early modern period, but also in relation to questions of identity in our own time, has become a widespread concern in recent years, and one cannot write on its matter without being affected by many other writers. My own concern with the person in early modern Europe goes back at least to *Tragedy and Truth* (1980) and *The Discourse of Modernism* (1982), some pages of which, rethought, are brought into Chapters 3, 9 and 10. Two paragraphs from my *Uncertainty of Analysis* have been put to different use in the Introduction. These earlier books profited much from writings of and conversations with not just Vernant but also Michel Foucault during his two-month stay in our Department in Montreal, when he was finishing *Surveiller et punir*, working on the middle ages and thinking about antiquity. This book clearly does too. During those same years, I was privileged to "direct" Line Beauchesne's Université de Laval doctoral dissertation on the twentieth-century "Droits de l'homme" debates, and remnants of our exchanges have made their way into this book. Questioning of modern western notions of person and identity is central to other writings in progress, and exchanges in correspondence and in person about such contemporary notions, the issues surrounding them and the divers implications deriving thence have inevitably affected *Mirages of the Selfe*.

For years, from 1973 until his death in 1996, I was able to shape thoughts about the European middle ages and more in conversation and correspondence with my Montreal friend and colleague, Paul Zumthor. I have benefited further from exchanges over thirty years with Gene Vance. I have been fortunate, too, to reengage exchange of views with Peter Haidu, part of a thirty-five-year conversation. To him I am also in debt for the chance to read an early long version of a book in progress, exploring broader implications of the political and personal changes in "subjection" first probed in his remarkable study of the *Chanson de Roland, The Subject of Violence* (topics raised here in Chapter 10). Ongoing exchanges with Kamau Brathwaite and Ngũgĩ wa Thiong'o have been especially challenging over the past few years and lie behind much of what follows. In this regard, I again thank Nuala Ní Dhomhnaill, who was kind enough to send me her own writings, as well as works of others difficult to get. Matthew Santirocco gave occasion to hear and talk with Adriana Cavarero and Richard Sorabji on many issues central to this book's Part 1. To learn that Sorabji is working on a book on the "self" in antiquity, that Gill is writing a sequel to the one named earlier and that others are doing so is to know how important the matter has become for western scholars and thinkers. To talk with Cavarero and read (only now!) her indispensable work is to joy in overlapping analyses which confirm that my meeting with antiquity is not the aberration I feared. I thank her, too, for her generosity in getting an essay that U.S. Interlibrary Loan systems seemed unusually unable to locate and, more, in reading the entire manuscript. Helen Tartar was thoughtfully enthusiastic and caring in shepherding the book from its depressingly broken halfway point to rebuilding and publication. I thank her for that and her editorial passion. I also again thank the Dean of Humanities at New York University for a small grant toward publication costs. I am very grateful to Tony Hicks for his careful production work, and to Paul Psoinos for his scrupulous proofreading.

I could only think of these many friends and colleagues when falling again on ibn Khaldūn's closing words to the Foreword of his *Muqaddimah*: "I am conscious of imperfections when I look at scholars of past and contemporary times. I confess my inability to penetrate so difficult a subject. I wish that people of scholarly competence and wide knowledge would look at the book with a critical, rather than a complacent eye, and silently correct and overlook the mistakes they come upon. The capital of knowledge that an individual scholar has to offer is small. Admission of one's shortcomings saves from censure. Kindness from colleagues is hoped for" (1.14). I doubt admission will obviate censure. Nor should it. I neither expect nor hope for silence. But I have tried to acknowledge the kindnesses already received, aware I have probably failed to make full use of some and even omitted others.

Most especially, I thank Patricia Penn Hilden. Her remarks on argument, claim and syntax have as always been indispensable. Our talk on things tied indirectly and directly to what follows have forced many rethinkings. Her too close encounter with the abuse, oppression and wars born from meetings, crossings and politics of cultures and identities has been an instructive, if dispiriting, experience. Giving meaning to the cliché "sadder and wiser," it makes one cynical of academic ethics, undiscriminating affirmative action and political decency (or have these always been oxymorons?). But the generosity and brilliance of her own work not only on and in spite of such abuse, oppression and conflict but on the enrichments and vitalities that can and do nonetheless arise from these meetings and crossings, at least in some circumstances and in some people's actions, continue to provoke and inspire. Above all, without her and her dialogue, on these matters and far more beside, the light would be different.

A Note on the Text

References give author and short title, if needed. Full title and publication information are given in the Bibliography—essentially a checklist of authors and works cited. This book, however, originally debated with more writers than published length allows, and I have left a few of these in the Secondary Sources to acknowledge and thank those with whose work what follows is in dialogue. The Index, besides topics and names, gives dates for all who lived before the nineteenth century. Unless otherwise noted, translations are my own; although a word needs saying about those from Greek, of which my knowledge is exiguous. But I could not evade the responsibility to deal with thought essential to the early modern writers with whom I began, even if they now find themselves in a different book from the one I had expected (most of them, too, had little or no Greek). I have used the Greek, the several translations indicated in the Bibliography and, more often than they doubtless wished, friends expert in the language. I had hoped to give all foreign-language quotations in full. Length again forbids, except for poetry and where language itself is discussed. I use B.C. and A.D. rather than B.C.E. and C.E. The former say who is speaking, the latter pretend it is everyone. After all: while useful in comparing dates across cultures, to whom are *these* eras "common"?

Mirages of the Selfe

Introduction

This book started life as the second volume of a pair discussing controversial issues in early modern European intellectual history. One appeared in 1997 as *Knowledge, Discovery and Imagination in Early Modern Europe*. The other was to study experiences and ideas of personhood—*whoness*—from Francesco Petrarca's time to René Descartes': "personhood" naming the sense a human might have had of *who* and *what* she or he was in everyday experience, in doing and being in the local world. Many years' work on the European seventeenth and earlier centuries had convinced me that this sense and its matching experiences differed radically from those dominant in the modern West, and that between the waning of the European sixteenth century and that of the seventeenth some (nonmonolithic) change solidified. Chapter 1 views reasons for the conviction, showing tensions in long-held experiences of the person and their historical origins. The book fills them out, but claims no abrupt shift. To the contrary, Part 2 shows that it jelled after centuries of now anxious, now tranquil tension. "Creation of conditions of possibility" for the change, writes Olivia Holmes, may go back to the twelfth and thirteenth centuries (*Assembling* 4). Peter Haidu has for years been arguing this case in detail, analyzing fictive writing against and with sociopolitical actualities (*Subject of Violence* and *Subject*). Caroline Bynum finds the age singular in its concern with "evolving notions of change and identity" (*Metamorphosis* 29)—though resisted by most. Change is, after all, multifold. This Introduction summarizes different experiences, suggests why they matter and charts theoretical assumptions grounding later arguments.

As the book's research advanced, it became clear that adequately to grasp early modern senses of the person, one had to return through the middle ages to views current in early and late antiquity with which later writers were saturated. Later people's experiences and concomitant ideas were unintelligible without the earlier. Ethical, social and political experiences and their expression were rooted in Cicero, Seneca and Plutarch, as well as Plato and Aristotle. Religious experience was grounded in a sensibility deriving from Augustine, Nemesius and others. Juridical mentality went back to Justinian and the centuries of work blended in the *Di-*

gest. Physical and medical analyses of the human lodged in tradition extending through the Arab doctors to Galen and the Hippocratic corpus. Obviously, actual experience could be so divided only for analysis. In life, these were interlocked facets of the experience of who and what one was.

Indeed, from antiquity these and other facets of being were experienced as mutually essential elements of at least one sense of what it was to be a person at all. It may not have been the only sense of personhood but it was a principal one, becoming centrally important for many, even most, early modern Europeans. From Greco-Roman tradition until much later (disregarding other changes for now), material world, society, family, animal being, rational mind, divine, named some of the "circles" which were a person. These *circles* or *spheres*—as Cicero, Seneca, Hierocles and Plutarch called them, cued by tradition reaching beyond Plato's *Republic, Timaeus* and *Statesman*—did not "surround" a person who somehow fit into them. They *were* what a person was: integral to my very substance. At the same time they were public and collective, common to everyone *qua* human. They named existential spheres to which the person enlaced in them was in a *reactive* relation.

Chapters 2 through 5, via Plato, the Hippocratics and Aristotle, Cicero, Seneca and Plutarch with glances at others, detail this relation and the sorts of experience involved, giving them their Latin name of *passibility*. This is not passivity. Passibility names experiences of being whose common denominator was a sense of being *embedded in and acted on by* these circles—including the material world and immediate biological, familial and social ambiences, as well as the soul's (or "animate") and cosmic, spiritual or divine life. Perhaps the circular nimbus or halo, ivy and laurel fillets and even the great semicircular hoplite helmet crest surrounding heads both sacred and secular on vase and frieze, statue and coin, painting and mosaic, connoted this multiple experience. In a sense, these circles *preceded* the person, which acted as *subjected to* forces working in complicated ways from "outside." But because of the embedding, that "outside" was manifest in all aspects and elements of "inside"—of *being* a person.

Human agency, for example, entailed "acceptance" of actions preceding and enveloping their doer, acceptance due to anything from imperative constraint to rational consent. Reasoning and knowing meant slotting oneself into reasons and knowledge already present in the universe, having "one's life shaped by a pre-existent rational order," writes Charles Taylor of Plato (*Sources* 124). Such experiences of doing and knowing grounded perceptions of the human capacities taken to enable them. *Will* did not name a capacity of an agent subject responsible for actions it alone chose. *Choice* did not name a solitary act of deliberation founded on personal rights preceding collective intention. *Intention* did not name a purposive individual claim on rational enunciation or instrumental action. Intelligence of the terms translated as *will, choice* and *intention*—as if essential to western experiences of the subject—depended on a communally embedded sense of being human. As to "will," for example, the Greek terms commonly translated as denoting willed or unwilled actions, *hekousia* and *akousia,* refer not to an agent's independent mental decision but to such actions and their actor being in or out of kilter with *ousia,* the soul's or universe's "substance" or "essence" (see Chapters 2 and 3). As to human body and material world, the embedding was physically literal: they were composed of the same matter flowing between them. At the same time, this body was of "divine design," *subjected to* purposes whose study was for Aristotle a "cosmic inquiry" and on which Galen's *Usefulness of the Parts* was "an epic meditation" inspired by "awe," remarks Shigehisa Kuriyama (157, 123; cf. Brain 3–7). These change how we understand, for instance, the active/passive "opposition" in Aristotle, Thomas Aquinas or even Descartes. Embeddedness was essential to these experiences of the person, different from anything familiar in the modern West—if not from other cultures' experiences.

This sense of personhood shows why it is risky to apply modern psychological and moral concepts like self, will, intention or action to antiquity. Understanding this sense helps us know, even *feel,* ancient concepts so translated. For this sense of who-ness, political society, family, cosmos, biological nature and the material world were not realms which a person could or could not join. They were not collective praxes in which a "self would function" or which were "implemented" in "the life of the individual" (Stock, *After* 10). Nor were they social roles or positions that "self" filled or adopted, as Thomas Greene has Petrarch doing in the fourteenth century ("Flexibility" 248: although Greene later injected doubt: "Petrarch"). These realms *were* what it was to be human. Their relations and elements were not, Alasdair MacIntyre remarks, "characteristics that belong[ed] to human beings accidentally, to be stripped away in order to discover 'the real me.' They [were] part of my substance defining partially at least and sometimes wholly my obligations and my duties" (*After* 33). There was no idea of a self free and independent in its will, intentions and choices; none of a separate, private individual. John Chioles recalls (personal communication) that no word exists for the last idea in ancient (or modern) Greek. The private, as an arena of the individual closed from the public and communal, seems to have been literally unthinkable until the first or second century A.D. at the earliest; even then thought of as aberrant perhaps still well into the European seventeenth century. Save perhaps for the dating little is unusual in this observation.

Nor does it concern me until later. I hope to find something of what *was*, not was not. For an Athenian to be out of community involved *shame* and radical *otherness*, marking *lack* in personhood. For a Roman, to be *priuatus* was to be *deprived* of something. Late sixteenth- and early seventeenth-century dictionaries still defined *priuatus* and its vernacular cognates *only* as someone holding no public office. To be a private soldier was to be not an officer.

MacIntyre applies his remark just quoted to "many pre-modern, traditional societies" (33), partly distinguishing these from a Greco-Roman tradition which Aristotle already encapsulated but which was "far older than" his work. In this tradition "man" named "a functional concept" describing a life in which "to be a man is to fill a set of roles each of which has its own point and purpose: member of a family, citizen, soldier, philosopher, servant of God." The modern West has lost this functional concept of the human, making it an entity "prior to and apart from all roles" (58–59). The older idea of the human compels moral claim. To say someone *is* family member, citizen, soldier, is to say what that someone *ought* to be and do, since family, city, army have ends entailing actions that are "good" insofar as they enable those ends. Aron Gurevich's remark that western medieval life stories told "not a whole life, but movement along a path to a goal that had been laid down in advance, ordained by Providence and which shall mark the high point in . . . spiritual growth" implies that the compaction of person and moral experience lasted for centuries (*Origins* 204). It did so at least into the European seventeenth century. Margaret O'Rourke Boyle notes that the "ages of man" cliché signified not "chronological age but . . . moral experience" (*Loyola's* 22). Human growth related less to time than to the circles of being that were its humanity. Here, MacIntyre's description may mislead. If it describes something different from the role-playing and "subject-position"-adopting typical of analyses of modern ("bureaucratic") societies, it depicts mutually separate roles among which their player moves as occasion requires. Even for Cicero, who did write of roles (*personae*), this misdirects attention. But MacIntyre's description avoids eliding diversities of societies different from the "modern," making them all versions of its putative "other."

Chapters 6 and 7 propose that people excluded from the goods enjoyed by the writers explored in earlier chapters, here women and slaves, shared their sense of who-ness. I had to defer inquiry until the experience at issue was clear, although Adriana Cavarero and John Winkler argue that half-hidden in men's writing lies women's experience, one rooted in a home where "they stay together quietly, exchanging looks and words rooted in the individual wholeness of their existence" (*In Spite* 30; cf.

Constraints 6–8, 129–61). This echoes experiences earlier chapters explore—less labored in the sensibility expressed, more fraught in the social oppressions suffered. In epic and tragedy, Helene Foley shows tenser portrayals of forthright women's agency, whose meaning is equivocal, whose fact is not (*Female*). Chapter 8 details further how person was *materially* embedded, through Galen, Plutarch, Nemesius, later Arab doctors and briefly the *Digest*. From these later centuries, Chapter 9 steps back to Augustine to plot a mutation. "Horizontal" embeddings became potentially hierarchical. Among its effects *may* be a "language of inwardness" that Taylor sees as Augustine's "crucial" contribution to "the modern identity" (139). If so, it entailed no sensibility most modern westerners would recognize. But the hierarchical adjustment created tensions in the experience, sensibility and thought of who-ness carried into the later middle ages glimpsed in Chapters 9 and 10. Here I retie these strands and begin to analyze whether, how and for how long they grounded later western European senses of who-ness. Part 2 follows them to other tensions needing new adjustments, that growth of "'today's' dissonance" that is "the consonance of 'tomorrow'"(Kandinsky 21).

However strained experiences of who-ness became, Part 2 argues that these experiences share little with a familiar "Renaissance idea of man." An embedded, passible "selfe" (often so called after the late middle ages), pervious and tied to divine, social, material spheres and historical community, underlay western experience from Petrarch until Michel de Montaigne, even as dissonances appeared. Early came a sense of the ineluctable inconstancy of "mind," with ancient forebears. This was joined by a sense of the situated impermeability of person, replacing perviousness. Women's situation (instanced especially but not only by Hélisenne de Crenne) expressed, if it could not yet fulfill, a peremptory need for other experience. Ending with Descartes, I do not infer creation of the self-possessive and right-endowed individual subject that he is held to have made almost *e nihilo*, despite clichés that "Descartes brought about a revolutionary change" (Taylor 142) and that a "Cartesian" subject characterized western senses of self till after Freud and beyond. Descartes is unintelligible without an experience of embedding in multiple worlds. On change's cusp, he confronted the divide certain reasons had made, urging moral, social and political need to keep all possible remains of known experience, of the "old house . . . to use in building a new one" (AT 6.29: *Discours de la méthode*, part 3).

If Part 1 depicts senses and experiences of who-ness in Greco-Roman antiquity, it also serves, then, as prolegomenon to later writers. But it does not try "to write a history of [later] identity," tracing "rise and development" of its core parts (Taylor ix, 111; Michel Foucault has another

genealogy). It offers "takes" on experiences of who-ness and their adjustment to historical circumstance. It does so by exploring writers vital to
those of the European fourteenth to seventeenth centuries. I do not hold
Plato, Hippocratics, Aristotle, Cicero, Seneca, Plutarch, Galen, Augustine
and others to build a whiggish history of experiences and ideas of personhood in the west (and disagree that Galenic physiology came to found
a "discourse of selfhood and agency": Schoenfeldt 11). Simply, they especially mattered to later writers. So certain issues arise, not others. But
scholars agree that soul, mind, reason, will, intention, imagination, memory, physical presence, rank, gender, social status and political role
rooted experiences of person. These terms and their enigmas signal pres-
ent-day debates that efforts to fathom the ancients cannot skirt. Their issues were also early moderns', if differently. Some schools of thought get
much notice, others (Epicurean, Neoplatonic) little or none. These chapters do not claim to give one account of ancient experiences of personhood. Such a project would be impossible simply from the dearth of material and complexity of what remains. It is surely impossible, too, as a
matter of fact. But we can attain soundings of vagaries, changes and continuities, proposals of fairly well-patterned pieces cut from an intricate
garment woven over centuries, to adopt Paul Veyne's image ("Introduction" 13). No doubt the garment was always a patchwork, and even if a
"communal" nature of personhood was habitual, it also had myriad
forms.

A drawback of treating prolegomenal experiences is that they risk
seeming to establish the whiggish teleology just denied. One should remember that they offer *aspects* of experiences of who-ness. They are,
though, aspects that ancients stressed and explored, not ones read back
from later centuries, even if parts of them became "fragments of future"
experience, to adopt Terence Cave's phrase (*Pré-histoires* 111–27,
143–76). To see them as fragments helps avoid offering a history sweeping from Plato through Augustine to Petrarch and on to Descartes and
the modern West. They echo in the shattered containers and mirrors of
Chapter 1, signaling how "the fractures in the mirror of history" let us
"rearrange its fragments," recover the lost and excluded along with the
familiar (Stolcke 272). They stay nonetheless key to experiences recorded
by Hildegard of Bingen and Ignatius Loyola, de Crenne and Montaigne,
Philip Melanchthon and Descartes, even as they underlie tensions, fractures and transformations many of these and their contemporaries expressed. They let us know persons, in Bynum's phrase, as "shapes with
stories, always changing but also always carrying traces of what [they]
were before" (*Metamorphosis* 188). And even as we seek commonalities,
we know that the plurality of circles, as well as the manifold different re-

lations to the social, political, legal, sexual, material, animate and divine, made who-ness as much tense and riven as staunch. Stable plenitude was more desired than achieved, disjunction more battled than overcome. If the stories told in the following chapters sometimes imply "dominant" experiences, they suggest neither that these were not accompanied by others nor that they were ever secure for good.

Even so, I offer these early stories with trepidation. I do so not because they may or may not be "true." What matters here is the effort to get at the nature of cultural differences, their "truths" being always in both senses partial. I do so for practical reasons. While I had the usual English public school (and beyond) training in Latin and less Greek, professional interests over the years making me continue using the first, I am not a classicist. This can be good in bringing unfamiliar views to bear. But poor knowledge of one needed language and short acquaintance with professional debates and arguments on these complex issues carry risks. I had thought two introductory chapters sufficient to ground the arguments about early modern experiences. But as I moved from primary texts to critical historical debates on them, it seemed that nowhere had this experience and sense of personhood received close analysis, let alone due weight. The chapters of Part 1, truly *essays*, try to give them that weight, not as a conclusive story but as ground for understanding early European experiences and explorations helpful to classical scholars.

The most detailed analysis of anything in antiquity near what I call personhood is Christopher Gill's *Personality in Greek Epic, Tragedy, and Philosophy*, published in 1996, after the essays of this book's Part 1 had already had several versions. It crowns many years' work and differs from this book in aim and argument. Gill sets his argument about personality between two poles of experience and understanding. One is Cartesian and Kantian, "subjectivist individualist." The other, "objectivist participant," has modern advocates in MacIntyre and Bernard Williams, ancient models in the matter his book studies. Gill does not see these as simple opposites. Each has many varieties. But they are sole archetypes. Debatable as a general proposition (echoing a distinction between "liberal" and "communitarian": Benhabib 2), this serves the side of Gill's project that sets ancient Greek ideas of personality against modern western ones. For *Personality* is also in dialogue with contemporary philosophers about what person and personality are, and in argument with classical commentators who have imposed a modern model on ancient Greek ideas.

The second of these projects overlaps with mine. But as Gill pursues it, it is inflected by his first. In the "objectivist participant" experience of personhood mental activities were bound in ethical action and choices.

The name describes the relation of these mental activities, *"reasons,"* to actions chosen and what that relation tells us of how people were. The reasons were "objective" in being independent of the person making them and available equally to all. They were elaborated in dialogue and by participation in divers sorts of social intercourse. I cannot summarize here the powerful argument of a book whose five hundred pages are necessitated by detailed readings of the epic, tragedy and philosophy of ancient Greece and of modern philosophers and critics. Gill's "objectivist participant" experience fits well with what I argue in the following chapters. But it is, I suggest, one aspect of a more complicated—or more *packed*—experience of "personhood" (an aspect Gill calls "personality," created in participatory dialogue).

What I mean by who-ness or personhood must await later chapters. They limn its experiences and understandings in diverse places and times. Weighing *passible* senses and experiences of who-ness seems to answer crucial enigmas in modern analyses of ancient writers, as approaches from modern western ideas of the person do not. So these inquiries differ from Taylor's search for basic elements of "the modern [western] identity": its "senses of inwardness, freedom, individuality, and being embedded in nature," one from Augustine, two from the Reformation, the last from Romanticism's idea of nature as "an inner moral source" (ix–x) quite other than the embedding named earlier. My chapters, I repeat, want to get at *different* experiences, an idea of what they were, not what they were not. At worst, these chapters may be useful in classicists' and philosophers' debates. At best, they may suggest rethinking aspects of antiquity. Maybe these and later chapters can help us "to reassess our habits of perceiving and feeling, and to imagine alternative possibilities of being—to experience the world afresh" (Kuriyama 272).

One problem just implied is that of approaching ages before a western present with the premise that its experiences are typical and universal. Many look in Greco-Latin antiquity and later for a "self" like "the dominant western fantasy of a singular, unified identity" (Singh 288). Not finding it or finding it "imperfectly," some see nothing odd in stating that the writers studied were just unable to grasp what subject or self *really* is. I take it, rather, that people's experience of subjectivity, of what it is to be a person, varies from culture to culture and over time. So does Taylor, reputing it "almost a truism" for "many historians, anthropologists, and others" (111). These experiences *are* subjectivity. They may differ radically. They may verge on the mutually unintelligible without large efforts of understanding. Here, early modern experiences can offer a filter against imposing modern western ones. This, too, is why I try to avoid the inaccuracy of naming all personhoods *subject* or *self*, as if cultural and historical differences were but clothes covering one universal human identity. Although no one thinking today about these issues deems "person," "subject" or "self" to be unaffected by cultural, historical, political and social contexts, most western thinkers tend to assume a core of personal being essentially one and unaltered by superstructural vagaries, which are held to overlay the real being of all humans. This core "subject" is one entity (often called "individual"), responsible for actions which are its "own." Even though it *reacts* to acts and events coming to it from "outside" these are quite apart from the "internal" essence of a core "which has no history" (Strawson 10): Jyotsna Singh's "western fantasy."

However untenable such universalist claims, their existence and implications are some reasons why this question of the person and these responses matter. They do so not just for knowledge of European antiquity or early modernity. These are not esoteric or antiquarian squabbles among scholars. They concern everyday political and educational matters, to say nothing of quotidian meetings of peoples with different cultural experiences. An examination of these issues sheds light on particular societies and their histories, here, historically distant European ones, but also on urgent current issues.

Western culture has claimed that views and experiences that developed after and out of early modern European society were a "progress" toward ways of knowing and ideas of the person which it has then asserted to be universally valid and tried to impose wherever dominion allowed. Much of the modern West uses this claim, explicitly and implicitly, to justify defense of what many of its members see as *the* canonical culture and to legitimate forms of disbarment that run a gamut from obligations to use one language, and do so "correctly," to economic oppression, political disenfranchisement and physical exclusion. Some of these have been hailed in United States political and educational forums in recent years with disturbing vehemence, but they have been enjoined with equally stormy acerbity in countries of all continents. Many have been made into law by state and national legislatures eager to close peoples' minds. These are among more "benign" forms of action about matters often provoking brutal violence. The violence is not unique to modern traditions, although its technical means are, but does make it a major contemporary issue for those within these traditions.

To "justify" these coercions, experiences and ideas of personhood are crucial, as the long debates over the United Nations' 1948 *Universal Declaration of Human Rights* show (Beauchesne). Arguments for diversity of personhood are used to warrant exclusions, those for identity and universality to exact conformity (a Benefaction drawing them into Advanc-

ing Civilization). The debates lasted for decades. One outcome was the
Organization of African Unity's *African Charter on Human and People's
Rights* of 1982, a document seeking to take account of different ideas of
the person. The framers of this Charter recognized that people agreed neither on what a "person" was nor, therefore, on what "rights" inhered in
one. The general applicability of both ideas was suspect: MacIntyre
rightly notes that the UN declaration just took them as given (69; cf. Taylor 11–12). During the early post-war UN debates, those who believed in
one universal humanness succeeded in reducing these vexed disagreements to one between political "East" and "West" at least on matters of
rights. Differences were "solved" by a principle of national sovereignty
and self-determination: Soviet arguments that work and housing were inalienable rights were separated from the West's rights of speech and association.

Such unity ignored questions about the nature of the person possessing
these rights. Here, East and West were in full accord. U.S.S.R. and liberal
West shared a single culture, both being, Leopoldo Zea agrees, "expressions of that culture in its growth and development" (*Role* 84). That was
why devolution to each nation of determination of specific rights was not
taken to impeach the Declaration's "Universality." West from Leningrad
to Paris and thence to Los Angeles, people shared individualist understanding of person and nation, based in a common culture. Once voices
from cultures previously excluded were raised, consensus began to melt.
Consider the cases of four peoples geographically relatively near together.
How do their experiences and ideas of who-ness fit with those "universal" assumptions about individual rights?

The Akans of Ghana, explains Kwame Gyekye, experience personhood as constituted of *ōkra* and *sunsum*. As with any complex cultural
experience, Akans disagree on the exact relation of these to each other
but not that *ōkra* is somehow part of *Onyame*, the supreme being. When
it leaves the body, a person dies. *Sunsum* also "derives ultimately from
Onyame." It is "a universal spirit, manifesting itself differently in the various beings and objects in the natural world." The essence of character,
sunsum is basic to each person's "thoughts, feelings, actions, etc." (*Essay*
47, 85, 73, 90). *Ōkra* is your life, *sunsum* the particular person you are.
It "is an innate faculty possessed by a person at birth" differing from one
to another. "Departure of the *ōkra* means the death of the person" but
sunsum can leave the body to wander among other spirits and places,
then to return. Indeed, the word *sunsum* also names deities ("spirits")
lesser than Onyame. However unlike, together "*ōkra* and *sunsum* are
constitutive of a spiritual unity, which survives after death" (62, 96–97,
88, 98). They are tied to Onyame, other spirits and human society.
Judged good in a person's *sunsum* are thought, feeling and action "which

promote . . . social welfare, solidarity and harmony in human relationships." "The good is identical with the welfare of the society." The "individual" person is inseparable from the community, is defined in it (132; and see 155–62).

Gyekye sees here a dualism not alien to western experiences of personhood—including that attributed to Descartes. For *ōkra/sunsum* together form a spiritual side of being "opposed" to *honam* or *nipadua*, body, although these constantly interact. Yet the experience of being a person by adhering at once to a complex supernatural world and a social community makes a whole very different from that lived by most modern western people. Actually, besides these lived bonds, Kwasi Wiredu asserts, the spiritual substances composing a person are in fact more complicated, being

(1) *ōkra* (soul, approximately), that whose departure from a man means death, (2) *sunsum*, that which gives rise to a man's character, (3) *ntoro*, something passed on from the father which is the basis of inherited characteristics and, finally, (4) *mogya*, something passed on from the mother which determines a man's clan identity and which at death becomes the *saman* (ghost). (*Philosophy* 47)

"The traditional Akan view," he writes elsewhere, is that "a human creature is not a human person except as a member of a community"—itself always multiple (*Cultural Universals* 19).

Not far eastward, in modern Nigeria, live the Yorubas. For them, explains Segun Gbadegesin:

destiny is construed as the meaning of a person—the purpose for which the individual [*orí*] exists as chosen by the other self [*èmí*, the vital life force that makes a human exist "before" becoming one with a particular "personality"—*orí*] and sealed by the deity. However, this purpose, though personal to him/her, cannot be separated from the social reality of which he/she is just a part . . . The purpose of individual existence is inextricably linked with the purpose of social existence, and cannot be adequately grasped outside it.

The person is utterly "intertwined" with the community of people and the life-world surrounding it (58). Gbadegesin shows how from before birth children are educated to communal ways of being (62), how the physical organization of space makes communal socialization (62–63) and how the kind of being these and other conditions create explains "the common reference to the typical African as saying 'I am because we are; I exist because the community exists'" (63–64). *Orí* is tied to the spirit world as well as to the human community and its material production (Drewal, Pemberton and Abiodun, *Yoruba*, esp. 13–42). Here, too, complexities make for interpretive variation, and Wole Soyinka equates *orí* with a person's thought, "essential conceptualization" (*Art* 111).

Orí is trained into *ìwà* (translated as "character"), where resides the core of a person's behavior, through the communal socialization of the person (81). In such conditions, to speak of rights inherent in an individual *as* individual is meaningless. Written in this Yoruba tradition, Soyinka's *Death and the King's Horseman* depicts the calamitous consequences of colonial efforts to force these sorts of rights on a community that ties this world to another and past time to future in these ways. Bonds of human to natural and spiritual worlds, of child to parent, of woman to man, of past to future and of community to person are shattered by western insistence that moral harm hurts the individual first and always worse than the community. Certainly, *Death and the King's Horseman* fails to query oppressive relations within the culture, as 'Zulu Ṣofọla observes. Those between men and women are especially vexed (Abeola James 145). Soyinka's Praise Singer and Horseman (Eleshin Oba) seize dominance over Iyaloja, "mother" of the market, while Eleshin claims unquestioned right to have his last "seed" before his death "take root / In the earth of [his] choice," who is the unnamed betrothed of Iyaloja's son (*Death* 21). Such other oppressions, notably in relations between women and men and masters and slaves, will get much attention in what follows. They need understanding in the context of their own culture's experience of personhood. Of the violence resulting from "traditionally" immoral behavior that ends her own play *Wedlock of the Gods*, Ṣofọla remarks that what matters is not something called "age-old traditions" but the fact that "those violent deaths are going to affect the families because of re-incarnation." They disrupt life immediately, but more importantly they provoke imbalance in the long-term course of the community and persons (James 148–49). That was Soyinka's point: these experiences of personhood involve lived bonds with past, present and future worlds which are all "part" of a person.

Writing from the other side of the continent, Ngũgĩ wa Thiong'o describes "oneness of nature as the underlying principle of the universe." For the Agĩkũyũ, all created things are "an expression of that nature." But, he continues, "nature as the primary order of being generates a second order, nurture, which is social being." Further,

beyond nature is the supernatural realm, the site of spiritual beings, the highest expression of which is God. And beyond nurture is the supernurtural realm, the site of spiritual life whose highest expression is the soul. . . . The four realms of being are another way of conceiving space. Space is a unity containing in itself the four realms: the natural, site of the material force; the supernatural, site of spirituality external to human; the nurtural, site of social force; and the supernurtural, site of human spirituality.

Their "interconnection" is key, but also that the interconnection is not just "spatial" but temporal, of past to present to future, of ancestor to living to unborn (*Penpoints* 116). A person, by definition and experience, is an element in, *an aspect of*, a "oneness" for which the word "community" seems too narrow. *Named* into this common culture, a person is deprived of *that* "who-ness," as Ngũgĩ translates Gĩkũyũ *ũnũũ*, if her name is changed (*Wizard* 468).

Ngũgĩ's compatriot Jomo Kenyatta recorded the *material actuality* of these relations. Analyzing land tenure, he told how Gĩkũyũ "communion with the ancestral spirits is perpetuated through contact with the soil in which the ancestors of the tribe lie buried" (*Facing* 21). He described communal socialization by parents, family and other groups. This did not mean no "individualist" existed but that s/he was aberrant, with "no name or reputation," "looked upon with suspicion and . . . given a nickname of *mwebongia*, one who works only for himself and is likely to end up as a wizard" (119). Religious practice and belief shared material actuality of "communal life . . . regulated by customs and traditions handed down from generation to generation," without "individualistic aspects embodied in Christian religion" (271). "According to Gikuyu ways of thinking," Kenyatta ended, "nobody is an isolated individual. Or rather, his uniqueness is a secondary fact about him: first and foremost he is several people's relative and several people's contemporary." Spiritually, socially and biologically, a person's life "is founded on this fact," daily work "is determined by it, and it is the basis of his sense of moral responsibility and social obligation. His personal needs, physical and psychological, are satisfied incidentally while he plays his part as member of" various communities. Individualism is associated with evil (309–10). Persons can of course be separated from others, but in normal conditions that is neither a principal nor a centrally interesting fact about them.

From the same Gĩkũyũ culture, Micere Githae Mugo sees this slighting of the individual as risky, especially as it could ground abuse of "individual" women and children in relation to men, but even so she agrees that usually rights were "respected" and "enforced by the collective group," from whom the rights *and* the people whose they were were inseparable (*African Orature* 15, 17). Indeed Mugo describes these social relations as so like aspects of what we will see in analyzing Greco-Roman antiquity that it is useful to cite her at length. Comparing "the relationship between the people and the social reality around them" to an "onion structure," she explains how this

begins with a nucleus, or inner core at the centre of its "being." The shape of this nucleus/core is round or circular. This is then surrounded by accumulating layers. . . . layers upon layers of increasing solidity. The layers also become larger and larger, or wider and wider in their "circularness" as we move outwards—away from the core/nucleus. These embracing and connecting circles or rings maintain tight contact with each other, harmoniously making one whole. If we were to peel off the outer layers of the onion, we would find that we had interfered with its completeness . . . .

There is the individual, the co-operate personality and the collective group. There is the family unit, the extended family, the clan and the community. There is the inner "world" of the personality—the sound, the heart, the intellect, the imagination, etc. There is also the outer "world" of being—the physical human appearance. Then there is the outside world—the environment, the natural world and the physical features that define it. The utmost circle of the outer world defines the world "up there"—the sun, the moon, the stars, the sky and the rest of the elements.

This world view also represents life in cyclic motions. The seasons rhythmically dance in and out of existence with: hoeing time, planting time, weeding time, harvesting time, resting time . . . The weather follows in similar rhythms with: hot weather, the dry season, wet weather, long (heavy) rains, short (light) rains, the cold season . . . The journey of life is depicted in terms of milestones which individuals and the collective group live through from birth, through second birth, initiation, marriage, elder status, into the sphere of ancestral spirits and the deity . . .

All the layers of the "human onion structure" must harmonize or the world will step out of measured rhythm and cause chaos. An individual can only fully *be* if he or she is a part of the collective group. (12–13)

No individual truly exists outside the community. The rights that some consider to inhere in such an individual, to take the doubts Mugo advances, are not separable from the collective. Her description is no metaphor. It renders a particular sense and experience of the order, context and embedded relations of human life. We shall see odd similarities with how Seneca, Plutarch and others formulated their sense of personhood. This does not make these experiences the same. But to acknowledge affinities in descriptions of senses of being very different from those commonly used to describe modern western experience may loosen conceptual prejudices. Sharpening awareness of differences and similarities, they may also help grasp experiences hidden in the hugely complex processes in debate when people talk of *individuals, selves, subjects* or *persons*. Different as it is from Akan and Yoruba experience, what Mugo, Kenyatta and Ngũgĩ describe differs still more from modern western experiences of the person.

Lastly, here is an example from the Ugandan Acholi writer Okot p'Bitek. In a well-known poem, he drew an image from cooking to catch an element common to Gĩkũyũ and these other experiences but again differing from modern western ones. He described the difference between the experience of being pervious to the world and that of being impermeable to and divided from it. So "the half-gourd / And the earthen dishes" breathe to the earth below them and the food on them, quite differently from "The white man's [porcelain] plates / [that] Look beautiful" but make warm food wet and cold:

> On my return home
> Give me water
> In a large half-gourd
> Water from the glass
> Is no use.
> It reaches nowhere. (*Song of Lawino* 61)

Western ideas of self applied to this experience twisted it hopelessly, seeing in it, Okot wrote elsewhere, universal mind distorted to incorporate "ghosts, spells[,] evil influences" and who knows what. The western self, said Okot, experienced mind as "a mysterious receptacle containing intellect, imagination, memory and wisdom[,] . . . the seat of consciousness and unconsciousness, the storehouse for the accumulated results of heredity, environment, training and experience; the abode of the *id* and *ego*" (*Africa's* 78–79).

This self was held distinct from all others and "born free," wrote one exemplary protagonist, Jean-Jacques Rousseau, by that very distinction. Okot disagreed. A person "is not born free" but "physically cut free" from its mother. Cutting the umbilical cord is a "symbolic" no less than "a biological act," intimating how "*upbringing*" will train one to a "full role as a member of society." "Rousseau was most correct when he added, 'but everywhere he is in chains'." A person "is incapable of being free," nor should one think that this idea of being "free" is some sort of good:

For only by being in *chains* can [a person] be and remain "human." What constitutes these chains? Man has a bundle of *duties* which are expected from him by society, as well as a bundle of *rights* and *privileges* that the society owes him. In African belief, even death does not free him. If he has been an important member of society while he lived, his ghost continues to be revered and fed; and he, in turn, is expected to guide and protect the living.

Persons remain in this ongoing relation across times, places and the many communal associations of which they stay always part and parcel (*Artist* 19).

All this, to return to the issue of rights, is why the African Charter was preceded by efforts to define the continent's cultures from within, by the 1969 Algiers *Panafrican Cultural Manifesto* and the 1976 Port Louis *Cultural Charter for Africa*. Both attend to personhood and sometimes have difficulty with concepts like self-expression and intellectual property. In most African cultures, Mugo recalls, the artist "belonged to the people and . . . his or her task was to articulate the aspirations of the people, drawing themes from them and keeping constant touch with them for inspiration." Performative interaction is inseparable from the practice of what the west calls "art." In this situation, works that the artist "composed were not personal property but a part of the communal heritage" (21). Ngũgĩ interprets the Gĩkũyũ concept and practice of *kĩrĩra* similarly, rendering it as "orature" because it involves verbal forms. But otherwise it approaches a broad western idea of "art" as "everything that enhances the human spiritual, moral, and aesthetic strivings" (*Penpoints* 119; cf. Reiss, *Against* 174–75, 178). A principal difference is that the activities *kĩrĩra* identifies are in all ways inseparable from community and its life. So whose "property" and expression are they?

These are just some voices among myriads now heard beyond the edges of their homes. Even here, proximate as these from Ghana and Nigeria, Kenya and Uganda may be, differences of idea and experience have always been evident and needed elaborating. If Akan *sunsum* and *ōkra* and Yoruba *orí* and *èmí* seem to overlap, the first are complicated by being part of *onyame*, universal spirit, and both pairs fit differently into series of collective relations, each with their histories. From another nearby people, Chinua Achebe calls Igbo *chi* a person's spirit being complementing human being; so overlapping in some way with both *ōkra* and *èmí*. But it, too, has its own divine, communal and personal dimensions and forms of existence (*Conversations* 84; Soyinka, *Art* 11). One could add endless cases showing essential differences between peoples' who-ness. Personhood is *in and of* those differences. It matters to grasp and detail differences of person; while recognizing that to talk with care between cultures calls, as Kamau Brathwaite pleads, for "miracle of tact and selfless grace" (*Contradictory Omens* 61). Crosscultural knowledge and experience demand attentive silences no less than speech, hard-listening efforts to know wholes before hoping to traverse differences. Of such wholes, the person is necessarily a major part.

To show that other personhoods have existed historically *in* western culture is equally urgent; less to show *how* its modern identity was *made* (Taylor's project) than what others there were. For the West's modern idea of self has too easily been read into its own distant pasts. It had to be, if it was to be universal. So historical claims echo cultural ones— partly addressed, too, in my *Against Autonomy*. *Mirages of the Selfe* offers reasons to reject the many forms of *historical* appropriation.

These polyvalent appropriations and confusions in debate about human difference require attention to some theoretical ramifications, if grounded historical discussion is to be offered of differing experiences of western personhood, their tensions and changes. It is not enough just to assert that human being differs by times and places, a claim no more surprising in the European sixteenth century than it is again now. Even twelve centuries before, during a contemplation whose aim was to elucidate the nature and final cause of personal being, Augustine remarked: "all things fit not only with their places, but also with their times" (*Confessions* VII.15). Belief in essential and universal sameness of person and its mind was a centuries-later European manufacture.

Many western foes of this view revel in nosing out a binary opposite, called "sacred," "primitive," "mythic"or "communal," opposed point-by-point to the "logic," "method" and "autonomy" of right reason. This is a racial strain (not inevitably ra*cist*) of a polarity whose familiar economic and political form is late nineteenth-century German sociology's *Gemeinschaft* versus *Gesellschaft*. It lives on in Marcel Gauchet's claim of a basic historical duality in all human cultural organization: religious/social versus political/statist. The former's "embryonic" technical growth now joins "highly sophisticated forms of social organization and powerfully elaborated thought systems." Perpetual, not "primitive," its "anteriority of the world and law of things" challenges the latter's "anteriority of humans and their creative activity." Whatever society's kinds, "history" shows one or other of these "founding dimensions" to ground all (*Désenchantement* viii, xiii, xiv). Complex as both are, their idea shares the familiar binary paradigm. Karl Morrison's "empathy" or "compassion" versus "empiricism" or rational disjunction seems an aesthetic (or "hermeneutic") version. Gill's *Personality* flirts with it, despite its acute analyses of reason, community and ethical action over a gamut of hard texts. The duality shows two faces of one coin. They compose an abstract money depicting "self" on its obverse, "other" on its reverse, struck in the mint whose fellow currencies oppose linearity to circularity, male to female, ice to fire, reason to emotion, Apollo to Dionysos, oral to literate.

Efforts to avoid these binarisms grow, but historicized versions also swarm. Sigmund Freud's and others' idea of analogous phylogenetic and ontogenetic psychological stages takes them to echo historical development of humans from primitive to advanced. In psychiatry the idea lingers in contrasts of symbolic order to semiotic *chōra* dear to Julia Kristeva and pupils of Lacanian reworkings of Freud—as she puts it: of the "philosophical or theoretical" to "the more archaic, more infantile, more feminine areas" (Riding 19). Historically, it begets awards to Petrarch as a "first modern man," aspiring, Gurevich says of the epistolaria discussed in Chapter 11, to beget "a new type of human individuality" (*Origins* 236). Interested, agrees Leo Spitzer, "in himself *qua* himself," he supposedly began a sequence that continued with "Montaigne and Goethe"—

temporal evolution completed by a south to north European developmental geography ("Note" 417). Marcel Mauss' historical and cross-cultural essay on the category *person* seems the acutest version of the idea. It crops up in Nietzschean tales of antiquity (Havelock), of Greek philosophy's hierarchical reorienting of a horizontal equability of race, sex and species (duBois, *Centaurs*). It joins phylogeny in Shakespeare's invention of the autonomous modern individual, Freudian (Bloom) or Lacanian (Fineman). These are chronological and largely "commonplace" post-Enlightenment versions (Pagden, *Fall* 2) of the old topological Chain of Being familiar to the age whose ideas on these issues occupy this book's Part 2. A chronological version was also familiar at the time. As Jaques declares in *As You Like It*:

> All the world's a stage,
> And all the men and women merely players;
> They have their exits and their entrances,
> And one man in his time plays many parts,
> His acts being seven ages. (II.vii.139–43)

At issue are ways of conceiving differences of personal being.

Non-primitive personhood is typically characterized as separate from contextual actuality, sharing rational mind and often *mentalité* (way of knowing the life-world common to people in a given place and time). A major disparity between mind and *mentalité* is that the one is thought always the same, the other different from culture to culture, age to age, place to place. That is why G. E. R. Lloyd rejects the second, arguing that differences in times (ancient Greece or modern Europe) and places (China or the West) of "styles" of thought show no debt to "some hypothesised . . . mentality." Rather, "important differences . . . relate more directly to differences in the prominence given to certain leading concepts and categories and to differences in the styles of interpersonal exchange, where, in turn, in each case, socio-political factors may be a crucial influence" (*Demystifying* 12). The dissent is well-taken. But it, too, assumes mind's isolation. Differences are not just of style, of prominence given to concepts and categories or of sociopolitical influence—which are anyway inner organs of person and mind, not outer clothes. The differences are of being, action, perception and knowledge. As Kuriyama compares physicians in ancient China and Greece, they "*knew* the body differently because they *felt* it differently" (55), in all senses of "felt." No *opposition* between human mind and sociopolitical or other behavior is at issue. They are inseparable.

To distinguish mind and *mentalité* is an artifice of the claim about mental independence decried by Okot. Even when people *think* mind or person separate from society, the forms of the corresponding social organization and its experience *depend* on and are bound to *that* way of perceiving and experiencing the subject and not to some other. For in western societies, too, person and community are no less imbricated than they are in those Acholi and Akan, Gĩkũyũ and Yoruba experiences alluded to before. The challenge is to understand manifest diversities of act and experience involving mind (or "soul") *and* society. Such diversities will always partly escape the onlooker, because the integration of mind and society, person and experience, is endlessly intricate. Difficult and tangled as are the resultant problems, there is, Moses Finley paraphrases Antonio Gramsci, no "immutable human nature, indifferent to social structure, values and status" (*Ancient Slavery* 108). As Jean-Pierre Vernant adds:

One cannot speak of humans outside the groups in which these humans are engaged, their precise social context; but, conversely, there is no social context without its "human," that is, mental, dimension, no institution that does not imply, as long as it lives, beliefs, values, emotions and passions, a whole set of representations and feelings. One does not find on one side isolated human individuals whom psychological study would elucidate, and on the other social realities as inert things, whose evolution would be subject to a kind of external determinism and which could be studied as objects. (*Entre mythe* 51)

Shakespeare's ages were not of mind alienated from life. Jaques eyed the thought and action of "infant," "schoolboy," "lover," "soldier," "judge," "old man" and senile second child. Each "mewled and puked," "whined," "sighed," swore, fought and sought glory, delivered sententious counsel, "piped and whistled" thoughts and fell into oblivion by age, nature *and* social place. None of these was just temporal. Tied to social actualities, the human ages of childhood, youth, maturity and senescence recorded movement in moral rather than temporal experience: which explains why children were painted with moral rather than chronological markers of difference from adults. To imagine mind and sociopolitical environment divided is to adopt Enlightenment fantasy of the autonomy, self-identity and universality of mind, and to ignore experiences of people dwelling in other times and places.

When Aristotle called humans social animals (*Politics* 1253a2–3) and Xenophon thought the *polis* "inherent in human nature" (Higgins 26), they meant that sociability *defined* the human. To be *politikon*, rational, a language user and a laugher (Aristotle added in *De partibus animalium* 673a9) were minimal properties of *being* human. The root unit of Athenian culture was named by the word *polis*, from which derived its constituent part, the *politēs*. Its opposite was the isolated shameful *idiōtēs*.

Communal life preceded the persons composing it. This helps explain
Socrates' refusal of exile. As Harold Donohue observes (personal communication), this may differ from the Roman case, where derivation of
civitas (state) from *civis* (citizen) seems to express an opposite relation, although my later proposal of similarities and continuities between Greece
and Rome argues that etymology is only a pointer requiring support from
thick context. (Equal wariness is needed for any parallel between Greek
idiōtēs and Gīkūyū *mwebongia*, of whom Kenyatta wrote.) Community
precedence is a view lost to "the modern liberal individualist world," says
MacIntyre: "we have no conception of such a form of community concerned . . . with the whole of life" (156). "The philosophers," Augustine
still asserted, "think that the wise man's life is social; a view we approve
much more fully" than ideas that the "highest good" lies in singular being. How could the City of God grow "if the saints' lives were not social?" Augustine was attacking the Stoics of his reductive account (*City
of God* XIX.5). Seneca's idea in the *De constantia* that the sage was one
able to shut off all ties of society and kin actually gave him major difficulties, as it strained to distinguish itself from more current views (*Moral
Essays* I.48–105). This Stoic sage, we see in Chapter 5, was peculiar both
in paradoxical argument and in uniqueness—even impossibility. Different as sixteenth-century European ideas of personhood were from those
of Augustine or Seneca, dependent as they yet were on traditions drawing
on ancient writings, they, too, were trammeled in social life and actuality.

The idea that consciousness precedes or is otherwise apart from public interpersonal exchange, sociopolitical activity and all forms of material activity and event, is relatively recent. It has also been much questioned. "The human essence," wrote Karl Marx in his sixth *Thesis on
Feuerbach*, is "the *ensemble* of social relations." "*Individual consciousness*," Valentin Vološinov elaborated, "*is a socio-ideological fact*" (*Marxism* 12). The view that person, its experiences and actions, are enlaced in
the social in ways essential to the nature of the person radically opposes
the idea of a self-contained isolated individual. Vološinov argued that
consciousness comes to exist only through the circulation of social, communicative "signs"—*all* and any activities and events that acquire meaning by social praxis. Person and society are mutually constructive events.
Gramsci simultaneously echoed Marx in writing that "there is no 'human
nature', fixed and immutable . . . , that human nature is the totality of
historically determined social relations, hence an historical fact which
can, within certain limits, be ascertained with the methods of philology
and criticism" ("Machiavelli and Marx" in *Selections from the Prison
Notebooks* 133). Through a series of western moments, that is what this
book's analyses attempt.

"Consciousness" exists only as engaged in the social circulation of signs that *are* the sociopolitical environment, essential to the nature and forms of mental activity and senses of personhood. The relation flows both ways, from environment to consciousness and consciousness to environment, both marked by a fundamental materiality—a fact whose local forms some later chapters stress. These events, processes, activities and experiences mutually determine each other:

Consciousness itself can arise and become a viable fact only in the material embodiment of signs. The understanding of a sign is, after all, an act of reference between the sign apprehended and other, already known signs; in other words, understanding is a response to a sign with signs . . . Signs emerge, after all, only in the process of interaction between one individual consciousness and another. And the individual consciousness itself is filled with signs. Consciousness becomes consciousness only once it has been filled with ideological (semiotic) content, consequently, only in the process of social interaction. (Vološinov, *Marxism* 11)

Unawares, Vološinov was repeating basic concepts of Charles Peirce's and Victoria Welby's work. They, too, saw consciousness as matter and product of signs entirely social (Reiss, "Significs" and *Uncertainty* 40–55). The "personhood of people," adds Wyatt MacGaffey, is not "given in nature" but comes "of a local, culturally specific" process (quoted in Ravenhill 44).

   None of this is to say that persons are wholly determined by context, that personal identities are socially, culturally and ideologically fashioned as mere semes of an overarching discourse, meanings made by a symbolics of power. Webbed, made and making in multiple contexts, personhood still has real agency (of endlessly varied sorts). I think of the poet Nuala Ní Dhomhnaill's proposal that a chronologically earlier sense of person lives in the Irish language because political oppression and military violence forbad that language's use in a new, English-language dominant culture in those very sixteenth–seventeenth centuries when modern experiences of self were developing ("Why" 27, and in personal communication, April 11, 1995). The poet does not recover that earlier sense by writing now in what became a "subjected" language, but makes something other by writing Irish against its English agonist: not alone, though, for her impulse is not lone. George Thomson clarified the relation in writing of how people living in the "traditional" poetic and conversational culture of the Blasket Islands on Ireland's west coast "adorned" their speech "with proverbial couplets and quatrains" or brought "from the same source some image or idea as though it were their own. This was all the easier," he remarks, "because the thoughts embodied in their poetry *were* their thoughts" (*Island* 40). Without traditional poetic images,

meanings and habits of thought, they would not be thinking at all. What
and how she thinks and says are *her* thinking and saying, not someone
else's, yet embedded in communal knowledge and experience *as such*.

"Audience participation" here (as in Mugo's argument about the
Gĩkũyũ case), cannot be divided from one poet's art. The collective is integral to personal action in poetry as in all human praxis (*Island* 59–60).
But one must beware of fusing times and places, ancient Greece, a "middle ages" generalized from Augustine to Dante, the early twentieth-century Blaskets and various contemporary cultures, into instances of "primitive" against "modern," or of setting them on an evolutionary spectrum
running from *their* Other to *our* Same. So, in Louis Dumont's analyses,
social organizations by caste as in India or archaic Greece, where an individual (like Greek *idiōtēs* or Gĩkũyũ *mwebongia*) is one renouncing social ties and living outside their hierarchies, ultimately evolve into societies where individuality has social value and "modern man" is born.
Still, even as this thesis adopts other/same and primitive/modern binaries,
it does consider sociohistorical context and opens gaps which Vernant
readily widens in reaction to this effort to make such organizations *evolve*
into "modern individualism" (Dumont, "A Modified View"). Vernant
notes the great "gulf" between the "I" of "Augustinian man" and the
"citizen of the classical city-state" or "*homo aequalis* of pagan antiquity," and between these and "the *homo hierarchicus* of Indian civilization" (*Mortals* 333).

Against this, fruitful starting terms are those Vernant uses to learn how
archaic Greeks may have grasped the notion of "body," divine and mortal. We may "direct our inquiry to the body," he writes,

no longer posited as a fact of nature, a constant and universal reality, but rather
viewed as an entirely problematic idea, a historical category, steeped in the imagination . . . , and one which must, in every case, be deciphered within a particular culture by defining the functions it assumes and the forms it takes within that
culture. (*Mortals* 28)

Comparing Chinese and Greek medical history, Kuriyama details accounts of the body that "frequently appear to describe mutually alien, almost unrelated worlds" (8). There are, as he says, "innumerable ways to
know the body" (118). These knowings correspond to different perceptions and ways of being. If even the "material fact" of the body is steeped
in the imagination, as he shows at length, how equally urgent is such understanding for the praxes of sense and sensibility, context and environment that forge who-ness?

These praxes may or may not be identifiable chronologically—which
is not to deny local or wider continuities, but to think them endlessly var-

ious. Such wider continuity, with variety, existed in the western under-standing of human physiology grounding experiences of the person for far longer than recent ideas of the subjective individual. Early modern Europe inherited this physiology from the Hippocratic corpus, Plato, Aristotle, Hellenistic writers and most directly Galen and his Arab and later medieval commentators. After Galen it provided a stable view of the human constitution as composed of the four elements, earth, water, air and fire, with their physiological counterparts in the four humors, black bile, phlegm, blood and yellow bile. Each of these mixed two of the four qualities present in the natural world: respectively cold and dry, cold and moist, warm and moist, warm and dry. Diet, climate, season, exercise, positions of stars and planets, choice of company and much else went into keeping the humoral balance needed for good health. Imbalance caused psychic no less than physical illness. The roots of this knowledge reached past Pythagoras. It was woven in a cosmology basic to western medicine and changing notions of person for over two millennia. With debate and changes, it lasted beyond the European sixteenth century, only then starting to be supplanted. It still underpinned John Evelyn's major treatise on gardens which had occupied him for fifty years when he died in 1706 (*Elysium* 36–64: bk.1, chs.3–9). Even later, in 1821–33, K. G. Kühn published his 22-volume Galen for practicing physicians, not antiquarians. But that the system grounded who-ness for so long does not mean its patterns never changed. Taylor finds modern experience of "in-wardness" prefigured in Augustine. Roger Smith finds other aspects in Christians' "immortal soul" or Roman law's positing "of individuals endowed with agency and hence responsibility" ("Self-Reflection" 50). None of these terms—not "soul," "individual," "agency" or "responsibility"—name entities or acts given once and for all.

Even so, the little brief authority of the modern west mocks so stable a system at its peril (besides, we still live with goodly parts of it). Yet it is also clear that this system could only have been imagined in a particular geography. Its seasons and its steadily repetitive qualities of cold and warm, dry and moist depended on the familiarities of a temperate climate. No tropical or semi-tropical culture could imagine this version of humans and their society in the physical world. This is not so say that geography and climate do (or do not) relate intimately to human nature and human activities. It is to say that in this instance they did relate indelibly to how people *thought about* the world and humankind and *experienced* who they were. In this two-thousand-year overarching system, we can trace endless variety and movement, deeply linked to wider and narrower contexts of home and society. To be a person can only ever be how people *think* their contexts and *experience* their *being* a person. Thought and

experience, understanding and being *may* be separable for some purposes. They cannot be in the case of what it is to be a person.

Just as these are in an inseparably intermingled knot, so person and
community, one cannot repeat too often, are in a mutually creative dialectic. The varieties of dialectic in diverse times and places are what it is
necessary and hard to capture. For none of this means that these differences and varieties are shut to each other or, with struggle, to understanding. This research began as an effort to get at least some idea of the
principal experience of personhood in, more or less, one such time and
place. It grew because it then needed to show how that experience was
based in continuities and differences going back through the European
middle ages to Greek and Latin antiquity.

These differences are why I use the words *Mirages* and *Patterns* in my
title. The divers personhoods are not unreal, but their exact nature and
boundaries of place and time are impossible to fix and slippery to hold.
They are not unreal, insofar as they are, have been, lived somewhere,
somewhen. They identify not just different concepts of what human persons *might* be, but actual human behaviors and practices, what who-ness
has been, is, in particular times and places. Yet they reach us (other times,
places, peoples) as variegated patterns, broken mirrors or like mirages,
imaged in another place and shimmeringly distorted by traversing milieus
different from their original as from ours. What is one to make, for example, of the 1402 miniature of my cover and frontispiece? Illuminating
a French manuscript of Giovanni Boccaccio's *De mulieribus claris*, it pictures the Roman artist Marcia looking in a mirror, painting her portrait.
Most simply it is a late medieval portrayal of an early first-century B.C.
person, although one biographical dictionary (Petteys) lists it as the actual self-portrait that Pliny the Elder recorded Marcia doing from a mirror. In Pliny she was Iaia of Cyzicus, working at Rome in Marcus Terentius Varro's youth. A fast worker, her paintings and engraved ivory
miniatures fetched higher prices than her contemporaries' (35.xl.148).
Boccaccio repeated Pliny, but made her Varro's daughter, dubbing her
"Marcia" (*Famous* 274–77: ch.66). Between her several names (including also Laia, Lala, Lerlao), Pliny's notorious unreliability and Boccaccio's and others' misreadings, who she was fades in and out.

The vellum miniature echoed Iaia's ivory miniatures. Whom and what
did it depict? Some think its illuminator was Anastaise, an artist known
to Christine de Pisan (*Livre de la cité des dames* 1.41). If she or another
painted herself, matters are further raveled. Showing the artist once in
profile and twice head on—first finished in a small mirror, second on a
larger canvas unfinished (she is still painting the lips)—the three portraits
are almost exercises. The heads are shared, the profile surmounting a

clothed body seen from right back, the canvas frontal topping a clothed upper torso, the mirror having just a face. The picture glosses difficulties of what follows here. In varying contexts, it could show ancient and later experiences of who-ness existing multiply via another's gaze, a community of women, fraught fragments, a Lacanian mirror stage of self learned by being seen as other, or a Platonic display of progressively distant simulacra viewed by a spectator comprehending a whole (Idea) outside the portrayed gaze of the painter. Autoportrait or not, the miniature is a show of the process of (its) creation and commentary on depicting persons. The trouble in interpreting the what, who and how of *single* cases—and knowing them collectively—explains the title *Mirages*. It also tells why contextual reality matters. This book tries to get at three or four such realities in what has been thought one place with a continuous history. To do so, it must avoid contemporary western concepts of subjectivity and their vocabulary. The latter sets an agenda impelling its user toward these same concepts, to approach others through them or overlay others with them. For if "person(hood)" and who-ness seem fairly neutral terms, "self," "subject" and "individual" are decidedly not.

So until I speak of a time when a modern concept began to share space with an older, I avoid using the word "individual." Unless otherwise specified, "subject," in a sixteenth-century context and earlier, means only the (public) subject of civic polity—as when one speaks of the "subject" of a queen. "No hay ser sujeto sino estando sujeto," to change an apocryphal maxim recorded by James Fernández: you can't be a subject without being subjected (*Apology* 1). For the same reasons, I have chosen to use the usual early modern spelling of "selfe" (except as suffix or prefix). I hope its quaintness is offset by its defamiliarizing effect. It just named whatever interior nature it was that made a person a human and no other kind of being. Only near the end of the ages this book studies did "selfe" start to refer to what made a person *that* person and not another, marking a "private" difference of something like individuality. "Self" refers only to a modern notion. One can probably never defeat misunderstandings, but care over vocabulary can be a start.

Essences of Glass, Histories of Humans

"To me," muses Günter Grass' contemporary hero, "Oskar's voice . . . was an ever-new proof of my existence; for as long as I sang glass to pieces, I existed, for as long as my purposeful breath took glass' breath away, there was still life in me" (*Blechtrommel* 449; *Tin Drum* 362, which omits the last phrase). Even in 1959, Oskar Matzerath's vocal assault on others and the world, establishing certitude of being by using his voice to smash and incise glass, was out of the ordinary. Yet it confirms his fixed sense of self so surely that he can multiply his names and voices, the variety of personal relations, ambiguity of events and uncertainties of history. None of these pluralities casts doubt on his intrinsic core of selfhood. On the contrary, all confirm it. To smash glass is to make *his* mark, to certify his particular existence as significant to the world. It is to certify it *against* the (Nazi) world. This does not so much parody the modern Western notion of a self-conscious singular subject, as emphasize that opposition and conflict are as fundamental to its idea and action as selfconsciousness and singularity.

Too, against an age-long background of destruction, Oskar's aggressively defensive isolation reminds us that the idea that we exist only to the extent that we are outside and against others was itself a cultural creation. It grew from—and against—different assumptions: ones involving community as integral to personhood, interdependence as essential to human being. This is not to adopt Jacob Burckhardt's familiar saw that medieval "man was conscious of himself only as a member of a race, people, party, family, or corporation—only through some general category" (*Civilization* 1.143). But it is to agree that such "membership" was *one* element in selfhood, although needing careful analysis. "Subject," one could still say with Montaigne in the 1580s or with various European "meditational" (in Louis Martz's word) or "metaphysical" poets yet later, was public citizen and divine soul, not private self. Burckhardt's view of the inception of the willful self was at best a simplification (as it is still in Charles Trinkaus' *In Our Image and Likeness*).

People today ascribe the "invention" of Oskar's condition to the thinker Descartes or some later agency named *Cartesianism*. Those earlier writers said to have set "the dignity and worth of the individual soul" against "impersonal and collectivist views of the older tradition," as John Herman Randall puts it (Introduction to Pomponazzi, *Immortality* 257), simply opened a path whose climax was Descartes. The "possessive individualism" basic to Hobbesian or Lockean sovereignty, to Smithian capitalism and Kantian rationalism and ethics, to copyright laws and ideas of an "author," no less than to Freudian psychology, was founded in a "subject" or "self" whose earliest clear formulation is said to be *cogito ergo sum*. The maxim is assumed to express the self-conscious awareness of an agent making its own expansive being from inside its isolated "desert." If it has seemed that Descartes did fabricate such a myth, one should also note that he used the Latin maxim only once, in a January 1642 letter to Regius quoting an attack on himself. Otherwise, in the corpus of his works, it is only in Frans Burman's conversations (written by Burman) and the posthumous Latin translation of the *Recherche de la vérité* (besides the early French of the *Discours*). It was, Marshall Brown reminds us, never his own phrase ("Kant's" 163). This matters, especially when we try and understand Descartes himself.

Further, whatever critics and historians *say*, most characterize persons prior to this time in terms of a self whose description is hardly distinguishable from that supposedly possessed only by those living later and in a different cultural environment. Or they anyway go looking for aspects of such a self: as if persons living in divers histories, geographies, societies and cultures had to be "progressive" steps to a more correct sense of self whose universal rectitude is defined by post-Enlightenment western assumptions about individual and society. Montaigne is deemed to have evoked a thinking self, as Loyola to have taught it to meditate a way to God. Martin Luther and Desiderius Erasmus are held to have freed it from authority and empowered it to right Scriptural exegesis, as Giovanni Pico della Mirandola to have given it angelic dignity—if Nicholas of Cusa or Marsilio Ficino had not already done so. Early Renaissance talk of human "dignity," "nobility" or "glory" (or their complementary counter of human misery) is conflated with later individualism, even though a figure so central to these claims as Petrarch urged that humans were "noble" only in their knowledge of the clear limits to their reason and action and of the exiguity of their place in a grander whole. Despite such difficulties, some scholars even urge that a modern self was vital by the twelfth century.

Polemically defending this last case, Lee Patterson rightly attacks those who, taking Cartesian and Burckhardtian claims as givens, embed them in pseudo-historical assertion ("On the Margin" esp. 95–101). Yet he accepts the binarism on which such arguments rely, plumping for early existence of modern "inward subjectivity" in play against "an external world that alienates it from both itself and its divine source" (100), as if personhood could only be a choice, again, between alienated individualism and enchanted embedding. His *Chaucer*, Haidu notes, effects this "return to a transcendent model of subjectivity" ("Althusser" 62). Others do, too. Natalie Zemon Davis argues that in specific sixteenth-century conditions people did make a "self" in community, objecting that "the greatest obstacle to self-definition was not embeddedness, but powerlessness and poverty." She suggests we see "the person as part of a field of relations" ("Boundaries" 53, 63). The last remark is fruitful, the first supposes that the rich and powerful *did* have a modern sense of self. Usually unavowed assumptions of a transcendent, universal model of self validate applying Freudian, Lacanian or other anachronistic schemata. This book engages these debates, Chapters 9 and 10 addressing those involving medievalists. Just to deny these claims is uninteresting. What matters is the effort to know what different familiar ideas of personal being existed, to show, too, how they stayed strong far into the seventeenth century. To attempt to understand as far as possible in people's own terms is hard, and must also account for facts like the medieval use of an adjective *subiectus*, the fame and familiarity of Augustine's *Confessions* and habitual recourse to the terms *selfe, selbst, soy-mesme, sí mismo, medesimo*, even perhaps *metipsimus*, through the middle ages and Renaissance.

Almost exactly 350 years before Grass, several authors central to the Western literary tradition had, however, used the same vitreous metaphor to capture quite other assumptions about human being and its condition. At the turn of the sixteenth century, glass figured the fearful fragility of any such thing as we might now want to call individual identity. To be sure, Miguel de Cervantes' *licenciado* Vidriera, terrified that people touching it would break his glass (*vidriera*) body, was judged by his fellows to be mad. But if madness it was, it was one he could not escape even after being "cured": those among whom he lived "decided" who he was and what he could do. Just so they removed his earlier peasant and *licenciado* name of Tomás Rodaja to make him glassy Vidriera. But he could escape their judgment of isolation only by flight to another community. In his case, we learn in the *novela*'s last sentence, that meant quitting the roles for which he had been educated and joining the Spanish army of Flanders. This choice was inscribed in his birth name, meaning not just a round of sausage or bread (as befitted his peasant state) but the rowel of a spur. In the army, Vidriera was again characterized only by communal role, leaving "the reputation at his death of a prudent and very brave soldier" (*El licenciado Vidriera, Novelas* 2.74). As Vidriera he was a fractured being dead to community as community was finally dead to him. The *Novelas ejemplares* were first published in 1613. This one seems to have been completed between 1604 and 1606.

In 1604, Shakespeare used the same metaphor to figure the human condition as Montaigne's *branloire perenne*, and especially to mark an error that involved confusing public communal role with anything like private being:

> but man, proud man,
> Dressed in a little brief authority,
> Most ignorant of what he's most assured—
> His glassy essence—like an angry ape
> Plays such fantastic tricks before high heaven
> As makes the angels weep . . . .

So Isabella in *Measure for Measure* (II.ii.117–22). Francis Bacon offered a similar view in the *Advancement of Learning* in 1605, saying that "the mind of man is far from the nature of a clear and equal glass, wherein the beams of things should reflect according to their true incidence; nay, it is rather like an enchanted glass, full of superstition and imposture." Bacon's hope was that this enchanted glass could be "delivered and reduced" (II.xiv.9: ed. Johnston 127). He was not altogether isolated in what was nonetheless just a hope, if Edward Taylor rightly understands Isabella's "glassy" as referring to the human soul as mirror image of God. This may be so and explain why the play's persons are tensed "between emblematic icon and naturalistic characterization," between "archetype" and singular (7, 12). He is certainly right to see character as secondary to action, as *not* representing individual psychologies, but figuring Dr. Johnson's Aristotelian "common humanity" (5). The issue returns in Chapter 3. This subjected "secondariness" is essential to the common experience of human being and its representation preceding the breakdown suggested in this chapter. In this breakdown, glass figured the frangibility and insecurity of human life and being; "glass" as often meaning a container as a mirror: sometimes ambiguously both, as it does in the last two cases.

In this regard, to think one was glass was madness acting out metaphor as reality. In 1607, Thomas Walkington's "ridiculous foole, of *Venice*, verily thought his shoulders and buttockes were made of britle glasse; wherefore he shunned all occurrents and never durst sitte downe to meat, lest he should haue broken his crackling hinderparts" (*Optick*

139). Walkington may have lifted this case from Levinus Lemnius, who in 1561 described a madman likewise believing "ex vitro sibi conflatos clunes" in a work whose Italian translation appeared in 1564 in Venice (*De habitu* 120v). But these could have been separate cases: like Tomaso Garzoni's later lunatic who, thinking he had "become glass, walked to Murano so as to throw himself in a furnace and have himself made into the form of a glass flagon" (*Il teatro* 101). In 1600, Simon Goulart wrote of melancholics who, "thinking they have become earthenware pots or of glass in all or part of their body, flee all company for fear of being broken" (*Thresor* 1.324: these last three from Hainsworth, "La source" 71–72 and note 12).

The psychosis was not rare. Caspar Barlaeus, famed poet-professor of Amsterdam, endured it a bit later. "He thought he was of glass and feared he would be broken in pieces" (Worp, in *Oud Holland* 7: 99; cf. Heckscher 78, and entry in Bayle). Caspar Barth, translator of *Celestina* and *Diana enamorada* in the 1620s, was once thought Vidriera's glassy origin. He was not Cervantes' model, but perhaps he, too, suffered the psychosis—unless it was just a case of confusion with his near homonym Barlaeus. In antiquity, Rufus of Ephesus (*Oeuvres* 355) and Galen had known of melancholics similarly fearing for their bodies as earthenware pots. In "De locis affectis" (III.x), Galen wrote of a person who "thought he was made of earthenware and drew away from all those around him lest he should be broken" (*Opera* 8.190). In the seventh century, Paulus Aegineta echoed him on people who imagined themselves "earthen vessels, and . . . frightened lest they be broken" (*Seven Books* III.xiv: 1.383; see, too, Siraisi, *Taddeo Alderotti* 233, and Neaman 18–19). Cases of people taking themselves for such fragile clay vases, literary or real, had been noted throughout the middle ages. In this form the madness was familiar. To know one's glassy essence, though, was to grasp the real nature of human being, the limits of identity and the proper place of individuality. Angelo and the Duke failed this test, taking public authority for private assurance, communal obligation and duty for personal right— *subiectus* as "lying under" for *subiectum* as prior agency. But glass figured insecurity even as to this "lying under," setting in doubt its provision of assurance either of being or of knowledge. So Bacon wrote of people's false idea of divination by "influxion . . . grounded upon the conceit that the mind, as a mirror or glass, should take illumination from the foreknowledge of God and spirits" (*Advancement* II.xi.2: ed. Johnston 115). Here, Bacon directly queried older experiences and ideas of the mind's relation to the universe, soul to immanent God, passible person to enveloping world.

One kind of person, and one alone, could identify public and communal authority with anything at all like private being, and suffer securely the soul's jointure of inside and outside. Such a person was the monarch, whose temporal being was in some sense coincident with society's being. The learned James I of England and Scotland did not fail to make the point, telling Parliament four days after the Gunpowder Plot: "I would wish with those ancient Philosophers, that there were a Christall window in my brest, wherein all my people might see the secretest thoughts of my heart." They would then see that the now reassured stability of the kingdom had its counterpart in there being "no alteration in [his] minde," save only to make him more determined in maintaining present authority (ed. Sommerville 153: November 9, 1605). The king was enamored enough of his idea to embroider it four and a half years later for the benefit of another Parliament:

So haue I now called you here, to recompense you againe with a great and a rare Present, which is a faire and a Christall Mirror; not such a Mirror wherein you may see your owne faces, or shadowes; but such a Mirror, or Christall, as through the transparantnesse thereof, you may see the heart of your King. The Philosophers wish, That euery mans breast were a Christall, where-through his heart might be seene, is vulgarly knowne, and I touched it in one of my former Speaches to you: But though it were impossible in the generall, yet will I now performe this for my part, That as it is a trew Axiome in Diuinitie, That *Cor Regis* is *in manu Domini*, So wil I now set *Cor Regis in oculis populi*. (ed. Sommerville 179: March 21, 1610)

Much might be said of the King's idea of all others' faces as "shadows" and of *their* inability to use their glassiness as he can, his gesture being "impossible in the generall"—not to speak of the question of the divine: matters that will return in later chapters. And it is worth recalling that James' point had had its negative version performed on stage in Shakespeare's *Tragedy of King Richard the Second* just ten or so years earlier, probably in 1595, in a scene taken sufficiently seriously by Elizabeth's censors to have been excised from the 1597 printed version. At the moment when Richard is dethroned, when he becomes a "private" person, he makes exactly the opposite gesture from James' future one, calling for a mirror to see how he has changed. Outwardly, he sees no mark. But this, he laments, must be a lie, for everything has changed. Repetitively invoking his face, visible outer shell, brittle and false image, Richard dramatizes the abyss carved into his being, no longer identifiable with state:

> Was this face the face
> That every day under his household roof
> Did keep ten thousand men? Was this the face

That like the sun did make beholders wink?
Was this the face that faced so many follies
And was at last outfaced by Bolingbroke?
A brittle glory shineth in this face.
As brittle as the glory is the face,
[*Dashes the glass to the floor*]
For there it is, cracked in a hundred shivers.
Mark, silent king, the moral of this sport—
How soon my sorrow hath destroyed my face.

(*Richard II* IV.i.281–91)

Richard, not at all mad, caught the "shadowy" brittleness of personal being. The identity of a monarch's personal and public being was unique, and confirmed, James would observe, by divine title. Just the same point was made by Aemilia Lanyer, dedicating her *Salve deus rex Judæorum* to Anne of Denmark in 1611, and telling her that as she presents the image of Christ sacrificed and risen again so that humans might be saved "and with him t'Eternitie" raised, so should the queen: "This pretious Passeover feed upon . . . [and] / Let your faire Virtues in my Glasse be seene." Her poem can represent the Princess Elizabeth just as exactly, and

Then shall I thinke my Glasse a glorious Skie,
When two such glittring Suns at once appeare;
The one repleat with Sov'raigne Majestie,
Both shining brighter than the clearest cleare:
And both reflecting comfort to my spirits,
To find their grace so much above my merits . . . .

(ll.88–102: *Poems* 7)

Only because the poet's "Mirrour" was imperfect, made not of "chrystall" but of "dym steele," did appearance fall short of the queen's virtuous reality (ll.37–41: *Poems* 5). Monarchs and those who shared monarchy were secure in their identity, giving true reflections and clear sight through their glass exterior.

But no other human shared so secure a bond of outside and inside. For others, their glassy essence was as the king implied. John Donne, writing in the same years, was imbued with Montaigne's sense of inconstancy, where mental activity was at issue and that of the imprisoned soul's yearning for heaven in respect of being itself. To live in the world was ever to experience this brittle fragility. The 1612 "Second Anniversary" expressed both aspects "Of the Progresse of the Soule," as the poem's title had it. "[W]hilst you think you bee / Constant, you'are hourely in inconstancie," lamented the poet (ll.399–400: *Poetical* 238). But until the soul had left the world and risen to heaven, no longer having to "peepe through lattices of eyes" (l.296: 235), it was necessarily set in a public arena, where a person could only be beleaguered and in peril even in, indeed because of, its most fundamental relations. Knowledge and feelings required that the soul touch the world, be moved by it through the senses. So, in the probably earlier "Aire and Angels" (*ca.* 1590s), Donne explored his overwhelming love for a woman who, like an angel, would be "some lovely glorious nothing" were it not that the "soule, whose child love is," took on "limmes of flesh." For the soul to feel love, to act in any way at all, it had to work through the senses, or "else could nothing doe." Just so, the poet wrote, love itself had to

> take a body too
> And therefore what thou wert, and who,
> I bid Love aske, and now
> That it assume thy body, I allow,
> And fix itself in thy lip, eye, and brow. (ll.7–14: 21)

As a result, the person was in constant danger. And that the soul could react only via the senses to objects and events outside it, though doing so in virtue of thoughts and feelings (here, love) lesser than the soul, their "parent," yet imprinted on it by "a voice," "a shapelesse flame" more "angelic" than it (ll.9, 3–4), explains the appearance in Donne of this same brittle image. All ordinary humans, he wrote in the 1611 "Funerall Elegie," were inevitably as encased in "glasse" (l.6: 221). In "The Broken Heart," the poet recorded how love, thus marking, we see, the jointure of inside and outside within the heart, "At one first blow did shiver it as glasse" (l.24: 44). One might think this agonizing love must have been unrequited, but it sufficed that love moved a person's interior into the exterior world. For it had always to work through the senses. Love, therefore, was not only necessarily short-lived, less than "an houre," able to take in "tenne" loves in that time, but equally always a shattering of the glassy heart, which each time retreated from the world by loving less:

> Therefore I thinke my breast hath all
> Those peeces still, though they be not unite;
> And now as broken glasses show
> A hundred lesser faces, so
> My ragges of heart can like, wish, and adore,
> But after one such love, can love no more. (ll.27–32)

For Donne, like unkinged Richard, not madness, but the habitually unstable, inconstant and brittle state of embodied soul in the world was ever at issue.

Donne's and Bacon's friend, George Herbert, was no less explicit in

The Temple, published posthumously in 1633. "While that my soul repairs to its devotions" in church, he wrote, flesh was there separately "intomb[ed]," that it might know itself just "this heap of dust." He apostrophized flesh directly as having to "learn," "while I do pray," how it was "but the glass, which holds the dust / That measures all our time, which also shall / Be crumbled into dust" ("Church-Monuments" 58–59: ll.2, 20–22). Hour-glass measuring years in its own dust, flesh was more generally the brittle case which would end as dust and whose surety on earth depended only and wholly on God. Even one ordained to preach God's word was secure only in God's grace:

> Lord, how can man preach thy eternal word?
> He is a brittle crazy glass:
> Yet in thy temple thou dost him afford
> This glorious and transcendent place,
> To be a window, through thy grace.
>
> But when thou does anneal in glass thy story,
> Making thy life to shine within
> The holy Preacher's; then the light and glory
> More rev'rend grows, and more doth win:
> Which else shows wat'rish, bleak, and thin.
>
> ("The Windows" ll.1–10: 61)

Grace was always momentary. Fragile, cracked ("crazy") humanity hovered in an anguished abyss:

> Broken in pieces all asunder,
> Lord, hunt me not,
> A thing forgot,
> Once a poor creature, now a wonder,
> A wonder tortured in the space
> Betwixt this world and that of grace. ("Affliction (4)" ll.1–6: 82)

Herbert's reference in this last, editors observe, was Psalm 31:14: "I am clean forgotten, as a dead man out of mind: I am become like a broken vessel." Appeal to God was never as satisfactory for ordinary mortals as it was for the monarch.

　　I don't pretend these cases are straightforward. Some see in Vidriera a desirous self blocked by the demands and obstacles of a society of fools: a view advanced with particular force by Otis Green, echoing many Spanish commentators. This misconstrues psycho-physiological premises underlying the *novela*. Others see the tale reflecting fascination with a quest for knowledge whose humanist archetype, Odysseus, echoed on through Petrarch, Erasmus, François Rabelais, Francisco Sanchez and

Pierre Charron, yet cast always in doubt as a poison or a *hubris* setting humans against God, the proper goal of a humanity whose wholeness made individualist claim matter for scorn—or worse, almost a mortal embodiment of blasphemy and the demonic (Forcione 228–96; Sampayo *passim*). Both cases anyway show a breakdown in identities founded on older assumptions of being. In this regard it is instructive to see that when Petrarch thrice wrote of his glassy being, it was without *any* sense of insecurity. On the contrary, for him it figured something like the later James I's clarity of the soul's expression, disconsolate in life as it might be:

> Certo, cristallo o vetro
> non mostrò mai di fore
> nascosto altro colore
> che l'alma sconsolata assai non mostri
> più chiari i pensier nostri
> et la fera dolcezza ch' è nel core
> per gli occhi. . . . (*Rime* 37, ll. 57–63)

> Sure, crystal or glass
> never showed on the outside
> its inside hidden hues
> more clearly than the disconsolate soul
> shows forth our thoughts
> and the sweet wildness in the heart
> through the eyes . . . .

In sonnet 95 Laura's light passes into him as directly as the sun penetrating clear glass (9–10). In 147 the soul expresses its truths "transparently as glass" (13). In a seeming counter instance (sonnet 124), hopes of love break like a mirror (*vetro*) falling from his hands (12–13). This is precisely *not* his being. The case further proves the instruction. Whereas for a Donne, love was marked by profound tensions between interior and exterior, for Petrarch, its *public* nature gave security. This fits, indeed, with the tradition of what C. Stephen Jaeger calls "ennobling love," a tradition of amity and love coming down from antiquity as "primarily a public experience" and sign of public virtue (*Ennobling* 6, 28; and see Eric Jager, who shows how the loving heart is inscribed from without—by the divinity or other agency). We shall see more of this in later chapters.

Against this tradition, Vidriera is a liminal figure, caught between communal and individual subject. We need to know the premises grounding the *novela*. Ruth El Saffar notes the "transparency" characterizing Rodaja's early trip through Italy and the Low Countries and its echo of a theory of temperaments tying understanding to dry humors (*Novel* 52–55). In his illness, poisoned by a mystery woman's philter, Rodaja "dried out . . . and became all skin and bones" (*Novelas* 2.53). This thin limpid transparency may have reflected the search for unencumbered knowledge earlier in his story. More importantly, it mirrored general medico-philosophical and psycho-physiological theories of the understanding.

In the 1575 *Examen de ingenios*, which made him celebrated, Juan Huarte de San Juan analyzed mind and temperament. Correcting it by Inquisitional order for the 1594 edition, he added an interesting passage about old people:

> Some natural philosophers held the opinion that the incorruptibility of the heavens, their diaphanousness and transparency, and the stars' brilliance, spring from the extreme dryness of their composition. For the same reason old people talk so well and sleep so badly: due to the great dryness of their brain, everything seems diaphanous and transparent, fantasies and images glow like stars. (387: addition to cap. vi, now cap. viii)

Yet more to the point, Huarte explained how Aristotle had based his physiology on the principle that "the body's accidents [i.e., its sensations] pass into the substance of the rational soul, and those of the soul into the body." "Principally," he went on:

> [he said] that those accidents by which the powers are altered are all spiritual, without body, quantity or matter; and so they multiply themselves instantaneously through the medium and pass through a glass window [*una vidriera*] without breaking it, and two contrary accidents can be in a same subject with all possible intensity. (158: cap. vii, suppressed in 1594)

A visual image, his editor Esteban Torres observes (158n17), "multiplied itself" in each individual who perceived it.

However now fragile, glass delimited outside and inside, as it did in all those others. Walkington, advising in 1607 on temperaments and their care, wrote that body enclosing "minde" needed tending like "a christall glass to saue it from cracking." Soul observing from body, "though it be not so blinde as a Batt, yet is it like an Owle, or Batt before the rayes of *Phoebus*, all dimmed & dazled: it sees as through a lattice window" (*Optick Glasse* 6, 21–22). Luisa Oliva Sabuco described in 1587 how eyes received external images via their "transparent glass" but had a wider aim: God having set highest in humans "two glasses or windows of the soul [*vidrieras ó ventanas del alma*], . . . that by opening these windows [*vidrieras*], it would see its homeland, the heavens, and rejoice in the vast variety created by Him, and watch out and see utmost afar to protect itself from this world's adversities" (*Coloquio* ch.lxii: 363; ch.lxvi: 367). In 1578, Guillaume du Bartas depicted soul's "flame" shining through the glass of "the body's lantern," God having set the soul "en un vaisseau de terre, / Plus liquide que l'eau, plus fresle que le verre" (in an earthen vase, More fluid than water, more brittle than glass): this in a poem that was perhaps the century's bestseller (*La sepmaine*, Sixieme jour, ll.933–34; Septieme jour, ll.367–68). These writers had a near precursor in Juan Luis Vives, in 1538 depicting mind in body "like one shut in a house, who has no opening to look from save a glass window [*una ventura de cristal*], and can see only what it allows: if it is clean, one will see more clearly; if covered with dust and mold, confusedly" (*Tratado* II.vi: 79).

However clichéd, embedded in a more or less Platonic vision of soul and body (anciently via Augustine or Cicero, whose *Tusculans* spoke of soul living in a home not its own, a "prison-cell" whose "chains" could not lawfully be broken [I.xxii.15; I.xxx.74], recently through Ficino or Pico) such remarks cast Vidriera's insanity in new light: as *subject to* the usual metaphor for fragility of personal being in community. As Petrarch had long since had "Augustine" put it to him (though not via glass): "No one is so mindless, unless he be irretrievably mad, as not to think sometimes of the fragility of his condition" (*Secretum* 48). The metaphor, that is to say (by no means just a metaphor, we see), signaled that selfe was always subordinate, on the one hand to Sabuco's divine world, on the other to this world's social actuality and materiality: this last caught to perfection in Donne's "Aire and Angels" and "The Broken Heart," but no less in Herbert's sundered "thing forgot."

There was, though, one use of the glass image throughout this period that both confirmed human nature as thus *subjected* and implied a particular sort of stability in being so. This was the common image in conduct books and more of "the wife as a mirror to her husband," as Ann Rosalind Jones puts it. The usage further confirms my points. On the one hand, "the mirror emblem totally suppresses any autonomy in the wife" (Jones 26–27), emphasizing being as subjection and *denying* (separate) interiority. On the other, its stability was in fact always uncertain: the very goal of the conduct books was to defeat the precarious and threatening nature of women in relation to men: we shall see how Hélisenne gave these male fears life. The mirror, *speculum*, as a good didactic reflection of things as they are, ought to be or will be (Grabes 39) had a pedigree dating from the early middle ages. Exploring the English case, Herbert Grabes finds it to peak "during the century 1550–1650" (221). On the whole, unlike the cases just seen, the traditional mirror involved remedial certitudes. Writing of a famous contemplative moment in Loyola's life, Boyle explains: "What Loyola sees reflected in the surface of the Cardoner is his image, much as his contemporaries viewed themselves in the moral mirror both realistically and correctively. Mirrors in literature could be factual, exemplary, prognostic, or fantastic. Exemplary mirrors, in analogy with their use for toiletry, were held up to the self for interior discernment and moral beautification" (*Loyola's* 139).

Mirrors as moral exemplars for princes, magistrates or wives, meant to be trusty. If they were at times "tricky," says Boyle, not their exemplarity but what they were correcting was the issue: "There were innumerable artistic examples of pride with a mirror. Who looks in the mirror—prudence or pride—when Loyola turns his face to the Cardoner river? Pride, as discerned by prudence" (*Loyola's* 140). One *can*, that is, rely on them provided one is sufficiently discerning. The glassy experiences just explored make that discernment categorically impossible. So although I am not concerned with mirrors *per se*, it matters that Grabes, after studying a vast corpus, observes that the trope of the *distorting* mirror became "enormously popular in English literature from the end of the sixteenth century to the middle of the seventeenth" (104). Its symptomatic implications are analogous to, if less drastic than, those of the fashion by the late sixteenth century of an illness whose sufferers felt themselves made of glass.

The dry, thin transparency of Cervantes' Vidriera signaled a state produced by a surplus of the fiery, warm and dry yellow bile. It was an illness that seemed somehow to make the window marking the soul's usual rational acquaintance with the material world extra tenuous and brittle, as if intellect were stretched and thinned to breaking point. This identification had a complex Greek medical and philosophical ancestry. For although Galen identified acuity of wit and intelligence with yellow bile, since Hippocrates a surplus of *black* bile, *melancholia*, had been associated with disease of the intellect. The *locus classicus* was Aristotle's *Problem* 30.1, whose first sentence gave a melancholy temperament to all those "eminent in philosophy or politics or poetry or the arts" (953a10–12). Too much black bile in this temperament tipped the intellect to madness. This bond between melancholy and intellect was broken until Galen's older second-century contemporary Rufus remade it. For him, mind's activity caused the illness of melancholy, not the other way about. Symptoms were almost the opposite of Vidriera's: bloating, swarthiness, lust and stuttering (*Oeuvres* 355). Galen disagreed a bit, noting symptoms of "leanness, darkness and hairiness" ("De locis affectis" III.x: *Opera* 8.182), a view Paulus Aegineta repeated in the seventh century (*Seven Books* III.xiv: 1.383). The disease's earthy dryness and *coldness* produced in its sufferers the delusion recorded by Rufus of being "an earthenware jar" (*Oeuvres* 355). Galen and Paulus agreed; but all three connected it less with frangibility than with earthiness.

In "The Soul's Dependence on the Body [That the Faculties of the Soul

Follow the Mixtures of the Body]," Galen similarly asked of intellect in old age, a period of life characterized by dryness and coldness: "why, then, do so many people lose their wits at the height of old age, a period of life which has been shown to be dry? This is not to be explained by dryness but by cold: for this quality manifestly damages all activities of the soul" (*Selected Works* 159). So, he said in "Mixtures" (Book II), Aristotle was right to have compared old age to "the drying out of a plant" with its aging. For it was clear, he wrote,

that old age is the driest time of life. That it is also the coldest is clearer still: this is a fact that has never been disputed. Old men appear obviously cold to the touch; they readily become chilled, turn black or leaden-coloured, and are prone to the cold illnesses: apoplexy, paralysis, numbness, tremor, convulsion, mucus, sore throats. They have lost nearly all the blood in their bodies, and with it the redness of complexion. (*Selected Works* 235)

Old age and melancholia clearly had certain attributes and causes in common for these doctors of antiquity. Both involved excess of bile. But what bile was its cause? And did—or how did—this affect symptoms and cures?

When Erasmus adopted these ideas on melancholia, early in the sixteenth century, emphasis and symptoms had both changed. Also linking the malady to overstrained mind, his famed 1528 *Ciceronianus* presented the scholar Nosoponus as among those who believed that they had "on scrawny necks great earthen heads sure to be broken if they move ever so little." One of his interlocutors would cure his lunacy by affecting to share it (*Ciceronianus* 20). In 1582, Lorenzo Selva told of a person imagining he was "una vettina da tener acqua," a water jar or urn (*cruche* in its French translation, says George Hainsworth), similarly cured by one simulating his malady and fear of fragility (*Della metamorfosi* 154; *La métamorphose* 196). Here, the symptoms were clearly closer to what Vidriera's were to be. We shall soon see how this *cruche* may further have its bearing on imagery in which Descartes importantly couched moments of his thinking.

Now, the Aristotelian *Problem* had noted that black bile could be either too cold or too hot, a duality marking the ambiguity of melancholia's results. Rufus had tried to clarify by arguing that black bile was not a basic humor. It was blood blackened by chilling or yellow bile by burning. The first gave cold black bile. The second was identified as *melancholia adusta*, always causing illness, bad regimen sufficing to cause insanity "through excessive burning of yellow bile" (*Oeuvres* 358). Galen adopted this view, as did Paulus, who found adust bile far worse than common black bile: "when the complaint is occasioned by yellow bile, which, by too much heat, has been turned into black, it will bring on the disease called mania, which occasions ungovernable madness, so that those affected with it will destroy persons who come near them unguardedly" (1.383: III.xiv). They were echoed by the Arab writer, Ishāq ibn 'Amrān, whose work grounded a monograph on melancholia by Constantinus Africanus. He, because of his close contacts "with the medical school of Salerno, had in turn a decisive influence on the development of medicine in the west during the Middle Ages" (Klibansky, Panofsky and Saxl 49). Paulus, too, was well known in Latin translation and via the Arabs, having been put into Arabic by the ninth-century physician Hunayn ibn Ishāq, known throughout the European middle ages as Joannitius, author of the celebrated and much-used Galenic *Isagoge* (Adams, Preface to Paulus, 1.xvi). Arab sources of western medicine argued the actual physical transformation of one humor to another and their always-possible mingling: a series of "coctions" changed foods into phlegm, black bile, yellow bile and blood in turn, and the "higher" could always degenerate to lower: as blood by chilling, for example, or yellow bile by burning. These changes lent themselves to vast complexities of symptom, we shall see in Chapter 8.

Melancholia adusta produced Vidriera's mania, the frenzy of Lemnius' glass-buttocked lunatic and Walkington's similar "ridiculous foole, of *Venice*," Garzoni's madman hoping to be refined to a frail glass flask, Goulart's timorous glass people, Barlaeus' fears of breaking, Selva's water jar and du Bartas' fluid earthen vase, "more brittle than glass." Indeed, as his verses caught the medical ambiguity of earthy black bile's symptoms and fiery yellow bile's "adust melancholy" so they caught the sense of teetering between solidity and brittleness, between mind grounded on earth, "safely" lodged in matter, and one whose walls had given way, whose "seething brain" had let its grasp on reality yield to "shaping fantasies" (*Midsummer Night's Dream* V.i.4–5). Not surprisingly, Don Quijote's melancholia was also depicted as due to a drying of the brain: "his brain dried up so that he lost his mind" (*Don Quijote* I.1: 1.73).

In its victims maybe, and for writers, this tension reflected the no less unsettling *branloire perenne* of the wider social, political and spiritual world, even what Cave calls "an epistemological uncertainty, an ontological or axiological anguish" (*Pré-histoires* 15). At the same time, as the container or vase metaphor denoted a prison for the soul, the fragility it betokened forbad belief in separable *self*. So did the fact that sensations, perceptions and *accidents* were shared (said Huarte) in some physically and mentally essential way by many selves. This grounded Montaigne's maxim: "All oddness and particularity in our behavior and circumstances is to be avoided as enemy of mutual exchange and society and as monstrous" (*Oeuvres* 1.26.166). "Humans," Vives had echoed Aristotle in 1531, "are born to society and cannot live thoroughly without it" (*On Education* I.v: 38; Aristotle, *Politics* 1253a1–18. The idea of shared feeling and knowing also drew on Aristotle, we shall see in the next chapter). Another link was Philip Melanchthon, "preceptor Germaniae." In his 1558 *Liber de anima* (revising his 1540 *Commentarius de anima*), he warned of the singularity made by variety, changeability and disturbance of humors. Especially one had to take account of these "in communal life, for preserving health, ordering behavior and being circumspect in relationships. Care is altogether needed to shun monstrous [*monstrosas*], overweening, malevolent, and perfidious natures" (87). The *Liber* was indebted to Aristotle, Galen and Vives (cf. Rump). Personhood was first social: not just *in* society but *defined* by (a particular) society.

All these analyses were grounded in the work of the physician who remained the solid foundation for practice and main sounding-board for theoretical debate even beyond the sixteenth century: Claudius Galenus (Galen). Behind him lay Hippocratic authority for the specific science of medicine, and Plato's and Aristotle's for the general knowledge of nature, world and being. Alongside were perennial theological and legal opinion and belief. I name these again because when we talk of "individuals," "persons," "selves," and "subjects" in historical context, we must know ideas and practices bearing on these notions in their context. If we want to talk of people, we need to know what "people" were. As Justinian's thousand-year-old but still basic legal textbook not unrelatedly began: "it is useless to know the law without knowing the persons for whose sake it was established" (*Institutes* 6: I.ii). The debates we have just glimpsed show that by the end of the sixteenth century, at least, deep tensions and grave pressures were felt in and on precisely thinking about the experience of what a "person" was. These widespread images of brittle glassiness in debates about human being, medical advice, poetry, theater and many actually lived experiences cry out for explanation of such a kind. One king's assertion that he, and he alone, could ignore such brittleness, and another's that he, unkinged, was reduced to it, simply confirm the point.

That Descartes used these images to mark the tenuity of human knowledge and precariousness of person at the outset of the 1641 *Meditations* further verifies that they embodied those tensions. Surely, he asked, although we know that the senses deceive us occasionally in the case of very small or distant objects, are there not others in which we cannot possibly have cause to question? If, for instance, I were to doubt knowledge and my presence here now, sitting by the fire, dressed in a winter gown and holding this paper in my hands, so much as to suggest that none of it were actually the case, and even "to deny that these hands and this whole body were mine," then I might rightly be compared to

those mad people whose brain is so undermined by the stubborn vapors of black bile that they perpetually maintain they are kings when they are poverty-stricken, or that they are dressed in purple when they are naked, or that their heads are earthenware, or that they are wholly gourds, or blown of glass [*vel caput habere fictile, vel se totos esse cucurbitas, vel ex vitro conflatos*]. (AT 7.18–19)

The word *conflatos*, translated here as "blown," meant to light a fire by blowing, to excite passions or to make something by mixing or melting things together. The participle let Descartes heighten the bond between humor (the fire-blackened bile of *melancholia adusta*), passion (melancholy), uncertainty of knowledge (the delusional series symptomizing madness) and insecurity of person (the earthenware or glass delusion and metaphor). Equally to the point, *cucurbita*, translated as "gourd," was also the word for the medical cupping-glass, a tool that by drawing blood served to nourish, quell pain and cure ills from the mildest to, Richard Gummere reminds us, "insanity and delirium." It was used, wrote Plutarch, to "draw the most virulent humor from the flesh" (Seneca, *Epistulae morales* 2.64: note a to Ep.lxx; Plutarch, *Moralia* 469b). Celsus wrote of just "two sorts of cup, bronze and horn" (*De medicina* II.11.1), but by the sixteenth century the tool was glass. The images Descartes put in play are even richer. For, he asked of his hands and body being "his": "quâ ratione posset negari?" "By what *reason* can it be denied?" If madness was just another reason, there were further dilemmas.

The 1647 French *Meditations*, authorized by Descartes, elided the phrase "vel caput habere fictile" with the next. *Fictile* means earthenware or clay. Joining it to *cucurbita* gave "s'imaginent être des cruches [believe themselves earthen jugs]" (AT 9.14). *Cucurbita* and *cruche* both meant "dolt" or imbecile as well as madman: one recalls Velázquez's celebrated 1630s portrait of the jester Calabazas, flanked on both sides by the gourds of his nickname, in a haunting painting of a "misbegotten man" whose very surroundings are distorted: nature's "cruel trick on this mindless fool" echoed "in the world around him" (Brown, *Velázquez* 148: see Figure 1). Also relevant is that Lemnius' maniac thought his buttocks "conflatos" of glass, while *cruche* was Selva's lunatic as *vettina*, to be cured by another feigning himself a *cruche*. Descartes probably did not find his *topoi* in these authors (although Selva's work was issued in Paris in 1611, where Goulart's had appeared in 1600, with several reprints elsewhere), but all were familiar. To use these images, signaling madness

Figure 1. Diego Velázquez. *Calabazas* (mid- to late 1630s). Photo: Museo del Prado, Madrid.

and its cure and incorporating a tradition stretching from Galen to Erasmus and into his own time, increased the intricacy of Descartes' discussion. They underscored edginess, the brittleness of border between reason and unreason, relative security and radical unrootedness—fear of an absence at mind's core. Not for nothing, my penultimate chapter argues, did Descartes adopt such familiar images of madness as threat *and* possible cure—trying to keep, "in knocking down an old house," we saw him say in the 1637 *Discours de la méthode,* "remnants to use in building a new one" (AT 6.29).

Far from spurning the fears they expressed, Descartes insisted that he was no less human than these who were thus called mad, subject to dreams, for instance, no different from their delusions—an association between dreams and madness also going back to Aristotle, whose writing *On Dreams* had stressed their similarity. Since he had no sure way to distinguish these sleeping from waking impressions and, therefore, "madness" from "reason"—or one kind of reason from another—recourse had to be had elsewhere: to something that *would* provide a firm bar between them. The ontological argument for God tried to do this. At the end of *his* story, Quijote's cure (and death) lay in the same familiar divinity, the knight waking from his last fevered sleep to cry: "Blessed be almighty God, who has granted me such great blessing! Indeed, his mercies are boundless, human sins do not limit or hinder them." He explained to his niece that God had made his "judgment now free and clear, without the misty shadows of ignorance," showing "their absurdities and deceits" and enabling at least some "light in the soul," even if there was not really enough time left to read such other books as "might enlighten my soul" (*Don Quijote* II.74: 2.587). For Donne and Herbert relief in the divine sphere from menacing doubts and instabilities was altogether less sure than Descartes and Quijote hoped, but in all cases the hope expressed an older familiarity.

For all these writers and thinkers, soul caught in its glassy or earthen prison sought a path to its original divine dwelling, striving to take "wing," wrote Herbert, though "pinioned with mortality, / As an entangled, hampered thing" ("Home" ll.61–63: 100). James I made it part of his secure condition here and now. But a king, especially one as convinced of his Divine Right as James, was God's present embodiment and representative on earth. Richard had forfeited that surety. Among James' "general shadows," even ordained ministers like Donne and Herbert never had it. Death alone, decked at doomsday "gay and glad," could close the gap between God's love and human pain (Herbert, "Death" ll.17–18: 175). Cervantes may have been ambivalent, but Descartes was proposing terms that would give in the material present a security of knowledge and person otherwise lost. Even so, they clung explicitly to older sureties, bound by them. His response to these fragilities was far from any the modern West and its avatars recognize (hence his recall of Aristotle). My final chapters explore these Cartesian moves. We now understand them as forged in age-old certainties pierced by the tensions we have glimpsed. Chance did not guide Descartes' use of these figurings to mark tenuity of human knowledge and precariousness of person at the outset of the 1641 *Meditations*. His choice verifies that they embodied new stresses. Contemporary analyses joined issues of personal identity to matters of wider political order. For its victims perhaps, and certainly for writers, glassy madness reflected tensions in personal identity and the equally unsettling *branloire perenne* of the wider social and political world. At the same time, as the glass container denoted a prison for the soul, the fragility it betokened forbad belief in separable *self*. Something had broken; with as yet no means of repair. What had broken is this book's topic.

In *Knowledge, Discovery and Imagination*, I noted that inquiry in the liberal arts changed social theory and practice and understanding of person, set in the world's fabric in firm intricate pattern. Since antiquity, music especially was thought to be a mathematical rule balancing a person's inner complexion as it did heaven's. Plato's Necessity turned a spindle whose whorl of eight star- and planet-bearing circular, nested "boxes," each with a Siren singing one note of an octave, was the well-tuned universe—upheld by a female principle (*Republic* 616c–17b). His analysis of the tie between divine, worldly and human by musical proportion in *Timaeus* 35a–37c was known to medieval Europe via Boethius, Macrobius and Martianus. In the *Republic, harmonia* grounded rulers' education, tuning the soul's "circuits." Robert Fludd still drew universe and person as monochords in his 1617 *Utriusque cosmi* (1.90, 2.275: in Hersey 54, 215). Music reset imbalance in the soul. It roused passions to resist contrary ones. Medical writers said that tunes in Phrygian mode quelled grief, in Dorian levity. Opening his 1575 *Chirurgie*, Ambroise Paré recalled fabled musical cures of tarantula bites, Asclepiades' tenet that music cured insanity, Theophrastus' and Aulus Gellius' claims that it eased sciatica and gout (1.94). These were proverbial. Evelyn retold the tarantula cure in the book in progress when he died in 1706 (303–4, 306). Music could disrupt temperament. Solemn Dorian and majestic Mixolydian modes accompanied tragic *choroi* to kindle pity and fear. Elsewhere, plaintive Lydian and "enervated" Ionian excited other passions (Plutarch, *Moralia* 1136c–37a). Music stirred anger, aggression (Plutarch 1140c–d, 1145e) or love, of whose musical food Duke Orsino in 1602 sought a surfeit that his "appetite [might] sicken, and so die"

(*Twelfth Night* I.i.1–3). Plutarch, Shakespeare's and Paré's source, said of the musical genera that "the chromatic relax[ed] the hearer, the enharmonic [made] him tense" (*Moralia* 1096b; cf. Martianus IX: 357–59). Such ideas were common, expressing older experiences as late as Evelyn, although in 1513, Raffaele Brandolini already saw them as highbrow entertainment no less than life's essence (12–41).

Apparently analogous experiences help contemporary profit margins: "companies have long known that ambient music affects shoppers— from subliminally discouraging theft to putting people in the mood to buy" (Flaherty C1). Restaurants play loud music to make people drink more, hospitals to relax them. But this music is a vague spur to individual emotion, not a rule susceptible of mathematical analysis. If, through the sixteenth century, music was credited with cures from banal to miraculous, it was because the world was still thought ruled by musical harmonies that fit the Aristotelian view that everything in the universe interlocked "in one system—as in a household" (*Metaphysics* 1075a18–19). Brandolini began his lesser claims by saying that the greater needed "natural philosophers'" skills, not his (13). Many sixteenth-century people hoped to revive its deeper usage. They thought it possible because their experiences of the human shared much with their ancestors', even if nostalgia tinted reality. Still, George Hersey shows how tightly imbricated music remained with geometry, light and architecture far into the eighteenth century (23–77). Nor did harmony alone tie music and physical human being. From the sixteenth to the eighteenth century, physicians and others sought to render the intimate relation between human pulse and *rhythm* on the musical staff and use it for knowledge and cure. This connection also went back to Greek antiquity (Kuriyama 81–91). Music's rule was braided in the general understanding of the world.

Late sixteenth-century frayings signaled an unraveling or dishevelment of thoughts and experiences of personhood whose weave, if not all details of their pattern, had come from one family of looms for almost two millennia, still found in Herbert's music of Providence hopefully "tuning" and "tempering" both the human and the infinite universe ("Providence" ll.37–44: 109). The warp and woof of their design were laid when Pythagoras and his followers in the Greek sixth and fifth centuries developed ideas of the rule of number in the universe. Especially important was the number four, taken to ground every aspect of the universe. As the eclectic but heavily Stoic-influenced Varro described it five hundred years later (*ca.* 47–45 B.C.):

Pythagoras the Samian says that the beginnings or seeds [*initia*] of all things are double, finite and infinite, good and bad, life and death, day and night. So, too, there are the two [basics], station and motion [each divided into four kinds]: what stands still or is moved is body, where it is moved is place, while it is moved is time, what is in its being moved is action. The fourfold division will be clearer as follows: body is, as it were, the runner, place is the racetrack where it runs, time is the period in which it runs, action is the running. (*On the Latin Language* V.11)

There could "never be time without motion" or motion without place and body: "Thus the four-horse chariot of first things is place and body, time and action."

"Just as the primal classes of things" were four, so were "those of words": the *lekta*, sayable things, of the *logos* underlying the universe (V.12–13). Varro did not expressly make the last point, but his etymologizing via these categories assumed this Stoic idea of the relation between words and things (of which we shall see more in Chapter 9). From thence came the tetradic categories corresponding to them, whose development we have begun to see: earth, water, air, fire; autumn, winter, spring, summer; moist, dry, cold, warm. Varro held the first "gods," powers or natures, to be "Caelum et Terra [Sky and Earth], quod anima et corpus [as soul/life-force and body]." Earth was damp and cold, sky dry and warm. Joined, they gave "birth to all things from themselves." Too much of any was destructive (V.59–61). Empedocles took these categories to define not just the universe or macrocosm but the human being or microcosm, and said that when the body's elements (earth, water, air, fire) harmonized a balanced temperament resulted. In the fourth century, Hippocratics, despite disagreement, put this physiology into more complex order. Earth and autumn had qualities of cold and dry and paralleled black bile among the body fluids; water and winter were cold and moist, matched by phlegm; air and spring were warm and moist, borne in blood; fire and summer were warm and dry, carried in yellow bile (see Figure 2). Human aspects of these categories are treated in Chapters 2 and especially 8. Music was a prime way to "retune" the body because the relations of these parts, powers, activities and instruments echoed universal numerical harmonies and proportions.

Medical and philosophical ideas of the person were obviously tied to those about moral "agency" and those about people as members of political and legal society. Here, matters get more complicated. With regard to the physiological constitution of the human animal, antiquity ultimately passed on something like an agreed model. The authors of the Hippocratic corpus (fifth-fourth century B.C.) had disagreed on many aspects of human life that concerned them, from the nature of soul to the constituents of body, from the etiology of disease to its treatment. Plato and the Hippocratics set the rational powers in the head, Aristotle and

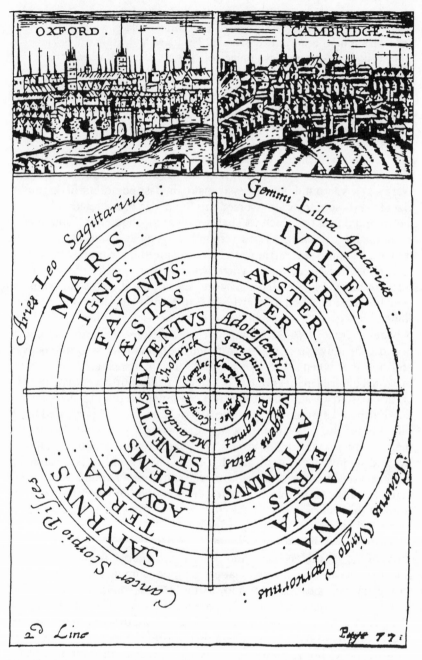

Figure 2. Frontispiece to Thomas Walkington, *The Optick Glasse of Hvmors* (1607).

early Stoics put them in the heart. After the second century A.D., the "Galenic takeover" erased most larger differences. Galen mauled authors who placed reason in the heart, for example, tasking Chrysippus especially with muddled thinking, sophistical argument, doctrinal chaos and anatomical ignorance, and approving what he called dissension from within the ranks by other Stoics like Cleanthes and Posidonius (*De placitis* II–V; see V.6.42 for sample summary remark: vol. 1.334/35). Galen's "Hippocrates" was a major source of medical knowledge even into the nineteenth century.

He was, at least, for such later historical intents and purposes as touch the Latin middle ages and European early modern era. According to Owsei Temkin, Galen's work was preponderant in Alexandria and the Greek East by the fourth century and entirely dominant there and among the Arab doctors by the sixth. In the Latin West, the methodist Soranus of Ephesus kept a strong voice until the spread of Arab influence moved him definitively to the background by the eleventh century (Soranus xxix; cf. King 231). Disagreement lasted, to be sure, over the exact locus of certain activities, the primacy of elemental qualities or elemental matter and many details of treatment. But the picture of what it was to be human was one and whole in its fundamentals. This continuity is worth emphasizing because it grounded the many differences, disputes and changes we shall be following.

For long there was less accord over moral and political implications. Socratic-Platonic ideas of personal *good* and sociopolitical legitimacy did not altogether mesh with Aristotelian ones. Both differed from more materialist Stoic and Epicurean argument (as Stoics' pneumatic concept of the soul did from Epicureans' generally atomistic one). Although Epicureanism had exiguous impact from the European fourteenth to sixteenth centuries, the other traditions were chief secular sources. By then, probably mostly due to the massively read eclectic Cicero, their diverse implications seemed hardly in conflict. There was overall agreement on the role of the moral person in the social order, in no small part because such a person was thought to be inseparable from that order; an assumption no less fundamental, albeit in material and physical ways, to medical explanation and treatment. This is not to say that there were not sharp debates. It is to say that such debates took place on shared ground.

Among other traditions (I include Arab commentators and practitioners under "Aristotle" and "Galen" and rather omit Jewish, heavily dependent on the Arabs, as Maimonides shows), one was for later European ages most important of all. Christianity had usually been less concerned with the human city than with that of God. In its debates, through Late Antiquity and the middle ages, secular moral agency had been a less immediate issue than grasping relations between human and divine intellect and will, evaluating the bond of the material and the spiritual, understanding the play between God's determining knowledge and order of all things and humans' free will and reason, and articulating personal incarnation with soul's immortality (although Paul Oskar Kristeller finds the last doctrinally unimportant until the fifteenth century: *Renaissance Concepts* 27–32). In these considerations, the person's place in social life was secondary, determined after personhood was situated in relation to the divine scheme. Still, it goes without saying that so drastically to separate the two spheres falsifies actuality for heuristic ends. The division is a logical or theological, rather than historical, one. Real life held them intertwined, as the medieval overlapping of Canon and Roman law more than hints. That intertwining of spheres is, of course, what I suggest is basic to ancient as to later experiences of who-ness, whatever otherwise their variety.

This reality is not affected by any one person's level of awareness of that who-ness or "selfe." The experiences grasped and being passed along were not particular to a tiny educated group of thinkers, even though they were the ones writing of it. One must be wary of the objection that most of this has to do with written records, and so not only by definition *public* and unsuitable, if not unable, to address such a "privacy" as the modern western self (whose absence would simply result from the written form and not from any radical cultural difference) but also produced by and for a particular "elite" group of people. The first point has been taken to mean that the who-ness these records express would necessarily be a public one (although one must observe that "public" and "communal" are not the same), the second that their ideas of personhood were probably not those experienced by "common people."

The reply to the first point is a ready one. Modern western writers (for instance) do not depict the same sense of person as those we shall examine. The self a Rousseau or later autobiographers depict in writing or other public medium is private in *essence* and as discrete as Lloyd and Okot hold. This self is injected into a public forum whose existence it precedes. The experience differs utterly from the person-in-community presented by Cicero or Seneca, Plutarch or Galen, Augustine or the Arab doctors, and early modern writers. "We are now known, read, judged [*Iam noscimur, legimur, iudicamur*]," Petrarch wrote to Philippe de Cabassole in his letter prefacing the *De vita solitaria*, "with no hope of escaping gossip and hiding mind [*voces evadendi celandique ingenium*], and whether going out in public or sitting at home one is bound to be on show [*apparendum est*]" (*Vita*, ed. Martellotti 290). All are/were for a public record that was not impediment, constraint or election, but the nature of being. "Impersonal" first person plural passive verbs, absence of personal pronouns, use of impersonal gerundives and gerund matter here, hard as they are to put in the vernacular. And translation is always an issue. Like most translations of Petrarch's Latin, Jacob Zeitlin's *Life of Solitude* (here 100) adjusts the language to a modern western sensibility, as usual making Petrarch the first to claim "as a principle the right of the human personality to express and realize itself according to its individual qualities" (Zeitlin, Introduction 87). The view guides translation, as it ignores the fact that the *Vita* was a tissue of classical citation and reference (more even than the many K. A. E. Enenkel identifies in his edition of Book One), a mode of composition requiring adjustment in any idea of "individual qualities." Public gaze was no obstacle to private insight. Public record was integral to the being experienced and expressed, which existed humanly first and foremost via relations the recording established and explored. It is not that Petrarch's experience was not "new" and different—of a sort, maybe, that lets David Wallace suggest that the choice of this "republican" from the Florentine "republican *patria*" to work for its Visconti enemies was "a typically self-contradictory, self-alienating act expressive of a new post-medieval individualism" (*Chaucerian* 53). There was no absence of tension, change and struggle, as Chapters 10, 11 and 12 show, but they characterized an experience in its essence "communal."

The second point, about the elite nature of the personhood expressed, raises more complex issues, many of which will come up again in the course of the following chapters. But they merit immediate quick inspection as laying these chapters' groundwork, being among the issues they raise—and seek to answer.

At the simplest level one can reply that it would be hard—now, for example—to find the divide this assumes between written documents and contemporary sensibility as to how people explain and experience being. "It is my opinion," railed one of the first Hippocratics, apparently in this spirit, "that all which has been written by doctors or sophists on Nature has more to do with painting than medicine," as if protesting irrelevance of written theory to actual practice ("Tradition in Medicine," *Hippocratic Writings* 83). Whether having in mind painting as Socrates' second-order simulacrum of nature's first-order copy of Ideas, told later in Platonic dialogues like *Phaedrus* (275d–e) or the *Republic* (596e–598c), or a simpler discrepancy between writing and doing, the physician was saying that medical theory did not describe real experience. But the polemic spoke to the issue of medical utility and not to that of human experience more widely—of which medicine was recognized as but a part. His colleagues (and he, too) clearly thought that collecting written data on ma-

terial nature, human physiology, diseases and their etiology was essential
to establishing medical classifications and enabling prevention and treatment.

In this wider regard, all agreed that they were echoing a shared understanding of shared experience. Modern commentators have shown that
this was why ancient medicine depended on a *dialogue* between the patient and a doctor, writes Jackie Pigeaud, who "had the patient remember the lived experience [*le vécu*] that would become meaningful": both
were undividedly [*indivis*] located in the same experience (*Maladie* 11).
Patient and doctor shared responsibility for treatment, Michael Frede
agrees, it being "the patient who must combat the disease with the help
of the doctor" ("Philosophy" 225–26). Plato, in a passage in *Laws*
(720c–e) to which we will return in Chapter 6, used the point to distinguish between the way free and slave physicians treated their patients, the
former in dialogue, the latter by command. Doctors—those who wrote
of such things—may have been treating wealthy people but no one
thought the nature of the human body, healthy or unhealthy, and its interaction with its surroundings differed thereby. Besides, the cases given
in the Hippocratic corpus recorded the condition of people from all ranks
and walks of life.

Maria Michela Sassi, exploring classifications of the human deployed
by the ancient Greeks across such "popular" domains as physiognomy,
astrology, medicine, economy and geography finds parallel evidence from
the most elite to the most popular writings. Such consensus must always
hold in general if not in detail even for those unable or not in a position
to write or otherwise express it. Society, large or small, is otherwise
unimaginable. Structures of feeling within a social organization are always, broadly speaking, shared. They must have been so in the early
modern ages of western Europe, say, if only because sermons, tales, diagnoses, trade, barter, work arrangements and the myriad other negotiations of everyday life between all levels of society would otherwise be
meaningless or inoperable. As Gramsci wrote of an analogous case, in an
expression readily allowing its extension to the present: "one might say
that every social group has a 'language' of its own, yet one should still
note that (rare exceptions apart) there is a continuous adhesion and exchange between popular language and that of the educated classes"
("Languages of the Arts" [*Quaderni* 6 §62], *Selections from Cultural
Writings* 120). This is only to say that in any society, conditions, events
and phenomena experienced, as well as analyses of them, presumably
made more or less similar sense to the real people embroiled in and addressed by them.

So while I agree with Winkler that one should beware of assigning to "philosophers" a "privileged position . . . in reconstructing a picture of ancient society," one should also not presume their disjunction from it (19). Gurevich reminds us that analyses like Vološinov's cited in my Introduction apply in this case no less thoroughly. Not only do societies ground individual senses of identity, indeed identities, but they do so for *all* their members. He adjusts Vološinov's thought to the middle ages:

> The medieval individual does, and indeed can, exist only within society. The medieval individual is absorbed into the social macrocosm via the microgroup— family, extended network of relatives, rural commune, parish, seigneury, feudal domain, monastic brotherhood, religious sect, urban *fraternitas* and so on. Each microgroup adheres to certain values which are, in part, specific to the social microcosm in question and in part common to a number of groups or for society as a whole, and the individual becomes part of that culture by assimilating those values. (*Origins* 89)

This language implies a modern western view that individuals preexist these groupings, threading between them to fix themselves in them. The ambiguity may be what Kuriyama calls "an artifact of translation" (48) from Russian. The point is that being a person is being always already inseparable from these groupings.

Studies like Carlo Ginzberg's *The Cheese and the Worms*, Gérard Simon's *Kepler astronome astrologue* or Anthony Parel's *The Machiavellian Cosmos* show that a sense of the human as enlaced in a living world from which the person was scarcely separable was also grounded in widespread animistic structures of feeling underlying everyday practice, no doubt beyond the sixteenth century. That the case applies to the Florentine statesman Niccolò Machiavelli and the Emperor's mathematician Johannes Kepler no less than to an uneducated miller of Friuli shows how one should beware of sharp distinctions between "elite" and "common" in these regards. For good cause, clear evidence is often hard to find and harder to construe—although Gurevich has tried to recover some of its commonalty from sermons, folktales and such (*Categories*; *Medieval*). Too, the glosses of Hildegard's *Scivias*, the lore of her *Physics*, the vernacular blend of her medical *Causae et curae*, her constant personification of world and universe here and in her visionary works, show how easily these ideas joined those deriving directly from "higher" Greco-Roman tradition, implying, from Hildegard to Kepler, the fallacy of any elite/commonalty split. Overall, Gurevich proposes that while intellectuals *might* increasingly be finding this experience problematic (*Origins* 74), most others did not. The point, though, is that this experience was/is everyone's or, at least, sufficiently widespread as to be the experience against which others would be measured. This will *always* be so.

So while we may put many questions about the person in its varieties called "woman," "man," "slave," "free," "black," "white," "noble," "peasant" or "barbarian," it is unclear how they touch what it is to be a *person at all*—as against varieties of interpersonal relations and sociopolitical treatment specifying this here-and-now person. The powerful "moral capacity" that Foley explores in Penelope and women protagonists of tragedy belongs to the first, "the female social role" to the second (*Female* 109). Young men in love, says Theseus in Euripides' *Hippolytus*, may be much as women, but their "standing as men," their male social role, alters consequences (968–70). In the same author's *Andromache*, the princess' slave agrees to do her will, despite danger: "What's my life, that I should care / What happens now? A slave's life, and a woman's" (89–90). It matters, Harold Donohue reminds me, that the phrase the slave uses to express the worthlessness of her life is *kou peribleptos*: unnoticed, her being is negated because unseen by others. But what do these things mean? Andromache had not so much been giving orders to her slave as trying to persuade her. Indeed taking one reply as a refusal she called the slave "a fair-weather friend" (87), as if admitting not only that the slave had her own opinions and could act on them, but could rightly do so. The same differing circles are at issue. Euripidean irony and that the exchange was *composed* by Euripides (a *man*), and not "neutrally" recorded, add ambiguities to which I shall return.

Save occasionally for "woman" and more rarely "slave," during the ages treated in Part 1 these terms leave little separate extant trace in debate on the specific issues of personhood, although otherwise very present. But this absence does not validate a supposal that women and slaves were considered non-persons—as the *Andromache* exchange implies. It does show that they were considered sociopolitically and sometimes morally different, but that is not at all the same. Following chapters attend in greater or lesser detail to implications of these traces. Naming sociopolitical determinants (and sometimes others), these were aspects of what person was, and we shall see, for instance, that Cicero took them into account when trying to characterize the nature of who-ness. Sexual, racial, rank or caste markers were variants, often, even usually, painful and oppressive, on the spectrum that was the experience of personhood. Their effect and kind are part of what I try to show. It clearly matters, Eva Cantarella holds, that "beginning in the seventh century the Greek city defined itself as a political community by means of the exclusion of two classes of people, slaves and women," on the grounds that "'nature' . . . made women and slaves different from, respectively, free man *qua* male and free man in the sense of human being" (*Pandora's* 38–39). As to personhood, just how it matters is developed in later chapters.

But first, it matters if such definitions and exclusions were clearly the case. Difficulties are lack of evidence, ambiguities not limited to imaginative texts and artifacts, and the exact nature of the exclusions. As Geoffrey de Ste. Croix observed, the idea of natural slavery virtually vanished after Aristotle (*Class Struggle* 418; "Slavery" 28–29). Too, if a claim of women's *physical* difference was widespread and not disreputable, its import was always unclear, other differential claims being even more so. Further, *if* the—or *a*—Greek city was grounded on such exclusions in the seventh century, in 451–50 Athenians passed Pericles' law limiting citizenship to children of two citizens, repassing it in 403. Obviously this meant that women *had* to be citizens. Since no new provisions were enacted to this end, this must always—or long—have been so. Citizenship differed. But if women's roles included participating "in public and private religious rituals and festivals," having "the capacity to bear children who would be citizens" and caretaking in households, these may underscore the importance of the *oikos*—the domestic arena where education first occurred and which all held the city's foundation (Sealey 14; Foley, *Female* 4, 7; cf. Patterson, "Hai Attikai"). People did so at least in the 150 years between the sixth-century move from "feudal" countryside to cities (whose political arrangements varied) and the last years of the Peloponnesian war. This urges a tale different from one having Aristotle tie men's ontological superiority to women's political inferiority, with noncitizenship principal (Lange 10). *Polis* and *oikos* may have shared importance. I shall argue that *Antigone* debates the proper foundation of the city and that the quarrel between Socrates and Thrasymachus in *Republic* I was over what institution, *oikos* and oligarchy or *polis* and single sovereignty, grounded the good city. No one, anyway, doubted the fundamental importance of the *oikoi* to the *polis*.

These facts imply that "exclusion from the political community" may be a phrase whose censorious tone entails anachronistic assumptions. Foley, wary of fusing art and life, notes that tragedy "not only collapses but blurs boundaries between public and private worlds" (*Female* 333). Here, neither wariness nor blurring seems needed. We shall see repeatedly that this public/private split is modern, not ancient: "our distinction between 'public' and 'private'," remarks Kate Cooper of Romans from late republic to late antiquity, "might have baffled men and women accustomed to perceiving the household as both the index and the end of men's struggle for position within the city." She expands the point: "the notion of a 'private' sphere divested of 'public' significance would have seemed impossible (and undesirable) to the ancient mind. The *domus*, along with its aspects of family and dynasty, was the primary unit of cultural identity, political significance, and economic production" (*Virgin* 4, 14). Homer shows these habits of perception to date from long before the Athenian fifth century. They have major consequences for persons.

Associated with this line of anachronistic understanding may be another, also involving social hierarchies. Page duBois, for example, sees a change between fifth and fourth centuries in expressions of relations between humans understood as sexually, racially or species diverse from one another. Interhuman relations held to differ along a horizontal spectrum—people having different spaces and roles, but not ones shaped exclusively by dominion and subservience—would have been reordered and fixed in a hierarchy by fourth-century thinkers (*Centaurs* esp. 138–45). The last point follows Gregory Vlastos' thesis that Plato first set slaves on a scale between humans and animals, lacking *logos*, and then took relations of subjection and dominance typified by the *social* fact of slavery as model for *all* human relations, speaking of all "sorts and conditions of political subordinates as *douloi*," slaves. "There is no difference in Plato's political theory between the relation of a master to his slave and of a sovereign to his subjects; or, as Aristotle put this Platonic doctrine: mastership (*despoteia*), statesmanship (*politikē*) and kingship (*basilikē*) are the same thing [Aristotle, *Politics* 1253b18, 1252a8]" ("Slavery" 137). Thucydides wrote of the Athenian League as a *douleia*. Yvon Garlan notes that for Plato the word *douleia* extended beyond slavery and political subjection to moral servitude and all forms of subordination: "of a body part to another, a child to its parents, a citizen to political and legal officers"—and, of course, of body to soul (*Esclaves* 32).

Here, too, anachronisms may be at work. We may need to rethink this picture of unrelievedly oppressive hierarchies. Agreeing that *douleia* was "used to describe any kind of subjection, whether to the government, to parents, or to the rule of law," within status groups, of body to soul, of the very structure of the soul, of the human to the cosmic world, Joseph Vogt poses the caveat that "this willingness to obey is considered to be beneficial to the subject" (*Ancient Slavery* 33: ref. to *Republic* 590c–d). And lest we jump too fast to belief that this benefit was just ideological justification, we should consider that this "obedience" was in fact basic to understanding the subjected, *passible* relation to the circles composing the person's being and bond with the worlds outside him or her, and that it involved an understanding of stability in the world—from metaphysical to "psychological"—wholly analogous to the *oikos/polis* stability in the political and social spheres. Anthony Long remarks that "Plato politicize[d] the mind" in holding it *subjected* "to the *rule* of reason" ("Ancient" 23). He was expressing, rather, the mere nature of human being. All this is why I can do no more in this introductory chapter than raise some of the issues involved in trying to include all persons in my examination. Fuller analysis has to wait until we have a clearer idea of just what *passibility* entails. Nonetheless, I raise these issues now so that they are in mind during the analyses of the next four chapters.

I must also note the matter raised by duBois (among many others) when she adds that Aristotle set women into this model and sealed their place for subsequent centuries when his philosophy dominated (*Centaurs* 145). The claims are problematic. Whatever Aristotle's eminence, for centuries his thinking did not dominate. Even "Peripatetics" differed often from the founding figure. Too, Aristotle's assertions about women and slaves were polemically argumentative replies to others. Many, perhaps most, of them actually had little or no afterlife. The "places" of both women and slaves were assuredly more ambiguous than all this proposes.

Besides the immense difference in relations from city to city, from Athens to Sparta or from Gortyn to Mytilene, further complicating things is that most men also had no role in politics. Precise population figures are lacking even for Athens, and subject to endless speculation. Vogt agrees with A. W. Gomme (*Population*) that in Athens' glory days, just before the Peloponnesian war, "there were about 115,000 slaves to 172,000 citizens and 28,000 metics" (*Ancient Slavery* 4). Perry Anderson follows Antony Andrewes (*The Greeks* 135) in supposing a figure of 80–100,000 slaves against 45,000 citizens, the last presumably referring only to heads of household—although Anderson does not suppose so (*Passages* 22–23n7, where he also notes the unreliability of all figures; cf. Winkler 224n2). The only exact figures are from a census taken a little over a century later, between 317 and 307. It showed 21,000 (male) citizens, 10,000 metics and 400,000 "*oiketai.*" Everyone writing on slavery gives these figures (e.g., Jones 3; Garlan 68; Westermann 76; Wiedemann 12). They are the only point of agreement. Were the 21,000 those who could vote? Those who could fight? Who were the *oiketai*? William Westermann is adamant that "the context makes it certain that . . . *oiketai* . . . means slaves" (76). Paul Cartledge observes (with others) that the term included "free domestics" (34). Thomas Wiedemann is equally sure that it may "refer to anyone who belongs to the household (*oikos*)," maybe including "male citizens' wives, children and free dependents" (13). How does one interpret the meaning of the figures for male citizens and metics? Should one take them to mean 31,000 free households, each with several members, whose total (of "how many mouths would have to be fed in the event of a siege," as Wiedemann puts it) was 400,000?

These debates demonstrate how even apparently straightforward indications yield no unambiguous conclusions. Be that as it may, for the moment, and to return to my point about male citizens' exclusion from political activities, the 21,000 certainly indicated something like heads of *oikoi*. Of these, writes Raphael Sealey, 12,000 were "beggars" who "tried to survive as hired laborers," most of the other 9000 "lacked resources" and had to engage "in toil." Three or four hundred were the "elite" rich who have left records of life and institutions—who built the last. If we may justly, however uncertainly, suppose "that the poor and the indigent borrowed the norms of the rich," this would surely be so as well in their sense of what it was to be a person at all (*Women* 9–11; on the elite, cf. Winkler 47). I will try to show that this was the case as much for women and slaves as for metics and indigent and wealthy citizens.

If some humans were taken not to be human at all, then under no circumstance could they be considered "persons" and contemporary descriptions would simply not apply—although later analysts would still want to extend the descriptions to such excluded humans. How such persons might have experienced *themselves* would be largely unknowable by other observers, since they would have had no access to the necessary media of expression. It *may* be the case that somewhere at some time some people may have taken some "humans" not to be human and that names like *woman, slave, black, yellow* or *red* may have been thought to describe radically different animals. They did not do so in ancient Greece or Rome (except for a very few Hippocratics and some others who tried to describe far less radical distinctions). Further, for reasons just advanced, it is hard to think that people inhabiting a single culture experience their being in ways radically different from each other and even harder to imagine human beings having no experience of their own personhood. Then, when nouns and adjectives like *slave* and *woman* were taken to name humans, it would seem that at least for Greco-Latin antiquity what made someone a person was generally the same regardless of exterior, even though one could only approach an interior by way of that exterior: which is why, we shall see, Greek auto-knowledge depended first on externals, and why Cicero was to write of soul speaking to soul. Such persons had different roles to play in the world, but their relation to their role depended on a personhood that was in the nature of what it was to be human at all. It was thus by and large the same for all. This is not to say that personhood was separate from or precedent to its multiple surroundings. It is to say that the person's embedding in its local and immediate social environs was governed by and grounded in its relation to a source whence its life force was supposed to have come.

Just so does Finley explain why in ancient Greece and Rome corporal punishment was restricted to slaves and their legal testimony admitted only if obtained under torture. Besides the simple use of "naked force," what mattered was to "degrade and undermine [the slave's] humanity": "If a slave [was] a property with a soul, a [political] nonperson and yet indubitably a biological human being, institutional procedures" to effect subordination were needed. But that a natural person was at issue is clear from the fact that when manumitted, a Roman slave became not just free but, if the owner was a citizen, a full citizen of Rome with all attendant rights. In Greece, the ex-slave was a metic, a free inhabitant lacking political rights, equal to any resident foreigner. It was, then, "fundamental that a slave could think, could act deliberately," use rational language and engage in doings from concerted revolt to authorized military and diplomatic acts. Slave and free, often the slave's master, worked beside each other as skilled artisans, diplomats, soldiers, medical aides in Greece, doctors in Rome and much more (Finley, *Ancient* 93–107; cf. Ehrenberg 181 and Vogt 114–20). In both Greece and Rome, among typical tasks, female slaves were nurses, responsible for children's early upbringing; male slaves were tutors, with "an even deeper effect on public life, because they molded the characters of young men" (Vogt 105–14: here 109). Although the master of an *oikos* assumed unlimited sexual access to his female slaves, Xenophon's Ischomachus remarked that compulsion was needed (*Oeconomicus* X.12). The remark said that the activity was recognized as a violent act. It supposed the thought that the slave was a person reacting humanly to oppression. Indeed throughout the *Oeconomicus*, Xenophon assumed that men and women, slave and free, shared equal virtues, vices, talents and rational abilities (cf. Pomeroy, *Xenophon* 66; Foley, *Female* 113).

I mostly defer wider discussion of slaves and women until Chapters 6 and 7, but *this* point is clear: however political and social condition varied, to be human was to be a person. To use force—beating, torture and sexual oppression (of both men and women)—made sense as a way to degrade, and *show* one was degrading, a person. That was why slaves, said Demosthenes (XXII.55), were "answerable with the body for all offences" (quoted in Finley, *Ancient* 93). If some writers from Herodotus on held them inferior that was surely not least because such ideological belief underpinned the system. Even so ambiguity ruled. Herodotus' tale, for instance, of returning Scythians defeating their warring slaves by showing them whips instead of swords (*Persian Wars* 4.1–4), Finley notwithstanding, is told deadpan and could have divers implications. Aristotle waffled. Like others he distinguished "natural slaves" from victims of military defeat (*Politics* 1255a4–b15; 1253b15–55b40 for full discussion). Often he contradicted himself about the former. A free person could possess the soul of a slave as a born slave a free soul (*Politics* 1254b27–37). Property as they were, slaves were no less *persons* with rational, embodied souls. Seemingly against this, he wrote that natural slaves lacked *to bouleutikon*, the deliberative faculty, and *prohairesis*, ex-

ercise of choice (*Politics* 1260a12). That *could* make them other than human, and *his* discussions on personhood, then, would simply not apply to
slaves (or any other non-human). But Aristotle could be "inconsistent
within the limits of one sentence," Robert Schlaifer notes, parsing *Politics*
1254b16ff to show how it "simultaneously grants to the slave a participation in reason and denies it to him utterly, making him a mere body."
The slave somehow shared in reason, but not fully, even while "it is a part
of the *psuchē* which is involved" ("Greek Theories" 121–22).

I will return to this in more detail once we have a clearer view of general ideas of personhood. Suffice it to say, for the moment, that this muddle betrays—at the least—unease with any claim that a slave was a different kind of animal from a free person. Corporal punishment, torture
and manumission belie such arguments and make them contortions of an
ideology faced with the indubitable fact that slaves were humans with a
soul, as Xenophon implied in writing of those who bought slaves to be
"fellow-workers" (*Memorabilia* 2.3.3). Citing this remark, Finley confirms its truth by reference to surviving numbers for those who built the
Erechtheum on the Athenian Acropolis at the end of the fifth century B.C.
(*Ancient* 81, 100). The remark and the numbers catch the reality of laboring citizens in their personhood, among other things. We shall see
how philosophical and dramatic texts may well need to be read less as
furnishing evidence of actual experience, however ambivalently, than as
revealing a complex negotiation between ethical norms, ontological expectations, rationalizing claims and the social fact of slavery. Slave torture, duBois remarks, reveals the "need to have a clear boundary between
servile and free, anxiety about the impossibility of maintaining this difference." Torture was a way to mark the boundary, an effort to allay anxiety and unease (*Torture* 41, 63–68; more generally 47–62).

In that sense boundaries could be crossed. They became fixed in classical Athens not in matters of who-ness but in those of civic roles; of
which an alien or ex-slave (for instance) could play none—the reason for
the suit brought by pseudo-Demosthenes against Neaira around 340 B.C.
(see Chapter 7). Records of Roman slave marriages show that half of
those whose duration is noted lasted thirty years, which, at the whim as
they could be of their master's control and economic advantage, implies
recognition of human feelings (especially, too, when one recalls that life
expectancies meant many shorter marriages). At Gortyn in Crete, earlier,
the "slave family was not merely a permitted union, but a full legal entity
with regular marriage" (Pomeroy, *Goddesses* 67–68, 193–94; Schlaifer
111). Personhood was unsurprisingly and clearly seen in all these:
"Who," Ngũgĩ has a later enslaved person cry to his oppressor, "deceived
you into thinking that the builder has no eyes, no head and no tongue?"

(*Matigari* 22). Xenophon could have said that he was not so deceived. Aristotle perhaps wanted to be. We shall have to see whether personhood in antiquity either required or depended on such deceptions.

Even so, in this regard, Aristotle may for the moment have a last word. For he was very clear on this distinction between civic role (natural or constructed) and inherent humanity when mentioning slaves in the context of his discussion of friendship in the *Nicomachean Ethics*. Insofar, he wrote, as there could be neither reciprocity nor equality between a slave as a "living tool" and a master, no friendship between them was possible, no *philia* with a slave *qua* slave. But with the slave as human being (*anthropos*) there emphatically could, because reciprocal relations of "justice" held between any who "can share in law and contract." This argument also made slaves fully rational (1161b4–8).

I use the generic "humans," not "men." It is no bias little to distinguish women from men until later eras this book examines. We can name Aspasia, Plutarch's daughter the thinker Asclepigeneia, Perpetua, Sosipatra, Hypatia, but only study Hroswitha, Héloïse, Hildegard, Margery Kempe and other later women who have left writings. Even when earlier women have done so, difficulties abound: Sappho, so supreme a poet as to be Antiquity's "tenth Muse," survives as but a body of lyric fragments. That these were kept and organized suggests weight given her experience of personhood. Still, for women leaving no writings, the problem is beyond difficult. They appear as written about by men, from whose beliefs we can scarcely disentangle them, with possible exceptions for some aspects of medical writing and fragments of poetry by women. "The real women of everyday Athens [for example] are inaccessible to historical research. None of their utterances has survived. The inscriptions on their tombstones were carved by men, and the vases which show their everyday activities were painted by men" (Sealey 4).

Claims like this, that only men carved and painted or never cut an epitaph penned by a woman surely reveal later prejudice. After the second century A.D., women of the Roman empire did, for example, write epitaphs. No evidence exists against them having done so before. To determine these things is hard, and knowing the later Roman case hardly erases practical difficulties. Modern research shows women's "inaccessibility" is not absolute, but to elude it requires concern and ingenuity. To lack both vitiates discussion of men, too, although translation often hides the fact. In W. G. Spencer's rendering of Celsus, for instance, "he" translates every third person singular verb, while *aliquis* (anyone, someone), *quis* (one, whoever, someone, anyone) and the like always become "a man"—a noun constantly used without warrant. In a random instance, Celsus wrote, "At in tabe sputum mixtum, purulentem, febris adsidua, quae et cibi tempora eripit et siti adfligit, in corpore tenui subesse periculum testantur": "But in tuberculosis, mixed purulent spittle and persistent fever that robs (appetite at) mealtimes and torments with thirst signal growing danger in a thin body." Spencer has: "But that in phthisis danger threatens a thin man is signified as follows: the expectoration is purulent with admixtures, a persistent fever robs him of his appetite at meal-times and afflicts him with thirst." The case is the more striking because a few lines later Celsus specifically set girls (*virgines*) and women (*mulieres*) among those so described (*De medicina* II.8.24–25: ed. Spencer 1.142–45). This is not to deny that Celsus *may* have taken men as generic humans but to note how sexual exclusivity has been introduced into a work from which it was largely absent. Much of Celsus' writing, far from emphasizing exclusion, did not even imply distinction. The same goes for Thomas Lodge's 1614 translation of Seneca, where use of "she" for all emotion words gendered feminine lets us say little about Seneca, and certainly not that he gendered "emotions feminine" and "reason and intellect" masculine (Gwynne Kennedy 1, 5); especially given feminine *ratio*. Such misprisions are, again, artifacts of translation.

Of course, that in extant writings from antiquity women were written of only by men is an obvious problem (ignoring for the moment what it means to set a group of people out of the historical record). One need but ponder Maria Dzielska's recent *Hypatia of Alexandria*. Rejecting the myriad myths and legends of the Western fifth to twentieth centuries, Dzielska hopes to recapture who Hypatia "really" was. To this end, however, she has nothing by Hypatia, only exchanges of letters between male students and disciples, avowedly misogynist and admiring their teacher for having risen above sexuality and "transformed the concept of womanhood" (60). These tell of the circles in which she moved, the veneration in which she was held, the plots and counterplots in which she may—or may not—have been involved. They tell nothing of how she may have experienced *who* she was. In the case of (later) women who have left writings the issue seems simpler. And in some sense it is, although paucity of numbers may be evidentially problematic. Even so, styles, not facts, of information about the person may be mostly what differs between men and women. We shall see that generally speaking recognized sexual differences in the human body did not affect its generic uniformity (and so etiology, diagnosis and cure of disease, or preventative hygiene, regimen and diet). We shall see that women and men did not differ in claims of relation to the divine or in their suppositions about the human person who underlay their diverse social roles.

There were many views about sexual differences and gender relations. And even if women were legally and economically in subjection to men throughout this western history, these views were not as universally misogynist as often alleged. Sassi advances much evidence in "popular" writing for demeaning views of women, but we shall see that Aristotle's questioning of their *personhood*—perhaps any in the case of slaves, full in that of women—seems to have been echoed only by a few Stoics and was always deeply ambiguous. No others queried their personhood. On the contrary, need for certain kinds of rules and constraints was dictated by the fact of being a person in community. Too, varieties of view on most of the issues involved were matched by varieties in the laws and customs of different places pertaining to these issues: classical Athens and early Rome may have been atypical. By and large, it does seem the case that the ground of who-ness underlying the diverse roles (*personae*, as Cicero called them) that a human played in life was taken to be one. This is because although it was always recognized that physical bodies differed, it was rarely held that the nature of *who* one was, in being and its relation with the several surroundings which composed the person, differed in any major way for any creature considered human, even though in Greco-Roman antiquity *some* did think that women or slaves might need more help fully to achieve the manifold possibilities of human nature. Still, while Aesop or Epictetus may have been socially anomalous, if far from unique, as a slave who became a venerated fabulist or revered teacher of philosophy, neither was *humanly* so. For their part, Hypatia and other women philosophers of late Hellenistic antiquity were neither humanly *nor* socially anomalous.

So in writing of "humans" in this respect rather than of "men" there is much evidence that one is following a principal track of antiquity. That men were on top, there is no question; any more than that they were there in often violent and oppressive ways. They were on top, too, in ways taken to fulfill demands of a given universal order engaging certain obligations. These involved a more or less set place in that order. All humans were in this fixed situation and could fulfill their humanity only via their place in it: but it was the same humanity. One's place in the order meant a *relation* to it that was the same for all *as a person*: what the *person* was felt to be was affected by the particularity of the relation but not changed in nature. One can of course never get under someone else's skin, not even that of those who have left records of thought and experience, let alone of those whom we know only by tale, like Socrates' Diotima "deeply versed in this and many other fields of knowledge" (Plato, *Symposium* 201c–212a)—whom David Halperin reads not as a woman but as Plato's "staging of 'femininity'" to rethink men's relations ("Why?" 291)—or of whom we know only that they existed. But people did communicate with each other. This entailed shared axioms as to who was doing the communicating and shared structures of feeling. Commerce, medicine and all forms of everyday intercourse, as I said, suppose agreement on such things. No one, under any circumstance, ever does any of this alone, either in place or in time.

Later chapters take up these topics in detail. They show that whatever uncertainties and ambiguities inevitably suffuse so complex a phenomenon as the sense of who-ness, and whatever the latter's *varieties*, few saw foundational differences. Still, if the story of women's personhood would be no "counter-history," nor is it just "a supplement" (O'Faolain and Martines xv). It alters perception of oppressions, understanding of agency, grasp of (misnamed) public and private spheres and much more, to say nothing of gender and social relations, making the picture more complicated and many-edged, shifting the effects if not the facts of commonly grounded who-ness. To the reader of Plato and Aristotle, the claim may seem harder where slaves were concerned. I think their case entails the same conclusion. In what follows, I hope to have made women's and slaves' cases as full a part of the story as possible. That until Chapters 6 and 7 only details occur is because the manifest difference of personhood from anything now familiar in the West meant that its characteristics had to be clarified before one could hope to know how gender, sexuality, rank or class might affect it, or them.

PART ONE

Assays and Arguments in Antiquity

A Cock for Asclepius

Plato, the Hippocratics and Aristotle

The earliest Greek medical writers, the Hippocratics, disagreed about men and women. Lesley Dean-Jones argues that they treated "exclusively . . . the male sex." Some dealt with women's diseases by opposing them to the dicta of male medicine, others specified when women were included. Overall, their diseases were taken to originate and be focused in reproductive functions and physiology. For the Hippocratics, she says, woman was "a radically different animal from man in structure and processes" (*Women's* 112, 117–19, 225). The unreliability of so bald a claim about Greek ideas of women and men and opacity of the texts are evident in Dean-Jones' contrary assertion that "despite the dichotomy which many Hippocratics would see in the treatment of men and women, the principles of health and disease were the same for both" (120). Bodies, sexual physiology aside, shared nature and substance and housed like sorts of person. Helen King shows that contradictions coexisted and claims of difference served later western medical ideologies (8–11, 249), which required seeing, said a Victorian obstetrician, that "the uterus is to the Race what the heart is to the Individual . . . the organ of the circulation to the species" (Poovey 145). Chapter 7 treats these issues. Their difficulty implies a need to see first what being a person was at all. For now, in their regard, I recall one Hippocratic's doubts about theory, opposing unreal copy of medical practice to real experience, image to engagement. Besides its warning about theoretical claim, this matter of actuality and image gives a useful entry to the who-ness of which we need a sense before asking questions of it.

For how far, asks Vernant, "did the ancient Greeks recognize an order of reality corresponding to what we call image, imagination, and the world of the imaginary?" (*Mortals* 164). Did they recognize an order of reality that along with belief in will, intention and auto-reflection is for modern western people vital to selfhood? At first, he agrees, the question seems pointless. Plato had, after all, a general theory of image making and its place in knowing the world. Before him, Xenophon held image making to define *mimēsis*. The issue is what these *eidōla*, images, did and what place they took in the mind, whose rational powers, by Aristotle's time, were described as memory, intellect and imagination. Each power was exactly located in the brain, the first at the back, the second in the middle, the third in the frontal lobe directly touching fibers bearing vital spirits moved by the senses. Two and a half millennia later, Fludd depicted these in circular perfection (Figure 3). How they worked, and the nature, presence or absence of experiences like those signaled by "intention," "will," "knowledge," "action" and "imagination," are among the hard questions needing attention.

While in the *Sophist* (235d–e) Plato differentiated two kinds of image, *eikōn* (first-order copy of Idea, like an actual bed) and *phantasma* (second-order copy, like a painting of a bed), he did not, finally, think the difference important for their relation to the true and the real: both were simulacra. These images registered in the imagination, *phantasia*, whose functioning Plato distinguished from that of "the intellect, at work in *dianoia*." *Dianoia* was an active operation, *phantasia* a passive recipient, "immersed in the flux of the sensible," although the adjective "active" will need serious qualification. While *phantasia* was a power of mind or soul, it was also an aspect of physical body, bound to it and, like it, a receiving container. Even so, *phantasia* was not *just* a place of images "resembling" what they "represented." Its contents needed interpreting: its *phantasmata* could concern more how things were perceived than how they really were. Because *phantasia* was already in mind, it was not *simply* "passive" (cf. Nussbaum, *Aristotle's* 221–69). We shall see how important this "active-passive" nexus is for understanding person as *possibly* set in the world.

However *eidōla, eikones* or *phantasmata* got into *phantasia* (explanation varied), they were "not apprehended in their aspect as facts of consciousness" (Vernant, *Mortals* 171). Using this language risks bias, though, as if "their aspect as facts of consciousness" were not itself a culturally created experience, or as if there were consciousness of a kind now familiar that then failed to cope properly with these images—or whose explanation did. Perhaps they were not apprehended or explained in this way because there was no such consciousness. *Phantasia* received images, it did not first make them. *Phantasia*, Vernant continues, "is that state of thought where spontaneous assent is given to the appearance of things in the form in which they are viewed" (173). Intellect could then work rationally on these images as they were in *phantasia* or memory could re-

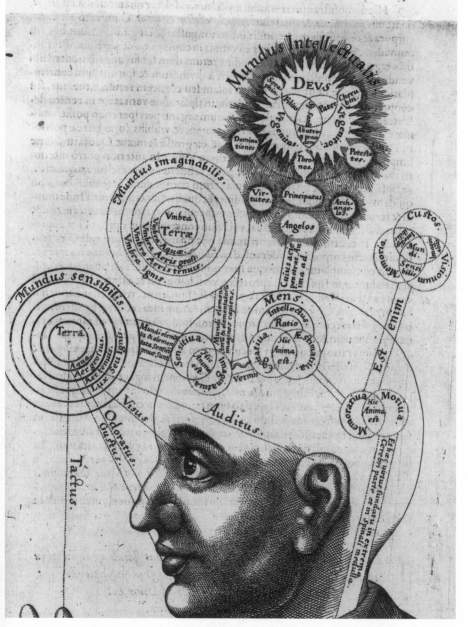

Figure 3. Robert Fludd, the three faculties of mind, from *Utriusque cosmi* (1619). Photo: Bancroft Library, University of California, Berkeley.

cover them. Neither involved imaginative consciousness of the kind dear
to the modern west, certainly not that personal imagination described as
"self-consciousness." That is why Sassi can show that "what might be
called the 'human sciences' of antiquity . . . focused on the appraisal of
visible signs, observed on the body" (xv). Mind functioning as introspective subject was not conceivable in idea or practicable in experience—
Oedipus not excepted, we shall see briefly in Chapter 3. The physical
placement of mind's operations, from *phantasia* through intellect to
memory, depicted a path from body through rational soul to the one faculty able to conduct the soul back toward the universe whence it came.
This physiology matched ideas and experiences of mental life foreign to
most modern westerners.

To recognize *phantasia*'s operation as sensuous matters, signaling how
directly tied was mental image-making to the sensible world. It helps explain how, far from "self-consciousness," apprehension of one's being as
a person occurred by *looking at* one's form, its presence. Just so did Aristotle explain the name of the human face:

> In humans the part between the head and neck is called *prosōpon*, a name de-
> rived, it seems, from its function. For the only animal that stands upright is also
> the only one that looks directly ahead and sends its voice forward. (*Parts of Ani-*
> *mals* 662b19)

Prosōpon meant both mask and face, referring primarily to outward appearance. Tying gaze to speech, Aristotle implied other people's presence
as partly defining the human. Vernant's translation catches this: "the only
one who looks you in the face and who speaks to you face to face" (*Mor-*
tals 142). Sassi observes how outward *prosōpon* implies that persons
were a condition of social relations, existing, *qua* persons, as a knot in
those relations. This was emphasized by the Greek sciences of color and
physiognomy, the latter showing how "the distinguishing features of a social or ethnic group [were] presented as natural and visibly inscribed on
the body" (33). Particularly were such features "concentrated in the description of the facial area," a point Aristotle emphasized (44, 73). At the
end of the *Odyssey*, Penelope, one protagonist who has made a story of
her own by her weaving and unweaving (unlike the swineherd Eumaeus,
father Laertes or the old nurse, whose stories are parts of Odysseus'), demanded that Odysseus *show, prove* who he was. Because once-familiar
relations no longer existed, they had to *see* each other anew. Doing so,
they and the community would *be* anew (cf. Cavarero, *In Spite* 12–14).
Winkler and Foley make similar points during broader arguments about
Penelope's agency and her equality with Odysseus in remaking the household (*Constraints* esp. 145–61; *Female* 127–43).

Cavarero expands the point apropos of the Demeter/Kore (Perse-
phone) myth. After Hades abducts her daughter Kore, Demeter "no
longer generates, rendering the whole earth sterile." Now, the whole
earth, nature, the "world's boundless mode of being," is *phusis*, a word
derived from the verb *phuein*, to be born. "Indeed, according to Aristotle, the first two meanings of the word *phusis* are: 'generating things that
are born' and 'the primary material element from which the thing that is
generated proceeds' (*Metaphysics* 1014b)." Cavarero adds that Latin
natura relates similarly to the verb *nasci*. The myth records not just the
sterility but the risk of literal nothingness that arises when Kore "is
snatched out of [her mother's] sight." "She wants to *see* her daughter, to
be seen by her, and to welcome Kore within her sight. *Phuein* becomes
possible only in this reciprocal visibility," Cavarero recalls Luce Irigaray
(*Sexes* 132). "When *visibility* is denied, *phuein* stops." This, Cavarero
concludes, "is the end of the world, precisely because the world is *phusis*"
(*In Spite* 59–61). Cavarero's argument concerns the threatened "desolation" of "the patriarchal order." Mine emphasizes that "Demeter produces [it] when her eyes grow desolate from the absence of her daughter's
gaze" (*In Spite* 65). The material point is that sense of being was attached
to sight, sound and external experience. We risk mistaking what was being apprehended if we name personal who-ness "oneself." It is not that
people had no sense of interiority, but that its understanding and, therefore, auto-apprehension depended firstly on external—reciprocal—experiences.

Not only in archaic Greece, Vernant adds, did "each person exist as a
function of others in the gaze and through the eyes of others." One still
did in later times. To experience one's personhood was to turn "outward,
not inward. Individuals seek and find themselves in others, in those mirrors reflecting their image, each of which is an *alter ego* for them—parents, children, friends" (Vernant, *Mortals* 85, 327; cf. *Entre mythe*
414–20, and Frontisi-Ducroux's *Dieu* and *Du masque*). This is what Andromache's slave meant: her being is unrecognized because unseen by
others, although her mistress' treatment belied the sentiment. It was the
point of Sophocles' *Philoctetes*. The protagonist's exile in shame and otherness *because* it was from the eyes of humankind was one "from the status of a human being: 'You left me friendless, solitary, without a city, a
corpse among the living,'" MacIntyre quotes, stressing "the idea that
friendship, company and a city-state are essential components of humanity" (135). It may be the deeper meaning of how the messenger in *Oedipus the King* tells of Oedipus gouging out his eyes, more exactly the
"joint of the spheres" (*arthron tōn kuklōn*), a phrase troubling to translators, who make it "eyeballs" or "eye sockets" (1270; 1405 in Fagles'

translation). Perhaps Sophocles named not just the eyes Oedipus destroyed, but disarticulation of his very spheres of being. To be human was to be present *to* and *for* others. *Presentness* to others was no accidental property of being human, a relation one could choose or not. It was essential to being. (Cavarero makes the same point, especially in *Tu che mi guardi, tu che mi racconti* [*Relating Narratives*].) Gurevich sees humans and human relations in terms still very similar to these in the later time he examines (*Origins* 90).

One begins to sense what it meant to think of a human as *zōon politikon*, as *first of all* socially embedded. And it is useful to recall that for the Greeks vision was itself an embedded exchange. The eye did not just receive light. Like the sun, "an eye in the sky," the human eye "radiated a kind of light": "The luminous ray, which emanate[d] from the object and render[ed] it visible, [was] of the same nature as the optical ray which originate[d] in the eye and render[ed] it capable of seeing." Sight was a signal element in "a complete reciprocity" between humans and their surroundings (Vernant, "Preface" 41).This was no doubt why colors, Sassi shows, were so important a classificatory device in reference to humans (1–33; as Kuriyama shows it was in ancient China: 167–92). But if whoness was ineluctably social, in historically different ways, it was rooted physiologically in the natural, material world, *phusis*. Human community and enveloping physical actuality were equally basic. So, too, human nature's "ensouled" or spiritual actuality was an essential dimension of who-ness for centuries stretching from Plato to medieval and early modern selves. The poverty of the term, "spiritual," and breadth of the realities it names will become clear.

In 399 B.C., Socrates was prosecuted by the Athenian oligarchs and sentenced to death by poison. Feeling his body grow numb and the poison reach his heart, he famously addressed a friend: "Crito, we owe a cock to Asclepius. Be sure to pay, and do not neglect it" (*Phaedo* 118a). The usual scholarly gloss is that Socrates was asking that the customary offering be made to the divine physician in thanks for his recovery from illness. His celestial soul was leaving its earthly prison to return to the higher life whence it came. This interpretation aids my argument. Now, it faces Glenn Most's refutations: (1) Asclepius was everywhere praised not for bringing eternal life through death but for restoring worldly life; (2) nowhere else in this dialogue did Socrates "adopt the view that life is an illness or that death is its cure"; (3) once he came close to denying it. Further, (4) Socrates' words imply that Asclepius had *already* cured the illness. Since Socrates was alive when he spoke, his words could not refer to his own death (although he is giving directions for afterwards). Most notes that the only ill person mentioned, briefly but strikingly, is Plato.

He concludes that the cock is thanks for Socrates' principal pupil's recovery from an illness serious enough to keep him even from his teacher's death ("Cock" 101, 103–4, 106–10).

Plato, then, *may* not have been thinking of Socrates' soul's return to eternal life when he asked that Asclepius be thanked. He certainly was in the dialogue in general, meaning to convince his followers not to worry for his immortal soul. Indeed, the usual interpretation was only ever possible because of the idea that the soul at death was reabsorbed into universal soul/*psuchē* returning to the place it occupied before entering a human body. Death was not just an end to life. It was a *desired* end to life (cf. Cavarero, *In Spite* 23–26). Most acknowledges, too, that while Socrates might have been told of Plato's illness, he could not have known his recovery. His knowledge of *that*, unless we think Plato simply careless, could be justified only by the widespread belief "that those about to die possessed special clairvoyant and prophetic powers" ("Cock" 108). This belief was tied to the idea that at death, on the verge of rejoining universal *psuchē*, reuniting with cosmic *ousia*, the soul began to recover knowledge lost at birth into its body. This idea, too, lies in the usual interpretation of Socrates' request for a sacrifice to Asclepius: that he was stressing the importance to remember such things; recalling his theory, evoked earlier, that "our learning is nothing else than recollection [*anamnēsis*]" (*Phaedo* 72e). Hugh Tredennick has Socrates' last words, "alla apodote kai mē amelēsēte," as, "see to it, and don't forget" (*Collected Dialogues* 98), a translation losing the first verb's meaning of paying a debt, but catching the second's implication of remembering (an obligation). Memory was not only the grounding form of knowledge but soul's recovery of its essence in the knowledge inherent in it before embodiment. The old interpretation may be wrong about the meaning Plato gave to Socrates' request for a sacrifice but not in matching the request to the dialogue's overall representation of the nature of embodied soul, its relation to the universal and the connection of both to memory, knowledge and being. But what exactly could "soul's recovery of its essence" mean?

Plato initially explored the idea in this dialogue (on *psuchē* earlier, see Claus). Here, the thought may have been imprecise and argumentative, but it was unambiguous, as Socrates' request that Asclepius be paid made clear:

The lovers of knowledge perceive that when philosophy first takes possession of their soul it is chained and fastened to the body and compelled to regard realities not directly but through prison bars, and is wallowing in utter ignorance. And philosophy sees how the imprisonment is cleverly effected by the prisoner's own active desire, which makes him first accessory to his own imprisonment.

So philosophy urged the soul to ignore the senses, to turn inward "to collect and concentrate itself in itself and to trust nothing except itself and its own abstract understanding of abstract existence [*autēn de eis hautēn sullegesthai kai hathroizesthai parakeleuomenē, pisteuein de mēdeni allōi all' ē autēn hautēi, hoti an noēsei autē kath' hautēn auto kath' hauto tōn ontōn*]" (82d–83b). The repeated "auto-reflexion" of Plato's sentence signals both soul's self-contained nature and its being part of universal *psuchē*. That "soul" perhaps just named the tuning or adjusting of the elemental matters or qualities composing the body was an idea given short shrift by Socrates: divine soul must be tuned before entering the body (86b–95a). His point related, too, to the connection between the harmonious soul/body, the harmony of the universe (whence comes the soul), the well-ordered society and the training in *harmonia* central to the *Republic*.

For the essence of soul was life—as its name, *psuchē*, indicated, meaning something like "life principle" (105c–e). Soul was thus defined as the opposite of death, and immortal. Human body came alive only when soul entered, and remained so as long as soul was present. Soul was life itself: "Then, Cebes, it is perfectly certain that the soul is immortal and imperishable, and our souls will exist somewhere in another world." The argument of *Phaedo* melds words and things, but to be able to name *psuchē* as the vital principle shared by all living things did mark soul as some sort of substance, although without saying what sort it was. This has led some exegetes to see *Phaedo*'s treatment of the soul as ambiguous. It did not stop Socrates offering a cock to Asclepius.

The simply topological relation of soul to body—its being in it—received an ethical dimension in *Gorgias*. Body was "under the control" of soul (465d). Fettered though soul was for its lifetime, its control was not in doubt. Each was trained by its proper art. To the soul belonged the "political," divided into *mathēsis* and *mathēma*, a potential and an actual, "legislation" and "justice." The unnamed art of bodily welfare was also twofold, "gymnastics" and "medicine." Each's two parts overlapped (464b–c). Their goal was to free body and soul of the evils to which they were subject: in the soul's case, injustice, intemperance, ignorance, cowardice and such, greatest of all evils because of soul's primacy (477b–479c). Its order and regularity were called "lawfulness and law" because through them people were "orderly and law-abiding," living by "justice and temperance" (504d). As *Gorgias* developed, Socrates stressed the relation between the "singular" embodied soul and the ordered nature of an entire state and society (506e–510e), finally using his story of the last judgment of famed evil leaders to show that death was "nothing else but the separation from one another of two things, soul and body" (524b)—a case implicitly echoed in that of social dissolution. That the soul was an essential bond between universe, person and society was as clear here as it would be in the *Republic*.

Phaedrus further complicated these thoughts. It did so partly by defining *psuchē* otherwise than by its name's first meaning, yet starting from the same point that

all soul is immortal. For that which is ever moving is immortal. . . . Only that which moves itself, since it does not leave itself, never ceases to move, and this is also the source and beginning of motion for all other things which are moved. (*Phaedrus* 245c)

The determining idea of soul was now that it provided motion from within. Life followed:

For every body which is moved from without is soulless [*apsuchon*], but that which is moved from within itself is besouled [*empsuchon*], since of such essence is the nature of the soul [*hōs tautēs ousēs phuseōs psuchēs*]. (245e)

This argument of internal motion gave Plato his image of the soul as a charioteer guiding two horses, one orderly and one unruly, itself the rational power controlling good and bad, sensitive and appetitive powers (246a–b). More importantly, if for now less clearly, it began to shed light on what the universe might be to which soul returned after the death of its body.

For in some sense, prime motion, "source and beginning of motion for all other things which have motion," was one and whole. Soul in body might have been momentarily split from that source, but only to be reabsorbed into it: "All soul has the care of all that is soulless, and traverses the whole universe" (246b–c). Embodied souls came from this ensouled universe, which, because it was soul, was also "Truth." It was the place of Idea, and so whither the soul's nature as *phusis* and site of recollected knowledge most drew it (248b–c). The philosopher's soul was nearest, but all soul was by nature capable of recollecting and dwelling in truth, justice, temperance and beauty (250a–d). This Idea-oriented argument about the nature and experience of the soul furthered Plato's use of the same terms in *Gorgias* to set the soul in its socially prudential context.

In the *Timaeus*, we learn how the creator made the natural universe intelligent, its rational soul making it "good" and "beautiful," the irrational being necessarily imperfect:

On which account, as he fashioned the all, he put reason in soul and soul in body, so that the work he was making would be of its nature most beautiful and best. So then, by the likely explanation, we may say that the cosmos came into being as a living creature truly endowed with soul and reason by god's providence. (*Timaeus* 30b–c)

Drawing together fire and earth, water and air (31b–32c), god fashioned the universe's matter that was to be ensouled by the living essence already created from being, the same and the different, organized and built according to geometrical and musical proportions (35e–36b). The creator centered soul in the world's spherical body, "diffused it through the whole and also enclosed the whole in it." He gave this world "the movement suited to its spherical form" and made it "a sphere turning in a circle" (34a1–b5). The demiurge or creator worked, says T. M. Robinson, "with a sort of soul-stuff, which he cut up into pieces in such a way that they form a scale or ratio," made as "a long band or strip" which was "then split lengthwise into two halves." The extremities of these were then joined to make each a circle. "One of the circular strips he placed inside the other—but not in the same plane" (77; *Timaeus* 36ff.). The outer strip was "the Same," the inner "the Different" (36c6–7). Later, from impure matter, lesser souls were made and assigned each its star, "as it were a chariot" (41e). *Phaedrus'* image of soul in human body was thus set in a wider scale, tying microcosm to macrocosm, characterized by "soul-stuff" ordered by circular motion in many planes, from human ones to the world's, visible in equator and ecliptic, to those of the stars where each soul lived when not embodied (*Timaeus* 36–42; cf. Robinson 78–88). God sowed these souls "in the instruments of time" (42d), instructing the lesser gods to frame the mortal bodies that were those instruments, which they also made from fire, earth, water and air. In these, "subject to inflow and outflow, they fastened the orbits of the immortal soul" (43a), on the pattern of soul orbiting in and around the world's body.

Here in Plato's story is one of the much-denigrated moments of Greek misogyny. The bodies in which souls were sown followed a descending order according to a soul's mortal achievements: male human body, female human body and on to various brutes (42b–c). Plato repeated himself at the dialogue's end: "cowards or immoralists may rightly be supposed to have changed into women's nature at their second birth." This was obscurely taken to explain sexual love between men and women (90e–91d). *Phaedrus* explained a similar descending cast of bodies in terms of (presumably male) ranks: philosopher, lawful king, statesman or trader, athlete or physician, priest, poet, artisan, sophist and tyrant (248d–e). In *Republic* III (395d–396b), Socrates had women head, Froma Zeitlin writes, "the long list of undesirable models for men that descends to the servile, the buffoonish, the bestial, and the non-human" ("Playing" 85). Chapter 7 takes up this issue.

For present purposes, it suffices that the point of these incarnations was that whatever its acts and however affected by its body, soul was unchanged. So Plutarch accurately explained later that Homer's "admirable interpretation of the soul's condition," by depicting Circe as changing Odysseus' crew's bodies without altering their minds, confirmed "what Plato and Pythagoras said about the soul": that although

imperishable of nature and eternal, it is in no way impassible [*apathēs*] or immutable, but at the times of its so-called death and destruction it experiences an alteration and recasting which brings it a change of outward bodily shape. (*Moralia* fr. 200: 15.368/69)

Diversely as bodies were evaluated, rational soul's incarnations would have made no sense if its essence did not stay the same. What did change were its embodied ways of being *materially* in the world (entailing, we shall see, Cicero's third and fourth *personae*, as the soul's basic nature did his first and second). As to the person present through soul, therefore, this story did not contradict the argument of *Republic* V (and *passim* in *Laws*), holding men and women to the same rational training and achievement.

Rapidly describing mortal body, Plato paused to show that it, too, drew ultimately on some ethereal essence, its four material elements variants of primordial substance. This unitary view may have come from Heraclitus, who saw the elements circling into one another: "Fire lives earth's death, air lives fire's, water air's, and earth water's" (Diels-Kranz 1.168, fr.76). In Plato, elemental substance was more abstract than material (49b–51d), shading into Idea or Form, one of three foundational essences, with Substance or Copy and Receptacle or Space (51d–52b). These underlay the universe, preceding its actualization. They begot four fundamental geometrical forms, four elements, the basic qualities of hot and cold, wet and dry (which Heraclitus saw also flowing into one another: Diels-Kranz 1.179, fr.126), heavy and light, rough and smooth, and so the sensations bodies experienced. These framed the lesser gods' making of mortal bodies:

They took over from him the immortal principle of the soul and, imitating him, encased it in a mortal physical globe, with the entire body as vehicle. In this they made another sort of soul, mortal and subject to terrible and irresistible passions [*pathēmata*]: pleasure, greatest incitement to evil; pain, which deters from good; rashness and fear, two foolish counselors; obstinate anger and credulous hope. They mixed these with irrational sensation and all-daring lust, and so by necessary laws compounded humans. (69c–d)

This composition was regardless of sex, indeed, before sexuality. It was what it was to be a person.

"Mortal nature" was set in a part of the body separated from the rational divine, situated in the head and divided from the mortal by the neck. The highest part of the mortal soul, the sensitive, "endowed with courage, warmth and ambition," was placed above the diaphragm where it could heed reason and constrain desires and appetites. The heart was a guard, passing reason's messages quickly through the body. The lower part of the mortal soul, the appetitive, dealing with nutrition and other bodily needs, was set below the diaphragm. Because it was inaccessible to reason and subject to images and phantasms, the bittersweet liver became its guard, through which warning images and sensations were sent (69e–71b). Whether these were aspects of one soul or three kinds of soul working together, divine/immortal/rational, mortal/sensitive, mortal/appetitive or nutritive (89e–90d), was unclear, but did not affect this organization's consequence that the body's diseases were understood to result from disarray of physical elements and qualities (81e–86a), the soul's from bodily disarray impinging on it through the passions (86b–87b).

This creation story's power is its tight imbrication of spiritual, material and human. The "operator" enabling the passage between these "orbits," bridging whatever divide lay between them, was *psuchē*. In the *Timaeus*, the word *psuchē* kept layers of meaning: generalized life force, universal rational and human cognitive principles, rational, sensitive and nutritive drives in humans and so source of moral action. In these regards, embodied human *psuchē* was not specific to the particular human being whom it "occupied" for the time of a life. Vernant remarks:

> The *psuchē* is truly Socrates but not Socrates' "ego," not the psychological Socrates. The *psuchē* is in each of us an impersonal or suprapersonal entity. It is *the* soul in me and not *my* soul. This is true first because this soul is defined by its radical opposition to the body and everything related to it. . . . Next, this is also true because this *psuchē* is a *daimōn* in us, a divine being, a supernatural force whose place and function in the universe goes beyond our single person. (*Mortals* 330; cf. *Entre mythe* 71)

As the *Timaeus* had it, the number of souls eternally equaled that of stars. After death of the temporal form in which it was embodied, the soul returned to its star until reincarnated. The story's interest is less its detail than its emphasis on the soul's non-particularity, its *impersonality*.

The spiritual aspect of human nature was distinct from its physical envelope, although embodied in and tied to it in intimate ways. Human reason was thus *not* particular, but embedded in the ubiquitous, eternal reason of the universe. *Psuchē* bonded the human, the material and the universal, and attained its highest good through the thinking or remembering that drew it back to the ordered truths of the rational universe. Philosophy was thus where soul's attraction to the universal played most forcefully. But *psuchē*'s bonding function was never so limited, as the contemporary pragmatic Hippocratic corpus made clear and as Plato agreed.

In *Phaedrus*, Socrates told how Hippocrates held that rhetorician and physician needed equally broad philosophical knowledge to treat soul and body. As without knowledge of the human body in general you could not heal a particular, so you could not treat one soul without knowing the general nature of soul. Where a simple object was concerned, you needed to know its active and passive functions, what it acted on, what acted on it and how. In the case of a complex, you had to know its number of parts and for each the nature of its functions in the same way as for simples, then explaining the complex object as one whole (*Phaedrus* 270c–d). For the physician, soul, spirit, mind or life principle was part of body, an element in analysis and treatment of a complex whole, essential to practical considerations about the everyday welfare of the body in which it functioned. Plato could have been answering the apparently anti-theoretical doctor whose views now recur. I also note, here in passing, how Galen reiterated Plato's view 550 years later by citing this passage (*Therapeutic Method* 1.2, §§7–8: 8–9). In *The Therapy of Desire*, Nussbaum probes the "medical" activity of philosophy as therapy "for the soul in distress" as "an important tool both of discovery and of justification" for the major philosophical schools of Greco-Roman antiquity (14). Galen's citation of Plato reconfirmed the experience underlying everyone's work: that of the soul's place between the goods of everyday practical living and those of the wider material world and widest rational universe. From Galen through Arab thinkers and physicians to later western practitioners, this assurance was basic. While the soul's role and exact "status" may have changed, some such sense stayed generally constant to the idea and experience of personhood. But this is to outrun discussion.

The writings of the Hippocratic corpus I will mention are contemporary with the fictive and actual times of Plato's dialogues. Their treatment of *psuchē* and its related elements did not differ greatly from more abstract Platonic theses, although writers of the corpus otherwise disagreed considerably. We have seen that *Ancient Medicine*, generally dated between 420/10 and 390/85 (Jouanna, Introduction to *De l'ancienne médecine* 74–85), rejected outright the medical utility of hypotheses about the mingling of the four "qualities," heat, cold, moisture and dryness as futile for a basis of treatment, which had to rely, said the writer, on practice and experience. Such hypotheses were needless and risked impeding successful cure, which required comprehensible dialogue between doctor and patient. Ordinary people might be unable to find the nature and etiology of their own diseases but could easily learn when a doctor explained them and themselves intervene in like events, using their own experience and understanding. So, "if anyone departs from what is popular knowledge and does not make himself intelligible to his audience, he is not being practical" (*Hippocratic Writings* 71).

On the other hand, however scornful of the practical utility of these hypotheses, the writer did not deny that the body worked by "coction" and mixture. Although not writing directly of the four qualities, he held that the body's mixing of humors, *chumoi*, was in order when no single *dunamis* predominated ([*Works*] 1.50–52; *Writings* 81–83). The word *dunamis* meant "force," "strength," "potential." It was also, in Plato and the Hippocratics, a technical term for some of the "substances" to which this power attached, especially those whose terms are regularly translated as "dry" (or "solid"), "wet" (or "fluid"), "hot" and "cold." The substance did not possess *dunamis* as a specific way of affecting a body. Such apparent effect was "described simply as the presence of the strong substance, and the remedy for it was to 'concoct' the strong substance or otherwise to bring it into a harmless condition by 'blending' it with other substances" (Peck, Introduction to Aristotle's *Parts of Animals* 31). Such adjustment of different *dunameis* was what even this writer was addressing. His objection was not that the body was not so made, but that the "new method" of medicine, hypothesizing clear relations between these elements, too grossly simplified complex relations between these *dunameis* and the body's *schēmata*, its structures of shape and texture, forms and function of its parts or "organs" ([*Works*] 1.34, 52, 56; *Writings* 77, 83, 84).

Unwillingness to distinguish matter and quality apropos of these elemental *dunameis* was not limited to Plato and the Hippocratics (and maybe Heraclitus). It reflected recognition of the complex interlacing of the world and the human on which Aristotle also insisted, noting the ambivalence of these terms as he used them to speak of the first, fundamental nature of animal bodies: "composition out of what some call the elements, that is earth, air, water, fire. Perhaps, however, it would be more accurate to say composition out of the elementary forces [*ek tōn dunameōn*] . . . the moist and the dry, the hot and the cold" (*Parts of Animals* 646a14–17). It was not that "elements" and "qualities" *could* not be separated, but that these terms named different aspects of the behavior of natural substance (*ousia*) or matter, at least where human bodies were concerned. Galen would still spend many pages of his *De elementis* debating whether or how elements and qualities could be held to differ (6.1–8, 10: pp.102–23). Plato's derivation in *Timaeus* of both soul and elements of body from primordial *ousia* marked an analogous imbrication. The import of these ambiguities will become apparent.

The writer of *Ancient Medicine*'s argument that the mixing of *dunameis* was utterly complex did not disagree with that of physicians wanting to ground diagnosis and cure in reliably ordered knowledge of the human being. He claimed that no disease resulted simply from dominance of one element or quality and could be treated as if it did. He set up a straw man. No extant text makes so reductive a claim. Lloyd suggests that the author was attacking Philolaus, and proposes that the word *hypothesis* in the sense of "unproven assumption" came from mathematics before its use in Plato's *Meno* ("Who?"). This could explain the author's reductiveness, inapplicable to medical practice *or* theory, where people's physical constitution, life circumstance, local conditions, geographical situation and much more had to be taken into account. Even in the first taken alone, dominance of one "substance" or one humor had an effect that differed from person to person according to their compositions, endless other factors aside.

The schematizing of the human body and its relations came to act as ground and sounding-board for successful practice, but no ancient writer took it to give generalized, one-time answers. On the contrary, its difficulty lay in adjusting it to cases: hence the Hippocratics' innumerable case studies. That far more were of men than women is a problem in assessing women's place in Hippocratic medicine, especially as the disproportion seems due no more to theoretical premises than to proprieties keeping male doctors from attending female patients—although a quarter of the corpus deals with women's illness (King 1). Even so, efforts to adjust universal order to separate instance tell us much about the understanding of human being and its place in the world, as it confirms that Plato's views may readily be seen as a philosophical version of those of "the common people" (as the early Hippocratic named them), of patients "in conversation" with doctors. The interweaving of the human in the world that the doctors faced in seeking causes, courses and cures coincided with Plato's exploration, as Dean-Jones puts it (*Women's* 8), of the boundlessly intricate "relationship and interaction between the human microcosm and the macrocosm of Nature." We cannot here examine the entire Hippocratic corpus, but three typical and well-known writings provide something close to its shared ideas: *The Sacred Disease, The Nature of the Human* and *Airs, Waters, Places*. They take us from the complications of material context to the particularities of person (*not* their singularities) and the universalities of *psuchē*.

Airs, Waters, Places told the aspiring doctor that knowledge of the seasons and their differences, of the winds (general in a country and specific to a locale), of situation of town or other place of habitation, of soil and waters typical to the place of practice, and of people's drinking, eating, associating, working and exercising habits, was essential for diagnosis, prognosis and cure. Beyond close study of these matters, the physician had to know what sorts of epidemics were prevalent in any place and at what time of year, what might be effects of change in life style, how the seasons progressed in the particular place and when the "stars" rose and set. Knowledge of astronomy was important because sidereal motions affected weather and season, in turn affecting diseases, their prevalence, nature and course.

The writer then provided examples of relations between geographical setting, weather, geological situation, general nature of the inhabitants of particular sorts of locales, styles of life, qualities of mind, states of body and the various upsets of temperament one could expect. A given geography and climate were thus linked to production of phlegm, the general flabbiness of mind and body that accompanied it and predominance of certain illnesses. The same went for bile and blood, although this writer left connections between the many factors rather vague as to their relation to particular humors, if not their vast complexity. He next emphasized details of differing effects of winds, waters and places, before ending with an analysis of racial differences found between peoples of "Europe" and "Asia" (Minor) due to these geographical, meteorological and geological variations. In this writing, contrary to *Ancient Medicine*, the qualities of cold and hot, moist and dry played a predominant role.

Airs, Waters, Places did not concern individual cases. But it shows how embedded the person was in the physical, material world. Not only bodily well- and ill-being depended on surroundings that stretched from immediate setting and local custom to geographical, climatic and astronomical context. So did mind and its sensitive and rational powers. One could not know their operations and conditions without the detail of the narrow and wide worlds from which they were inseparable. These bonds were no less at issue in the many case studies. While those entitled *Epidemics* described diseases suffered by individuals, they always began, however rapidly, by setting the person in a locale and explaining seasonal and other conditions. This was because, by nature, the elements of any human body were in contagious flow with the *same* elements in the world: a person could thus communicate his or her disease directly to the air (say), whence it could communicate equally directly with other persons. This provided an epidemiology that lasted even beyond the European sixteenth century, explaining, for instance, measures like those of sealing up in their houses victims of bubonic plague and their households, cutting off, it was thought, all contiguity.

Such a view was expressed even more clearly in what seems to have been a work aimed at a lay audience, perhaps a public talk on *The Nature of the Human*. This work's author also rejected simple explanations for the human body, insisting that its complexity lay in its constitution from mixture of blood, phlegm, yellow bile and black bile, although it is unclear whether each of these mixed the qualities of hot and cold, moist and dry, or was identified with one of them (the consensus held that while an element and a quality predominated in any humor—as in the body's temperament as a whole—each was a mixture). Body and mind were in good health "when these constituent substances are duly proportioned to one another in strength and quantity, and are well mixed" ([*Works*] 4.10; *Writings* 262). Pain and illness were produced by imbalance in these substances. The tendency of one to predominate was much affected by the seasons.

In winter, phlegm was at highest level, and while it stayed high in spring, blood also increased, doing so yet more in the summer, as cold retreated further and rains increased. As summer advanced, bile began to increase, although blood remained strong. As summer drew to autumn, bile came to predominate, at first yellow, then black. This balance of qualities and substances, we already know, was no less affected by diet, air and general "regimen" ([*Works*] 4.23–27; *Writings* 264–67). The last included all the affecting events and conditions we have seen. This is clear in the work entitled *Peri diaitēs*, concerning way or style of life—or, as it is translated, *Regimen*. Here, after again insisting that food, drink, exercise, climate, geography and the rest combined the different forces of wet and dry, cold and moist, the author argued in detail how all of these (especially nutrition), along with bathing, oiling, vomiting, repose, exercise and everything else in one's place, time and habits were inseparable aspects of who one was and how one lived ([*Works*] 4.224–447). This applied to women and men. Their regimen might differ, insofar as at least in rich households women would in theory be indoors, but her various business and labors, we learn from Xenophon's *Oeconomicus*, also served to keep the body healthy.

This intimate relationship between the human and the world was also emphasized by the writer of *The Sacred Disease*, a work attacking popular (and medical) beliefs about epilepsy, asserting that it should be understood not as resulting from divine intervention but as due entirely to physical causes. After noting how human constitution (here, mental) and the surrounding natural world were bound together, their balance playing off each other ([*Works*] xi.21–23: 2.162; xvi.1–46: 170–72), the author then described the physical situation of the brain in the body and went on to emphasize its centrality to all activities properly and particularly human:

It ought to be generally known that from the brain, and from the brain only, come our pleasures, joys, laughter and amusement, as well as our griefs, pains, anxieties and tears. Through it, especially, we think, see, hear and distinguish the ugly from the beautiful, bad from good, pleasant from unpleasant, in some cases judging by custom, in others by perceptions of utility. (*[Works]* xvii.1–9: 2.174)

The brain's proper functioning was upset and became unhealthy when it suffered from abnormal warmth or coldness, moisture or dryness, or any other unnatural "affection [*pathos*]." The dampness of phlegm and differing powers of bile and blood had their distinct symptoms, not only their precise forms of madness but their exact *pathēmata* as well.

All these things showed the brain to be "the most powerful organ of the human body." It was the "messenger of intelligence," which derived from the amount of air (*aēr*) the body took in. This went first to the brain to leave its fullest vigor, enabling consciousness and intelligence, before being distributed by the brain to the rest of the body. If air were to go first to the body it would become impure before it could give the brain its keenness: "Wherefore I assert that the brain is the interpreter of consciousness," the author repeated, dismissing the common view that the diaphragm served that purpose (*[Works]* xix.1–21, xx.1–6: 2.178). The writer shared this view with Plato (but not with Aristotle).

Air was one manifestation of the life force in nature and the universe (and see Kuriyama 233–72). The vigor with which it informed the mind was partly that life force; which was why the author concluded that no specific intervention was needed to explain the sacred disease. The flow of vital force *was* presence of the "divine." This, too, went back to Presocratics, Anaximenes writing: "As our soul, being air, holds us together, so breath and air surround the whole universe" (Diels-Kranz 1.95, fr.2). In that sense, all illness was divine and human, caused by imbalances in nature, *phusis* and the human constitution (*[Works]* xxi.2–8: 2.182). This explains why a Hippocratic work on dreams construed them as the soul's recovery of usual waking functions: clear, they indicated good health; confused, illness and disorder (*[Works]* 4.420–47). During sleep, the soul flowed through the body, giving clear or unclear sight like the pure or impure air which in some way it was. Nearly two millennia later, Petrarch exactly echoed this view in the *De vita solitaria* (I.ii: 318).

We find ourselves back at Plato's union of spiritual, human and material. In the Hippocratic works, too, rational soul was united inextricably with the physical world and with the vital natural force setting life in the universe. A person was inseparable from the complex contexts, potentially unlimitedly varied, in which it was enlaced. The human person experienced being, *was* a person and a human in virtue of its surroundings. Illness, therefore, was not just imbalance in the body, but between the human and its whole environment. As Pigeaud remarks, the goal of the successful medical cure was to "reintegrate the illness (difference) into the cultural and historical process" (11).

In the frame of their differing goals, then, the one seeking philosophical understanding, the others practical treatment and prevention of illness, the view of being human offered by the Hippocratics and Plato was essentially one. Medicine wanting cures and philosophy the highest good sought to overcome a basic imbalance of the ensouled body. Set between universe and nature, every human's healthy balance was always tenuous in the wider scheme of existence. These writings set the relation between soul and body as firstly "agonistic," even if only potentially. This has stayed a constant in western thought to the present day; including in the post- (not *propter*) "Cartesian" mind/body division—which for Descartes was never his final thinking on the matter, as my final chapters show (and see Reiss, "Denying"). Perhaps we are seeing, also, processes of taming that divisive agon (perhaps just displaced, since western tragedy, for example, is a "cultural instrument" embodying this agon and becoming a way to urge it on other cultures: Reiss, *Against*, chap. 3).

For we see how the distinction between outer and inner that Vernant urges needs emphases that modern westerners may see as quite undermining it, or anyway making it more ambivalent. Those airs and waters that flowed into, around and through body and mind, to say nothing of all the other manifestations and aspects of nature which lodged them, mean that this outer/inner distinction must be unsettled. Above all, nature and universe (by definition) preceded the singular human being and person, *making* and giving it life from outside. That, of course, is not quite right either. But the point remains that principles of life and intellect entered body and mind from without. Personal and interpersonal understanding, I quoted Vernant, worked in the same way, "each person exist[ing] as a function of others in the gaze and through the eyes of others"—which also brings us back to *phantasia* as receptor and interpreter of images. People related to one another, that is, as the natural world and the universe related to them.

The gaze and the discourse enabling cure or understanding to occur through the exchange between doctor and patient can be seen, as well, to take us to the sort of pragmatic interests emphasized by Plato's most renowned student. Son of a doctor who doubtless shared the usual bent of medical philosophy and practice, Aristotle adjusted his teacher's views

to such pragmatism, even as he kept many of their seemingly less pragmatic aspects: although as we try to know an unfamiliar idea of personhood we shall see "seemingly" as the appropriate qualification. To reach
this idea and get at least a general sense of the adjustment, I highlight the
De anima, partly because it was a work that eventually acquired a huge
and varied readership in the early modern era (varied if only because of
differences in its many translations), becoming a fundamental text from
the late middle ages. It was kept alive by endless commentaries (see
Cranz). But it was also vital in the Aristotelian corpus as the jointure between the physical, biological and human sciences. Not seldom it edged
on metaphysics, proposing at its outset that "knowledge of the soul" contributed to those of Truth in general and Nature in particular. For the
soul was "in a sense the principle of animal life" (Aristotle, *On the Soul*
402a5–7).

So the first issue raised as problematic was exactly that of the relation
between soul and body. Aristotle asked whether the soul was singular or
plural and whether "affections of the soul [*ta pathē tēs psuchēs*]" depended on the compound of soul and body or whether any were "peculiar to the soul by itself" (403a3–5). If the latter was never the case, then
equally one could never consider embodied soul separately from ensouled
body, not, anyway, in regard to humans while they lived. The Philosopher
immediately asserted that the soul could have no affections separate from
the body (403b18–19).

Aiming his first question at incarnate physical being, Aristotle thus
started from the basic agonistic relation just recorded. And because he
asked his question less in terms of philosophical abstraction than in those
of physical analysis, he began by considering soul as already present in
and united with body. Plato had begun with world soul and its creation
into body. That soul, Taylor observes, scarcely needed body at all (146).
Aristotle began with ensouled body. Too, although he got to something
like "soul-in-body" (not always unlike some form of rational mind), he
could never think it wholly out of body—any more than he could think
person out of social, "political," context. Soul and person were ineluctably characterized by their surroundings. Logic might let one consider soul apart, not nature. Soul and body, spirit (life) and matter could
doubtless be conceived separately in theory; they could not be examined
in such a way, since no one could so experience them in life: which helps
explain why Aristotle and many others ascribed quasi-vital properties to
inanimate things (see, e.g., Arthur John Brock's comment in Galen, *On
the Natural Faculties* 3n1).

Aristotle broached his problem, as usual, by examining stock views of
the soul's nature, to reject them outright or make them so doubtful as to

necessitate complete reexamination. Everyone, he averred, agreed that soul had "movement, sensation and incorporeality" (405b11–12). Beyond that, dissent was near total: soul being understood as atoms, air, fire, water or ceaseless flux. Aristotle first attacked the areas of consent, two of which anyway required dubious premises. Firstly, soul's "sensation" clearly needed bodily senses. Secondly, whatever the nature of elemental fire, water or air, atoms were corporeal, attenuated as philosophers might make them for argumentative purpose. The claims about sensation and incorporeality actually fell before Aristotle's basic contention that the soul had no motion of its own separate from that of the body in which it was (405b27–407b26). Sensation was a kind of movement produced in the soul via the body. To the extent it needed reminiscence it was in the soul, but each needed the other and their action depended on their union (408b2–17). Corporeality was an inseparable aspect of the body to which soul was united. To suppose that soul was just its *opposite*, even to put the issue in such agonistic terms, was to beg the question, taking soul a priori for what body was not. Like Plato, Aristotle also rejected the idea that soul was just the name given to body's harmony (407b27–408a30). Finally, he dismissed all the ideas about the soul's elemental composition (409a31–411b30).

Given all this, wrote Aristotle, one had to start over. Of whatever exists, there was one sort of thing defined as "substance," *tēn ousian*. Such *ousia* was divided into three: matter, considered as such and not as any particular; shape or form/essence, by which particularity was established; the compound of the two. As such, matter was potentiality (*dunamis*); form or essence was actuality (*entelecheia*); and actuality was twofold, for example, as knowledge (*epistēmē*) and as its exercise or as reflection on it (*theōrein*) (412a6–10). People thought of bodies first as substances (*ousiai*). Of bodies, some did not have life, others did: with auto-nutrition, growth and decay. Such a body was "not something predicated of something else. Rather [was] it that of which something was predicated [*hupokeimenon*]" (412a18–20). As matter, that is, it was *subject* (*subiectus*) *to* attributes that (in this case) made it *actual*.

This passage has proven difficult for translators, who always give *hupokeimenon* as "subject." Typical are sentences like Lawson-Tancred's: "the body, far from being one of the things said of a subject, stands rather itself as subject and is matter" (157). Hett translates: "the body is not something predicated of a subject, but rather is itself to be regarded as a subject, *i.e.*, as matter" (67–69); while Smith has: "for the body is the subject or matter, not what is attributed to it" (1.656). To imply that body, matter, was an agent or at all *active* at best misleads: "Ou gar esti tōn kath' hupokeimenou to sōma, mallon d' hōs hupokeimenon kai hulē." Body was the kind of *ousia* that could *receive* attributes, be "subject to" them. Hence, Aristotle went on, soul had to be *ousia* in the sense of being "the form of a natural body potentially having life." Such "*ousia* was actuality, *entelecheia*," and soul was "the actuality of the body thus described" (412a20–22). In this sense, soul no more realized its actuality separate from body than body realized its potentiality without soul. And soul was the first kind of actuality indicated before, analogous to presence of knowledge rather than its exercise, like Plato's *mathēsis* and *mathēma*: "Thus the soul is the first kind of actuality of a natural body potentially possessing life" (412a27–28). Soul, as Nussbaum sums up Aristotle's view, was "the form of the living body" and it was "wrongheaded even to *ask* whether the soul and the body are one" (*Aristotle's* 68). We shall soon see why the explanation necessarily took this form. It may here seem especially complex because it was tied to a quite different idea and experience of mind and person from anything now familiar to western people. To speak of "body" *or* "soul" as *subject* is to distort that notion and experience toward this later familiarity.

Aristotle thus concluded, Nussbaum adds, that "soul and body ma[d]e a living creature," and that at least some of the soul's parts were inseparable from the body's. Such were those where "their actuality [was] that of the parts themselves," like vision of the eye. Some parts might not be so imbricated, but to know it needed further inquiry. For as the body's form, soul was best defined as "the set of vital capacities, the functional organization, in virtue of which [the living creature] lives and acts" (*Aristotle's* 71). In the meantime, said Aristotle, this rough definition sufficed to enable a closer look at what one could now analyze as manifestations of soul in body (413a4–10). It allowed, indeed, an understanding of the plurality of the soul's functions and of which were needed for each kind of living creature.

Many different functions let one call a thing living, among them intellect, perception, motion, certain sorts of rest, and movement associated with nutrition, growth and decay. The last was why plants were said to be alive, for their power of auto-nutrition pointed to their potential (*dunamin*) and principle for increase and decrease in all spatial directions. This power of auto-nutrition could be separated from all other powers, not they from it. Auto-nutrition was basic to all living things (413a25–34). After this was sensation, whose possession defined a living thing as an animal. Of the sensitive (or perceptive) functions, touch was fundamental, shared even by the lowliest of animals and separable from the other senses as the nutritive power was separable from the other powers (413b2–6). This suggested that the functions of living bodies could be set in an order running from the minimum for *any* life to those present in living creatures whose complexity increased with the number of functions present, "earlier" ones being progressively necessary to "later" ones. So soul could be considered the origin of all the phenomena Aristotle had first named and was, indeed, defined by them: nutritive, sensitive and intellectual powers, and movement.

Aristotle used his analysis to start answering the questions raised in the first book of the De anima, where he had rejected or doubted his predecessors' views. One such question was whether these powers were each a separate soul or parts of one. Another was how far any of them could be separated from the body. In the case of the nutritive, this query answered itself, since only bodies fed and reproduced. Clearly, too, sensation and movement were inseparable from the body. What had sensation had to have imagination (store of sensed images), as well as appetite, motion, pleasure, pain and desire (413b21–24). The cases of mind (nous) and thinking power (theōrētikē dunamis) were less clear, although at first sight they seemed distinct from body (413b25–29). In the maybe later (Nussbaum thinks: 10–12) De motu animalium, Aristotle was more certain: "the [necessary] movers of the animal are reasoning and phantasia and choice and wish and appetite. And all of these can be reduced to thought and desire" (700b17–19).

In De anima, this first step in the analysis of what living physical bodies did in actuality brought him to state more firmly that "the soul [was] that whereby we primarily live, perceive and think," and then to reestablish his earlier complex explanation: "it follows that soul must be the notion and form and not the matter or subiectus [hulē . . . kai to hupokeimenon]" (414a14–15). Matter, he repeated, was potentiality, form actuality, the first two sorts of substance, ousia, of which the third was compound. Now, he could suggest something of the nature of the compound about which he had earlier remained silent:

Since the composite here is the ensouled thing, the body is not the actuality of the soul but the soul is the actuality of some body. Hence the rightness of the view that soul is not without body, but is not a body. It is not body, but is relative to body. That is why it is in a body, and a body of a particular kind. (414a17–23)

No doubt this lacked precision. But Aristotle confronted a sort of Catch 22: trying to understand and define an entity the nature and status of whose very existence was unclear. Further knowledge of soul/body required that selfsame knowledge: the play between observation of soul/body functions, analysis of efficient powers and understanding of causes was delicate.

So for the moment, Aristotle continued analyzing the enumerated powers, nutritive, appetitive, sensitive, locomotive and intellective, plants having only the first, animals at least the sensitive as well. But any creature possessing the sensitive had to have the appetitive, which included desire, passion and wish. For anything perceived produced corresponding pleasure or pain, and to these in turn corresponded desire (or hatred). This was so even for animals with the minimal sense of touch: through this they sensed the dry, wet, hot and cold on which all living things were nurtured, and for these they felt the desires called hunger and thirst (414a32–b9). Imagination's status remained unclear and questions about it had to await, thought Aristotle, a later stage of analysis. He did reassert that only humans and beings superior to them had powers of thought and intellect (414b19). These were essential features of the human's ability to achieve its *logos*, the fullest realized "form or functional organization" of its species and of what it was to be human and not some other kind of creature (Nussbaum, *Aristotle's* 78. Cf. 61).

At the same time, he definitively answered one of his earlier questions: the diverse powers were not several souls but one. Just as more complicated geometric figures contained simpler ones, so more complex soul contained logically earlier functions: a triangle was in a rectangle as nutritive power was in sensitive (414b20–32). This answer corresponded, as well, to the concept of actualization of which we have seen Aristotle gradually making more: each more complex soul corresponded to the actualizing of the potentiality of the particular body to which it related. That was why he immediately explained that the only way to analyze, compose, the real nature of body/soul was to study the exercise of its functions, resolving them into its powers (415a14–20). Only so could one achieve the delicacy needed to attain knowledge of an unknown actual: "resolving" its visible functions into its inherent powers, "composing" the latter into "causes" explaining the being of the soul and the body to which it inseparably related.

One looked, that is to say, at the second kind of actuality, the *ousia* corresponding to the exercise of knowledge, in order to find the first kind, that matching the presence of knowledge. By this means one attained knowledge of the nature of the soul and the sort of living body peculiar to it (415a14–20). But as he repeated that the nutritive was "the first and most widely shared power of the soul, through which all have life" (415a23–25), he added a new and important rider. All living things had this power of nutrition and reproduction so that all might "share in the eternal and the divine [*tou aei kai tou theiou*]" as "all creatures [strove] to do" (415a29–b1). The grounding actuality of soul, as was explicit in Plato and implicit in the Hippocratic *Sacred Disease*, was its yearning toward the eternal and universal. The full weight of this assertion in establishing the meaning of personhood and grasping its experience will be clear at the end of this exploration of the *De anima*. We shall then see it pattern everything from notions we tend to identify as pertaining to the "will" to experiences of knowledge and action, as well as simple questions of being with others in the world.

The idea of soul as body's actuality in these ways offered Aristotle another recapping halt. Whether such pauses and repetitions are his, a student's or a follower's does not matter. Actually, the more these views represent consensus and not one person's finding, the stronger the support they give the thought that they express, in philosophical vocabulary, habitual experience, familiar feelings, ordinary sensibilities:

The soul is the cause and first principle of the living body. . . . The soul is the cause of the body alike in all three senses we have defined. For the soul is the cause as source of movement, as end and as substance [*ousia*] of the ensouled body. It is this last because for all things their *ousia* is the cause of their being, and living is the being of living things, and of their being and living the soul in them is cause and principle. Again, the actuality is the essential notion or formula [*logos*] of whatever potentially is. (415b9–15)

Soul was thus formal cause. It was also efficient cause of locomotion and change of state (415b22–27). It was final cause in that "all natural bodies [were] instruments/organs of the soul." They existed for the sake of the soul in the sense that soul itself was focus of natural body's functions and that they carried out its purposes (415b16–21). Aristotle had already made "the eternal and the divine" a first desire of all living things, and so the soul's first purpose.

In the *De anima*, Aristotle found no need to supply any force to link motions of passible soul to material and physical activities of body. In the *De motu*, however, after repeating the thought that the soul originated all motion in body, he explained that for soul to do so, another unmoved mover was needed to explain, for instance, simultaneous movements that did not simply annul each other (by applying equal and opposite force). Living bodies had to have a "secondary" mover called "connate [*sumphuton*] pneuma*" from which they drew "strength [*ischun*]" (*De motu* 703a1–9). Although Aristotle never fully explained the operation or nature of this "innate breath," it was also important in the *De generatione* and *Parva naturalia*. In the *De motu*, he set it near the heart, whence it operated to let functions of mind effect material motion, being one with "the *archē* of life-activities" (703a11) but enabling these "mental" processes to move physical ones. Elsewhere he contended that *pneuma*'s vital heat was what transmitted sensitive soul to the fetus, *pneuma* then being like "the element of the stars" (*De generatione* 736b37). The exact status of this element, ether (only here, once, did Aristotle link it to *pneuma*), was unclear, but the next chapters show the immense importance it was to acquire in the tradition, from Stoics to Avicenna and into the European early modern era.

At this point in the *De anima*, Aristotle returned to his analysis of the soul's functioning, applying the actuality argument to sensation. Again using the analogy of knowledge, he explained that particular knowledge and knowing how to order knowledge were both potential: the ongoing exercise of knowledge was alone actual. The only flaw in this analogy, he said, was that knowledge was actualized by an inner power (applying the analogy to the soul was what made *pneuma* necessary in the *De motu* as, exactly, that "inner power"), whereas the sensitive power could be activated only from without: a sensible object had to be present, and some medium, whether air, fire, water or even earth (in the case of touch, for example), had also to be activated (416b32–424b18). Information accumulated by the senses then entered into contact with the soul's other powers, judging or practical thinking and understanding or speculative thinking, both divisible into several activities and separate from but connected to imagining, as the place and practice of calling up images (427b19–20) and "a movement resulting from the actual exercise of a sensation" (429a1–2), all three likewise separate from but connected to perceiving or sensing (425b12–429a9). So Aristotle finally reached the rational soul, thinking mind itself.

He began by urging that since all and anything could become object of thought, mind was nothing but a pure capacity to receive: "that in the soul which thinks is, before it thinks, not in actuality any existing thing, and so cannot reasonably be mixed with body" (429a21–25). "It was therefore good," he added, "to say that the soul is the place of forms, at least so far as its thinking is concerned and as the forms occupy it potentially, not actually" (429a28–30). This apparent detachment from body was unique to thought, a power that further differed from sensation in being unable to be overwhelmed by stimuli, which just pushed it to further accomplishment (429a29–b4). Mind in this sense was what it was because it became all things. But in another sense, it made all things (430a10–25): it "is separable, impassible [*apathēs*], unmixed, for it is in its essence activity" (430a17–18). So, he ended:

Actual knowledge is identical with its object. In the individual, potential knowledge is prior, but absolutely it is not. Mind does not sometimes think and sometimes not. When separated it is alone just what it is, and this is deathless and eternal, although we do not remember because while this [last] is impassible [our] passible mind is perishable, but without [impassible mind] nothing thinks. (430a20–25)

Mind was arena and form of both kinds of "art" discussed at the beginning of the *Nicomachean Ethics*: those that taught how to produce something else and those whose end was themselves. It was equivalent to the "principal" of all, since it contained within it the final cause of its own striving, the divine and eternal. It did so because it was both separate and not separate from body. Embodied and perishable, it still shared in reason and always bore the hope of recovering through memory something of the highest good represented by the perfection of eternal and impassible soul. United with body, it suffered all those ill and good attributes to which body was subject, but its *ousia* was that of the eternal. The highest capacity of mind, then, like *phantasia*, was simultaneously active and passive. This combination was the essence of *passibility*, that "reactive" nature to which I will return at this chapter's end as fundamental to who-ness, and which underlies the rest of this book's analyses.

But I must return to the active mind as auto-existent, eternal *ousia*. This substance was able first to think of "indivisibles," forms about which issues of truth and falsehood did not arise. Although the point was unclear, these seem to have been thoughts always present in deathless and eternal impassible intellect. Only once the mind started to compound thoughts did matters of truth and falsehood, of growth and decay, one may say, become an issue (430a26–29). The compounding of thoughts moved intellect ever further from the eternal into the material, for it was an operation of passible and perishable embodied mind. The analysis corresponded closely to Plato's narrative in the *Timaeus* of the abstract-becoming-concrete "divisions" of originary *ousia*. For Aristotle, the soul— rational, sensitive and nutritive—was "all existing things": sense was the form of sensible things as thought the form of forms (432a2–3). But it was only potentially so. To actualize it would require thought to pass into the realm of impassible eternal intellect, able to be conceived but never experienced (in life), although it was the ultimate object of embodied soul's striving.

How are we to understand all this? Perhaps modern westerners grasp such ideas of mind and person more in the fact of their difference than the how of their experience. This trouble need not be everyone's. Experiences of mind, person and society usual among peoples named in my Introduction, and analogous ones elsewhere, however unlike those just described, nonetheless share traits. Greek experiences of mind and person are one of those mirages glimpsed before, distorted by the milieus through which they have passed. Even so, beyond diversities, we have seen much that makes this experience of who-ness. If we cannot live or feel *of* the experience, we can feel *for* it. Hippocratics, Plato and Aristotle pondered essentially one idea of being, life and who-ness. Assumptions converged. Primary was that of the person as enlaced in associative life, from the rational eternal *living* of the universe to political and social community, from humanity to physical environment. Neither experience nor thought split these surroundings from the person. Parmenides and Empedocles already (Diels-Kranz 1.238–39, 242–43, frs.8, 12; 1.324, 327, frs.28, 35), Sophocles maybe, certainly Plato, and others later, called them literally *circles* or *spheres* that began with the Demiurge's "eternal auto-rotation" (*Statesman* 269e5), continued in the circles and musical harmonies of stars and planets (*Republic* 616–17) and through world and human souls, forms and motions, to include every *circum*stance that was what it was to be human. Fulfillment of human *logos* depended on all these.

Oedipus, I offered, perhaps felt his breach with them as disarticulating his "spheres" of being, again literally. Did the halo-like helmet crests around Athena's divine head and another's heroic one, the laurel around Hercules', and the several circular shields on a mid-sixth-century Athenian krater depicting a group of warriors at ease in the world, limn that experience—especially as the krater's other side gave the world awry of Apollo and Artemis slaying Niobe's children (Figure 4)? Many similar artifacts may do likewise. Marthe Collinet-Guérin sees in the halo an "emanation of [the stars'] refulgent atmosphere" of the divine (191), a symbol uniting "the divinity with the human being by a bond at once supernatural and natural, invisible and visible" (694). Imaging the sun's light and (soul-like) auto-moving power (34), it also evinced the sun's relation to eye and vision that we saw earlier. Besides the divine, it marked "physical energy" and "moral force" (323), reflecting material and social circumstances. As to the last, iconographic ties of halo to Greco-Roman ivy and laurel fillets are shown by Adolf Krücke, Walter Weber and especially Marianne Bergmann, notably on round coins, with their wreathed and nimbused heads and circling of letter, number and image. The circularity of vases, urns, kraters, bowls, amphoras and their shaping of the flow of form and figure possibly made them particularly appropriate media to represent these imbricated relations.

These relations are clear in the *Nicomachean Ethics* or the *Politics*, showing persons always already rooted in the social and political. Victor Ehrenberg writes of people so experiencing life that "in a Greek Polis no citizen can be said to have been a private" person (*People* 26)—nor any non-citizen. In all these writings, *ēthos*, "character," was as much enlaced with social custom, habit, *nomos*, history and place as bodily welfare. Not only were the moral excellences essential to the good life impressed on humans like all passibly received affects, because "we are adapted by nature to receive them," but citizens (women and men) were made good by being educated into appropriate "habits": "it is in this that a good [political] constitution differs from a bad one" (*Nicomachean Ethics*

Figure 4. Niobid krater (Athens, mid–sixth century B.C.). Musée du Louvre, Paris. Photo: Département des Antiquités Grecques, Etrusques et Romaines, cratère G341, face A.

1103a25–b7). As habits (*hexeis*) were *received* by a human, so was their excellence, trained into one by the city (1106a12). This gave doing and identifying voluntary and/or involuntary acts their lawful and moral order: human *prohairesis* educated to the good (1109b30–1113a22).

To be excellent as a person inevitably involved "excellence as a citizen and *vice versa*" (MacIntyre 141). The *phronēsis*, practical wisdom or prudence, into which one was trained, "accorded with right rule [*logos*]" because *logos* was common to the well-ordered city as to the world *and* the purpose of human life (*Nicomachean Ethics* 1144b23). Excellence varied following people's different roles in the city. Being passibly trained to it did not. In *De motu*, Aristotle internalized this thought that persons were trained from without to and by the city:

We should consider the organization of an animal to resemble that of a city well-governed by laws. For once order is established in a city, there is no need of a separate monarch to preside over every activity; each person does his own work as assigned, and one thing follows another because of habit. (703a29–34)

The experience of the human as embedded in surroundings, here political and social, to which it reacted passibly, could hardly get a more dramatic image. But the same conception and experience were evident in physical works like *Parts of Animals*, which began with a surely direct reference to the *De anima*: "If the form of the living being is soul, part of soul or something that without soul cannot exist . . . , then it is the natural philosopher's business to inform himself about the soul" (641a18–22). "Body as a whole," the text later added, "must exist for the sake of some complex action." Since soul was the body's form, this could only mean—by the arguments of the *De anima*—that "in some way the body exists for the soul, and the parts of it each to some work for which it is naturally adapted" (645b16–17). The relation was again that of "reactive" passibility.

Reading this work of biology, we recall that the soul whose working was the final cause of body's existence had its own finality to share in the eternal, divine, rational universe itself. That this understanding of the soul had to underpin natural philosophy and be present in its explorers' minds was explicit. So, for example, Aristotle's discussion of the three levels of the composition of animals must be seen as engaged in this context. To speak of their composition from elements or qualities, from earth, water, air or fire, or from dry, wet, cold or hot (646a14–18), was also to set these events in the wider universal context which Plato had explored in the *Timaeus*, which had put these elements in god's hands simultaneously with mind. But as Aristotle immediately went on to examine the other kinds of composition (of the homogeneous parts of animals, bone, flesh . . . , and of their heterogeneous parts, face, hands . . .), a reader or listener had to recall, as well, the physical and material surroundings explored in places like the Hippocratic writings.

All this says that understanding and experiencing a person's acts and thinking were far from modern western ones. We now see, for instance, that what has often been called the "passive" functioning of *phantasia* with which this chapter began, typified all activities of embodied soul. The very word *passive* is caught—with its opposite, *active*—in modern notions of agency and will. We better use the old term of art, *passible*: Latin *passibilis*, rendering Greek *pathētikos*. These words named any aspect of the soul able to be affected by something. Latin distinguished the realm where they applied from that of the active/passive. These last terms and their opposition described aspects of the world as Aristotle divided it into *energeia* and *entelecheia* (activity and fulfillment), and *dunamis*, itself divided into active and passive—*potentia activa vel passiva*, wrote Aquinas (*Summa theologiae* 1a.77.3). They did not readily apply to humans, in whom active and passive intertwined to compose their *reactive* passible nature—for which Aquinas used the terms *passio* and *passibilis* (1a.97.2). These transcribed Aristotle's words, and modern translators falsify in using "passive" for both *passivus* and *passibilis* (still an issue in Descartes, whose *passio* is too often translated as "passivity"). *Passions*, or affections, were motions perturbing the embodied soul (to use Cicero's term for them: *perturbationes*). But as Aristotle showed in the *De anima*, *every* aspect of that soul was passible. Thus was it distinguished from eternal, universal/divine *im*passible soul.

Passibility was the fundamental nature of the human being *as* human. Its relation to the endlessly multiple matter, qualities and events of its surroundings—divine, animate, social, physical—was one of being always and constantly affected by simply being in them, more exactly, being *of* them. *Passibility* names the relation as *passivity* does not. And because it was *of* them, effects were not one way. As body and soul changed each other in respect of the passions, so passible mind was somehow *with* impassible mind, the living body affected its physical surroundings as they affected it (as a diseased person infected air which infected others, producing an epidemic), unhealthy people showed unhealthy environs (and vice versa) but as part of them, a person's *ethos* was inseparable from social *nomos*. Action and passion were essentially interactive. *Passibility* named a different experience of the human in the world from those familiar in the modern west. This is doubtless why we no longer have the word. So the experience and ideas it names help us understand what otherwise seem the curiosities of ancient notions of "will" (the term is ours, not theirs), reason, intention and action, as well as of the nature and place of person in its worlds. They also alter understanding of the implications of different sex and of differing gender, social status and conditions.

CHAPTER THREE

Excursus on Will and Passibility

To modern western thinking, individual *will* and associated notions are essential to human being and action. By the late seventeenth century, *will* joined a wholly human *reason* of which it was guide and efficient cause: inverting older ideas setting will below reason, as David Hume would later anticipate Freud by holding reason and will both subject to passions (*Treatise* 2.III.iii). On these understandings, *will*, as a separate mental ability to decide acts, was vital to self-identity. Its operation was altered by later ideas of the unconscious, its existence was not. Will is inseparable from the *action* matching its *intentions* and the *knowledge* enabling both intentions and the power to effect them—which is why Gilbert Ryle's denial of a discrete faculty of will, with attendant "volitions," was controversial (*Concept* 61–80). Indeed, what the West calls "free" societies and "free" world are so called because they claim actively to foster this will's actions, fulfillment of its intentions and acquisition of the knowledge needed. To medievals before Aquinas, ruled in this matter much by experiences and views exemplarily expressed by Augustine, *will* (*voluntas*) without divine grace was tied to (bad) passions and opposed to a rational intellect whose function was to lead one toward God. Untrammeled human will, misused without grace, brought error and falsehood. If divine charity embraced the soul, will could lead back to God. Left alone, reacting to "concupiscent" love of one's own being, will was evil: "Recta itaque voluntas est bonus amor [caritas] et voluntas perversa malus amor [cupiditas]" (*City of God* XIV.7: 4.290). In the earthly city the last was usual.

This experience entered later European thought and sensibility. In its Augustinian form, it perhaps drew on a dispute pitting Stoic against Peripatetic belief—insofar as Alexander of Aphrodisias, "the greatest of the Aristotelian commentators" (Frede, "Philosophy" 241), represents that tradition as it was around 200 A.D. In the *De fato* he held that freedom of human "will" meant ability to choose between contradictory possibilities of thought and action, although at the end of Chapter 8 we shall see that for him *all* choices assumed passibility. He was probably disputing Stoic belief that freedom did not mean "choice" but any created being's ability to fulfill the inherent potential of a nature always bound by the rational order of the whole natural and supernatural world. But we need not pit Aristotelian and Platonic pluralism against Stoic monism, the ones allowing degrees of virtue, the third "an all or nothing" obedience to "right action" by a will guided by "cosmic order" and "law" (MacIntyre 168–69). Passibility undoes such "oppositions." Stoic will concerned "the power to adapt or fail to adapt one's actions and goals to the natural course of events" (Long, "Freedom" 190). It involved issues not of freedom and determinism, but of humans' "fit" and *sense of fitting* their multiple surroundings, of being at home in the world. The Stoics named this *oikeiōsis*, a difficult idea entailing most other parts of Stoic thought (see Chapter 4). In their own way, too, Epicurean ethical views appear "remarkably similar to" Stoic ones (Cottingham 32). Julia Annas, often making this point, draws tentative conclusions entirely commensurate with passible being: as agents, humans and some animals "are those beings that can respond to their environment in flexible and discriminating ways, and can learn from their interactions with it" ("Epicurus" 71).

These seem different ideas of freedom from Alexander's, holding humans free in their purposeful adjustment to complex surroundings. Alexander did take a materialist view of the soul, closer to the Stoics than Aristotle, and possibly derived, Pierre Thillet suggests in his edition of the *De fato* (ci–civ), from Galen, on whom he wrote repeatedly. Urging essential freedom as that of choice, he can be interpreted as asserting an idea of freedom setting deciding will *against* such adjustment. From there to Augustine's Christian censure of this will was not far. (The saint also attacked Seneca's Stoic sage—whose problematic status Chapter 5 addresses—even as he embraced other aspects of Stoicism.) I argue later that Alexander's will and choice were in *no* sense modern. Stoics perhaps stayed closer to earlier sensibilities, but agreement was wide as to the grounds of who-ness. Many Greek and Roman familiarities then lasted beyond the European middle ages, not least those named by terms translated as "will," "purposive choice," "deliberation" and their fellows. These denoted experiences very different from modern western ones.

The sense of person and *psuchē* as passible involved particular sorts of relation with every aspect of their surroundings—surroundings that included action and knowledge. As to the second, full knowledge and wisdom were only in impassible mind. Whatever of these a person had was achieved, Socrates asserted in *Phaedo*, by recollection. So passible mind *put itself in a posture to be affected by* impassible mind, to receive elements of knowledge as imagination did sensations. Various prompts induced recollection, especially the analysis of words, concepts, actions and events that was philosophy, love of wisdom. For Plato and Aristotle, thought and words were intimately joined, sharing commemorative purpose—a view Stoics explored and expanded. Verbal interpretation later grounded Alexandrian wisdom and education, whose teacher, said the polymath Eratosthenes, was the *philologue*, lover of *logos* (Pfeiffer 156, 158–59). Such ideas of words' power were absorbed by Augustine and others, to permeate medieval thinking and beyond.

The Alexandrians called their goal *enkuklios paideia*, encircling knowledge, encyclopedia (Pfeiffer 253; cf. Dionysius 25: 222–23; Quintilian I.X.1). Just as Aristotle scorned the fallacy of taking the epic "cycle," *kuklos*, geometrically (*Posterior Analytics* 77b32; *Sophistical Refutations* 171a10), so one doubtless cannot link all circles to person and world. But epic is not indifferent: not only was Homer bearer of all-encompassing knowledge, but Alexandrian learning started with analysis of the poets. Until Aristotle, *kuklos* approvingly named Homer and a "Homeric" corpus of Trojan and Theban epics encompassing the Greek past. Aristotle dismissed all but the *Iliad* and *Odyssey* as imperfect, calling them "not Homeric" or "*kuklikos*," a view and terminology the Alexandrians adopted (Pfeiffer 229–30). However now pejorative, *kuklos* had nonetheless originally named these poems as together bearers of "encircling" knowledge. That most were now seen *not* to be did not prevent the Hellenistic thinkers from envisaging full knowledge *and* the verbal analysis enabling it as *enkuklios*. Although the word often now translates as "everyday," clearly, here, it affirmed something far broader and more powerful.

Using a view expressed in the *De anima*, the *Posterior Analytics* began as an effort to answer the Platonic puzzle noted in the *Meno* (80d): How can you learn anything new if you don't know what you're seeking? But if you know what you're seeking, you aren't learning. So either you learn nothing or what you already know. Aristotle found the dilemma false. The analyses of the *Posterior Analytics* would enable discovery of "already existing knowledge," first principles of true science, in one's mind. His first example was to be a cliché of western claims about the nature of thought: that the angles of a triangle equal two right angles. Two kinds of knowing were involved: "You understand it universally—but you do not understand it *simpliciter*." Deductive, demonstrable knowledge *was subject* to premises that were "true and primitive and immediate and more familiar than and prior to and explanatory of the conclusion." They were the "indivisibles" of the *De anima*: "primitive and non-demonstrable" (*Posterior Analytics* 71a1–b27).

The *De anima* showed these elements of knowledge to be in passible mind insofar as they were recovered from impassible mind. To passible mind, primary indemonstrable premises were potentials held in universal mind, parts of the rational order that even the creative demiurge could not violate (Dihle 1–2). Through commemorative operations—words or other prompts—they were actualized in embodied mind. This was not so very far from Platonic *Idea*. An important passage of the *De anima* reads:

Actual knowledge is identical with its object. In the individual, potential knowledge is prior, but absolutely it is not. Mind does not sometimes think and sometimes not. When separated it is alone just what it is, and this is deathless and eternal, although we do not remember because while this [last] is impassible [our] passible mind is perishable, but without [impassible mind] nothing thinks. (430a20–25)

Passible embodied mind *received* (or could receive) whatever was thinkable: first among such things, the true, primitive, immediate and *familiar* premises of all particular knowledge. Passible mind's relation to *action* repeated this pattern. To get to it, we must first examine "will."

Many have observed that ancient Greek could not express the idea of will as a reasoned process toward action. Pierre Gravel argues that Sophocles' tragedies never made anything like a "subject." Froma Zeitlin notes how *Oedipus the King* insisted in plot and language on the multiple nature of Oedipus' "self" ("Thebes" 111). Elsewhere, she shows how staged equivocations in gender, genre and mimesis itself created analogous effects ("Playing," "Power" and "Travesties"). Personal will was no more isolated still in Aristotle's moral thinking than it was in available vocabulary. On this, Albrecht Dihle's analysis (20–67) goes back to Hesiod. Vernant takes it to Aeschylus ("Ébauches" 48–54). He shows that the word *hekōn*, usually translated as "voluntarily" or "by an act of will," simply meant "willingly" or even "wittingly," in opposition to *akōn*, "in spite of oneself" or "unwittingly." It applied to *any* action not externally imposed or entirely fortuitous. An animal, too, could act *hekōn*. No English word well names the relation at issue. Drawing attention to *Rhetoric* 1347b4–10, *Nicomachean Ethics* 1135a15–36a9 and *Poetics*, Gerald Else found analogous properties in acts that were *hekousia* or *akousia* (*Aristotle's* 380).

Ousia, I recall, the word naming that with or without which such acts occurred, was also the word naming soul actualizing human body. These acts had to do with whether or not they had *affected* the *ousia* that was soul-in-body, whether they did or did not become that soul's attributes through what Charlotte Stough, in a usual modern characterization of Stoicism, calls "intelligent assent" (224). An act was not *hekōn* or *akōn* in virtue of a purely internal decision, but because of a *relation* where "outside" pressure weighed most ("outside" and "assent" also need determining).

Frede's analysis of Aristotle at first seems at odds with this. He argues that the verb *boulesthai*, the closest form to "willing" in Plato or Aristotle (its noun, *boulēsis*, appearing later), denoted "a highly specific form of wanting or desiring, in fact a form of wanting which we no longer recognize, for which we tend to have no place in our conceptual scheme." It named "a form of desire which is specific to reason." Conceiving a good, reason desired it and undertook the actions judged to attain it. *Boulesthai* denoted only this "desire of reason." "Socrates, Plato, Aristotle, the Stoics and their later followers" all agreed: "reason, just as it is attracted by truth, also is attracted by, and attached to, the good, and tries to attain it." Plato and Aristotle saw this "willing" in context of a tripartite soul subject to "radically different forms of motivation." These forms could conflict with one another (contrary to Socrates' view that no one acted against their rational knowledge and belief). But the anger or lust of the sensitive or appetitive powers which might for the time of their acts pre-empt rational desire entailed no mental act, whether of willing or anything else. "Aristotle explicitly characterizes these cases as cases in which one acts against one's choice *(prohairesis)*, rather than as cases in which one chooses to act against reason." One does so because "in the past one has failed to submit oneself to the training, practice, exercise, discipline, reflection" that make obeying reason's choice automatic *(Freewill* chap. 1, 19–22), reacting to, reinforcing and producing a collective practice of the rational and the good. The centrality of this communal and objective reasoning to all human action and the "desire" preceding it comprise a principal theme of Gill's *Personality*. We have seen this training of reason to habit, and shall again.

Under certain conditions the rational desire (of *boulesthai*) might conflict with non-rational desire or appetite. No "further instance which could adjudicate or resolve the conflict" existed, such as might approach a later idea of will. Aristotle does, Frede agrees, distinguish "between things we do *hekontes* and things we do *akontes*." His view, too, distinguishes things done wittingly from those done by force or in ignorance. An action done *hekōn* reflected the actor's "motivation." Says Frede: "we must have acted in this way, because in one way or another we were motivated to act in this way, that is either by a rational desire, or a non-rational desire, or both" *(Freewill* 23). This repeats the pattern traced before. Motivation is either affection moving the sensitive or appetitive powers or souls, or trained *hexis* moving reason to a right *prohairesis*. Whether one acts against or with that "choice" (as Frede renders *prohairesis*) does not change the fact that one is "*reacting*" passibly to passion or training coming from "outside." In Aristotle such choices resulted from natural or trained attachment to the good: "natural" because of rational soul's relation to universal reason, "trained" because embodied soul had lost that relation's immediacy.

In like vein, Anthony Kenny notes that the pairs, "voluntary" and "involuntary," "voluntarily" and "involuntarily," which usually translate the Greek terms into English, owe more to Latin *voluntarium* and *involuntarium*, "used in the medieval translations of Aristotle," than to a Greek vocabulary to which they are inadequate. The crucial term *prohairesis* can only be rendered clumsily as "purposive choice," a clumsiness reflecting "the fact that no natural English concept corresponds to Aristotle's." Indeed, "many of the traditional English expressions for Aristotelian concepts are misleading." His many references to continental scholars generalize this to all European vernaculars (*Aristotle's* 27, 69n1, 111). Frede echoes the point (*Freewill* 18–19). Charles Kahn adds that while *voluntas* and *volo* are tied like *boulēsis* and *boulomai*, other connections differed entirely. *Voluntarii*, for example, was the usual noun for military volunteers, connoting absence of economic, political, physical or legal "compulsion" rather than presence of "will." The Greek word *ethelontēs* lacked even that "voluntariness." *Volo*, *voluntas* and *voluntarium* are tied "in an essential way . . . ." But though Cicero naturally used *voluntarium* for *hekousion*, "nothing in Greek connects *hekousion* with *boulēsis*" (or *ethelontēs*) (241). These disparities are rife, and matter.

Most of those just named are uninterested in the usual assertion that Aristotle had no theory of the will. Dihle suggests that Aristotle's practical reason, distinguished from his theoretical, did incorporate a circumstantial notion of "will" simply ignored by subsequent Greek thinkers (58–60). Kenny, rejecting the "no-will" assertion as "a commonplace of Aristotelian scholarship," holds that the philosopher had such a theory, but a wrong one (*Aristotle's* vii). He posits a modern western notion as the right one (a view attracting both Dihle and Gill in *Personality*). John Cottingham argues analogously that Aristotle lacked proper understanding of "our innermost motivations and their . . . relationship to our overt actions," replacing "will" with "innermost motivations" because he sees ancient *and* modern, analytical-philosophical, notions of rational will alike flawed by lack of a "modern concept of the unconscious" (47). Ryle found Plato and Aristotle lacking concepts of will and volition, but not because they had failed to "discover" them. Rather, they had no need to anticipate their later unnecessary postulation (64).

These analyses do not show that Aristotle and others had no theory of will, but that ways of being, acting and thinking so differed from modern western ones as to need different explanatory focus. No active and separate *will* was particular to humans and qualitatively different from the general faculty allowing any action: embodied mind/soul, said the *De anima*, was by nature passible. Aristotle, uniquely, distinguished deliberate practical action from passible intellect's theoretical reason. But this action came from immediate material pressures and assent to it was inseparable from the events to which it responded and the reasoning processes engaged in and by them (Dihle 59). This is explored further in a moment.

Vernant suggests that an idea of "free will" was not fixed in the vocabulary until between Diodorus Siculus (first century B.C.) and Epictetus (first century A.D.) ("Ébauches" 53n20). Kahn flatly ascribes a quite "modern" idea to Epictetus, said to have seen the Stoic's life as "a continual process of self-definition, of identification with the inner world that is 'in our power,' of deliberate detachment from the body and from the external world that lies beyond our control" (253). This misleads, ignoring the human *embeddedness* that my next chapters explore. Urging a like case, Frede makes room for play by noting that Epictetus used old terms but narrowed them to capture the fact that while *prohairesis* might be "up to us," *eph' hēmin*, its event never was. To "assent" to the "impression" corresponding to choice did not guarantee the resultant act: in Epictetus, trained *prohairesis* was not "a disposition . . . to choose to act in a certain way, because we do not have that choice, but rather a disposition to choose to deal with one's impressions in a certain way" (*Freewill* chap. 2, 12–13). This is not modern "will." Kuriyama finds voluntary choice of "what we do and when and how" in the opening sentence of Galen's *Peri muōn kinēseōs* (On the movement of muscles), defining muscles as "the organs of voluntary motion," *instrumenta motus voluntarii* in Kühn's translation (*Opera* 4.367). The words were from Rufus of Ephesus, so again first century (144–46). But they actually said, "the muscles are organs of motion *kath' hormēn*," naming forceful impulse or desire, not *will*.

I note in passing that this dating of an independent will approximates the one some scholars give for a new notion of imagination. "It is not until the end of the second century of our era," writes Vernant, "that we can find the idea of imagination" as a power for forging images, adding *sophia* to *mimēsis* in a *phantasia* that represents what it has never seen (*Mortals* 185). Gerard Watson argues that Philostratus took Platonic-Aristotelian *phantasia* in this direction, influenced by Stoic views about *phantasia*'s ability to forge images not obtained via external senses ("Discovering"). This development was not yet in Cicero, for instance, who often translated *phantasia* as *impressio*. For him and the Stoics (until Epictetus anyway), rational impulse required "passive" impression and "active" assent to it, as Frede remarks (*Freewill* chap. 2, 6–10). This exactly echoes the definition of passibility given before. However "willed" a choice might be it was always a matter of rational assent to an impression or to trained or innate habit.

Like Dihle, Myles Burnyeat argues that although Aristotle did suggest an idea of freedom implying humans to be "by nature" able to act independently (*Politics* 1255b6), even that slim proposal set the notion in a familiar practical *political* context of freedom from collective oppression having nothing to do with individual will. Everyone anyway ignored the idea, implying that it matched no experience. In Crates, Burnyeat proposes, then in Zeno and notably Chrysippus, one begins to find a notion of person able to act *against* an oppressive collectivity. But developing Stoic focus was on choosing actions compatible with a providentially ordered and determinate universe ("Ancient"). The oppressive collectivity would be out of kilter with the providential universe whose order the person, on the contrary, would be following.

Such was the meaning of the simile attributed to Zeno and Chrysippus:

Just as a dog tied to a wagon, if it is willing to follow, follows as it is also being pulled, making its own autonomy coincide with necessity; whereas if it is unwilling to follow, it will in any event be compelled. So it is too with human beings. (Arnim, *Svf* 2.975)

Seneca reported Cleanthes as asserting that "ducunt volentem fata, nolentem trahunt," the fates lead the willing [soul], drag the unwilling (*Epistulae morales* cvii.11; *Svf*, Cleanthes frag. 527). Cleanthes' poem was quoted repeatedly through antiquity, past Epictetus (*Enchiridion* 53) to Augustine (*City of God* V.8). Willing entailed fitting actions, thoughts and experience to universal order. "'To will' in Greek thought," Long agrees, "is not to exercise some independent mental faculty called 'the will' but to adopt a pro-attitude to some specific object, and for the Stoics this object is given and necessary" ("Freedom" 192). The process of intelligent assent mentioned earlier was what enabled a person to adopt this attitude.

None of this argues absence of moral choice or variable intention. It asserts that they occurred in surroundings determined by the *logos* of a providential universe, the state (*diathesis*) of a person's soul, limiting assent to propositions and acts compatible with it, and the relation between them. Gérard Verbeke has shown how the Stoic idea of *pneuma*, running from life force to a kind of divine afflatus in the person, after Cleanthes usually took the form of a divine power enabling one to achieve acts, in accord with a determining universe, that would otherwise exceed human power. For Stoics, human soul shared in "world soul" (*Evolution* 512–17, 528–32; cf. Annas, *Hellenistic* 43, 50–56). Virtues and vices were among the soul's *diatheseis*. A person was habituated over time to certain dispositions to act—*hexeis* (Latin *habitus*). These elements fixed the bounds of human acts in the Stoics' determinate universe, whose "constraints" on action and "implacable law" (MacIntyre 170) have received vast scholarly attention (e.g., Adkins 230–31; Inwood 66–91, 106–11; Long, *Hellenistic* 164–70; Rist, *Stoic* 112–32, and essays by Gould, Long, Reesor, Sparshott and Stough). The issue arises in all writing on the Stoics. It was what stirred Alexander's acerbic criticism in his *De fato*. But to these diversities of soul and universe, we must add other "surroundings" we have only begun to see. The sorts of action selectable were constituted by the nature of the universe, the human soul and the many other spheres of which it partook. These actions had to do, said the post-Stoic Origen, with mind's assent to "certain plausibilities" inherent in its being "*about the world*" and in the world. "On the Stoic view," Troels Engberg-Pedersen adds, "human beings are bound to the world and so is human reason" ("Stoic" 131, 133). The actions that the soul selected reflected its possible give and take in the universe. We shall see how important this was to Cicero's conception of human action.

Whatever the word translated as *will*, it connoted a faculty by which humans adapted to the world's demand. To Greek thinking, *prohairesis* was not a power of mind like memory, intellect or *phantasia*, but a faculty to be learned and practiced (Dihle 134; Frede, *Freewill* chap. 2, 15). In this, it shared *modus operandi* with *hexis* (*habitus*), allied in accomplishment of action and alike in being subject to learning and practice. For Aristotle, the same applied to all virtues, including *phronēsis*, master virtue of humans-in-the-world, practical wisdom or prudence. Trained *prohairesis* and *hexis* gave passible acts their reasons, allowed intelligent assent to them. On this, Cicero recalled Zeno's pupil Ariston urging that when all but the good or evil of virtuous or non-virtuous action was at stake, the human could only be unmoved, *adiaphoros*, good and virtuous action necessarily being ruled by the ordered reason of universal nature. The areas of intelligent assent were those of moral experience and act. In other domains, humans could not so much resist their passible natures as disregard their manifestations. He noted that Pyrrho had demanded more, requiring one wholly to ignore such things, maintaining a state of *apatheia* (*Academica* II.xlii.130).

That anyone could attain this impassibility was unlikely, for the human's relation to its surroundings was that of a possibility corresponding, Cicero held, to "nature's reason itself, which is divine and human law" (*De officiis* III.v.23). Since the first two books of the *De officiis* paraphrased the old Stoic Panaetius (III.ii.7), Cicero was apparently giving wider views. Most believed that such impassibility could only ever be an unreached ideal. Its utility was to offer a pattern of adjustment to the rational universe and let humans achieve at least the partial wisdom of reaching for and moving toward it. Even "Chrysippus, the third head of the [Stoic] school, confessed that he had never known a Wise Man" (Rackham, in Cicero, *De finibus* xxiii). The finished sage, all agreed, was rare as the phoenix. True wisdom lay most in taking the ideal as guide to action and outlook on being that could set one at home in the world (cf. Long, "Logical" 151; "Greek Ethics" 177). To attain impassibility would make one literally inhuman, requiring "that one become one with the world" (Engberg-Pedersen, "Discovering" 183). It could thus easily change into Neoplatonic striving for absorption in the One or Christian hope for union with God. Chapter 5 argues that an effort to demonstrate actual attainment of the ideal mooted by a Pyrrhonian thesis let Seneca show enigmas beyond paradox in this idea of the sage. Belying basic claims about the bond of person to world and society, it was counterintuitive for all who shared this sensibility. The experience behind these contentions was general.

So actions that went against an oppressive collectivity, for instance, were not done in the name of or for an individual, or even *by* one, but for and by the ideal community in its alignment with the rational universe. At least for early Stoics, the virtuous life meant always choosing "the things in accordance with nature" (quoted by E. M. Atkins in Cicero, *On Duties* xxxv). Citing Chrysippus and Cleanthes, Diogenes Laertius was to write that "our life" had to coincide with nature in general and human nature in particular (the second anyway part of the first), and that virtue was a "harmonious state of mind" (*diathesis*) fitting it to "the whole of life" (*Lives* VII.89). Human acts were a matter of "fitting" *with* the universe; better, of being fitted to it. So Alexander of Aphrodisias observed: "the Stoics, although removing the possibility that man has the power to choose and perform one of the contradictories [cases of moral choice], say that that which happens through us is attributable to us [*eph' hēmin*]" (*Svf* 2.979).

The remark specifies assent to passible actions: things happening through us. Such assent was a focal idea of old and late Stoicism. We should beware of fusing it with modern will, as Charles Taylor does in saying that by it, "we do control our all-things-considered rational intention," and adding: "Epictetus developed a similar doctrine using the Aristotelian term '*prohairesis*,' which one might translate 'moral choice,' [a faculty] utterly under my control" (137). This suggests an "I" controlling *prohairesis* and all on which it operated or, rather, on which "I" operated by way of *prohairesis*. But Epictetus still used the word to mean a trained ability to fit *all and any* actions to things one *received* from without. *Prohairesis* was not a "reflective consciousness" separate from its experiences, some "free-floating ego." It named "the way assent" used representations set in mind by the natural world to live in accordance with it—and them (Long, "Representation" 282). Kahn also makes *eph' hēmin*, naming acts "up to us," a basic element of Epictetus' understanding of *prohairesis*, but observes that Epictetus took this latter faculty to be "a part of God which he has given to us" (*Discourses* I.17.27; "Discovering" 240, 253–54). Being "up to us" meant assenting to *prohairesis* working *through* us. That Epictetus took *prohairesis* and *eph' hēmin* to name "choice" as assent to an impression subject to "God's providential plan" is also Frede's view (*Freewill* chap. 2, 12), who nonetheless sees Epictetus as the first ancient philosopher to elaborate a notion of "free will" (chap. 3, 9ff.). If so, it was neither ever normative nor of a kind familiar to any "modern idea of self-consciousness" (Gill, *Personality* 405–6; dilemmas of *eph' hēmin* return at the end of Chapter 8).

Passible soul received its actions. Like Zeno's dog, it could form them to its *logos*, through *hexis* and *prohairesis* trained to fit the universe's *logos*, or it could be dragged by main force, resisting and falling into the evil folly that Cleanthes blamed in his *Hymn to Zeus*: "Nor does any act occur without you, lord [Zeus], not in the divine aetherial heaven nor on the sea, except what is done by evil men through their folly" (*Svf* 1.537.11–13). Even in Epictetus, *prohairesis* was trained to assure actions matching one's place in the world and life. Others were false and improper, like the evils knowingly committed by Euripides' Medea (*Discourses* I.xxviii.7–8). This idea of evil as a falling from divine reason may have found its way to Augustine and on to early modern sensibilities (Rist, *Augustine* 186–88 and Chapter 9 below). Even so, in *Medea* and Galen's commentary in *Doctrines* III.3, Medea was shown as *subjected* to *thumos*, "spirit" or "anger" (Gill, *Personality* 120, 154–74, 216–39). Her assent is rational, if as "a kind of malfunctioning" (Gill, "Did?" 140; cf. Foley, *Female* 244–68). Assent to appetitive or sensitive affections against reason is the same passible schema.

Only the Aristotelian Alexander, says Burnyeat, offers a rare proposal that the wise man might be able freely to act against fate's compulsion ("Ancient": *De fato* 200.2–7; cf. Frede, *Freewill* chap. 3, 24–30). This was not a good or usual form of action but a kind of freedom able to be *imagined* to characterize at least one sort of person. Addressing his *De fato* to the emperors Septimius Severus and Caracalla in thanks for his appointment as professor of Peripatetic philosophy (presumably at Athens), Alexander had a political goal. To assert human freedom of choice was to justify imperial actions whose possibility, and certainly whose good, were denied by Stoicism's democratic contentions. By now, the issue was edging toward absorption into Christian and Neoplatonic debates, perhaps engaging another experience of personhood. Certainly before this, neither Stoics nor their opponents approached a notion of soul, mind or person that western moderns would recognize. Annas observes that no aspect or element of mind was ever "taken to be accessible to introspection by privileged inner view." Nor were its "contents" ever found "epistemologically basic [or] in any interesting sense private" (*Hellenistic* 64). Even Stoics did not allot mind "any ineradicably subjective content . . . , whatever content it ha[d] was thought by them to be in principle public and accessible to rational discourse." The mind's content was always "objective" in the sense that it belonged to a rational stock held in common by all persons (Engberg-Pedersen, "Stoic" 122, 125). This is again who-ness as adhering in a process of passible relations.

Thought and experience surely varied over five hundred years. Yet here and later we see that basic beliefs and experience of personhood stayed widely shared and assured. Little had changed, it seems, since the sophist Thrasymachus, who, although regularly "taken to represent egotism— myself versus the rest," in fact "clearly [had] a theory of 'us' versus others: *oikeiou agatha* [the goods of the *domus*] connects with *oikia*, not with individual atoms" (Burnyeat, personal letter, October 16, 1996). In Plato's *Republic*, the debaters anyway rejected even this idea of the more limited group championed by Thrasymachus, who had protested angrily that the person they called the "just" leader had to let "his own affairs [*ta . . . oikeia*] fall into disorder" and "become hateful to friends and acquaintances alike [*tois te oikeiois kai tois gnōrimois*]" (*Republic* 343e). Even here, the most intimate experience, "rooted in [his] very nature," as G. B. Kerford puts it ("Search" 181), was fundamentally social and "public," bound to the *oikeioi*.

The hard paradox that Thrasymachus was posing, ignored by his interlocutors, was that the *oikoi* (we shall see more in Chapter 7) were the city's basic units and could not therefore be at odds with it; or, if they were, perils to the welfare of communities both large and small were fundamental. He was surely echoing a view that Sophocles' *Antigone* rendered dramatically: Antigone maintaining traditional values of the *oikos* and its divine foundations, Creon taking rights of the *polis* and its authority to the extreme of tyranny—ill-judgedly, as he finally laments. To see Antigone as a "rebellious nay-sayer" (as it has been put to me) is a post-Hegelian romanticizing. She denied Creon not in the name of any personal right but in that of the rights (and rites) of the household, of a traditional *nomos* that he rejected in the name of a political law he claimed to personify. MacIntyre concurs that in *Antigone* "the life of the clan and the life of the city are weighed against each other" (132; cf. Foley, *Female* 172–89). Similarly, Athena's intervention at the end of Aeschylus' *Oresteia* "and the resolution of the issue between her and Apollo, establish a conception of justice which shifts the center of authority in moral questions from the family and the household to the *polis*" (144).

In the *Republic* Plato offered the vision of a city where the *oikoi* were replaced by a seamless whole community. Socrates' and his friends' silencing and ungenerous scorn of Thrasymachus marked their claim— hope?—that he belonged to a bygone age. We have already begun to see that that was unclear. In any case, for both sides in the quarrel, "myself" seems to have been unthinkable except as Vernant's "soul in me." As for the concept of *will* in the earlier time, he adds that the opposition *akōn/hekōn* was actually a juridical one, bearing, we saw before, on practical reason deciding action. It was not at all

based in its principle on the distinction between the voluntary and the involuntary. It rests on the distinction made by the social conscience under specific historical conditions between fully reprehensible action and excusable action, which, besides legitimate action, are posited as a pair of antithetical values. ("Ébauches" 54)

Even so, not agent but action was this judgment's object: "The agent is caught in the action. It is not its author. It remains included in it" (56). For Aristotle, too, to act "virtuously" was to re-act to things impressed on mind from without, to live, Diogenes Laertius cited Chrysippus, "in accord with experience of the actual course of nature" (*Lives* VII.87: this remark's fuller context is given in another translation at Chapter 4's end). Here was the same pattern of reason, knowledge and imagination. The possibility of the human mind/soul characterized all aspects of its functioning; it was its fundamental nature. In this instance, the "agent" was part of a whole for which its "responsibility" was decidedly limited. Had circumstances differed the person would have done otherwise because the potentially suitable actions would have been otherwise. Although a person was responsible (in ways to be defined) for its actions in given circumstances, it had qualified control over the circumstances or the extent of its knowledge of them.

This makes a notion of the unconscious wholly unnecessary, since the internal lacks and lapses it explains were not internal but lay in the relation between passible soul and universe. Passibility, and the passions, explain the relation between how the mind/soul *reacts* to objects, events, actions and ideas, the motions in soul/body that result and, then, the actions of soul, mind and body that ensue. What else does the notion of the unconscious seek to explain? It is needed to explain how an agent subject can act—it seems—"against" (or whatever word one prefers) what it perceives as its agency. Passibility supposes a different concept of what a person is, one subsuming "conscious" *and* "unconscious" under passible soul and obviating Gill's "puzzling" contradiction between "agency" and "passivity" (*Personality* 97). The polarity did not exist. One may precisely say that for the passible soul action was inherent in circumstance rather than in an agent effecting such action. This conception was, again, entirely coherent with that of the passible mind "imprinted" with actual knowledge. It remained coherent with it through Stoicism, into the Christian middle ages and beyond—although the experience became increasingly fraught and uncertain.

Vernant refines his case by continuing Émile Benveniste's analysis of the two endings that attach to Greek agent-nouns. Those in *-tēr* signal that "the agent is immersed in its action, which is conceived as a function; it blends with an activity to which that agent is unavoidably given up and in which, by destiny, aptitude or necessity it is as if shut up." Endings in *-tōr* show that "the agent possesses, in the form of a quality belonging to it, the act seen as already accomplished, completely carried out." There were thus two sorts of action and of relations between action and agent. In the first, "the activity viewed in its functional aspect is superior to the agent, primary in relation to it." It was a *technē* inherent in a metier and operating *through* the agent, just as actual knowledge was the imprint of preexistent potential knowledge on passible, embodied mind. In the second, action was still neither "inherent to the agent nor [was] the agent present to its action." The action did not concern the "series of productive operations that the artisan develop[ed] in the course of his work; it dwel[t] in the made object, the produced piece of work." Whatever the status of such a concept of action, it precluded experience or treatment of an agent "as source and origin of its actions" ("Catégories" 88–89, 91–92). This was clearly so for both modalities of action and actor.

Kenny agrees that action is "out there," awaiting me:

"*Hekousion*" for Aristotle is not a predicate reserved for actions; both what happens around us and what we can do can be divided into things which are *hekousia* and *akousia*. If I see a child drowning and don't jump in when I can and should, then, Aristotle would say, the child's drowning, as far as I am concerned, is voluntary, or perhaps rather, is voluntary for me.

One again recalls Vernant's remark about it not being "my soul" but rather the soul "in me." The ideas are exact analogues. Kenny adds that

in the *Nicomachean Ethics* something was defined as "voluntary with respect to a particular agent if there is no compulsion, if there is an appropriate degree of knowledge, and if the originating cause of the situation
(the *archē*) is in the agent" (*Will* 15). Making this argument, Aristotle
had insisted contrariwise that involuntary acts were those "which take
place by force or through ignorance," or, he added later, in madness
(1109b35, 1111a6).

Aristotle's definition of *hamartia* in the *Poetics* flagged absence of these
qualities of voluntariness. *Hamartia* was not a "fault" or "tragic flaw"
marking failure of will, but rather "unwittingness." Kenny observes, precisely, that in *Topics* (148a8) and the *Nicomachean Ethics* (1110b29),
Aristotle recorded *hamartia* as one kind of *agnoia* (*Aristotle's* 49n1). This
involved a "responsibility" quite different from one presupposing willed
accomplishment of an intention. One could assent to certain kinds of
"*reaction*" but the action to which they responded felt like a process into
which the actor was "absorbed," to which the protagonist was, again, fitted. One recalls blind Oedipus' cry in *Oedipus the King*:

> Apollo, friends, Apollo—
> he ordained my agonies—these my pains on pains!
> But the hand that struck my eyes was mine,
> mine alone—no one else—
> I did it all myself! (ll.1329–33)

The sentiment and experience exactly fit Alexander of Aphrodisias' later
gloss that Stoic belief in the restriction of the sorts of choice open to humans accompanied their claim "that that which happens through us is attributable to us." Oedipus *acceded* to a choice suiting the trained and
practiced disposition of *his* soul. This experience of who-ness agrees with
its being tied to those *outside* him whose looks and speech make him
who he is—as his do them, in the relation noted in the last chapter
(Cavarero, *Relating* 11–15; cf. "Oedipus"). That, too, is why Odysseus
can tell his story only *after* he has heard it begun by the blind rhapsode at
the Phaecian court (*Relating* 17–31). The story of the actions that have
happened through them and their choices now become "theirs."

This experience of acceding to actions is explained by the protagonist
of *Oedipus at Colonus*: "my acts / have been sufferings more than actions
outright" (ll.266–67). Bruno Snell and E. R. Dodds are eloquent on the
lack of a notion of agent "self" among the ancient Greeks. One recalls
Dodds' analysis of Agamemnon explaining his theft of Achilles' captive in
the *Iliad*, overcome by "wild *atē*" (*The Greeks* chap. 1). Hercules and
Ajax, too, famously suffered *atē*. Years later, Cicero used the same cases
of frenzy to fault Greeks who made melancholia the root of all *furor*

rather than passions like "wrath or fear or pain, by which kind we say Athamas, Alcmaeon, Ajax and Orestes were enraged" (*Tusculan Disputations* III.v.11). *All* passions, said Cicero, affected a person in this way, echoing a view by now generations-old. Madness and rational action were opposite ends of a single spectrum of possibility.

These cases clarify a well-known crux concerning action and person, Aristotle's insistence that the focus of drama was the ordering, *muthos*, of action, *praxis*. Character, *ēthos*, not only did not precede action but came *out of, from* action (*Poetics* 1449b36–50a22). Singularity of "character" or person was of no concern—not even to be avoided, since not conceived. Actions made the *ēthos* the spectators saw. Place, time, custom and condition came before, if with, temperament and singular reason, possibility of action before, if with, singular fulfillment. People's *ēthos* was their "set dispositions to behave" in a certain way (MacIntyre 38). It was visible *in* actions and made *by* actions. Foley's remark about the difficulty of separating tragic "characters from the action, from the social roles and expectations of their community, from the dialogic form of drama, in which each character is defined in interaction with others" (*Female* 16), is also true of life. That is why "Cicero invented 'moralis' to translate the Greek word [*ēthikos*] in the *De fato*," MacIntyre observes in the passage just quoted, meaning those "set dispositions" of behavior and the circumstances making them (Edward Taylor, we saw, found the same effect still in Shakespeare's *Measure for Measure*).

Like Vernant and others (including Aristotle), Kenny remarks that the account of *will* that all this supposed could clearly include animals. He deems this a "failure" of thought and explanation. So, referring to an argument advanced by G. E. M. Anscombe that Aristotle failed to see deliberation as "a key concept in the theory of action" ("Thought" 147), Kenny approves her implication that "the weakness in Aristotle's account is a lack of the concept of intention"—another rendering of *prohairesis* (*Will* 16). He renews the criticism in his later book on the will where, writing of a passage in the *Nicomachean Ethics* that does not distinguish between classes of action and individual actions (a constant view, we now know), he continues:

A bizarre metaphysic seems implied, according to which one and the same individual action may have certain properties before being performed and others while being performed, and may have certain properties if it is performed and different properties if not performed.

At the very least, Aristotle's "mode of expression is clumsy" (*Aristotle's* 31). Is it?

This experience *does* agree with the kind of relation we see between surroundings—material, social, rational, divine or pertaining to thought, action and sense—and possible person. Such a metaphysic would not describe events and actions experienced or conceived as static objects "out there" to be acted on. It would not describe them as possessing fixed, once-and-for-all knowable ontological status. Rather would it describe *praxis* as an ongoing process acquiring meaning as it went, as *it* acted on passible being ("je peins le passage," Montaigne was to write many centuries later, expressing a sensibility few find "bizarre" or difficult of sympathetic access). One wonders, indeed, why this should be thought "bizarre." An action's properties surely do depend on when, how, why, where and, yes, whether, it is "performed"—and much else besides? The enacting of an action is vital to its nature. We might also recall the Hippocratics seeing bodily effects become meaningful *symptoms* in actual interaction between patient and physician. Passible being fitted into action, reason, knowledge, all the surroundings that were its varied worlds, as into spheres of doing that already potentially existed. They became actual once the "fitting" was established. Precisely the "processive" nature of the relationship between passible mind and surrounding world is why no concept of unconscious is needed in counterpart to one of rational mind. Again, the lacks and lapses of passible mind are necessary aspects of its embedding in the world.

To call analysis of this a "weakness," dismissing its discussion as "clumsy" and its metaphysic as "bizarre," is to want to assert the singular truth of modern western concepts of *will* and unconscious and to claim that Aristotle was unable adequately to theorize them. But lack of modern western concepts of *will* and *intention*, with the actions, events and experiences following from them, may better indicate different social and personal praxes, human ways of being and doing, born from different historical and social times. All the preceding suggests as much. Kenny asserts another view, arguing further that although Aquinas "greatly improved" Aristotle's account, the later one was also "wrong," for if it admirably developed a concept of intention, its notion of "deliberate action" still inadequately accounted for permanent human realities familiar to us as they should have been to Aquinas—and Aristotle before him (*Will* 19–21). In other ways, Aquinas' view just repeated Aristotle's (24–25). These permanent human realities have no place for passibility and its many consequences.

Like Kenny and Lloyd, Bernard Williams also influentially argues that whatever difficulties of understanding are posed by thinkers and dramatists like Plato or Sophocles, scholars wrongly imagine that these difficulties arise from essential differences of being. At first he claims a middle way, saying of action, intentions and normal minds that "these really are universal materials. What we must not suppose is that they are always related to one another in the same way or, indeed, that there is one ideal way in which they should be related to one another" (*Shame* 56). This is like saying that everyone has a body and everyone experiences death. The *way* in which body (to echo Vernant and Kuriyama) or death is experienced is a cultural creation related to a web of social and cultural being. This way in which they are related *is* their being and experience. What is felt and thought inherent in them is inseparable from the tissue of whose warp and weft they are. A time's and a place's real world, the one people experience, is always woven up in its possible worlds: Williams' "universal materials" are but blunt threads which those in the carpet can never see separated out (he is in a carpet, too). They are never static objects out there to do with as we will.

Yet that is what Williams comes to say of them: they are universals separable from their relational worlds, and *we* can so know them. He thus recasts the specific responsibility borne by Oedipus in *Oedipus at Colonus*, understandable in the ways we have been following, into a model of "universal" responsibility:

Suppose that we lay aside the idea of pollution; lay aside, too, the conceptions that shape the end of the play [that Oedipus becomes a healing force]. . . . Lay aside any idea that the difference made by his actions is that they gave him new causal powers, for ill or for good. All this laid aside, it is still a truth about him that he has done these things, and it is a truth in the present tense: he is the person who did those things. (*Shame* 71)

Well, no doubt it is. But it is a truth so incomplete as to tell us nothing about *this* play, *this* time, *this* place. Pollution, healing and causal powers (to name only Williams' own exclusions) were essential to doing "these things." Remove them, and you do what you wish with what remains. Similarly, Williams remarks that the Guardians of Plato's *Republic* did, or rather "do"—the present tense is not innocent—not need an "internalised other" to know shame, because they carry in them something else: "a paradigm of justice gained from their intellectual formation (more exactly, revived in them by it)" (99).

First, education is other than superstructural decoration on universal mind. Training *hexeis*, we have seen, entailed particular experiences of being. Second, the parenthesis, even its *being* a parenthesis, speaks volumes, bearing a load analogous to the earlier "lay asides." That the actor's internal knowledge of justice was *revival* of a *memory* matters hugely, again involving complete or incomplete truth. Remains are indeed being detailed. We have seen the sense of such memory in Chapter 2. Williams says that the parenthesis merely indicates that knowledge-as-

memory does not affect his point. How can it not? The paradigm of justice that the Guardians carry is not "theirs" and entails no familiar "in-
ternalisation." Their "intellectual formation" *depended* on their recovering—on their teachers' recovering—access to the universal reason where
Ideas were. This is the "recovery" of knowledge mentioned at the start of
this chapter and in the previous one as essential no less to Aristotle's notion of mind than to Plato's and Socrates'. It was one natural effect of the
passibility fundamental to the philosophers' and the Guardians' humanity, to whom they were *as* humans. It was *natural* in the fullest possible
way. What does it then mean to say "they carry in them"? Nothing remotely similar, at least, to what a modern westerner would mean.

At stake is the place of these "pieces" in a whole culture, hard as this
last may be to know. They are not separate "materials." To split the
whole into autonomous, discrete parts transforms everything. Williams
resisted this in the first passage quoted, but not later: "The fact that we
can honestly and not just as tourists respond to the tragedies is almost
enough in itself to show that ethically we have more in common with the
audience of the tragedies than the progressivist story" told by his "opponents" allows (18). Setting aside that the precisions his "opponents"
(Vernant and others) pursue have nothing to do with "progressivism" but
offer a subtler play of continuity and difference, our response to the
tragedies shows no such ethical commonality.

The claim holds our response identical or closely comparable to that
of a first audience. It belittles, even dismisses, audience differences no less
than an artwork's capacity to be reread. This does not mean it is understood always in the same way. It means it responds to diverse sensibilities
and experiences (Kermode, *Classic*; Reiss, *Meaning* 226–62). What
causes our common response, Williams asserts, is that "Greek tragedy
precisely refuses to present human beings who are ideally in harmony
with their world, and has no room for a world that, if it were understood
well enough, could instruct us how to be in harmony with it." Our responses to these universal truths are not touristic, because disharmonies
are equally vital in the modern world, if manifest in other ways: "we" live
in a world where "social reality" has replaced "supernatural necessities"
(*Shame* 165). These are superstructures set atop an invariable infrastruc-
ture, clothes worn by universal humanity. The notions that tragedy shows
humans that they live in a dissonant world, that they must always be in a
conflictual relation with it (even if they can learn how to live *with* disharmonies) and that this is ever and everywhere the case for all humans have
been commonplaces since the European Renaissance. Tragedy has been a
"cultural instrument" interpreting western culture from within and
grasping other cultures in ways and with purposes never overly obscure

(Reiss, *Against* chap. 3). Tragedy, too, belongs in webs of experience and sensibility that do not remain the same.

"Supernatural necessities," demands of memory, experiences of "pollution," "healing forces," "divine" powers, disharmony and harmony, possibility are pieces of a cultural experience that one needs to weave together, not reject as curiosities, anomalies or barbarities. If the Greeks lacked modern concepts of *will* and *intention*, if Aquinas omitted a notion of *deliberate action* and thought the end of humans in God and passible soul essentially mediation of the divine, this was not because Aristotle was insufficiently intelligent to see that he "ought" to have elaborated deliberation as "a key concept in the theory of action" or Aquinas too obtuse to have given a fuller "account of practical reason." Rather was it because they did not need such theories and accounts. We should also beware of taking Aristotle's (or Plato's) analysis of *akrasia*, the weakness or loss of control allowing irrational actions, as wrong, because "lacking the modern concept of the unconscious, [he did] not have a philosophy of mind sophisticated enough to explain" the loss of control or the difference between a "surface" knowledge of the facts of intentional action and "a deeper understanding of their emotional and symbolic significance" (Cottingham, *Philosophy* 47). The concept is not needed to explain operations of passible mind, which is certainly no less "sophisticated" an explanation of human nature than that to which Cottingham is referring.

Universalizing reactions are a refusal to take differences seriously. They split them into broken details because they want instantly to adjust them to "our" local familiarities. But human action, relations, experience and being, these other ways of expressing them urge, were and are different. What does it mean to say that "in a certain sense" all people "have the same concept of truth," their different theories merely showing how they "misrepresent their grasp of the concept" (Williams, "What" 9–10)? "In a certain sense"? The fact that "truth" does not always play a same vital cultural role is already fundamentally important. More vital in antiquity was a quite different concept and experience, one that Kenny recognizes when he speaks of both Aristotle and Aquinas as basing their concepts of practical reasoning on a first premise that assumes reasoning to be transmitting an objective and universal value or plan of life—the good. "Such a line of thought," he says, "is very alien." It is more alien than Kenny wants. As Nussbaum observes, "the good" or "happiness" was no final objective state, feeling or truth. *Eudaimonia* placed "emphasis on *activity*, and on completeness of life" (*Therapy* 15n5, her italics). Like all action, it was a process and essential, *as* process, to becoming completely human.

We should surely then start by supposing that Aristotle and Aquinas were talking of something that moderns need to make an estranging effort to understand. We would better say with Seneca, seeking new explanations for lightning, that he however did "not presume the ancients were so dull that they believed Jupiter had ill-will or at least unreliable skill" (*Naturales quaestiones* II.42.2). His phrase is wise. Only cultural arrogance lets us assert that ancients were unsuccessful in their attempt to describe experiences and phenomena familiar both to them and us because a permanent part of things human. It is more useful to assume that they were at least as successful as analytical philosophy may be at describing a human praxis that differed as much from what we find familiar as does their account of it. Kenny "solves" his difficulty by arguing that in the *Eudemian Ethics* Aristotle's views "bear a remarkable resemblance" to those of philosophers like Ryle and Ludwig Wittgenstein (*Aristotle's* vii–viii). Williams reacts by splintering whole practice into shards then brought to resemble readier familiarities. Cottingham wants to make a map of the human mind (insufficient as any single one always is) by associating traces from different mappings.

The view Rousseau advanced in his *Discourse on the Origin of Inequality* is preferable and more accurate: "Humankind of one age is not the humankind of another, and the reason why Diogenes did not find the [kind of] man [he sought] is that he was looking among his contemporaries for a man of a time that was no more" (*Discours* 91). Rousseau might have been thinking of Augustine's maxim, quoted in my Introduction, to the effect that however general human nature was, what people were nonetheless depended on particular social and cultural realities, fitting "not only with their places, but also with their times" (*Confessions* VII.15). We may recall my epigraph from ibn Khaldūn, or the concluding analysis of the Hippocratic *Airs, Waters, Places* about the essential differences between peoples of Europe and Asia Minor due to varieties of land, weather, society and the rest. This does not necessarily make them mutually incomprehensible. It does mean that comprehension takes work, efforts to know complex wholes, as well as Brathwaite's tact and grace.

Will, intention and the unconscious, following ancient argument and evidence adduced by many scholars, are products of particular sociohistorical organization—along with other "affections." Rousseau, adopting views of many illustrious predecessors, was insisting that human sensibility, thought and practice undergo such radical changes as to make people of one cultural place and age exceedingly hard for those of another to comprehend. Thus, writing of the inextricable bond between rationality, feelings, senses and modes of expression like language and music, he noted the folly of trying to make ancient Greek music comprehensible to eighteenth-century French academicians by simply transposing its nota-tion. Similarly, the French music that stirred the latter would be "only worthless noise to a Carib's ear." The quite different system of musical consonance used by North American Indians confirmed these vast disparities. To think that their system or the Greeks', and above all the processes of reason and sensibility accompanying them, needed correcting by "our" reasonings in the matter was mere universalist "prejudice" (*Essai* 143–45, 165, 181–83). The view was not unique to Rousseau in this height of the Enlightenment. In *Knowledge*, I quoted Edward Gibbon on what universalists could learn from "an Iroquois work" (197–98). Will, intention and other concepts are not permanent givens, proper to the human species, fundamental to its reality and part of its definition. The term translated as "will" (*boulēsis*) signifies, rather, a discourse and experiences unfamiliar to modern western people, ones where "agent" was an actor *within* the action, a knower *within* the knowable, passible being in constraining surroundings.

Such was the grounding condition of man and woman, slave and free, independently of diversities of actually manifest surroundings. We must try to interpret that world in its terms, not in those of our later time and place: in terms according to which the human has no dominant control over that of which it is a part. *Will* now names the action of a *subject* enunciating the predicative discourse of analysis and reference and experiencing the grasp entailed (see my *Discourse of Modernism* and *passim* in *Uncertainty*). As I began to suggest, no view approaching this can be ascribed to later ancient thought and practice, certainly not to earlier. Writings from that later era mattered even more to the ongoing tradition than some of those just discussed. It is to these that I turn in the rest of Part 1. I discuss mainly works by writers who seem typical on questions of personhood and who were to be generally exemplary in later times. Cicero and Galen absorbed, recorded and transmitted a remarkably eclectic atmosphere of thought and practice. Early European moderns found Seneca's and Plutarch's essays especially congenial for pedagogical exercise and ethical training. They and, in Chapters 6 and 7, an eclectic group of early and late ancients used to approach issues of slavery and gender, also open the debate toward other medical, theological and legal writers, as well as Augustine, next to Cicero, possibly most important of all for the tradition.

CHAPTER FOUR

Cicero's Person, Passible Minds and Real Worlds

From the fourteenth century, Cicero's *Tusculan Disputations* and *De officiis* were basic to debates about the person and a person's place in society. Their ground was Greek experience, on which Cicero was marshalling divergent thinkers. *Tusculans*, he said, gave several schools' views on person and soul, *De officiis* mostly paraphrased the Stoic Panaetius. How much and how faithfully he rendered Panaetius' work on "moral obligation," despite offering "some correction" (*De officiis* III.ii.7), has incited controversy. That scarcely matters here. What does is how far these works show even opposing views to rest on widely agreed assumptions.

In *Tusculans*, Cicero first gave a description rather more Platonic than Peripatetic, although he would see them in no fundamental opposition:

To me, in thinking about the nature of the soul, it seems far harder and more unsure to grasp what the soul may be in the body, as if in an alien home [*tamquam alienae domui*], than what it may be when it has left and come into free heaven as if into its own home [*quasi domum suam*]. For unless we are unable to understand what something we have never seen may be, assuredly we can compose an idea of god himself and of the divine soul freed from the body. (I.xxii.51)

A difficulty was that soul in body was inevitably opaque to the intellect. Plato, too, was clearer about soul out of body than he ever was about embodied soul. To a degree, the same went for Aristotle's impassible and passible souls, but for him and early Stoics, embodied and universal soul were on a continuum in a way Plato's seemed not to be. This hardly simplified Cicero's difficulty. For, he said, to function and act in the world, humans had first to know themselves. How could they, if one was human only in virtue of an embodiment whose creaturely nature blocked the soul's transparency to its own being and made knowledge, especially of *that*, so very hard?

First, one had to clarify what it meant to know oneself, one's who-ness, one's person. Second, one had to know what person was. Third, one had to know the relations to the plural surroundings that were a person. For Cicero, like his predecessors, to be human was to be enlaced in these, to exist only *as part* of them. To know *who* one was was to know *where* one was. So, he wrote in the *De oratore* (another text central to later education), the illustrious dead were right to have

> said that all things above and below are one and held together by one force and harmony of nature [*una vi atque consensione naturae*], for there is no class of things which can stand by itself, cut off from the rest or which the rest may do without and still be able to maintain their own force and eternal being. (*De oratore* III.v.20)

All persons and surroundings were conjoined, aided by unifying rational knowledge (*doctrina*), "in a single bond of association [*uno quodam societatis vinculo*]," all meanings, difference and causes grounded in a "wonderful agreement and harmony [*mirus . . . consensus . . . concentusque*] of all areas and forms of knowing" (*De oratore* III.vi.21).

Within this overall union, Cicero further agreed with his predecessors that one had to consider the person in relation to the divine before all. One had to know that soul was a divine substance free of body both before and after its temporary embodiment. It was, too, the only source of intellect and reason. To speak of "I"—or rather, "you"—was to speak *only* of the soul:

> It is of utmost importance that soul sees by soul itself. And surely this is the force of Apollo's maxim advising that each know oneself [*ut se quisque noscat*]. For I do not think it meant that we should know our limbs, our height or our shape; since we are not our bodies, nor, speaking to you thus, do I speak to your body. So when he says: "Know yourself [*Nosce te*]," he says this: "Know your soul [*Nosce animum tuum*]. For the body is a sort of jar [*vas*] or a kind of container of soul [*animi receptaculum*]: whatever is done by your soul, that is done by you [*ab animo tuo quidquid agitur, id agitur a te*]." (*Tusculans* I.xxii.52)

Soul, in this sense, he concluded Platonically, was self-moving and eternal (I.xxiii.53–54): "the soul feels that it is moved [*se moveri*], and when it feels this, it also feels that it is moved by its own power not by any other [*sentit se vi sua, non aliena moveri*], and that it could never occur that it be left by itself [*ut ipse umquam a se deseratur*]" (I.xxiii.55).

A first bond of the soul was still to the universal: "deus ipse," said Cicero in this chapter's first citation. So the truly wise person "will joyfully pass from the darkness here to the light there, though he will not break the chains of his prison-cell" prematurely (I.xxx.74). The soul, he elsewhere recalled Socrates, was the immortal auto-moving part retaining memory of the substance whence it came and whither it would return, as well as potentially remembered knowledge of all inventions, sciences and arts. He thus approved how Xenophon had described Cyrus the Elder bidding his sons farewell at his death by reminding them that the soul was simply being set free of his body (*De senectute* xxi–xxii, 78–81; Xenophon, *Cyropaedia* viii.7.17–22).

At the same time, soul was embedded in the humors, bones, nerves, veins, organs, muscles and flesh of a body moved by life processes shared with vines and trees and by sensations producing appetites and desires shared with beasts (*Tusculans* I.xxiv.56). While soul had memory, invention and reason—set divinely in the head (another Platonic, but also Hippocratic, touch)—it was also bound to all the affections stirred by the sensations (I.xxiv.57–xxix.70). This led Cicero to a more or less Stoic analysis of soul's relation to body through the passions or, in his term, *perturbationes*. Embodied soul could not achieve the good without using reason to control its passibility, a view of "the role of right reason" that Cicero, "not least," passed on to Augustine and others (Rist, *Augustine* 168). *Tusculans'* third, fourth and fifth books gave Cicero's analysis of how soul thus "used" reason.

If *Tusculans* ordered the universal and the physically human as first and last surroundings of soul-in-body, its second book studied environs narrower than the first, wider than the last. These were social. Immortal soul accorded with nature in effecting its duties in this sphere. Even were it mortal, virtue's prime source would still lie in social life: to live well in "strength and greatness of soul, in disdain and scorn for all things human [in the sense of any personal interest] and in all virtue" was to live for public *fama, laus* or *gloria* (I.xlv.109–xlvi.110). (Foley says the same of Homer's Penelope: *Female* 127–43.) Public renown confirmed our soul's fulfilment of its public duties and preparation for the heavenly "haven and place of refuge readied for us" (I.xlix.118). Here we see that the person's duties to and absorption in *generis humani societate*, as he repeatedly put it in the *De officiis*, were fully part of its bond with the universal. Nonetheless, *public* failures were the worst evil, marked by "disgrace [*dedecore*], crime and turpitude" (II.v.14). *Tusculans* attended rather little to these failures of duty. They, especially those of *decorum*, received detailed analysis in the *De officiis*, a writing of towering importance throughout the European Renaissance.

Tusculans began with soul's very nature and its relation to the universal. *De officiis* took as its domain what it began by suggesting was almost more important:

Since, as it was splendidly put by Plato, we are not born for us alone [*non nobis solum nati sumus*], but our country claims part of us and our friends part, and

since . . . humans are born for the sake of humans, so that they may be able mutually to serve each other [*ut ipsi inter se aliis alii prodesse possent*], so in this we
ought to follow nature as our guide, to contribute to the common stock things of
general benefit [*communes utilitates in medium afferre*] by exchanges of duties
[*mutationes officiorum*], by giving and receiving, and so by expertise, labors and
talents to bind fast the fellowship of humans to humans [*devincire hominum inter homines societatem*]. (I.vii.22)

The *De officiis* made the social bond preeminent. For humans, it was
something like a fundamental law of nature: for souls embodied, that is
to say, as opposed to souls considered in relation to the universal or in the
particularity of their relation to the physical body.

Asserting *societas* to be the ground of the human meant that Cicero
had to account for the relation between the collective and the personal,
indeed, for what "personal" was in such a context—never forgetting that
the personal was embodied soul. The debate offered in the *De officiis* regarding the play of person and society was complex. We best get to it by
first showing the extent of Cicero's insistence that fellowship (*societas*)
defined the human:

But perhaps the natural principles of community and fellowship [*communitatis et
societatis humanae*] should be further recalled. And first is that which is seen in
the fellowship of the whole human race [*in universi generis humani societate*],
whose bond is reason and speech, which unites humans through teaching, learning, communicating, debating and judging, and joins them in a sort of natural fellowship [*naturali quadam societate*]. (I.xvi.50)

We saw him make this point in the *De oratore*. Because of their natural
societas and *communitas* and because they are "rationis et orationis ex-
pertes"—share in reason and speech—humans, unlike other animals,
have "justice, equity and goodness."

Cicero was rather vague about the embedding in language of which he
continually wrote, but at least one ancient author is said to have understood languages too (in their variety) as differing surroundings also composing personhood. "Quintus Ennius used to say," wrote Aulus Gellius,
"that he had three hearts [*tria corda*], because he could speak Greek, Os-
can and Latin" (XVII.xvii.1). E. H. Warmington proposes translating
"tria corda" as "three brains" (*Remains of Old Latin* I: xviii.8 note *a*).
The phrase referred to affections received in the sensitive soul or powers
and adds another dimension to the ways in which person existed passibly
in the world. For Cicero all these specifically human conditions, circumstances and attributes inhered in and confirmed a total bond: "This is the
fellowship extending most widely to humans among one another and to
all with all [*latissime quidem patens hominibus inter ipsos, omnibus inter
omnes societas haec est*]" (*De officiis* I.xvi.51).

Humans, he wrote (echoing Aristotle), were like bees:

Just as swarms of bees do not congregate in order to make honeycombs but make honeycombs because they are gregarious by nature, so humans, and to a much greater extent, gathered together by nature, exercise their resourcefulness in acting and thinking.

Human association and community, "consociatio hominum atque communitas," confirmed by bonds of *justitia* keeping and marking balance among its members, grounded all other conditions and claims (I.xliv.157). *Communitas*, sociability, "which most conforms to nature," ruled. Even when extreme need seemed to justify an apparently unsocial act—for example, to save one's country—a closer look showed that such anti-communal acts were impossible or illegitimate (I.xlv.149): either *communitas* and need would actually be seen to coincide, or the action either would not save one's country or in "saving" it would destroy *communitas*. So if ever duties seemed in conflict, those "grounded in human fellowship [*hominum societate*]" should be chosen because they were *necessarily* right (I.xlv.150). Justice balanced person in society, the whole being first. Anything else shattered "what most accords with nature, the fellowship of humankind [*eam quae maxime est secundum naturam, humani generis societatem*]; as a person would die if parts of its body were to grow and separate at the expense of other parts" (III.v.21–22).

To liken human to bee *societas* generated interesting resonances. Nicole Loraux observes: "throughout Greek tradition, the bee [*melissa*] [was] the paradigm for the model wife" (*Children* 78). Xenophon's Ischomachus in the *Oeconomicus* compared the *oikos*, ground of the city, to a beehive where female slaves were worker bees and the mistress queen. There they "wove" raw materials into "combs"—textiles in particular, the well-run household in general (*Oeconomicus* VII.33–38). Pomeroy notes that the elder Pliny used *textum*, woven cloth, and *tela*, web, to describe hive-building (*Natural History* 11.x.22; *Oeconomicus* 63). Penelope weaving, unweaving and reweaving her shroud to stave off the suitors and to maintain the royal household's integrity exemplified this role. Exactly analogous was her weaving tales to prevent the suitors from murdering Telemachus. Winkler analyzes Penelope's seduction of the suitors into giving her yet more gifts—before Odysseus' admiring and rejoicing gaze—as evidence of her and Odysseus' like-minded attention to "enriching the household." "This is," he adds, "an important case of that mental similarity or *homophrosunē* which characterizes their marriage" (*Constraints* 147). Not just her fidelity but Penelope's attention to the welfare of the *oikos* grounded the universal admiration in which Penelope was held throughout antiquity. Winkler joins others in noting her centrality to the story and goal of the *Odyssey*, and does not disagree with John Finley's remark that Homer came close to "making our *Odysseia* a *Penelopeia*" (132–33; Finley, *Homer's* 3). Foley argues similarly, adding how the "web of relationships and responsibilities" which she is place her agency beyond such boundaries as "public" and "private" (*Female* 127–43, here 141).

Xenophon's *Oeconomicus* likewise emphasized the harmonious household and partnership of husband and wife in its daily organization, maintenance and welfare. It was at once civil society in little and ground of that wider society. The conjunction gave Cicero a soft spot for Xenophon's analysis. He chose the *De officiis*, his study of political behavior and interest, to recall translating it forty years earlier. It showed, he wrote, the managers' duty to save and increase household wealth by "diligentia et parsimonia [care and thrift]" and so serenely to expand its well-being (II.xxiv.87). In this wife and husband were little different from the careful managers of society at large.

Plato notwithstanding, the sense that the *oikos/domus* was constitutive of the *polis/civitas*, manifest in Antigone and Thrasymachus, lived on powerfully and long: "it was well understood," says Cooper of the Roman first century B.C. on, "that a man's claim to [political] power was in fact a claim on behalf of his household and family line." The claim was not in *his* name, but in that of a collective past and future also assuring stability of the political order as a whole, no modern distinction being made between "private" and "public" (*Virgin* 3). Cooper argues that this stayed the case into late Roman antiquity, but that from around the fourth century Christianity introduced acute tensions into this conjunction of family and society. It set the household "in the shadow of an otherworldly ideal, one that asks men and women to think of themselves as autonomous, detachable individuals with a spiritual fate independent of kin or class" (144). Veyne also identifies a "passage from 'civic man' to 'interior man'" between early Roman empire and later Christianity ("Introduction" 13). Peter Brown is more reserved. Of any such change during the 350 years from Marcus Aurelius to Justinian, he remarks that one can write neither of interior man nor of detachable individual nor of private family life: to do so is to adopt "the fatal anachronism that involves isolating the 'private' world from the public context that gave it its meaning throughout these centuries." "The principal change during this period of late antiquity," he adds, "is the slow evolution from one form of public community to another, from the ancient city to the Christian church" (*Antiquité* 226).

The matter returns in later chapters, but the force and durability of these irreducibly communal experiences needs keeping in mind. In *De senectute* (xvii.59), responding directly to Plato (whose *Republic* he also translated), Cicero has the elder Cato laud the *Oeconomicus* via a passage (IV.20–25) where Xenophon made Cyrus the Younger care for his household's order as the image of the whole kingdom's welfare. Perhaps this link between state and *domus* was what made Cicero's translation popular among Roman writers, Varro, Columella, Pliny, Quintilian and others all citing it over the original. Pomeroy remarks that their citations suggest that Cicero did not so much translate the work as make a version, adding matter of his own (*Xenophon* 70). One would like to know if he further stressed the state/*domus* link, but his version is long lost.

Xenophon's work is noteworthy, too (over its pseudo-Aristotelian counterpart) for the extent of its making women and men partners in the *oikos*—a point not foreign even to Aristotle (see Chapter 7). For Cicero, over the thirty-four years of their marriage, his wife Terentia had been just such a wise household manager and financial director. Further, of wealthy family, she was of substantial political importance to him. The state/*domus* tie was thus notable in her own person. Given, too, Cicero's love for his daughter Tullia it is reasonable to think that the *domus* was for him, as for the Greeks, model of the well-run city. Choosing Dolabella, profligate and eventual supporter of Caesar, as Tullia's third husband during Cicero's forced absence in 50 B.C., and maybe pursuing financial ventures of which he disapproved, Terentia might seem to have derogated from the model: hence their divorce. That did not change the standard of order or roles of husband and wife in patterns of duties and authority—even if Simon Goldhill is right in speculating that Xenophon's readers knew Ischomachus' wife Chrysilla an adulteress, him a pompous fool, the dialogue a malicious joke (*Foucault's* 140–41, 177n68). Perhaps some such odor attached to Xenophon's original was why others cited Cicero's "translation," which they certainly took as seriously as he did.

This just society agreed with the law of nations, "iure gentium," and with the laws of peoples, "legibus populorum," "by which the common weal of separate cities is maintained." But its deepest foundation was set in nature: "Again, *nature's reason itself, which is divine and human law*, begets [the just society] far more." Thus, "loftiness and greatness of spirit, and courtesy [*comitas*], justice and liberality accord more with nature than pleasure, life and riches" (*De officiis* III.v.23: my italics). It followed that "hominem naturae obœdientem homini nocere non posse"— "a human obeying nature cannot harm a human" (III.v.25). This is the view we saw that passible humanity and the rationally ordered world were naturally in a relation of "virtue," the "rightness" agreeing with the nature of things—a view much echoed by Seneca. Here we have already joined the issue of the relation between "singular" person and *communi-*

tas, a complicated consideration central to the *De officiis*, involving Cicero's familiar discussion of the four *personae* inherent in all human persons. *Personae* were actual behaviors and traits impressed on a soul readied to respond to necessities of natural and social being, enabling its embodied functioning in the world. *Persona* shared meanings with Greek *prosōpon*, but this usage seems original to the notoriously unoriginal Cicero, which has made Phillip De Lacy derive them (dubiously) from Panaetius ("The Four" 166–68; cf. Gill, "Personhood") and Long tie them to Aristotelian functionalism, stressing both the practical side of Stoic wisdom and its agreement with areas of Aristotelian ethics ("Greek Ethics" 164–66).

Humans, Cicero began, had two *personae*: "we have been dressed by nature as it were for two characters [*personis*]," one "common," the other "singular."

The common came from our shared reason and the superiority that set us above beasts, "from which [reason and superiority] derived everything *honestum decorumque*" (I.xxx.107). At issue here was the rational soul defining the essence of the human person. Cicero strikingly held that the four cardinal virtues, *sapientia, justitia, fortitudo* and *temperantia*, belonged to the human at this first level, combined under a wider idea of *honestas* or "moral rectitude," itself incorporating *verecundia*, the sense of shame or restraint. Cicero agreed here with the Stoic thinking that saw virtues (and vices) as *diatheseis*, ingrained states of the soul natural to the fact of being human.

Their condition of being fundamental states of the soul *qua* embodied meant that their combination enabled humans always to accord with the claims of *societas*, for it meant that a person could always control its relation to the whole by keeping the same balance at the micro-level, so to speak, as was kept at the macro-: "temperance and modesty and complete calming of passions of mind [*perturbationum animi*] and measure in things." He went further:

Under this heading is included what in Latin can be called *decorum*, for in Greek it is called *prepon*. Its essence is that it cannot be separated from moral rightness [*ab honesto*]; for what is seemly is morally right, what is morally right is seemly [*quod decet, honestum est et, quod honestum est, decet*]. (I.xxvii.93–94)

The *honestum* came first but was inseparable from *decorum*; and these accompanied every aspect of moral rectitude no matter which particular virtue was considered. In practice, *decorum* was inseparable from the virtues, themselves part of the foundationally human (I. xxvii.95). Its typical definition was: "*decorum* is that which agrees with human excellence in that by which its nature differs from that of other creatures"

(I.xxvii.96). Human nature lay under the *naturae ratio*, the *lex divina et humana* which gave the grounds of all *societas*. So *decorum* meant those ways of acting, in accordance with the *honestum*, through the four cardinal virtues which fitted the person to and by the social. In *De inventione*, Cicero had been quite clear that *honestum* contained everything referred to as *virtus* (there divided first into *prudentia*—wisdom, *iustitia*, *fortitudo* and *temperantia*) and how it named "a habit of mind [*animi habitus*] in harmony with reason and the order of nature" (II.lii.159). More specifically, he added, *prudentia* named the virtue of knowing good and bad and included *memoria, intelligentia, providentia* (foresight). *Iustitia* named the "habit of mind which gives each their due while preserving the common advantage," proceeding from nature and including *religio, pietas* (duty), *gratia* (gratitude), *vindicatio* (revenge), *observantia* (reverence). *Fortitudo* was divided into *magnificentia* (high-mindedness), *fidentia* (confidence), *patientia, perseverantia*. *Temperantia* included *continentia, clementia*, and *modestia* (II.lii.160–65). All this agreed with those Stoic beliefs of which we earlier saw a little. Such was the first *persona* of the human person.

The second "role" (like others, Cicero stressed the theatrical meanings of *persona*) was more particular. "Assigned specifically to persons [*singulis*]," it involved people's different mental and physical abilities, temperaments, inclinations of spirit and habits (*hexeis, habitus*) of action (I.xxx.108–9). Thus, it largely corresponded to the temperamental explorations of *Tusculans* books 3 to 5. These "singular" differences within the human were, though, also social: *decorum* controlled them, too. Its action now meant that whatever the differences of ability, temperament, inclination and habit, their practice and use never contravened "universal nature" (I.xxx.110). So everyone had to know their talents and properly judge their qualities and faults, like actors choosing roles (*personae*) best suited to them (I.xxxi.114). We recall *Tusculans* insisting that such knowledge was knowledge of the soul (I.xxii.52): that again which made humans humans—here, it seems, male or female, slave or free. The judgment by which a person estimated its nature required recourse both to the fundamental *persona*, the essentially human, and to "universal nature," the one embedded in, the other embedding, *societas* and *communitas*.

These *personae* were followed by two more, one imposed by chance or circumstance ("*casus aliqui aut tempus*"), the other adopted by decision. The third involved things like social, political or economic status by birth. Social surroundings were its essence—with a certain added weight of history. Here, *decorum* meant that a person's actions had to be adjusted to constraints that were even more evidently social than in that of the second *persona*. The fourth concerned "what role we ourselves may wish to assume, deriv[ing] from our will [*a nostra voluntate*]"—career choice, for example. Even now, despite what de Lacy implies in writing of this *persona* as "a matter of voluntary choice" ("The Four" 165), such *voluntas* was not simply "free." Not only was it caught up in the bonds of the first three *personae*, but it was again constrained by *decorum*, which meant that not only the "initial" choice but ongoing practice always had to follow socially educated and experienced *habitus* and the natural order of things (I.xxxi.115). Nature (the first and second *personae*) was primary and to act under its direction "the essence of seemliness, decorum"—"id enim maxime decet" (I.xxxiii.120). Such decorum was constraining, but also the essence of being *zōion politikon*, a human being. That Terentia could break with that seemliness was itself evidence of her humanity and personhood, even though shown by a bad choice (if it was) at the level of the fourth *persona*.

Personal or "singular" action was thus inseparable from the social, and all practice, behavior and habit were fitted by and to the claims of "community." Cicero even seemed to suggest other names for the cardinal virtues, *sapientia, justitia, fortitudo* and *temperantia*, to capture their functioning more particularly in relation to the social: respectively, *cognitio* (sometimes *prudentia*), *communitas, magnanimitas, moderatio* (I.xliii.152). Efforts to systematize the virtues were not always very clear. This suggestion from the *De officiis* clearly differed from the relationships of the virtues offered in *De inventione*. In the *Partitiones oratoriae* (§76), Cicero defined *prudentia* and *sapientia* as mildly differing aspects of one virtue. *De officiis* presumably gave Cicero's more mature idea that the same virtue could usefully be given different names to signal its application in different circles of personhood. *Sapientia* thus indicated an "attitude"—disposition, habit or *hexis*—of the person to the rational-natural wholly analogous to that indicated by *prudentia* in the sociopolitical: ability to know the good and the bad and act on them appropriately in both spheres. Just so did *iustitia* signal a person's knowing the balance of goods in rational nature and *communitas* that of singular worth and common benefit in social and political life; similarly for the cases of *fortitudo/magnanimitas* and *temperantia/moderatio*.

At the same time the reason and law of nature in whose ambit person and society could alone be understood were intimately joined to the sphere beyond the embodied human called the universe, the divine or the impassible. It was not just that soul released from body would "happily" come to "its own home" amid the stars, at last fulfilling its being by "seeing the truth" (*Tusculans* I.xix.43–44). Nor was it only that the truly wise person would "joyfully pass from the darkness here to the light there" (*Tusculans* I.xxx.74). To the point was Cicero's addition to the last remark that, even so, that person would not commit suicide but would "leave when called and released by god as if by a magistrate or some other lawful authority." Divine and social orders were *by nature* identical. That the relation with the divine could spontaneously be put in secular social terms shows the degree to which these spheres were also mutually enlaced. This gave the grounds on which Cicero asserted that the laws of societal and communal bonds between humans manifest in any given *civitas* extended to foreigners as much as to its citizens. To deny their attachment to all humans everywhere and always would be to "tear apart the common fellowship of humankind [*communem humani generis societatem*]." More, those who destroyed these bonds were

to be judged blasphemous even against the immortal gods. For they overthrow the fellowship among humans [*inter homines*] that the gods established, and the tightest bond of that fellowship is that it be judged more against nature for one human [*hominem*] to deprive another human [*homini*] for one's own gain than to endure every disadvantage, whether to externals, the body or even the soul itself, so long as it does not touch on justice—for this virtue is ruler and queen of all virtues. (*De officiis* III.vi.28)

These bonds were fundamental. Elsewhere, writing of Stoic *oikeiōsis* (of which more in a moment) and of the specific idea that by nature "children were loved by their parents . . . and from this source we trace the developed communal association of humankind," Cicero agreed with the Stoics that this further corresponded to the relations that held at all levels between persons and society, society and nature, nature and the divine, society and the divine, persons and the divine and indeed between all those circles of being that we have seen:

They also hold that the universe is ruled by the power of the gods, that it is a kind of common city and state of humans and gods [*quasi communem urbem et civitatem hominum et deorum*] and that each of us is part of this universe; from which it follows by nature that we put the common benefit before our own. For as the laws put the safety of all before the safety of singulars, so the man [*vir*] who is good, wise, law-abiding and aware of civic duty consults the benefit of all more than any one other's or his own. (*De finibus* III.xix.62, 64)

The last point did not mean that one person could have no benefit, but that *iustitia* and *communitas* balanced them with the social, natural, universal and divine. Cicero's remarks on Xenophon's *Oeconomicus* and long partnership with Terentia suggest that he would readily apply these assertions to women (should he think them needed)—as his general use here of *homo* rather than *vir* may imply.

In such passages, the thorough place of the person in the divine, in nature, in *societas* (society, fellowship, community) and in material world (*externa*) was comprehensively summarized: person was inseparable from the multiple surroundings that also constituted its passible essence or substance (*ousia*). It was no more separable either, said Cicero in the last-quoted *De officiis* passage, from the actuality of body (*corporis*), composed of the four elements and their qualities—as he recalled them elsewhere: "terrena, humida, ignea, animalis," earthy, moist, fiery, and of the soul or life itself (*anima*) (*Tusculans* I.xvii.40). And if in the texts just mentioned Cicero did not go far into the surroundings composed by the materiality of bodies (touching on but not detailing it when writing at length of the passions), he did in other writings. For him, too, ensouled body was related to physical world as to another of those surroundings intimate with—woven with—the human.

This experience of who-ness as embedded in interwoven and multiple surroundings was given in *Tusculans* and *De officiis* as Cicero's own—a personal, as well as a common, experience of human being. Even where exact descriptions might disagree, these multifold circumscriptions remained the underlying ground for him as for others. In the *De fato*, he held that the connection of the functions of soul and mind to the surrounding physical world duplicated their connection to the human body in which they were: subject to its functioning by a trained process of intelligent assent. Humors, temperament and character of the surrounding world were of a piece with those of the person, to be addressed by the same trained *prohairesis* and *hexis* as always gave passible acts their reasons, enabling mind to adjust circumstance to virtue and the world's natural order:

We see how great is the difference between the natures of places: some are healthy, others unhealthy, in some, people are phlegmatic and as if overfull with moisture, in others they are parched and arid; and many other things differ vastly from one place to another. Athens has rarified air, for which reason Athenians are thought sharper of wit, Thebes has dense, so Thebans are stout and vigorous. Yet the rarified air will not affect whether one listens to Zeno, Arcesilaus or Theophrastus, nor the dense whether one seeks victory at Nemea or the Isthmus. (*De fato* iv.7–8)

The nature of a locality only partly affected the sorts and times of actions, company chosen, general regime and behavior. It affected the first two *personae* directly, these marking the ground of humanity. It affected the third, one's social condition, somewhat, the fourth not at all. Interestingly, Galen, we shall see in Chapter 7, discussing the roles of female and male in generation, gave a biological explanation for something very like Cicero's first three *personae*. From such material cause, wrote Cicero, the motions of stars and planets affected some things but not others.

While the person was passibly subject to all its surroundings, the relation between them was also always subject to intelligent assent. Exactly that accord between surroundings and person, wrote Cicero, characterized the "wise" person living in freedom. For such a one knew that *libertas* was rightly defined as "potestas vivendi ut velis [the power to live as you will]." But who, Cicero asked,

lives as one wills except one who follows the things that are right [*recta*], who delights in duty [*officio*], who has a well-thought path of life mapped out ahead, who does not obey the laws from fear but follows and esteems them from judging that most salutary, who says nothing, does nothing or thinks nothing except voluntarily and freely [*libenter ac libere*], whose aims and courses of action start from and bear on oneself [*ab ipso proficiscuntur eodemque referuntur*], nothing counting more with that person than its own will and judgment [*quam ipsius voluntas atque iudicium*]? (*Paradoxa stoicorum* 34)

Such will and judgment were, then, perfectly adjusted to the natural orders of society, of material human being, of the physical world surrounding that being, of the universe and of the divine realm of things. All were equally rational, and while they differed from each other materially, so to speak, they were in fine-tuned sympathy as to their ordered processes—assuming reason, right, virtue, *decorum, honestum* and the rest. When all was rightly ordered, as it was in this instance of the sage, passible soul was in harmony with god or impassible soul or universal nature, person was internally in concord, soul with body, intellect with affects or passions, humors with senses, mind with society, body with physical milieu, particular with the general of what it was to be physiologically and mentally human. When Seneca advised that the "highest good was harmony of soul [or mind: *animi concordiam*], since the virtues must be where agreement and unity are" (*De vita beata* viii.6), and that the ideal being of thought, action and experience was to "agree with the nature of things" (iii.3), he had in mind these imbricated relations (*Moral Essays* 2.120, 106). In these circumstances, Gill agrees, there could be no "conflict between pursuing your own happiness and meeting the ethical claim of other people" (*Personality* 321). They necessarily coincided. The exact nature of the relations and its and their meaning for what a person was and what its actions and experiences could be were of major concern. They were at root the same, if different in third and fourth *personae* surroundings, we saw of relations of city and household, for Marcus Tullius or Terentia, Dolabella or Tullia.

In *De finibus* III, Cicero rendered the experience of these relations in Stoic terms, giving Latin translations for *oikeiōsis* (*commendatio*) and its associated concepts. At birth, a living creature felt "an attachment for itself [*ipsum sibi conciliari*], a *commendation* toward preserving itself and feeling affection [*diligere*] for its constitution [*status*] and the things tending to preserve that constitution." The result was that newborns desired things useful for their welfare and recoiled from their opposites. But they could have no such desire "nisi sensum haberent sui eoque se diligerent [unless they had a sense of and felt affection for their selfe]" (III.v.16). Useful things were those "which in accordance with nature are to be taken for their own sake" (III.vi.20). An act using these to preserve one's constitution was called, said Cicero, an "*officium* (for so I translate *kathēkon*)." By such acts humans came to know that these things, he repeated, "in accordance with nature" were part of the harmony in which they lived, joining them to nature and being their "highest good" (III.vi.20–21). Adult humans (as against newborns) thus became aware of being, as the etymology of *oikeiōsis* says, at *home* in the world, aware of their harmonious relation to all of "nature." *Officia* were the acts sustaining that harmony, being essential wisdom (*ipsam sapientiam*), the mark of "reason." They held alike in *domus* and *civitas* (III.v–vii.16–25).

These propositions have provoked wide debate over the past years. I shall not detail it. Suffice it to say that principal points of controversy have developed between those, like Troels Engberg-Pedersen and to a degree Gisela Striker ("Role"; but see "Following"), trying to analyze parts of a holistic system, and others, notably Long, striving to keep it whole (see esp. "Logical" as reprinted in *Hellenistic* 172–73, 185–88, chapters of *Stoic Studies*, and "Stoic Philosophers," 25–29). My point, anyway, is not whether one grants contemporary philosophical "validity" to the Stoics' argument, but what they actually say. Besides the Cicero passage, with an echo from Greek sources in Aulus Gellius (*Attic Nights* XII.5.7), two others are most often cited, one from Diogenes Laertius, the other from a fragmented papyrus of Hierocles discovered in 1901, which gives the first three hundred lines of an *Elements of Ethics* (English extracts in Long and Sedley). Like Cicero, Diogenes seems to have been citing Chrysippus:

The Stoics say that an animal has auto-protection as the object of its primary impulse, since Nature from the beginning endears it to itself [*oikeiousēi hautōi*], as Chrysippus says in his first book *On Goals*: "The first thing which is dear [*prōton oikeion*] to every animal is its own constitution and awareness of this; for it was not likely that Nature estranged the animal from itself, nor that, having made it, Nature gave it no attitude of estrangement or endearment. It follows that having constituted the animal, Nature endeared it to itself; for so the animal rejects what is harmful and pursues what is suitable (or akin) to itself."

The assertion that pleasure is the object of animals' primary impulse is proved to be false by the Stoics. For pleasure, they claim, if it really exists, is a secondary product only when Nature on its own has searched out and adopted the things which are suitable to the animals' constitution—like the flourishing of animals and bloom of plants. Nature made no absolute distinction between plants and animals, for it directs plants too, though without impulse and sensation, while in us some processes of a vegetative kind take place. But animals have the added faculty of impulse, through the use of which they go for what is suitable to them; so it accords with Nature for animals to be directed by impulse. And since reason has been given to rational beings for more complete authority, so for them it accords with Nature rightly to live according to reason—for reason supervenes as the craftsman of impulse.

Hence Zeno in his *On Human Nature* was first to say that the goal is to live consistently with Nature, that is to say, according to virtue; for Nature directs us towards virtue. . . . Again, life according to virtue is equivalent to living in accordance with experience of Natural events, as Chrysippus says in book one of his *On Goals*. For our natures are parts of the Nature of the universe. Hence the goal is to live in accordance with Nature, that is, in accordance with one's own nature and that of the universe, being active in no way usually forbidden by the common law, which is the right reason pervading everything and identical to Zeus, lord of the ordering of all that is. And the virtue of the happy person and a good flow of life consist in this: doing everything according to the agreement of each person's guardian spirit [*daimonos*] with the will of the director of the universe. (*Lives* VII.85–88: translation from Long, "Logical" 151–52, and Annas, *Morality* 159–60)

Annas observes that the emphasis on "cosmic nature" (Long's "Nature") appears to be found mostly in late Stoic writers—an appearance possibly due, as Long counters ("Logical" 155), both to "the fluidity of Stoicism in the hands of its ancient interpreters" and to the fragmentary nature of the sources. There is, too, the further problem about "late Stoic writers" that Cicero, Seneca, Hierocles, Diogenes Laertius and others claimed to be citing or paraphrasing earlier Stoics like Zeno, Cleanthes and Chrysippus, and did so, as far as one knows, directly from now lost texts independently of one another. More importantly, Annas argues that the view expressed here has little to do with "an *ethical* position at all," not only because virtue was "simply" conformity to Nature but because to suppose (as all ancients did) that ethics concerned an *end* in happiness meant that an agent had to reflect on its being and aims even as the appeal to cosmic nature pulled "the agent away from the kind of attachment to her own concerns which is needed for useful reflection on her final end to be possible" (*Morality* 160–62).

Firstly however conformity to nature per se involved a most unsimple rational process of reflection—whose very possibility was seen as indicating processes common to all and all-embracing but no less (re-)acted on/to by separate minds/persons. Secondly, to say that the Stoics did not separate value and fact in a providential universe is right. However "weak" (or not) may have been their arguments that that was how the universe was did not change the fact of the experience they sought to explain. This verdict of weakness may rather show a commentator's inability, *now*, not to assume such separation or to share a sense of being enlaced in such a universe. Indeed their non-separation is central to MacIntyre's argument about the flaws of modern western ethical supposition. For thirdly, to define "the ethical" foremost in terms of individual agency *is* a modern, even post-Kantian, move falsifying any ethics grounded, exactly, in a non-individualist sense of personhood. As Annas herself insists, one needs to set aside one's "own [modern] expectations of what an ethical theory is and should do" (*Morality* 3).

I do not want this trespass in specialist debate to distract us from the goal of observing such ancient thought and experience as was absorbed by these and later writers—for whom arguments in Cicero, Seneca's works and person and remarks in some Church Fathers were what Stoicism was. But I am of course making a claim even about what it was *possible* for later writers to absorb; and part of that claim concerns the absence of anything at all like the individualism just referred to. A point is that the "appeal to cosmic nature" was *no less* an "attachment to one's own concerns." In that sense, it hardly matters (here) whether or how Stoics before Cicero conceived of "cosmic nature" since the later views were certainly what got passed on. That said, it does seem to matter that allied experiences were in fact expressed, we saw, by Plato and Aristotle. That is also why it is unnecessary to emphasize recurrence of "cosmic nature" in Hierocles—or even Epictetus and Marcus Aurelius (the last two known to later Europeans only from the fifteenth and sixteenth centuries, Hierocles mostly for but a century: see Praechter for earlier). The general pattern into which a person fit—that sense of being passibly inscribed in multiple surroundings—appears readily able to be grasped and to have nothing to do with modern individualisms.

Most modern commentators agree that the teleological thrust of this thinking—the natural urge toward a rational good whose source and end were in the very order of nature—was foundational of the sense of personal identity, of the idea that virtue lay in achieving natural goods and of the claim that moral worth was revealed in magnanimous and just actions toward humans as a whole. Some assert such teleology unproven at best, at worst incoherent (as Descartes did in writing to the Princess Elisabeth [AT IV.273–74: August 18, 1645]). Some try to make Stoics' statements mean something other than what they nonetheless agree they really do seem to have said. My interest is in what they tell us of the *experience* of being that these expressed. In this regard, Simon Pembroke rightly notes how Stoic argument, that the newborn's *sense* of what was useful depended on the *oikeiōsis* it felt toward its own being and status, meant that they saw *oikeiōsis* and its opposite, *allotriōsis*, as "the conditions without which consciousness could not arise" (140). But that "consciousness" was not any sort of "self-love": reason did not stop at some "self," but took rational being on to nature and on to others, both integrally related to the person.

Consciousness so understood, as Diogenes Laertius' citations from Chrysippus and Zeno said, rested on the assumption that nature had implanted in mind a reason not "identical" *with* nature but a part of the same reason *in* nature. It thus led *naturally* through awareness of one's own being to that of one's part in nature. Engberg-Pedersen urges that this shows Stoics building "wholly from within practical thought itself an argument proper for their view of the human telos that nowhere relies on any premise outside human seeing," and avers that "the telos is quite concretely anybody's individual telos" (*Stoic* 43–44). From here to the claim that Stoics had an almost modern western view of human identity or counterwise that they were weak in lacking one, is not far. André-Jean Voelke *has* argued that the Stoics did elaborate concepts like will, individual, deliberation and self in ways directly presaging "Cartesian" thinking. Not only does he treat the Old, Middle and New Stoas as if they were simultaneous (claiming to reconstruct older texts from later ones "without deforming" them: *Idée* 7) but picks and chooses carefully. Even so he has to conclude that the idea of will—of person—changed markedly around the first century B.C.—which recalls others' remarks we saw about Diodorus Siculus and Epictetus. Too, while proposing nothing like Voelke's claim, Taylor implies that the Stoics were much farther along a steady path to modern views than the evidence I am adducing shows.

Long avers that such views ignore "the physical and theological underpinnings of Stoic ethics" ("Logical" 155). Indeed, Teun Tieleman faults Engberg-Pedersen's rejection of these foundations, showing that it forces him to ignore clear contrary evidence (esp. 229–32). The rejection parallels in impulse and effect Williams' series of rejections discussed in Chapter 3. "The Stoics philosophised about the mind," Long writes, but they never saw this as an "inquiry separate from their interests in logic, physics and ethics. . . . Attention to this point is essential for any sympathetic understanding of their significant contributions to what *we* call 'philosophy of mind'" ("Representation" 264); or again: "no clear distinction can be drawn in Stoicism between physics and ethics, between factual and moral statements" ("Language" 103). Marcia Colish notes that the Stoics identified "mind and matter with each other and with God [*logos*]." Reality was "totally unitary." Mind and body were "completely translatable into each other," "simply two ways of viewing the content within [a] continuum" (*Stoic Tradition* 1.23: she records analogous views in Aall 1.7–167; Heinze 9–172, and Kelber 44–88). There was no unimpeded path to "modernity": which does not mean that later views and experiences could not find emergent shapes and fragments in earlier ones.

Understanding one's personal relation to "nature," the harmony within and without one's own body and soul, as well as the natural affection between parents and offspring, led to feeling an equally natural attachment to other people. As one reasoned through one's being to rational nature, coming also "to perceive, know and understand wider and wider circles centered upon [us], we come not only to feel affection for others, we also make them part . . . of our own identity" (Kerford 195). Reasoning to Nature made one see how others sharing the same reason were of one's being. *Oikeiōsis* named "the tendency we have both toward developing self-concern and towards developing other-concern" (Annas, *Morality* 263; cf. Nussbaum, *Therapy* 342–43). For modern westerners these are discrete. For the Stoics they fell under one concept naming a life faculty fundamental to being a rational person. Just as to be a person was to be imbricate with nature, so it was to be imbricate with others. That was why Cicero insisted that "nunquam privatum esse sapientem," the fully rational being was never a private or isolated individual (*Tusculans* IV.xxiii.51). There is, he wrote elsewhere: "communis hominum inter homines naturalis . . . commendatio, ut oporteat hominem ab homine ob id ipsum quod homo sit non alienum videri," a natural common *oikeiōsis* of humans among humans, so that a human cannot be considered alien by another human, simply because one is human (*De finibus* III.xix.63)

Cicero's source extended this to the assertion that "we are thus by nature fitted for unions, societies, states [*ad coetus, concilia, civitates*]." Virtuous action involved acting always to benefit the wide community of humans. Just as one drew from awareness of one's own nature an awareness of one's harmony with the universe so one drew from antipathy against being alone an awareness that "nos ad coniunctionem congregationemque hominum et ad naturalem communitatem esse natos," we are born for association, mutual human union and natural community (*De finibus* III.xix–xx.63–65). All commentators agree that *oikeiōsis* toward people was no less fundamental than those inward toward one's being and outward toward material nature and the universal. The *officia* maintaining harmony in this domain were those Cicero studied in the work so titled. Justice, friendship and their concordant virtues were the marks of this community, all of them confirming the universality of the harmonious rational order in which humans participated. *Oikeiōsis* in this aspect was, Striker remarks, "the foundation of justice" ("Role" 161). Engberg-Pedersen concurs ("Discovering" 175–83). At least as to these aspects of a person Cicero was in full agreement with the Stoics.

If they developed and thickened these ideas, the Stoics surely did not originate them. Books Eight and Nine of the *Nicomachean Ethics*, "abruptly" applied to an exploration of friendship, have not seldom been seen as an interpolation from another work, disunited from the preceding books. But if one considers that the goal of the *Ethics* is to explore the nature of the good life, that the good life is defined as fulfilment of true nature and that human nature is above all defined in terms of reason and sociality, friendship is clearly the epitome of the good life: the *polis* or community in little. Friendship, said Aristotle, was a communal association based in justice; different sorts of friendships echoed different sorts of communities (1159b30–32, 1160a30); the forms of friendship echoed the forms of a person's relationship to oneself, to the determination to retain life, security, the rational part of being and the accomplishment of virtue (1166a1–35). True "selfe-love" for Aristotle was very much like these descriptions of *oikeiōsis*. It involved a sense of being in the world, a need to fulfill one's humanity to the full, knowledge that one did this through *decorum, prudentia, phronēsis*, and that these lock one into—as it were—the world and all the forms of one's community, iterated in little in those of friendship (1168a28–1169b1). The good person was *philauton*, a lover of selfe. This person was defined as also of most aid to the community, in fact and as example. If everyone fully achieved their humanity in this way, then "the common welfare would be realized to the full and all would obtain the greatest goods, since virtue is the greatest good" (1169a10–12). Cicero appears to have been summing up, perhaps bringing together, a number of traditional strands.

CHAPTER FIVE

Senecan Surroundings

At the start of his *De providentia*, Seneca took up Cicero's and the Stoics' intimate binding of the divine, natural and human: "between good men and the gods is a friendship brought about by virtue." This statement, he continued, actually fell short of the case. The bond was nearer identity. With the gods, humans shared not just virtues, but reason and speech, being and fortune, wisdom and life. Only the "time" experienced by the gods differed. "Do I say friendship?" he exclaimed: "Rather is it a matter of necessity and likeness, for a good person differs from god only in the element of time, [being] his pupil, emulator and true progeny, whom his glorious parent, no mild overseer of virtues, raises as do strict fathers with much severity" (*De providentia* I.5: *Moral Essays* 1.6). The gap between eternity and history would be vital in Augustine's thinking about human existence and the nature of being. For Seneca, like most Stoics, it signaled the only difference between eternal and embodied souls, which otherwise echoed one another's *logos*. Indeed, the Stoic sage (*sapiens*) was one who sought to reduce the gap to nothing. That search proved particularly problematic.

Like Cicero and other precursors, Seneca experienced person (soul, mind, being) as webbed in crowded surroundings: divine and universal, pertaining directly to *anima*, human, social and materially worldly, to name the clearest. A person's enlacement in these surroundings was usual to being human, implying particular behaviors. That people's everyday behavior sometimes seemed to ignore the fact made *that* behavior deviant and corrupted their humanity. Seneca's moral advice did not propose behavior attainable only in an imaginary world. It aimed to make people *humanior*, more human—even if "the majority of people fail[ed] to accord" most of the time with the natural rule of their surroundings (Long, "Logical" 138). Seneca urged changes in behavior, not in humanity. He urged behavior *more* in accord with the experience of being human, not less. Moral behavior required proper adjustment of the person to these surroundings—which I explore in the order just given: universe, *anima* (*animus*), human, society, material world, although doing so falsifies their experience as inseparably joined.

The human mind operated as it did because its intentions and deliberations worked to an end "to which the divine ruler [*rector*] directed them, by whom form was given to things" (*De beneficiis* I.vi.2: *Moral Essays* 3.24). Mind was an integral part of the universe: "universorum enim pars sum" (*De beneficiis* VI.xx.1). When mind (*animus*) "touched" the "immense spaces" which surrounded it, it was returning "to its origin as if released from chains [of the body]," to "dwell there not as among alien things but as among its own, proof of its divinity being the pleasure divine things gave it" (*Naturales quaestiones* [NQ] I, Pref. 12). As the universe moved, so did soul or mind. Nature, god, divine reason, fate and fortune were one, and humans part and aspect of it. These several names given to the universal whole were analogous to those given to one mind: "So, then, you may speak of nature, fate, fortune; they are all names of the same god who uses his power in various ways. And justice, honesty, prudence, courage and temperance are goods of one mind" (*De beneficiis* IV.viii.3).

This echoed the diversity of terms Cicero used to name the widest sphere—the divine, universal, impassible, Nature—by which the human was surrounded, *circumdatus*. You would not be wrong, said Seneca, to call whatever was the principal rational power, "ruler and guardian of the universe," whether "Jupiter" or another, "fate," "providence," "nature," or "universe," all of them just different names for the various qualities, capacities and events rationally operating in *ousia* (NQ II.45.1–3). He reiterated the point, asserting that it was all one to say that "it is all-powerful god, or incorporeal reason builder of vast works, or divine spirit diffused with equal energy through all things greatest and smallest, or fate and an immutable sequence of causes bound to one another" (*Ad Helviam matrem* viii.3: *Moral Essays* 2.440). We shall return often to the *spiritus* named here. It was essential as well to the human per se and to the place of the person in the material natural world (cf. Delatte et al.). Just now, I am concerned with the relation of mind to the divine: a bond Seneca never tired of stressing, fundamental as it was to the very nature of person as rational.

Not surprisingly, as the just-quoted passages hint, Seneca insisted that the human mind could be given the same set of names: like god over the universe, mind was "the director and ruler of us." So none could say what best to call it: "One will say it is spirit, another some harmony, another a divine force and part of god, another the subtlest part of the soul, another an incorporeal power; there will not be lacking someone to call it blood, or another to call it heat" (NQ VII.25.2). Rational mind did not just "echo" the reason of nature or of god. It was the same thing. Reason that was "cause" in nature was reason in mind. When working at its best, it was by an "art" (*ars, technē*) that was an *imitatio* of nature (*Epistulae morales* [Ep] lxv.2). This *imitatio* did not just copy objects in the world. It iterated the process by which "divine" reason ordered the universe, nature, fate, providence or life force. Prime cause was god, "ratio faciens [creative reason]." Human reason did not just image it in little. It was *of* it (Ep lxv.12–14). As the anti-Stoic Plutarch was to echo Seneca, naming Plato in *Timaeus*: "the human soul . . . is a portion or copy [*mimēma*] of the soul of the universe and joined together on principles and in proportions congruous with those governing the universe" ("On Moral Virtue," *Moralia* 441ff: 6.26/27). Or again: "The soul, however, when it has partaken of intelligence and reason and concord, is not merely a work but also part of god and has come to be not by his agency but both from him as source and out of his substance" ("Platonic Questions" 1001c: 13¹:1.32–35).

Divine reason ("divina ratio") was "set over all things," "beneath none": "our [reason] is the same because it is from it" (Ep xcii.1). The mind in which this reason lay (the two often synonymous) humans could "set in dominion over all things and make possessor of the universe." Its boundaries were the same as those of the gods (Ep xcii.32). Reason acting so was "keeping to the road that nature prescribed for us, not swerving from it" (Ep cxxii.19). Reason being of the divine, rational action was "imitation of nature [*naturae imitatio*]" and led to "the highest good"— which was "to conduct oneself according to the will of nature [*ex naturae voluntate*]" (Ep lxvi.39).

For, finally, "right reason is single and of one sort." Material things decayed, not reason, which "is nothing else than a part of the divine spirit set in human body" (Ep lxvi.12). So the good peculiar to humans was to attain "perfect reason" (Ep lxxvi.9). Because reason defined nature's universal order, the genuine happy life for humans, apex of *being* human, was to be at one with rational nature (Ep cxxiv.14): having a "clear and flawless mind, rival of god's." As a rational animal, a human's highest good lay in identity with nature (Ep cxxiv.23–24); nature that was also the universe, the divine, fate, impassible substance.

To obey god was therefore freedom, "deo parere libertas est" (*De vita beata* xv.7: *Moral Essays* 2.140). To do so put one in unison with the universe, was "to live according to the nature of things and follow the example of the gods" (*De beneficiis* IV.xxv.1). To be in the natural material world necessarily tied the human to the divine, "would move your soul/mind [*animum*] with a certain intimation of the divine"—which was why people venerated so much of the natural world (Ep xli.3). "The universe," Plutarch agreed, "is a most holy temple and most worthy of a god; into it man is introduced through birth" to know the depths of the "divine mind" ("Tranquillity of Mind," *Moralia* 477c: 6.238/39). To reach to the "immensum [the boundless universe]" was not only to be in concord with nature, but to live fully the "great and noble thing [that] was the human soul," without limits "save those shared with the gods" (Seneca, Ep cii.21). Whoever did so would have become the sage, bathed in an aura of "divinity, heavenliness and grandeur," reaching the soul's supreme good (Ep lxxxvii.19–20). The way to this achievement lay through the many difficulties entailed by the soul's embodiment, whose defeat was the job of philosophy. Harder yet, to approach the gods was to depart from, deny and risk losing, the characteristics fundamental to being human.

Alexander of Aphrodisias, around the year 200, offered some version of "willed" being. A century and a half before, Seneca addressed a short treatise on the sage to his younger relative and friend Annaeus Serenus. The idea got tangled in perplexities beyond the paradoxes of Stoic philosophy. For Seneca's *sapiens* was wise to the exact degree of his disjunction from all social and communal ties. Even Seneca, addressing the same recipient elsewhere, queried the idea on grounds that Stoics asserted: "We shall engage in affairs to the very end of life, we shall never cease to work for the common good, to help each and all, to give aid even to our enemies when our hand is feeble with age" (*De otio* I.4: *Moral Essays* 2.183). He argued that people belonged to several societies (*res publicas*), from the vast one embracing humans and gods, bounded not by the earth but by the "path of the sun," to the smaller one of the "city" and yet smaller ones of family, friends and other communities—a thought Descartes would elaborate. All or each of these life circles or spheres could satisfy the demands of engagement, as did both action and contemplation, depending on one's condition and state of life (*De otio* iv.1–2). Here and in the *De vita beata*, Seneca argued that the indifference he praised was not to these areas where principles of *virtus* and *dedecus* were in play, but to worldly wealth, which impeded them.

One might think arguments of this sort convincing enough. Worldly wealth, however pleasant and enjoyable, was indeed inessential to the natural communities, human and other, that Stoics held essential to life. But this was not Seneca's argument in his *De constantia sapientis*, which took the first of Cicero's *Paradoxa Stoicorum* a contradictory step further. The republican had argued that the truly wise man, like Bias of Priene, was unmoved at losing all his belongings: he did not consider such "toys of fortune" among his goods. Cicero had then given a list of truly wise Romans, a list limited to those who lost or risked their lives to benefit the Roman people (*Paradoxa* 8–13). This was more or less what Seneca argued in the *De vita beata*. The *De constantia* advanced a radically different idea.

The sage, he argued in a straightforward syllogism, was one who could live wholly impassibly: "For if injury is the suffering [*alicuius mali patientia*] of some harm, and if the sage is one who suffers no harm [*nullius mali est patiens*], no injury is attributable to the sage" (*De constantia* v.3). This person wise in impassibility (*impatiens*) did not just obey the gods and conform to the nature of things, but "stood nearest neighbor to the gods and like a god except for being mortal and living in time" (viii.2). Such a person would be wholly impervious to the world—a demand that explains why the *sapiens* was so rare that even Chrysippus had never known one. Only loss of *virtus*, said Seneca, could harm the *sapiens*. Virtue, usually the contrary of *dedecus* but here more like a resolve to impassibility, was also the only thing for which a human could be responsible. Unlike other goods, virtue was in the hands of a person rather than of *fortuna* (v.4–5). That was why the sage led a wholly ascetic life, nothing of fortune crossing his threshold (xv.5): a barrenness perhaps depicting the tautology of an argument from impassibility that necessarily meant that whatever "virtue" lay behind it had to be disjoined from the world. Seneca did not shrink from the violence of its implications.

He told the exemplary story of the impassible philosopher Stilbo, whose home city of Megara had been sacked by hostile forces. Asked by the victor whether he had lost anything, Stilbo responded that he had not, all his goods were with him: "omnia mea mecum sunt." Seneca added that his estate had been plundered, his daughters raped, his country taken by foreigners, he himself now interrogated by a hostile king in arms. Yet, he ended: "he wrested victory from him and bore witness that although his city had been captured, he was not only undefeated but unharmed" (v.6–7). He was, to put the earlier syllogism's phrase affirmatively rather than negatively, "ullius mali impatiens." To be so, he had not just to ignore loss of material belongings, but be utterly cut off from all social relations: even the rape of his daughters was counted as affecting "things" wholly "*adventicia*" (v.7). This extreme of sagacity was a problem in the very work in which Seneca offered it. He ended by stating that one should always strive for such wisdom: that there be "something undefeated, someone against whom fortune can do nothing, is to the good of the commonwealth of humankind" (xix.4). This good required, though, that the human be loosed from the ties that alone made it human. Here was no reasoning for intelligent assent to passibility, but for denial of humans' passible nature.

Defeating fortune, he said elsewhere, humans achieved the "knowledge of selfe and nature [*sui naturaeque cognitio*]," and of reason's being, source and relation to the world, that defined the wise person (Ep lxxxii.6). Doing so exemplified the sage (Ep xcviii). The Stilbo case went much further, and Seneca worried it again in a letter which began by noting Epicurus' protest at its claim that "the highest good . . . is an impassible soul [*animus impatiens*]" (Ep ix.1). He replied by arguing that the idea that the wise person was auto-sufficient ("se ipso esse contentum" or "se contentus est sapiens": Ep ix.1, 13) had been badly interpreted. At one level no one could be so, all being dependent on "friends" and a general relation to society (Ep ix.13–15). At another, the wise person was auto-sufficient in attaining interior happiness and peace through knowledge of the nature of human reason and its coherence with that of the universe (Ep ix.21). Such was Stilbo's achievement.

Part of the trouble, said Seneca, was that *impatientia* was a poor rendering of Greek *apatheia*. It mixed not feeling with ability to ignore feeling (Ep ix.2). This just complicated things. As we shall see, he had to face the issue of whether or not passions were diseases of reason, to be cured and voided, or irrational motions of the soul, to be controlled (or ignored). Most Stoics held the first. If Seneca agreed, he was indeed talking about not feeling the affects of human and social ties. Letter ix asserted the lesser case, arguing that Stilbo tamed these affects. *De constantia* urged rather that he had cured the malady of the soul that they were, voiding them utterly—but cutting human ties. Aulus Gellius was to record his Platonist teacher Calvisius Taurus saying that the sage could endure harmful affects but "not altogether not admit them to his awareness." "*Analgēsia*" and "*apatheia*," insensibility and impassibility, were "censured and rejected" by such as the wise and learned Panaetius (*Attic Nights* XII.v.10). Diogenes Laertius held early Stoics to have thought the sage "*apathē*," impassible, though not to the extent of becoming "cruel and hardhearted." Yet *apathē* also described *ton phaulon*, the bad, mean, thoughtless or indifferent person (*Lives* VII.117). Fifteen centuries later Descartes surely intended both meanings when he told Elisabeth: "I'm not one of those cruel philosophers who want their sage to be unfeeling" (AT IV.201–2: May 18, 1645).

It was this fruit of *apatheia* that Seneca had "Stilbo's disciple" Crates reject in his tenth letter, on grounds that to live alone, commune with one's own mind and be absorbed in one's own singularity of reason was to be engrossed "cum malo homine [with a bad/evil man]" (Ep x.1). It was to combat nature, isolating oneself from one's worlds. To be sure, "soul and reason perfected in the soul" were "proper to the human," indeed the highest good—humans being rational animals and their perfection lying in living rationally according to nature (Ep xli.8–9). In these last terms was the rub. Seneca, too, after all, knew that to be human was to be enlaced in natural and divine surroundings. These included the social, and in another letter he replied directly to the Stilbo case as opposing the "common feeling, humanity and sociability" with all humans that it was philosophy's goal to further. It failed if it taught "unlikeness," *dissimilitudo*, if it urged, as the *De constantia* did, disjunction from human ties (Ep v.4): this was the later "monstrosity" glimpsed in Chapter 1.

Seneca agreed, above all, that to be human was to be woven in social bonds. Without them one was not human. That was why of all passions Seneca decried anger as most furthering the disunion he seemed to praise in *De constantia*. The angry soul was not just unable to rule itself. It was "forgetful of decency [*decoris*], unmindful of ties [*necessitudinum*], shut to reason and counsel, unfit to discern the right and true" (*De ira* I.i.2: *Moral Essays* 1.106). "Ruining" those it seized, making them *non sanos*, anger destroyed the decorum, ties, reason and understanding that defined the human. Speech, too, final defining trait of humanity, anger reduced to unintelligibility (I.i.4). From Hesiod to Homer and beyond, Leonard Muellner shows, the anger of *mēnis* menaced and destroyed societies and culture. The very word was taboo (*Anger*). More recently, in *Restraining Rage*, William Harris has explored the reasons why the ancients thought that anger had to be curbed and the ways in which it might be. (His book appeared too late for me to give it full due.) Anger, says Gill of Aeneas' killing Turnus at the end of the *Aeneid*, was "a certain kind of madness." He finds exemplars in Seneca's *Phaedra* and *Medea* ("Passion" 213, 215–28). We saw other cases in Chapter 3. The traits and habits from which anger disjoined a person were those essential to humanity. They also ran counter to the "virtue" praised in the *De constantia*. But Seneca famously ended the *De ira* by demanding them: "let us cultivate humanity," "colamus humanitatem." He called for love for all humans and care for one's own humanity—meanings not synonymous but implying each other. Anger should not turn us from life to inhabit past wrongs, from helping to hurting (III.xliii.5). Aristotelians held that some anger—as at vile acts—was in fact a mark of humanity. So Taurus urged that lack of anger, *aorgēsia*, differed from insensibility, *analgēsia*: a just measure was good (Gellius, *Attic Nights* I.xxvi.10–11). Seneca's examples pro and con suggest that he never resolved these tensions (on the contexts, polemics and psychophysiology of the *De ira*, see Fillion-Lahille; on its humane tensions, see Nussbaum, *Therapy* 402–38).

Anger was above all not "secundum naturam," in accord with nature.

It erased the "mildness" basic to a person when "habitus" was "in right state of mind." In "cruelty" it acted directly against the grounding human trait of being "loving of others." In hostility, it negated a person's being "born for mutual help and desiring togetherness [congregari]." Humans had to be of use (prodesse) to others, to succor even strangers, to "expend themselves for the good of others." Anything else went against nature at large and human nature in particular: "For human life is established in mutual services [beneficiis] and concord and is tied communally into a compact and shared resource [in foedus auxiliumque commune constringitur], not by terror but mutual love" (De ira I.v.2–3). Right action meant always working for society and community (I.xi.5). The "most certain virtue" was that "which examined the selfe closely, deeply and at length, dominated it and proceeded slowly and purposefully" toward right fulfillment of its nature (I.xi.8). That was why Seneca sought to give Serenus the peace of mind that would enable him to be "more serviceable and useful to friends, relatives, all citizens and then all humankind" (De tranquillitate animi I.10: Moral Essays 2.206). To cherish humanity in all ranks and kinds, Cicero's native and foreigner, woman and man (maybe free and slave), was one with cultivating one's own humanity. That was why domus and civitas, oikos and polis were mutually intricate, with implications and consequences we began to see in Chapters 3 and 4 and explore more in Chapter 7.

Humans acted rightly when they did as the law did, echoing in personal action the reasoned social order that itself matched the rational processes of the universe (De ira I.xvi.6). Any passion let loose—anger, luxury, avarice, lust, ambition—was wrong insofar as it took a person away from the calmness of ordered "lofty and sublime virtue" (I.xxi.1–4). "Born to a given state and temperament of body," certain feelings were natural to a person (Ep xi.6). Where needed, however, these could be overcome and changed by example and teaching, inculcating new habit and intention. People could be moved toward the humanness from which they had derogated. They could be made more human, humaniores, as Seneca put it. To attain this control over selfe, mind was to be trained, habitus fixed, prohairesis given rule: "Education calls for the greatest and most beneficial attention; for it is easy to set tender minds in order, but vices that have grown with us are cut back with difficulty" (De ira I.xviii.2).

"We should begin to shape and rebuild our soul," he wrote elsewhere, before depravity hardened it (Ep l.5). All shared the idea of habitus, will and intention as faculties to be bred to their full humanity (for auto- and other-care). Long notes Seneca's younger contemporary Epictetus constantly stressing "the need for suitable education." The view was basic to all schools of philosophy, not just the Stoic ("Freedom" 191)—an idea illumined by Nussbaum's trope of educating a woman philosopher that organizes her *Therapy*. "How else can this be achieved," asked Epictetus' contemporary, Plutarch, "except through reason . . . carefully trained quickly to hold back the passionate and irrational part of the soul when it breaks bounds?" ("Tranquillity of Mind" 465b: 6.168/69). By such training, the virtues that were those of law in the social sphere were set in the educable faculties of mind as rule of duty—no abstract duty, such as Enlightened Europeans would know, but one as practical as Seneca's *De ira* samples project. These virtues would become natural *habitus*, inbuilt guide to reasoned assent. Their rule conduced far more to a person's right reason and right action in the world than did that of law as an outside demand to be obeyed ("Quanto latius officiorum patet quam iuris regula!"). Well-trained *habitus* would react aright and *prohairesis* reason in unison with nature when "pietas, humanitas, liberalitas, iustitia, fides" were thus ingrained (*De ira* II.xxviii. 2): names of qualities whose part and place in *animus*, we saw, were analogous to that of god's powers in the universe.

This education would make sure that person was in a natural relation with its surroundings, from the widest to the most singular. For just as one should strive to accomplish one's "identity" with gods of the divine realm, so one should live to the full the bonds of one's community and its members and be certain, too, that one's internal order was in harmony *qua* human. All these relations together were what it meant to say that humans were "born for communal association [*ad coetum*]." Society (*societas*) could not be kept "secure except by the mutual protection and love of the parts" (*De ira* II.xxxi.7). The internal order of which Seneca spoke here was literally that of the body's physical members. But among these, he had said earlier, was also the mind: "For the mind is not set apart and does not view the passions from without, so that it may not suffer [*patiatur*] them to go further than they ought, but is itself changed into the passion and so cannot recover its useful and saving power, now betrayed and weakened" (*De ira* I.viii.2).

This argument seems to have been directed against Aristotle and others, like Cicero, who agreed that the passions belonged in an irrational part of the soul and hence could be brought under reason's control. In *Academica* (I.x.38–39), Cicero had observed how this disagreed with the views of the Stoics (and see Plutarch, "On Moral Virtue" 440d–442c: 6.18–29), like whom Seneca was on the contrary proposing that the passions were an "infirmity" of reason and required an altogether different order of educated control: reason had to be "cured" of them (and see Frede, "Stoic"; Fillion-Lahille 203–20; Nussbaum, *Therapy* 78–101,

359–438). The vices of which he wrote were a cancer in the rational soul: "passion and reason are only changes in mind toward the better or worse, they do not have separate and distinct sites" (*De ira* I.viii.3). Both live "in the breast" (II.xix.4). To be sure, he did not always make this claim, insisting elsewhere, for example, that he had "often spoken of the difference between the diseases [*morbos*] of the mind and the passions [*adfectus*]," the ones being hardened vices, the others sudden impulses (Ep lxxv.11ff.). He also spoke of rational and irrational parts of the soul (Ep xcii.1).

The difference should have affected educational requisites, understanding of the distribution of the soul's faculties and the rule one could have (or not) over the passions. In practice, Seneca's many hesitations imply, the difference hardly changed any of these. Human nature stayed the same whether one argued with Socrates, doubted with Carneades, relaxed with Epicurus, battled with Stoics, overshot with Cynics or argued with Zeno, Pythagoras, Democritus, Aristotle or Theophrastus (*De brevitate vitae* xiv.2–xv.4: *Moral Essays* 2.334–38). Whatever difference lay between their views of the details of human being it little touched the fact of the passible person's fit with its surrounding worlds and the many consequences making that experience unfamiliar to the modern western mind.

The difference between conceiving the passions as wholly irrational or as an infirmity of reason did not affect soul or mind in itself or in its bond with the universal. It did not mean any the less that "the whole body served the mind," which stayed hidden within, commanding the body according to temperamental characteristics (*De clementia* I.iii.5: *Moral Essays* I.366). It might be that "this body is a weight and punishment on the soul," crushing it and holding it "in chains." Yet reason always kept the soul tied to its divine origin, able to think selfe away from that servitude (*mancipium*) and the shackle of a body otherwise binding its freedom (Ep lxv.16, 21). It might be that "this little body, prison and chain of the soul, is tossed to and fro," but soul was "sacred and eternal," and on it "no hand could be laid." Hidden in body it yet ranged over all space and time, past, present and future. Unable to suffer "exile" mind was "free and akin to the gods and at home in every world and every age" (*Ad Helviam* xi.7). The wondrous beauties of nature had "as their highest glory mind as its surveyor and admirer," and because of their mutual integration and constant exchange of capacities and qualities, the person could: "never be in exile in the world, or anything in the world alien to a human" (*Ad Helviam* viii.4). He repeated this toward the end of his life in the penultimate book of the *De beneficiis* (VI.xxiii.5–7).

The difference of views about control or eviction of the passions, about the relation between affections and rational mind, did not mean, either, that the "virtues" to which one was trained were any less what made a person "more human" (*humanior*): the training just fortifying the fact that a "human is a social being born for the common good" (*De clementia* I.iii.2). Indeed that was what the seven books of the *De beneficiis* were about: reciprocity of services, intricate exchange of giving and receiving, and elaborate courtesies governing transfer of benefits essential to the welfare and stability of community and society—household business, municipal affairs, city politics and imperial organization alike. One infers that Seneca's lost *De officiis* taught similar lessons, although St. Martin of Braga's possible sixth-century epitome of that work implied that it most stressed the human virtues, *officia*, as Martin had them, necessary for the well-lived life. Nor did the difference with regard to the passions mean any less that whatever the pressures one lived under, one's first, second and third resources were always to seek the many varieties of social and communal intercourse and succor in the city, country, many countries and the world; but at home too, among friends, even in the study (*De tranquillitate animi* iv.1–8).

Here is Seneca's version of Ciceronian *honestum*, the "moral worth" that defined the good person's action and being in community. Embodying reason, nature, truth, *fides*, worthiness, order and temperance, *honestum* drew together the four cardinal virtues of wisdom, justice, courage and fortitude (Cicero, *De finibus* II.xiv.45–48; also *De inventione* II.lii.159–65). Above all it named the balance of personal reason and moral behavior in society. Seneca, who defined the "supreme good" as achievement of "perfect reason," further defined it as "that which is morally worthy [*honestum*]." Here was "the unique good," all others being "falsa et adulterina," alloyed and debased (Ep lxxi.4–5). To follow the *honestum* was to follow god, nature, soul and society. To be happy was to know that the "unique good" was found in the *honestum* (Ep lxxiv.10). To act according to this moral virtue was for instance to die for the community (*pro re publica*) on the spot, if one knew one ought to do so. It was to purchase the "safety of all one's fellow-citizens" at the cost of one's own and be supremely happy in doing so. This *honestum* revealed the "perfect soul" (Ep lxxvi.27, 30). It was, Seneca repeated, the "perfect good" (Ep cxviii.10) and necessarily so (Ep cxx.3).

Here, discussion merits exploitation of the probable epitome of Seneca's *De officiis* that was Martin of Braga's *Formula vitae honestae*. Claude Barlow traces long speculation that this condensed the *De officiis* as elsewhere Martin had the *De ira* (Martin, *Opera* 206). Marcia Colish takes it for granted (*Stoic* 2.297). Through the European middle ages into the sixteenth century Martin's work, also known as the *De quattuor virtutibus*, had a huge afterlife, with more than 635 known Latin and vernacular manuscripts, many commentaries and then printed editions (Barlow in *Opera* 7, 232). Since the work is found unidentified in so many manuscripts, Hans Haselbach is surely right to think that far more copies must survive than are presently known (*Seneque* 155–56).

Written between 570 and 579, Martin's treatise explored the import of the four cardinal virtues of *prudentia, magnanimitas, continentia* and *iustitia*, "adorned by which the human spirit could attain moral worthiness of life [*honestatem vitae*]." Each of these "duties" or "services" (*his officiis*) was intricately tied to the others, making a person "morally worthy and endowed with a good character" (*Opera* 237). Prudence meant living by "right reason," judging things not by others' opinion but their "nature," overvaluing nothing, fixing oneself as one and the same but flexible to circumstance and demand, ever acting advisedly, never in ignorance or impotence, living soberly with those about one and knowing one's limits, abilities and surroundings (238–41). Magnanimity or fortitude meant courage to do what circumstance required and restraint in neither bullying nor overreaching (241). Continence meant cutting superfluities from around one (*circumcide*[*re*] *superflua*), limiting appetite in property, acts and emotions, finding measure in relations with others and in speech (242–46). On the last, Martin was expansive (243–45), echoing Cicero's—and Ennius'—regard for language as another circumstance "around one," essential to a person's being. Justice was "a silent agreement of nature made for the mutual aid of the multitude," not a human but "divine law and bond of human society" (246).

These four virtues made one "a perfect man" (247), provided one kept them in measure; provided, that is, one followed not the Stilbo of *De constantia* but the sage of *De vita beata* or *De tranquillitate*. For "prudence" could become cunning or deceit, "magnanimity" pride, "continence" meanness and "justice" pitiless zealotry (247–49). Measure kept the balance that alone assured a person's "perfection" and society's stability, by proper attention to and use of these *officia*. Even if the work was not an epitome of the *De officiis*, it was Senecan through and through. Indeed, while the first extant mention of the work (by Isidore of Seville) named Martin as its author, from the twelfth to early sixteenth centuries, this vastly popular essay was almost universally thought by Seneca, though already in his *Epistolae rerum senili* (II.4; *Letters* 1.66), Petrarch told his "Lelio" that the text was Martin's (Barlow in *Opera* 204–5). The *Formula* was a principal mediator into the middle ages of Stoic thought in general and Senecan thought in particular. Colish calls it the "first pseudo-Senecan handbook of the middle ages," with myriad progeny. She in fact ends her study of ancient Stoic thought with Martin's writing (*Stoic* 2.297–302: here 298). It spelled out the necessity of the four virtues as human and social "duties" essential to a life whose goodness lay in a measured and balanced relation with the world and people around one. It was a vademecum to core aspects of Stoic thought, including the centrality of right language that Martin stressed and that by his time had been important at least since Augustine.

We saw it begin to gain this weight in Cicero. It did so yet more in Varro, for whom language was central to right knowledge and action. For Seneca the proper balance between the personal and the social, revealed through morally worthy action in the civic arena, also appeared in the identity of *ratio* and *oratio*. For, "*oratio* [speech/style] is the *cultus* [clothing] of mind." *Cultus* was actually a term of wider meanings than "clothing" suggests: while it means ornamentation or adornment, it principally denotes education, cultivation, habitation, even devotion (whether in amity or religion). In this passage Seneca argued that superficiality in language use always showed absence of the cardinal virtues, no less than of others like frugality, moderation, endurance, refinement, sociability and humanity (Ep cxv.2–3). It showed a mind in which reason was far from its natural fulfillment. Speech was one aspect of how one inhabited being, an attribute of *persona*. How one appeared to others signaled how integrated one was in one's surroundings. Seneca called this appearance *oratio*. Its first meaning was "speech," but here it also denoted gesture, dress, habit, behavior: the material acts of contact between persons (Ep cxiv.1–27). Their corruption had equivalents at a wider social level in "luxurious banquets," "elaborate dress" and such (cxiv.11). *Oratio* showed ability or inability rationally to order relations between inside and outside, between mind and the circumambiences in which it was enlaced. *Honesta* action showed the soul in something of its natural balance. Because it meant that personal, natural and social reason were in harmony it was by definition "voluntary": "Omne honestum voluntarium est" (Ep lxvi.16).

So the *honestum* was the best indication that the soul had attained rational assent to integration in its surroundings. It showed, acted and described equilibrium in the divine, natural and human world. If the soul stayed "tossed to and fro," it was because reason did not keep it in hand. This would be why "nothing private and nothing public is stable, that the destinies both of humans and of cities reel" (Ep xci.7). To yield to fickleness of fortune was to counter the soul's true good. To reach perfection might always only be a goal, in life, but to reach for it was incarnate soul's nature, seeking social and personal "happiness." To live was thus always to be in battle, "vivere . . . militare est" (Ep xcvi.5), giving here a metaphor and there an idea of perennial motion one day integral to Petrarch's sense of selfe and world. The martial metaphor was, Marcus Wilson recalls (after others), ubiquitous in Seneca ("Subjugation" 63). To instability and war, death offered a quiet port (Ep lxx.3). Alive, soul fought to defeat instability. The mind unadapted to social and other surroundings, inapt for moral collective life, lacking *prudentia* (*animus inprudens*), was *defined* by changeability: "it shows now this now that and, than which I think nothing worse, is unlike/unstable in itself [*impar sibi est*]." While only the sage was perfect, all others being "multiform" (Ep cxx.22), all could fight the battle.

Indeed "the greatest proof of an evil mind is instability [*fluctuatio*]" (Ep cxx.20). To remain in such a state was to yield up the rational order that made one human. Fighting the battle could bring the soul to rule the body and all its surroundings as one whole: "So this vast crowd surrounding the soul of one person [*haec immensa multitudo unius animae circumdata*] is ruled by its spirit, guided by its reason, and would crush and smash itself by its own powers were it not upheld by educated reason" (*De clementia* I.iii.5). The evil of yielding to instability was the pole opposite the evil of absolute impassibility. This was why, like Cicero, Seneca argued that to know who one was meant the soul's grasping what its own "good" was: "Let mind discover mind's good" (*De vita beata* ii.2). Doing so it would know that in "the best life," pleasure (*voluptas*) was not director "of right and good will," *rectae ac bonae voluntatis*, but companion (*De vita* viii.1). Pleasure followed trained will's agreement with the nature of things, its reasoned assent to possible presence in the world and concord of person with its crowded surroundings. Instability was lack of these.

Plutarch, indeed, thought mind's instability echoed and embodied an entirely wider experience of evil in the universe: the subsistence of stochastic chaos even in the well-tempered world of body and soul made by god. He quoted Plato to the effect that the universe, created from the chaos of body by the addition of divine rational soul and set in motion by the demiurge, slowly forgot its instructions, so that aspects of primordial body grew ever stronger. Virtue in the universe came entirely from god's rational soul, while "from its primal chaotic condition [came] all the wrongs and evils—evils which it engenders in turn in the living creatures within it." As the universe aged, so discord and chaos regained ground. Finally, lest it be "dissolved again into the boundless region of dissimilitude" and become anew wholly "irregular," god intervened ("On the Generation of the Soul in the *Timaeus*" 1015c–d: 13¹.194/95, quoting Plato, *Politicus* 273b–e). The same instability in humans identically required intervention of that part of the divine which was rational soul. This may have been Platonic but it clearly catches the same experience and sense of person as that explained by Seneca.

A person's soul was like god's, in its surroundings and understanding. For "god, all-embracing world and ruler of the universe [*mundus . . . complectens rectorque universi deus*], reaches out to exterior things but thence, too, returns inward into himself" (*De vita beata* viii.4). These patterns of identity between a person's many surroundings built the harmony that was not just the highest good of the soul, but of society, world, universe and nature. Too, "where accord and unity are, there must the virtues be" (*De vita* viii.6). These established, even things indifferent could be more or less desirable goods, icing on the cake, as long as they did not upset the essential ingredients of nature (*De vita* xxii.4–5; xxvi.4). To that extent, they too became parts of "the highest good of living according to nature" (*De otio* v.1).

These highest goods, perfecting reason, acting *honeste* and living according to nature, described humans' relation to what the Greeks called "*ousia*, essential substance [*res necessaria*], nature holding the foundation of everything" (Ep lviii.6). Tentatively translating it by *essentia*, Seneca then discussed the equally hard noun, *to on*, for which he complained of having to use a verbal phrase, *quod est*, and split into six categories of existents (*ibid.* 8–22). This was the fix he tried to resolve by using "god," "fate," "nature," "providence" and the rest. The several names given to the highest good were ways to describe humans' relation to different aspects of *ousia*. It was *all* these "surroundings" that determined life and being: "when all the circumstances [*perihestēkota*] surrounding the cause and effect were the same, it would be impossible for things to turn out now one way, now another." This did mean "*totality* of circumstances," including a person's internal motions: among them the reason matching that which ruled the surroundings (Sorabji, "Causation" 253–54). In this, Stoics rightly saw no conflict of freedom and determinism: to be and act rationally in one's many worlds fulfilled one's nature. Wisdom, Seneca echoed Cicero, tuned the selfe to the world's natural demands. "Wisdom," Plutarch agreed, made "such a life best and most pleasant" ("On Tranquillity of Mind," 466ff.).

To live in these ways according to nature was not only a matter for mind or soul, spirit and reason, divinity and society. As human soul was intricate with body, so physical body was intricate with material world. Nature had set humans in the center of the universe and given them a gaze to sweep its length and breadth. Nature had made humans erect so that they could readily contemplate it, and set a head atop their body on a flexible neck so as to follow the stars and turn their face with the whole as it revolved. By this actual presence in nature humans could (and should) "yield themselves entirely to it," knowing, admiring and revering it, thereby living "in accord with nature" (*De otio* v.4, 8). Seneca's concern for the physical body and its real placement—house, city, geography, climate—graphically shows the experience of perviousness to the surrounding world, physical manifestation of all-encircling *ousia*. As the grounding experience of being a passible human person, this would be unaffected by sex, race, rank or socioeconomic condition.

A mind's temper depended on its body's particular composition of elements and qualities, but also on their composition in the places (*loci*) surrounding the person whose mind/soul it was and in the many other material externals in contact with it. As mind's temper was characterized by whichever element and quality dominated so was it affected by age, food, drink, momentary condition of the body, specific activities and desires, company—the endless varieties of surrounding substance (*De ira* II.xix–xx). Too, like all Stoics, Seneca saw the earth as infused with *spiritus* (*pneuma*) joining every part, animate and inanimate, and nourishing all things. This same *spiritus*, or *aer*, as he also named it (synonymously now to mean atmospheric air) filled and nourished "all heaven" and the "highest part of the universe," breathed out to them, as it were, from earth's body (NQ VI.16.1–4). *Spiritus* created the tension (*intentio*) in material things that held them together but that also created motion— and so growth and becoming (NQ II.6.6; see Arnold 160–61). *Aer* was essential in the universe, binding all material things, smaller things like trees and animals being *quasi pars* of the universe and the earth part and material of it (NQ II.4.1–6.4), just as human reason was *of* divine reason. Earth was infused with the matter and *spiritus* that fed and underlay the universe and governed by nature much like human bodies: with liquids flowing through "veins," with exhalations, decoctions and decomposings (NQ III.15.1–8).

Not just air, *spiritus*, was thought of as life infusing. Water and fire were creative forces (NQ V.5.2; 6.1). All four elements flowed and changed each into each other (NQ III.10.1), every part of the universe interacting with every other. That was why states of animals and the motions of planets and stars predicted events—never disagreeing (NQ II.32.5; 34.3). These behaviors were tied to all other motions in nature. Like humans', animals' bodies were endowed with a *sensus* making them *feel* their presence and actions in the world. Vegetation, too, sharing *spiritus*, not only shared aspects of growth and development analogous to humans', but "fit" the world analogously (Ep cxxi.9, 15). More broadly, one could say that sun, moon and stars moved "for me," who am intricate with their universe (*De beneficiis* VI.xx–xxii), that one was "in debt to the sun and moon, to the seasons" with which one changes (Ep lxxiii.6) and to the geography which one inhabits: so that even those living in the harshest terrain and climate relished their harmony with them

(*De providentia* iv.14–16). Changing seasons altered our bodies as did fluctuations in local weather or place. This "law" our soul, intricate with body, "had to be adjusted to, had to follow and obey" (Ep cvii.7, 9).

The human body as such, some say, was of small concern to Seneca and other Stoics (Arnold 257–59). In the sense that they allotted many bodily functions to soul and had little interest in human physiology, this may be so. But since (like soul) the human body was pervious to body in general, part and aspect of *to on*, to treat the one was in many ways to treat the other. Lack of separate attention may be due to the experience of person as passible and more evidence for it (although care is needed over such claims, and Galen found it endlessly worthwhile to reprove Stoic views of human physiology). It is in terms of this intimate interweaving that we can best understand how Seneca discussed the soul as a living thing (*animal*) and many of its active attributes as "corporeal," although he did so with irony toward those who would take the argument too far.

To describe the soul, *anima*, as "animal" at first seems little more than a tautology. It got the name *anima*, as it did Greek *psuchē*, because this "life force" named the basic difference between animate and inanimate substance. One should recall, though, that *anima* or *psuchē* was itself one form of *ousia*. Slightly sardonically perhaps, Seneca took the name itself as proof: the soul was *animal* because it "makes us living things [*animalia*]." Now, virtue was soul in a certain condition, so it, too, was *animal*. Virtue was "active," and all action needed "impetus." To have "impetus," a thing had to be "animal," so virtue was also a living thing (Ep cxiii.2). Seneca was almost as sarcastic as Plutarch (apropos of Chrysippus in "On Moral Virtue" 441b: 6.20–23) about those who sought to ascribe "animality" to every separate trait of the soul and every singular virtue (ibid. 6–9). But he meant what he said of virtue as a whole: the good.

For, we have seen, the good characterized all actions that affected *honeste* one's surroundings—"the good acts, for it is useful." "What acts is body" because only so could it have an effect on other things. The good, Seneca went on, "moves the soul [*animus*] and in a manner shapes and enfolds what is essential to the body. The goods of the body are bodily; so therefore are those of the soul. For it, too, is a body. Human good is necessarily corporeal, since the human itself is corporeal" (Ep cvi.5). We Stoics, he wrote, hold: "what is good is a body, because what is good, acts; whatever acts is a body." Moreover what was good was "useful," and to be so had to act. Again: whatever acted was a body (cxvii.2–3). "Corpus," here, was clearly a form of *ousia*, another mark of the way in which all aspects of being human were aspects of its perviousness to the material world in particular and to all manifestations of *ousia* in general: the divine or universal, the "animate," the human, society and the material world.

These surroundings and others composed, then, a series of interlocking spheres or circles from which person was inseparable, as Plato had offered. Seneca took the thought to depict a person's life span, which "orbes habet circumductos maiores minoribus," has greater globes encircling smaller (Ep xii.6). The greatest, whose diameter ran from birth to death, "surrounded and bound all the rest." The others encircled decreasingly large parts of a person's life down to day and hour. These spheres matched natural cycles just as a day went "from sunrise to sunset." Seneca's globes within globes clearly repeated those of the heavens, as a person's mind and soul repeated universal mind and soul. Using this same idea to refer to the form and function of this surrounding world, an ancient commentator on the poet Aratus called the four elements or qualities themselves separate circumambient spheres: "so there are four spheres [*sphairai*], which the ancients call stoicheia, elements"(Campbell, ed. 2.420/21).

Plutarch adopted the idea to show the tight relation between universal and personal soul:

in one part it is ever governed in uniformity and revolves in but one and the same order, which maintains control, yet in another part it is split into movements and circles which go in contrariety to each other and wander about.

The difference between the order of the fixed sphere and the more complex relative motions of the lower ones, giving rise "to the beginnings of differentiation and change and dissimilarity in those things which come into being and pass away on earth," was exactly echoed in the difference between a person's rational soul and the passions ("On Moral Virtue" 441ff.). Too, the idea nicely described the play between rational soul and unstable passions that we saw Seneca condemn as necessarily harmful. Plutarch was much attached to the idea, repeating it in an elaborate play on the name Circe (*Kirkē*) in a fragmentary passage we saw before, praising Homer for depicting the true nature of the soul's permanence as it passed from body to body. Undergoing this "cyclical revolution [*en kuklōi perihodon*] and recurrence of rebirth that Homer called *Kirkē*," said Plutarch, and returning repeatedly to "her" brew (*kukeōn*) where birth stirred (*kukeōsēs*) and bewitched it back into life's cycles, the soul learned how to act by reason and control the passions (*Moralia* fr. 200: 15.368–71).

Contemporaneously with Plutarch, Hierocles (in a definition known via Stobaeus) explained mutual relations between a person and surrounding communities:

Each one of us is as it were entirely encompassed by many circles, some smaller, others larger, the latter enclosing the former on the basis of their different and unequal dispositions relative to one another. The first and closest circle is the one which a person has drawn as though around a center, one's own mind. This circle encloses the body and everything taken for the sake of the body. For it is virtually the smallest circle, and almost touches the very center.

From thence the circles move out to immediate family, close relatives, distant relatives, neighbors, "tribe," fellow townspeople, regional community, country, and finally to "the outermost and largest circle, which encompasses all the rest, . . . that of the whole human race." The full life of the "well-tempered" person kept these circles together, at once being and encompassment (Long and Sedley 57G: 1.349).

Plutarch further explained that *failure* to heed the experience of being in these concentric circles or spheres was a failure to know a person at all. He faulted Epicurus for ignoring the wholeness of the person's surroundings and reducing them to one false core. Such people,

as it were describing a circle with the belly as center and radius, circumscribe in it the whole area of pleasure, whereas delight that is magnificent and kingly and engenders high spirit and a luminous serenity that truly diffuses itself to all humans is beyond the reach of those who set up as honorable and pleasing a cloistered life, estranged from public duty, indifferent to human welfare, untouched by any spark of the divine.

This was to abjure full human life. So paltry and false a view took person out of the "cycles [*perihodous*] of time and place" and the goods accompanying them "and thus constricts our nature and casts it down into a narrow space . . . where the mind delights in nothing but the flesh, as if human nature had no higher good than escape from evil" ("Epicurus Actually Makes a Pleasant Life Impossible" 1098d, 1107c: 14.94, 148). These cases go beyond metaphor. They express a real experience of whoness as embedded in, defined by, its surroundings—of which the universal, "animate," human, social and material have so far been just the most evident.

Philostratus' story of the first-century Pythagorean Apollonius of Tyana may be related. Seeking greater wisdom, Apollonius went to study Brahmanism at its Indian center. Told to start with any question, he asked the Brahmans' leader "whether they knew themselves," expecting the reply that this knowledge was hardest of all. But Iarchas replied: "We know everything, just because we begin by knowing ourselves" (*Life* III.xviii). Because he was not asked to pursue the issue, Iarchas' meaning went unexplained. He surely had in mind nothing so unusual as an independent, willful subject. The phrasing fits perfectly with the idea that the person, as such, was a focus where the aforesaid circles met. If anything,

Iarchas' final sentence on the matter confirms it: "We consider ourselves gods . . . because we are good people [*anthrōpoi*]" (III.xviii). As we have sufficiently seen, the best and wisest person was one who integrated all the circles of being. To do so was to be as god.

Later in life, jailed by Domitian, Apollonius consoled his fellow prisoners by saying: "Humans are in a prison all this time we choose to call life. For this our soul, being bound and fettered in a perishable body, has to suffer many things and be the slave of all the affections which visit humanity." Moreover, we are confined in the family circles centered on our houses, the social surroundings of our cities, the natural environs made of rivers and such and the farther natural boundaries of "encompassing ocean" (VII.xxvi). Immured in his body and these circles, Apollonius told the emperor at his trial, the good person was "honored by the title of god" to signal harmony achieved in these mortal constraints. Such a one's soul could be mortally touched not even by Domitian (VIII.v). It was for "being a good person" that Apollo considered Lycurgus "a god." Such people were of "godlike composition" in harmonizing these circles and creating tranquility about them (VIII.vii). Pythagorean Apollonius and sophist Philostratus apparently shared this Stoic experience of person and surroundings.

One was *humanior* in striving for harmony in these circles. Only a god might reach it. Coeval with most of those just named, a fresco of the Casa del Citarista at Pompeii shows such resetting of the world in Dionysos finding sleeping Ariadne, abandoned by Theseus (Figure 5). The god's cloak blows in the Naxos sea breeze, crafted into a circle about his head and shoulders. The curve of Ariadne's right side, her extended right arm and the tops of the heads of two figures above her form the arc of a circle whose circumference seems to continue through figures in severely damaged sections above and whose diameter is made of the round faces of the god's retinue, aligned from the composition's lower right to the top of Dionysos' cloak at upper left. A fresco from the Casa di Sircio shows wounded Aeneas being cured by Iapyx, a doctor trained by Apollo himself (*Aeneid* 12.391–429), in which a round shield at shoulder height on the right lies behind Iulus' head, while to the left and slightly higher Venus' cloak forms another perfect circle about her head and torso, both circles frame recovering Aeneas (Figure 6). Circular composition, faces, cloaks, shields, suggest a harmony found in a double herm from the Casa dei Papiri with Dionysos' head on one side, Ariadne's on the other, as if illustrating the spherical person of Plato's *Symposium*, remade by true love (repeated in a sculpture at the Villa dei Vetti: such doubles have many subjects, male and female). Not for nothing did Seneca take the circu-

Figure 5. Fresco from the Casa del Citarista at Pompeii, Ariadne and Dionysos on Naxos (1st century A.D.). Museo Archeologico Nazionale di Napoli, inv. 9009. Photo MN0777, Luciano Pedicini / Archivio dell'Arte.

lar dance of the three Gratiae as emblematic of the well-tempered society of generous exchange, giving, receiving and returning, moving in a continuous and unbroken ring that endlessly turns upon itself (*De beneficiis*, I.iii.4–5).

Now that we have an idea of this experience, though, the hard ques-

Figure 6. Fresco from the Casa di Sircio at Pompeii, wounded Aeneas being cured by Iapyx (1st century A.D.). Museo Archeologico Nazionale di Napoli, inv. 9286. Photo, MN0604: Luciano Pedicini / Archivio dell'Arte.

tion we must pursue is whether it was shared by others than these wealthy educated men. Did women and slaves experience the same sense of who-ness as that which these men described? Can one know? Did these writers then include women and slaves in their description? Was this who-ness experienced as including sex and gender, slave and free as integral members of those circles and surroundings? My answers are affirmative. Of course, "integral" does not mean "equal" (as the fragmentation or nonexistence of women's and slaves' writing itself shows), and if, in regard to the universal, animate, human and material circles, experience may have been the same or similar, endless room for oppressions and violence remained in economic, social and political surroundings. What "integral" does mean is that whatever the latter case, grounds of personhood were the same and these persons themselves mutually essential.

CHAPTER SIX

How Were Slaves Persons?

That passibility and essential engagement in multiple surroundings grounded who-ness clearly affects gender, slavery and all sociopolitical and economic relations. I had felt, though, able to add little about personhood apropos of slavery, beyond the remarks at the end of Chapter 1. Documentation seemed scant, and subject to only speculative interpretation. It was at least clear that whatever Aristotle said about "natural slaves," the mere fact that slaves were manumitted to become metics (at Athens) or citizens (at Rome) showed that being property and being a person were not at odds. Aristotle said as much in a widely discussed passage: to be a slave permitted no automatic inference about the nature of the person enslaved (*Politics* 1254b27–37).

Indeed, we saw Aristotle assert that if master and slave could not share friendship *qua* master and slave, they certainly could as humans (*anthropoi*). Reciprocal relations of "justice" existed between any who could "share in law and contract" (*Nicomachean Ethics* 1161b4–8). We can now fill this out a bit from Aristotle himself: for this clearly made slaves sharers in that rational rule of the universe and human relations fulfilled as the good life by the virtuous *hexeis* available to all good humans— slaves among them. People like Alcman, Terence, Epictetus, philosophers named by Gellius (II.18), including Socrates' and Plato's "close friend" Phaedo of Elis, and many powerful imperial favorites (slave and freed) were not exceptions proving a rule but evidence that social and legal status were aspects of a personal being whose core *nature* was the same. They would so have experienced it. At issue here is whether commentators extended this same personhood to those whom some modern critics of the age call their or its "others."

The circles in which the latter were engaged and rank they held differed from those of the writers discussed. Forms of engagement in those circles compassed oppression, deprivation and exploitation. But the surroundings and engagement were still those of a person, whose fact and nature may well not have differed. Even so, to speak of a "core," as I just did, may mislead. Personhood and its surroundings or circles, "inside" and "outside," were inescapably enmeshed (Chapter 8 shows this as one reason why the modern western concept and experience of "private" are recent). We may come to find that for both slaves and women (as for everyone else) differences lay in the sorts of circles (but social, political and economic rather than universal, human and material), not in the fact or even the nature of engagement with them. Whether and how this engagement inflected personhood is among the things this and the next chapter hope to clarify.

This remains to be shown. There is no question but that a slave was property. She or he was owned entirely by another. As Peter Garnsey puts it:

The slaveowner's rights over his slave-property were total, covering the person as well as the labour of the slave. The slave was kinless, stripped of his or her old social identity in the process of capture, sale and deracination, and denied the capacity to forge new bonds of kinship through marriage alliance. These are the three basic components of slavery. (1)

The slave's "person," adds Wiedemann, "is absolutely under the control of another; he is another's property, part of the household unit to which his owner belongs (the owner may not be the head of that household, but a wife, son or even another slave)." A slave was legally wholly "rightless" (*Greek* 1–2, 9). Garnsey and others hold that this chattel slavery was the case in fifth- to fourth-century Athens and in Rome after the third century B.C., whatever the actual numbers. Garnsey's "three basic components" allowed for much variety. Even had they not, and even under the brutal conditions these remarks describe and further imply, the question of personhood would remain open.

We can start with no expositor better than Seneca. Stoic as he was, he also joined experiences and strands from what are generally thought very different traditions. That he wrote on the personhood of slaves was unusual. At least, besides Aristotle's curt remarks in the first book of the *Politics*, mentioned before, only Seneca's writings on the issue survive from early antiquity (many do from later, not least scattered through the *Digest*). This matters. Garnsey recalls that "the tradition refers to a lost work *On Liberty and Slavery* by Antisthenes, an associate of Socrates." A scholiast on Aristotle's *Rhetoric* 1373b18 said that what "Alcidamas said in the Messeniac Oration," referenced but not quoted by Aristotle, was: "The deity gave liberty to all people, and nature created no one a slave" (*Ideas* 12n23, 75). Perhaps he shared views with Antisthenes, a founder of the Cynics who taught simplicity, poverty and virtue as alone needed in life. Aristotle himself declared that he was writing against those who criticized slavery.

Was Seneca advancing a polemical, oppositional view? Or was he expressing one more usual? Perhaps Aristotle's had always been minority. Certainly Seneca seems to have been adopting Homeric and Platonic suggestions, soon claimed and embroidered by Plutarch, to the effect that while soul was *affected* by the body in which it was incarnated its nature stayed the same (*Moralia* fr. 200: commentary on Circe). So I start by analyzing some of the arguments Seneca advanced in the third book of the *De beneficiis* and in *Epistula* xlvii, both because of the present book's continuity and because they give a clear sounding-board against which to test earlier arguments, both Roman and Greek.

In the *De beneficiis* Seneca asked "whether a slave could give a benefit to [her or his] master" (III.xviii.1). A benefit differed from duty or service. A duty (*officium*) involved rational actions toward nature, the *oikos* or *domus*, the *polis* and indeed all circles of personhood, whose virtuous source lay in the nature of being human. A service (*ministerium*) was what a slave did for a master. A *beneficium* differed from these in that it presupposed the person giving it not to be constrained to do so, able to *choose* against it. It presupposed the giver to have the educable power of *prohairesis* and inherent power of deliberation. These were exactly the abilities that Aristotle had denied slaves—or at least "natural slaves." So it mattered that Seneca gave an immediate and unhesitant affirmative response:

Further, whoever denies that a slave sometimes gives a benefit to a master is ignorant of human law [*iuris humani*]; for it is the soul (or mind) not the status of the one who gives that counts. Virtue is closed to no one; it is open to all, admits all, attracts all, freeborn and freed, slaves and kings and exiles; it selects not by household or property, is satisfied with the naked human being. (III.xviii.2)

Virtue inhered potentially in all human beings *qua* human beings. It was, we saw, what enabled a life in accord with nature and the universe. It was signaled by the proper accomplishment of the *officiorum* necessary to life. It enabled a person to *choose* to give a *beneficium*. If authority meant that a slave could give no benefit to a master, it meant that a subject could give none to a king and a soldier none to a general, since not the kind but the fact of authority would be constraining. If the ones could, so could the other (III.xviii.3). No one denied that subjects and soldiers could give a benefit to those in authority over them. So could a slave. These very comparisons supposed equivalence of personhood. Like anyone else "a slave can be just, can be brave, can be great-souled; so can give a benefit, for that is also part of virtue" (xviii.4). Seneca did not hesitate to apply to slaves the dictum that we saw him write in the essay *Ad Helviam* (xi.7), to the effect that mind or soul was not shackled to the body but "free and akin to the gods and at home in every world and every age." Thus he continued in the *De beneficiis*:

> Whoever thinks that servitude penetrates the whole human being is wrong. Its better part is exempt. Bodies are answerable and belong to masters; but mind is under its own law, and is so free and moving that it cannot be restrained even by this prison [of the body] in which it is shut, but which cannot stop it using its power, doing mighty deeds and moving off into the infinite in company with the gods. So it is the body that fortune has handed over to a master; this he buys, this he sells; that inner part cannot be taken possession of. Whatever comes from this is free; further, we cannot command all things nor are slaves compelled to obey in all things. (III.xx.1–2)

So the slave could act on her or his choice whether giving a benefit or doing anything else unrelated to the slave's duty or master's order. Such acts, said Seneca, were done *ex voluntate* (xxi.2), apparently deriving his term directly from the Greek debates followed in Chapter 2. Regarding these acts, it was not a master being benefited by a slave, but a human by a human, *homo ab homine* (xxii.4). Seneca exactly applied Cicero's thought of speaking "soul to soul" to the relation between master and slave, which, here, became one between persons equal as human beings. The social status of a human being could not diminish the worth of a free act of choice (xxviii.1). Such an act showed, rather, that the moral worth of a human was separate from his or her social rank or status. One had always to remember that the person "whom you call your slave is born from the same stock, blessed with the same sky, breathes, lives and dies in just the same way as you do" (Ep xlvii.10).

The epistle just quoted may be thought less clear-cut than the essay. The slave's soul, he wrote in imaginary dialogue, is *perhaps* (*fortasse*) that of a free person. To his imaginary interlocutor's flat response, "servus est," Seneca replied:

> Show me anyone who is not. One is slave to lust, another to greed, another to ambition, all to fear. I will give you an ex-consul slave to an old woman; I will give you a plutocrat slave to a slave girl; I will show you the noblest youths in servitude to pantomime players. No slavery is worse than that by choice. (Ep xlvii.17)

This may seem as specious as the opening of the letter seems condescending: "I am glad to know that you live on familiar terms with your slaves" (xlvii.1). That this opened naturally onto the argument that slaves were humans like their owner and any other free person is beside the point if they were so only in the sense that all humans were "slaves" to passions. The claim would be a metaphor dependent on the social reality of slavery: part of the extension of the notion of *douleia* that I noted earlier. It is not the same as the fact that to be a Roman or Greek slave meant being owned and controlled by a master or mistress in legal and physical ways quite different from the moral ones of being "enslaved" by passions, although we recall that everyone was in some sense in this bonded, passible, relation to surroundings. *This* usage is not metaphorical.

That in Rome "slaves were legally defined as property, and . . . not entitled to own property," "were strictly non-persons" and "did not own themselves" are grounds on which Long specifies the uniqueness of Stoic arguments for the equality of all humans, "regardless of social position, gender or race." These arguments belying the legal situation show their "fundamental part in generating an idea of persons—i.e., human beings to whom common attributes of morality, responsibility, interest and justice apply simply because they are human" ("Stoic Philosophers" 16; cf. Griffin 459–60, Vogt 138–40). Whether or not Stoic arguments were unique, they surely had nothing to do with the legal status of slaves, nor does Long suggest they did. My point is that no Stoic was addressing slaves' legal status as non-persons and non-owners of themselves. That status lay among *adiaphora*, things indifferent. Seneca was not questioning the legitimacy of slavery as a social institution, but observing that slaves' status as *legal* non-persons did not affect their human condition as *moral* persons. That is why we should not see his analogy of people being enslaved to passions as specious elucubrations or just an analogy with real slavery. The point was not so much that in this sense all humans were slaves but that all humans have the same souls, minds, passions, feelings and rational capacities. They had these *regardless* of social (or gender) actualities. Their conditions of daily life were affected by these actualities, not their nature as human beings.

Elsewhere he said exactly this: that while all people were equally humans yet they were chained by "Fortune," by the circles in which they lived, to which they were born or into which they were set by circumstance. For some, he acknowledged, "the chain is made of gold and is loose, for others it is tight and filthy" (*De tranquillitate* X.3). Had Seneca been arguing against the social institution of slavery he would have been unusual. Far from doing so, he asserted, rather, that considerations of the moral and ontological equality of humans were separate from those of social and legal actuality, as "human law" from that of peoples or states. Domestic slaves, he thus wrote, had long, if not always, been thought endowed with the same human attributes as their masters. That was why "our ancestors" were careful to have masters act without ill-will and without insulting their slaves—a moral stance that did not affect their rights to punish, torture and exploit their slaves. That was why they fixed a holiday when masters and slaves shared a meal, why they "let slaves receive honors in the household, pronounce judgment [*ius dicere*] and [why] they considered the household to be a commonwealth in little" (Ep xlvii.14). Seneca was claiming that in the *domus* or *oikos*, slaves, like free members, had always been the equivalent of citizens in the *polis*, *civitas* or *res publica*. The carnival holiday recognized the difference between "civic" status and human being. Because commentators habitually assimilate legal non-personhood and social oppression to moral and ontological non-personhood and because everyone is aware of Aristotle's arguments about natural slaves' lack of rational deliberative capacities, Seneca's assertion may seem unfounded. Thus we need to ask whether it was as controversial as it now appears. In this regard, even if Seneca was exceptional in joining them, none of his arguments was new. Too much ancient writing is lost to know whether he was exceptional, but the materials Garnsey collates deny such an evaluation. Basic questioning of the institution of slavery was rare. The sense that it involved brutal oppression of *fellow human persons* was not.

It has, however, become common claim that fifth-century Greeks, Athenians anyway, thought slaves of a different nature from free people. Further, they supposedly took this difference as a standard against which to measure all relations between the free Greek male citizen at the top of the human heap and others, whether women, aliens, slaves or barbarians. The last two were then set at the same level. Barbarians by nature lived in political slavery, their ruler alone being free, as Euripides' eponymous protagonist said in *Helen* (412 B.C.): "All Barbary is slave except a single man" (276). The remark may deliberately have echoed the best-known claim of this sort: Herodotus' description of an interview between Spartan ambassadors and the Persian satrap Hydarnes. Invited to become friends with the Persian king and submit to him, the Greeks replied by asserting that Hydarnes could not grasp their condition: "A slave's life you understand, but never having tasted liberty, you cannot tell whether it be sweet or no" (VII.135). In the same century one finds similar assertions in Aeschylus' *Persians* 241–42, Euripides' *Iphigenia in Aulis* 1400–1401, and elsewhere. We have seen arguments that this hierarchical ordering of human relations was fixed in Greek imagination and practice by the end of the fifth century at least. The sweeping nature of this perception of human relations hints that the Greeks could not even have *conceived* of the differences enshrined in their hierarchization except in terms of some *otherness*. Such is what most commentators assert.

One work establishing terms of this otherness with special clarity was

the Hippocratic *Airs, Waters, Places*. It did so not by reference to slavery
(save by implication) but to an opposition between barbarians and
Greeks, Europeans and Asians (meaning those of the eastern and south-
eastern Mediterranean littoral from the southern Black Sea to Egypt). It
grounded their differences in the nature of the physical world and rational
universe of which it was part. The difference, wrote the author, was large,
for "everything in Asia grows to far greater beauty and size," the human
beings (*anthrōpoi*) are "of very fine physique and very tall, differing from
one another but little either in physique or stature." Because of the region's temperate character and seasonal mildness, its inhabitants necessarily lacked "courage, endurance, industry and high spirit" (even Greek
immigrants to Asia Minor were quickly affected by these surroundings to
acquire the same characteristics). Pleasure inevitably reigned supreme
(*Airs* xii.10–45). Although there were varieties among Asian peoples,
apart from their slightly differing physique they all shared this "lack of
spirit and courage." Temperateness of land and seasons meant that there
occurred "no mental shocks nor violent physical change, which are more
likely to steel the temper and impart to it a fierce passion." Such temper
needing change and movement, without them Asians were "feeble." This
was why they were mostly ruled by kings. People's feebleness, cowardly
character and inclination to idleness and pleasure reinforced each other
and monarchical constitutions. So much so that even those born brave,
high-spirited and industrious were transformed with little ado (like the
Greek immigrants) to the same character (xvi.1–30).

The Hippocratic's argument, then, was that these surroundings formed
their peoples to be natural slaves. So, at least, it has been taken. But how
rightly? *Airs, Waters, Places* is not without contradictions. On the one
hand, peoples of the littoral did vary widely. On the other, climate, season, geography, health regimen and all such conditions did not themselves suffice to create "natural" servility. Having asserted that "with regard to the lack of spirit and courage among the inhabitants, the chief
reason why Asiatics [were] less warlike and more gentle in character than
Europeans [was] the uniformity of the seasons" (xvi.3–6), the writer then
changed tack altogether, declaring that peoples' character was due entirely to their humanly instituted sociopolitical organization, their politically despotic constitutions. Of this, he said, he could "give clear proof":

All the inhabitants of Asia, whether Greek or barbarian, who are not ruled by
despots, but are independent, toiling for their own advantage, are the most warlike of all people. For it is for their own sakes that they run their risks, and in their
own persons do they receive the rewards of their valour as likewise the penalty of
their cowardice.

It being thus "proven" that servility was induced entirely by human institutions and so was not at all "natural" did not prevent the Hippocratic
from returning immediately to the contradictory claim that "the reason
for this, as I said before, is the seasons" (xvi.33–43).

The contradiction was not due to inattention. It was systemic. Concluding his analysis of European peoples, which, as one would expect,
emphasized how variety of climate, season and geography made them
courageous, wild, high-spirited and industrious, the author returned to
the play between physical world and human institutions:

For uniformity engenders slackness, while variation fosters endurance in both
body and soul; rest and slackness are food for cowardice, endurance and exertion
for bravery. Wherefore Europeans are more warlike, and also because of their institutions, not being under kings as are Asiatics. For as I said above, where there
are kings, there must be the greatest cowards. For men's souls are enslaved, and
refuse to run risks readily and recklessly to increase the power of somebody else.
But independent people, taking risks on their own behalf and not on behalf of
others, are willing and eager to go into danger, for they themselves enjoy the reward of victory.

Having again shown the prime importance of human institutions the
writer tried nonetheless to reinforce the claim of natural servility by ending with the lame assertion: "so institutions contribute a great deal to the
formation of courageousness" (xxiii.25–41). But servitude itself (and
with it "appropriate" character) was wholly the creation of monarchy or
despotism.

Over half a millennium later, Galen glossed these claims by saying that
the human "rule," of which "Hippocrates" wrote and which *Airs, Waters, Places* held to change notions of how people were "by nature,"
"clearly mean[t] the way of life that comes to be 'the rule' in any given
country, under which should be included nurture, education, and local
custom." By and large he seems right, although he wants to insist on the
primacy of the physical qualities of hot and cold, dry and wet. Still, the
word used by the Hippocratic, highlighted by Galen, was the rather ambiguous *nomos* (xxiv.21), signifying anything from law to custom. In the
work quoted, explaining the importance of all aspects of physical surroundings to what a person was, not to physical being alone but soul as
well, Galen held that the "rule" in question related to everything involving health ("The Soul's Dependence on the Body [That the Faculties of
the Soul Follow the Mixtures of the Body]," *Selected Works* 166). The
Hippocratic, I suggest, was playing on the several meanings of *nomos*,
signaling, to be sure, the play between nature and human institutions, but
stressing above all the force of political institutions. The distinction mat-

ters little to my point here. The singular importance of any human institution to the making of what a person was undermined any claim about
essential differences drawn by nature. And how to explain, in this regard,
someone like the lyric poet Alcman, freed apparently because of his talent, but born into a slave family and so the closest anyone could imagine
to a "natural" slave (Campbell, ed., *Greek Lyric* 2.337, 347: *Testimonia*
1 and 12)?

The ambiguities of *Airs, Waters, Places* (xii–xxiv) summed up tensions
between the social fact of slavery, the need to justify and legitimate it and
the moral anxiety that accompanied the fact and the need. If Euripides
could have Greek Helen observe barbarians' natural servility, he could
also remark that noble-souled people were found in all lands, as one fragment says (Nauck 902). Schlaifer's claim that Euripides "let" Helen express views opposite his own and that "it is clear that his own sentiments
are shown in the fragment" has no direct basis (97). Rather, in expressing both views the dramatist was catching a crucial insolubility in Greek
experience and the Greeks' thought about it. Still, in his lost *Alexander*
(*Paris*), Euripides may have written a play whose main theme concerned
the equal personhood of slaves. Enough is known of the play to reconstruct its plot, enough fragments exist to sketch its debates. I follow Jean
Christian Dumont's presentation (*Servus* 540–54).

At Troy Priam and Hecuba organized expiatory games to honor a
child whom they had exposed to avoid evil foretold should it have lived.
A young slave, Paris/Alexander, claimed the right to participate and won,
defeating the Trojan princes. Deiphobos sought to have his victory reversed on grounds that a slave had no right to enter the stadium and participate in the games. Deiphobos and Paris defended their cases in turn
before Priam. The Trojan king accepted the latter's arguments and declared him a legitimate participant and the games' victor. The many surviving fragments show Deiphobos arguing that moral worthlessness defined slaves, Paris that people's moral equality was unaffected by one's
being legally a slave. Paris' arguments agreed with the common view that
to be a slave was entirely a matter of accident. The force of Priam's agreement with Paris' arguments may be offset by the sense that Euripides un-
dercut them (as he did in *Ion*) by having the "slave" found to be of royal
birth—in Paris' case, an exposed child of the Trojan king and queen. But
even that suggests how deeply vexed the issue was felt to be, then and for
years. Half a millennium later, Dio Chrysostom's Discourse 15 ("On
Slavery and Freedom II") gives a dialogue between a "slave" and a "citizen" echoing *Alexander* (2.143–73). So close are they that Euripides'
very terms seem to have resonated down the centuries. Scholars propose
that Dio drew on Antisthenes (see Cohoon, in Dio 2.143). If so, the con-

juncture of Euripides, Socrates and Antisthenes (see above) hints that such arguments were common at the end of the Athenian fifth century. Xenophon expressed like views. They seem to have been majority ones both before and after Aristotle (Ste. Croix, "Slavery" 29).

The same tension traversed the debates in which, for non-specialist posterity, the major participants were Plato and Aristotle. These were conflicts in which we see that more people may have opposed than favored any idea of difference in the humanity of slave and free. Democritus had urged (not unequivocally) that the Greek/barbarian and by implication slave/free divide was flawed: "the wise person walks over the entire earth; all the universe is homeland [*patris*] to the noble soul" (Diels-Kranz 2.194, fr.247). Aristotle in *Politics* I presumably correctly summarized his sophist opponents' views in saying, "that the rule of a master over slaves is contrary to nature, and that the distinction between slave and free exists by convention only, and not by nature; and being an interference with nature is therefore unjust" (1253b20–23). Among extant sophist comment, Antiphon's is most categorical: "Barbarians and Greeks have all been created with a nature in every respect identical" (Diels-Kranz 2.353, fr.44 B2). The view was constant, the *Digest* holding a millennium later that to be enslaved to another was "contrary to the natural order" (I.5).

Throughout the fifth century and into the fourth this debate was not simply one of ideas. It was caught up in the struggles over political authority and social order in Athens and other Greek cities that ultimately became military. As Socrates' execution shows, Xenophon, Plato, Aristotle and others were addressing issues of power, participation and order. Of these three, the second actually had rather little to say on the topic of slaves beyond scattered fragmentary remarks. Among them the fullest is the comparison between kinds of lawmakers and kinds of physicians to which I referred in Chapter 1:

Now have you further observed [asks the Athenian] that, as there are slaves as well as free people among the patients of our communities, the slaves, to speak generally, are treated by slaves, who pay them a hurried visit, or receive them in dispensaries? A physician of this kind never gives a servant any account of his complaint, nor asks him for any; he gives him some empirical injunction with an air of finished knowledge, in the brusque fashion of a dictator, and then is off in hot haste to the next ailing servant—that is how he lightens his master's medical labours for him. The free practitioner, who, for the most part, attends free people, treats their diseases by going into things thoroughly from the beginning in a scientific way, and takes the patient and family into his confidence. Thus he learns something from the sufferers, and at the same time instructs the invalid to the best of his powers. He does not give his prescriptions until he has won the patient's support, and when he has done so, he steadily aims at producing complete restoration to health by persuading the sufferer into compliance. (*Laws* 720c–e, trans. A. E. Taylor, *Collected Dialogues* 1310–11)

The distinction between using reasons to restore people to health or states to political stability and imposing despotic or slavish order is clear enough. Less clear is what it means as to any natural difference between slave and free, and so as to any basic difference in their humanity.

Certainly the passage implies that the free physician used reasons to coax his patient to health, perhaps not least because physician was often of lesser rank than patient. Did Plato therefore suggest that the slave was mentally or morally incapable of using such reasons? Or was it just that the slave patient, not worth that sort of attention, was to be treated with all speed? As to incapacity the slave physician him- or herself had at least to be capable of learning from the free physician just as the free patient did. Like the Hippocratic earlier, Plato was insisting on a *sociopolitical* condition—which was, after all, the point of his simile to start with. Slave physicians did not use reasons to persuade not because they were morally or ontologically unable to do so but because they were legally and politically disenfranchised. Plato was saying that the state whose law-makers were always engaged in public debate was better than one where despotism simply imposed its authority. That was *not* a natural condition. Many, indeed, thought Athens at the peak of political progress precisely because it had achieved that condition by civic endeavor, if not alone, at least better than anyone else had so far done. What better simile than one using the everyday case of those who were particularly *disallowed* from participating in that polity? Contrary to Vlastos' assertion, nothing in the simile suggests that Plato was arguing that slaves were "incapable of . . . reasonable intercourse" (133).

Perhaps he did elsewhere. The difficulty is that the fragmentary brevity of what are always passing asides impedes interpretation. For what can we really make of the later one in *Laws* XII (966b), replying to the Athenian's asking whether the state's "guardians" could understand the unity of the different virtues and truths but not "give any articulate demonstration of it." "Out of the question!" Clinias exclaimed: "A condition only fit for a slave!" Was Clinias saying that slaves were incapable of reason? Or asserting that they had no political or legal right to do such a thing? After all Plato's point was that the rulers, and only the rulers, ultimately had the role of interpreting and authorizing civil society; which is why he immediately went on to explain that free members of society had to accept the guardians' reasoning as well. He had made the same argument in *Republic* IX, saying that those who lacked highest wisdom, and were, indeed, at least partly ruled by baser instincts, were better off controlled by those who did have highest wisdom (the guardians). Here, the people who should be so controlled, he actually called "slaves." Plato was not writing of legal slaves but of legitimate political subjects (*Republic* 590c–d). So how can we interpret these passages? Vlastos, chiefly from the simile in *Laws* IV, concludes that slaves were capable of *doxa*, not of *logos*. They could "learn by experience (*empeiria*) and external prescription (*epitaxis*)," but "neither give nor follow a rational account." They were "therefore susceptible to persuasion." And that, he argues, was the reverse of reason which, said Plato in *Timaeus* (51e), was "unmoved by persuasion" (133–34).

The trouble with this analysis is not just that it takes the simile for a general statement about slaves, but that it makes the free physician's patients into slaves, since they, too, were persuaded by the doctor. That is clearly wrong. But so, then, is the extrapolation from *Timaeus*. It was not that reason was unmoved by persuasion but that it could exchange reasons, judging whether persuasion was good or bad. Whether or not Plato held that slaves could not do this is simply unclear, although Socrates drawing from a slave boy remembered knowledge of geometrical relations is clear enough (*Meno* 82b–86b). He evidently felt that some could do it qualitatively better than others—as those apt to be guardians could be educated as others could not, thus distinguishing in this regard some free citizens from other free citizens. But such understanding obviously depended on the sense that all were persons varying, like all humans, in abilities. Perhaps it is not that fifth- to fourth-century notions of hierarchies were formed on the basis of master-slave relations but that these last were increasingly analyzed to fit such ideas: *douleia*'s wide meaning—*any* relation of dominance and subjection—preceding its precise narrow meaning of slavery. Slaves were legally and socially different from all free citizens. Plato nowhere clearly proposed that they differed *humanly*, any more than did variously abled citizens. Slaves in Athens lacked "legal personality" and could not, for instance, bring suit or be sued. In this, they were like metics or other foreigners. They were property, but not property like any other, for they were humans "and possessed of all the characteristics inherent in [humans] as such" (Schlaifer 110). There was always, Wiedemann notes, "tension between the slave's total rightlessness in law and the fact that he [or she] was a human being," between their being "chattel slaves" and "human beings," between their legal disabilities and their abilities as person (*Greek* 9, 15). *That*, of course, is what is at issue.

Here, Aristotle is always advanced as the prosecution's chief witness, polemicist as he was against those who held slavery "contrary to nature" (*Politics* 1253b20). But he, too, as we saw near the end of Chapter 1, was full of contradictions on the issue, giving the slave reason with one hand, removing it with the other. As a slave, a person could do one sort of thing; as a human being, another. Schlaifer has detailed the contortions into which Aristotle's doctrine led. I can do little better than quote Schlaifer's summary, echoing his caveat that it gives the philosopher's doctrine a consistency it never had, and elides glaring internal contradictions:

The natural slave is a being having that part of the soul [the *pathētikon morion*; *to alogon*] which shares in reason [*logou koinōnein*] to the extent of perceiving it [*aisthanesthai*]; he lacks that part [*to bouleutikon*] which possesses reason fully [*logon echein*] and enables moral choice [*prohairesis*] in advance of action [*tēi dianoiai prohoran*]. Thus he is neither a man, who is distinguished by full possession of the soul, nor a beast [*thērion*], which is distinguished by its absence, but is sui generis. His whole function is to be a tool [*organon*] and possession [*ktēma*] of his master; considered in this aspect he is a part [*meros*] of his master, and, since he performs only physical tasks, a part only of the master's physical nature [*sōma*]. But since he is a self-acting tool, he differs from other tools, and even in his actions in that capacity employs his *psuchē*. (196: I have transcribed the Greek)

Any consistent definition such as this garner offers has difficulties. Not least is that the *organon* was *empsuchon*, animate, ensouled. Thus, wrote Aristotle, a master could not be friends with a slave *qua* slave, who was only a tool. But if the slave is an *empsuchon organon*, they could be friends as humans, both being ensouled, and so sharing "a system of law," an ability to be "parties to agreements" and a humanity making them "equal [and with] much in common" (*Nicomachean Ethics* 1161b4–9). We have thrice seen this crucial passage. Schlaifer's summary poses the further difficulty that everyone knew slaves did *not* do only physical tasks. As nurses they did more than just feed infants, as doctors they did more than just keep people healthy, as tutors they helped educate them. Everyone knew that in households whose production sought to satisfy all their own needs even everyday "physical" tasks implied a use of *psuchē* far exceeding the limitations Aristotle sometimes implied. It is no surprise that "the theory of 'natural slavery' [was] not at all prominent in antiquity after Aristotle's time" or that by the Hellenistic era almost all thought only that "the state of slavery—like poverty and war, or liberty, riches and peace—[was] the result of accident, of Fortune rather than of Nature" (Ste. Croix, *Class* 417, 418). Did only Aristotle make contrary arguments? Ste. Croix calls them "intellectually disreputable" (418), "the most inadequate section of his great work, the *Politics*, and perhaps the feeblest part of his whole magnificent philosophical output" ("Slavery" 28). Their lack of posterity suggests this was also antiquity's view.

Certainly Aristotle's polemical arguments, if not Plato's fragmented asides, are vehement. But what do even they tell us? Their contortions suggest them to be symptoms of an uneasy reaction to the social fact of slavery, efforts to legitimate or at least negotiate a repressively brutal reality that affronted proud claims about democracy. The now too-familiar perception of slaves among the Greeks as non-persons was not simply questioned. It was specifically and continually contested. This is not to say that anyone contested the institution of slavery.

The slave's life was oppressed and always threatened with violence. We do not, says Wiedemann, "have to believe that owners frequently executed or sold their slaves, or did so out of spite, the fact that it was allowed at all will have been a powerful enough incentive for slaves to repress their feelings and act to please their masters, except under the severest provocation" (*Slavery* 27). Nor do we have to think that many were as sadistic as the emperor Augustus' friend, the freedman Vedius Pollio, "allowed to punish his slaves by throwing them into his fishpond as food for his lampreys with complete impunity" (Vogt 104). The point was that the law tolerated such behavior, indeed, in cases of the trial of a free person, *imposed* torture on slaves (and only on slaves) when they were thought to possess evidence in a case.

Aristophanes was probably hardly at all exaggerating when his slave protagonist Xanthias, having switched garments and roles with his master Dionysos, told Aeacus that they might try and prove his "slave" Dionysos guilty of assaulting an officer in the underworld:

> Aeacus: What may we do to him?
>
> Xanthias: Why, anything!
> The rack, the wheel, the whip . . . Skin him alive . . .
> Vinegar up his nose . . . bricks on his chest . . .
> Or hang him by his thumbs . . . what have you . . .
>
> (*Frogs* [405 b.c.], ed. Hadas 388)

Slaves did die under torture (some authors praising them for signal loyalty). Flogging and other savage punishments were usual. In the Laurium silver mines serving Athens, conditions (shared by freemen) were infamously lethal. In law, slaves' bodies belonged absolutely to their masters: "a man's body, such is fate," said Aristophanes' Cario, "belongs / Not to himself, but to whoe'er has bought it" (*Plutus* [388 b.c.], ed. Hadas 465; for other examples, see Wiedemann, *Greek* 167–87). The laws of Greek cities, as of Rome, not only allowed but regulated these conditions. But whatever the legal impositions, perversities like Pollio's were not allowed, *pace* Vogt, "with impunity." The tale of Pollio throwing slaves to his fish continued that once, while entertaining Augustus, he was about to do this to a slave who broke a crystal glass. When he refused the emperor's request that he spare the slave, Augustus freed the latter and had the fishpond filled. As an illustration of bestial behavior, the story was told and retold. For Seneca it showed inhumanity in the strongest sense: Pollio's sadistic anger made him no longer human (*De ira* III.xl).

Matters are not straightforward. Were ancient Greek and Roman societies slave economies? Were they, that is, wholly dependent on slavery for their economic and political existence, let alone well-being? Controversy continues. Partly it depends on the definition. Ste. Croix insists that it does not have to do with "how the bulk of the labour of production is done," but with "how the dominant propertied classes . . . ensure the extraction of the surplus which makes their leisured existence possible" ("Slavery" 20). This proposal may owe more to the fact that we are now pretty sure that slave production was never the principal form of economic productivity in ancient Greece or Rome, although Anderson (18–28) and Garnsey (3–8) assert it to have been (at times, for the latter). Certainly, whatever were the numbers of slaves in any era, whether a quarter, third, half or even more of the total population of Athens, everyone agrees that slavery was, as Moses Finley says, "a basic element in Greek civilization" ("Was?" 69). It was not *the* basic element. Finley accepts Westermann's conclusion that "Greek culture was not founded upon slavery" in the sense that "the enslaved population predominated over the free or that the Greek city-states displayed the mentality of a slave-ridden society" ("Athenaeus" 92). Slavery was one element of their economies and polities, not their foundation. The "bulk of production," agrees Ste. Croix, was not slave: "the combined production of free peasants and artisans must have exceeded that of unfree agricultural and industrial producers in most places at all times, at any rate until the fourth century of the Christian era" (*Class* 133). Garnsey adds that the extent of slave production of course varied over time. All this has consequences for arguments about slaves and personhood.

It suggests and evidence shows that free and slave worked alongside, not just in the household but in public spaces as well. We earlier noted records of such co-working in the building of the Erechtheum and saw Xenophon write of people buying slaves so as to have "fellow-workers." Both imply relations recognizing people as souls, not tools. At Athens there were, as Ehrenberg sums up many sources, "public slaves who worked in the courts and offices, for instance in the mint. They were a group of real importance, 'the only non-elective and permanent Civil Service'," he cites Humfrey Michell (*Economics* 358). Many slaves, he further observes, "approximated the standard of" many citizens' lives (*People* 174, 189. For ancient materials about slaves of the *polis*, see

Wiedemann, *Greek* 154–66). These points matter as suggesting that the clear-cut opposition between slave and free that we have let Aristotle (and the *Digest*) draw for us did not hold in real life. We have seen vast ancient opposition to it and even how Aristotle's own arguments betrayed an inability to sustain the view. One must agree with Finley, that between the two wholly "hypothetical extremes" of "the slave as property and nothing else" and "the perfectly free" person there is "a whole range or spectrum of positions":

A person possesses or lacks rights, privileges, claims and duties in many respects: he may be free to retain the surplus of his labour after payment of dues, rents and taxes, but not be free to choose the nature and place of his work or domicile; he may be free to select his occupation but not his place of work; he may have certain civil rights but no political rights; he may have political rights but no property rights so long as he is, in Roman terms, *in potestate*; he may or may not have the right (or obligation) of military service, at his own or public expense; and so on. (*Ancient Economy* 67–68; cf. Garlan 99–133)

This splendidly helps understand Aristotle's distinction of the slave as ensouled human being and as owned tool. The one was natural, Cicero's first and second *personae*, the other social, Cicero's third *persona* (the slave had no *chosen* fourth, by status, not reason). Finley's spectrum offers one set of circles composing personhood: sociopolitical and economic surroundings in which person is differently embedded. It makes us understand why in Rome manumitted slaves could and did become citizens, why in Athens they could and did get, however sometimes precariously, the same status as foreigners and metics—indeed there, too, if on rare occasions, citizen rank (Ste. Croix, *Class* 174; Garlan 94–97: *one occasion of such citizenship would suffice to evidence the sense of equal humanity*). Neither in Greece nor in Rome was it rare to free slaves—on the contrary. It is the case that "most freed slaves were obliged to provide their erstwhile masters with a range of services which had the effect of making the freedman's status one of dependence just as tight, if not as exacting, as that of the slave" (Wiedemann, *Slavery* 28). But let us not forget that in Greek city states, as in Rome, the free citizen had obligations of military service, taxation, ritual participation and others that were also forms of subjection, *douleia*. All these signal equivalent *personhood* of free person and slave.

Ancient poetic and dramatic texts add evidence. Certainly, these works or even inscriptions are not transparent documents. Mosaics, statues and pottery are not straightforward representations. Specific genre conventions and rules apply. Speakers in dramas, figures on jars depict no unequivocal claim or argument. Matters involving slave characters are further complicated by the realities just seen. These aspects of plays by

Euripides, Aristophanes, Menander, Plautus, Terence, are manifestations of vexed negotiations between social fact, moral unease and perhaps even metaphysical anxiety.

Much ancient tragedy, especially Euripides', inferred that slavery was always unnaturally imposed on vital personhood. Choruses in *Suppliants*, *Trojan Women* and *Phoenician Women* amply noted slavery's oppressions. *Hecuba* could be taken to be as much about enslavement as *Alexander*. Many suggested that the slave was no less a person than someone who, by whatever accident, finds themselves free:

> A slave bears only this
> Disgrace: the name. In every other way
> An honest slave is equal to the free.

So the old man in *Ion* (420–410 B.C.?: 854–56, trans. Willetts), a play as much about the transformation of a high-born person into a slave (and back again) as the above-mentioned choruses. "Many slaves," wrote Euripides elsewhere, "are unworthy only in name, while their soul is freer than that of non-slaves." "The name 'slave' does not exclude worth. Many slaves are worth more than free people" (Nauck frs.831, 511, quoted in Garlan 140). What of Menelaus' slave in *Helen* (412 B.C.)?

> He is a poor thing who does not feel as his masters do,
> grieve in their grief, be happy in their happiness.
> I, though I wear the name of lackey, yet aspire
> to be counted in the number of the generous
> slaves, for I do not have the name of liberty
> but have the heart. Better this, than for a single man
> to have the double evil of an evil spirit
> and to be named by those about him as a slave.
>
> (728–33: trans. Lattimore)

In *Iphigenia in Aulis* (405 B.C.) as much as in the lost *Alexander*, Euripides implied equality of slave and free, and claims of absolute difference due only to self-interest. *Iphigenia* showed a web of deceit and trickery, betrayal and violence. Just before being sacrificed, Iphigenia apparently succeeded in persuading Clytemnestra and Achilles that her death would indeed accomplish the gods' will. By now she was fully aware of the lies and cheating behind her present circumstances. So it is hard to see anything but irony in her conclusion that the sacrifice would rightly allow Greeks to rule over barbarians:

> It is right,
> And why? They are bondsmen and slaves, and we,
> Mother, are Greeks and are free. (1401–2: trans. Walker)

The point is not whether Euripides was urging his view or an opponent's. Rather is it that the play's action has removed clarity, certitude and, even more, rectitude from the claim. Too, if *douleia* was the issue, then the obligation laid on Agamemnon by the gods, its imposition of moral blindness or deprivation of moral choice (as Clytemnestra and Achilles assert), showed that only sardonically could one call the Greeks free. And if one *could* nonetheless speak of freedom, what then was it to be a slave?

Nor, to go from tragedy to comedy, can we know just what may have been signaled by what Yvon Garlan calls "the more complex typology" of Menander's slaves over Aristophanes', or "their more active participation in the progress of the action" (29). The last is true in the sense that Xanthias in *Frogs*, to take him again, however active in the telling, was not vital to the plot as many of Menander's or Plautus' slave protagonists were, without whom the plot could not advance. Menander's Daos in *Aspis* and Onesimos in *Epitrepontes* were surely fully human beings? And what of the slave *hetaira* Habroton, exclaiming that the only reward she wants for reuniting Chairesis, Pamphile and their child is a free life: "Freedom's all I want, dear gods!" (*Epitrepontes* 548: Menander 1.457). We cannot know whether such instances as these echoed widely held views or criticized them. We cannot know what sort of change, if any, such characters may have represented: we have no access to enough of the dramatic corpus.

David Wiles takes Menander's theater to legitimize slavery, reasserting Aristotle's claim for natural slavery (64). The view is untenable: it is not the case (as he argues) that a slave is not the main protagonist in so many of his plays. Their very complexities evidence their humanity, their whoness. Against this view, Wiles asserts that at least no such conclusions can be drawn from Plautus' slaves (supposed transcriptions of Menander's), being no more than "a kind of algebraic symbol for the underdog in Roman society" (66). Even *were* this the case, how the plays present this "underdog" matters. They are certainly far from mere tools of their masters. J.-C. Dumont also disagrees diametrically with Wiles' view regarding both Menander and Plautus (*Servus* 557–606). Ancient comedy offered a complex spectrum of slaves and slavery. It clearly shared in ongoing debate, expressing, at the very least, a sense that whatever was the social fact of slavery, the sense of what it was to be a person was not changed by it, though the person was obviously *affected* by the oppressions it involved.

This is confirmed in practice by the wide variety of actual legal and political slave conditions in different city states. Such variety shows the *practical* awareness that slavery was a social, legal and political disability, not moral or ontological. At Gortyn, for example, by laws dating from the mid-fifth century, "enslavement did not automatically involve the loss of civil rights." Indeed, "the Gortynian system" granted "to the slave certain personal privileges which are now thought of as belonging by right to the human being *qua* human, and not to the citizen only." One cannot now know, Schlaifer adds, whether slaves had these privileges in cognizance of such right, as a better way of control or from "pure humanitarianism." Whatever the case, for reasons probably associated with these conditions, the slave there could acquire considerably "more property in his own right than was usual at Athens" and, we saw, Gortyn slave families were full legal entities "with regular marriage" (105, 110–11). Whether the reasons for these abilities were interested or disinterested, they anyway show that on the ground slaves were persons like anyone else.

So, too, does the argument recorded over the status and history of the Greek colony of Locris in southern Italy. Aristotle explained that because the colony had been founded by slaves and their children by free women, they had instituted matrilineal descent to signal their free origins and hide their slave ones. The historian Timaeus vigorously protested this "insulting" account, but was later taken to task by Polybius, defending Aristotle. Polybius did so, however, in terms that the Aristotle of now-familiar accounts could hardly have accepted since, echoing Menelaus' slave in *Helen*, he assumed people's souls to be equal:

To suppose, with Timaeus, that it was unlikely that men, who had been the slaves of the allies of the Lacedaemonians, would continue the kindly feelings and adopt the friendships of their late masters is foolish. For when they have had the good fortune to recover their freedom, and a certain time has elapsed, men, who have been slaves, not only endeavour to adopt the friendships of their late masters, but also their ties of hospitality and blood; in fact, their aim is to keep them up even more than the ties of nature, for the express purpose of thereby wiping out the remembrance of their former degradation and humble position, because they wish to pose as the descendants of their masters rather than as their freedmen. (Polybius fr. 12.6a, quoted in Finley, "Was?" 163)

That they could do this did not contradict Aristotle's history; it did his arguments about natural slavery. So too did the fact that this story was debatable at all in the terms Polybius used. The same weight of institutions over nature in establishing slavery, to echo our earlier Hippocratic, and so sense that *persons* did not differ in essential being, was evinced in the differing situations of slave populations subjected by ethnicity, like the Helots of Sparta, the Penestai of Thessaly and others. Ongoing scholarly dispute over whether such groups should be thought serfs (tied to an owner's land in return for specified services and production) or slaves (totally owned) may echo contemporary unease about personhood. If we can get this last straight, we may see serfdom and slavery as two varieties of the ways in which Cicero's third *persona* was socially circumscribed. The relation of *persona* and social surrounding may have involved a flexibility forbidding so clear-cut a division as that between slavery and serfdom. The facts of slavery spoke against it as against the idea of natural inhumanity: hence the "fellowship" of slave and free laborer.

By nature all humans were endowed with similar capacities of feeling, acting and reasoning, their varieties not having to do *per se* with their sociopolitical or economic status. The first-century A.D. Latin fabulist, Phaedrus—apparently once a slave—explained Aesopian fables as being precisely the means by which slaves had been able to express their humanity and its capacities in these conditions of social, political and legal disenfranchisement and oppression:

> Now why the genre of the fable was discovered
> briefly I'll explain. Always liable to harm, the slave,
> not daring to speak outright what s/he wished,
> translated their own affections into fables,
> and so eluded censure with made-up jestings.
>
> (Book III, Prologue 33–37)

Almost any of Phaedrus' or others' fables offers evidence for this claim.

Further, the thinker now increasingly seen as either originator or consolidator of a sense of person somehow self-contained, self-reflexive and experiencing "willful" choice, spent his youth and beyond as a slave. Epictetus' personal experience as he expressed it in his teachings confirmed Seneca's analysis. Perhaps it confirms Phaedrus' assertion, itself echoing strong claims for universal personhood in Menander, Plautus and others. Were slaves thought "moral inferiors" (Wiedemann, *Greek* 61–77)? Evidence suggests so. Evidence suggests ambivalent shame at thinking so. The shame implies cognizance that human beings were at issue, and humans *qua* humans were equal. The very contortions show people in fact agreeing that a person was a person, regardless of social circumstance. Not even Aristotle managed always to disagree.

CHAPTER SEVEN

How Was Personhood Gendered?

I want to argue that the same was so for women. So much work has been done on women in antiquity in the past generation that account is possible and needed before analysis of personhood can continue. The work has yielded conflicting interpretations. Some claim misogyny so ineluctably deep-seated in ancient Greece and Rome as to make women non-persons to the men whose writings survive. Considered social "pollutants" (Carson), denigrated, segregated, dominated and raped, women would have been just non-human slaves by another name—or twice over. If women were indeed non-persons then what is said of personhood in the preceding and following chapters on antiquity would simply not apply to them, any more than it would have done to slaves. Others argue that however women were oppressed by and subordinated to men they yet experienced high levels of emancipation in various times and places, if never equality. (Whether "emancipation" and "equality" or their contraries are categories usefully applied to societies as different as Greek and Roman were from the European post-Enlightenment that made the categories is itself a question that some of what follows may help resolve.)

Remembering again that the present discussion's focus is on personhood, it is not the level or nature of such "emancipation" (if true) that counts but its mere fact: it assumed possession of abilities general and common to all humans. I shall actually argue that this more or less "negative" trace is just a bottom line and that more than enough evidence shows that when the men whose work is detailed in these chapters envisaged persons they did not exclude women any more than slaves (with the possible, but very ambivalent, exception of Aristotle, who seems at least to have *wished* to exclude both). As before, being oppressed and being a person were not at odds. Strictly speaking we need to know how women felt such oppression, this very term being our modern interpretation of a condition to whose passible sentiment we have no direct access. Again, needed records are sparse or nonexistent, which itself says a lot about status and (non)representation. Further, we need to recall that Greek and Latin had words for humankind, *anthrōpos* and *homo*, distinct from the words specifying gender, *anēr* and *vir*, *gynē* and *mulier*. In modern European vernaculars the first four of these have been and are usually translated as "man" or its equivalent. This makes care necessary in using even the finest editions and translations: throughout De Lacy's model edition of Galen's *De elementis*, for example, *anthrōpos* is translated as "man." Only at the very end is it once or twice "person" or "human being" (151).

Certainly, Cavarero rightly says that the "universal-neutral valence that is supposed to indicate humankind as a whole" is here "named in the masculine singular" of the noun *anthrōpos* (*In Spite* 38). She adds that "all the ancient texts at our disposal describe *anthrōpos* with masculine attributes." This strikes me as needing nuancing, especially the claim that "since she is devoid of these attributes, woman is an *anthrōpos* of a lower level." Given what we have seen, it is not clear what attributes are at issue or to what level of being they adhere. And to jump to Aristotle as proof seems risky (123–24n5). Later, Cavarero does nuance her point, arguing less that the gender of *"anthrōpos"* reduced women to inferior beings than that its valence had an "abstracting effect" with regard to all humans. It "dematerialized" unique singulars into universals, moving them from material life into a realm of "pure thought" (51). This certainly inflects the origins and course of western philosophy and how certain things are thought. How it affects experiences of who-ness is unclear.

Recognizing these limitations and strictures, this chapter takes up a further challenge. It evokes social actualities which, with all change and variety, held largely from the fifth and fourth centuries B.C. to the fifth and sixth centuries A.D. (and perhaps beyond—at least as to what they tell us about and how they relate to personhood). Unsatisfactory as this is for general historical debate, I hope to show it less threadbare respecting the specific questions this book addresses. I certainly do not mean that there were no changes in status or condition over these more than a thousand years or across diversities of place. I do mean that while changes affected adjustments of the person to differences of circumstance and surrounding, to the circles composing the person (adjustments whose *exact* ways we cannot know, for silence mostly reigns), they little affected the fact and nature of the person. The circles differed, not their place and role in being a person. That is what the present chapter tries to make convincing.

Through Chapter 5, I studied ancients as if they had presented all humans as equal, heedless of whether slave or free, man or woman. The last chapter sought to show that what was generally held to differ was not a person's humanity (the first and second *personae*) but her or his sociopolitical insertion in the world (aspects of the third *persona* and the whole of the fourth). However inferior Aristotle did hold women to be in energy, strength and certain other capacities, even he yet thought that the common characteristics Chapters 2 through 5 explained belonged to both women and men as persons. Certainly, as he moved from the universal to the physical, material and social, he introduced restrictions. Still he did not make women into different beings. He saw them as lesser humans; and not always that, despite most commentators' unanimity. We need to know not just what his restrictions were, but their general import: whether specific to Aristotle and members of his school or widely agreed. Evidence suggests they were the former, never the latter, and even for the school were deeply ambiguous. To that end this chapter looks again at Aristotle, more at others and some of the realities in which people lived. It means to show that this book discusses a broad majority of its European peoples, not just half of them.

Whatever ambiguities inhered in Plato's variable view of women, Aristotle has been the main butt of anti-misogynist ire—largely because his views have been held to rule antiquity. Yet among major schools of Greek philosophy only his Lyceum had no record of teaching women, seeming thus to imply difference in the mind or soul that was personhood's core. "His philosophical views," says Nussbaum, "according to which women are incapable of practical wisdom [*Politics* 1260a13], appear to support this practice" (*Therapy* 54). But she adds both, with G. E. R. Lloyd (*Science*), that Aristotle may have lagged behind wider intellectual opinion, and that to include women in his school would have opened him to perilous ridicule and criticism. Socially, politically, economically and rationally, women were held to serve society not in the *polis* at large, but by their place and activities in the *oikos*, founding unit of the *polis*: a vastly serious fact gravely complicating modern western perceptions of "emancipation," "equality" or "oppression." Plato, with his aristocratic connections, was shielded (as Epicurus later was not) but, as a resident alien in Athens without civic, religious or property rights and further suspect by his Macedonian origins and ties, Aristotle could ill afford even mildly unconventional steps.

Aristotle's writings sometimes suggest that he held women in scant respect. But if he said that women were in some ways "lesser" men, he restricted implications of such statements to specific areas and matters. A statement's context needs weighing, though Lynda Lange argues that his "theory of sex difference is . . . interwoven" so consistently "into the fabric of his philosophy . . . that it can[not] simply be cut away" ("Woman"

2). Elizabeth Spelman judges similarly a correspondence between subjection of the irrational to the rational part of the soul and "natural" authority of men over women—and children and slaves. Eva Keuls ties analogous remarks to the extravagant assertion that "Aristotle was one of the fiercest misogynists of all times, obsessed with the need to prove that women played no genetic part in reproduction" (405). Roger Just takes more or less "Aristotelian" "attributes of gender" to have been widely understood and practiced in classical Athens (153–93).

Critics must always use the same two passages of the *De generatione* and *Politics*, boosting them with comments in the *De anima* and *Nicomachean Ethics* about rational and irrational parts of the soul (sometimes instancing slaves but not women, the connection having to be made by the critic). This is small evidence in so large a mass of writing—especially when honest critics like Lange and Spelman have to acknowledge that these claims make Aristotle as unsteady in belief and incoherent in argument about women as we have seen him about slaves—which does not invalidate the claims but suggests, at the very least, that even he was unclear.

Winkler has usefully annotated the too-often-disregarded "threefold comparison of household authority-relations to forms of political authority" used by Aristotle in *Politics* 1.12, exemplifying "the revealing gap between prescriptive discourse and social reality." Aristotle asserted that the relation of master to slave was like a tyranny: master giving orders in his interests, slave having to obey. A father's relation to his children was like that of a lawful monarch to subjects over whom he ruled in everyone's interests. Under this same patriarchal governance "the relation of husband to wife, says Aristotle, is like a democracy. In a democracy all citizens are equal in rights and are equally eligible for office. Those elected to office are invested with insignia marking their temporary and purely conventional difference from the rest of the citizens." The only difference "is that in the case of husband and wife the distinction is permanent." Still, Winkler rightly remarks, given usual claims about Aristotle's views, "this is mind-boggling." He had, after all, "no need . . . to compare the relation of husband and wife to democratic equality, no need to raise the thought that wives might, if elected, govern the household in turn with their husbands, and no need to conjure up the paradoxical image of a democratic system in which the same citizens always hold office." Winkler suggests that Aristotle was "off guard" here, "processing descriptive data into his legislative system." Women *did* contribute at least equally to the welfare of the *oikos*, and were recognized as doing so. Aristotle here acknowledged this fact of actual living, even as his discourse strained against it (*Constraints* 7). Even the idea that the "distinction is permanent" could not readily be grounded in anything other than social habit. One can easily read belittling biological and other remarks as efforts to make social construction into essential nature.

Now one notices that such remarks in *De generatione* concerned the female role in biological reproduction, not women as persons. As animals without "testes are deficient in this part . . . not because it is better to be so but simply because of necessity," so females have "a certain incapacity" in being unable to concoct "the nutriment in its last stage into semen." Without this species could not reproduce (717b34, 728a17–20). Aristotle held that menstrual blood was the imperfect female equivalent to male semen in lacking the element of *psuchē*; in this degree women could be described as "deformed" males (737a). In Aristotle's hierarchical teleology of living creatures, women were one place further from the divine than men. Biology reflected this. Did mind and personality? His answer was: "yes, partly." The price was intellectual contortion and disagreement on the biology with almost everyone

Aristotle said that active, warm males provided the formal and efficient causes of life, passive, cold females the material only (729b1–20). The male principle was superior to the female, though both were essential. For him, writes Dean-Jones, woman was biologically "a substandard man whose body only approximate[d] to the ideal in human structure and processes" (*Women's* 225). The consequent point that women's social role differed from men's did not affect the core of who-ness. Women lacked men's "authority" over their own desires but they were rational and equally persons (*Politics* 1260a14; cf. Sealey 41). One can argue that Aristotle was giving ideological justification for segregating women into a domestic sphere, denying them not reason but "authority" (cf. Sassi 11). Perhaps so, but matters were more complex, as Aristotle's acknowledgment of married "democracy" suggests. In Greece and Rome, the household was not just in thrall to the city. Thrasymachus' anger over the destructive effect of believing that it was may not have been given its due weight by Socrates, but Xenophon advanced the same usual view less vehemently long before it was echoed by Cicero and the many who approved his version of the *Oeconomicus*.

Further, Aristotle's biology did not signal a consensus. Danielle Gourevitch insists that his work in this discipline gave the chief philosophical bases of Roman medicine (13–14). Dean-Jones claims that his medical model dominated Hellenistic and Roman times (*Women's* 21). If so, it was in a form vastly altered by various eclecticisms. Dean-Jones adds that judges of ancient medicine's supposed misogyny should remember that the model was adopted "during a period in which women were being admitted into more and more activities—including the profession of medicine."

The model's adoption would have to be explained against women's actual emancipation in the craft most held to sustain the prejudice. K. C. Hurd-Mead gives many names of Hellenistic and Roman women physicians from Pliny and others: Agnodice, a fourth/third–century follower of Hippocrates whose acquittal for practicing fraudulently got women physicians the right to study with whom they chose and wear what they wanted; her coeval Philista or Elephantis, Pyrrhus' sister, who wrote and taught on medicine; Salpe of Lemnos, who wrote on eye diseases, Olympias of Thebes (a contemporary of Pliny); divers Laises, Antiochises, Olympiases, Aspasias and Cleopatras ("Introduction," 189–91, 281–305; cf. Dean-Jones, "Excursus"). Real medical practice would deny its theory. Aristotelianism would have functioned more as ideological apparatus (cf. Hanson 313) than reflection of actual experience, far less its guide.

But to assert an Aristotelian consensus is a stretch. When Aristotle was teaching, generation was much disputed (Lange 3). So it was before and after. Things were settled, more or less, not in Aristotle's favor. A glaring example is women's supposed physiological passivity and Aristotle's claim that women provided only the receptacle of the uterus and the matter of its contents, her blood. Most medical practitioners, from the Hippocratics on, held that women actively gave a necessary seed. The Hippocratic writings on the "Seed" and the "Nature of the Child" were explicit that female and male provided seed and that these joined in the uterus. Galen's later *De semine* explicitly denied Aristotle (and two others) on the point, appealing equally explicitly to his version of Hippocratic authority. The male's semen, he argued, joined the female's semen in the uterus and was fed by it. Pneuma contained in male semen was freed only by its interaction with female seed (*De semine* I.5.18, 7.5, 7.6; II.4.19). Galen explained that though female sperm was "thinner" than male, it was a "food" naturally matching it, wetter and cooler being drawn to thicker and hotter for a perfect balance—food of natural affection, "*oikeia trophē*" (II.4.19). That male sperm needed the "congenial materials, blood and pneuma" (I.5.2) of the mother to draw it in was not all. Apart from her seed the female supplied the blood furnishing the major part of the pneuma, generated in the heart and flowing through the arteries (I.7.1; cf. De Lacy's commentary 214, to 82, 15).

Refuting others, Galen said that in trying to echo Aristotle, Athenaeus in fact agreed that "the offspring ha[d] more from the mother than from the father" (II.1.45). Both gave seed but the mother provided two of three matters and powers (*dunameis*) needed to make fetus, blood and one of the two seeds: "let these things be said," added Galen wryly, "for the sake of Athenaeus and Aristotle, since they take delight in scientific demonstrations and are eager to use them" (II.1.73). Seed and blood were active matter and power (*dunamis*) (II.2.15). Galen ended by arguing that these interactive powers created beings whose similarities and differences could be defined much as Cicero did his first three *personae*: those being explained in social circumstance, these in biological. First was just being human rather than some other living being, second were differences between humans (these exactly analogous to Cicero's first two), third were differences and similarities involved in being female or male (II.5.20–22), enacted in the social sphere. The first was due to the substance of seed and blood, the second to the motion of seed, the last to specific mingling, *kraseōs*, of seed and blood (II.5.75). This biological exegesis of the experience of Cicero's *personae* gave women more part than men in generation and, more importantly, explained the spheres of essential sameness and lesser spheres of difference.

In all this, Galen claimed Hippocratic authority, even as he did not hesitate to add Aristotelian authority for this anti-Aristotelian position: "Aristotle, too, believes that the soul's faculties depend upon the mixture of the mother's blood, from which, in his opinion, our blood derives" ("The Soul's Dependence on the Body," *Selected* 161). The last point was accurate enough, the first was equivocally Aristotelian. Aristotle denied it, saying that *psuchē* was only in male semen, but Galen quoted the *De partibus animalium*: "The thicker and warmer the blood, the more it makes for strength; the thinner and colder, the more it conduces to sensation and intelligence" (II.ii.648a2–4). Galen had the philosopher in a contradiction. Having always insisted that the mother contributed only blood to the child's origin and growth, Aristotle here made blood responsible for intelligence, a faculty specific and central to rational soul. Referring next to the *Historia animalium*'s claims about visible physical evidence "of the relation between soul characteristics and bodily mixture" (491b–492b: I.viii–xi), Galen added:

His opinion here is that the construction of the whole body is, in each kind of animal, especially fitted to the characteristics and faculties of that animal's soul. For example, in blooded animals birth comes about from the mother's blood, and the soul's characteristics are dependent on the mixture of that blood, as was made clear in the statements cited above. But the construction of the organic parts of the body, too, is fitted to the soul's characteristics. (*Selected* 163)

Galen's clarity was much later, but Aristotle's contradictions are akin to those in his arguments about slaves (and married "democracy"), and show the same signs of confusion, ambiguity and tension.

Soranus also held that women supplied the fetus with "blood and pneuma" during growth, and so with life force or soul. For as Galen said, "without it the living creature cannot exist" (*De elementis* 5.24: 98), pneuma being a medium of the soul's rational and spirited parts (De Lacy's commentary 198 to 98.16–17). Soranus found the point important enough to repeat when writing of cutting the umbilical cord to avoid hemorrhage: "since the vessels have served to convey the blood and pneuma from the [pregnant woman] to the body of the infant" (*Gynecology* I.10§38: 37; II.7§11[80]: 81). "The uterus, that is, the *mētra*, according to the Greeks," Aetios of Amida (Justinian's court physician) confirmed in the sixth century, "is called the matrix, because out of it all living souls develop as from a mother" (*Gynaecology* 15: *Tetrabiblon* 16.i).

If these were efforts to explain the source of "connate pneuma," Aristotle's power enabling soul to function in body, it is the more striking that all these late writers insist that it was via women's physiology that this active fundamental power entered the human body. Women did not just transmit pneuma. They fed it to the fetus as they did blood. Certainly Aristotle had agreed that women supplied nutritive and sensitive faculties of soul, these being matter and so provided by the blood. What blood could not provide was the rational (Lange 6). This distinction got hard once one said (with Aristotle) that these were powers of the *same* soul. It was largely invalidated by analyses incorporating women's seed and common pneuma. Consequently, neither Aristotle's view of the uniqueness of male seed nor this distinction got attention in medical writings or for practical purposes. We have also just seen that on at least one occasion (Galen claims more), Aristotle *did* in fact write that blood provided the rational faculty. Aristotle's contradictions signal vexed confrontation with social actuality. Certainly, his views were not dominant.

Some, it is said, held the uterus to be an "animal" distinct from the women in whose body it lived. If so, supply of blood and pneuma might be thought independent of the woman in whose body the fetus was. Difficulties strain such claims. One is that "animal" (*zōion*) simply means something with life in it, and to speak thus of the uterus is just to speak of a living element of a living body. Another is that no ancient clearly made such an argument, including Plato in the *Timaeus*. No Hippocratic did, and care is needed over what is read into Plato (cf. King 222–24). Plato told a story to explain humans' peremptory biological urge to reproduce: if the womb was alive with demands uncontrollable by women, the penis was likewise "an animal disobedient to reason" in men (91b–c). Men and women shared the disability. The tale evoked the urge to procreate, not physiological realities (in a circular universe upheld by a female principle). For his part Galen construed these lines of the *Timaeus* to mean "the illness named suffocation of the uterus," ignoring errant animals but adding, un-Galenically, that God made humans want intercourse, gave women wombs and men semen (*Compendium* 95). The divine intervention was a later interpolation by Hunayn ibn Ishāq (or his school), whose Christianized Arabic rendering of this work (cited from the Latin translation) was not straight Galen. Nor did Galen hold that women had wombs in which men's semen just grew, but otherwise this medical interpretation of Plato became standard. After ibn Ishāq, Razes (famed in the European middle ages) noted Galen's commentary when writing of the cause of suffocation of the womb (Galen, *In Platonis* 34).

Galen's main point was a normal "correction" of Plato. When Hippocratics wrote of the uterus raised, lowered or otherwise moved, they had no need to imagine an *animal* to explain what they saw as "a real and organic condition: the movement of the womb to other parts of the body" (King 209). Like most later writers, some were relating effects of tautened or slackened ligaments or muscles, of illness, regimen, intercourse, pregnancy and menstrual suppression on the reproductive organs and through the body (214). Some analyses, like that opening the Hippocratic *Diseases of Women* (2.123), are hard to interpret: "When the womb turns to the head [*trapōsin hai hysterai*] and suffocation stops there, the head is heavy" (ed. Littré 8.266; King 36, 216). Did this mean the womb *moved* to the head or that it *affected* the head? No such passages require interpreting the womb as an independent animal. Taking it as read, Mary Lefkowitz explores Hippocratic claim that celibacy caused uterine movement, charging it to their ideological bias and goals (*Heroines* 12–25). One might better credit the idea that women get ill from light sexual activity to male fantasy, even as one grows to feel that a literal reading of the *Timaeus* has ruled interpretation of the Hippocratics. King suggests this (224), arguing that ancient debate about male and female difference was tilted by medieval to modern western practitioners for ideological aim and to justify medical subjection of women. The ostensibly typical wandering womb was not in Aetios, any more than it had been in Rufus, Galen or Soranus, to name a few figures vital to the tradition. The uterus was a live part of a live body, in or out of balance with the whole, like *all* organs, members and humors. For most writers, not the male, far less a separate animal uterus, but the female was *essential* for the soul's passage into the growing fetus. Whether it did so under separate impetus or by means of the mother's pneuma was not clear, but the implications are. Women were mostly thought as active as men in conception and more so in the fetus' growth.

These views did not originate in the first centuries A.D. All these specialists referred to previous authorities. The very facts that in his first-century medical encyclopedia Celsus nowhere proposed any animal uterus and treated women's physiology in ways agreeing with its analysis by those just named shows that medically speaking, at least, Aristotle's opinions were not the more but the less usual.

Most medical texts do seem to take men as their standard—although, again, one must take care to distinguish *anthrōpos* and *anēr, homo* and *vir*, and beware of translations that introduce their own prejudices. Still Dean-Jones appears right to say of the Hippocratic corpus that by and large its works seemed to make men the standard. But three cautions may usefully be advanced.

First, as Dean-Jones remarks, a good part of the apparent focus on men in the classical Greek treatises may have been grounded in the medical reason that "a woman's reproductive system" was taken to act "as her own natural purging process." While a woman's health was held generally more precarious than a man's, it was thus also thought that she "succomb[ed] less often to, and recuperat[ed] more quickly from, serious disease." This natural purging meant that since women did not need men's plethora of therapies, general medicine's descriptions targeted primarily men (*Women's* 146–47). This contention reflects aspects of ancient Greek medical opinion, but is quite speculative and may overdraw belief in difference between men's and women's bodies that evidence does not always support.

The second caution is simpler. Writers on these topics observe that social and moral proprieties prevented male physicians (authors, it seems, of all the most ancient surviving works) from examining women patients save in the gravest cases. The result was rare case reports and scanty hearsay evidence for non-critical conditions. This gives a social explanation for belief in women's auto-purgation. Called in only for critical cases, male physicians supposed everyday health. Their explanation for this fortunate condition, however, presupposed human bodies to be alike: but for auto-purging women would suffer the same ills as men. King rightly says that natural purgation made women "men with a bonus" (51).

The third caution is this one's counterpart. If the male body was therefore taken as a model, the foundations of human physiology were still given as the same in men and women. Humans (*anthrōpoi*) varied as men or women only in their reproductive organs. Everything else applied to all. Differences required specifying only where differences were. Women and men shared basic elements and qualities of the human body, its relations with the physical and social world and its general regimen and diet, as Hippocratics and later writers held (see Chapters 2 and 8). Differences in regimen, diet and diagnosis accounting for differences in sex were on a par with those accounting for differences in temperament, humors and myriad other conditions. Physicians indeed said so when listing these *differentia*.

Few, if any, male physicians writing on women made differences generic. Soranus dismissed Aristotle's assertion of women's difference from men by saying that whatever the sexual specificity of an organ, here the uterus, it was "woven from the same stuff as the other parts, and it [was] regulated by the same forces, and it [had] available to it the same substances, and . . . suffer[ed] disease from the same causes." Hygiene and cure, etiology and regimen varied with the local conditions of an organ but were "generically the same" (III [Preface] §§3–5.129, 132). We earlier saw Celsus insist on identity of symptoms in women and men with tuberculosis (II.8.24–25). When Rufus wrote of kidney and bladder diseases, stones for instance, he took equal care to specify what applied differently in the nature of the stones and treatment for women *and* men, because of their body parts ("Kidney and Bladder Diseases" 3.5–8, *Oeuvres* 22–24). Writing of curing melancholy and need for phlebotomy and purging "downward," Galen added that both meant promoting "hemorrhoidal and menstrual" bleeding, being equivalent ways of getting humors back in balance. His analysis and his treatments, he said, came from Hippocrates ("De locis affectis" III.x, *Opera* 8.183). Paulus Aegineta echoed the same advice four centuries later (III.xiv: 1.384). The body's parts were sexually different, their composition was not.

Trotula, best-known of many women doctors at Salerno half a millennium later, wrote likewise of the relation between sexually specific organs and general distribution of humors. Like all others, she took physiology of elements, qualities, humors and passions in women to be simply human, explaining excessive menstruation, for example, in strict accord with Galenic theory:

Yellow bile pouring back from the gall bladder makes the blood feverish to such an extent that it cannot be contained in the veins. Sometimes a salty phlegm is mixed with the blood and thins it and makes it burst forth outside. If the blood which comes becomes yellowish or inclines to a yellow colour, it is due to the bile. If it inclines towards a whitish color it is due to the phlegm. If to a red color it is from the blood. (*Diseases* 9; Latin in *Malattie* 58)

This is to get far ahead of things, but virtually identical accounts were given by Paulus (III.lxiii: 1.617–18), Aetios (*Tetrabiblon* 16.lxv.66) and earlier writers back to the Hippocratics (Adams in Paulus 1.618–19).

All this strongly suggests that through most of antiquity and even down to the later European middle ages Aristotle's opinion of female physiology was not standard. The dominant view was of sexual differences on a ground of human sameness: men and women were sexed variants of one human species. That is what it certainly *became*. Dean-Jones shows that in later "Graeco-Roman medicine" a woman's body was thought so close to a man's that its auto-purgation was felt unnecessary, it being found, therefore, that "it would have been better for [the process of menstruation] to cease altogether" (*Women's* 250). Gillian Clark similarly argues that by the first and second centuries A.D., medical texts "tend[ed] to emphasize the similarity of male and female" (71). I am suggesting that between ancient Greece and the first Hellenistic and Roman centuries B.C./A.D. no fundamental change occurred, and that no opinion involving basic difference ever held authoritative sway. Sexual organs differed, the body's foundations, composition and non-reproductive functions did not. Not for nothing could Tiresias move between being male and female, knowing both in their similar who-ness. As to the physical body, diverse in some parts but not in "the stuff from which it was woven," in the forces ruling or substances composing it, nothing in medical debate stopped women experiencing a common human personhood: *contra*, for a moment, whatever was implied by varieties of social and legal role, condition and status.

In these non-biological and non-physiological areas of experience and debate realities are also hard to touch. If Aristotle and a few Stoics set women under men's ("democratic"?) authority, Socrates said he bowed to women's advice, many being wiser than he, Aspasia above all. Plato's *Menexenus* praised her as teacher of the greatest Athenian orators and had Socrates repeat a funeral oration by her (235e–249e). In *De inventione* (I.xxxi.51–52), Cicero quoted dialogue by Aeschines Socraticus where Aspasia displayed her renowned moral wisdom: showing Xenophon and his wife the impact of envy and a desire for abstract perfection on the real affection of their union, and insisting, as Héloïse would remark to Abelard, that true union needed mutually recognized merit—merit increased by the very recognition (Héloïse, ed. Monfrin 115). Xenophon related an exchange between the *hetaira* Xenodote and Socrates in which, duBois notes, women were represented "as attracting, as capable of speech and humor, as present and engaging in conversations with the philosopher" (*Memorabilia* 3.11.10; duBois, *Sappho* 94). Certainly these are men speaking for women. There is, too, an abyss between Aspasia's advice and Socrates' authority. Women read and wrote. Did their writings circulate? That almost none survive implies that they were rated less important than men's; which matters as a marker of women's social *personae*. At present, my concern is personhood's core, not relative social position and status.

Xenophon's *Oeconomicus* gave the view, apparently not unlike Aristotle's "democracy," that a well-educated wife would have authority over her husband in the *oikos* (his main responsibilities lying elsewhere). Soul's qualities were "neither immutable nor predetermined by gender: men and women [were] equal in their ability to exercise memory, diligence, moderation, and discretion" (Pomeroy, *Xenophon* 37; cf. Just, 114–18, 135–36, 151–52). Women and men shared memory, care, reason, self-control and the various other natural aptitudes (as "endurance" and "timidity"), showing that nature planned for the "partnership" and bond between them to be the stronger and closer for its necessity (*Oeconomicus* VII.22–32). Foley finds a contemporary counter to Xenophon's fortunate intimacy. In a fragment, the sophist Antiphon, after quickly noting fear of a bad marriage, enlarged on the anxiety of a good, saying that a husband's and wife's mutual esteem, love and desire to care equally for two beings as one (or more, if they had children) increased anxiety unlimitedly, since care for one's own being alone caused despair. Foley sees here a misogynist view of women as a "threat" (*Female* 80; Antiphon fr.49). This seems an odd reading, but even if women *were* a threat, it was precisely because their who-ness was the same as men's. The fragment strongly endorses the sense of women as no less moral and social agents than men, hence the anxiety.

Antisthenes, founder of the Cynics, held that men and women had "the same virtues." So too did his pupil Diogenes and his follower Crates who traveled everywhere with his disciple Hipparchia. Aristippus' daughter Arētē became head of the Cyrenaic school of philosophy founded by her father (Wider 48–49), although her leadership was presumably "unofficial" since it appears to have been her son Aristippus the Younger who formalized the school's teaching. Besides Cynics and Academics in part, Epicurus and his followers "believed in the equality of women." Stoic theory in general held men and women equal, a view stressed notably by the Romans, Seneca and Musonius Rufus (Colish, *Stoic Tradition* 1.36–38; Wider 51–52). In *Republic* V Plato argued for equality of education and domain in the public sphere, saying that the soul and its faculties were unaffected by sex, although elsewhere he argued the opposite—ambiguously in *Laws*, less so in *Timaeus* (his views were equivocal even within the *Republic*, as Froma Zeitlin notes: "Playing" 84–85, and see Wender). Pythagoreans held women apt and able to govern and share fully in political life. Perhaps this did not touch such real-life facts as that in ancient Athens women were segregated in the *oikos*, confined to domestic work and subject in public life to a husband's, father's or brother's legal power as her guardian (*kurios*). It does not touch the fact that in texts like Xenophon's *Oeconomicus* wives were nameless, husbands named. That this reflected social niceties (*hetairai*, prostitutes and women being insulted were often named) underscores social differences. Perhaps it touches not at all claims that "the possible social positions of women were as wives, concubines, heterae, or prostitutes" (Cantarella, *Pandora's* 56–57, 50; cf. Wider 26–40).

Perhaps. But these roles may reflect some wealthy males' fantasies more than reality. Pseudo-Demosthenes' often quoted remark—"we have mistresses for our enjoyment, concubines to serve our person, and wives for the bearing of legitimate children" ("In Neaeram" LIX.122), usually censured as recording usual misogyny, can only with care be generalized beyond one wealthy Athenian man's view. It may not even be that, since it recapped a plaintiff's avowedly vengeful attack on a woman and man said to have flouted all rules of household, city and religion, illegally mixing diverse civic spaces for their own advantage, making themselves asocial individuals. What it lets us extrapolate beyond forensic rhetoric or an individual's view is unclear. Scholarly dispute boils over what the distinction of charge for women and men, domestic versus public, meant in fact. Even at Athens men and women were thought essential to the welfare of the community as a whole (cf. Pomeroy, *Goddesses* 58–60).

In ancient Athens the *oikos* was ground of the city's stability, wealth and well-being. Only the wealthiest households could segregate women. The familiar idea of women's separation from Athenian life, echoing a fact about *political* participation (in practice the same for many men), did not and could not hold true in general other than in the richest *oikoi*. Perhaps this was the point of Plutarch's later supposed quotation of the Spartan king Areus, since its claim seems otherwise misapplied to Sparta, where women were not segregated as in Athens. Areus was quoted as having said of men who even commended "other men's wives," that "there ought to be no random talk about fair and noble women, and the qualities they happen to have should be totally unknown to all save those who live with them" ("Sayings of Spartans," *Moralia* 217ff.). Whatever this meant more generally (if anything) it clearly specified that gossip "peri tōn kalōn kagathōn gunaikōn" was what was to be disallowed and that it was particularly "gentlewomen" who were to be known only to members of their household. At the same time it insisted equally clearly on their qualities of personhood.

Poor women went about for many purposes, as did the wealthy, if we credit imaginative art and writing where scenes of women publicly socializing also imply that they did not just dash furtively from and to the family home with downcast eyes. Country women shared agricultural work. A large majority circulated out of the household. Evidence shows women from diverse households mingling for all kinds of reasons and doing many tasks from which laws ostensibly excluded them (Fantham et al. 106–12). Actuality was not limited to a wealthy minority varying in the fifth and fourth centuries between two and four hundred families (Sealey 161–64). Even about them care is needed. Galen told a story of one Phryne who, during a game, made a fool of other women present at "a drinking party." Even if these were *hetairai*, the many admiring tales about them show that no one doubted *their* status as persons. They may have been at an all-women's party; even so they had to get there and were not "confined." Galen gave no date, just narrating it as a past tale he had read. The event itself was no surprise. Indeed, since the story made Phryne the acme of natural true beauty it would have lost its point if the occasion were a unique oddity ("An Exhortation to Study the Arts," *Selected* 46). Although we know nothing of its place or time the tale offers a minor counter-indication to claims about women in purdah, as does artwork at Pompeii and elsewhere. Historians need to observe actual roles and capacities of women and men before declaiming against putatively general misogyny or, even more, assuming women to have been considered non-persons (Foley summarizes economic, social and legal conditions of Athenian marriage and household in *Female* 61–79. Patterson's work is especially important).

The segregation of women in wealthy households matters in regard to *political* emancipation, these being the families that ran the state. It matters differently for the sense of who-ness. The spheres of the person differed, its fact and feeling will have varied far less if only because daily exchange would then have been impossibly insecure. Women were excluded from direct participation in "the secular affairs of state." They were essential and recognized in "the structure of the *polis* as members necessary for its perpetuation and cohesion as a closed community" (Just 25). The *oikoi*, not individuals, were the fundamental units of the state; the domestic economy was bound to "the political structure," its success basic to the state's welfare. Economically, the "dichotomy between public and private that appears in industrialized societies" did not characterize ancient Athens (Pomeroy, *Xenophon* 52).

Free people of either sex could choose which sphere they served. But "public" and "domestic" were equally vital grounds of the *polis*. In this context actual relations between women and men, where meaningful records exist in writing or art, often show a closeness of feeling and shared responsibilities dependent on both being persons, even in classical Athens (hardly surprisingly). Fourth-century grave stelai likewise "indicate a concern for emotional relationships among family members" (Pomeroy 33; cf. John Gould 44–51). These things may seem not to need saying but given usual belief that Athenian women (and slaves) were excluded and segregated to the point of becoming—literally—non-persons, such counter-evidence of recognized and experienced personhood is needed along with some sense of the different organization of economic, political and social space that was its background.

Dean-Jones notes that modern western views of the inferiority of domestic to public life come from long dominion of male views; others could well valorize the domestic sphere, marginalizing those outside (avoiding prejudgment; not saying that Athenians did so—although Thrasymachus came close). Both assumed full degrees of personhood. It is, too, unclear that written laws and customs held even in Athens. Dean-Jones gives two indicative cases from the Hippocratic *Epidemics*. In one, a doctor, called by a head of household to attend a young niece, records not knowing if she had "had a child," avoiding inquiry. Solonic law decreed that such a person be sold into slavery. The physician clearly "thought it was conceivable that a young unmarried girl might give birth and be protected by her family." In the other case, a doctor attended a twenty-year-old woman, described as beautiful, who had been hit on the head while playing with friends and taken home. "This shows that not all Greek women were married at fourteen and that they sometimes left their homes for reasons other than religious festivals" (*Women's* 39, 27n80). Like much art and writing, these cases show that real legal, economic and leisure demands were far more flexible than written law and ideological claim make appear.

Clearly, the *oikos* was valorized *differently* from the city. It did not inevitably have lesser status. Plato's Thrasymachus thought it outweighed political life even for one who led the city. We need not think that those concerned principally with the household and spending most of their time in or around it would think it the lesser place. Besides the foundational role of the *oikos* in the wealth and stability of the city, it was a main site of interpersonal relations and chief visible assurance of a family's historical and economic cohesion. That is why a vast majority of extant legal debates and rulings treat relations in or between *oikoi*: inheritance, infringements of household rights, domestic credit and debt, affirmation of family standing and legitimacy.

A late fifth-century Athenian tale addresses these issues. Much commented upon as evidence of the oddity of Greek thinking, its overwhelming misogyny or simply concern for the legitimacy of household and family, it bears witness, too, not only to women's personhood but to the very personhood we have been seeing.

Lysias wrote the tale for Euphiletos to defend himself for the murder of Eratosthenes, who had seduced his wife, "corrupting her and inflicting disgrace on my children and outrage on me by entering my house [*tēn oikian*]" ("On the Murder of Eratosthenes: Defense" §4: 17). Euphiletos told how he and his wife began their marriage happily, and how, after a first child's birth they reordered their sleeping arrangements and the men's and women's quarters of the house, moving the latter downstairs to make it easier for his wife to feed the baby at night, accompanied by the slaves who looked after it. They lived "in perfect intimacy" until the death of his mother, at whose funeral Eratosthenes saw his wife and "in time corrupted her" (6, 8). Keuls calls this "a telling detail" (for Euphiletos' view of women): that his wife and Eratosthenes could strike this "first flirtatious spark" proves how "evidently Euphiletos did not attend [the funeral] himself" (91). This would be just silly, but hides the serious fact that Euphiletos sought to stress that his wife was not initially party to a seduction which victimized her, him and the *oikos*, that it took time and that Eratosthenes was, he said, a habitual and practiced seducer of married women (17). After a long time, Euphiletos realized that his wife was regularly bringing Eratosthenes into the house at night and, interrogating a slave girl, discovered "how my wife was in time persuaded" to yield to the seducer (20). One night, after a male friend whom he had been entertaining had gone home, the slave girl alerted Euphiletos to Eratosthenes' presence. Having gone to get some friends, with them he then caught his wife and Eratosthenes *in flagrante*. As one legal way out the latter offered Euphiletos money. But the husband chose rather to kill him on the spot in accordance, he told the judges, with "our city's law," and with the witness of "so many persons" as "were in the house" (23–26).

Euphiletos explained that he had killed the adulterer rather than taken money from him because the city's law imposed a severer penalty on those using persuasion than on those using force (32). For the latter were "hated by the persons forced," whereas the former

thereby corrupted their victims' souls [*psuchas*], so making others' wives more closely attached [*oikeioteras*: "more householdish"] to them than to their husbands, got the whole house [*pasan . . . tēn oikian*] into their hands and caused uncertainty about whose the children really were, the husband's or the seducer's. (§33)

The seducer utterly muddled lines of descent and inheritance within the *oikos* and sureties of citizenship without it, and thus future relations with other households and the children's status in and duties toward the city. Therefore, the law decreed his death (§34). This was why Euphiletos concluded his plea by asserting that his action had been in the interest "of the whole city" (§47).

The plea has two points of special interest. One involves Lysias' care to assure the household's good name. He did so by noting the close ties between husband and wife until after a clearly legitimate baby was born. He certified the last by dating it before the grandmother's death and funeral, when the two adulterers first met. The relation between the *oikos* and the city's laws had been carefully upheld. Euphiletos had not stalked his man. Rather was he so little prepared as to have been entertaining that evening, bidding his friend goodbye and getting ready for bed. Only when the slave followed his orders to tell him of Eratosthenes' presence had he hurried to gather what few friends he could and bring them as witnesses. His decision to exact the law's full penalty was because while a rape victim would spurn her attacker, a person seduced put the household and its pillars of legitimacy in her lover's hands and would pass off a child as legitimate. That was why, obeying the law, Euphiletos was acting in the city's interests. He was doing so many times over: Eratosthenes, he insisted, had been a habitual seducer of married women, a wide danger to legitimacy of marriage, inheritance and citizenship (on some of this, see Blundell 125–26; Dover, *Greek Popular* 147; Fantham 113–14; Just 68–70; Lacey 115).

Since the plea was a defense of Euphiletos, it did not say what penalty might be exacted of the seduced wife. Under the law, she could be excluded from the *oikos*, and so deprived of the ability to fulfill her duty (and citizen right) to bear and raise children for the household and city. This punishment would also remove the risk of her giving the household an illegitimate child, with which she might be pregnant. What is above all clear in Lysias' story are the carefully complex protections that surrounded the bounds of a household whose legitimacy and welfare mattered deeply both to its own existence and tranquility and to those of the city. Equally clear is the interaction between household and city, whose laws (here) existed to assure a legitimacy in the one essential to the security of the other. "The offenses, in other words," says Sue Blundell, "were treated as public ones, a good indication that the protection of the integrity of the *oikos* was considered to be in the interests of the community as a whole" (125).

The second aspect of interest in Lysias' plea involves personhood. Cantarella takes the speech as yet another sign of Athenian sexism and misogyny. The wife, she says, was held wholly passive in the affair, not "considered an adulterer but rather 'adulterated.' She was *moicheutheisa*, or 'corrupted,' as Lysias says." Cantarella adds that "she was a victim even if she had consented, because in the final analysis she was unfit to make up her own mind, whether for good or bad" (*Pandora's* 41). This may be too easy. As Raphael Sealey says of the same sentences in Lysias' speech, they insisted, rather, that seduction was worse than rape just because it seduced "the woman's mind and alienated her affections from her husband" (28). It taught her, we may now say, to give reasoned assent. Her soul (*psuchē*) was corrupted because in giving such assent she sapped the very foundations of the *oikos*, replacing it by a surrogate household (signaled in the word Lysias used to describe such new affections: *oikeioteras*).

Lysias twice accented alienation of the partner's affections, once when justifying the killing in general terms of the law, once when explaining to the judges the specific "perfect intimacy" between husband and wife until Eratosthenes' advent. This may remind us of the married partners' intimacy in Xenophon's *Oeconomicus*. The seducer persuaded the woman to replace that intimacy with another of the same sort (*oikeioteras*). He did so by getting her affected by an action as we have seen it described from Aristotle on. An action was not forced on her, like rape. Rather did she react *passibly*, accepting it by the assent common to all actions in which one acquiesced. This was no different from the passibility typifying *all* human action for those describing it throughout antiquity. It says, exactly, that women *did* have a mind, and that it acted just like a man's. (Eratosthenes can likewise be said to have acquiesced in an action of seduction that was only potential until he accepted it.) The insistence on intimacy and partnerlike relations in the household makes it further clear that Lysias was presenting the wife as a person like the husband: making the seduction all the worse.

This is one of the more melodramatic of surviving disputes. We do not know what happened to the unnamed spouse, but the very fact that she remained unnamed suggests that for the plea's duration, at least, she was to be considered wife, mother and partner in the *oikos*—its respectability upheld by the very murder whose legality was being asserted. To name a woman in a trial was deliberately to insult her, marking her as *déclassée* (cf. Goldhill 177n67). This was done to the main protagonist in another familiar case, one saying perhaps less about personhood (except that the accused woman and man were neither better nor worse than one another) but yet more about the tight imbrication of the *oikos* and all aspects of the *polis*. Doing so, it further stresses the importance of women's responsible control over it. The case is pseudo-Demosthenes against Neaira, brought shortly before 340 B.C. by Theomnestos and his brother-in-law Apollodoros, who, Louis Gernet thinks, probably wrote the speech (Demosthenes, *Plaidoyers* 66, 69). Although Neaira was named as defendant, her accusers were avowedly wanting vengeance on the entire household, especially the husband.

Stephanos, this husband, had attacked Apollodoros in 349 B.C. for having sought an illegal edict to use leftover military funds, of which Apollodoros then had charge. Theomnestos said that Stephanos, having brought this false charge, had tried to ruin Apollodoros and his household by demanding a huge fine of fifteen talents. The judges had levied one talent, still a big sum for a man who his defender said was worth only three talents (Murray ed. 3–8). Not satisfied, Stephanos had then sought Apollodoros' exile by bringing a false murder charge, that was rejected (9–10). None of their family had ever harmed Stephanos, said

Theomnestos. They could not explain these attacks, but had to safeguard their threatened households. They would prove that Athenian Stephanos had illegally wed alien Neaira, and both broken many state laws (13–14). The penalty for such marriage was that the alien, man or woman, would be sold into slavery, the husband, in the latter case, fined a thousand drachmas (16). They would further prove many crimes involving "their" daughters (13), including their passing for Stephanos' own and as Athenian citizens, being married to Athenians, one of them even taking part in the most sacred and secret religious rites. Theomnestos now handed the case over to Apollodoros.

Apollodoros told a sordid story, doing his best to underline its caste aspects. Neaira had been a slave, bought as a young girl by a freedwoman, Nikarēte, married to the cook of her one-time master. The evidence and witnesses showed that by 375 B.C. or so Neaira was working as a prostitute at Corinth and then for a couple more years at Megara, where she met Stephanos around the end of the decade (18, 23–37). From thence he returned with her and her three daughters to Athens where they lived as husband and wife, she continuing to work as a prostitute, he trading in blackmail by threatening some of her clients with what we have just seen as the potentially deadly accusation of adultery. During this time a daughter Phano, married off as Stephanos', had been repudiated by her husband Phrastor, after she had become pregnant, as being non-Athenian (one of her parents not being a citizen). Stephanos chose not to fight the issue, coming to an arrangement with Phrastor. Sometime later Phrastor took ill, and allowed Phano and their son to return to his house. He then tried to have his son declared Athenian by enrolling him in his phratry—which refused, on grounds that the son was not a citizen. All this was offered as proof that Neaira was long known a foreigner and Stephanos therefore equally long known to have been breaking the law.

Matters got worse. Apollodoros told how Stephanos had "wormed his way into the favor" of the man drawn by lot to become king-archon. He married another of Neaira's daughters to him, passing her off as his own. He did this knowing that the wife of the king-archon had the most sacred duties to perform during the year of his archonship, becoming the symbolic bride of Dionysos and administering the oath to the god's priestesses, duties that could be performed only by the most noble and respectable Athenian women (72–73). Here, Apollodoros gave a history of the Anthesteria festival, its symbolizing the union of god and people (74–85). He noted that as a slave or foreigner she would not have been excluded from the rites (but could not have played the role she did); as an adulterer she would: in this regard she and her sisters, Apollodoros said, followed their mother (85–87). The plaintiff then returned to the gravity and exclusivity of the rites, emphasizing how even those closest to the Athenians were not admitted to their affirmation of the city's and people's fully harmonious circumstances (88–107).

The proofs that Neaira had been a prostitute and foreign slave, Apollodoros summed up, were manifold. Stephanos could not claim that he had not said he and she were married since he had married off their daughters as Athenians, legitimately born of two Athenian citizens (118–19). If Stephanos now said, as he apparently intended, that they had only been living together as man and concubine, and that the children were his by another woman, not only could contrary proof be brought but he, Apollodoros, had already offered to have Neaira's two slaves testify under torture that the three daughters were really Stephanos'- the latter had refused (120–25). The case, he said, was amply proven "against these people who have acted lawlessly" (126). Indeed. Apollodoros' prosecution had proven far more than it needed to indict Neaira and Stephanos.

As much as anything, the speaker seems to have been showing the extent to which *oikos* and *polis* were bound to one another. Stephanos' and Neaira's usurpation of civic rights had led to a series of breaches in law and custom. Stephanos' breach of the public sphere was demonstrated in his false accusations against Apollodoros in the past. Neaira's breach of the household sphere was shown by her using it not only as a place of prostitution but as one of fraudulent claims of citizenship. *Oikos* and *polis* met; Neaira and Stephanos were equally guilty, equally "these people" who had flouted the laws. Doing so they had harmed other *oikoi* by confusing genealogies, the *polis* by trying to alter the composition of deme and phratry, and religion by placing a slave, adulterer, prostitute and alien in charge of the sacred harmonizing rites of Dionysos. Few things could better show how these many spheres were integral and essential to one another's welfare than a case such as this. That, too, was why Theomnestos began their plea by insisting that the harm done was not to individuals but to two households especially recognized by the people and city of Athens (1–2). Neaira and Stephanos had played equally fraudulent roles in city and household. Besides these wider implications the case shows both as equally able in interpersonal manipulation and that as persons before the law they were deemed equally capable of rational assent to actions. Both were in multiply woven circles "of relationships and responsibilities," and clearly shared "the same values and moral capacities." And while it may often be correct to say, with Foley, that even under such conditions men and women "act under different constraints and with different priorities" (*Female* 141), it certainly seems not to have been so here.

Actually the many cases that record struggles between heirs show clearly that in their relations with women—citizens, metics and slaves—men had no doubt that they were dealing with the same sort of person as themselves. By law a woman might be given in marriage by her guardian (rather than by her "choice"), she might not be allowed to engage in economic transactions beyond small amounts, she might not hold land in her own right but only for transmission of the *oikos* between generations (and so be forbidden from transactions with it), she might be unable to make a will. Even in classical Athens extant speeches show that many of these proscriptions were flexible. Sealey cites an early speech of Demosthenes listing actions in a case from the first quarter of the fourth century. He recorded a woman having lent a large sum of money (whether it was a loan or some other transaction, such as receipt of an inheritance, does not matter: it was forensically plausible that she could have made the loan). The same woman and her daughters were accepted as legitimate witnesses. When the woman's earlier deceased husband had written his will the debtor sent his wife in his stead as capable of representing his interests (Demosthenes XLI; Sealey 38–40).

Cases of Athenian women's ability legally to testify can readily be found. Too, as Sealey adds, in "forensic speeches women are said to take action at law in order to assert rights to property." Their relation to their attendant *kurios* "was the same as that of a modern litigant to his attorney. It would be mistaken to say that a litigant lacks personality because he has an attorney to represent him." Women accused of murder, wrongful marriage and other crimes were tried in a law court where they could also sue and be sued: "it follows that the law recognized women as persons." Athenian law recognized them as such precisely in holding them responsible for actions it saw them as controlling, contrary to claims that it assumed women unable to make up their own minds (Sealey 44, 48–49). Everywhere women participated in religious rituals. And if Keuls, concluding an argument about the relentless oppression and nonpersonhood of women, is right to propose that it was women exploiting their freedom during the festival of Adonis who castrated the Herms of Athens in the summer of 415 B.C. in protest against male violence and the risks, especially for Athenian women, of failure in the coming military campaign against Sicily, this would only be further evidence of women's experienced personhood (17, 383–95).

No doubt few but the highest ranking women of ancient Athens were educated. But literacy rates among women *or* men are unknown (vase art shows women reading): both were perhaps evenly illiterate. Outside Athens things seem to have been very different. Sappho's society of young women at Mytilene on Lesbos was one of many on the Asia Minor coast and mainland Greece (including Sparta) and many critics note records of women poets, for example, from the fifth to third centuries all over the Greek world, save Attica (Pomeroy, *Goddesses* 52–56; Cantarella, *Pandora's* 71–76; Fantham 163–68). Galen said that in his day "everyone understood" that "Sappho" and "Homer" were used equivalently to name the classes of female and male poets ("The Soul's Dependence on the Body," *Selected* 152). Reading Sappho on love and loss, amity and absence, soul and association, one little doubts that later philosophers' accounts of who-ness could have applied equally well to her understanding of who and what she was. For duBois, she marked a new turn in "the development of subjectivity," "the thinking of existence" (*Sappho* 6–7, 16–17). Others say the same. That the "existence" was akin to what we have seen is implied by Claude Calame's analysis of the "quasi-juridical language" of certain of her poems, stressing the "institutional bond with the members of her circle." The point is akin to Vernant's that we saw earlier about *akōn* and *hekōn* marking an essentially legal and *public* understanding of "will" and the mind's functioning more generally.

More concretely, Lacedemonian law codes, says Sarah Pomeroy, show that at Sparta certainly from the seventh century to the fourth, a mother's roles in reproduction, childcare and education were seen as "at least as important as" the father's (*Goddesses* 36). Women were educated and, with the difference that men were trained to be soldiers while women were trained rather to reproduce and raise children, had the same obligations toward and freedoms in the overriding community as men. Pomeroy shows, too, that under the laws of Gortyn in Crete, women's situation and status there during about the same period were quite comparable. At Gortyn, unlike Athens, women could hold property legally recognized as fully theirs, not held *in loco heredis* (35–42; cf. Sealey 80; Schaps *passim*; Savalli 51–59; Blundell 150–59). We have seen that slaves' rights in Gortyn had similar recognition.

In Macedonia and elsewhere even such distinctions did not hold. Macedonian women after the era of Philip II shared much the same activities as men, including hunting and fighting on horseback, for example. As at Sparta, women owned land and often controlled "very substantial territories." This stayed the case certainly through Hellenistic times in Egypt. Its weight is clearer when one recalls how central was land ownership to the ancient economy (Pomeroy, *Women* 4–9, 14, 148–73). In similar vein abundant manumission-inscriptions across mainland Greece from the third and second centuries prove that women could free slaves, and so own them (Schaps 7). Apollodoros said that Neaira was bought, owned and sold by the freedwoman Nikaretē in the northern Peloponnese early in the fourth century ("Against Neaira" 18–29). In *Women in Hellenistic Times*, Pomeroy shows that freedoms

like these increased for women throughout the Hellenistic world, especially in Ptolemaic Egypt (that is, after the death of Alexander the Great).
During this era women's equality with men seems to have been greater
(Pomeroy, *Goddesses* 120–48; *Xenophon* 58). Cantarella agrees that
things altered in Hellenistic times, women less oppressed, more liberated,
while still stereotyped (*Pandora's* 90–98). Riet van Bremen also much
agrees but urges that if, "during the late Hellenistic and Roman periods,
female members of local ruling elites played a prominent and visible role
in public life," it did not mean that "women had formal access to political power and had administrative and deliberative duties to carry out"—
their public acts were chiefly "ritual and ceremonial," even when secularized (*Limits* 1, 4). Most writers concur that by the second century A.D.
(at least) a combination of wealth, "family tradition, the preservation of
status, political ambitions, and even ideological developments" made it
"no longer new or unusual for women to imitate" men. But they still
"crucially belonged" in the familial sphere (*Limits* 299, 302)—a sphere,
though, we have seen, integral to the social and political community as a
whole.

All this suggests that while Athens changed as Greece fell under Macedonian dominion, it may have done so in the direction and by the push of
wider Greek custom, the more so as the "changes" in question went back
to the mid-fourth century B.C.: which hardly suggests a break between
them and the then active debates between the various philosophical
schools with which this chapter began. Similar ambiguities hold for the
Roman world. Cantarella contends that under the monarchy and early
republic women were entirely men's property. This improved slightly under the empire, when women had the major task of educating (as well as
raising) their children. But they stayed shut in the domestic realm, under
the inescapable rule of *patris potestas*. Whatever minor gains there may
have been were anyway reversed for centuries under Christianity (*Pandora's* 113–70). Gourevitch also argues that under the late republic and
empire, despite some women's emancipation, they were thought (by some
wealthy men anyway) not just inferior, but creatures who at best might
mechanically imitate men (261–76).

Lately adjusting her estimate a bit, Cantarella states that under Augustus at least some Roman women, far from a majority, were emanci-
pated, though still without power. But in arguing that their subaltern
roles resulted from an "autocensura," she confirms my point about personhood, presupposed by such autocensorship (*Passato* 133–36,
145–46). Further, the Greek case and the ambivalence of the Roman,
even in Gourevitch's and Cantarella's especially harsh estimate (for at the
very least, if women could educate their children to take their proper

place in the *civitas*, they had to be rational persons), suggest again that legal supposition did not entirely match social realities and experiences of who-ness. We have seen that they seem not to have matched medical practice either. Our problem is to know how women experienced and understood their personhood in regard to the circles they inhabited. To do this properly would require women's writings that have not survived or never were, forcing one to infer similarities or differences from men's: although such Greek and Roman writings by women as *have* survived certainly suggest no difference in experience and sense of personhood.

　　For some texts from Hellenistic times and before do in fact seem further to confirm sameness of personhood among women and men. A treatise for women purporting to be by Plato's mother, but probably later, explains "the harmonious woman to be one who is well endowed with wisdom and self-restraint" and if she had to put up with her husband's behavior, this itself was just more evidence of her "sagacity and temperance" (Pomeroy, *Goddesses* 134–36 for the treatise's text). A marriage contract of 311 B.C. drawn between two Greeks living in Egypt, recognizing the partners' different but equal roles, emphasized their shared "social and moral rights and obligations." Several other marriage agreements surviving from later times in more or less the same area incorporated similar stipulations (127–28; cf. Pomeroy, *Women* 87–89; Fantham 136–82). The point is not that women and men participated equally or similarly in all spheres of life. They evidently did not. But both were clearly persons. Sealey credibly proposes that the original reason for women's civic disabilities lay not in beliefs about differences of rational and sensible being but in "an assumption about the incapacity of women to bear arms," dating from a time before the laws' codification, when people depended on "self-help" (155).

　　Cantarella's and Gourevitch's caustic view of Rome differs from that of Margaret Alic (30) and Pomeroy (*Goddesses* 149–89), who think that women's situation improved quite dramatically under the Roman empire both as to education and as to wider participation (cf. Fantham 216–394). Conditions may be more complicated. Among other things, Larissa Bonfante has argued in a number of essays, gender-egalitarian Etruscan society had a profound effect on early and later Roman views. Although Etruscan culture was fully absorbed into Roman by the fifth to fourth centuries, habits and mores may have lived on in memory and experience. John Evans shows that Rome's constant imperial wars deeply affected women's status, emancipating some wealthier women and forcing many peasant women off the land into various precarious town and city jobs, menial and worse, but nonetheless implying assumptions and feelings of rational ability and independence (cf. Cantarella, *Passato* 135).

The fact of oppression, I repeat, is not the same as denial of who-ness. It is rather the opposite. Ramsay MacMullen mentions records dating back to the second quarter of the second century B.C., referring to women being punished by their husbands for "conversing or being seen out of the house with any but their own immediate family" ("Women" 208). Such incidents record oppressive acts like those mentioned in Chapters 1 and 6 apropos of slaves: they are ways of controlling persons with their own minds and passions. Even in the political and legal arena stressed by Cantarella and mostly thought to confirm women's non-personality, strong evidence counters the assumption (Sealey shows that some of Cantarella's claims require omissive or slanted reading of the legal evidence: 166–68). In the *Digest*, Ulpian was noted as having observed the injustice of different moral expectations for men and women (XXXXVIII.5.14 [13].5). Too, the *Digest* considered marriage to be based on "the consent of a man and a woman to live together as husband and wife. This principle recognize[d] the personality of the woman": "Marriage is constituted," it said, "not by corporeal union but by joint consent" (Sealey 33, 159, citing XXXV.1.15 and L.17.30). Besides the laws' explicit recognition of equality of personhood in mutual consent, the Justinian code, MacMullen recalls, "contain[ed] hundreds of imperial responses to women litigants," treating "civic status, obligations of freed condition, marriage, divorce, support, dowry, minority status and child custody." He remarks that these were all essentially "private matters," though without explaining that the only distinction made by the code in this regard was that public law involved offices of state and public religion, *everything* else being "private law" (see end of Chapter 8 below). Thus, he does add, these matters were "among those most often of concern to men, too." He also notes that many of the cases involving women dealt with often large financial transactions, again confirming what we have just now been seeing (210).

What Cicero made of Xenophon's *Oeconomicus* early in the first century B.C. also implies interwoven social and political personhood. The seeming popularity of his Latin version suggests that he was not alone in his view of the imbrication of *domus* and *civitas* and the homogeneity of women's role in the beehive of the first with men's in the beehive of the second. Overlappings could be closer. In 42 B.C., Hortensia gave a renowned speech in the Roman forum successfully defeating an edict to tax wealthy women whose male relatives had been proscribed (Pomeroy, *Goddesses* 175–76; cf. Bauman 81–83). At Pompeii, wall graffiti of political support list names of women and men of all social levels. Shop walls record names of many different kinds of businesswomen (MacMullen 209–10). Such social, political and economic "emancipation" seems to have been ordinary in all levels of society. Whatever it meant as to freedom from oppression, it implied a personhood shared by all humans. In a pedagogical context, Quintilian urged: "As regards parents, I should like to see them as highly educated as possible, and I do not restrict this remark to fathers alone" (*Institutio* I.1.6). Gourevitch (264–66) takes Catullus' misogynistic satire and Pliny the Younger's crass condescension toward his "childlike" third wife to show women's common condition, but such contrary views as these and many others suggest that the poet and the advocate may rather have been betraying male wishful thinking and particular fears roused by an opposite reality (though Pliny's wife certainly *was* very young). Women's surviving writings suggest as much, even if, on some imaginary spectrum of consideration and treatment of women, their authors were probably as unusual in lying at its opposite end (for a good overview of Roman women writers, see Snyder 122–51). The truth doubtless lies, as often, somewhere in the middle.

In the first century A.D. Soranus could write not only that a suitable "midwife" had to "be literate, with her wits about her, possessed of a good memory," but that the best

is trained in all branches of therapy (for some cases must be treated by diet, others by surgery, while still others must be cured by drugs); ... she is moreover able to prescribe hygienic regulations for her patients, to observe the general and individual features of the case, and from this to find out what is expedient. (I.1§3; I.2§4: 5)

Soranus' demand that midwives be expert in the use of diet, drugs and surgery echoed the definition of the "art of medicine" given by Celsus, indeed the very plan of his eight books (Proemium 9). Soranus' best midwife, that is, was trained as a doctor. How much Soranus' case would apply in Rome (at a time long after the age when Roman medicine was still in the hands of slaves) we do not know. Many names of Greek women physicians from Hellenistic times and later have survived (as have two gynecological treatises attributed to women, one from the fifth century A.D. but one from Hellenistic times). In Rome and around its empire women were trained to be *medici* through written texts and by association with other practitioners.

During this later era, from empire to late antiquity, women engaged not just in these activities. They served, as they always had, as cult priestesses. Across Italy and the provinces, women—not just those of the highest social standing—served as "patrons" of men's groups and in the highest positions in municipal politics, in posts secular and religious. There is, says MacMullen, no way to know what these officeholders did, but the "deference secured from one's fellow citizens," appearing in public, holding a title, having one's statue erected—"memorialized in stone in the forum"—clearly attached to a person (211–15). Again if women held such positions less frequently than men—though not *in*frequently—the mere fact of such practices shows that women and men were equally persons, and persons of the same sort. The same is indicated not only by so unusual a work as Perpetua's prison "diary" of early 203 A.D. but by the many tomb inscriptions written by women extant from this period on—although some seem more likely done self-servingly by men and most suggest subordinate relations (Dronke, *Women* 2–4, 21–26). Hardly less unusual than Perpetua's record were the third-century Proba's poem on Creation and the life, death and resurrection of Christ, and the fourth-century *Itinerarium Egeriae*—"diary" of a three-year journey to Jerusalem by a woman who was possibly a nun from the Spanish northwest (Snyder 136–39, 141–51). We shall never know how unusual these were. Women were certainly also and at the same time subjected by men to oppression, exploitation and violence, but they were so in the context of the fact and experience of being persons of like kind.

Whatever may have been the legal and economic cases, differing in place and time and never free of debate and flexibility, the vaguer arenas of sensibility and culture were far more constant. And the first were never free of debate, one might think, just because this equal sense of personhood meant that there was a gap between law and sensibility, economic rule and cultural give and take. Whatever women's legal and economic standing, in actual practice they clearly always saw themselves and were seen by men as endowed with the same sort of *who-ness*. Aristotle and some few followers may have tried to engage in powerful wishful thinking. Others did not find that disabilities before the law made women less rational than men; their reason served other social tasks. This affected the person's stance to the law (for example). It did not change the nature of personhood. Indeed, as the early Lysias case shows ("early" as to the debates we have been following, it being contemporary with Xenophon and Plato), that person was exactly of the sort examined by Aristotle.

He may have wished to exclude women as persons. Few others seem to have felt it necessary or worthwhile, far less useful or true. It is, I think, simply not the case that most sought to do so, whatever the levels of misogyny and worse. Clark agrees that whatever Aristotle's views, "Platonists and Stoics disagreed: they argued that women may have more to contend with, and *qua* female are obviously inferior, but men and women share a common human nature and aim at a common excellence (*aretē*)." Both could be trained to virtue (121). In general, that "obviously inferior" was never so evident, and in real daily life matters were just more complicated. Too, we must remember that misogyny, exploitation and violence were not the same as belief in the absence of personhood. In this last regard medical and philosophical analyses not only had always to apply to women as well as men, but did indeed do so in practice and theory. Returning to Cicero's four *personae* and Galen's threefold biological explanation of identities and varieties of being human, we understand that differences of sex (or slavery) make no difference to the first two *personae* or varieties.

The first was that level of the human covering its relation to the universal (*ousia* and impassible soul), its existence as an ensouled being (what I have called the animate) and its physical humanity (elements, qualities, temperaments, humors and so on). Within the human's relations to these circles at this level fell also its moral life: we saw Cicero ascribe to this first level humans' endowment with the four cardinal virtues, *justitia, prudentia, temperantia* and *fortitudo*. The second *persona*, for Cicero and Galen, was that of differences in humans *qua* humans: in mental capacities, physical strengths, spiritual sensitivities and other abilities born with them as members of the species. At neither of these levels was sex a delimiting factor (if Aristotle sometimes said that women had lesser rational capacities than men, most did not). Cicero's third *persona* involved the social and economic level into which one was born, Galen's the biological distinction between men and women. They matched to the degree in which women and men had, by sex, different social and political roles. For Cicero and others, these were equivalent and analogous and both essential to the community as a whole. They were also, of course, places of various oppressions and exclusions. But again, as the circles which helped compose personhood, the relation to them was shared.

Cicero's fourth *persona* had no pair in Galen, for the clear reason that as it involved things like choice of work and career, its connection with the biological was mostly indirect. Here, too, evidence abounds that such "choice" applied to women and men alike. Wealthy, high-born Apollodoros may have thought Athenian women existed to be his and his peers' whores, concubines or wives (*if* he did). In everyone else's real life they occupied the many places one would expect, no less than they did in Hellenistic Egypt or imperial Rome. The evidence is inarguable that in ancient Athens women suffered oppressions of many different kinds and equally varied violence. This certainly meant that women's relation to the social and economic circles of the person differed from that of the men whose writings we have been seeing—if not from that of the less wealthy and less well-born. These circles were no less integral to their person. It surely gave women "more to contend with," making it harder for them to follow the path toward the good life of harmony with nature, internal and external: although the women portrayed in Plato's *Menexenus* and *Symposium* and in Xenophon's *Oeconomicus* and *Memorabilia* were presumably on their way to achieving it, for all their different social arenas. Violent oppression was undoubtedly built into women's experience of personhood as part of its integration with some of the circles emphasized by writers on the matter. But the experience of what it was to be a person would be a common *human* one.

Even were violence as universal as some claim, it would not alter the fact and experience of who-ness. To be human was to be composed as an ensouled creature woven in the universal, animate, human, social, economic and material. This would be *affected* (as by *passio, affectio* or *perturbatio*) but not altered by particular behaviors ruling interpersonal relations. These would be practices to which Seneca's *humanior* would have to offer a response. For the idea and experience of personhood could only but be always separate from whether or how it achieved what was thought of as its ideal form. The point is however that *that* ideal could only be centered on actual experience.

Earlier chapters did not focus on material circles. This one has shown how crucial they were to understanding personhood. We can get no clearer idea of their importance than by taking a closer look at Galen, the celebrated physician who lived a century or so after Seneca and whose work was destined to form the *material* ground of the idea of the human in the Christian and Arab worlds for more than the next millennium and a half. Deeply influenced by the Stoics (even as he vehemently criticized their approach to human psycho-physiology), unlike them he was most concerned with human physiology and (its relation with) the material world. But if this was his principal interest, he did not hesitate at the same time to draw the same connections with the many other circles of personhood as his predecessors. His views and others' in these areas provided much of the ground for later thinking about the person. And if, of Aristotle's account of freedom, one is right to think no one took it up because it matched no one's experience (as his contortions over women and slaves imply), we must, on the contrary, imagine that Galen's account of human physiology, of its relation to the world and of the simple materiality of bodies, overwhelmingly adopted by later commentators, did correspond to people's experience. He drew his account of that experience directly from those examined in this and preceding chapters. His elaboration takes us far toward later analyses and experiences.

CHAPTER EIGHT

The Public Materiality of Being Human

Galen and Medical Traditions

The passible idea and experience of the human was clear and fixed in most details. It was the ground from which future experience of the person would be projected and its understanding evolved. This chapter and the next explore three other writers—traditions—vital in bearing and moving this sense of who-ness. Galen stressed the human and material, Justinian the sociolegal, Augustine the divine and animate. This division was evidently not entire. As people had held for centuries, human, material and universal were wholly interwoven. All moved beyond their direct area of concern to set who-ness in the totality of surroundings, the wide ambit of circumstancing spheres. Still, for future readers, writers and thinkers, they could be thought so to have split the complex pie. It is worth adding, too, that these three spheres (as I saw absurdly long after realizing this ancient division) were those of the higher faculties in medieval and Renaissance western European universities: medicine, law and theology.

Galen was by and large right to repeat that philosophers and physicians were in "complete agreement" on these matters, referring, for example, to the familiar argument of Plato's *Phaedrus* (*Therapeutic Method* [TM] I.2.7). Cicero said the same: "Philosophy . . . cures souls" (*Tusculans* II.iv.11). Seneca and the Stoics held the very goal of education in wisdom to be such cure. (This shared view is Nussbaum's insight in her *Therapy of Desire*, tracing the idea in Hellenistic times in Peripatetics, Epicureans, Academics, Stoics and Seneca.) Revisiting the question worried by Seneca and others as to whether passions were diseases of the soul to be cured or irrational aberrations to be controlled or tamed, Galen accused some Stoics of breaching that wide accord. Such a breach opposed one premise common to all his polemics on medicine and philosophy. He was sure that the views he put together were ultimately one and the same view of the human and its place in the world. It mattered to him that philosophical and practical medicine be able to rely—for obvious reasons—on an experience and idea of personhood shown as generally agreed and true for *all* humans. Such agreement threaded its way through his many works: one of its primary bequests to the future.

Most of the first four books of the *Doctrines of Hippocrates and Plato* were to show agreement between the two on the main issues of body, soul and affections, and less their discord with Stoics than the continual self-contradiction of *one* Stoic: Chrysippus. Arguing that the latter's idea that the passions inhered in "the reasoning power" and so "irrational animals [and children] had no share in them" was clearly false "in the face of facts," Galen approved the attack on such views by Chrysippus' later heir, Posidonius (like Cicero, a close reader of Panaetius). Galen's survey of the dispute much concerned the nature of body and soul and agreement of philosophy and medicine. For finally, he said: "that affection is an unnatural and irrational motion of the soul is acknowledged not only by the ancients but also by Chrysippus" (*Doctrines* [DHP] V.1.10–2.2: 1.295). To put the matter thus actually eluded the debated issues since it said nothing on whether affection was the motion of an irrational impulse *on* the soul or a deformation *of* the soul's very nature. As usual, Galen asserted his own view to be derived from all and generally accepted: which was, I repeat, how Galenism was received for the next fifteen hundred years.

Seneca's younger contemporary Plutarch had taken Plato's familiar image of charioteer and two-horse team to refute the extreme Stoic view. Arguing that the difference they asserted between "temperance" (*sōphrosunē*) and "self-control" (*engkrateia*) held up only if one thought of the rational and the irrational as quite separate, he objected:

temperance belongs to the sphere where reason guides and manages the passionate element, like a gentle animal obedient to the reins, making it yielding in its desires and willingly receptive of moderation and propriety; but the auto-controlled man, while indeed directing desire by the strength and mastery of reason, yet does so not without pain, nor by persuasion, but as it plunges sideways and resists, as if with blow and curb forcibly subduing it and holding it in, being the while full of internal struggle and turmoil. Such a conflict Plato portrays in his simile of the horses of the soul, where the worse horse struggles against his better yoke-fellow and at the same time disconcerts the charioteer, who is ever forced to hold out against him and with might and main to rein him in. ("On Moral Virtue," *Moralia* 445b–c)

For Plutarch, the fact that such different forms of control could be thought to operate readily proved how separate were a person's rational and irrational elements. But modification of something like the second of these forms gave Galen a way to use the same image to show the nature of possible personhood as *necessarily* perilously balanced between action and passion. This, too, he could have got from Plutarch's extension of the metaphor: "It is, in fact, the rebellious kicking and plunging of oxen and horses that men do away with, not their movements and activities; even so reason makes use of the emotions when they have been subdued and are tame" (451d). Reason actively played against passions.

Galen's remark about affection as "an unnatural and irrational motion," echoed in Plutarch's plunging and resisting horse, seemed to contradict—or be modified by—what he said elsewhere: that affections were tied to "natural" motions. The point was that they moved the soul from the ideal oneness with nature so many argued. But in another sense it was natural to be so moved. The two remarks captured the "twofold" nature of the human person and indicate the complex dialectic involved in the "active" and "passive" functioning of the possible.

Chrysippus and Posidonius, Galen continued in *Doctrines*, agreed that souls of "good" people were free of such motion. They disagreed on souls of "inferiors." The first argued that their souls were diseased—because prone always to passions as body to fevers. The second retorted that these souls were simply like healthy bodies. Indeed, said Posidonius, so to compare souls and bodies was misleading, for while one sort of soul, that of the wise person, was immune to these harms, no body was. One could compare body only with souls belonging to all *but* the wise. Galen approved Posidonius' view but thought he did not go far enough: the state of such "lesser" souls should not be called "disease" at all. The extreme rarity of the virtuous sage might be compared to the equal rarity of "bodies immune to disease," an idea that strengthened Galen's account of the equation of soul being to passion as body to illness. One had to set aside altogether these rare cases, so special and particular as to be "not germane to the analogy now before us." Then, one could construct a precise comparison:

the souls of those progressing in virtue should be compared to bodies of robust constitution, souls of intermediate persons to bodies that are healthy without being robust, souls of the multitude of ordinary humans to bodies that become ill at a slight cause, and souls of humans who are angry or enraged or in any affected state whatever to bodies that are actually diseased. (DHP V.2.9: 1.197)

The question of an unreason external or internal to the soul has faded. Galen has rewritten the issue to stress the analogy of philosophy and medicine regarding soul and body and, more importantly for my purposes, the agreement of all parties on the general processes of the human person. Galen just conflated the two ("The Affections and Errors of the Soul," *Selected* [SW] 100–149). The very fact that Stoics habitually analogized soul and body showed accord on the first point; their contradictions and opacity on the second showed that their seeming disagreements countered accepted fact and common experience. Even by Chrysippus' own account, Galen ironized, bodily elements (hot, cold, dry, wet) could be equated with Plato's "spirited, rational, and desiderative" parts of the soul, saving the analogy "in every respect" (DHP V.2.20–38: 1.301–3). Jubilantly summing up his case, he detailed reasons for not confusing disease of soul with vulnerability of body, the soul's beauty with its health (as Chrysippus had avoided apropos of body, the one involving proportions of members, the other of elements) and for being able to distinguish, with Plato, proportions of the soul's parts from those of its acts, the ones equated with health or illness, the others with beauty or ugliness (DHP V.3.12–31: 1.309–13).

For Galen the issue was no longer that of either controlling irrational passions or removing them altogether by a full therapy of the rational soul. Rather was it to describe and then balance the *fact* and necessary *interplay* of health and harm, equilibrium and disequilibrium, to enable the healthy and good life. The series of comparisons derived from his predecessors naturally inclined him to pursue his theme by returning to inquiry we saw in Diogenes Laertius and Hierocles about the work of *oikeiōsis* and growth of body and soul. This let him shift emphasis from debate in philosophy and medicine to what he told as observation and experience of the human. Like his two near-contemporaries, he noted that "all children rush untaught toward pleasures and turn and flee from pain." People had a natural kinship with "pleasure, through the desiderative (form); victory, through the spirited (form); and what is morally excellent, through the rational (form)" of the soul or life force. Epicurus, he added, saw only our kinship with the worst, Chrysippus with the best. These extremes further confirmed commonly agreed patterns of personal experience (DHP V.4.3–8: 1.317–19). *Oikeiōsis* had certainly to do with the growth and eventual disposition of the soul, but simultaneously concerned those of the body, if only because the soul was ineluctably bound in body's matter ("The Soul's Dependence on the Body," SW 150–76). One could not understand the one without knowing the other, or treat their relation without knowing them to be subject to such comparative analyses—just because they were so conjoined. General agreement on these things mattered, because a doctor's efficacy depended on everyone concurring in this way on what the *person* was to which treatment was directed.

As people agreed on soul, affections, body and health—the nature of being human—so too, Galen urged, they agreed on their bond with the other surroundings to which *oikeiōsis* drew them. Of special interest to him as a physician was the nature of the material world, in itself and as related to the person, for as elements and qualities embedded soul in body, so they embedded humans in the physical world ("Mixtures," SW 202–89). He often observed that all the major philosophies (Academic, Hippocratic, Peripatetic and Stoic in what follows) agreed that "everything [was] blended from these things [the four qualities], that they act and react on each other and that nature is constructive [*technikos*]": a repetition of the usual Stoic idea of nature as "rational artisan" (cf. *On the Natural Faculties* [NF] II.iii.81–82). In this context of nature blending and "constructively" interacting, added Galen, one had to know, again with Aristotle and the Stoics, that "the whole [human] body breathed and flowed in concert, and that all the parts of animals were in sympathy." For Aristotle, this flowing involved only qualities, for Stoics it concerned "actual substances," but the distinction was "superfluous" to the doctor and of no meaning in experience (TM I.2.10–11). He repeated these arguments virtually word for word elsewhere, insisting that anyone still in doubt could read the Hippocratics, Aristotle *and* Chrysippus, and that the basic intermixing of all material existents and its consequences was unaffected by debate over whether "*substances* as well as their *qualities* under[went] this intimate mingling" (NF I.ii.5–6).

Analyzing nearly identical variations in Seneca, I suggested that they did not affect a common experience of who-ness. So Galen asserted here, like Seneca linking these writers as holding identical views of the human, their accord untouched by debate on detail. So he began *On the Natural Faculties* by noting what was shared by all things able to change, inanimate or animate. With Hippocrates and Aristotle (and Chrysippus, he said), he posited that "there are, in all, four mutually interacting qualities, and that to the operation of these is due the genesis and destruction of all things that come into and pass out of being" (NF I.ii.5). Balance and mix were health and growth in the world and bodies, imbalance and friction disease and decay. The qualities were those of hot and cold, dry and moist. Some theorists saw the last two as passive, under the first two as active. Galen held them to mix equally and criticized Aristotle's ambivalence on the issue, for since he "used the four qualities to explain the genesis of the elements, he ought rightly to have upgraded and focused [*anagein*] in these principles the causes of all the things we are to consider." Galen insisted that these four were the primary instance regardless of the material level where one set them. His point was to stress their universal presence and efficacy, a case he repeated constantly, ascribing it now to Aristotle (TM I.2.10), now to Hippocratics and Stoics and to Plato, quoting from *Timaeus* (82a):

As there are four things from which the body has been compounded, earth, fire, water and air, the occurrence of unnatural excess and deficiency of these, and change of place from their own to an alien one, and again—since fire and the others happen to be more than one—the accretion of any part of the one that is not proper to it, and all things of that kind, produce disorders and diseases. (DHP VIII.2.15–16: 2.493–95)

For Galen, then, as for Hippocrates and Plato, usually for Aristotle and always for Cicero and Seneca, the four qualities or substances were the ground of "genesis, growth and nutrition," as of all "alteration and shaping" and the forms these changes could take: foundational in the universe as in particular animate and inanimate bodies. Hot and cold, dry and moist were, or composed, the four elements (fire, air, water and earth), as they did the four humors (blood, yellow bile, phlegm and black bile), the temperaments (sanguine, choleric or bilious, phlegmatic and melancholic or atrabilious) and correspondent senses: sight corresponding to fire, hearing and smell to air, taste to water, touch to earth:

We shall say, therefore, that it was needful that the organ of sight be luminous, the organ of hearing airy, that of smell vaporous, that of taste moist, that of touch earthy. It was not possible for them to be otherwise, for they required the alteration caused by similars; and this is what Empedocles meant when he said,

> By earth we perceive earth; by water, water;
> air by shining air; and consuming fire by fire.

(DHP VII.5.42–43: 2.463)

They matched different foods, minerals, herbs and the four human ages. "Adolescency," to use Thomas Elyot's later terms, was hot and wet, going to twenty-five; "Iuventute," to forty, was hot and dry; "senectute," maturity, up to sixty, was cold and wet; "Age decrepite," beyond sixty, was cold and dry (*Castel* sig. 13r). These came from antiquity. Ages varied slightly, divisions did not. They had their counterparts in the skies (Jove, Moon, Saturn, Mars), seasons (Spring, Summer, Autumn, Winter) and winds, where disagreement ruled. But Hildegard of Bingen and Thomas Walkington, later, would not have thought they disagreed with usual opinion, one saying in the twelfth century that east wind related to air, west to water, south to fire and north less clearly to earth (*Causae* I [§15]: 4), the other holding in 1607 that east wind related to water, west to fire, south to air and north to earth (see fig.2). Did these variations echo those of seasonally prevailing winds? Stressing the "regional" nature of the arguments they again show the specifically European nature of these concepts. Winds were an element of these correspondences liable to local variations, geological and topographical ones had the same effects wherever met, as the Hippocratic explained apropos of Europe and "Asia," as Marco Polo observed (see Chapter 13) and as a late sixteenth-century Jesuit assumed in making what Charles Boxer calls "the rather curious comment that [Brazil] was 'somewhat melancholic,'" a temper "he attributed to the heavy rainfall and the numerous flowing rivers" (91–92). The comment was predictable.

The exact relation of the originating qualities or elements to the bodily humors that were their physical manifestation was often unclear. Galen's criticism of Aristotle's failure to give each due weight and depth implied that they could be securely identified at *no* simple level. First, the elements from which body was said to be generated might correspond one on one to the qualities or themselves be characterized as a mixture of the qualities. Second, these qualities were

in the body potentially, not in actuality; in actuality are rather the things generated from the qualities by means of nutriment: blood, phlegm, yellow and black bile. Yellow bile is analogous to fire, black bile to earth, and phlegm to water; therefore yellow bile, like fire, is hot and dry in power [*tēn dunamin*], black bile is cold and dry, similar to earth, and phlegm is cold and moist like water. Only the airlike element [*to aeroeides stoicheion*] in the bodies of animals is observed to be close to its nature.

The "airlike element" was blood, linked here to respiration, pulse, illness "attended by throbbing," emphysemas, tumors and flatulence. "The balanced mixture of all four elements generates blood in the precise sense" (DHP VIII.4.20–22: 2.503). For this last reason, third, since all animals naturally made blood when their heat was "well blended and moderately moist," it could be said that blood was "a *virtually* warm and moist humor, and similarly also that yellow bile is warm and dry, even though for the most part it appears moist." So for the other humors (NF II.ix. 129–31).

These uncertainties and differences enabled Galen to appeal again to wide agreement on causes of imbalance or balance in the body's powers, saying that those who thought theory did not matter to real practice were refuted by myriad ancient practitioners, Pneumatic, Dogmatic, Empiric, above all those based in (or originating) the Hippocratic tradition. Still, those believing in the need to ground practice only in theoretical agreement should

call Athenaeus, Mnesitheus, Diocles, Pleistonicus, Hippocrates, and Philistion, and countless others of this calibre as witnesses; if the dispute must be settled by witnesses, they will win by a large margin. For they can bring forward not only Hippocrates and all the other doctors, but Plato, Aristotle, Theophrastus, Zeno, Chrysippus, and every philosopher of note as witnesses for the claim that there are many different species of morbid disposition, and that there is a distinct therapy for each of them. All the philosophers and doctors I have just mentioned held that one cannot either discover anything about the *differentiae* of diseases or arrive at cures for them in the proper way without first having made accurate discoveries about the nature of the body; and, by Zeus, they . . . offered demonstrations of it. (TM II.5.11)

Such insistence again shows that Galen's appeal to general theoretical agreement posited common experience. However necessary to convince theoretical opponents, for practitioner and patient theory supposed the common experience that was, in any event, its real ground.

Although the mix of elements, qualities and humors might only be *explained* by philosophical and medical theories, their exact details were of small importance in practice. At whatever level they began, qualitative mixings, unbalanced or balanced, were experienced and observed in ways whose materiality let them be maintained or readjusted by applying reagents according to the latters' warmth, dryness, coldness or moisture. Because element, quality and humor shared these characteristics neither the efficacy of the reagent nor its explanation was changed by the details of the grounding analysis (as Galen often said). "Humor" was just the name given to the substances in which the four powers were materialized in the body and whose mixture explained present state, diagnosis and possible prevention. It explained, for example, the importance of diverse foods, balancing humors according to their own predominant power and to be taken to suit one's present circumstance (NF II.viii.117). Food matched condition and age of the person taking it: "at birth we are first nourished by milk, which takes its origin from blood, and later on by the same foods as adults, from which blood, phlegm, yellow and black bile are again generated" (DHP VIII.3.6: 2.499).

As age affected the fitness of foods so, for the same reason of fluctuation in elemental, qualitative or humoral balance, it changed the diseases to which one was prone (DHP VIII.6.25–32: 2.519). Too, since diseases were related directly to one or other of the four powers, they were moved by the seasons. Diseases occurred anytime, their causes being in body, food, age, planetary motion and indeed in any passibly received affect, but season was a great factor:

In the spring melancholia, madness, epilepsy, flowing of blood, sore throats, colds, hoarseness, coughing, leprosy, skin eruptions, white patches and ulcerous pustules are most numerous, and tumours and diseases of the joints. In summer some of the aforegoing and also continuous fevers, burning fevers, tertian fevers, quartan fevers, vomiting, diarrhoea, ophthalmia, earaches, ulcers of the mouth, putrefaction of the genitals and heat spots. In the fall most of the summer diseases, and also quartan fevers, irregular fevers, affections of the spleen, dropsy, consumption, strangury, lientery, dysentery, throat infections, asthma, intestinal obstructions, epilepsy, madness, and melancholia. In the winter pleuresy, pneumonia, colds, lethargy, hoarseness, coughing, pains in the chest and sides and loins, headaches, dizziness, apoplexy. (DHP VIII.6.20–24: 2.517–19)

Thus did Galen agree with Hippocrates that diseases matched Spring (warm and moist), Summer (warm and dry), Autumn (cold and moist) and Winter (cold and dry). So, too, they were provoked by their proximate humors (blood, yellow bile, phlegm and black bile):

for the humours are clearly observed causing diseases wherever they settle in the body. Yellow bile causes erysipelas and shingles; black bile causes cancer; phlegm causes tumours; and blood in time produces corruption in the lungs and between thorax and lungs when it pours out of its proper organs and stands rotting. (DHP VIII.4.32: 2.505)

Of these sympathies affecting the state of the person and its well-being, Galen thus summed up that they involved differences not just of food or age but of "occupations also, localities and seasons, and above all of natures themselves [tōn phuseōn autōn], the colder more phlegmatic and the warmer more bilious" (NF II.viii.118). Nature's fundamental qualities or powers occurred globally in "modes of life, regions, constitutions and diseases" (NF II.ix.131). No aspect of a person's existing in the world could be separated from what it shared with all aspects of its surroundings. Being was indivisible from a total ecosystem experienced by Galen and his posterity, as by Hippocratics, Plato, Aristotle, Cicero and Seneca earlier, as a universe of sympathies among these surroundings. With whatever variants, the tie between human constitution and character, nutrition, physical condition, climate, geographic place, planets and zodiac was axiomatic. And from at least Chrysippus, phusis was both human nature and nature in general: to be in accord with one was to be in accord with the other (Long, "Logical Basis" 141). This principal was Galen's medical one no less than the others' philosophical one.

"Bodies act on and are acted on by each other," wrote Galen, "in virtue of the Warm, Cold, Moist and Dry" (NF II.viii.126). Just how they did so depended on their internal balance prior to any specific relation and on the general surrounding conditions and circumstances as and when they did so. For these changes and adjustments, the material world's blending, breathing and flowing depended on "everything throughout nature" (NF II.ix.134). That was why the "airlike" humor of blood was taken to be at once a humor like the others and something more: in balance, the very basis of health. That was why breathing and pulse were so central to diagnosis: they showed the state of the body's fit in the all-flowing pneuma or spiritus that filled the world. That was why Galen wrote repeatedly on pulse: seven separate treatises, nearly 1000 pages of the *Opera*. And because *spiritus* was so crucial to human life, pulse stayed a vital medical concern to later practitioners and commentators (cf. Kuriyama 18–60).

The fit of body and soul in the world's *pneuma* was why sight was the primary sense, directly connecting with air and light without and with bodily *pneuma* (possibly the soul's living force) within:

what difficulty is there in supposing that the sunlight is sensitive, much as the pneuma in the eyes that is brought in from the brain is clearly seen to be? For it is luminous. And if we must speak of the substance of the soul, we must say one of two things: we must say either that it is this, as it were, bright and ethereal body, a view to which the Stoics and Aristotle are carried in spite of themselves, as the logical consequence (of their teachings), or that it is (itself) an incorporeal substance and this body is its first vehicle, by means of which it establishes partnership with other bodies. We must say, then, that this (pneuma) itself extends through all the brain, and that by partnership with it the optical pneuma becomes luminous. (DHP VII.7.24–26: 2.474/75)

Inside the body *pneuma* was distributed not just to sight but to all sense organs "through a single power common to all sense organs which flows to them from the ruling part." This ruling part (*archē*) was the brain (DHP VII.8.2–3: 2.474–76). Nor did it matter, said Galen, whether one thought soul incorporeal or corporeal. For as to the *pneuma* in the ventricles of the brain (whence it was distributed through the body), "if the soul is incorporeal, the pneuma is, so to speak, its first home; or if the soul is corporeal, this very thing is the soul" (DHP VII.3.19: 2.442/43–44/45). In a way, it was a matter of words whether one considered soul to be *pneuma* itself or just "lodged" in *pneuma*.

In the brain, *pneuma* was motive force of the rational powers, working "to provide imagination and memory and recollection, knowledge and thought and ratiocination." It guided the senses, too, and "motion of the parts that move voluntarily." For *pneuma* flowed in the two other seats of vital power: the heart, where it provided the tension (*tonos*) of the soul, its constancy in acts enjoined by reason and right response to passions stirred by impressions; and the liver, where it provided everything involving nutrition, production of blood (in animals) and pleasures. These were the seats of the three aspects of soul in humans: rational in the brain, sensitive in the heart, nutritive in the liver (DHP VII.3.2–3: 2.438–40; cf. VI.2.13–14: 2.370–72). As to *pneuma*'s action, Walter Pagel seems to me to have introduced confusions, especially where brain and rational powers are concerned, whose import will be clear when we come to Nemesius, the Arab doctors and the Christian West. He argues that Galen did not locate specific processes in specific brain ventricles but in "brain substance" (97). But while Galen did not set *soul* in any ventri-

cle (as he said Herophilus had done), he agreed with tradition that memory, intellect and imagination were so sited, set physically in the body, as
we saw earlier, in intimate relation to the senses' contact with the world
(imagination), internal reasoning (intellect) and the substance of the universe itself (memory). One should rather say that for Galen specific *powers*, rational, sensitive and nutritive, were located in specific places, brain
ventricles, heart and liver, and *activated* by *pneuma*. In the human body,
in *practice, pneuma* and soul could be treated as one (which is why Descartes could later insist that soul was both unique *and* tied to the whole
body).

Pneuma or *spiritus* was the essential material force by which human
bodies were in the same passible relation with their physical surroundings
as they were with all their others. This was why, to name diseases again,
epidemics like plague, smallpox, cholera, dysentery, typhoid or, for the
European fifteenth and sixteenth centuries, syphilis, were thought (even
beyond these centuries) to spread through the air by what can only be
called "spiritual contagion," interpenetration of *spiritus*. This it was that
bound exterior and interior together, as it also—as soul or soul's
power—tied embodied soul to whatever greater force might be thought
of as impassible and eternal soul. That is why, to return to the issues of
soul and body with which this chapter began, Galen stated that the affections, contrary to what a few misguided "moderns" tried to argue, were
not to be thought of as having to do only with "unnatural changes," but
concerned "all changes of a natural type, at least those which were not
active in nature" (TM II.3.6).

For the "active" was their "opposite": affections were what were *received* by passible substance and hence were also called "passions" (TM
II.3.9). All bodily motions could thus be both active and passive, active
insofar as the particular force in the body was actually producing a motion (the sensitive in the heart in a case of anger, say; the nutritive or
"desiderative" in the liver in one of lust), passive insofar as they were *re-*
acting to an appearance or impression from elsewhere *and* as the other
forces in the soul/body were *moved* by the first. This give-and-take defined the passible nature of the person, as Galen explored often and at
length. He did so most memorably, it may be, in discussing the interplay
between the three different seats, forms and forces by which the human
animal functioned, observing how the rational, the sensitive and the nutritive each had its own affections, while being always in some active/re-
active relation with those of the others (DHP VI.1.5–27: 2.360–66). To
this end he also adopted Plato's image of the soul in *Phaedrus*. Plato's
guiding charioteer of two horses became the person, torn between two
teams of horses figuring interplay of *energeia* and *pathos*, activity and af-

fection: passibility (DHP VI.1.17–19: 2.364). It had no doubt been the image's power to depict the shared generative play of active and passive that let Varro use it to signify the "four-horse chariot of first things . . . place and body, time and action" guided presumably by god or the demiurge. Galen repeated such themes over and over. They show the material and physiological counterparts of the diversity and complexity of the passible soul's other circles and the manner in which ideas of the person (and of soul) assumed its nature and functioning to be inextricably bound to, involved in, them.

Indeed, the triple nature of the human soul itself corresponds to a basic division in those circles. The nutritive (or vegetative or desiderative) involved the simple materiality of the surrounding world. The sensitive tied into the social sphere, where the person touched other reactive, passible beings. The rational related not only to this last, but to worlds of knowledge, memory and the universal or "divine." The rational contained a similar division of sympathetic functions. Imagination was immediate contact with material images (*phantasiai*) of and from the world. Intellect was the processing of one's place and action in a rational organization in which one lived. Memory reached toward wherever the "soul" had come from and, for some, wherever it was going. Too, while *spiritus* flowed throughout the body, it was also thought of as divided into three sorts: natural, corresponding to the nutritive powers; vital, to the sensitive; and animal, to the rational—a division that was later to cause much debate.

In large degree, as my earlier separation of these analyses into something like three "traditions" proposed, this triple arena of the person guided later conceptions. So, for instance, two centuries after Galen, the Christian bishop Nemesius of Emesa in Syria, who wrote his *Treatise on the Nature of Man* [TNM] to clarify the relation of humans to the divine, grounded his thinking in the physical arguments of Galen and a material understanding of the person that came to him, as well, from Aristotle and Stoic debate. If he rejected Stoic ideas of the soul's corporeality on grounds that need for exact placement would prevent its being the body's unifying principle (to say nothing of the substantial problem of its immortality) he did give it a kind of tempered materiality (TNM 257–60; cf. Verbeke, *Presence* 32). Nemesius' work was one of the major strands bringing these traditions into the European middle ages and Renaissance (through two medieval and three Renaissance Latin translations, besides an Italian and an English, to say nothing of much earlier Armenian, Arabic and Georgian ones).

Nemesius began by rejecting Plotinus' division of humans into body, mind and soul (which would have given him the same ready tool to separate the material from the divine as it gave Plotinus), urging rather that they were grounded in the four elements, whose material being they shared with things inanimate. This led to the very different threefold division adopted by Galen. Humans shared "faculties of self-nutriment and generation" with plants. They shared "a range of voluntary movements, together with the faculties of appetite, anger, feeling and respiration," with "irrational animals." They shared with "incorporeal rational intelligences the prerogative of applying, to whatever be, will, reason, understanding and judgement" (TNM 228–29: Telfer translates from Matthei's Greek edition, to which I refer as M, with page and sometimes line). This was Aristotelian, but also Stoic and Galenic.

Like Galen and the others, Nemesius sited these activities of mind in the brain ventricles, each answerable for one faculty: imagination and sensation being in the soft and moist anterior, thought in the warm and dryer middle, memory in the cold and dry posterior. Unlike Galen, the Christian Nemesius could not leave the problem of the soul's corporeality undecided. So he specified that it could not be identified with any of these nor directly with the *pneuma* moving them: either would mean that it died when body did. Still, despite Pagel's claim (98), Nemesius did *not* write of the soul's "incorporeality" but of something quite different. To follow Nemesius' argument, drawn straight from Galen, depends on knowledge of passibility and its contexts.

In His wisdom, said Nemesius, God had tied "intelligible and phenomenal" natures in humans. For that reason pursuit of virtue involved both body and soul (whatever this might precisely be), while pursuit of "godliness or philosophic contemplation" was for the soul alone (TNM 236). For the first, care of the body and of its place in the material and social world was primary (TNM 240–42). But this body, by its relation to embodied soul, "though mortal, is [thereby] immortalized" (TNM 255). Thence came the grandeur of the human, placed between the irrational, rational and divine. It joined these "in se ipso [in its own person]," bore all aspects of creation "in its very own nature [*in sui ipsius natura*]" and so was "rightly called 'the world in little' [*mikros kosmos*]" (TNM 255; M 63). I give Burgundio of Pisa's 1165 Latin (referred to hereafter as VM), widely known in Western Europe, because it here implies an evaluation of the human that was to come into early modern deliberation. And Nemesius did now give a long panegyric of the human. Still, we must recognize that humans' embedding in matter was vital to what they were and Nemesius' phrase, further, clearly recalled ones seen representatively in writers like Seneca and Plutarch. Materiality was essential to human "dignity" along with the many troubles and difficulties it posed. Indeed to be aware of and act within the *limits* set on the human by its material condition was just what would define human dignity—in Petrarch's case for example (contrary to later claims made about him as the "first modern man," going beyond those limits). The soul, then, could not be simply corporeal. That agreed, opinions, allowed Nemesius, were countless. Even if soul was not corporeal, yet the body of "the living creature is ensouled throughout": "totum est animatum," Burgundio translated (TNM 268; M 69; VM 30). Soul, in human experience and analysis, was inseparably entangled in body: one had, then, "to show that the soul is a real entity." That, at least, is William Telfer's translation, apparently not understanding the passage (TNM 269–70). Burgundio was more accurate, saying that the soul was "neque insubstantialis" (VM 30). Nemesius had written that it was "ouden anousias," "not at all insubstantial," based, that is, in *ousia* (M 82.14). We recognize the appeal back not just to Aristotle but, as Nemesius elaborated, to the Plato of the *Phaedo*. For *ousia*, substance or essence, whatever its nature once embodied in the person, was what humans reached by recollection; preexisting the person, it was nonetheless bodied in the person (TNM 270). Embodied soul was not *located* in any specific place, but its bond to the impassible depended on a mental process through the separate *physical* stages of the brain: exactly what we saw when examining Plato and Aristotle, and then Galen. For Nemesius soul was self-subsisting, rational, living and the integrator of the person, *in* matter not just *of* matter (TNM 275–80). This clearly agreed with such as Plutarch and Cicero, as it did with Seneca and less dogmatic Stoics.

Because in the living person what was called soul was indivisible from body, it was essential to know the body's physical mechanisms—no person alive could *experience* soul without body. Nemesius thus moved to a long discussion, drawn from Hippocrates and Galen, of elements, qualities and humors with their relation to the physical world; of the soul's faculties (memory, intellect and imagination) and their link to that world through the sense organs; of the nature of animal *spiritus*; of the bond between the senses and the elements; of the division of powers between the nutritive, sensitive and rational and of passions between the liver and the heart as controlled by the brain; finally coming to the importance of pulse and respiration, sign of the presence of *pneuma* or *spiritus* in the body, and so another *physical* sign of the soul's embodiment (TNM 305–82). Nemesius then discussed the nature of will, free-will, the relation of humans to providence and providence itself (TNM 382–452). I will note elements of this discussion later. I have wanted to emphasize here how deeply this Christianized discussion of the person was embedded in a Galenic view of the materiality of human existence.

So it was natural for Nemesius to be among those translated during the great ninth- to eleventh-century Arab enterprise that (along with Byzantium) kept alive the Aristotelian-Galenic tradition. The work's ninth-tenth-century translator, Ishāq ibn Hunayn, was a Nestorian Christian, son of Hunayn ibn Ishāq, whose vital work is discussed shortly. The son translated Plato, Aristotle, Euclid, Archimedes, Ptolemy, Alexander of Aphrodisias, Galen, Paulus and others essential to later western thought. The Aristotelian-Galenic tradition itself entered the medieval Latin West via the medical practitioners and eventual school of Salerno— already famous, Kristeller thinks, by the second half of the eleventh century ("School" 143–44)—and thence to early European modernity. In the eleventh century, Nicolaus Alfanus, future archbishop of Salerno, came there from Montecassino, where he had been abbot. Besides writing his own treatise on the four humors, he put Nemesius into Latin, minus the chapters on will and destiny (naming it *Premnon physicon*, Key to Nature), translating the material, Galenic, chapters just described, clearly found useful to a practicing physician (TNM 217–18; Kristeller, "School" 149–52, VM lxxxvi). Between the times of these two renderings and the sixteenth century, Nemesius was to be put into Latin at least four times, besides other languages, with many manuscripts and editions, the *Treatise* becoming a kind of "bestseller" (TNM 219–20). Influential as it was, though, the Arab doctors were themselves the principal continuers of the Galenic tradition.

Probably the most important medical work for the Latin middle ages was an anthology called the *Articella* or *Ars medicinae*. This originated in Salerno and was used everywhere for more than half a millennium, printed frequently in the fifteenth and sixteenth centuries. By 1280, says Owsei Temkin, it was "required reading in Paris, Naples, and Salerno" (100). To these one may add Bologna and Montpellier, both founded in the twelfth century, the former the premier university and medical school of Europe by the second half of the thirteenth century. In the fourteenth, in medical faculties founded at Padua, Pavia and other Italian universities, the same texts were adopted. What is indicated here is not simply the wide acceptance throughout medieval Europe of a single view of what it was to be human, materially speaking, but, no less importantly, the fact that at least in Italian medical faculties, medicine and philosophy were joined: a practice that came through the Arab doctors directly from Galen and antiquity more generally (see Frede, "Philosophy"; Kristeller, "Philosophy" 31–32, 35). This explains why many early modern philosophers were also physicians (for the pattern of the link in medieval and Renaissance universities, see especially Siraisi, *Taddeo* 72–95, 147–236, *Avicenna* 221–93, and Schmitt, "Aristotle"). The relation emphasizes how fundamental were medical practice and its experience of the physical body to understanding and experience of mind in particular and person in general.

The *Articella*'s contents varied, but always included two works: Galen's *Ars medica*, called the *Tegni* or *Microtegni* (*Ars parva*), and the *Isagoge* of the ninth-century Arab writer known to the middle ages as Joannitius: Hunayn ibn Ishāq. Among the first Arab transmitters of the Galenic tradition, ibn Ishāq sketched a division of medicine like the *Tegni*'s: into theory and practice. Theory was subdivided into study of things natural ("basic science"), things non-natural ("hygiene") and things contranatural ("pathology"). Natural things were all aspects of the person proper to physical body itself: the four elements, nine complexions or temperaments (these were the equable, rarely if ever found in practice, those corresponding to the four qualities separately and those composed of the qualities mixed: dry and warm, dry and cold, moist and cold, moist and warm), humors, parts of the body, and its faculties, functions and spirits (some writers, said ibn Ishāq, added age, color, form and sexual difference). Some scholars claim that the Galenic-Arab doctrine of *crases*, complexions composed of the four qualities or their compounds, measured against ideal but never-achieved equable perfection, differed from late Latin and medieval ideas making humor and temperament basic (Klibansky, Panofsky and Saxl 100–101, Ottosson 129–54). This supposed clarity of distinction misleads. Both are in Galen, we have seen, as in the Arabs, especially Avicenna (Soubiran 62, 65–68).

By non-natural things ("res non naturales") the physicians meant all material things that were not just in or of the body but that related it to the material world outside it: "air, food and drink, sleep and watch, motion and rest, evacuation and repletion, and the passions of the mind" (Ottosson 253–54). Of these, scholastic commentaries of the *Isagoge* and the *Tegni* would later emphasize air (*spiritus*) and passions. Contranatural were disease, causes of disease and the accidents following from disease.

The *Isagoge* was well-known in the Latin West by late twelfth century. It had been written three centuries earlier. A few years after ibn Ishāq, Qustā ibn Lūqā wrote a short work also destined to be a main source for the middle ages. This was Latinized as *De differentia animae et spiritus* (DD) by the twelfth century, early adopted in Salerno, passed into later debate and became widely used in the West (Harvey 37–39). Ibn Lūqā ostentatiously set his work in the Greek tradition, declaring that his data came from Plato's *Phaedo* and *Timaeus*, Aristotle's *Physics*, Theophrastus and Galen, an Arab go-between of uncertain name, with some Hippocrates and more Plato (DD 120). He then explained that *spiritus* was a "certain tenuous body" (*corpus subtile*) that arose in the heart and flowed out by the venous pulse vitalizing and breathing life into the body. To the body it brought "life, breath and pulse." Similarly it arose (or appeared: *oritur*) in the brain and nerves. But basically both blood and spirit were in and from the heart, more of the former in the right ventricle, of the latter in the left (DD 121). When *spiritus* left the heart the body died (DD 123).

Spiritus was also responsible for all rational, intellectual operations: "In fact intellect, reasoning [*cogitatio*], foresight and understanding result from *spiritus*, which is in the ventricle that is among the two ventricles in the anterior brain" (DD 126). So there were two kinds of *spiritus*. One was the "vital," nourished on air taken through the lungs and proceeding from the heart to flow by *pulsus* in the veins to the rest of the body. The other was the "animal," nourished on vital spirit and functioning through the brain, enabling sense and motion by means of the nerves, and letting soul function in a way yet to be explained (DD 123, 130).

So ibn Lūqā now discussed Plato's and Aristotle's views of the soul, finally agreeing with the latter: "It is well and finely said that the soul is the first perfection of natural body instrumental in living, potentially, and this definition is universal, full and sufficient for every soul that may be in corruptible and dissoluble body, universally" (DD 136). This soul had three powers (*virtutes*), forms or genera: vegetative, sensible and rational. The vegetative or seminal (Galen had called it vegetative, nutritive or reproductive) was common "to us as to trees, grasses and animals." The sensible or vital was "common to us and animals." The rational was only in humans. The vegetative was characterized by four natural powers: "attractive, retentive, digestive and expulsive." The sensible or vital had seven faculties: five senses, *phantasia* and "voluntary local motion." The rational had five faculties or powers: "reasoning and foresight, judgment and dubitation, and memory" (DD 137). It is easy to see how these powers and faculties of the soul fit with the vital and animal spirits (DD 137). Their difference, said ibn Lūqā, was that spirit was corporeal, soul incorporeal. Spirit was "held tight" (*comprehenditur*) in body, soul was not. Spirit could not survive separated from body, soul did. Spirit moved body, senses and vivifying motions directly, soul did so through spirit. The spirits were, then, the proximate cause of all the body's motions, the soul a more distant but infinitely greater cause. Spirits, finally, inhered in body in much the same way as did the humors (DD 138).

One sees why this work was so popular in the Christian middle ages. Distinguishing life force, as material spirits, from the soul, it clarified a difficulty left over from Galen and his many predecessors which Nemesius had tried to clarify in a not dissimilar, but less successful, way. If *spi-*

ritus or *pneuma*, as present in the body, was *the same* as a universal divine afflatus, and if both were somehow *psuchē* ("life force" and soul), how could its apparently necessary materiality, as "air" for example, be adjusted to the soul's immortality? Ibn Lūqā gave another way to separate them, even though medieval ideas of *spiritus* stayed confused (Hamesse). Only much later, after the mid-sixteenth century, did most practicing and theoretical physicians start to reject ideas of vital and animal spirits as physico-rational or ensouled motion in the body—Jean Fernel being a notable exception (Siraisi, *Avicenna* 337–41; Walker). As a physiological explanation of what one would now perhaps consider neural impulses they would live on.

Many other Arab doctors' work was used. Four were notably familiar during the Latin middle ages: Razes, a contemporary of ibn Lūqā; Haly Abbas, author of a widely used *Pantegni*; Constantinus Africanus, who came to Salerno about 1077, taught at nearby Montecassino and whose translations of Hippocrates and Galen tied Greek past, Arab present and Latin future; and Avicenna. My aim here is not to give their history, but a sense of how and in what form material emplacement of the person came to early modern Europe. The greatest of Galen's Arab heirs, his work incomparably crucial to later centuries, was Avicenna, working in years when Salerno was just beginning. His *Canon*, systematizing Aristotelian-Galenic medical tradition, had fourteen different Latin renderings by the fifteenth century, further translations, more than sixty complete or partial editions and countless commentaries through the seventeenth century (Soubiran 166; Siraisi, "Changing Fortunes" and *Avicenna* 43–76). Its poetic epitome, the *Cantica Avicennae*, was used as a readily memorizable manual: Latinized in the twelfth century, established as hugely popular by the late thirteenth and still used in some universities beyond the sixteenth. Its earliest known commentator was Avicenna's Arab rival in celebrity in the Latin West, the philosopher Averroes (Avicenna, *Poème* ix; cf. Temkin 104). For the poem was no less popular in the Arab world than in the Latin, and ibn Khaldūn, for instance, discussing the effects of air and general climate on color, character, mind and manners of humans, did not hesitate to cite its authority as to the effect of the earth's extreme hot and cold zones on skin color:

> Where the Zanj live is a heat that changes their bodies
> Until their skins are covered all over with black.
> The Slavs acquire whiteness
> Until their skins turn soft. (1.171; cf. 174–76)

Every "Arab systematization," including ibn Ishāq's earlier *Isagoge* and those of the others just named, began by reviewing the elements and nine complexions or temperaments of the body (Browne, *Arabian* 119). Avicenna was no exception to the rule, taken supposedly from a physician antedating the Hippocratics, Alcmeon of Crotona, more immediately from his closest precursor, Haly Abbas (*Poème* 7). Drawing directly on Galen, Avicenna continued his first book by systematizing the "naturals." He held that temperaments came first "from the mutual interaction and interpassion of the four contrary primary qualities residing within the . . . elements" (*Treatise* [TCA] §27), although he speculated on a fifth, driest, element, the ethereal (§50). Temperament was also affected by age (adolescence—to thirty, subdivided into babyhood, infancy, childhood, puberty and youth; prime—to thirty-five or forty; senescence—to sixty; and senility), sex, geography and occupation (§§51–52; §§63–65). Since the qualities composing temperament were found not only in the elements but also in the seasons, the natural kingdoms (animal, vegetable and mineral), places and so on, all these had a role in balancing complexions. Above all *'ustuqus*, "primal principle constitutive of the body," had to be balanced (*Poème* 12–13). What *'ustuqus* was is unclear. It seems to have been equivalent to *pneuma/spiritus*. Could it have been a transposition of *ischus*, strength, of which we saw Aristotle write in the *De motu animalium* as present in the body through *pneuma*?

Like everyone, Avicenna held that among the seasons winter corresponded to phlegm, spring to blood, summer to yellow bile and autumn to black bile. Whatever one's temperament it thus varied in interaction with time of year. So it did by diet. For foods, divided into mineral, vegetable, animal, and then into how their kinds beat illness and aided healthy growth, were also endowed with temperament and corresponded to the humors. Taste showed their qualities: sweet, salty and bitter were chiefly dry; spicy were hot; sharp, acrid and astringent were dry and cold; fatty were wet and hot; insipidly pleasant were cold and wet. A person's age affected temper. Childhood and adolescence were hot—the former wet, the latter drier. Prime was mostly cold. During senescence one grew yet colder. In senility humors became coarser. As to sex, male was mainly hot and dry, female cold and wet. Body form also evinced temperament, fat and fleshy marking a cold and wet, bony and lean a dry. This was why ibn Khaldūn later insisted that those on a harsh and light diet and living in hard surroundings would be healthier and mentally sharper than others who were fleshy and wet (1.179; cf. 2.376–77). If veins were visible, said Avicenna, the body was warm-tempered, cold if not. Climate and place affected the body's color, its health and the temper that color revealed: a yellowish complexion showed biliousness or choler, a dark brown marked atrabiliousness or melancholy, reddish sanguinity, white or ivory phlegm. White and red mixed suggested a body in balance. The humors corresponding to these temperaments were not wholly fixed. Blood could degenerate to phlegm as imperfect "natural" blood, to yellow bile as blood's natural "foam" (by some, like Moses Maimonides, named red bile) or to black bile as its "sediment," although each of these humors also existed in separate, distinct form (*Poème* 14–16; TCA §§73–86).

The imbrication of the physical body in the material world remained essential to understanding what and who a person was. Avicenna was in wide company. In his *Paradise of Wisdom* (*ca.* 850), 'Alī ibn Rabbān al-Tabarī analyzed something like an "opposite" process. In nutrition, a first digestion or "coction" produced chyle—becoming phlegm with no particular location. A second coction in the liver made a "scum" of yellow bile and a "sediment" of black bile. A third coction took place in the blood vessels, refining the blood on its way to the heart and a fourth refining coction. He thus held the humors to be normally mixed, with a reserve of yellow bile in the gall bladder, of black in the spleen (Browne, *Arabian* 121–22). A Syriac Christian contemporary of ibn Ishāq, al-Tabarī's work was much used by Razes and others. Later, more generally yet, Hildegard held the four elements to be themselves virtually forms of each other, shading into one another following proportionate changes in their qualities (*Causae* II.[§15]: 39). She was perhaps developing Ambrose and, more, Isidore of Seville's well-read *De natura rerum*, whose eleventh chapter noted how elemental qualities overlapped. All may have drawn on Stoic ideas of the elements' mutual interpenetrability (Colish, *Stoic* 1.24–25). But ibn Khaldūn was similarly to argue that the elements were arranged in "an ascending order, from earth to water, from water to air, and from air to fire. Each one of the elements is prepared to be transformed into the next higher or lower one, and sometimes is transformed" (1.194). He thought the same of relations between mineral, vegetable and animal kingdoms and, more remarkably, but by the same axioms, between species: "The higher stage of man is reached from the world of the monkeys, in which both sagacity and perception are found, but which has not yet reached the stage of actual reflection and thinking" (1.195).

Imbrication of physical body and material world (both synchronically and diachronically, one sees) was always evident. So was its huge complexity, although we have barely begun to approach it. I have mentioned the seasons, nutrition, age, sex, geography, climate and occupation. Drawing mostly, if not entirely, on Galen, Avicenna added countless material aspects: the effect of stars and planets on the atmosphere, differences of air by country, sea, mountains and wind, the impact of variations in the land (whether marsh, lake, rocks, desert, hilly, etc.), the importance of clothing, scents, colors (those around one, not just those of one's temper), exercise, regimen, evacuation and repletion, state of the passions, music and far more (*Poème* 20–25; for music, TCA §698; §1084). All had their signs, symptoms, cures and prevention, their etiology, symptomatology and pathology (*Poème* 25–61). Only once all this was known in theory could doctor (and teacher) give consideration to medical practice (*Poème* 62–99).

Even so, if one accounted only for these one would still fall short of one's material enlacement. One had to consider not only that the four humors had their subvarieties but that all these things had varied effects not just in the whole body but in its members: the four principal organs (brain, heart, liver and reproductive gland), their auxiliary organs (respectively the senses, lungs, stomach and intestine), the direct auxiliaries of these last (nerves, arteries, gall bladder/spleen/kidneys and genitals) and their remote auxiliaries (bones/muscles, flesh/fat and intestinal tract—the reproductive gland having none). Each of these had its temperament, although certain humors, qualities and elements were basic to each, indeed produced in some of them (TCA §§114–35; *Poème* 17–18). To the organs corresponded the three sorts of spirits that came down from Galen through Nemesius and ibn Lūqā. The natural was reproductive and nutritive and focused in the reproductive gland and liver, the vital controlled breath, sensation and motion and was centered in the heart and its associated organs, the animal ordered all things associated with reason and was concentrated in the brain (TCA §§136–41; *Poème* 18).

The first two spirits controlled the body's seven forces. To the natural belonged formless action on seed, action giving form, height and organs, action of attraction and growth and action of retention and expulsion—these "actions" could also be divided in three, as generative, nutritive and augmentative (Avicenna, *De anima*: Harvey 41). The vital ruled dilation and constriction of pulse and the feelings that made the reactions called affections, the things having to do with elevation or baseness of soul. These were the "motive" powers, the latter being "appetitive" (divided into concupiscible and irascible), the former affecting actual motion through nerves and muscles. The animal spirits controlled the soul's nine faculties: those of the five senses, the nervous, and—in ventricular turn, so to speak—imagination, reflection and memory (*Poème* 18–19; TCA §§174–90).

In non-medical works Avicenna was more exact on these last faculties. He matched the five physical senses with five inward faculties. He got these by seeing reflection act in two ways. What he called the (physiological) "nervous" faculty in medical works, he elsewhere called common sense or *phantasia*, where sense data converged. He sited it in the front of the head, followed by imagination in the anterior cavity. Next was the estimative faculty, present through the brain but focused in the middle cavity, and imaginative or cogitative according to use. Memory lay in the posterior cavity (*Livre* 317–23). In his *De anima*, Avicenna separated faculties from their location and the middle became intellect (imaginative or cogitative) and judgment (estimative) (Harvey 41–46). The spirits moving them were a "divine emanation" from god entering the body as soul and taking its varied forms, animal ruling the others (TCA §§168–70). We have traced this view's growth from Aristotle through Galen, Nemesius and Avicenna's Arab precursors. The emanation from impassible "active Intellect" was embodied as rational soul, with "intelligibles" already implanted by its creator. Possession of these—the source of reason—and awareness of possessing them was the soul's "perfection," both dependent on impassible *intellectus agens* (*Livre* 6, cf. 42–43; Harvey 41, 47–48 for *De anima*). Perhaps this idea of the soul's perfection influenced Descartes' similar concept of "generosity."

This order was exactly adopted by ibn Khaldūn, saying that "the common sense transfers the perceptions to the imagination, which is the power that pictures an object of sensual perception in the soul." These two were in "the first cavity of the brain. The front part of that cavity is for the common sense, and the back part for the imagination" (1.196–97). Imagination led to "the estimative power and the power of memory." The first of these "perceived abstract ideas that refer to individualities, such as the hostility of Zayd, the friendship of 'Amr, the compassion of the father, or the savagery of the wolf." Memory was a "repository" or a "storehouse" "for all objects of perception . . . imagined or not." Ibn Khaldūn located these two powers in "the back cavity of the brain," whose "front part" was "for the estimative power, and the back for the power of memory." Together, these powers led "to the power of thinking," situated in "the middle cavity of the brain." This was power that set "reflection . . . in motion" and led "toward intellection." "The soul [was] constantly moved by it, as the result of its constitutional desire to think" (1.197). Trammeled as it was in body, "perception and intellection bec[a]me the actual form of the soul" through its constant working with what was given it by the body, through perception, imagination and memory. Doing so, it drew ever closer to its potential as it had been at its placement in body (1.215). This, too, looked back to Avicenna, Aristotle and beyond.

For the soul, wrote Avicenna Platonically in verses on the subject, was reluctantly sent down into its human prison, there to stay until released by the body's death ("Poem"). But even in human life it could reason back to that knowledge of perfection we have seen so important to the

Greeks. For the rational soul had not only an active power whose materiality we have seen but a contemplative one too. This had three stages. First was the "material intellect" that simply directed the soul toward intelligibles. Avicenna likened this to "the recess" where stood the "lamp" of the soul's faculty once moved by first intelligibles—perhaps these in some way matched *phantasia* and imagination. Next came the faculty of reflection or intellectual intuition, unrefined "olive" if the weak former, inflammable "oil" if the strong latter—corresponding to the estimative faculty as divided into imaginative or cogitative. Last came the *intellectus in habitu*, the whole "glass" of the lamp itself (matching in position the site of memory?), the faculty ripe for lighting and being brought to perfection by *intellectus agens* (*Livre* 324–26). However much this was a commentary on the Qur'ān (xxiv.35), clearly, even when writing of the most abstract level of soul, Avicenna emphasized its materiality (here, via a glassiness with a considerable future, we saw in Chapter 1).

The importance of these Arab writings (excepting ibn Khaldūn) to the European middle ages cannot be overestimated. They gave a foundation to medical theory and practice and to philosophy of the person, notwithstanding their non-Christian source. Too, similar views on these matters were later importantly passed on in works of Maimonides, such as his 1194 Arabic *Guide to the Perplexed*, limning complexities of soul in ways very like these, and his vastly popular *Medical Aphorisms* (Maimonides was court physician to Saladin). Also written in Arabic, from 1187 to 1190, this work, say its recent translators, was "the most widely known and desired repertorium of Galen from the 13th to 15th centuries" (*Medical* 10). Like Galen's *Tegni*, ibn Ishāq's *Isagoge* and the *Cantica* Avicenna, and even though it was considerably longer, this work no doubt owed its popularity to its summarizing of by now entirely familiar doctrine, besides giving grist for a teacher's mill in a "twenty-fifth" and last treatise listing aphorisms "pertaining to some of the doubts that arise from the words of Galen."

Medical tradition, for clear cause, emphasized the material world and its interaction with the human body and person in *their* materiality—not just as to phenomena subject to medical attention, whether preventively by exercise, diet and general regimen, or therapeutically. I offer two last cases, one early one late both lowly, of this comprehensive sympathy between human body, natural "instinct," habitation, seasonal changes, food, exercise, material world and elemental nature:

What is the meaning of our demand for a yearly change of habitation? In winter we retreat to the loftiest parts of our houses, those farthest from the earth, while in summer we require the lowest parts, submerging ourselves and going in quest of comfortable retreats, as we make the best of a life in the embrace of mother earth. Since we do this, are we not guided to the earth by our perception of its coldness? Do we not recognize it as the natural seat of primordial cold? And surely our living by the sea in the winter is, in a way, an escape from the earth, since we abandon the land as far as possible because of the frost and wrap ourselves in salt sea air because it is warm. Again, in the summer by reason of the heat, we long for earth-born, upland air, not because it is itself chilly, but because it has sprung from the naturally and primordially cold and been imbued with its earthy power, as steel is tempered by being plunged in water.

So Plutarch in "The Principle of Cold" (*Moralia* 954b–c). My other example is from Constantinus Africanus, a millennium later, offering this time a cure:

The melancholic's dwelling should face the east and lie open to it; to counteract the dry nature of the "atra bilia," preference should be given to moist things in his diet, such as fresh fish, honey, all manner of fruit, and, with regard to meat, the flesh of very young and, if possible, female, animals, like yearling lambs, young hens and female partridges (vegetables, on the contrary, are to be avoided, because of wind); above all, his digestion is to be aided by means of diet, as well as of early morning walks in cheerful dry surroundings, massage with warm and moist ointments, and daily infusions of lukewarm (or cold, in summer) water. (*Opera* [Basle, 1536] 1.291ff., paraphrased by Klibansky, Panofsky and Saxl 85)

(Constantinus' brief *De coitu*, widely disseminated in the middle ages, assailed by Geoffrey Chaucer, is available in English and offers a good sense of how every aspect of life was ruled by these relations.)

Both of these, Avicenna's complexities show, were simple versions. John Sutton catches well the sense of material connectedness marking what it was to be a person, still far later: "the body was by nature open, the internal environment always in dynamic interrelation with the external environment." Its well-being required regulating its relation to and place in non-naturals, carefully monitoring and balancing naturals and warding off contranaturals. "Urgent steps could be taken to close off its vents and windows, barring the orifices by which external dangers could intrude. But this seasonal body was always vulnerable to climatic effects, and permeated by the environment right through to its cognitive capacities" (95–96). Sutton believes that Descartes still felt something of this sensibility. My last two chapters argue that he remained embedded in it. Small wonder if Montaigne devoted an entire essay (2.37) to the difficulties of medicine: the doctor "needs too many factors, considerations and circumstances; he must know his patient's complexion, his temperament, his humors, his inclinations, his actions, even his thoughts and his fancies; he must take account of external circumstances, the nature of the locale, condition of the air and the weather, the position of the planets and their influences; he must know the disease's causes, symptoms, affections, critical days; the drug's weight, power, country of origin, appearance, age, dosage," how to combine all these things, and yet more besides (2.37.752–53).

Medical writers dwelt on material world and physical body. Others, by partiality or purpose, stressed the rational and divine; yet others the rational and social. These were varieties of emphasis, not of understanding and experience. Nemesius' material embedding of the person, we saw, for instance, buttressed its enlacing in the divine. No less was person webbed in the social and political: "man is a naturally sociable animal, and made for citizenship. No single person is in all ways self-sufficient. And so it is clear, how that cities exist for the sake of intercourse and for the sake of learning from each other" (TNM 243). Burgundio's rendering of this passage made its links with Latin antiquity clear: "Natura enim gregarium et civile animal factus est homo; unus enim nullus sufficiens est sibi ipsi ad universa. Manifestum est igitur quod civitates propter negotiationes et disciplinas constitutae sunt" (VM 14; M 26). Exchange of Ciceronian duties and Senecan learning depended on the person's imbrication in the *polis* in an utterly essential way. Who-ness stayed inseparable from sociopolitical community. Ensouled persons inhabited interwoven surroundings, material and social, political and divine, epistemological and biological, physical and ethical, economic and historical. These defined experiences of personhood and all thinking *about* personhood. Here we need to come back in time from the story of medicine and its interests to those of the divine and rational and the rational and social. The first is approached in the next chapter via Augustine, the second concludes this chapter.

As these circles were basic to what a person was, it matters to realize that the modern western distinction between public and personally private was inconceivable. Every aspect that one might want to take as "personal" was inseparably woven in its surroundings: divine or universal, animate, rational, social, human, material. All were further divisible: the last included location, climate, geography, planetary and stellar motion, winds, waters and seasons; the human included age, sex, social status, temperament, humoral composition; at their "interface" were food, exercise, air, regimen; the social included political relations, leisure activities, education, career, one's social "circles"; the animate involved various levels of soul, the rational faculties and parts of mind, divine harmonies, god, agent intellect, primordial substance. Such surroundings meant that *no* aspect of the person was "private" in any way meaningful to modern westerners. The person's place in the sociolegal sphere is one circle whose exploration gives many clues to understanding this publicness in other areas of the person.

Here, absence of *this* "private" was such that it had no word: "Publicum ius," Justinian's *Digest* opened, "est quod ad statum rei Romanae spectat, priuatum quod ad singulorum utilitatem [public law is what relates to the state of the Roman commonwealth, private to utility of persons]." The distinction was clarified. Public law covered "religious matters, the priesthood, state offices" (*Digest* I.1.1: 1.1). Private law was split into precepts drawn from nature, *gentes* and the civil arena. *Ius naturale* was law common to *all* animals (such as the union of male and female). *Ius gentium* was common to all nations and specific to humans. Civil law was particular to a nation and case (I.1.6: 1.2). *Ius civile*, the *Digest* specified, was that of a given *civitas, ius gentium,* common to all peoples, was established by natural reason (I.1.9: 1.2). Laws of nature, peoples and nation, then, were all parts of private law, *ius priuatum*: hardly what modern westerners would think of as "private." But for the sixth-century *Digest* these were private in that they ruled relations of "singulars" to one another and to the society in which they were organized *by* these laws (adopting the word "individuals" for *singulares*, the translators have diverted the meaning toward much later ideas of a person). Quite analogously, we saw that for Martin of Braga (a contemporary of the *Digest*'s compilers) what we would think private virtues inherent in the person were public *officia* in act, affect and outcome. Richard Tuck's analysis of the meaning of *ius* in Roman law is thus not surprising. The general idea of *ius* and the separate *iura* to which the word applied were "the product of agreements or promises made between specific and independent parties" (opposed to *dominium* which involved no mutuality). Contrary to later claim (of the fourteenth and fifteenth centuries and again the seventeenth), *ius* did not inhere in a person. It marked a social arrangement (10).

If the sacred and the "official" somehow eluded human control (as the interface of the human and divine), civil law on the contrary was that which came "in the form of statutes, plebiscites, *senatus consulta*, imperial decrees, or authoritative juristic statements" (I.1.7: 1.2). These divers agreements formed the body of *ius*. Produced by human counsel, they overlapped: "A statute [*lex*] is a communal directive [*commune praeceptum*], a resolution of wise men [*uirorum prudentium consultum*], a forcible reaction to crimes committed either voluntarily or in ignorance, a communal covenant of the state [*communis rei publicae sponsio*]" (I.3.1: 1.11). The very breadth of what was defined as *priuatum* can be seen here. It was not "individual" or "particular" but always "collective" (*commune/communis*). It belonged in communal decision about singulars (persons) made for civic *prudential* reasons, by *viri prudentes*. Indeed Ulpian was cited to this very effect: "Iura non in singulas personas, sed generaliter constituuntur [Laws are established not for singular persons, but generally]" (I.3.8: 1.12). The "singular person" involved an "external" personhood able to fall under public jurisdiction: like Cicero's *persona* of the *De officiis*. As to personal status before the law, the great divide was not between public and private, external and internal but between slavery and freedom: "omnes homines aut liberi sunt aut serui," even though the former could be made or born free (1.5.3/5: 1.15).

Ulpian raised the matter of a false understanding of "public" at the turn of the second to third century: "The goods of a community are wrongly called 'public' [*Bona ciuitatis abusiue 'publica' dicta sunt*]; for only those things are public that belong to the Roman people" (L.16.15: 4.934). "Public" named *only* matters of state and religion. Even those of a particular *ciuitas* were private. A tax collector for the Roman people was called *publicanus*, it was explained, because "the designation 'public' relates in a number of cases to the Roman people; since communities [*ciuitates*] are regarded as being in the position of private people [*priuatorum loco*]" (L.16.16: 4.935). "Private" things and "public" things were *both* public in a modern sense. They simply named different levels of publicness.

Still, what Ulpian was said to have seen as an error clearly raises the question of whether the habit of calling such things "public" did not reflect some other habit opposing them to things "private" and so at least to *some* idea of the personally private that might quite simply not be the business of the law. At one level, certainly, such public things were naturally opposed to the goods of the *domus*, the household—another community. Were they ever opposed to some individual privacy? Here, as far as these legal texts are concerned, it could surely only be seen, if at all, where matters of will and intention arose: did the distinction between things done involuntarily and things done willfully not imply separate subjectivity? This returns us to the arguments of Chapter 3 and how far they match what is found in the *Digest*: they lead us again to Alexander of Aphrodisias and Nemesius, and directly to Augustine.

The *Digest* had a lot to say about legal culpability and will. First, someone doing something in error could not be held to have consented to it; ignorance vacated *all* willing: "those who are in error do not consent: for what is so contrary to consent as an error that shows ignorance?" (II.1.15: 1.41). It is worth noting that the error here was mistaken identification of which state officer (praetor) had a given jurisdiction. The ignorance was not personal, as it were, but civil/*legal* ignorance. Second, acts done in fear or by force, and so contrary to the will, were not subject to legal pursuit (IV.2.1–23: 1.113–19). Nothing, Ulpian was quoted as having said, was "so contrary to consent, which sustains cases of good faith [*bonae fidei*], as force or duress." (We shall see later the huge *public* force of *fides*.) He repeated, here, that error never entailed consent (L.17.116: 4.963). Third, someone could only refuse to do something (and be held responsible for having done it, in not so refusing) who was in a position to will it ("Eius est nolle, qui potest velle"): a person legally obedient to a father or master, for example, could not will. A person in tutor- or guardianship could legally speak, but the tutor or guardian would author the speech. Fourth, a mad person could not be held to understand *or* to will; such a person was legally "absent" (L.17.3–5, 124: 4.957, 964). To be willing or unwilling (*uolens* or *inuitus*) always required legal ability. In general Ulpian's contemporary Papinian had said, "all things which are to be done intentionally [*quae animi destinatione agenda sunt*] cannot be done [*non . . . perfici possunt*] except with true and certain knowledge" (L.17.76: 4.961). The Aristotelian and passible descent of all this is clear.

Collected in the sixth century, the texts cited came mostly from the time when Alexander of Aphrodisias was flourishing, and the experience they record seems to have much in common with his views. The primacy of private and public *ius* in determining the willful or unwillful nature of an act set it entirely in our passible circles. It matched Alexander's assertion that it was less that an "agent" brought something about than that things did or did not "come to be by the agency of the doer." The oddity of the more "literal" English phrase is marked by the translator's adding it only as a note correcting his translation (*On Fate*, chap.iv [167.22–23]: 44, 127, 181). It parallels the "agenda sunt" and "perfici possunt" of my last *Digest* quotation. For Alexander, issues of deliberation (*to bouleuesthai*) and responsibility were of massive importance, no less in the *De fato* (chaps.xi–xv) than in his *De anima* and *Quaestiones* (given in Robert Sharples' edition and translation). He noted that there could be no responsibility—as the law recognized—for acts done "*involuntarily*" (*akousiōs*) (xix [189.13]: 67, 196).

Too, things "*voluntary*" and things "dependent on us" (*to te hekousion kai to eph' hēmin*) differed: "For what depends on us is not [to be found] in [creatures] yielding of their own accord to an appearance [*phantasia*] when it impinges on them and exercising impulse toward what has appeared, but this perhaps is what constitutes and indicates the voluntary." Here is exactly the person as passible: external *phantasia* impressed itself on that person. The voluntary, he said, was assent to anything "not enforced" (by the voluntariness, for example, by which a person in tutorship willingly spoke but whose tutor was author of their words). What "depends on us [*eph' hēmin*]" was what was done by "reason and judgment." Everything *eph' hēmin* was voluntary, not everything voluntary was *eph' hēmin*. "For irrational living creatures, too, which act in accord with impulse and assent in them, act voluntarily," as he said before. Only humans could do things *eph' hēmin*: by deliberation and choice (as Sharples has *prohairesis*): that choice that was to be trained, said the Stoics, to right rational assent. Alexander was supposedly arguing against them, but it is unclear that there is any great difference here, however often he rejected his opponents as "absurd" and their arguments as "absurdities" (*On Fate*, Chap. xiv [183.24–35]: 61, 192). Many scholars have observed how much the *Digest*, including its notion of natural law, owed to Stoic thought. Too, these descriptions matched no less the kind of explanation for the behavior of Euphiletos' wife and the corresponding laws noted in Lysias' speech of five centuries before than they did the sort of thing Nemesius was saying two centuries later.

He also set rational, chosen, voluntary acts, those done *hekōn*, against acts *akousia* (TNM 382–83; VM 118–19; M 263–65). Referring to *Nicomachean Ethics* (1109b–1113a), he defined involuntary acts as those done "under constraint or those done unknowingly" (TNM 383–86). He could have named Ulpian and Papinian. Like Alexander, he separated ignorant involuntary acts from voluntary acts (TNM 386–91) and chosen acts—done via *prohairesis*, in the last case again referring to *Nicomachean Ethics* (1113a–b; TNM 391–93). This was Alexander's division of *akōn* from *eph' hēmin*. There was then no such thing as pure personal will: there was agency that was no agency, ignorant, forced, legally minor or mad; agency that "received" the motion of passible effect; and agency using collectively educated and trained *prohairesis* to intelligent assent to such effect. "Will," "choice," "intention" were bedded in their surroundings, accepting acts done in accordance with *ousia* (*hekōn*), not without it (*akousia*), Seneca's, Plutarch's and Hierocles' circles within circles. The terms stayed the same for Nemesius' contemporary Augustine, bishop of Hippo, however he may have realigned their traces.

CHAPTER NINE

Two-Timed Ipseities and Speaking Their Mind

Augustine

The Greek and Latin words translated as "will," "choice" and "intention," then, named ideas and experiences altogether distant from modern western ones. They involved experiences of agency in actions that enveloped their doer, of knowing within the knowable, of passible being woven in multi-layered surroundings, being whose spectrum of affect ran from imperative constraint to educated rational assent. Will, choice and intention are only three aspects of a later concept of the person—itself a term and concept whose own difficulty has been shown by the way Cicero and the *Digest* used *persona* to mean strictly public being. Long has analyzed developments in the meaning of *persona, prosōpon* and *anthrōpos*, showing their move from denoting "roles" or status (social, political, legal), through Epictetus' *anthrōpos*, meaning a rational, auto-knowing, morally aware actor in a community, to usage of *persona* in Boethius, who went "some way towards anticipating the word's later development," naming (after the seventeenth century) either "the conditions of an individual human identity through time, or the attribution to an individual human being of psychological, social and ethical properties": all absent from *persona* in classical or early Christian Latin ("Stoic Philosophers" 14). Colin Morris also observes how hard it is now to understand the ancient Greeks, Hellenistic philosophy and the Greek fathers mostly because "they had no equivalent to our concept 'person,' while their vocabulary was rich in words which express community of being, such as *ousia*, which in our usage can be translated only by the almost meaningless word 'substance'" (*Discovery* 2).

This word was the principal component of those now commonly

translated as "willful" and "nonwillful," "willingly" and "unwillingly." It was also matter of soul, passible and impassible, and of surrounding "essence" or "substance" from which being sprang, in which it stayed embedded and into which it would be reabsorbed. The concept stayed central. But before concentrating on Augustine, it is worth briefly advancing again to the later middle ages for which he was so crucially important. Doing so lets me stress aspects of his writing that show continuities he helped enable, among them especially elements drawing on Stoic themes concerning relations between language, reason and possible being (critical as he was of parts of Stoic ethical thought). He was not alone in mediating this tradition. Colish notes that "the Christian apologists and Church Fathers, starting in the second century," gave Seneca, notably his "ethical works," reputation and influence that "reached new heights during the Carolingian renaissance and attained [their] medieval apogee in the twelfth century" (*Stoic* 1.17). Others find a deep gap between Jerome and Augustine, imbued with Stoic thought, and the European twelfth century (Reynolds 83–84, 104–24; Verbeke, *Presence, passim*) and the continuities we will see suggest marked *dis*continuity from *modern* European thinking on and experience of these matters.

For, as Morris says, the "nearest equivalents" to the modern "individual" (a central term for this later thinking) were words like "*individuum, individualis*, and *singularis*, but these terms belonged to logic rather than to human relations"—to law, too, we have seen in the last case. Here, human relations were subaltern to logical terms (contained by and based on them): "a central problem of medieval philosophy was the relation of the individual object (*unum singulare*) with the general or universal class to which it belonged, and humanity was often taken as a test case in this argument" (64). Haidu argues (in personal exchange) that while this may be true for philosophical debate, it could not be so "if the reference were either social life or vernacular fiction." He has analyzed the latter and, to a degree, the former from these points of view in *The Subject of Violence* and *The Subject*. How far one can know past "social life" outside vernacular fiction, other writing and philosophical debate is anyway matter of contention. The legal case just mentioned and the argument till now show that one cannot automatically assume the nature of personhood involved and that it is all too easy to read modern western supposals into quite different relations. Implications of the "logical" relation Morris observes were considerable. A (Neoplatonic?) belief in the reality of universals, as in Anselm for instance, held that individuals were indivisibly and integrally part of them. The ontological argument advanced in the *Proslogium* and *Reply to Gaunilon* may be comprehensible only in such a light. If one took universals to be primary existents, words were then present as mental concepts only as they held the reality of these universals. Only so does association between the concept of a Perfect Being (whose perfection must include existence) and the Divinity's actual existence become not just comprehensible but *essential*. They become yet more so if we take them as *remembered* concepts in embodied, possible soul bound to the reasons of impassible soul, universal *ousia*, by possible rational faculties. Words and concepts can in no way be detached from other aspects of a person (including the sociopolitical: see 296–98 below).

Anselm's argument assumed an Augustinian and Stoic framework and background and the experience of "conjunctive" surroundings. The difficulty modern westerners have in grasping this view helps explain why we may have more sympathy for a thinker like Peter Abelard whose tendency toward nominalism seemed more to stress the "individual." Even here, *pace* many contemporary arguers, we may not find too much similarity with modern western experience. I argue in the next chapter that even the collection of medieval writings most often taken by scholars to reveal a nearly modern self—at least incipiently—actually shows who-ness well within the experiences so far explored. Abelard's *Historia calamitatum* and the exchange of letters between him and Héloïse finely illustrate a possible relation to the divine as to the material. One can set it in a Ciceronian and Galenic tale of *personae*. The surest early manuscripts, indeed, giving the *Historia* the ancient or *ars dictandi* title, *Abelardi ad amicum suum consolatoria* ("Abelard's consolatory [letter] to his friend"), offered a further embedding circle: a literate intellectual tradition, a collective history of writing that will later become for some a basic mark of personhood. That said, it may be that Abelard signals entry of something new: less by his "rebellious behavior" than by his assertion of personal authority. Haidu observes (again in personal exchange) that Abelard's abuse at the hands of Bernard of Clairvaux and others shows that they felt his urging of "new opinions on his own authority . . . as an individual thinker against the constitutive tradition" to be a "gross misuse" of the intellectual tradition. His "individualism" entered the stage of history "with a negative marker." But that Abelard may evince new kinds of experience does not mean he was not part of the familiar. The fact is among the "tensions" named in the next chapter's title. If he did mark emergent sensibility, he did so negatively in a tradition exemplified and typified by Augustine, which saw soul and/or mind as *essentially* tied to universal *ousia* or, in Christianized terms, divine "intellectus agens."

For, despite modern commentators' claims, Augustine's *Confessions* did not depict a willful self fully responsible for its "individual" life. It portrayed discovery of the divine through reflection. It did not affirm an individual. It showed absorption of the human into the divine. The human person was significant to the degree that it became visible as part of and path toward God, the ultimate "universal." Memory of internal (imprinted, passible) knowledge was sacred memory of sacred history. Augustine's narrated life *had* to end in spiritual interpretation of the start of all life recounted in Genesis. Scriptural memory of the passage from the divine to the material grounded Augustine's telling of human passage from the material back to the divine. This Augustinian trace and bond of human to divine explains why much later John of Salisbury ended his *Metalogicon*, a book defending the trivium of language arts as the ground of education, with lament over the world's decay and call to prayer (addressed to Thomas à Becket) that the reader might be joined with Christ. Just as speech (grammar, rhetoric and logic in this instance) proceeded from the divine so it led, like memory, back to it. Hildegard's *Scivias*, unique as it was, was also a cry for speech to draw humans from a decayed world back to Christ: its very title said as much, *Scito vias Domini*: "Know the ways of the Lord." Its stress on using right words to express the Word of God, show His meaning and remember the angelic praise with which this work also ended, redoubled this aspect. Written between 1141 and 1151, *Scivias* was exactly contemporary with John's *Metalogicon*. The exemplary earlier texts were Augustine's *Confessions* and *De trinitate*, providing bridges to and through medieval experiences that would long remain at the root of early modern ones.

Retrieval of divine memory lay through the word, in speech and language. Augustine was major in passing this memory culture from antiquity to the middle ages, figuring behind Abelard and endless others: "Augustine was to the intellectual history of the middle ages what classical civilization was to its political and cultural history, a creative source, whose recovery and study spurred new directions of thought and controversy down through the Reformation of the sixteenth century" (Ozment 2). An Abelard could find in the saint's writing both the source of his own story of misfortunes and the path from those miseries: "all humans, as long as they are mortals, must needs be also wretched," and only Jesus' mediation could bring them "from mortal misery to blessed immortality" (*City of God* [CG] IX.15: 3.204). Verbeke notes how deeply Stoicism influenced this striving for perfection (*Presence* 48). The sentiment and experience it reflected were a Christianized version of Seneca's "life as a battle."

For Augustine had a like relation to his predecessors, gathering elements from sources direct and indirect, even so crucial a one as that of memory: "key passages of the *Meno* about knowledge as recollection seem to have reached him via Cicero's *Tusculan Disputations* (I.xxiv.

57–58)," writes John Rist (*Augustine* 9). Cicero was, with Seneca, "the principal Latin source for Stoic ethics," who, partly due to Christian writers of the second century and after, became "the most widely read and the most influential ancient Latin prose author during the Middle Ages" (Colish, *Stoic* 1.126, 158). Cicero's mediation of Greek experience kept its force for more than one and a half millennia, an integral part of cultural memory, deeply marked as well by his own work on language and speech. For Augustine, as later for Abelard, Aquinas and a tradition lasting as an urgent cast of experience through Loyola and St. Teresa, memory gave access to presence of the divine in humans, "the right road which [led] to the vision of God and to eternal union with him" (CG X.32: 3.418–20).

This road, joined closely to memory, gave the high middle ages its sense of language's weight, a sense Augustine may have drawn mostly from Stoicism, which bound the human soul via reason and language to divine and earthly surroundings. Claude Imbert tells how Stoics gave the term *logos*

three interconnected meanings: those of divine reason organizing matter, of human reason and of discourse. The qualifier *logike* reminds us that representation gets its discursive state from the human reason that gives it birth, and that this reason is a fragment of divine reason, and so able to penetrate the physical organization of sensible appearances. ("Théorie" 226)

The tight bond between human language, human reason and divine order of the universe echoes what we have been seeing. The assumptions and experiences underlying it presupposed passible relation of being to overarching totality. So it is exact to say, with Long: "*Logos* itself is a term interchangeable in its cosmic sense with destiny" ("Freedom" 178). The totality was made up of imbricated surroundings. Like reason, knowledge, understanding and action, so passible *logos* was reactive: able to penetrate material reality because passibly affected by that rational reality and the divine *logos* ordering it. *Logos* as rational human discourse was productive in the same sense as reason and knowledge, understanding and action: marking the human as passibly reacting between the divine and the material.

In some versions this idea of *logos* was given an almost blunt-minded material existence, as, for example, when Plutarch envisaged Socrates' *daimōn* as a direct giver of interior speech and reason ("On the Sign of Socrates," *Moralia* 588b–589f). He proposed that the voice Socrates said intervened at vital moments to guide him on the path of virtuous reason was to be understood as due to a division in soul's matter: *psuchē* naming what was submerged in body, *daimōn* what remained uncorrupted on its star. Its voice in Socrates' mind was thus that "fragment of divine" reason of which Imbert speaks: *logos* present in human mind. Further, said Plutarch, who was not alone, over several cycles of human life, *psuchē* could be helped by its *daimōn* to be free from need of further incarnation, rejoining divine reason (591e–f, 593d–594a: another version of the same divisions of the soul is in "Concerning the Face Which Appears in the Orb of the Moon" 943a–e). The echo of *Phaedrus* and *Timaeus* was patent, even if such tales literalized the myth in an un-Platonic manner. We may prefer to read these not literally but as allegories of the kind of relation of human to universal *logos* analyzed by Imbert and Long, although Peter Brown argues that these opinions exemplified an experience of a multi-layering of soul typical of late antiquity: a physicalizing of the passibility we have been exploring (*Making* 68–69).

Such views show an experience of human reason and discourse ruled by and from the divine, parts of its overarching totality. The Christianized variant fits divers streams of this experience rising in antiquity, Platonic, Aristotelian or Stoic. At the same time these views stressed the productive role of discourse: *logos* and reason, speech and understanding. John of Salisbury spoke of the Stoics in ways similar to the modern writers just named. He remarked that his contemporaries would do well to adopt a practice of etymologizing, enabling them to reach back to the "truth," acting according to Stoic habit: "who are concerned with the etymology or resemblance of words, for [Latin] *uerum* [true] is from the Greek *heron*, which means firm and stable or certain and clear" (IV.34: 171).

Such a technique, John wrote, enabled the interpreter to work back to the divine origin, even though the Stoics strayed in "believ[ing] matter and idea to be coeternal with God." John denied the belief, agreeing with Bernard of Chartres, "the most accomplished among Platonists of our era," that God preceded and made both matter and idea. For John, analysis of words was a way back to the divine, but no direct one: it had to *pass through* lesser matter and idea to reach it. He separated his view from that of the Stoics on grounds that for them discovery of matter and idea, through the etymon, was concomitantly that of the divine (IV.35: 173–74). John's argument backs Imbert's and Long's analyses. And although he now saw a hierarchical distance in the relations within *logos*, he situated his arguments (as he said) by reference to and close to Stoic theory. In this, he was certainly a reader also of Isidore of Seville, whose *Originum sive etymologiarum libri XX* (*ca.* 600) made just such assumptions about the relation between words, concepts, ideas and the divine; and practiced them. This, too, was the view, distilled and simplified, that Isidore had read in Martin of Braga's call for measured language in a world balanced by the cardinal virtues.

Whatever the hierarchies introduced, that divine and human reason were identified with each other in Stoic and post-Stoic theory is of prime importance. Discourse was seen as self-sufficient and, in a way, "autoreferential"; the fact of that autoproduction was an adequate *presentation* of reality (it, too, being part of possible intellect). The very utterance, *as* utterance, presented the interconnection:

It follows that discourse has no claim to express external reality, save only to the extent that it refers to a representation of internal language, to a thought [itself tied to divine reason]. Properly speaking, there is therefore [in Stoic theory] no semantics to bind the parts of speech to some division or other of physical reality; no discursive truth outside the situation in which the protagonists state or interpret it. (Imbert, "Théorie" 241)

This description of language is strikingly like that description of action we saw in Chapter 3 as causing some moderns such difficulties. Kenny thought this ancient description of action implied "a bizarre metaphysic" in which the properties of actions differed according to whether they were executed or not and, if the former, to whether the action was ongoing or finished. In the same way linguistic meaning and discursive truth hung on time, process and context of utterance.

As Imbert observes, following Erwin Panofsky (and John of Salisbury), this was not Platonic. It did not ascribe the possibility of intellection to Idea but to incessant and indivisible interplay of divine and human reason and discourse. Such a description of language could seem even more bizarre than its counterpart of action, seeming to deny access to fixed meaning or truth. But it cohered fully with the overall experience of humans' possible relation to their surroundings. The description held meaning and truth to depend on the ways in which *this* here-and-now utterance was embedded in the circles in which alone human action and thought made sense — or better, perhaps, on how this utterance incorporated and expressed the embedding of this (these) human(s) in those circles. That was how statements about the real imaged its order: "statements themselves do not exist as material objects, but the bodies [including events] which true statements describe instantiate the causal shaping power of cosmic *logos* which can express itself in *lekta*" (Long, "Representation" 95). Such *lekta* were in some sense contained in John of Salisbury's etymon. And although he opposed Stoic theory to Platonic on grounds that in the latter (which he praised) God preceded and created matter and idea, it may have been just this interplay that made medieval theories of interpretation notably responsive to those aspects of Stoic aesthetic theory relating language and meaning to the multiple circumambients of being.

This theory, says Imbert, started with a "presentation" able to "go proxy for a feeble perception and prepare a commentary suitable for God." This presentation shared aspects of Platonic views. It was (1) a "reflection" presenting "a vision of reality, less rough than that given in sensory contact or simple sense-impression, and containing only the essential differentiating properties (*notae*) of the object." It was (2) like a mirror in composing "fictional presentations," especially focused or synthesized images of the real. It was (3) like an "eye" in linking "rays of external light with the inner movements of the soul: cutting through appearances, it identifies its object under the bright light of revelation." This gave "a paradigm of cognitive activity." The view is similar to Augustine's concept of the intellectual "eye" that emitted a point (*acies*) of vision letting it be informed with remembered intelligibles. In Stoic thinking, the theoretical movement began with wonder, progressed to analysis, "interpretation by a master, which involve[d] a detour into things divine," and ended with initiation into "the truth behind appearances" ("Stoic Logic" 183, 200–201, 204–5). This was essentially John of Salisbury's thinking. It was the order Hildegard pursued in her visionary writings: from wonder of the vision itself, to analytical description, more or less lengthy interpretation and finally the uncovering of relations between the worldly and the divine in praise or prayer. Hildegard insisted on this sequence, specifying its stages by name.

This Stoic theoretical movement anticipated the usual medieval theory of interpretation: from literal ("Jerusalem" naming a city geographically located in Palestine: Stoic *reflection*) to allegorical ("Jerusalem" as the Church Triumphant: Stoic *analysis*) through tropological or moral ("Jerusalem" as the human soul: Stoic *interpretation*) to anagogical ("Jerusalem" as divine union in Paradise: Stoic *initiation*). From spiritual allegorical readings of Scripture, which Augustine's *On Christian Doctrine* exemplified, to interpretations of secular poetry popularized by Boccaccio (see *Boccaccio on Poetry*), the theory was standard. Dante explained:

In order to make this manner of treatment clear, it can be applied to the following verses: "When Israel went out of Egypt, the house of Jacob from a barbarous people, Judea was made his sanctuary, Israel his dominion." Now if we look at the letter alone, what is signified to us is the departure of the sons of Israel from Egypt during the time of Moses; if at the allegory, what is signified to us is our redemption through Christ; if at the moral sense, what is signified to us is the conversion of the soul from the sorrow and misery of sin to the state of grace; if at the anagogical, what is signified to us is the departure of the sanctified soul from bondage to the corruption of this world into the freedom of eternal glory. ("The Letter to Can Grande," Dante 99)

A more celebrated and much longer exposition is in the *Convivio* (112–14). A remarkable example of anagogical Jerusalem was Hildegard's hymn, "O Ierusalem," praising the union of St. Rupert (and all believers) with Christ (*Symphonia* 192–94: Hymn 49).

This interpretive passage embraced several circles of personal circumstance. And, despite what some assert to be the "individualistic" root effect of vernaculars, Dante urged their use in the "Letter to Can Grande" and elsewhere the better to know both multiple circumstance and this ascending path of the *vita beata*—or *nuova*. For, concurrently, this echoed the good life's path as traced in Augustine and an *imitatio Christi* like that of Abelard. This sense of writing and speech as forging a road to the divine was to subsist in Petrarch and beyond. Its remnant lived on, hollowed-out perhaps, into writings like Erasmus' *Adagia* or Montaigne's *Essais*, although *writing*'s divine source and goal (if not *life*'s) had by then much dropped away. Dante's and others' hermeneutics was a Christianized version of Stoic theory. In the *De lingua latina*, a text heavily influenced by Stoic linguistic theory, Varro had written:

> Now I shall set forth the origins of the individual words, of which there are four levels of explanation. The lowest is that to which even the common folk has come. . . . The second is that to which old-time grammar has mounted, which shows how the poet has made each word which he has fashioned and derived. . . .
> The third level is that to which philosophy ascended, and on arrival began to reveal the nature of those words which are in common use. . . . The fourth is where the sanctuary is, and the mysteries of the high priest. (V.7–8: 1.9)

Although an exiguous part of Varro's voluminous writings survive, Augustine was able fully to use his renowned *Antiquitates rerum divinarum* in the *City of God*, describing and analyzing the sixteen books of its second part (CG VI.2–12, VII.1–28) and glancing at the twenty-five books of its first, the *Antiquitates rerum humanarum*. Varro was a towering figure. His "*Disciplinarum libri IX*," says Martin Irvine, "which began with a now lost *De grammatica*, was the most influential encyclopedia in the Roman world" (51). Its disciplines modulated into the medieval trivium and quadrivium, becoming authoritative via Boethius and Isidore. There is every reason to think that the *De grammatica* expanded the brief comments just quoted from the *De lingua latina*. Augustine said that Varro believed that there was one god only: the soul governing the universe by motion and reason (CG IV.31). He had explained that human soul and body were not like a horseman riding a horse or a drink contained in a cup but a unit. A person's highest good thus joined the material, social and universal. The virtuous life enabled this. Augustine added that Varro drew these views from "his and Cicero's teacher," Antiochus, a philosopher upholding the Platonism of the Old Academy but who, according to Cicero, drew more from the Stoics (CG XIX.3). Certainly, as Augustine presented them, Varro's beliefs were principally Stoic. So it matters that Augustine used them so massively.

For the bishop of Hippo, like his predecessors (and successors), words were commemorative. Speaking was reminding, understanding was remembering: "Regarding, however, all those things which we understand, it is not a speaker who utters sounds exteriorly whom we consult, but it is truth that resides within, over the mind itself" (De magistro 177). The concepts behind this were those of the Aristotelian relation between passible and impassible mind, the one born from and dependent on the other, and of the Platonic relation between embodied and universal soul. Words reminded us of truths present in the universal and eternal, forgotten by the perishable and passible. In Augustine's Christian version, words let one rediscover in truth "[Him] who is said to dwell in the inner man, He it is who teaches—Christ—that is, the unchangeable Power of God and everlasting Wisdom" (177). Christ, like soul itself, mediated between realities. So Augustine added that a person was taught not by mere words "but by the realities themselves made manifest in him by God revealing them to his inner selfe" (179). Words were arbitrary (ad placitum), in having no inherent tie to specific res, but that did not affect their commemorative action: res, for Latin and later exegetes of language, meaning anything non-linguistic which words denoted, connoted or referred to. Teachers (all speakers) drew their pupils (all listeners) to gaze "attentively at that interior truth" ever potentially able to be "unveiled" through memory (185). This unveiling was enabled in master and pupil by divine illumination activating memory, reconnecting passible with impassible mind.

While this was far from a (non-theological) modern order of thought, it was close to elements of Stoic thinking as well as to Plato and aspects of Aristotle. Understanding Augustine's phrases in this connection, like ad placitum and voluntas significare, needs care. Words were learned by humans, not given. They were arbitrary in not inhering in the thing signified. But their meaning was not arbitrarily determined by humans. They were pointers to an inner truth set in humans by the divine: "Although I can lift my finger to point something out, I cannot supply the vision by means of which either this gesture or what it indicates can be seen" (On Christian 4). Augustine was speaking here of using words to interpret Scripture, so one hesitates to recall Oedipus' cry to Apollo at the end of Oedipus tyrannus, but its sentiment more than flickers behind this. Voluntas raised the finger, something else was needed to see it and its object: understanding granted by the impassible divine and reason educated by the same source to ground *voluntas*, whose meaning was clearly akin to that of *hekousia*. Marcia Colish observes that for Augustine

words may represent really existing things truly, if partially, and . . . they function either commemoratively or indicatively in the subject's mind, depending on his previous relationship to the object. Although seen as an epistemological necessity, verbal signs are never held to be cognitive in the first instance. They must be energized by the action of God in the mind of the knower in order for them to conduce to the knowledge of their significata. (*Mirror* 84)

Words depended on objects for their meaning not the reverse: being preceded knowing. But the object (*res*) was an "inner" object imprinted on mind and retrievable via memory activated by the verbal sign. In this sense, the sign, Augustine wrote in the *De magistro*, was learned through the "object" not the object through the sign (cf. Panaccio, "Métaphysique"). Again we see the familiar passible relationship.

This was how the child learned from adults, as told at the start of the *Confessions*. The child learned names of objects by combining in its memory adults' physical motions, objects toward which they gestured and names they related to these objects. But everything the child so learned depended on God's grace of mind (*mens*) and memory (*memoria*). And if the child associated names and objects by capacities granted by God, adults communicated them only by similarly implanted capacities to relate names and objects in a slowly recovered memory. Signs were learned from objects, but the connections needed for that to happen preceded their human use. To use language was to recover knowledge of connections and contents that birth had overwhelmed in "the darkness of forgetfulness" (*Confessions* I.7–8). These very connections were divine seeds of memory in the soul, whose meaning was released by language. From this opening, the *Confessions* are a long *speaking* or *telling* of the path back to God, an effort to find *right logos*: "the right path leading to sight of God and eternal union with him" (CG X.32: 3.418–20). Only by God's grace did child's memory and adult's actions reconnecting language to objects enable the spiritual path to be engaged.

Words were not to be confused with things, for then they would be immediately cognitive. But clearly some natural relationship enabled the combination of verbal signs and divine action to evoke true knowledge of the object: "Augustine also follows the Stoics in arguing that the natural significance of words provides a basis for the science of etymology" (Colish, "Stoic Theory" 25–26). The natural significance was that of human and divine *logos in mente*. Anselm's discussion of "*grammaticus*" in his *De grammatico*, seven centuries later, still shared much with all this. This relation and all signification involved a natural tie between individual words and their "objective significata." The signified might be a real or a conceptual *res*, but either was considered an "entity identifiable outside any relation and susceptible of being designated by its name, in such a way that not only [was] every word a name, but every name [was] the proper name of something in the mind," Claude Panaccio writes of Augustine's conception of naming ("Métaphysique" 271; for Augustine on language, cf. Rist, *Augustine* 23–40 and Stock, *Augustine*). Anselm's ontological argument depended on the assumption that such natural tie and properness both supposed and were guaranteed by the priority of universals.

Augustine's and others' distinction between natural and conventional signification is entirely misunderstood if we try to interpret it in terms of modern western theories. In Augustine the distinction depended on the "intentional or unintentional character" of signs:

His natural signs are unintentional. A fire signifies its presence unintentionally through the smoke it produces; a man signifies his feelings unintentionally through his facial expression. These signs do indeed signify physical and psychological realities, but they do so involuntarily. Augustine's conventional signs also correspond truly with the things they signify. But they are signs used deliberately by animate or intelligent beings to express their ideas, intentions, and feelings to other beings. (Colish, "Stoic Theory" 29)

They were used "deliberately" because God set in mind the powers, habits and impetus so to use them.

The concepts of voluntary and involuntary involved here were directly in the tradition summed up at the end of the last chapter via Alexander and Nemesius. They named a particular way in which humans experienced their being of the substance, *ousia*, of the universe. The role of mind and right reason was to draw passible soul back toward impassible soul. The child's accession to language and memory was a first step to defeating forgetfulness and to reunion with God. In this regard, the bishop took a word from Cicero to name the mix of body and soul, doing so in a letter of 411 A.D. and again in the *De trinitate* (written 404–420s): "The 'mixture'," Rist writes, was "now, mysteriously, a *persona*." Augustine paired the *persona* which was "the union of body and soul with the *persona* which [was] the union in Christ of God and man. The word *persona* seems expressly chosen to indicate a union of substances." The union made "one *persona*" (*Augustine* 100: *Letter* 137 and *De trinitate* XII.12.18). For Augustine, person was "aliquid singulare atque individuum [something singular and individual]." "One person" was an "I" using "memory, understanding, and love" to undertake and achieve its path back to the divine (*On the Holy Trinity* [HT] VII.6.11: 112;

XV.22.42: 221). Gurevich finds such a view of the meaning and experience of *persona* fundamental still in Aquinas and even in Cusa in the fifteenth century (*Origins* 96–97).

Augustine's usage was clearly linked to the sense of *persona* woven in its surroundings found in Cicero and more materially and physiologically in Galen, involving four levels of engagement with the world. The first was analogous to Augustine's *persona* here, naming humanity's bond via rational soul to its formative *ousia*. It partly subsumed Cicero's second *persona*, the particularized human, but that and the social third and fourth *personae* had their real equivalents in people's activities in the earthly city. In Galen the third involved sexual differences between women and men. This also had its place in Augustine's thinking: at the level of life in the world, not at that of the first *persona*'s union of human and universal substances nor at that of the second, marked by the varieties of powers, strengths, talents and other capacities of humans *qua* humans. The issue of sexuality will return. Suffice it for now to say that for Augustine the first *persona* was core, where right reason ruled according to divine order. Here, women and men were equally in God's image. It was in this sense that Seneca had opened the *De providentia* by explaining that humans shared the gods' virtues: *logos* (reason and speech), being and fortune, wisdom and life. What alone they did not share was time. Augustine also took this up, to bind together these divers concepts of *logos* and will, material and social, soul and the divine.

In Book 11 of the *Confessions*, he moved the reader from worldly dealings to those of eternity. The soul had traced its history through earthly temptations and grasped the possibility of union with the divine. Now it sought to know the actual paths and nature of such union. Embodied life was a long wandering from God, when selfe was all too present: "quamdiu peregrinor abs te, mihi sum praesentior quam tibi [as long as I am wandering without/away from you, I am more present to me than to you]" (*Confessions* X.5: 2.84). Such *presence* to whatever one was as living in the world was *absence* from God. It was actuality of what Augustine named "evil," which grew the further one wandered from God. In this state, whoever one was experienced a real fragmentation, division from one's soul: "and behold, you were within and I outside [*intus eras et ego foris*], and there I sought you, and, unlovely, rushed on those lovely things you had made" (X.27: 2.146). "Et ubi ego eram," he had cried earlier, "quando te quaerebam? et tu eras ante me, ego autem et a me discesseram nec me inveniebam: quanto minus te!" "Where was I when I sought after you? You were there before me, but I was divided from me and did not find me; much less you!" (V.2: 1.210). The verb *discedere* marked the force of the experience of fragmentation. It meant to be divided, dispersed, away from, split up. For soul to know or "be present" to itself required that the process be reversed: "I shall seek you that my soul may live. For my body lives by my soul, and my soul lives by you" (X.20: 2.128). The soul's objective had to be that of being joined "to you with all of me," when: "my life shall be alive wholly filled with you" (X.128: 2.146).

Nearing a sense of its own first state, soul needed to find an idea of God apart from the physical materiality of the created world, always a distraction for embodied creatures living in and surrounded by it. Soul had to know God as He was beyond His creation, "in the beginning": hence the meditation on this opening phrase of Genesis that followed the summation of Augustine's converted state in the world in Book 10. Up to now the *Confessions* had traced soul's movement in created time back toward the eternity whence it came, reversing the order of Creation itself. Augustine was showing not just that a single soul was an image of others or, rather, embodied presence of divine soul, but that it was image and sign of Creation itself. The created time and history of one human soul iterated those of all human souls in their relation to eternity: "This is so for the whole life of a human, of which all human actions are parts, this is so for the whole history of the human race, of which all the lives of humans are parts" (XI.28: 2.278). However debated Augustine's general account of time may be (Rist, *Augustine* 73–76), he clearly saw the soul as participating in two times: God's eternity and worldly history. It participated as well in two places, we learn in Book 12: the heaven and earth whose separation was also made at Creation. Book 12 gave the topological counterpart of the chronological analysis.

Creation's six days peaked in that of humans, setting them in historical time and material place, soul "falling" into them: "defluxit angelus, defluxit anima hominis"—the angel fell, human soul fell. So they "showed in what utter darkness would have been the abyss of the whole spiritual creation had God not said: Let there be light" (XIII.8: 2.388). This light imaged final reunion, as elsewhere in Augustine it did Christ and redemption from earthly temptation. So Creation also symbolized possibility of soul's rational rule over bodily passions, again beginning a return to the divine (XIII.34). Creation's last day figured that eternity, rest and changelessness: "quietem ex tempore"—rest out of time. Creation was the macrocosmic image of the microcosmic progress of soul (XIII.37–38: 2.472–74). Its analysis climaxed Augustine's story of the soul, showing how it now dwelt in time and the world—seeing "through a glass darkly," in a favorite Pauline phrase—but would pass back through Creation to live in eternity and know God "face to face," as the Greeks knew one another, by looking at outer presence: here the presences facing one another were not material embodiments but those of soul to Soul (as Cicero envisaged soul speaking to soul, or as Augustine's teacher and pupil shared "interior truth").

Such was the ultimate aim of embodied soul, dwelling in time but come from the eternal. The *Confessions* showed selfe's rediscovery of the divine via memory, reflection and the writing of human reason, *logos* (cf. Stock, *After* 103–4). They showed, Brian Stock observes, an effort to ascend toward God that was about "spiritual interdependencies," and in no sense "about an individual self" (*Augustine* 18). They did not affirm an individual but showed the way for person to be absorbed into the divine: "I would therefore not be, my God," Augustine thus began his *Confessions*, "I would not be at all, unless you were in me [*Non ergo essem, deus meus, non omnino essem, nisi esses in me*]. Or, rather, would I not be, unless I were in you [*An potius non essem, nisi essem in te*], from whom, through whom and in whom are all things?" (I.ii: 1.4). This was written *after* the spiritual journey Augustine was about to tell. But the string of subjunctives and interrogative caught the uncertainties embodied life set in the sense of being, readying reader and writer for the hard traveling away from the vicissitudes of mortal existence through speaking and writing to the certainties of divine *Logos*. Until these God-given gifts could reach that end doubt and fear of purgatory prevailed: "shall I call it dying life or living death?" (I.vi: 1.12/13).

The human and social certainly mattered, for the soul lived in the world by divine authority—a constant theme of the *City of God*'s opposition between "Rome" and "Jerusalem." But it mattered fully to the degree that it was known as part of and path toward God. Platonic and Aristotelian memory of internal ("imprinted") knowledge had become this sacred memory of sacred history, and to fall away from it was the absence of forgetfulness, absence from the Good that was evil, that was "to withdraw further from you, loving my ways and not yours, loving my runaway freedom" (III.3: 1.106). Evil was to fragment being by moving from memory of the divine to "all those things that disagree with one another but agree with the lower part of things that we call earth" (VII.13: 1.378). It was "a perversity of the will which is turned away from you, God, the supreme substance [*substantia* = *ousia*], and toward lower things, casting away its inward things and swelling for outward ones" (VII.16: 1.382).

So a first step to knowing one's fallen state was to know the inner source of this worldliness, presence of *will* and its abuse: "And when therefore I did either will or nill anything, I was most sure of it that no other than I did will or nill: and there was the cause of my sin" (VII.3: 1.342). Evil, he said in *The City of God*, was not an "efficiency" but a "deficiency": "so no one should look for an efficient cause of evil will [*malae voluntatis*], for [the cause] is not efficient but deficient, just as [evil will] is not an effect but a defect" (CG XII.7: 4.32). It was will's general "falling away [*defectus*] from the work of God to its own works, rather than any one deed" (XIV.11: 4.568).

Evil was "pure" passibility, passibility where no *prohairesis* had been trained to give reasons. This was the idea of evil advanced by the Stoic Cleanthes in the *Hymn to Zeus*. The deeds consequent on will's falling away, "were evil [*mala*] because they followed it, and did not follow God, so that will itself was like the evil tree [*arbor mala*] bearer of evil fruits [*fructuum malorum*] of those deeds, or man himself was the tree, to the extent of his evil will [*malae voluntatis*]" (CG XIV.11: 4.324). The play on *malum*, apple (plural: *mala*), source of the Fall by Satan's persuasion, broadens the point. So elsewhere Augustine said: "when man lives according to man and not according to God, he is like the devil" (CG XIV.4: 4.274). What was called the "devil" was utter absence, total forgetfulness of soul's origins. The *Confessions* could well be taken as that education of the faculty of *prohairesis* essential to virtuous life. In Christian terms, ultimate virtue was recovery of the soul's union with the divine. This was achieved only by the Creator's will guiding passible human will, since, alone, it *always* tended away from God toward the world. That was why the witness of Augustine's life that is the *Confessions* had to end in the spiritual exegesis of the beginning of all life as told in Genesis, performing the road back across Creation to full jointure with the divine, reestablishment of *anima* in the impassible.

Language was tied in essential ways to the soul's rational faculties. John of Salisbury later said of Augustine's "dialectic" that it did not matter whether its name stressed the act of speaking or fact of verbal meaning: "since to examine the force of speech or truth and sense of what is said is the same, or nearly the same. A word's force is its sense. If deprived of this, a word is empty, useless and, so to say, dead, just as body is ripened into life by soul [*in uitam uegetatur ab anima*], so the sense of a word helps it to a kind of life" (II.4: 61). Augustine and later medieval thinkers shared Platonic, Aristotelian and Stoic experience of the impartible bond between human language and reason, political, social and ethical life, and the divine order of the universe.

Anima was a kind of mediating prism between the human and its many surroundings, refractor of divine and earthly *personae*. It was where one set of relations modulated into others. That was no doubt why *anima* was used ever more indifferently to mean both a person's spiritual being ("soul") and its rational ("mind"). Awareness of being a human person was inseparable from a sense of participation in the divine. God, said Augustine with so many others, dwelt in the soul and therefore discovery of what and who one was was the necessary and only "path to God" (Morris 65–66). We have seen marks of this process in some later writers and a trace of the mediatory *anima* in John of Salisbury. In passible being lay the imprint of impassible divine intellect. That was why Augustine had "no term for the elusive notion of the self, frequently designating it by pronouns (*se, ipse*) or by *mens, animus, anima*, or *spiritus*." But he was not "inconsistent" in writing of anything approaching such a notion (Stock, *Augustine* 260). These terms named different relations of passible being to its different surroundings. Augustine, again, was clearest on the role played by *anima* here.

In the *Confessions* he related how he gradually discovered this right path to God, remarking that he came across certain Platonic writings which, though pagan, were able to give him a true idea of the relation between *anima* and God: "for the human *anima*, though it bears witness to light, yet is not light itself, but the word, *deus ipse*, is the true light that lights every human who comes into this world" (VII.9: 1.366). The soul bore witness to the light by figuring in itself a form of the Trinity: in its earliest version offered as a trinity of being, knowing and willing. Being was in matter, knowing was in mind (above all in memory), willing was a potentially divine faculty (guiding one toward presence in God). The first could be called "life" (*vita*), the second "mind" (*mens*), the third "essence" (*essentia* = *ousia*): three that were inseparably one in the human person (XIII.11: 2.394; on memory see X.8: 2.92–98). Before achieving that unity, living with will divided from the other faculties, one dwelt in the evil or temptation of evil told in the *Confessions'* first nine books. The journey away from that was also part of the spiritual adventure they recounted. This first analysis of the triad gave Augustine a way to explore the soul's relation to the divine for which the central text was the *De trinitate*.

There, Augustine taught that memory, understanding and will (differently placed in this new accounting) were three faculties of *anima*, itself the image of God, as revelation taught. This relation between the soul and its faculties adopted a definition of God, widespread in Augustine's time, to which he constantly referred as "mia ousia, treis hupostaseis." This virtually untranslatable definition (one universal substance, three actual existents), again highlighting the word *ousia* whose difficulty we have so often seen, was rendered by Augustine as "a trinity of persons mutually interrelated, and a unity of equal essence" (HT IX.1.1: 125). He recast the *Confessions'* essence, mind and life as memory, understanding and will (running physiologically from the back to the front of the head). Using these, the second eight books of the *De trinitate* set out to show how human *anima* was a mediation to the divine. To explain this Trinity, Augustine began by going through will (passions) to reason, faith and hope of redemption. It was the interior nature of this tying of *anima* to the divine that made Ephraem Hendrikx view the *De trinitate* as "the most personal of all Augustine's works"; for if the bishop was introducing "us at once to the mystery of God's inner life [*vie intime*]," he was concomitantly introducing "the inner life of his own soul": the two were inextricably bound (*La trinité* 15.10, 12).

The *De trinitate* is an exemplary exploration of the Christian setting of the human in its divine circle. It had immense influence—perhaps the most read of Augustine's works throughout the middle ages. Hendrikx notes that more than 230 manuscripts of the Latin text still exist, most dating from the twelfth to the fourteenth century. Twenty manuscripts of an early fourteenth-century Greek translation are extant. Besides this evidence of wide popularity during the birth and heyday of Thomism, the work at once originated and typified scholasticism, in its dialectical interrogation of the texts in its search for true knowledge of God, its logical and "psychological" interpretation of them and its submission of both activities to the necessity of faith (Hendrikx, *La trinité* 14–17).

In the second half of this text (chiefly books IX, X and XIV), Augustine offered other triads seeking to show in what way the human soul was image and mediation of God. The first was *mens, notitia, amor*: mind or spirit, knowledge, love (or possibly will or desire). This triad, he said, was an incomplete analogy with the Trinity because Father, Son and Holy Spirit were three equal "substances" (*hupostaseis*) of one "essence" (*ousia*) whereas *mens* was substance (*anima*), *notitia* and *amor* its acts. The second triad was more satisfactory: *memoria* (*sui*), *intelligentia, voluntas*. Here some intuitive memory of one's real nature (what the *Confessions* spoke of forgetting) was both foundation of and equal to understanding and will, and the three were united in forming *anima*.

The third and last analogy and mark of divine presence in the soul was the triad *memoria* (*Dei*), *intelligentia* (*Dei*), *amor* (*in Deum*). Properly speaking this was no longer just an analogy. This was the image of the soul that had come to know God, to know its being as manifestation of and participation in the divine. Awareness of one's own nature, one's own knowledge and one's own will or desire or love had become awareness of God, knowledge of God and love of God. As elsewhere, Augustine practiced what he preached: search for truth, for full knowledge of "one's own" being, led to the divine. Mind given to itself and its own "willfulness"—the very definition of *absence* from God—could only fall into error, falsehood and diabolical subversion, as the *De trinitate* also continually insisted.

A person's final grasp of its being was the unveiling of God's image in the soul. "Know thy selfe" urged toward that particular understanding.

In life there could be no more than a continuous passage *toward* that goal, for the last unveiling could only be achieved by the soul's end in God. The final prayer of the *De trinitate* still named a distance that only death could overcome, even as it named continuation of the process to union through mediation, through *anima*:

And when the last day of life shall have found any one holding fast faith in the Mediator in such progress and growth as this, he will be welcomed by the holy angels, to be led to God, whom he has worshipped, and to be made perfect by Him; and so he will receive in the end of the world an incorruptible body, in order not to punishment but to glory. For the likeness of God will then be perfected in this image, when the sight of God shall be perfected. And of this the Apostle Paul speaks: "Now we see through a glass, in an enigma, but then face to face." (HT XIV.17.23: 196)

The *Divina commedia* was the exemplary medieval "interpretation" of that Augustinian process. But echoing it were innumerable meditational texts, from Pseudo-Dionysius to Bonaventure to Hildegard's visionary path from Creation to Redemption and Salvation in *Scivias*.

As such, embodied soul could not achieve the path to the eternal. But that was just one, if for Augustine the highest, of many surroundings. Unsurprisingly, his *voluntas* echoed Greek experiences of acting *hekōn*, marking a person's fit in mutually mediating circles. Ernest Barker describes Augustine's "concentric circles" of human society: the *domus, civitas, orbis terrae* (the earth and humanity) and *mundus* (God's whole universe) (240). Embodied *anima* dwelt in another time, indeed, in other *times*: worldly history was plural. It dwelt, too, in other places. These times and places in turn were made of multiple material actualities, societies and human realities. Weber shows many cases of early Christian and Byzantine art complexly weaving imbricated circles, showing, for example, a haloed Christ sitting or standing embedded in the aureola of a circled or multi-circled firmament, reminiscent of designs of zodiac and planets, often set in overlapping physical and spiritual circles (*Symbolik*). In the world, soul had to work to be adapted wisely, virtuously and decorously to these endlessly multiple surroundings.

From late antiquity to the middle ages the final (Christian) goal of this adaptation was soul's union with the divine. Collinet-Guérin agrees with most scholars that from the fourth and fifth centuries A.D., the nimbus was iconographic "sign of a nature superior to the human" (333–34): giving pictorial confirmation to a new hierarchy of surroundings we begin to see in writers from Augustine to John of Salisbury. Despite this, while a sense of the unworldly as *anima*'s finality was always present, it was one circle of many. The others still all had their virtues, wisdoms, decorums and beauties. A person's relation to them also meant using the soul's faculties to train intentions and dispositions to react "well" in the world. To know the soul's functions, to reason, speak and act rightly, were as essential to those living in the earthly city as to those hoping successfully to fulfill their pilgrimage back to the city of God. That is why Augustine began the *Confessions* by explaining how the child learned reason and language from adults, how the prohairetic faculty was trained from infancy for "the violently stormy fellowship [*procellosam societatem*] of human life" (I.8: 1.26): intimations again of Seneca's "battle."

Language, spoken and written, had always been for the Greeks and Latins chief mediator of the sociability and reason central to their experiences of the human. This circle, too, Augustine took over. For if the divine was the end of the soul's peregrination on earth, the pilgrimage was nonetheless in the world: hence the two cities. But each had its specific "peace": "There is actually one city of humans wanting [*volentium*] to live following the flesh, another following the spirit, each in their own kind of peace and, when they get what they desire, living in their own kind of peace" (CG XIV.1: 4.260/61). Just as the person could fall from the path of rectitude, so could society as a whole: the worldly city all too easily, for, "in the one, love of God prevails, in the other love of selfe [*amor sui*]" (XIV.13: 4.340). This could only lead to the same evil as that of separated will: "two loves thus made two cities, love of selfe [*amor sui*] reaching to contempt of God made the earthly, love of God reaching to contempt of selfe [*ad contemptum sui*] made the heavenly" (XIV.28: 4.404).

Augustine in no way saw the earthly city as inevitably or wholly evil. Besides the evil city there was an earthly city made up of those who, working back to the divine, composed a city of the world (*saeculi*) which, "as far as humankind was concerned," was as a *peregrina*, alien (CG XVIII.1: 5.362). Yet another city existed that was not just a "pilgrim in the world," but satisfied "in its temporal peace and happiness" (CG XV.17: 4.510). This city dwelt by God's law (*logos?*), adapting virtuous persons and the good city to particular worldly conditions, as Augustine said he had learned: "Nor did I know true inward justice, which judges not according to custom but to the most rightful law of God almighty, by which mores of places and times are shaped [*formarentur*] for places and times, although [that law] is everywhere and always one and not different in the ones or the others" (*Confessions* III.7: 1.122). There could, then, be a well-ordered, virtuous and peaceful worldly city, differing from the heavenly city not as evil from good, but as temporal prudence from holy wisdom, both with their right place and behavior: "All use of temporal things in the earthly city is related to the enjoyment of earthly peace, but in the celestial city it is related to the enjoyment of eternal peace" (CG XIX.14: 6.180).

This context offers the best understanding of Augustine's rather few comments about women and gender. With his contemporaries, he held women physically weaker than and legally subordinate to men in the social world (*saeculum*). He was clear that in mind, soul and their relation to body and all surroundings save the social, women did not differ from men. As humans in respect of the divine city of God, women and men were equal. The rational mind of both was in God's image. This is how one should read Augustine's notorious gloss on Genesis 1 and God's creation of man and woman: "male and female created He them." He interpreted: "that human nature itself, which is complete in both sexes, was made in the image of God; and does not separate the woman from the image of God which it signifies." Woman and man together were the image of God, "but when she is referred separately to her quality of *help-meet*, which regards the woman herself alone, then she is not the image of God; but as regards the man alone, he is the image of God as fully and completely as when the woman too is joined with him in one" (HT XII.vii. 158b–159a). One had to distinguish between women and men in relation to the divine world and women and men in relation to the fallen temporal world. In one women were "fellow-heirs of grace," in the other they were subject "to the government of temporal things" which their bodies figured (XII.vii.160a).

At the level of Cicero's first *persona*, that of being human in relation both to nature and to the divine, men and women were the same. So they were at the level of Cicero's second *persona* (humans differing in talents and abilities) although matters were less clear since worldly life began to come into play. There was no ambiguity as to the third *persona*: here differences between women and men joined various social and legal abilities and disabilities (distinguished from human equalities as persons). Clark observes that women's "bodily veiling" represented "the part of the mind which is directed to temporal things." Since women also had rational minds, they could "of course . . . contemplate eternal truths just as men" could (123). This was also what Augustine wrote in the *Confessions*:

Just as in the human soul there is one part which rules by making decisions and another which is made subject that it may obey, so in bodily relation to man was made woman, who has the same nature [*parem naturam*] as to mind's rational intelligence but in sex of body is subject to the male sex, just as impulse for action is subject to deriving from mental reason its skill in acting rightly. (XIII.32: 2.464)

Like others, Augustine distinguished social disabilities and oppressions from the core nature of passible who-ness. That was not gendered.

Whatever the disabling implications of sexual difference in the sociolegal and political world nowhere did Augustine imply women to be defective men. As Rist notes: "sexual differentiation [was] part of human nature as originally planned by God—so that the problems facing women in recovering their personal identity and wholeness [were] morally and spiritually identical to those facing men" (*Augustine* 115–21, here 117: referring to CG XXII.17). As far as mind, soul and their powers were concerned, sexual difference did not apply: mind was neither female nor male. Clark argues that this was a general view among most early writers: "The Christian consensus, too, was that the soul was not sexed. Christians believed that God created human beings in God's own image—and God is not limited by human categories, including the categories of male and female." Among those asserting this view, she names Basil of Caesarea, Gregory Nazianzen and Gregory of Nyssa (121).

Again, what made the issue so volatile and controversial was conflict between inequities of sociopolitical exploitation and wider equalities of personhood itself. Certainly, vehement claims later opposed this Augustinian strain. Some of the harshest were in the Church's own law code. In Gratian's *Decretals*, the Church's *Corpus iuris canonici*, a series of glosses directly contradicted Augustine: man, said one, was "imago et gloria Dei," image and glory of God, woman was neither: "non est gloria aut imago Dei" (C.33, q.5, c.13: vol.1. pt.2:). An equally bald assertion preceded it: "the natural order among humans is that women should serve men" (C.33, q.5, c.12). For these reasons, "the law decreed that women be subject to men and wives be almost as servants" (C.33, q.5, c.14). By twelfth century the Church had become a male bastion as far as its hierarchies and internal rule were concerned.

Canon Law was institutionally specific and we must be wary of generalizing such views. They directly opposed, for example, the secular ones of the *Corpus iuris civilis*. They were not yet dominant even in the later church. As to mind, writes Barbara Newman, "most twelfth-century theologians, however, held to the equality of the senses in this regard." Since Augustine, "virtually all Western writers" set "the locus of the image [of God] in the rational mind" (*Sister* 91, 92–93). Among other examples, she quotes Rupert of Deutz "stat[ing] plainly that 'God made woman no less than man to his own image.'" The line was actually Rupert's final summation of his longer argument supporting this contention (*In Genesim* II.6–7: 189–91). Although the matter was continuously debated, Augustine's view seems to have long prevailed: with regard to divine surroundings, universal nature, the powers of the soul and human being *per se*, women and men were no different. In the fallen worldly city, where all wandered exiled and homeless in suffering, other kinds of exclusion acted. This was so whether in evil Babylon or better Rome. However much the temporal prudence of the well-ordered, virtuous and peaceful worldly city managed to engage the Word of God it could yet only ever be through a glass darkly, demanding the inequalities of constraining social obligations and surroundings.

God's Word, *logos* or *lex*, was the animating expression of all society. So the heavenly city embodying that law was under any circumstance incomparably above even the finest earthly one—of a quite other order. Indeed, facts on the ground made Augustine gradually less assured of the earthly city's meager achievement. The sack of Rome by Alaric's Goths in 410 and growing threat from Spain of Genseric's Vandals to his own Hippo Regius, culminating in the city's siege in 430, during which he died, did not foster a strong sense of secular security. The ineluctable condition of the earthly city was instability and unsafety, perhaps *because* it was God-created to give impetus to search for higher truths. In that search, as Augustine used the circumstance and guidance of his own mother Monnica to show in the *Confessions*, women and men shared "parem naturam." Too, one learned language and started to recover lost memory from adults of both sexes.

Words were the communicative cement of God-given society, at its best the place of a first step on the pilgrim's path back to fulfillment of human nature. Language came from the naming of things, an activity produced and enabled by the divine. So the arts of language had two goals. The first, said Hugh of St. Victor in the 1130s, was to recall the divine source of human *logos*, to "restore within us the divine likeness, a likeness which to us is a form but to God is his nature. The more we are conformed to the divine nature, the more do we possess Wisdom, for then there begins to shine forth again in us what has forever existed in the divine Idea or Pattern, coming and going in us but standing changeless in God" (II.1: 61). The second goal was to bring humans to fulfill their social and material being. Hugh showed how the soul's rational power made use of the nutritive and sensitive powers to bind together the material, human and divine, words operating to order the mind and realize community:

But the third power of the soul appropriates the prior nutritional and sense-perceiving powers, using them, so to speak, as its domestics and servants. It is rooted entirely in reason, and it exercises itself either in the most unfaltering grasp of things present, or in the understanding of things absent, or in the investigation of things unknown. This power belongs to humankind alone. It not only takes in sense impressions and images which are perfect and well founded, but, by a complete act of the understanding, it explains and confirms what imagination has only suggested. And, as has been said, this divine nature is not content with the knowledge of those things alone which it perceives spread before its senses, but, in addition, it is able to provide even for things removed from it names which imagination has conceived from the sensible world, and it makes known, by arrangements of words, what it has grasped by reason of its understanding. (I.3: 49–50)

John of Salisbury also echoed Augustine in arguing that while word-use was *ad placitum*, it obeyed nature—human "choice" guided by mind's possible relation to God and sense impressions: "For in execution of the purpose of divine dispensation and to establish verbal intercourse among people, humanity first gave names to those things which lay before it, formed by the hand of nature" (I.14: 33). Anyone who attacked this animating and mediating use of language accepted immense responsibility:

he subverts all liberal studies, assails the entire structure of all philosophy, tears apart the bond of human society and leaves no place for social love and mutual exchange of services. Deprived of the gift of speech humans would grow brutish and the very cities would seem more like cattlepens than a community of people joined by a certain bond so as to live by the aforementioned law in sharing of services and friendly mutual exchange. (I.1: 13–14)

That was why, Aquinas said, differences of language made it hard for peoples to live together. For

if a human was by nature a solitary animal the passions of the soul by which it was conformed to things so as to have knowledge of them would be sufficient for it; but since it is by nature a political and social animal it was necessary that its conceptions be made known to others. This people do through vocal sounds. Therefore there had to be significant vocal sounds in order that humans might live together. Whence those who speak different languages find it difficult to live together in social unity. (*Commentary*, Aristotle, *On Interpretation* 24)

That could be overcome. But all agreed that to misuse language was to subvert humanity in its being as a social animal, and to blaspheme, since society, language and the soul they expressed were divinely instituted. Without language, asked John, how could any *contractus* be properly concluded or any instruction given "in faith or right mores [*fidei aut morum*]" (I.1: 14). Correct language use united souls not just in Augustinian mediation with the divine but with one another in the virtuous earthly city. Particular speech might be tied to particular time and place, but it was bound by the right meaning of words as guaranteed by the divine Word. For what let one talk of "right meaning" and of "misuse" of language? How could one judge them? Here, too, Augustine gave the standard.

The judgment had two elements. First, words were given by nature and God. Only their use and ordering depended on society and persons. Mind received them passibly and sent them forth in reaction to divine, social and material action. That was why, second, one could know right meaning through the "ear of the heart." That, said Augustine, was a faculty of *anima* and confirmed in its operation by God's *Logos*. The relation was that of soul to body: words were tied by their material existence as expressions of society, and guaranteed by their place in *Logos*. So Augustine wrote that the "mouth of the heart" could not lie: it "doth reach to the hearing of the Spirit of the Lord, Who hath filled the whole earth." Human passions might turn heart's voice to a lie when it was embodied in utterance or set in material action, but in its being the heart's mouth uttered God's truth (*On Lying* 471). This was "impressed in [humans'] hearts in the image of God" (Jager 31: quoting *De spiritu et littera* 17.48). Here was the root of true discourse and society. All things human after the Fall were corrupt and fallible by their existence in the world, but their *logos* was perfectible in virtue of Creation and the dispensation of Grace—an idea, however Christianized, that was profoundly Stoic.

The "sacred" relation of meaning and knowledge had its counterpart at the sociopolitical level. Walter Ullmann notes that the joining of Christian doctrine with Roman social and legal tenets meant in the middle ages that "the Christian was a member of the all-embracing, comprehensive corporation, the Church." Of this one became a full member by baptism, not "merely a liturgical or a sacramental act," but a political one that made baptized persons "reborn" members of society and recognized them as participants "of the divine attributes themselves." They became *fideles*, obedient to law represented and concretized by "those who were instituted *over* [them] by divinity" (*Individual* 7–10). Thus, for example, an 828 decree of the emperor Louis the Pious used the word of merchants "described as the ruler's 'vassals' (*fideles*)," considered to belong to his household (Duby 100). The term named the *fides* owed to God (which misuse of language would ruin, said John) and the Senecan and Ciceronian *fides* owed to society, guaranteeing that surety in exchange of duties which also upheld the *Digest*. Echoing more "personal" mediations the *ius* sustaining these bonds was often called society's *anima* (Ullmann, *Individual* 46–50). Understanding and experience of sociopolitical relations were analogous to those of spiritual and logico-epistemological ones.

The bonds between the divine and the human person (*anima*), between the divine and society as a whole, mediated by Law (*anima*), and between person and society, mediated by baptism, matched the bond holding between the divine and the word, secured by *anima*, and the word and society, secured by right language use—*anima* could thus mean, says Ullmann, immortal law, society itself, King, God, soul or society's laws (46–50). Similarly, *ius* could refer to law as divine institution or to human "will" to do right, to act in accordance with educated *fides*. For natural law and universal reason (*logos*) were one (Vinogradoff 107; Verbeke, *Presence* 56). These interconnections were why Hugh of St. Victor defined "practical" arts in terms of each other and their respective yet coincident concerns with the singular and personal, the larger household (*domus*) and society at large (*civitas*):

The practical is divided into solitary, private, and public; or, put differently, into ethical, economic, and political; or, still differently, into moral, managerial, and civil. Solitary, ethical, and moral are one; as also are private, economic, and managerial; and public, political, and civil. *Oeconomus* means manager, whence economic science is called managerial. *Polis* is the Greek word for the Latin *civitas*, or state, whence politics, the civil science, derives its name. And when we speak of ethics as a subdivision of the practical, we must reserve the word for the moral conduct of the person, so that ethical science and solitary science are the same. (II.19: 74)

Here were familiar human, social and material circles. Not surprisingly Hugh wrote of medicine here in terms drawn directly from the Galenic-Arab tradition, simply quoting Joannitius' *Isagoge* (II.26: 78).

These forms of *logos* were imprinted on passible intellect, if not by celestial influence, as Plutarch proposed, yet by grace of impassible divine intellect (Aquinas, *Summa contra Gentiles* III.84: 3². 13–18). The soul was "subject to knowledge," it *lay under* the intelligibles in the mind of God (ST 1a.75.5.2). The senses were subject to *sensibilia* in the same passible way. Humans chose the reactions of both but always in response either to intelligibles illuminated for the human mind by light cast from divine *intellectus agens* or to lawful *sensibilia* received from a material world in turn ordered by divine law or yet again to verbal communication subject to the mediating *anima*. This experience of who-ness and its many-braided environments was in many ways continuous with the Greco-Roman sense of being. It was also growing tensed, as Hildegard explained in laying out the visionary path of the *Scivias*, seven hundred years after Augustine, contemporaneously with Hugh, a century before Aquinas. Loss of knowledge of God's Word had brought the world to dissolution. The human city was in decay:

But now the Catholic faith wavers among the nations [*fides in populis uacillat*] and the Gospel limps among the people [*in eisdem hominibus*]; and the mighty books in which the excelling doctors had summed up knowledge with great care go unread from shameful apathy, and the food of life, which is the divine Scriptures, cools to tepidity. For this reason, I [God] now speak through a person [Hildegard] who is not eloquent [*loquor per non loquentem*] in the Scriptures or taught by an earthly teacher. (*Scivias* III.xi.18: 2.586; trans. Hart and Bishop [HB] 499)

Excursus on the Middle Ages

CHAPTER TEN

Measuring Tensions in the Medieval Microcosm

For the mutualities of these environments have changed, their relative weight modulated and reconfigured. Augustine had spoken a mind split from its source. He had stressed the soul's agon in the worldly city, its passible exile in fear and misery from the city of God and consequent life-long pilgrimage from created time and place back to the timeless no-where of the impassible divine. The Platonic agon of soul in body had become that of human society and all human life in the world. From Aristotle through Stoic debate and on to Cicero, Seneca and later, the circles of human personhood were in some sort of equilibrium: not that they were of equal "weight," but they balanced each other in what it was to be a person. To be ensouled, rational, social, endowed with speech, made of material elements and qualities, embedded in the physical world and enlaced in the surroundings that went with these characteristics all weighed equally in who-ness.

Augustine's writing, its popularity and influence imply that the Christian West experienced something like a core of being: soul's bond with the divine now constituted the ground of person. Although still composed *essentially* of all those other circles, personhood was now founded on its relation with the divine. A new, strong ontological and moral hierarchy had been introduced into the circles of personhood (between divine and mundane, good and evil, healthy and harmful, life and death). This also held for society as a whole, Paul Vinogradoff, Ullmann and others show, and is no doubt visible in architecture of church-centered medieval towns for example. This made for tensions in who-ness and the many circles composing it. But these tensions did not install what Mary McLaughlin calls a "new sense of personality," an "autonomous individual who carrie[d] his world within," defining "himself" through strictly "private decisions

and dilemmas," an "individual who by choice and action shape[d] himself" (488)—claims echoed in Robert Hanning's "private" being, "private destiny," individual "self-fulfillment," "personal, self-chosen destiny,
and therefore an inner-determined identity" (4). These are notably clear
statements of a now-usual view, partly recurring in Stock's idea that in the
eleventh and twelfth centuries reading, writing and a new sense of inten-
tionality "helped to define the boundaries of an independent notion of
the self in contrast to types of interdependency based on considerations of
race, family, lineage, historical devolution, or cosmology" (*After* 59). No
being was forged similar to what the post-Enlightenment West meant by
these terms. Nor did appearance in texts of "wit and ingenuity to shape
encounters with the world outside themselves" show that such "individuals" had been created, any more than did "mimetic rendering of" and
"personal perspective" on that world or "emphasis on the characters' inner life" (Hanning 12).

The last fit passible encircled personhood perfectly well. "Private being," individuality and self-chosen identity do not. Hanning and others
take these to have evolved in the twelfth century against social experience
of person as the *type* of a divine, institutional, historical or other *model*.
Hanning sees the evolution as brief, "stretching only from 1165 or 1170
to 1190 or 1195" (234). What could that mean? A generation of modern
individualism? Did it hide, to reappear half a millennium later? With
such oddities, these critics see ideas of a modeled community lingering in
twelfth-century writing. As Bynum notes, they take "typological thinking
and . . . sense of modeling oneself on earlier examples" as "vestige of an
earlier mentality that simply [got] in the way of a sense of individual
quest, experience, and self-expression" ("Did?" 84–85). Gurevich shows
that people did incorporate, or reincorporate, themselves in community
by absorbing models inherent in a community's auto-understanding (*Origins* 83, 87, 197): the late case of "Martin Guerre" was exemplary (see
Chapter 14 below). Even as twelfth-century romances showed characters
evolving "psychologically," they did so "to fill a given social role and become better versions of virtuous selves" (Bynum, *Metamorphosis* 23). Yet
to reduce intricate webs of passible being to types and models does not
just lose a sense of the who-ness involved but forfeits hope of knowing
just when and what changes in it may have occurred. The reduction sets
up some "other" of modern western "private identity" to serve as a stick
figure against which the self is then supposed to have grown. People like
Abelard, Héloïse and Christina of Markyate, held to have enacted this
self, are praised as "advanced members of that culture" (Hanning 20).
But experiences of who-ness have their own realities, not to be seen as the
"other" or "opposite" of some now more familiar self. Even to start by
wishing to see in them similarities or differences is to risk losing sight of

them. This is not to say that new experiences were not emergent, even slightly odd "outpouring[s] of individuality" on "the fringes" of "Christian medieval culture" (Gurevich, *Origins* 244).

To have brought into experiences of who-ness a sense of primary grounding in a specific core of being may eventually have created contradictions and ambiguities, but they took long to develop to a pitch of possible meltdown. Hildegard, Hugh of St. Victor and John of Salisbury in the twelfth century echoed Augustine on language, memory and the divine. Other elements lived on, the same or altered. Hroswitha's late tenth-century plays manifest sentiments and experiences that also went back to antiquity: "Oh Thou," prayed the eponymous protagonist of *Paphnutius*, asking God to take Thais' soul back to union with the "heavenly host,"

> Who art Thyself uncreated,
> Thou art true Form without Matter
> Thou whose uncompounded Essence created
> Man—not of like substance—
> Out of several elements.

As Paphnutius explained to his disciples, "the macrocosm [was] made up of four elements" which, "though contrary," the Creator had joined "in an harmonious order." These and the "even more contrary parts" of body and soul made up the human being (*Plays* 145–46, 106–7).

Hroswitha's harmonies matched Plato's and Varro's numbers and musicians' measures, for God, she wrote in *Sapientia*, "created all things out of nothing, / And . . . distributed all things with number and measure and weight" (157). Creation was marked by the spheres' celestial music and the human music that measured out proportions of soul, mind, temperament and body. If the first was imperceptible to humans, the second was the very sign of concordant personhood:

> In the harmonious connection between body and soul,
> And in the deep bass or high-pitched soprano of voices,
> . . . in the rhythmic throbbing of our veins,
> And in the measure and proportion of each of our limbs,
> As for example in the joints of our fingers,
> For which we find the same proportions
> when we measure off their sections. (112: *Paphnutius*)

Music, Paphnutius explained, linked the circles of the soul and all elements of the physical human body. It extended to the social sphere, joining the many "unlike" voices of humans. Hroswitha's plays showed without exception that life's goal was to reunite the soul with the divine. There lay the core of human life. But it also lay through the harmonies of the "microcosm," whose measures related the many surroundings that defined humans.

Hroswitha may be thought to signal a "homelier" experience than the likes of Augustine, Hugh of St. Victor or John of Salisbury because, as a woman, she was less educated, less free to circulate, less powerful. She may do so, too, because her plays and hagiographic poems targeted in good part a less educated and powerless public. That she voiced the same experience as these writers matters, therefore. Much the same may be said of Hildegard's writings, aimed at a variety of readers, from popes and kings to abbesses and abbots to ordinary monks, nuns and laypeople. She, too, presented a harmonious universe in which the Creator had made visible in time and place the timeless and invisible: making "all things by His will" and "showing in them not just the things that are visible and temporal but also the things that are invisible and eternal" (*Scivias* I.iii.1: 1.41–42; HB 94). The temporal world was created by "the Word of God, by whom all things were made, itself born before time from the heart of the Father." The Word was manifest in creation, kept in memory by the patriarchs and prophets and made incarnate in Christ, its living memory (III.iv.1: 2.392; HB 358. Here and later, I sometimes change HB slightly).

The church continued this memory work in the Eucharist, "reminding me in faithful [*fideli*] memory" of Jesus' sacrifice that the Word could live amid humans (II.vi.11: 1.240; HB 243). He was named Word because he was sown by God "among local and transitory human dust." As "a teacher's commands are understood *prudenter* [with civic prudence] by people who know and foresee the reason the command was given," so God's power and timelessness were kept in people's memory (II.i.4: 1.114; HB 151). As in Augustine the Word dwelt or could be retrieved in the soul in suitable human words. So Hildegard ended every vision in Book III of *Scivias*: "But let whoever has sharp ears of interior intellect, in ardent love of my reflection [*speculi*], pant for these words and inscribe them in the conscience of his soul [*animi*]." Incarnate soul could never fully recall the Word. So Hildegard said in a well-known letter to Guibert of Gembloux (*ca.* 1175), she could only see darkly and receive visions as a lowly vessel by God's grace. For, she began traditionally, "rational soul [*anima*] is inserted into body as into an earthen jar [*fictili uasi*]," adding: "I cannot know perfectly the things I see while I am in bodily service [*in corporali officio*] and invisible soul [*anima invisibile*]" (*Epistolarium* CIIIR 6: 2.259; CIIIR 59–60: 2.261).

The Word was at once memory of the divine in human mind and soul, reminder that on earth a human was *peregrina*, pilgrim "in the shadow of death" pacing the "road of error," and the language that could lead back to the divine (*Scivias* I.iv.1: 1.62; HB 109). That was the force of *officium* in the letter quoted, connoting the body as an obligatory set of duties on the path to God, involving (we shall see) all the non-divine circles weaving the human person. Earth, Hildegard agreed, was a "tearful exile," a longing to "see [Christ] and remain with [him]" (*Symphonia* 220: Hymn 57, "O dulcissime amator"). Memory dwelt in the "living breath [*vivens spiraculum*]" that was the soul, which, however, incarnate, bent all too easily to worldly pleasures and temptations (*Scivias* I.iv.1: 1.62; HB 109). For, she wrote of her vision of Christ and Creation (Figure 7), the

soul turns around in earthly affairs [*anima circuit in terrenis causis*], laboring through many changes as fleshly behavior demands. But the spirit lifts itself [*spiritus uero erigit se*] in two ways: sighing, moaning and desiring God; and choosing among options in various matters as if by a rule, for the soul has discernment in reason. Hence the human holds within the likeness of heaven and earth. It has a circle [*circulum*] where live perspicuity, breath and reason, as the skies have their lights, air and flying creatures; and it has a receptacle containing humidity, germination and birth, as the earth contains fertility, fruition and animals. (II.i.2: 1.113; HB 151)

Like Nemesius and his predecessors, Hildegard thought the human literally the microcosm. Isidore of Seville, too, after explaining in his *De natura rerum* (written in 612–14, diffused far and wide) that "the world is the total entirety [*mundus est uniuersitas omnis*] that is made from heaven and earth," wrote untranslatably that "mundus conpetenter homo significatur": world is mutually signified human (and vice versa), for "as the former is constituted from the four elements, so is the latter made from the four humors mingled in one temperament." The Greek language showed that "the ancients held the human to be in intimate union [*communio*] with the world's fabric, since in Greek the world was called *cosmos* and the human *micros cosmos*, that is, lesser world" (cap. ix: 207). Buttressing this linguistic claim, the Latin phrase just quoted used the nominative case of *mundus* and *homo* to make them interchangeable subjects or complements of the passive singular *significatur*: syntactically equal. This mutual signifying of world and human led Isidore to outline the world as a person, as Hildegard always did. The *De natura* was further noteworthy because in it Isidore made such vast use of images of circles and wheels that the work was known in many of its manuscripts as the *Liber rotarum* (*De natura*, introduction 15). Seven figures illustrated it. Six were wheels depicting (1) the sequence of months, (2) seasons of the year, (3) zones of the earth, (4) qualities and elements of the world, seasons and humors, (5) times of planetary orbits and (6) the four cardinal and eight tributary winds. The first, third, fifth and six had a human face at the center to show how these circles also constituted the human (to the fourth, incorporating the second, the human was anyway integral).

Figure 7. Hildegard of Bingen, *Scivias* (1141–51), Book 2, Vision 1, "The Redeemer." Photo: Abtei St. Hildegard.

Like the *Etymologiae,* Isidore wrote the *De natura* at the request of the highly lettered Visigothic king Sisebut, the first an accessible compendium of general knowledge, the second a practical manual on cosmology and the physical world (Riché 258–62, 300, 390). Though faulted in some circles as too pagan, the *De natura* was almost as successful as the massive *Etymologiae,* said to have been, after the Bible, the work most read and copied during the middle ages (*De natura,* chart following 83). The shorter work expounded plainly a complex sense of the world and the human in the world, with easy-to-grasp visual aids vividly showing the person integrated in the series of physical circles that were the work's concern. The work scanted any Augustinian sense of the grounding nature of the divine. Its clarity and secularity carried on a Stoic tradition earlier taken up by Martin of Braga, Isidore's predecessor prelate in Suevic Spain (modern Galicia more or less), whose *Formula* was as widely distributed as Isidore's *De natura*.

For Hildegard, humans were the image of God in their place in the world and jointure of soul and body: of Christ, Word made flesh, rather than of the Creator directly. Given Isidore and the legacy traced earlier, that she stressed being's materiality is no surprise. But now she set the physical circles of the person in a hierarchy from the divine through soul to its faculties and on to body and its surroundings. The divine worked in the soul through memory and the soul's rational faculties. Thus, of good works, Hildegard said: "will activates the work and mind receives it and reason produces it." Intellect, "knowing good and evil," knew the value and means of such works. It, in part of the soul, will, in another, were soul's "arms." They acted on mind, directly liable for human action. Soul moved will and intellect via reason—"the soul's loud sound [*sonitus animae*], which makes known every work of God and human. For sound takes the word aloft, as wind lifts the eagle that it might fly" (*Scivias* I.iv.20–23: 1.80–82; HB 121–23). Word and reason (*logos* or *ratio*/*oratio*) again tied soul and the divine. The first vision of the *Liber divinorum operum* (LDO) was of human Caritas as a fiery wind, "like soul's breath [*sicut . . . spiramen animae*]," putting life in all things in the natural universe, and rational life in creatures, "having the wind of the sounding word [*uentum sonantis uerbi*]" (I.i.2: 48). This "wind" (*ventus*) joined humans to a further circle of the person, where the divine worked on the soul in another way.

The images Hildegard used to explain the motion of the embodied soul on earth (*circuit*), the form of the rational mind (*circulum*) and even maybe the shape of the womb (*receptaculum*), picked up the usual ancient trope to tell aspects of personal being. Peter Dronke adds that "one of Hildegard's favorite wordplays" was the "circling circle [*circuiens circulus*]" (LDO, introduction xxv–vi). Isidore's was just one of its readily accessible versions. Hildegard's illuminations used circular figures exhaustively: for choirs of angels (1.vi), the Redeemer (2.i), the Trinity (2.ii), God enthroned (3.i), Salvation (3.ii) and others, including the universe (1.iii: Figure 8). She used an equally common image when writing of how soul was embodied:

For the soul is a fruitful power, which makes the whole person live by moving with it; and just as a person puts on and wears cloth woven from threads [*panno*

Figure 8. Hildegard of Bingen, *Scivias*, Book 1, Vision 3, "The Universe." Photo: Abtei St. Hildegard.

ex filis texto], so the soul, putting on as a garment all the works that it performed with the person, is covered with them, whether good or bad, as it is by the body in which it lives. (LDO I.iv.72: 203)

Soul in body woven from its colored threads worked, "with the person like the air [*in similitudine aeris cum homine operatur*]." Air, she wrote elsewhere, was "in human breath and reason":

For by the living breath [*viventi spiramine*], which is the soul, it [*aer*] ministers to the human who carries it and is born on its wing, whereby a person draws in and expels breath to be able to live. And the soul is fire that pervades the whole body and makes the human live. Air also ignites fire, and fire burns in all things by means of air. In humans, air appears as dew in emission, green vigor in excitation, wind in motion and heat in increase [*in dilatatione*]. (*Causae* II.[§26]: 43)

Hildegard was applying to the human body what she called air's four powers in general: "dew in emitting, all vigor in exciting, wind in moving, since by its means it raises up flowers, heat in increasing [*dilatando*], since by its means it makes all things ripen: just as it is spread [*dilatatur*] through the four parts of the world" (*Causae* I.[§43]: 20). Other aspects of her description of the human body fit her description of the elemental universe: "since fire is like the body of air and air like the viscera and, as it were, the wings and feathers of fire" (*Causae* II.[§15]: 39). Unfamiliar as her imagination may be, its parts were entirely coherent among themselves and always stressed the cohesiveness and interdependency of all parts of the created world. Contrary to some claims, the imagery and logic of *Causae et curae* show it clearly by Hildegard, though much of its Book 1 and many of its cures may have come from Isidore (Hurd-Mead, *History* 191; Engbring 781). He was also a practical exemplar in having built "an immense hospital of 580 beds on the banks of the Tagus and staffed it with men and women doctors and teachers from the school of the Nestorians at Gondashapur," writing a medical encyclopedia for their use (Hurd-Mead, "Introduction" 492).

Unfamiliar as is *Causae*'s imaginative expression, its content was familiar. Hildegard was echoing that experience of the soul incarnate, its body embedded in the world, that was common to medical writers (say) from Hippocratics on. In these very terms, she enlaced microcosm and macrocosm even more deeply:

The firmament possesses fire, sun, moon, stars and winds, by all of which things it is composed and by whose qualities it is made firm, so as not to be broken asunder. For as the soul holds together the whole human body, so the winds sustain the whole firmament, so that it not be shattered, and they are invisible as the soul is invisible, coming from the mystery of God. And just as a house does not stand without its cornerstones, so neither firmament, nor earth nor abyss nor the whole world with all its components may exist without these winds, since all these are composed and held together by them.

For the whole earth would be rent and shattered if these winds did not exist, just as the whole human body would be rent if it did not have bones. (*Causae* I.[§21]: 5)

These winds and air in body as *spiritus* and breath (*spiraculum* or *spiramen*), soul's means of operation and its nature, reached Hildegard from many sources. Jacqueline Hamesse writes that in the twelfth and thirteenth centuries, *spiritus* was a vital concept, with multiple senses: physical (air), biological (breath), animate (vital spirits, or soul) and theological (divine spirit, Holy Ghost, the Word, God-in-the-world) (*"Spiritus"*). A century earlier, *spiritus*, and other elements offered by Hildegard's many sources, tied the human as much to the world as to the divine, although her world was anyway imbued with the divine, here further weaving person into the world:

Because as the earth produces and nourishes humankind and as it sustains and feeds all the other things which are in service to humanity, so it seems the flower of beauty and adornment of the rightful virtue [*honestatis virtutis*] of God, disposing all things well and justly in his virtue, so the power of God should be honored throughout the earth: since it preserves humankind, who ought to praise and magnify the Lord all the time, and since it even sustains the rest which are meant for human use, when it makes itself available to them for their nourishment.

All creatures came from earth "since even humankind animated [*animatus*] by reason and the spirit of understanding is made from earth" (*Liber vite meritorum* IV.xx: 184). Prefacing her *Physica* (that Laurence Moulinier argues started as one with *Causae*), she echoed Genesis: "terra dabat viriditatem suam"—"the earth gave its vigor [or humanity's, if *suam* refers to *homo* in the previous sentence], according to kind and nature and customs and all the surroundings [*circumitionem*] of humanity" (1125). The *circumitiones* were plants, elements, trees, stones, fishes, birds, mammals, reptiles, metals discussed in the work, all part of and tied to humans in divers ways. This was fully in Galenic-Arab tradition, and Dronke shows decisively that Hildegard knew the "new learning of the Arab writers, at least that of Constantinus Africanus" (LDO, introduction xv–xvi).

Hildegard's equivocal remarks on women came from this understanding of humans' bond to the material and divine worlds. All humans were by nature rational and material, and if she sometimes asserted that man was "the sower [*seminator*]" and woman "the receiver of the seed [*sus-*

ceptrix seminis]," yet mutually essential like "hardness of stone to softness of earth" (*Scivias* I.ii.11: 1.20; HB 77), and twice flatly endorsed the view that woman "semen non habet" (*Causae* II.[§74]: 60; II.[§167]: 104), at others she took the Galenic view of her close precursor Trotula, that both had seed. Trotula explained, for instance, that a usual cause of suffocation of the womb in virgins was that their seed had amassed because not "drawn out by means of the male"; "from this superabundant and spoiled seed a certain cold vapor is loosed" (*Diseases* 11; *Malattie* 62: cap.IIII). Hildegard usually held people (*homo*) to have seed in diverse strengths (*Causae* II[§3]: 33). Since, here, she instantly spoke of other differences of man (*masculus*) and woman (*mulier*) (II.[§4]: 33), this *homo* clearly described something shared: as shown in a fuller discussion of the results of stronger or weaker male semen in conception, where she again distinguished man (*vir, masculus*) and woman (*mulier*) (II.[§8]: 35). Male/female diversity, stronger and weaker, mutually essential, caused different sexes and capacities of offspring (*Scivias* I.iv.13: 1.75–76; HB 118). She adopted the usual view we saw in Chapter 7 that soul was infused into the growing fetus via the mother (*Causae* II.[§75]: 61–65). But the diversity was why women could not be priests: as a woman conceived not alone but "through a man, as the ground [was] ploughed not by itself but by a farmer" (an image repeated in *Causae* II.[§169]: 104), so she could not "consecrate the body and blood of Christ." She had a finer role to play as His bride (*Scivias* II.vi.76: 1.290, HB 278). In women as brides of Christ (soul) yet born of earth (body), "the whole human race lay hidden." Neither man nor woman was human without the other; as *personae*, some of their *officia* differed.

Adopting the fourfold medieval hermeneutics evoked in Chapter 9, that Hildegard used in her Genesis commentary (LDO Lib. II. Visio i), one can say that *in a literal sense* men and women were alike rational and physical, embedded in the world. Trotula had made the point in opening her Prologue to the *Diseases of Women*. At Creation, God dignified the human race above other creatures by giving its members "freedom of reason and of intellect." He also made it "male and female" so that in their physical embraces cold and moist and hot and dry would complement, "soothe" and "assuage" each other's elemental excesses (*Diseases* 1; *Malattie* 46). Trotula and Hildegard saw the relation as one of comparative "strength" and "weakness," not of superiority and inferiority, unlike such as Hugh of St. Victor, who wrote of

the human body, over which the rational soul presides, and which four footmen carry—that is, the four elements of which the two upper ones, namely fire and air, are masculine in function and in gender, and the two lower, earth and water, feminine. (III.17: 100).

Even so, for Trotula, Hildegard and Hugh, men and women were complementary human persons, ensouled and rational, differing physiologically in their way of embedding in the material world.

Like Galen and Nemesius, Hildegard thought mental functions physically embedded. "In humans [*homine*]," she wrote, "are will, deliberation, power and consent [*voluntas, consideratio, potestas et consensus*]." Will enabled one to choose "to do this or that." *Consideratio* scanned the propriety and morality of each side. Power let a deed actually be done. Consent closed the series: "quia opus non potest perfici, quin consensus laudet, ut consentiat," since a deed cannot be done unless consent approve, so that it give assent. The terms were the ancient ones of reasoned assent to passibly affected action. Hildegard insisted that these functions were materially grounded in the four elements and what she called the four humors: "will" in fire and dryness, *consideratio* in air and moisture, power in water and *spuma* (foam), consent in earth and heat (*Causae* II.[§74]:59–60). The strangeness of some of Hildegard's terms does not alter the materiality of her argument, their sources and unorthodoxy not being of concern here.

Still in this literal exegesis, Hildegard saw women as more thoroughly taken in the world than men were. Their elemental qualities set them more deeply in the earth's elements: "Woman's temperament, which sensitized her to any spiritual forces that happened to be 'in the air' [because of greater moisture], also made her body more sensitive to the physical environment" (*Causae* II.[§170]: 105; Newman's paraphrase: *Sister* 129). She explained that women were "open like a wooden frame in which strings have been fastened for plucking or, again, like windows and exposed to the winds [*fenestrales et ventosae*], so that the elements affect them more vehemently than men, and the humours too are more abundant in them" (II.[§170]: 105). That was why Hildegard thought that the sicknesses she had suffered from birth, "in all her veins, inmost parts and flesh," came to her "from the air, from the rain and the wind, and from all stormy weather" (LDO III.v.38: 462). She typically emphasized the connections between veins and air, vitals and rain, flesh and winds, bodily sicknesses and storms. If Hildegard made a special case of women's engagement in the world, her understanding of it was that of body to world, detailed by medical writers from Hippocrates through Galen to the Arabs. Hildegard's emphasis here was tied to what she saw as women's particular relation to God.

Besides material and rational being that set them *literally* in the world, humans knew and experienced in other ways. *Allegorically*, "man signifie[d] the divinity of the Son of God, woman His humanity" (LDO I.iv.100: 243). To be human was to inhabit body in the world, and women were both more human than men (Seneca's *humanior*) and expressive of Christ's "two" persons. Women represented the church as the virgin mother of Christ or his bride. *Morally*, humans were rational and divine soul occupying and acting through body for the time of a life. Soul was set in a human by God to "make it living and rational" until it left the body again either to return "to its first life" or to suffer "eternally the torments of death" (*Causae* II.[§43]: 21). *Anagogically*, men and women both figured the possible path to the divine and final union with God. Hildegard thus answered the "Augustinian" problem of how women were in "the image of God" in terms of their "role as vessel of the Incarnation" (Newman 93), their rationality and their enlacement in God's material world—source of the human race but also mark of Christ's humanity. Sexual difference made no difference in the deep nature of personhood. It made a difference in the worldly activities of male and female *personae*, and so in how the circles of the person related to one another. The fourfold hermeneutics precisely fit this imbricated scheme of things, and Hildegard authorized it as a way to understand these relations: naming the first three steps in the *Liber divinorum operum*, where the type of exegesis, *littera, allegoria* or *moralitas*, was written in chapter margins from II.i.23 on (291ff.). Their names were in the Table of Contents from II.i.17 on (29–33) but not named in the text. Albert Derolez notes that the Table was by or supervised by Hildegard, as were the manuscript marginal comments and other corrections (LDO, introduction xcv, cxi). Table and marginal additions anyway merely named her actual textual practice. Anagogy was the final end of all the visions. It did not need naming.

This understanding of the human person, and the technique used for it, corresponded fully to what were now "descending" circles of the human person. Just as all humans experienced being and were perceived in terms of their relation to the divine, their animate, rational souls and minds, their physical being as humans, their social prudential roles and their embedding in the material world, so women (and men), were known as "singular" being only in such circles. Hildegard's *oeuvre* echoed this perception: eschatological story (creation, redemption and salvation) and divine and human works in the world in the three visionary writings, pilgrimage tales (worldly humans making a way back to God) in the hagiographies, human biology in *Causae* and material explanation in the *Physica*. One can add her correspondence, dealing not just with theological and mystical matters, but with issues social, civic and political (ecclesiastic and secular), unhesitant in chiding emperors, princes and counts, popes, bishops and abbots, eager to embed the highest interests in the lowliest material practices, a gardener's gathering informing a cardinal's duties, a herbalist's a king's, Hildegard at home in all.

Charles Singer is quite wrong to say that she saw "no distinction between physical events, moral truths, and spiritual experiences" (203–4). Hildegard gave an ordered hierarchical exegesis of traditional forms of understanding and experience of familiar circles of the person: divine and universal, animate and rational, social and moral, physiological, natural and material. Setting them in tiers under the divine, she offered a pattern of who-ness little different in essentials from that of Augustine and his many heirs, whose work she knew well, as Dronke shows (LDO, introduction xxiii and *apparatus fontium, passim*; and "Cidades"). Hildegard's knowledge of the human in the material world echoed that of philosophers and physicians ancient and contemporary. Isidore embedded humans in physical circles. Their temperaments combined seasons, elements, humors, qualities and more. He, too, saw all as subject to the divine, if less precisely than she (*De natura* cap. xi: 213–17). Hugh of Folieto, Hildegard's and Hugh of St. Victor's coeval, detailed relations between the four elements, humors and seasons and the identical distribution of qualities in each ("elements exactly match humors and humors seasons"), saying that "the soul is said to have its elements in the same way": "pro igne utitur intellectus subtilitate; pro aere, mentis puritate; pro terra rationis stabilitate; pro aqua ingenii mobilitate," as for fire, it works by subtlety of intellect, air by purity of mind, earth by stability of reason, water by mobility of wit. Thereby soul (*animus*) could perceive faith rightly by the intellect, understand purely, believe firmly, obey precepts of faith swiftly and by doing good works live well: "subtlety would be tempered [*temperetur*] by purity, purity by subtlety, stability by mobility, mobility by stability" (*De medicina* cap. ii: 1184–85). Hugh of Folieto, like Galen, Nemesius, Isidore and certainly his contemporary Hildegard, grounded powers of soul and acts of moral assent in elemental physicality.

Hugh's *ingenium*, even more his *mobilitas ingenii*, was a vital term in late twelfth-century courtly poetry, *engin* in French. Hanning argues that it not only marked Abelard's individualistic ability to manipulate his world (29–32), but became a focus of the free subjective action of the romantic courtly hero characterized by "exercise of untrammeled, improvisatory *ingenium*" (105–38, 235). Sarah Kay takes up his analysis to show how *engin* operated in the slightly later *Roman de Guillaume de Dole* (ca. 1225), but suggests it was caught far more in group activities than he allows (184–98). She does not wholly disagree with Hanning, since he avers that the individual freedom he espies vanished after 1190–95 under growing new institutional pressures exemplified by the Fourth Lateran Council (1215). Bynum, confuting Hanning's arguments, proposes that the Council had a different effect: "individual experience [then] breaks away from or undercuts, rather than issues in or coincides with, community" ("Did?" 109). The overall experience was of building *new* communities, individualities being, again, negative markers (and see *Metamorphosis, passim*).

The patterns set forth by Hugh and Hildegard indeed show that *ingenium* was a faculty of mind (or soul) acting as much in the "public" circles of personhood as all other human powers and doings. Like elements, said Hugh of Folieto, each mental or animate power, including *ingenium*, had its site (higher, middle or lower) in the order and rule of being. As *animus* corresponded to the elements so it did to the humors: "blood in sweetness, red bile in bitterness, black bile in grief, phlegm in settled mind." So, he ended, moral behavior also fit orders of mind, humors, elements, seasons and so on, wholly affected by and interacting with them: "the soul [*anima*] that safeguards its temperament lives cleanly" (*De medicina* cap. ii: 1185). All matched *ingenium* as well.

Still, when Jean Courtecuisse translated Martin of Braga's *Formula* in 1403 (as *Seneque des IIII vertus*), he used *ingenium* to stress how the very goal of the virtues in their *offices* was to maintain what one might call the public equilibrium of person in the world. Here, he did use *engin* when marking activity that drew one from such equilibrium: "if," he translated Martin's closing exhortation, "you exceed the measure of prudence, you will be heated and of dreadful wit [*caut et de espouantable engin*]." "Callidus et pavendi acuminis eris," Martin had written (247; Haselbach, *Seneque* 447). But here, not *acumen* (or *ingenium*) but its misuse was the problem. Martin and Courtecuisse were insisting that it belonged inextricably with the virtues as an aspect of *prudentia*. These virtues in turn were woven in community. Excess, for Martin, as for Plutarch or Seneca, was the imbalance that marked an evil life, a person out of sync with being. Right behavior in the world was the path back to impassible being along the courses of memory of the Word and the virtues it embodied. It was also memory of ancient ideas and experiences of the person seeking to live the life of virtue, *vita beata*. In popular literature, this *misuse* of *engin* or *ingenium* may be taken as the very ground of the *Roman de Renart*, his *engin* a constant threat and provocation to the community. Renart depicted ways of acting against surrounding collectivities, imperiling their security. Their reactions—like the reactions to a real-life person like Abelard—show awareness of the threat posed by such figures to normative behavior and common experience: the individual, again, as negative marker.

This sense of who-ness was not limited to writers on religious, philosophical, medical and other "professional" matters. Nor was it much changed by vernacular writers, even if they surely complicated understanding and experience. So, Eugene Vance, writing of the twelfth-century *Chanson de Roland*, recalls that the voice of the "individual" was not that of "an individualizing psychology." The formula of conquest spoken by Roland before he dies "belongs to a repertory of deeds that are not his alone, and his voice becomes more and more that of history itself speaking to us." Here, too, was commemorative affect based in the divine: Roland's "silent interlocutor" at this moment was his sword Durendal, given to Charlemagne by God (through an angel), brilliant "with the light of good works that originate, ultimately, with the Father in heaven" ("Roland and the Poetics" 389; *Mervelous* 67). As he writes elsewhere: "Roland's heroism was always to have remembered Charlemagne in his ordeal at Ronceval; then, as he died, to have remembered God" ("Love's" 41). The pattern is familiar. At the same time, Vance sees *Roland* as signaling a twelfth-century change from this comprehension of the human condition. He is not alone.

Haidu analyzes a moment during Roland's death scene further confirming these points. Noting how, after his death God sent the angels "Cherubin," "saint Michael" and "Gabriel" to "bear the count's soul to paradise" (*Chanson* ll.2393–96), Haidu also stresses that so far the poet had emphasized essentially secular aspects, ending in Roland's offering God his glove: the gesture of feudal vassal to overlord. The critic avers that the metaphor gives politics "ontological priority" over religion (*Subject of Violence* 18–19, here 19). But the angelic conclusion, with the ascension of Roland's soul, keeps the hierarchy of circles we have seen (it would be illuminating to examine the poem's huge emphasis on material place and body). The feudal metaphor did not mark priority but rather the identity of relation that marked person's place in the circles of being. This identity between politics and theology was a variant in a long tradition. Haidu further shows that until this death all gestures had involved secular feudal politics and the status of the warrior noble in these politics, noting, too, that in the *actual* processes of state-construction depicted in many vernacular texts, religion is invoked, if at all, as a legitimating ideology, the real work of social and political change being dominated by secular codes (personal exchanges, but these arguments are detailed in *The Subject of Violence*, in *The Subject* and other work in progress).

Two moments are of special interest to me inasmuch as they concerned what Haidu refers to as "subjectivity." The first occurred when the dying Roland displayed his body and the marks of his authority—his sword and horn (*s'espee e l'olifan*) in a particular way:

> Pur ço l'at fait que il voelt veirement
> Que Carles diet e trestute sa gent,
> Li gentilz cuens, qu'il fut mort cunquerant. (ll.2361–63)

> He did it so, because he truly wants
> Charles to say, and all his men as well,
> the noble knight, he died a conqueror. (trans. Haidu)

Later Charlemagne would tell his nobles that this did make him *remember* an earlier moment when Roland had told him that should he ever die in a foreign land he would turn his head and show himself in such a way that he would be seen to have died "cunquerrantment" (l.2867). The second moment came earlier. As the rearguard's defeat was becoming apparent Roland's intimate friend Oliver upbraided him for "foolishly" and "thoughtlessly" not having sounded his horn when it would have done some good, and so having failed in his feudal obligation, by present defeat and future inability, to give Charlemagne their aid (ll.1725–36). Shortly after, Oliver, blinded by his own blood, struck Roland with his sword on his helmet's nosepiece. At this Roland cried out:

> Sire cumpain, faites le vos de gred?
> Ja est ço Rollant, ki tant vos soelt amer!
> Par nule guise ne m'aviez desfiét! (ll.2000–2002)

> My lord companion, do you do this willingly?
> For this is Roland, who always loved you dearly!
> You have not challenged me in any way! (trans. Haidu)

Both these moments stressed their protagonists' place in the social, political order. At the same time, Haidu adds that the author attributed "willfulness and intent to the actor: 'pur ço l'at fait que il voelt veirement.'" This, and Roland's asking if Oliver did his action "de gred," are taken to imply action of a subjectivity threatening to the (feudal) collectivity (*Subject of Violence* 25–34, here 26 and 33). In the second case, Roland's reaction asserted what would have been the right way to do things: like the reader, he doubtless recalled Oliver's earlier judgment of his behavior, criticizing his foolhardiness but admiring his "proecce" (l.1731), the courage that was essential to the feudal warrior. In its terms the right way to enforce his criticism would have been through the proper ritual of a challenge. There was no doubt of Oliver's adherence to the codes, so Roland's question answered itself: he had not struck Roland "de gred." In now familiar terms, we can say that he had not *accepted, assented to* a particular action. What he did he did in ignorance (since he could not see that his opponent was Roland). A similar reading applies to the first case. Roland indeed "truly wanted" to be seen in death as having fulfilled his feudal duties, as being properly and fully embedded in a particular sociopolitical surrounding. He was assenting to an action that was, so to speak, "out there" for him to carry out, forged in the long-ago exchange between him and his king. As a feudal subject of Charlemagne he was "subjected to" the actions and forms of understanding properly affecting one of his rank in the system. This is not to say that one cannot speak of "willfulness and intent." It *is* to say that they were assent and trained *reaction* to a given set of patterns. They implied no unambiguous break with the feudal community.

For Vance, Charlemagne's presence interrupted, even did away with efficacious memory. The end of *Roland* was marked by a kind of dispersion of signification, where language was no longer clear and joyous but opaque, dark and painful, sign of the old not yet replaced by a new totalizing form of human being and understanding. Voice, poetry, words lost familiar meaning and with it their life. Agreeing in general, Haidu is more precise about what *Roland* indicated. His ground is insistence that *Roland*'s protagonists, including the two rival rulers, were never "simply individuals. The narrative subjects [were] rather the collectivities to which each belong[ed], and in which each [was] simply *primus inter pares.*" Suitably adjusted, the point applies to all the epic's protagonists. Such seemingly personal emotions as that of honor were ones "that each individual share[d] with his specific collectivity" or, better, marked adherence to that collectivity. The critic is simply wrong who, "bound by classical presuppositions regarding the psychological unity of character," wants to see these protagonists' emotional reactions as signaling such unity instead of regarding apparently "contradictory" successive *laisses* as telling the changing passible demands of successive actions. Characters were embedded in the demands of action, place, collective need and understanding. We must understand "the public nature of subjectivity" shown in the *Roland* (Haidu, *Subject of Violence* 75, 77).

The first half of the epic, up to the destruction of the rearguard and violent deaths of the twelve *pairs*, with aristocratic warriors and leaders always potential rivals of each other and their emperor, signaled collapse of a particular feudal order, Haidu shows. Here, Roland reveals a form of aristocratic feudal "individualism" that threatened the familiar political collectivity. The second half, where Charlemagne became sole ruler and victor over the Saracens, signaled "reconstruction of the collectivity after a disaster which call[ed] its very values into question." It would therefore be a *different collectivity*, needing new forms of "subjectivation." "Monarchical law" now claimed "priority over the rule of feudal law." Haidu proposes that *Roland* adumbrated new forms of subjecthood and made visible the need for "the subject that will be the subject of the nation-state," which was not—nor could be—"yet portrayed or constructed in that text": "Neither the polity nor the subject it require[d] yet exist[ed]." Because their existence lay "in some futurity" they were necessarily signaled "imprecisely," but this was the changing pattern "indexed" by *Roland* (129, 165, 186–87). While this seems to give too exclusively a political dimension to the "subject," the precision is well-taken. It was not that the epic ended in some vague dissolution of language. It was that it demanded a new "language": as began to develop, perhaps, in romances of Chrétien de Troyes and others (Vance, *From*; Haidu, *Aesthetic, Lion*; Bynum, *Metamorphosis* 23). With that language (but much later) would come new polities, new histories, new forms of analysis, new selves: at present, as Bynum observed against Hanning, they identified themselves as communal. The tensions adopted familiar patterns, corresponding still to (now hierarchized) circles of person.

For the movement that *Roland* marked was not toward experience whose center would be some self-identity. Of Gace Brulé, for another secular case from the (late) twelfth century, Vance warns against reifying "the authorial figure of Gace into any kind of subjective principle, into any kind of unifying 'original' presence, in terms of which his poems might take on 'meaning': indeed, the flatly conventional surface of these poems discourages any such temptations." In Gace, the *je* was almost always negated, a fact matching a wider condition: "The *je* of medieval lyric is merely the index of a basic principle of activity, and no more" ("Love's" 42, 50). The presence of *je* just as a mark of enunciation in the lyric was Paul Zumthor's constant point (*Langue* 165–213, *Essai* 68–70, 172–74), which, queried by modernizers, here, along with the "dispersion" of meaning that Vance sees in *Roland*, gains a new sense in Vance's reading of Chaucer's *Troilus*, a poem made of "concentric layers of fiction that correspond to the different spheres making up the onionlike universe of his poems." Here, too, he traces decay of language, truth and meaning. Finally the reader was placed before the only guarantor of "truth," the Divine, in "prayer" and "illumination" (*Mervelous* 308–10). To draw humans back to God was no new commemorative aim of language. That this drawing now resulted, at least in these secular writings, from a sense of language's *in*sufficiency signaled perhaps the tensions of emergent—as yet phantom—forms of community, but as yet comported no major changes in patterns of personhood.

More generally, Kay confirms these readings of a *trouvère* like Gace or a later poet like Chaucer, analyzing uses of irony and other techniques in troubadour poetry where, she observes: "the conflict of meanings [was] achieved by playing off existing registers of language . . . against each other," "Christian and secular" for example (18–19). These did not so much play against one another as reflect two of the circles of person (apparent, too, in *Troilus*' "spheres" of meaning). They were not in conflict but part of person's passible multiplicity. Kay writes of a poetic "subject position" that was never singularized because it stayed "caught in the play of voices" (20). The "first-person position" of troubadour lyric was "inseparable from rhetorical complexity" (49). But these techniques should not be taken to mean that "this subject is protean, lacking in boundaries, and divided within itself" (89). Rather was it the multiply encircled person "bound up with group identities of various kinds, such as gender, social peer groups, patrons and audiences" (84). This was Haidu's argument no less than Bynum's. And these just name the person's social circles. We must still add those, clearly depicted, of material world, animate soul and a love quest linked with the soul's pining toward God, to say nothing of the context of oral performance and its visible relating of the poetic to the feudal and legal (Kay 132–70, 111–27, 136; cf. on the last, Bloch).

Considering texts like these, it is necessary to address common claims that vernaculars marked a new subjectivity, in their use of first person pronouns, their making writing available to more people or their representing new forms of political and economic organization. Michel Zink claims this importance of "subjectivité" in the vernaculars (173), as does Sarah Spence. She also suggests, as the main thesis of a book, that the vernacular gave a greater sense of the body in the world (*passim*). But this was an essential aspect of who-ness from Greek antiquity. Dronke has anyway observed that vernaculars were important from centuries before the twelfth (*Poetic* 3–7). Too, no one who lived in Latin could feel disembodied in it, as Gramsci observed, mocking those opposing an abstract "dream" Latin to "vernacular-historical reality" (*Selections from Cultural Writings* 233–34). Dante's arguments for vernaculars and the "*stile comico*" associated with them concerned the "variety" and "polyglotism," diversity and multiplicity (dialectal for instance) that gave the *stilnovisti* poets "a varied tonality with which [they] . . . adapted to different states of the soul and different places and times": to the surroundings of passible being (Schiaffini 49–50, trans. Cirigliano, in Cavalcanti xxvii). Vernaculars at first offered a *better* way to express the person's place in its manifold surroundings. That ultimately they expressed and produced a growing sense of "fragmentation" was part of an emerging process both of whose concurrently "nostalgic" and "prospective" aspects deeply engaged a poet and epistolarian like Petrarch.

In this same spirit, lyric was not "individualizing." It tended to "categorize rather than particularize" (Kay 161). In the live lyric performance, what Kay calls the subject position was "constructed by its complex links with the historical circumstances of medieval authors [legal, feudal, theological and the rest] and by the elaborate rhetoric that engage[d] audience response" (170). Under some conditions it might be associated with "the body of the performer," after all present in the performance space, so that this "subject position" might be taken in performance as related "to an ontological entity" (213). But that is always a condition of physical performance. In that sense, people always and everywhere have bodies separating them from other people. The fact by no means rules the sort of personhood associated with it. The "subject" of twelfth-century lyric, Kay proposes, could only be defined as "subject to factors which overdetermine it" (212): though to talk of "overdetermining" also risks misplacing the subject For these "factors" were the many circles that *were* the person. They were the person, with all the growing tensions, regardless of whether religious or noble, peasant or burgher, courtier or troubadour, man or woman.

My three last cases show that these categories overlapped. Abelard, Héloïse and Christina of Markyate show the play of these circles at the intersection of noble and religious in such a way that the very intersection needed resolution. Especially was this Christina's case. I take these, though, because they are regularly given as proof of twelfth-century evolution of a modern self; its very "heroes," in Gurevich's ironic noun (*Origins* 6). Evidence for the first two is Abelard's *Historia calamitatum* and the four personal and three directional letters subsequently exchanged by him and Héloïse—one could now add the "lost love letters" identified as theirs by Ewald Könsgen, Constant Mews and others (see also, Ward and Chiavaroli). The familiar eight letters were written between 1132 and Abelard's death in 1142. J. T. Muckle plausibly dates Abelard's first letter between 1131 and 1136 ("Abelard's" 173). Whether all were written then, whether all were genuine and what was their status are questions asked since their appearance in manuscripts whose oldest is early thirteenth century: one now in the Paris Bibliothèque Nationale, with notes by Petrarch, its owner from about 1337. Zink states flatly that the letters are a thirteenth-century work which cannot be "wholly authentic" since it adopted conventions of twelfth-century lyric and writing like Guibert of Nogent's to forge the "subjective representation of a life. Formalized stereotypes of lyric poetry, rhetorical rules of spiritual letters, demands of penitential writing, the rule of the confession are all assimilated, blended, rethought by a consciousness making of them so many tools for contemplation and the expression of self" (240–41, 247). Héloïse and Abelard lived with all these developments, so none negates the letters' authenticity. Scholarly consensus, as evinced notably in Bonnie Wheeler's collection on Héloïse and the evaluation of new letters, now leans strongly in favor of authenticity.

It hardly matters here whether the letters are genuine, since they would anyway reveal an experience of personal being shared by people of their time. In that regard, Haidu observes, one may hold the *Letters* to be in some sense of *both* twelfth *and* thirteenth centuries, insofar as the earliest extant version was put together and written in the latter. There are, too, problems in such associations as that with Guibert of Nogent, however often taken as evidencing some new sense of autographic self. For one is constrained to agree with Gurevich, who suggests that Guibert's story is *without* a (self-conscious) person, save only as being in surrounding worlds. Of Guibert's *Vita*, the first book was really an "Augustinian" confession, witness to his becoming a monk and reaching God. The second showed that person "absorbed into the surrounding world," although Gurevich's description is rather that there *is* no person except as being of that world. The third book dwells wholly on various communities (*Origins* 117–23). The evidence for Zink's "subjective representation of a life," modeling Héloïse and Abelard is scant. But I shall discuss them after Christina, whose biography certainly *was* written in the twelfth century, recorded in a manuscript dating more or less from her time.

Whoever wrote it talked closely with her of her childhood, her vow to dedicate her life to Christ, her parents' brutal efforts to marry her off, her break with them, her anchoritic experiences and her temptations. The manuscript, though, is severely damaged and a second half is missing: whether or not it ever existed. What exists tells the first forty or so years of Christina's life, drawing her as a person bound by its circles. Contrary to Hanning's thesis, it did not make her life a subjective choice between "bad" and "good," but a locus where demands of the world and time met those of God and eternity. Whether or not a struggle between "God and the devil," this is not reducible to some modern intergenerational, self-interested squabble between Christina and her parents (39). At issue were Augustinian Jerusalem and Rome, although the parents did make the last a Babylon for Christina. Yet their wish was to defend and expand, through the marriage of an unusually able elder daughter, interests not of just one noble family but of an entire Anglo-Saxon aristocracy, gravely, even terminally, menaced, Hanning agrees (38), by Norman political and economic assault after an invasion barely fifty years past. The family's tenacity in holding its place (matched, said her biographer, by Christina's humor) and hope that a child, in whom "shone forth such moral integrity, such decorum, such grace" and who had "such acuteness of perception, such providence in affairs and efficacy in carrying things out," would sustain and further it, surely came in part from these broad pressures (Talbot, *Life* 66–68: translations mine). The memoirist agreed that family interests in expanding wealth and assuring posterity was a usual aspect of the good earthly city, albeit here in conflict with the interests of the city of God (67–69).

These explained their violent usage of her. But they were not individual decisions any more than was Christina's demand that she remain a virgin dedicated to Christ. Her act was a refusal to accept her parents' judgment as to which circle of being most mattered. It was not a move toward individuality—still less individualism. Echoing familiar patterns and experiences of who-ness, she held divine and human orders concordant: "I shall not be disobedient to my parents against the precepts of the Lord if I do all I can to fulfil my vow to Christ" (62/63). Electing "Augustinian" emphasis on the central import of a divine core of being, refusing the worldly city, she was not "choosing" selfhood. She stressed memory and reminding. From early on Christ as memory was basic: "renew in me [*reformes in michi*]," she prayed, "the image of Thy Son: who lives and reigns with Thee in the unity of the Holy Spirit God" (40/41). Memory of the Virgin, too, enabled the soul's journey back to God. Denied access by her parents to the monastery of Our Lady as part of their pressure that she marry, she replied: "you will surely never tear its sweet memory from my breast" (46/47). When they tried to use an orgiastic feast to make her yield to her betrothed's lust she fixed "the Mother of God in memory" (48/49), helped by seeing the monastery through one of the doors of the hall in which the feast was taking place, the monastery on whose door, in her childhood, she had scratched a cross to seal her vow about virginity as a sign that "she had hidden [for eventual recall] especially in that monastery her affection" (38/39).

In *imitatio Christi* (or *Augustini*) style, her emphasis was on battle against the world, the flesh (always sexual) and the devil. The last took a series of temptational forms: a lustful bishop of Durham, her weak betrothed, her worldly family—especially father and mother—a corrupt bishop of Lincoln and his bribers, later, her sexual desires when alone with a certain holy person over a long period, then a series of calumnies. Each was defeated in turn, usually with the help of others, lay and religious. In the penultimate case the two "victims" seconded each other and God finally reassured her that it sufficed just to have stayed a virgin. As "she considered all temporal goods a shadow" (38/39), "despis[ing] transitory things" (the writer insisted: 156/57, trans. Talbot), her sense was that she might here have given too much to them.

The path to the divine by memory over battle with the animate, human, social and material worldly circles and the place of the person in them was expressed in similar ways by Augustine, but closer by Hroswitha, Hildegard and Richard of St. Victor, as it would be by Bonaventure and Marguerite Porete, limning changes in the world-embedded soul itself, or even later by Margery Kempe, tracing her path from the human to the divine. Where one perhaps catches glimmers of tension was in the *gap* between the earthly and heavenly cities that in Christina seems potentially emergent. That gap would not open seriously for some centuries but it was a seed of eventually new growth, one to add to that planted by the secular *Roland*. It may also be seen in Héloïse's first letters to Abelard, agonizing over the ongoing desires that seemed to cut her off from heaven. Such agonizing is why I disagree with Luiz Costa Lima's evaluation—apparently based only on the *Historia calamitatum*—that at the time of these writings human internal "conflicts and anxieties had not yet been thematized as psychological material" (77). Whatever Costa Lima's "not thematized" means, such conflicts and anxieties are even clearer in the lost letters. The *different* psychology at issue did not exclude internal anxieties and conflicts.

Despite Héloïse's agonizing, her and Abelard's tale was one, overall, of defeating any gap between worldly and divine circles, defeating human frailty (especially of women, she wrote) and adjusting passions to reason (first letter to Abelard, ed. Monfrin [M] 113; trans. Radice [R] 111; second letter to Abelard, ed. Jourdain and Despois [JD] 90; R133. All JD referrals are to volume 1). One can read the original eight letters in terms of Cicero's or Galen's *personae*: the human relative to the divine, the nature of being animate (Héloïse on the passions: JD93–94, R138–39), humans in their differences (Abelard's sense of his superior intellect: JD107, R160), women differing from men—needing attention for instance to menstruation and other "weaknesses" (JD109, R163) and social choices, like becoming a teacher or taking the cowl: the last bringing us full circle back to the divine. Even though Héloïse feared the gap (M116, R117; JD89–90, R133), it was her vanquishing of it that the correspondence was about (JD101, R150; JD104, R154), and it was by gathering into the person these several *personae* that wholeness could be renewed: in a context drawn overwhelmingly from Old and New Testaments, Ciceronian citations and allusions were not chance. Zink scolds Abelard's "high opinion of himself and the bitterness of his rancors" (240), Spence his marking "his differen[ce] from other men," his "alienation" (65), "textual decentering" (73) and "detachment" (75). The latter allows that while he "may have intended to evoke Augustine . . . the thrust of his story is entirely different" (57). Zink denies even the intention: "his project is not at all inspired by St Augustine's" (240). McLaughlin is equally peremptory: "[Augustine's *Confessions*] seems, indeed, to have exerted not the slightest influence on Abelard" (471). This seems wrong. Abelard's wholeness was achieved in an Augustinian context and his letters counseled Héloïse along this path. Her last letter showed that she was following it. Further, Abelard's first consolatory letter to a friend, the *Historia calamitatum*, signals enlacement in another circle: that of a classicizing literate history stretching from Cicero and Seneca to his own age, part of what it was to be *this* person.

Passible encircled experience and ways of thinking dominated in Abelard. Although Morris and many others argue that Abelard possessed something like a modern sense of self, neither he nor anyone else could have viewed his experience of personhood in so radical a light. Whatever the person's "center of knowing" might be (some sense of an internal "responsible" focus) that center still conceived of its fulfillment as lying only in some sort of union with the divine even if, in a case like that of Christina, to achieve it implied a break in the circles that were those of the person. In the meantime it stayed subject to (not of) all its surroundings: as Kay says, "the subject is *subject* to factors which overdetermine it" (212). "Overdetermine," as I said, is a misleading word, but the general point is well-taken. Robert Elbaz suggests that Abelard's letters vacillated between a view emphasizing God's control over all human lives and one accentuating humans' responsibility for their own decisions (48–58, here 49). This is also the opinion of so important an interpreter of Abelard as Jean Jolivet (*passim*). Yet it is clear at the end of Abelard's first letter that his life's process as he had just recorded it was to be seen as figured in Christ's, exemplifying human suffering on earth within a divine plan, making himself into an Augustinian *persona*. This was why Abelard took as his own St. Jerome's view of *his* being as figured in Christ:

St. Jerome, whose heir I consider myself as regards slanders and false accusations, wrote in his letter to Nepotian: "'If I still sought men's favor,' says the Apostle, 'I should be no servant of Christ.' He has ceased to seek men's favor and is become the servant of Christ" (*Epistulae* lii.13). He also wrote to Asella, concerning false friends, "Thank God I have deserved the hatred of the world" (xlv.6; xiv.4). (M108, R105)

In light of this view, Abelard's "vacillation" was the very image of the ambiguities inherent in the concept of Christ as the Divine Word made flesh. And if the Eucharist was the means by which humans could reverse that process (through flesh to union with God), Abelard's written letters imaged that means. They did not just relate Abelard's own passage through suffering of the flesh to identification with Christ's divinity but that of the reader (especially if the main reader was meant to be Héloïse). Not only in the *Historia* was Abelard so figured. His last "personal" letter, for example, first set him among the "martyrs" and Héloïse among those who helped them reach the divine sphere (JD98, R145), enabling escape from the world's "Charybdis" (JD99, R147). But finally it reassociated him with Christ (JD102, R151) and transformed their worldly relationship into a divine one, setting him through *imitatio* as the person of Jesus and her as Christ's bride (JD104, R154). Héloïse might then be taken to image the suffering of the human and an incarnate Christ who has still to overcome abandonment: a figuration echoing Hildegard's explanations of women, her sufferings and her "identification" with Christ in her abandonment. An "ontological similarity," as Bynum calls it, is built into these associations (*Metamorphosis* 53).

The "eucharistic" value of Abelard's letters and their aspect of *imitatio Christi* bring us again face to face with the central importance of *memory* in Western thought and practice at least since Socrates. Vance observes the "special importance" of "the faculty of memory" in medieval culture: the "commemorative paradigm" was vital to the culture's experience and understanding (*Mervelous* 51). So it long remained. Mary Carruthers shows the matter in fine detail (her *Book of Memory* now the primary source for these matters). I would not return to this were it not that memory was a constant and unbroken motif in Abelard's letters, and that this further explains the meaning of Abelard's well-known insistence on separating intention and act in the judgment of sin. This matters here because Abelard's use of such intention (*intentio*) and will (*uoluntas*) has often been taken as a signal that for him the human was a self-organizing and self-responsible subject. "It is always open to the will," as MacIntyre puts it, "to assent to or dissent from" the urgings of a person's mixed dispositions. "Even the possession of a vice does not necessitate the performance of a particular wrong action" (168). This is surely right, but it describes acts of a quite different sort of person from the subject that it is regularly taken to represent. Abelard distinguished four things:

> the vice of the mind which makes us prone to sinning and then the sin itself which we fixed in consent to evil or contempt of God, next the will for evil and the doing of evil. Just as, indeed, to will and to fulfil the will are not the same, so to sin and to perform the sin are not the same. We should understand the former to relate to the consent of the mind by which we sin, the latter to the performance of the action when we fulfil in a deed what we have previously consented to.

These in turn were to be thought as responses to "suggestion, pleasure, and consent" (*Ethics* 33).

These terms can be compared directly to those of Alexander of Aphrodisias, Nemesius and the *Digest*. Intention was inseparably and integrally linked to "*consensus animi.*" It was reasoned assent to (in this case) a sin, *peccatum*, which was "out there" ready for a person to perform if he or she consented to do so, *peccatum perficere*. That is why Abelard insisted,

Marilyn Adams notes, on locating "sin in *consent* rather than in the deed" and on the thought that "*consent* is sufficient" for sin, whether or not any outward act is committed (*Ethical*, "introduction" xix, xxi). Contrariwise, one could therefore, under certain conditions, "sin" by accident, doing the deed without meaning to or knowing its sense or effect. Or one could knowingly accept, "will," the deed "against God's commandment." In this case one accepted a particular action *affected* on one by the world (or Satan).The spectrum between memory and assent to evil marked the distance from the divine to the world, from Jerusalem to Rome and Babylon. Abelard's and Héloïse's letters sought a path in the opposite direction. For similarly a "good intention" was acceptance of a deed "pleasing to God" that brought with it "the whole mass of [good] works coming from it"—whose circumstance proved the goodness of the deed effectuated—a deed from our memory of works that would "please God" (*Ethics* 53–55). To avoid sin was simply to avoid that "contempt of God" which was our "consent to evil" (69).

One could do this by keeping His memory in mind, essential ground for acting always according to "*prudentia*," the principal virtue: "Prudence, that is, discernment of good and evil, is the mother of virtues rather than a virtue" (128–29). Here was another piece of a familiar post-Stoic puzzle, essential in the world, essential in the internal balance of a person, essential to one's understanding of one's relation to the divine. Abelard's *Ethics* were far from proposing a willful modern subject, ruler of its individually judged and performed intentions. They offered a person well within familiar patterns, although Abelard's having to assent to a course of penitential auto-subjection traced for him by institutional codes to bring his experience back into the fold suggests that he threatened aspects of those familiarities. The principle of the penitential was that sin was "understood here as a sickness, as something that has 'befallen' the human soul from without" (Gurevich, *Medieval* 29; cf. 78–103). Tensions were becoming visible. Indeed, the confessional's growing importance may be understood as in part a response to such tensions.

Communal public confession had been used since the earliest Christian years. Gurevich notes: "as late as the thirteenth century, public chastisement of sinners was practised, along with auricular confession." Increasingly "confession in the presence of the community" was replaced "by private conversations between priest and penitent" (*Medieval* 24). This stayed irregular until the Fourth Lateran Council and Pope Innocent III imposed annual confession for "every *fidelis* of both sexes" (Tambling 37; cf. Lea and Tentler). This may suggest a "transformation of the ethical status of the individual" (Gurevich, *Medieval* 24). But this confession did not explore and reveal an interior subjectivity. First, confession was *impersonal*: you confessed *qua* fallen human, not as independent individual (in response to a standard list of questions, the "Penitential," applicable to all). Second, confession was expressly to cast off sins drawing one from God, to remember His bounty and reset the soul in the divine order. Third, you were *subjected to* a priestly interlocutor's authority, his subjected to God's. The Lateran's Canon 21 on confession was, fourth, part of the Council's insistent institutionalizing of Christian life, Church affairs and relations with its flock. The Lateran's establishment of "private" confession matched its establishment of the Inquisition "which made the individual subject the target of a host of invasive ecclesiastical and political investigations and thus shaped his conscious as a potentially secret site of truth," Elizabeth Hanson remarks (4).

For long, she urges (it is her book's main topic), a conflict—or *potential* conflict—existed between the sense that this "truth" of the soul was answerable only to God and the "disciplinary effect" created by the demands of church and/or state. The conflict was between two spheres of *subjection*. Certainly, if they were *potentially* experienced as not just fragmented but in conflict, none of this excludes the likelihood that over time and with other practices (like the Inquisition), the confessional may have helped establish a personalized private individual: not the least of these practices arising much later from confession itself, in the invention of the closed confessional box from the 1550s (Tambling 66–69). (More exactly, it may have helped create the *telling* of such a person. Nicholas Paige finds such an effect in French Catholic confessional writings from the late sixteenth century, but no real sense of private selfhood before the second third of the seventeenth century. Philippe Lejeune urges a still later time, that of "industrial civilization and the bourgeoisie coming to power," dating autobiography's beginnings as late as 1760 [*L'autobiographie* 10, 43]. Dates similar to these are agreed by scholars for England [Folkenflik, Lyons, Mascuch, J. Morris, F. Nussbaum, Pascal, Shumaker, Spacks], France [Beaujour, Lejeune], Spain [Fernández] and elsewhere. Such tellings and the experience behind them, we shall see, may be not far from being chronologically coincident.)

In the second half of the thirteenth century, some of these tensions were made further public by Étienne Tempier's condemnation (December 10, 1269) of views of which the Averroist Siger of Brabant was thought chief proponent. The bishop rejected thirteen theses asserted to claim, *inter alia*, "the unicity of the human intellect, determinism of the will, the eternity of the world, the mortal nature of the soul, the complete detachment of God from all knowledge of the universe, and the negation of divine providence" (Knowles 272–73). Averroes held that rational soul was part of and returned to universal soul. Lacking separate immortality, it was part of a whole. Still, as embodiment was what made the human human, it was partly defined by distance from that universal: for the time of a life. Even if no one actually held the views as condemned their statement clearly mooted fears and caught elements like the gap between the world and the divine or growing ambiguities in ideas of will. In just over seven years these fears grew: Tempier's March 7, 1277, renewal of the condemnation increased the number of propositions to 219.

But even the radical William of Ockham "totally accepted the [familiar] regularities of nature and the constancy of moral norms. If his was a universe of individuals they were not self-contained or discrete" (Leff xxiii). And that held only for logic. In the human sphere, says Gordon Leff, "Ockham like virtually every Christian thinker accepts St. Augustine's view of the soul as formed in the image of the uncreated Trinity" (529–30). The soul's likeness to God was partly in its substance as image, but mainly "through the soul's conjunction with its acts of knowing and willing." He then discusses the Eucharist as center and end of Ockham's thinking (596–613). For him, no less than for Augustine, Hildegard, Christina or Abelard, the Divine was completion of nature, attained by commemorative illumination. The dominant experience of who-ness stayed that of being in collective circles. Beside these, we can set public cases closer to what is suggested by *Roland* or lyric performance, such that Ullmann can speak of "the absorption of the individual by the community or by society," shown by such "collective punishments . . . as the interdict of a locality or the amercements of towns, villages, or hundreds" (*Individual* 32). "Society was pictured as a large organism in which each member had been allotted a special function which he pursued for the common good" (40). Fixed estates (what a human was born to) and personal vocation (social *persona*) were society's "characteristic facts" (41–43). A "member," though, was not "allotted": person was always already defined by this and other "public" circles, and "common good" corresponded inseparably to personal good, ineluctable elements of the *vita beata*.

But this understanding and the experience it represented may well no longer have been entirely stable. A still dominant theocratic discourse (corresponding to Augustine's or Hildegard's hierarchy of circles) may have confronted actually experienced practices that partly contradicted it. Ullmann sees the first as setting God at the summit in His plenitude with, immediately below, His anointed king. The king was set over a society whose members, *fideles*, were "incorporated" and conjoined in a fixed, hierarchically ordered totality. Against this was a feudal practice giving much "freedom" to the individual and also including the customary practices of everyday life (*Medieval* 189–219, *Individual* 130–44, and see Ganshof, *passim*). Karsten Harries explores Tempier's condemnation as signaling a growing space for new thinking about the world and the human (129–42). Janet Coleman sees similar change in advent of a sense (and law) of rights. She proposes that in England Magna Carta was thought of, if not yet in the thirteenth century, yet from the fourteenth to the seventeenth (when Edward Coke and his fellows began to interpret it in terms of individualist rights) "as fundamental law enshrining equal rights of all subjects." These rights or liberties, though, "were still to be considered grants, tied to the Common Law and its courts and to the increasing power of Parliament." No one took them to inhere in an individual *qua* individual. They depended on "consent and consensus" among the variously ranked members of the commonweal. Between the thirteenth and seventeenth centuries, "we can observe, then, a language of rights and liberties that is generated from an understanding that individual rights can only be political rights, dependent on individuals becoming [being] legally recognized subjects of a sovereign State" ("The Individual" 12; cf. Holt 292, Reiss, *Discourse* 96–97n75).

Such movements give us a glimpse of how to understand stresses of changing experience slowly working their way into becoming both means to understand that experience and, but not separably, elements of what will be felt as "new" experiences. These are possibilities composed, Hanson says, as "improvisations around the fissures between the material conditions of life and the conceptual resources already in place in a culture. Therefore new ways of knowing are often profoundly at odds with the consciously held commitments of the people who begin to articulate them, emerging not as principles from which a world order can be derived, but as contradictions in discourse and social practice" (*Discovering* 3). Nothing in the new experience was inevitable. No necessary "modern self" was growing as an inevitable product of human history. Differences and changes in analysis and practice, understanding and experience, out of sync with each other, created tensions. No sudden fracture occurred, rather a long bending of patterns which, after two or three centuries, became something qualitatively and recognizably different. These patterns inevitably affected every sphere of human praxis, including the personhood that was part of it.

Overall, the general sense of who-ness was still that which José Ortega y Gasset described as usual from European antiquity to the middle ages, seeing the human person as some concrete relation with the physical and rational world (of Platonic ideas, for example). For this "ancient conception of the world," "'being' means to know oneself (*hallarse*) a thing among things. These exist by resting one in another to shape the grand architecture of the universe. The [human] subject is nothing more than one among so many things immersed in the great 'sea of being' of which Dante spoke" ("Las dos" 259). Spitzer's thought that Dante and others "dealt not with the individual but with mankind," less interested in an "empirical person" than in "the generally human capacity for cognizing the supramundane," fingers analogous ideas ("Note" 415, 417). However impressionistic and vague these expressions, they clearly coincide with what previous chapters have described more precisely. This one has shown that by the twelfth to thirteenth centuries and even earlier, the sea was no longer so calm. The unease scholars have seen in *Roland*, Chrétien's romances, Gace, lyric poetry or Chaucer, shows beginnings of multiple tensions. These and matching strains in a wider public world have been interpreted as aspects of emergent "capitalist" praxis. This is not to say that capitalist experience and analysis were latently present, but that bits and pieces of what circumstances would one day consolidate as such were being forged in these tensions. "Events," to use Jacques Lezra's term, were in the making that could *one day* acquire meanings. They were marked by pressures erupting in forms of commercial and military conflict, reorganizations of political boundaries, struggles between pope, emperor and other secular princes and more. Nowhere, perhaps, were they experienced more up close than in Italy, ravaged from the twelfth through the sixteenth century by varyingly heated and often puzzlingly intricate conflicts between popes and emperors, by the internecine squabbles of its city-states and by the errant brutality of *condottiere* armies.

We shall not be surprised, then, that it took a Petrarch to express most clearly both the familiar experience of who-ness and the sources of the pressures tending to introduce new needs. Petrarch was a poet and scholar as intimate with the secular ancients as he was with Augustine, who admired Xenophon's *Oeconomicus* and recognized implications of its being translated by Cicero and so recalled in the broadly civic *De officiis* (*Le familiari* 3.18), who consciously played his own poetry off against such immediate precursors as Dante and the lyricists of Sicily, Tuscany and Provence, who owned and annotated the letters of Héloïse and Abelard. Petrarch experienced and commented on times so disturbed that he did not hesitate to pillory the supposed center of the divine in the world, the papal court of Avignon, reviling it as the opponent of an idealized Rome and embodiment of Babylon. At the same time this experience was bound to the particular concerns of the patrons with whom he was associated, for whom he labored and who made him a wealthy man, whether the Colonna family of his beginnings—magnates in Rome, closely tied to papal interests—or later, from 1353 to 1361, the Visconti rulers of a Milan that in those very years became one of the more rampant and rapacious of the peninsula's expansive city-states. Thus, whether we agree with Wallace that "the final effect of Petrarchan humanism and Petrarchan poetics [was] to announce and embellish the will of the state as embodied in the person of a single masculine ruler" (*Chaucerian* 262), his commentary could certainly never be innocent of particular interest, as Boccaccio did not hesitate to accuse him. Petrarch, slightly younger contemporary of Ockham, was reacting directly and precisely to these traditional experiences, these tensions, these new pressures. His strong sense of the desirable stability of familiar forms of personal being is all the more striking.

PART TWO

Petrarch through Descartes

CHAPTER ELEVEN

"Multum a me ipso differre compulsus sum"

Closely to read Petrarch is to sense an experience of personhood still near what we have been seeing and far from any familiar to a modern Europe of which he has long been depicted the first exemplar (Trinkaus, *Poet*, and Tripet can stand for this tradition). Giuseppe Mazzotta has much tempered this myth of Petrarch's modernist "psychological profile" (as have Ascoli, "Petrarch's Middle," and Waller, whose different views square with what follows), but my topic requires a return to his subject. For "subject," in any modern or even slightly earlier western sense, one does not find in Petrarch. Not for him belief in a Dignity of Man pitted alone against Nature and Fortune, responsible for his fate, ennobled by Promethean individualism. Not for him even modest belief in humans as essentially characterized by distinct singular interiority. Not for him plain reprise of Augustinian or later medieval experiences. Aspects of ancient who-ness, capacious in its multicircular embedding, now Christianized and hierarchized, lived on in Petrarch's experience, but tensed by poten- tial antinomies, by novel and many-directional pressures. Were they tensed enough to license Freccero's glimpse of Petrarch as new heroic sub- ject, if only in poetic device ("Fig Tree")? Or even Wallace's of "typically self-contradictory, self-alienating act[s] expressive of a new, postmedieval individualism" (to repeat a phrase cited in Chapter 1)? Were they beyond "tensed," forging an "egoism," says Thomas Greene, "so monumental and acute that it was an event in European intellectual history"? But he also saw it "explicitly challeng[ing] . . . the radical stasis of the medieval personality," a view I have already argued to be too uncomplicated, du- alistic and anachronistic ("Flexibility" 246).

The following analysis argues that even the first goes too far, but ef- fects of these pressures appear notably in an experience of "personal dispersion"—which Greene also thinks vital to Petrarch's experience, marked as "essentially new" by the *"varietas"* of his writings and above all "of the roles [he] improvised successfully upon the stage of European politics and letters" ("Flexibility" 247–48). That, I think, doesn't catch it either, but this "dispersion" is the most useful place to begin. Greene later stressed dispersion and "errancy" over egoism, noting a "radical ambivalence" as "the more constant principle throughout most of Petrarch's writing," and even talking of "all spheres of human effort in Petrarch's imagination" and "an inner threshold" projecting its sensibilities "outward in increasingly wide concentric circles"—of home, of country ("Petrarch" 35, 39, 47). Seeing these spheres and circles as just artifacts of a language that is "a kind of extension of the self into all that is not the self," Greene still pines for egoism and views Petrarch as similarly pining "to be truly and profoundly free, the disencumbered traveller of a Renaissance" (49, 57). Yet it is clear that another perception of being human is now shading the anachronistic imposition of a later western one. So we need to catch particularities of the "dispersion" now seeming to bespeak that earlier perception, its fundamental differences from modern western self-consciousness. We need, that is, to place that perception in its own context, not ours.

It has doubtless seemed to many moderns that in the opening letter of the *Familiari*, addressing his "Socrates" (Ludwig van Kempen), Petrarch wrote of the need, Aldo S. Bernardo translates, "to know the mind and heart of one's interlocutor [*nosse collocutoris sui animum*]," "to be accustomed to the personality of one person, to know what he likes to hear, and what you should say [*unius assuevisse ingenio, scire quid illum audire iuvet, quid te loqui deceat*]" (*Le familiari* 1.7; *Letters on Familiar Matters* 1.7. References, henceforth indicated by F, are first to Rossi's Latin, second to Bernardo's English, usually retranslated for reasons discussion makes clear. Latin and arabic numerals indicate Petrarch's book and letter, arabic, after a colon, volume and page).

Caveats are in order. To translate *animus* as "mind and heart" implies an individual interiority that the Latin did not. The same applies to interpreting *unius ingenio* as "to the personality of one person." *Ingenium* did mean "mental powers," "disposition," "temperament," even by now, the last chapter showed, "wit" (often abusive). It had nothing of the individualism connoted by the word "personality." *Unius* ("of one") let Petrarch avoid exactly the sort of specification asserted by a phrase like "of one person." The impersonal syntax of the two final clauses emphasized the *absence* of "personality": "to know what may please (or benefit) him to hear, what may become you to say." Translation is not just into foreign words but into foreign, inhabitual and sometimes unknown ways of conceptualizing. Its consequent difficulty is not more easily—or more of-ten—resolved for being a familiar one.

Petrarch was making a couple of points that this kind of translation obscures. A first was that the exact knowledge of others required of his letter-writer was impossible, especially for him as a wandering "Ulysses" facing constant changes of place and fortune, endless movement and dis-ruption, perpetual swings between calamity and prosperity. Just compare "Ulixeos errores erroribus meis [Ulysses' wanderings (or errors) to my wanderings]." One's very selfe was ceaseless errancy. Movement, peril, burdens, storms, fear, misdirection, doubt, crossings of known borders (*patrios fines*)—akin to lifelong "actual warfare" (Seneca's "battle")—were "common to all" (F 1.7–8, 1.8–9). People *had* no fixed individual personality at any rate partly because they experienced no stable situation or condition (quite aside from the many other elements we shall see com-plicating the sense of personhood). People were either, as Augustine had many times put it in *The City of God*, "alien wanderers" in the human city or, if given over to it entirely, tied to its everlasting vicissitudes (e.g. CG XV.1: 4.412–14). In this last case, one was, he said in the *Confes-sions*, a "spiritus ambulans," wandering spirit, one who "ambulando am-bulaba[t] in ea, quae non sunt neque in te neque in me neque in corpore [wandered wandering among those things which are neither in You, nor in me nor in body]," exiled (*exulaba[t]*) from one's "fellow citizens of the city of god" (IV.15: 1.192–94). The repeated negatives here underscore absence and uncertainty.

Humanity might be "the most industrious and noblest inhabitant of the earth," but not at all in any sense favored by Enlightenment histori-ans. This "nobility" was no willful glorying in powerful solitude. On the contrary, Petrarch wrote to Guido Sette, humans were "noble" only to the limit of their rational ability to understand the bounds set on them by the fact that "all things change condition: lands, seas, heaven itself," as well as everything in them. Human "fate is always shaky, always the mind [*mens*] is stirred by passions, body by places, mind [*animus*] dimin-ishes daily, memory ages, mental skill grows blunt, health is weakened, strength impaired, agility is dulled, beauty devoured, youth perishes, death stalks, life flees" (F XVII.3: 3.238, 3.14). As if these vicissitudes did not suffice, humans had always to suffer "fluctuation of Fortune, swiftest of all." Just remember, he wrote in a long letter on the *tempus fugit* and *ubi sunt* themes to the same correspondent around 1367, how all the places and people of our childhood, youth and maturity have changed—and with what drama and speed: "But I do not at all complain," he told Sette, "knowing that from the beginning of time everything turns, noth-ing stands still" (*Senili* X.2: 110b, *Letters of Old Age* 2.371. For the

Latin of I.1–7, I use the Nota/Dotti edition, of the rest, the *Epistole rerum senilium* in the 1501 Works, aided by much inferior 1554 and 1581 editions in expanding abbreviations. An S before numerical references indicates this work; an a or b after the *Epistole* page indicates column).

Not only was humans' situation in the world subject to ceaseless change, they had no stability of "interior" selfe either. One had to marvel, said Petrarch to his brother Gherardo, at how "desires of one and the same person [*hominis*] conflicted," at how they changed with age, season, even days, hours and minutes (F X.5: 2.314, 2.79). Opening the last book of the *Familiari* with another letter on the *tempus fugit* topos to his friend Philippe de Cabassole, Petrarch recalled feelings of thirty years before, observing how short a span sufficed for utter change in his habits of mind, customs and behavior, interests and studies: "nothing is to me now as it was then; I do not mean when I wrote that letter, but when I began to write this one" (F XXIV.1: 4.219, 3.312). A common figure of speech, this was also a deeply lived reality. Montaigne's *branloire perenne* was already by his later time a long-familiar experience of who-ness.

So another point was that even were it possible, plain knowledge of others would be undesirable. Not only were everyone's mental shape and style always moving with milieu, event, social circumstance and fugitive need, but "differences between people were infinite." "Good God!" he exclaimed to Gherardo, "how great their diversity, how many their pursuits, how dissimilar their taste, their opinions . . . what a business of myriad crafts, how varied the shape of affairs, how different the diligence!" (F X.5: 2.311–12, 2.77). This might seem to imply individual "personalities," even if untold variety impeded knowledge. It did not. Petrarch related an experience of people *depending* on one another in the strongest sense: their very being, we shall see, was mutually determined. To believe otherwise was to believe in an ipseity that, as Augustine had said, was the devil's work and drew one from God (Chapter 9 above).

These many enigmas meant that in writing series of letters you had to discuss endless variety of matters (including your own shifting mind: F I.1: 1.12–13, 1.11–13), alter mind and style, weave them "with multicolored threads" (1.14, 1.14). Petrarch iterated this in closing the collection: "so you have," he wrote to his "Socrates," "a book woven from my trifles with great disparity of things and words" (F XXIV.13: 4.264, 3.351). One was "compelled," Bernardo translates a crucial sentence of the opening letter, "to be very inconsistent." Its terms were more arresting: "Quibus ego difficultatibus multum a me ipso differe compulsus sum": "By these difficulties I was forced to differ much from my selfe" (1.9, 1.9). The play on *differe* and *difficultates* and *ego* set within *quibus* . . . *difficultates* amplify the sense of the infinitive as a constant "taking away" of *ego* from *me ipso*, "I" marked pronominally but as the first person of a passive verb, selfe ever readjusted to the ceaseless stir of conditions and *errorum*. Petrarch was clear in this prefatory letter that he was not offering—could not offer—a single, unified personality, his own or others'. This, too, recalled Augustine who, writing the *Confessions* as a worldly wanderer desperately seeking God, asked, we saw, "where was I?"; lamenting, "ego autem et a me discesseram nec me inveniebam [but I had gone from me and did not find me]" (V.2: 1.210). It is only in this sense that we can accept Wallace's phrase about Petrarch's reader that "we are interchangeable with any other member of the posterity that Petrarch [was] addressing" (*Chaucerian* 266). Each is a singular (not "individual") reader but each shares, as addressed by Petrarch, in a collective experience of fluidity and dispersion—as did he.

This lived reality was echoed in Petrarch's epistolary form and styles. Their collections fell into the *dictamina* tradition of letter manuals for diplomat, scholar or epistolarily challenged. They showed *types* of writing styles, of event and experience, of address and relation. One should not be surprised, therefore, at how many of them scholars have been able to show to be "fictitious." Here, the adjective means that the letters, as collected, were less "real" ones—sent—than *dictamina* samples; except that they "were invented" for "artistic" causes and "to provide the collection with the impression of a distinct chronology" (Bernardo, "Introduction," *Letters on Familiar Matters* 2.xviii; cf. "Letter-Splitting"). It makes clearer how far speaker and recipient, "I" and "thou," were mutually made in and by public (and publicly sanctioned forms of) exchange. While their originals *were* (usually?) sent and circulated, collected letters' dates, addressees and contents were, Petrarch said in his first letter, rewritten and reordered. Scholarship continues to show how much. Petrarch claimed, for instance, to have written the famous "Ascent of Mont Ventoux" (F IV.1) in April 1336 "ex tempore" after his descent. Clearly he did not, since he made much of Gherardo becoming a Carthusian in 1343. Scholars now argue that it "was actually written (or rewritten) as late as 1353." This makes its addressee, Dionigi da Borgo San Sepolcro, also fictitious, having died in 1342. The letter spoke to one "from a tomb," like others addressed to the illustrious dead (Ascoli, "Petrarch's Middle" 32, 39).

The letters incorporated particulars, but functioned as *exempla*, illustrating what we might call the representative *muthoi* of human existence. The Aristotelian term is anachronistic, since the *Poetics* was rediscovered only a century after Petrarch's death (although he could have known Averroes' commentary), but it well names the exemplary but familiar forms of action and experience the letters illustrated. In this regard, one should recall how the letters' public nature emphasized their *representative* character. Although most were addressed to individuals, even when they were not "invented" for the collection they were meant as public documents, to be read aloud and passed from hand to hand—precisely indeed as had occurred with Abelard's consolatory letter, the *Historia calamitatum*, and as Petrarch had experienced his and Héloïse's entire correspondence in the manuscript he possessed of it, the earliest now known. (Much later, Hélisenne de Crenne would produce her "novels" from the same ground.) For Petrarch, his own letters' diversities of style and instance meant, among other things, to give norms of civic counsel and public behavior—public and civic here being no less "unius," of the one, than of the many.

Probably in late July 1347, Petrarch made the point in a letter to Cola di Rienzo:

Do not imagine for a moment that the letters that you write from Rome remain long in the possession of those to whom they are addressed. On the contrary, everyone rushes to make a copy of them with as much earnestness, and circulates them around the pontiff's court with as much zeal, as if they were sent not by a man of our own race but by an inhabitant of another world or of the antipodes. All press around to interpret your epistles; and never was an oracle of the Delphic Apollo turned and twisted into so many different meanings.

Indeed in the present circumstances of conflict between Cola in Rome and the papal curia in Avignon, he warned his republican hero to remember that this public nature of writing could endanger him. "Always write," he advised, "as if everyone were to read, and not merely read, but as if they were about to set out from every shore and bear your message to every land" (*Variae* 38: Petrarch, *Revolution* 55. The Latin can be found in, e.g., *Epistolae*, and my bibliography's editions of the *Opera*). The warning did not concern Cola's "individual" safety, the well-being of "unius," in any simple, one-dimensional way. For Petrarch the self-styled "tribune of Rome" embodied Roman community past, present and future, as well as hopes for a peaceful and united Italy. The counsel reflected Petrarch's own intentions and experience of life's publicness. The exceptionality of this instance and its principal player did not prevent them from being like any other human being and event in letting norms of civic counsel and public behavior be particularized and applied to actual practice. If anything their seeming uniqueness had a contrary role. It showed how all human experience was subject to common norms.

The letters' diversities of style and instance were increased by continual citation of earlier writers, their author moving between *personae*. Story, counsel, commentary and rebuke thereby acquired particular authority. The assertion draws another caveat. For "authority," as used of medieval and early Renaissance writers' and thinkers' relation to precursors, however familiar an idea, still generates a misleading account of what was involved: not *auctoritas* of one writer or text, but *auctoritas* of settled doctrine and belief, which author(s) and text(s) then exemplified. The point, again, was that human knowledge and wisdom were cumulative, best and most often thought of as recovered or remembered. Thought and its matter built a treasury held by all in common. Even to say that risks to mislead. For to modern Western readers, "all in common" suggests individuals united by circumstance or condition for some useful goal—as if those composing the commonality preceded and had chosen to join it. For Petrarch and his contemporaries, a human being out of community would still have been problematic: to be human was to be in community—in many communities. Passible soul, mind, person dwelt in historically accumulated *auctoritas* as in any other of its surroundings. In that sense, to call the treasury of knowledge "built" also tends to misapprehension: what was "built" was its presence to human minds. The knowledge was always already *there* for recovery by human memory and passible reaction—of which an interesting case occurs in the "Ascent of Mont Ventoux." This letter's first paragraph recorded a passage in Livy: "apud Livium forte ille michi locus occurrerat." Ascoli translates: "by chance I came across that place in Livy" ("Petrarch's Middle" 27). The Latin actually says: "in Livy by chance that place came across me."

Passibility and community are reasons why concepts like "plagiarism" and "sincerity" are newer inventions, produced by other norms of human social being and relations. They assume individuals with stable cores of "personality," essential internal realities of "who they are" that proper ("truthful") human relations should reveal and depend on. They assume, too, that among the stabilizing essences are all the things set under the name of "property" as being one such individual's, not another's. So they help define "personality." The modern West has believed these and associated attributes to be universal and constant components of human being. It is a belief that has more to do with control than understanding.

Petrarch titled a letter to his friend Francesco Nelli: "fidem sufficere in amicorum colloquiis nec querendum stilum"; in Bernardo: "that sincerity suffices for corresponding with friends, and that no special style is necessary" (F XVIII.8: 3.287, 3.56). Modern expectations make this version seem unexceptionable. Closer attention shows otherwise. *Fides* meant trust, honesty, good faith. It mirrored no modern sense of a transparently secure rendering of "interior" being. It named a more "external" virtue (momentarily to use misleading adjectives) better fitting a civic, even legal, paradigm: loyalty, sense of duty, reliability, honor, worthiness of belief, credit. It did not name stable "truths" of personality but fulfillment of legitimate expectation and mutual obligation: "For the foundation of justice is good faith, *fides*," Cicero had written, "that is, truth and devotion [*constantia*] to promises and agreements" (*De officiis* I.vii.23). Justice was one of those primary virtues, along with *prudentia, fortitudo* (or *magnanimitas*) and *temperantia* (or *continentia*) whose proper balance was named *decorum* in the sociopolitical world and *sapientia* in the human being as a whole. Here, *fides* was their guarantor.

Through late antiquity and the middle ages, we saw in Chapters 9 and 10, this Roman civic virtue had been a central tenet of the legal, political and religious spheres, the *anima* of society. *Fides* named a constant adherence to stable sets of communal relations connecting persons to their many surroundings. We may usefully recall the syntactic "impersonality" that Petrarch used to express the relation between writer and recipient. *Fides* connoted fidelity to the common "treasury," here, expectations of ethical human action and speech, the aforementioned *muthoi*, not to any individual singularity. It was the name of access to one area of the common inherited wealth that was knowledge. Gathering *auctoritates* was thus an attribute of good writing, and *imitatio*, creating new savors from others' rhetorical flowers in emulation of Seneca's honey bees, the foundation of true knowledge and proper letters (Petrarch, F I.8; XXIII.19). The treasury was a whole not subject to "personal," let alone unimaginably individualist, choice.

"But see, lest you think me bound to anyone's argument," Petrarch observed to Boccaccio after expounding views on human life and death, "I have neutrally, knowingly and willingly collected conflicting authors and arguments [*sententias*] and you choose, as will seem fitting [*ut visum erit*], and truth will stand in its place" (S I.5: 1.50, 1.20). One could not choose one "truth," given once and for all. But more, while "visum erit" can be translated as a passive form of *video* (as here), it can also be a clause composed of *erit* with the noun *visum* as complement: "as its appearance shall be," "according to what will be before your eyes." *Auctores et sententias* together made one *visum* and that *visum* was *veritas*. Truth lay in authors and their arguments inasmuch as they *were* plurally collected, and *seen* to be. No one human could decide the rightness of any element of knowledge. So Augustine had argued toward the end of the *Confessions*: "In this diversity of arguments [*sententiarum*], let truth itself bring concord, and our God have pity on us, that we may use the law lawfully" (XII.30: 2.364). Truths, he explained in the next chapter (XII.31), were many. They were all right and single in God alone. Humans needed their multitude. For that very reason, *not* to heed one's precursors was to incur almost criminal loss and to fall into darkest ignorance.

The absence of trained and intelligent scribes and writers, Petrarch lamented to Jacopo Fiorentino, had resulted not just in the unintelligibility of past works, but in their actual disappearance: "Thus our times have gradually been bereft of the richest and sweetest fruits of letters and of the vigils and labors of famous minds, than which I would assert that there is assuredly nothing on earth more precious" (F XVIII.12: 4.295, 3.63). To know the thought of others' minds was basic to one's humanity. Incessant citation of earlier writers was not just search for support in greater, more reliable or more accepted authority. Nor was it just that differing *personae* marked a writer's changing selves. Enveloping presences inseparably grounded any selfe. So did the overall context of knowledge, wisdom, condition, place, in which everyone dwelt (or had dwelt). *No one* could be thought a self-contained entity. That was why, no less than their addressees (and their writer), the letters' characters were portrayed as defined by social, material and other relations.

In a real and deeply felt way no *person* was solitary. The experience of *being* in a public community held for all circumstances. Thus the *De vita solitaria* was not an exploration of solitude, but of what were the firmest surroundings for the life of wisdom. "I believe," Petrarch began, "that a noble soul/mind [*animum*] will never find repose except in God where is our end, except in itself and its secret thoughts, or except in some soul/mind [*animum*] united to it by much likeness" (*De vita solitaria* I.i: 296 [DVS]; Zeitlin trans. LS 105, but all translations mine). Potential perfection of person involved (here) three possible sets of relationships: with the divine, the animate and the human. Little needs saying of the first for the moment. I shall return to it. The others require a bit more precision. The second in particular seems to offer a certain sort of individualism. But what were this "selfe" and "its secret thoughts"? If they at all concerned what the *Vita* propounded, as we must suppose, they were marked indelibly and essentially by community.

Here, the community was the historical one named in previous chapters: that of the writers in which Petrarch rooted his authorial being. His secret thoughts were those of accumulated *auctoritates*. The *Vita*, I recalled, was an intricate fabric woven of references and citations. Enenkel's edition and exegesis of the *Vita*'s first book shows it composed almost wholly of such matter. His gloss does not exhaust the references. The *Vita* was a rich instance of such a treasury as Petrarch elsewhere praised and advocated. The value of "solitary" life and its representation lay in exchanges with past authorities—always, Giorgio Ficara adds, in *places* vibrant with local life (71–98; cf. Reiss, "Perioddity" 439–40). The second book, citing their multitudes over times and places—holy people and saints, Asian and Biblical luminaries, popes and scholars, philosophers and poets—names the participants. Exchanges with present interlocutors

mattered no less. Petrarch addressed the *Vita* to Cabassole as a long letter, even a conversation in which he was speaking, he said, his friend's
thoughts in his, Petrarch's, words: "tu in verbis meis tuam sententiam
agnoscas" (I.i: DVS 296; LS 106).

He did say that he had been led "in this treatise mostly by [his] sole experience," as following "[his] mind with a freer, if perhaps more insecure,
step than another's traces" (I.i: DVS 298; LS 106–7). But he was not at
all thinking himself some solitary individual agent of novelty. In fact, he
set "angelic solitude" (his and Cabassole's together, but including, too,
like-minded interlocutors) against "that Tartarean clamor" with which
they were only too familiar from the hellish Avignon papal court (I.i:
DVS 298; LS 107). Not isolated individuals but the right sort of community was the issue: the calm of Seneca's good sage against the evil fool's
unruly instability. The purpose of a "life of solitude" was to achieve the
sage's calm. Three kinds of personal relation enabled it: the divine, the
soul's intercourse with the historical *auctoritates* of wisdom and its ongoing dialogue with present sage interlocutors. Much of this will return.
Let it suffice for now to say that here, too, soul and mind were unthinkable apart from the circles of a person's being. To be sure, these and other
relations were now ineluctably hierarchical. In another letter to Cabassole, Petrarch talks of rejoicing "alone" in a landscape whose ruler his
friend is and whose peasants' consequent respect is part of his joy. Wallace rightly takes this to signal the hierarchy and the poet's exultingly
complacent experience of his high place in it (*Chaucerian* 272: ref. to S
X.2). This changes the *shape* of the collective experience of personhood.
It does not change its collective nature.

This was so even for the greatest and most "singular"—as a tale of
Charlemagne's infatuation for "a certain ordinary woman" shows. Even
after her death, the king's besottedness kept him by her, ignoring all duties. A "bishop from Cologne, . . . outstanding for his sanctity and wisdom," found a magic jeweled ring under her tongue and removed it.
Finding that Charles, freed of the corpse's charms, was now attached to
him, the holy man threw the ring into a marsh near where Charles and
his court then were. This was Aix, and the King grew so fond of the
marsh and its surroundings as to build a palace and church there, making it his kingdom's capital and the place where his successors would be
crowned (F I.4: 1.25–27, 1.26–28).

This was doubtless an extreme example—if not slightly tongue-in-
cheek—but Petrarch shows how personhood was not at all simply internal or singular. He gives us a king, among the greatest, a human at the
pinnacle of earthly creatures, whose person (*animus* and *ingenium*)—its
behavior, experience and very being—was ruled, made, by external ma-

teriality. It does not matter whether Petrarch or his readers believed the tale of the magic ring to recount historical fact. The point is the idea and feeling of what established a person's nature. It does matter that an especially holy and wise bishop broke the king's harmful attachment to the earthly things taking him from his duties as mediator among his people and between them and the divine. The latter role was also the bishop's. We have already begun to see that the soul's return to its origins was for Petrarch, too, a fundamental aspect of the nature of personhood.

The theme was constant in Petrarch as in everyone. He gave it a Platonic slant in *Familiari* II.5, the first of four consolations addressed around 1336–37 to the Dominican Giovanni Colonna, forced to leave Avignon. Petrarch likened his journey to that of life itself, in which "one must suffer many things until that day . . . when this mortal garment and the fetters of this gloomy dwelling are cast off from minds striving for heaven" (F 1.81, 1.87). God was in the soul, which stayed attached to the divine world: "seek and you shall find in your soul Him you love; there is no need to wander outside to rejoice in Him" (F II.7:1.88, 1.95). Yet, he wrote to Dionigi, the soul could not achieve "the blessed life" while "in this prison of the body [*in hoc corporis ergastulo*]" (F IV.2: 1.162, 1.181). *Ergastulum* named a household's prison-cum-workshop for recalcitrant slaves. The prison was "brighter" only for divinely chosen mediators, like Dom Jean Birel, Prior of the Grand Charterhouse at Garignano where Petrarch often stayed, to whom one might talk as if to "Christ, who undoubtedly inhabits your breast as a beatific guest. For the soul of the righteous is the seat of God. It is his gift that amid the sinful men with whom the globe abounds you shine like a new star [*nouum . . . sidus effulges*] on the world, through the darkest shadows of our times, having an angel's life and angelic reputation" (S XVI.8: 182b, 2.633). Such men were exceptions, as Petrarch's talk of angels made clear, although, as the "angelic solitude" which he and Cabassole sought implied, a community of the wise could legitimately hope for the same. For most, the *ergastulum* was enveloping. All human experience followed from these assumptions about the nature of soul and body and what each made of the other.

Some fancied they could avoid the "blows of the passions [*passionum insultibus*]" resulting from soul's bond with body. This was specious: "A law was imposed on me together with my body when I was born, that from its association with me I must suffer many things which I would not suffer otherwise [*Hec michi nascenti lex cum corpore data est, ut ex eius consortio multa patiar, aliter non passurus*]" (F II.5: 1.81, 1.87). The dictum is better translated: "This law was imposed on me when born with a body, that from association with it I should suffer many things I otherwise would not suffer" (remembering that no "I" was expressed save by verbal inflection). Petrarch quoted *Aeneid* vi.730–34 in explanation:

When Virgil said that a certain burning force and heavenly origin inhered in human souls [*ubi animabus humanis inesse quendam igneum vigorem et celestem dixit originem*], he added this reservation: "so far as harmful bodies do not slow them nor earthen organs and mortal members dull them; whence they fear and desire, suffer and rejoice, and do not recognize the heavens, shut as they are in darkness and a blind prison." (F 1.81, 1.87–88)

For Petrarch and his compeers these were not dead metaphors but the vitally characterized experience of human existence. At the same time, these figures powerfully marked people's place in a historical human community. This dialogue with Virgil was simultaneously with Augustine, who had used this thought and the same citation to discuss human sin and the nature of evil as inherent in a mind that abused God-given will as if able to act as isolated authority (CG XIV.3: 4.270): ability Petrarch denied in the *De vita solitaria*, but which was nonetheless part of the Senecan battle of being human.

The *exemplum* of suffering from soul's birth in human body was of course Christ, personifying suffering that included struggle in every circle of a person's being, from material through mental to the spiritual war against various temptations to do or think evil. Petrarch wrote to his brother:

To this end it was undertaken by decision of the inaccessible and ineffable Trinity that the eternal and immortal and omnipotent son of God should don the robe of our mortality, so that, since there was no proportion between God and human, he would clearly be mediator between God and humans, perfectly uniting both natures in himself, and would draw humans to God, incline God to humans and enable mortal sight to be fixed on God robed in mortal flesh. (F X.3: 2.299, 2.67)

Of the Trinity, the mortal Jesus was at the same time the model for human life, as Christian contemplatives never ceased to observe. That embodiment in Christ—*as* Christ—was an essential part of the medieval West's experience, which was why the *imitatio Christi* was so commonplace a textual figure, from Bonaventure's or Richard of St. Victor's divine meditations to Christina's life-story and Abelard's letters.

Nor was Petrarch merely exercising rhetoric when he rebuked Giovanni Colonna for chafing at delays on a journey, dismissing among other arguments the wish to be buried in one's native land:

if you consider the body, it matters to you not at all where a thing once possessed by you may be, whether you were amenable to its abandonment or resisted its removal. But if you are truly thinking of the soul [*animum*], no strait place confines it, no great place enhances it; and from wherever it starts, whether for ascending to the heavens or descending to hell, the toil [*labor*] is the same. (F II.7: 1.87, 1.94)

Augustine's mother Monnica had said the same. Leaving Ostia to go home, she replied to her companions' worry lest she die abroad instead of at home, that wherever the body was, for the soul "nothing is far from God" (*Confessions* IX.11: 2.54). Experience of body and mind/soul as not just distinct but *really* adherent to different spheres of being, hard as that may be for most modern westerners to envisage, far less feel, was lived actuality. The circles stayed entwined in complex and often obscure ways but the gap between them had grown, powerfully increasing the experience of life as a battle. Still, when Petrarch used the pronoun *me* or *ego*, or a first person of the verb (too frequently translated as *I*), he expressed a "selfeness," an ipseity, understood and felt first of all as mind/soul, *animus/anima*. So we see him write, and must suppose he spoke the same way, unless we imagine the two activities completely disjunct.

This separation of soul and body lets one grasp how the soul's essential adherence to the divine now related to its born insertion in mundane actuality and human community. These made two spheres distinct by the differing extent of their necessary association with material—even corporeal—reality. The first was the arena of that *"labor"* by which the soul struggled through and against embodied life back to its place of origin. Here it was "enslaved" by its corporeal incarceration and its now being of a really different and inferior nature to the divine whence it came—just as the slave was to the fully human citizen. Our love, Petrarch wrote to the papal secretary Francesco Bruni, was not for *any* beings seen. For when "we think we see them, we see not them but their dwellings and, more truthfully, their prisons [*ergastula*]. For indeed, what we call bodies are chains, and had they not been granted us dissoluble and breakable human anguish would be eternal" (S I.7: 1.80, 1.31). He echoed Cicero's thought that "real" human intercourse was soul to soul, bodies being a concealing imprisoning shell (*Tusculans* I.xxii. 52: see Chapter 4 above).

Worldly "habit" (*consuetudo*) was real "slavery" (*servitus*), he wrote to his old friend Sette, from which only God "will deliver wretched me." "My body's guest, badly in harmony with it [*hospes corporis mei, secum male concordans*], wages an implacable struggle." "I was truly born for greater things," he ended, "than to be slave of my body [*mancipium corporis mei*]." In this sense, "what is called our life, is death" (F V.18: 2.42, 1.276–77). The poet combined these to ask Neri Morando: "What else in truth is this short life save prolonged death? what else this earthly dwelling save a vile prison of oppressive slavery and dark house of unbroken grief?" (F XX.1: 4.4, 3.123). A letter to Lombardo da Serico, written near the end of his life (November 1370), reached a sort of paroxysm, simply listing for a page and a half all the evils human life could be compared to or was: Rabelaisian, one might say, were it not quite without humorous intent. Even that, he ended, failed to capture the matter: "For [life] is much worse and more wretched than can be said by me or anyone among humans. . . . [O]ne good thing lies in all the bad: unless the right path is abandoned, it is the way to the good and eternal life" (S XI.11: 121b, 2.415).

Petrarch's view was sometimes slightly less bleak. He told "Socrates": "The life we lead is a sleep, and whatever happens in it is most like a dream. Death alone dispels the sleep and the dreams." Still, he wailed: "O if only it were given to wake earlier!" (F VIII.8: 2.180, 1.421). To Boccaccio, he repeated: "Indeed, life led here is smoke, shadow, dream, illusion, nothing, finally, except a cell of grief and toil; that has one thing of good: it is the way to another life" (S I.5: 1.44, 1.18). Typically gathering various authors' arguments as to whether human life was death or not, and refusing to "choose" among them, he concluded that having been born one should make the most of life; to have stayed unborn would have been better. Christians had at least been redeemed, the chains breakable (S I.5: 1.46–52, 1.19–21). He endlessly mulled these thoughts: "as seems right to wiser people," he reminded "Socrates," "nothing is better or more just than death, which frees them utterly from these shackles into eternal liberty" (F X.2: 2.284, 2.55). Petrarch never tired of this theme. Besides others, *Familiari* XVI.5 and XXII.12, *Senili* I.5, I.7 and XVI.8, in their entirety, recur to it. In a sense, much of the *Senili* was a series of variations on the theme.

Body was the "great enemy and prison of the soul [*animae . . . ergastulum*]," Petrarch summarized, as if in passing, to his doctor and close friend, the renowned physician Giovanni Dondi, in November 1370 (S XII.2: 139b, 2.474). Here, too, we can spot a different trace of growing divisions to be overcome.

We saw before that body, its biology and physiology, was one further integral sphere of personal being. For Petrarch this seems to have been no longer simply given. We must not forget to whom he was writing. Giovanni Dondi Dall'Orologio was an eminent medical man. Besides his important practice, he lectured at the Padua Studio on Galen's *Tegni* in 1356–57, on the first book of Avicenna's *Canon* in 1359–60, on Hippocrates' *Aphorisms* in 1360–61 (*Dizionario* 41.97a). Petrarch designedly, then, earlier in the letter dismissed precisely some of the authorities central to Dondi's medical teaching and practice:

Before closing, I ask a favor of you: that you keep your Arab authorities in banishment from any advice to me; I hate the entire race. I know that the Greeks were once the most ingenious and eloquent men; they produced many philosophers, the greatest poets and outstanding orators and mathematicians. That part of the world gave birth to the chief physicians. But you know what sort of physicians the Arabs are. And I know what kind of poets they are. Nothing is more charming, nothing softer, nothing more lax, nothing, in a word, more base . . . I shall scarcely be persuaded that anything good can come from Arabia; but you learned men, through some strange mental illness, celebrate them with great and, unless I am mistaken, undeserved trumpeting. (S XII.2: 138b–39a; 2.471–72)

This may have been partly a bit heavy-handed humor at Dondi's expense, criticizing his advice to Petrarch "especially about fasting" (S 139b, 2.474). It also seems to widen divisions in the circles of the person. Petrarch questioned whether the kind of easiness with the biological and material envelope of the person that had been the Greco-Arab ideal was even possible. Apropos of diet, regimen and one's relation to geographical surroundings, he railed to Lombardo: "Wherever you turn, man is the most ferocious animal, and at the same time the weakest and softest, and, to put it briefly, the most wretched." Not only did many groups of people live off each other and commit other vilenesses, but humans were rarely at ease in their physical environment. To these difficulties "one can add what also pertains to our subject: that no animal's gluttony is more troubled or more restless [than humans']; while for all animals one food suffices, for humans alone all foods do not suffice" (S XV.3: 164b, 2.563). Less readily and firmly enlaced in the world, the body and the medicine and regimen used to treat it now seemed more caught in the *branloire* and mutability of human life, worried by urgent errancies of person and a feel of the body as obstacle.

This makes it legitimate to understand him as conflating his "exile" in France with the soul's exile on earth. He wrote to his relative and friend Giovanni dell'Incisa of another's death: "never more to be seeing him in the exile, to me, of this pilgrimage" (F VII.12: 2.118, 1.362). He made the link explicit to his brother, who had made him see: "by how great a distance I am absent in my misery from Jerusalem our homeland, for which we always yearn in this exile, unless our dark and filthy prison makes us forgetful [*nisi nos nostri immemores fuscus et luteus carcer facit*]" (F X.5: 2.310, 2.76). Later (*ca.*1366–67), he repeated the conflation to Urban V in urging him to return to Rome, calling Avignon and the false reasons given for staying there, "the inextricable knot fettering hearts, the prison banishing the view of a better fatherland [*patria*]" (S VII.1: 73b, 1.244). Here, *patria* was both Rome and heaven, a conceit that grounded the entire letter collection forming the savage anti-Avignon polemic issued anonymously as the *Liber sine nomine*.

Petrarch's spontaneous recourse to the conflation to capture his own, the pope's, the church's and humans' condition more generally, again underscores the inseparably common and shared nature of that condition, how the personal and the civic (whether of family, friends or the more widely political) were one. All shared the same boat, even so blessed a person as Dom Jean. Humans—*everything* human—were exiled from the source of all about them able to be thought "holy, religious, pious, excellent." All this came from God. From Him came "soul, life, intellect, desire for the good and freedom of judgment." Everything tied to body was worse even than Shakespeare's later "quintessence of dust." "What even is a father, if not worthless semen? what, a mother, if not a foul habitation?" (F X.5: 2.311, 2.76). And yet . . . And yet . . .

For this was also the letter praising the great variety of human nature, human occupations, abilities and minds, and arguing the worth of the "threefold" human pursuits of pleasure, of "wealth, honors and power," and of "wisdom and contemplation" (F 2.312, 2.77). None of these could be undertaken by any person alone. None could be undertaken by God-given members separate from the body and its physical and material surroundings. To be "born with a body" was to suffer the flesh in one's person. So Petrarch wrote to Boccaccio after having his leg badly broken by a horse's kick and the wound putrefy: "Hardly ever have I recognized [*cognovi*] in another's corpse as now in my own flesh what a nothing, or, more precisely, what a wretched and vile animal man is." But he added an immediate qualification: "unless he redeems baseness of body with loftiness of soul" (F XI.1: 2.323, 2.85–86).

The new distinctness (fragmentation, even?) of the spheres of human being was less clear than my earlier bald claim said. On the one hand, the *cognition* Petrarch named here showed that all circles of being determined *experience*. Their distinction by reason opened a path to "redemption" via that knowledge of human subjection to change and decay whose confines exactly delimited any notion of human "nobility." On the other hand, incarnation dimmed and obscured the soul's cognitive function. Being human embodied experience of the distinctness of these spheres even as it impeded full awareness of the experience. Born in body, the soul's incessant struggle with the flesh was sufficient mark of its divinity. That experience itself signaled the distinctness of at least these spheres. Perhaps the divine could be fully *experienced* as distinct only in the deepest meditation, for one would have to make oneself almost inhuman (by definition) to achieve it. In its complexity, incarnation itself offered paths to redemption.

The latter, material, circles were where person was constructed as reactive subject of community, by which it was defined and by whose conditions it was adjusted and changed. Here, *"subject"* had its etymological sense of "lying under." But no longer was it despised as a miserable slavery. On the contrary, servitude there took on positive values. Put into medical terms, for example, the construction, adjustment and change were named by the unbreakable bond between temperament and passions and surroundings, from climate and geography, to food and exercise, occupation and social position, and all else: despite the difficult hesitations we saw him advance on occasion. It included treatment of mind as well as body. With regard to this, Petrarch remarked, it had to seek "help from heaven." Such cure also had a triple path, for of those who treat minds, "some undertake cure of one person, some of the family, some of the state," objects respectively of ethics, economics and politics, though poets also addressed these (F X.5: 2.313, 2.78). My next chapter traces this.

Each had their "servitudes." In ethics, they were named by the four cardinal virtues, justice, prudence, temperance and fortitude, each naming not just an "internal" virtue, but a norm of responsible relation to others. In the area of the family, they were named by the different kinds of obligation and responsibility every member of the household had for every other. In the political sphere, they had names like *officium* and *prudentia*, service, obligation, duty (different exercise of the cardinal virtues functioned in all three realms). We saw how Hugh of St. Victor (and many more distant predecessors) had named these in just this way, reflecting our circles of the human, the social and the material. Petrarch's tale of Charlemagne and the magic ring (F I.4) narrated these material and ethico-political sets of ties, as did a later letter of April 1364 to the condottiere Luchino dal Verme, concerning the qualities of great military leaders (S IV.1). The mutuality of human relations and worldly affairs, despite all, remained total. Personal or wider changes in fortune were not just the way of the world, but caused, he told Pierre Bersuire, by changes in social practices and tradition (especially military ones): "de mutatione Fortune eamque ex morum et presertim rei militaris mutatione procedere" (F XXII.14: 4.138, 3.242). Things "are so much in common to us," Petrarch reminded the Dominican Giovanni Colonna,

that nothing can be said not to belong to another, for what is another's is ours. This can be said the case not only of close friendships, but also of the common society of humans, as [Juvenal] the Satirist said when he taught that to the good man no evil is another's and that tears are given to humankind by nature as sign of mutual sympathy [*pietatis*]. [Terence] the Comic had said this long before: "I am a man, I think nothing human foreign to me." I certainly do not deny this to be true, yet in this public obligation of mutual love there are levels whereby from the widest sphere of humanity [*ex amplissima . . . humanitatis area*], so to speak, we reduce it to the narrows of kinship and amity, and universal love for all is compressed to a certain particular love and friendship for a few. (F VI.3: 2.60–61, 1.296)

The narrow [*angustus*] did not replace the broad. It worked the more firmly against its background—more precisely, as integral part of it. Each was an essential aspect of the other.

Petrarch thus moved easily from widest political interests to quieter advice to more humble friends and acquaintances (no less than had Hildegard before). He sent severe ethico-political counsel to Cola di Rienzo, "Tribune of Rome" (F VII.7), as well as regular personal and political encomia and inspiration: enough to strain his friendships and relations with the Avignon papal court and some of its members. He gave warm advice to Luchino Visconti, duke of Milan, on the merit and utility of learned and wise princes, although this may also have been ironic reprimand, more interested as the duke was in military expansion than learning or wisdom (F VII.15; and see below). He wrote as directly to the emperor Charles IV, whom he got to know. Charged with the diplomatic office of winning him back to Italy, he begged him to come to stop its warfare and reunite it (F X.1, XII.1), accused him of sloth, political ineptitude and less magnanimity than lowborn Rienzo (F XVIII.1), cheered his tardy arrival (F XIX.1), bewailed and scorned his breakneck departure (F XIX.12). He narrated these aims and ultimate failure in two letters to Francesco Nelli (F XIX.13, 14) and in another tone to "Lelius" (F XIX.3). Later letters to Charles returned to biting criticism of the emperor's failure to raise Rome to its ancient glory as capital of empire (F XXIII.2, 15, 21). These writings balanced the ambitious political goal of renewing "Augustan" Rome to lead a united Italy and forge a worldwide Pax Romana with personal reproof and advice. His lament to Pierre de Rainzeville on Charles' early failure to come to Italy deplored as much the emperor's moral weakness as his political ineptitude and indifference (F XV.5).

Commentary on the sad state of Italy and demands that something be done about it, whether about the war between Venice and Genoa (F XVII.3, 6; XVIII.16), or Naples, Sicily, Rome and Pavia (F XIX.18), and on the generally war-torn state of the known world (F XV.7; XIX.9), was always a part of more singularly aimed thoughts. Petrarch always mingled ethics and politics, as he did to his friend Philippe de Vitry about the diplomatic mission of Gui de Boulogne, whose chaplain Philippe was (as well as Pope John XXII's). Petrarch used the excuse of wide political interests to offer personal ethical advice. Philippe had written bewailing Gui's "exile" from France. Petrarch took the opportunity, via praise of

Gui's person and of the success and necessity of his diplomatic missions in Hungary, the German lands and the Italian states, to criticize Philippe's "provincialism" and assert the need always to join the "local" to the universal. The "citizen of the world" perpetually balanced the broad against the narrow, benefiting humankind in the "personal" *and* "political." These were not separable. To turn merely "inward" would in the long run bring public calamity (F IX.13: 2.246–56, 2.35–44). But the ethical and the political, the cure of "one person," of the family and of the state, also needed the "help of heaven," we saw.

Petrarch (like Hildegard or others) always tackled the play of these circles of the social, worldly and public with the eschatological, eternal and contemplative. The terms remain awkward, but we must shun anachronistic contrasts like private/public, interior/exterior, personal/social, individual/communal. Both circles, like those of widest humanity and tightest kinship, were best qualified by the second terms of these contrasts, as we already saw toward the end of Chapter 8. The poet displayed his convictions and feelings in a letter to Marco Portonario (F III.12) treating exactly the idea that "even those who serve the state can live piously and purely, and beyond its uproar can approach the silence of a higher life" (1.128, 1.145). What mattered was that Marco keep a first vow to "love God in every circumstance, cling to Him, worship Him and yearn for Him with concentrated effort of the whole mind," "through the storms of public life" arising from "the charge of [his] citizens that [he] administers." Between the two was "a well-trodden path." Although, while on it, one might seem to tread a "side and, as the Pythagoreans call it, a left-hand road," civic duty was not "opposed to the divine grace you seek." On the contrary, as Scipio said in Cicero's *Somnium*, "for all who have saved, strengthened and sustained their homeland, there is certainly a definite place in heaven where the blessed rejoice through eternity" (*De republica* VI.13.13). Petrarch added: "Nothing more pleases the supreme God who rules the whole world than the assemblies and gatherings of men united by law that are called states" (1.129–30, 1.145–46). None of those "busied in any honorable activity" was barred from the goal supposedly more hospitable to contemplation. As Plotinus held, Petrarch ended, one "may be blessed not only by purifying virtues and those of a purified mind, but by civic ones [*politicis*]" (1.130, 1.146).

That was why in the public sphere the very aspects of person that seemed opposed to fixing it in any certainty and security could actually be made useful to the civic interest. Petrarch thus advised Zanobi Mazzuoli da Strada that his abilities in the arts should be better used than to teach grammar. Humility and retreat might be of contemplative benefit under some circumstances, but to adopt a more publicly useful art when one was capable was "more glorious" (F XII.3: 3.21, 2.144). As he told Elie de Talleyrand, public benefit and its ultimate divine worthiness offset "hardships and dangers of the higher life," as a letter's title had it (F XIV.1). This prospectively answered "Augustine"'s criticism:

> When you boast of having fled from cities and become enamored of woods, it shows not excuse but a change of guilt. By many paths one reaches one end, and you, believe me, although you have left the path trodden by the crowd, still strive by a side path toward the same ambition you say you have scorned. Repose, solitude, total indifference to human affairs and your very intellectual activities lead you on this path, but their ultimate end is glory. (*Secretum* 96)

Even were the series of accusations applicable to Petrarch, such "glory," Petrarch iterated elsewhere, was not inevitably a yielding to Babylonian evil. It reflected civic virtue in Augustine's own good worldly city.

This was again the *Vita solitaria*'s argument, opposing the civic virtues of the citizen of Augustine's Rome to the evil ones of Babylon. Solitude, in Petrarch's communal sense, fortified the good person in the virtues of civic welfare and public service (I.iii: DVS 322–24, LS 126–27). To choose the civic ("political") life was to elect a *persona*. What *persona* was available depended on one's particular human *natura*. Here, the four virtues were set in an ascending order of use: in the ethico-political world they mitigated passions, in the "purgatorial" (naming the philosopher's activities) they removed them, in the realm "of perfection" they let one rejoice in freedom from them, only in the mind of God could they be exemplary (I.iv: DVS 332–34, LS 133–34). The first three were all human and all good in their appropriate spheres of action. The first and second characterized "Rome," the third, with the help "of Christ," defined "the towns of Jerusalem against the army of Babylon" (I.v: DVS 346, LS 142). "Solitude" was flight from the noise and turbulence of evil cities, not from the amity of good (I.vii: DVS 374–78, LS 162–66). To him who yielded to city chaos, "conscience stood for hell"; he was attacked by Furies "begot in hell of an infernal father" (I.ii: DVS 310–12, LS 116–17). Such people were hardly persons at all, wholly separate, as it were, from themselves:

> Omnia illis aliena sunt: alienum limen, alienum tectum, alienus somnus, alienus cibus, et, quod est maximum, aliena mens, aliena frons; non suo iudicio flent et rident, sed abiectis propriis alienos induunt affectus, denique aliena tractant, alienum cogitant, alieno vivunt.

> To them everything is foreign: their door is another's, their roof another's, their sleep another's, their food another's, and, what is worst, their mind is another's, their countenance another's; they do not weep and laugh by their own judgment,

but having cast off their own and put on another's passions, they do, in sum, another's business, think another's thoughts, live through another. (I.iii: DVS 318, LS 122)

The sentiment was Senecan: "For the person involved in many affairs never a day goes by so fortunately that some upset is not provoked by a person or circumstance. Just as one hurrying through the crowded places of a city is bound to collide with many people, and in one place to slip, in another to be held back, in another to be splashed, so in this varied and restless activity of life many hindrances befall and many causes for complaint" (Seneca, *De ira* III.vi.3–4). Petrarch could well have taken the theme of the *Vita solitaria* from what could be Seneca's own commentary on the view expressed here: "I think Democritus had this in mind when he began: 'Whoever wants to live tranquilly should not engage in many affairs either privately or publicly'" (*De tranquillitate animi* xiii.1). The key word for Petrarch, perhaps, was *multa*, many. One had to strike a balance between interior and exterior, between being a person and letting one become—or be used as—something else. Petrarch knew Stoic teaching not just through Augustine. The first named fourteenth-century Stoic teacher was Barlaam of Seminara, author of a manual of moral philosophy. He taught mostly in Greece, "but in 1342 was present at the pontifical court at Avignon, where his friend Petrarch was his pupil." Verbeke adds that he may have induced Petrarch's extensive use of the Stoics in the *De remediis utriusque fortunae* (*Presence* 12). Petrarch seemed to need little encouragement.

Because the sociopolitical realm yielded all too readily to such (non)people, the good person had a duty to engage in it. Thus did Petrarch justify to Andrea Dandolo the very mobility which the collection's prefatory letter had suggested was incapacitating (F XV.4). The same point was readjusted in remarks to Francesco Calvo on the glories of an active life. Taking up his earlier observation about always differing from his selfe, Petrarch warned that those who adopted this motion must beware of being "everywhere but with themselves [*apud semet ipsos*]; they often speak with others, never with themselves" (F XIII.4: 3.60, 2.181). He went on to reverse the meaning of his return to Ithaca topos. Ulysses' travels now connoted the wish for knowledge that alone made humans fully human. He could have lived tranquilly, "if only the insatiable desire to know many things had not driven him to every shore and land [*nisi inexplebile desiderium multa noscendi cunctis illum litoribus terrisque raptaret*]." Now the topos depicted "laboriosa virtus"; laborious virtue, but "illustrious and celebrated, and one that joined labor to love and wonder" (F 3.61, 2.182). It was this "overpowering love of study," he told Boccaccio, repeating Cicero and another favorite, Valerius Maximus, this "love of learning, that drove Pythagoras, Democritus, Anaxagoras and Plato over lands and seas, oblivious of dangers and toils" (S I.5: 1.60, 1.24; see *De finibus* V.19.50; and Valerius, *Factorum et dictorum memorabilium libri* VIII.7, ext. 2–4, 6, in *Opera* 2.105–8). The labor it took was in every way an echo of the struggle of the soul back toward its divine origin.

Petrarch's letters on civic affairs, even with their wider views—renewal of Rome, pacification of warring city-states, unification of Italy—always focused, too, on personal ethical behavior, although Tuscan friends, Boccaccio most bitterly, accused him of not escaping reproach in this regard, by having accepted the patronage of the Visconti, tyrannical rulers of Milan (he feebly replied that this signaled his human fallibility). His political stances were not unequivocal, Albert Ascoli observes ("Petrarch's Private" 2). To Wallace they clearly favored individualist rule, even to tyrannous result (262–71). He might reply that his counsel checked Visconti violence. So he advised Manfredo Pio, lord of Carpi and Modena to link public duties and contemplative path: "so that you should willingly commit your selfe and your affairs [*te ipsum et res tuas*] to divine judgement and raise the mind to heaven, and fix in Him the anchor of hope" (F IX.1: 2.212, 2.2). Similar in tone were letters to Andrea Dandolo, doge of Venice (F XI.8) and to his enemies, the doge Giovanni di Valente and Council of Genoa (F XIV.5, 6). Genoa was a prey of the Visconti, who became its rulers by treaty in 1355 after the city turned to them in its defeat by Venice two years earlier. Here, as well, Petrarch's advice moved on several levels of interest and disinterest. Such letters, we saw, joined moral dicta to piety and the political counsel that these political and military actors set their energies to peace in Italy and war with foreigners for commercial and political reasons (F XI.8; XIV.6).

The endless agitation and fluctuation of the personal, social and political was, then, one form of the soul's struggle with the flesh, precisely as it operated "against" the background of the eternal. In a letter to Gherardo, the thought became the nub of the reply to his wide question: "Now what do you think should be said by me about laws?" After running through names recalling well-known human ones, "Phoroneus for Argos, Lycurgus for the Spartans, Solon for the Athenians," Roman improvements on these, the Twelve Tables, senate decrees, plebiscites and more, Petrarch added: "Yet all these laws and others, as they are of human making so they suffer human change, from the vicissitudes of times and the changed passions and dispositions of humans on which they were based; for it is common that one law corrects another." Permanent law, he insisted, had to be set on an "eternal foundation": not just the law of

Moses given to the Jews, but the "grace of fulfilling the law through Jesus" (F XVII.1: 3.225–26, 3.4). Again the singular and the social were fulfilled in the eternal.

That the political and ethical, the communal and "singular" necessarily worked together did mean that failure was calamitous. The Pythagorean left-hand path, he wrote to his son's teacher Giberto Baiardi, might lead so far astray as to take one to hell (F VII.17: 2.133, 1.380): to that "hellish conscience" of which he wrote in the *Vita solitaria*. Petrarch always fought a temptation to keep the contemplative, pertaining to soul, distinct from the civic, pertaining to body and mind incarnate. One could set praise of monastic life written to his brother (F X.3–5) against many letters on civic subjects, or Gherardo's Carthusian vows of 1343 against his own 1341 laurel coronation, what critics often call the "Christian" versus the "classical." For Petrarch, the clearest case of failing to temper the civic with the contemplative, of taking the left-hand path to hell, was that of papal Avignon. Increasingly he grieved, as he did to Boccaccio, that "this Western Babylon, worst of places and most like Hell," was too near (F XI.6: 2.336, 2.97). To go there from his dear home on the Sorgue was, he told Giovanni Aretino, to cross "that Tartarean threshold of nearby Babylon" (F XI.9: 2.349, 2.109). He could never stay long enough in his idyll, he grieved to Fiorentino. All too soon "the Babylonian hook was again thrown into [him] and [he] was drawn back to Hell" (F XII.8: 3.31, 2.154). One could go on. The complaint was a commonplace far beyond Petrarch, whose readers have always known his ever-growing hatred of Avignon as it tore against his love for his Vaucluse retreat.

Avignon embodied the Babylon to which Augustine had referred as the "city . . . called Confusion." Indeed, the bishop had written, the very name "Babylon was translated as confusion." Babylon was "empty human presumption" setting itself "against God" (CG XVI.4: 5.26–28). For Petrarch, Avignon was the evil world that Augustine set not just against the city of God, but against the good civic world of ideal Rome:

In this wicked world, in these evil times, the Church by present humiliation is preparing for future exaltation, trained by stings of fear, tortures of sorrow, distresses of hardship and dangers of temptation . . . many reprobates are mixed in the Church with the good. (CG XVIII.49: 6.60)

Petrarch looked on Avignon without any such reassurance of its possible recovery.

Countering the Curia's calamitous failure, which had dragged soul itself not just into the world, but beyond it to hell, was a vision of earthly utopia which a purified Rome would center. The first allowed the

worldly clamor of sectarian strife, vicious ambition and personal greed
to replace contemplative silence and religious values of any sort. The
second would reunite the generously public and communal with the contemplative, bringing body "up" to soul, not soul "down" to body. This
was Petrarch's hope for Cola's revolt, on whose failure he still dwelt
with deep sorrow in the mid-1350s (F XIII.6). Brought to Avignon, Cola
was charged by Babylon with the crime "that he wanted the republic
safe and free and matters of the Roman imperium and Roman powers to
be dealt with in Rome" (F XIII.6: 3.76, 2.196). This vision had caused
Petrarch to support Cola. It was the topic of letters to the four cardinals
whom Clement VI named to reform Roman government, entrusted with
protecting the "liberty of Rome" and reinstating the city as "queen" of
an equitable world, purifying it of barons who continued their ravages
and "foreigners" who refused to let the citizens share in the civic community (F XI.16, 17). This aim lay behind his defense of Rome's glory
to "Lelius" (F XV.9), and appeals to him to pursue Roman reform (F
XV.1) and to Niccolò Acciaiuoli to purify Italy by, among other things,
removing foreigners (F XI.13). Foreignness in the social and political
sphere was as evil for Rome as alienation from one's person was in
those who related to the civic in a disorderly way. It broke with the "justice" tying the human to the divine, which alone could make Rome the
ideal worldly city: as Augustine had thought impossible in pagan times,
since it needed the divine justice of a Christian God (CG XIX.21:
6.206).

Petrarch never lost concern not just with the ancient debate over balancing the contemplative and the active life, but with the samenesses and
differences in the kinds of who-ness they implied. That is why he tied
these matters of profoundly "civic interest [*communis utilitas*]" to personal circumstance (F XII.16: 3.46, 2.168). This *utilitas* was subject of a
letter addressed to Acciaiuoli and Giovanni Barrili, leaders in Naples,
begging them to mend their friendship, broader peace depending on it.
The matter was sufficiently urgent that Petrarch wrote to Zanobi, another
well-placed friend, to help bring them together (F XII.17).

The pairing of personal and civic, ethical and political, contemplative
and public, selfe as "subject" of the state and community and selfe as
soul, preoccupied Petrarch. It was the subject of the *Secretum* as of the
letter to Dionigi known as "The Ascent of Mont Ventoux" (F IV.1), especially when its surrounding letters are taken into account. Out of this
context, the letter seems to move Petrarch from the material world and its
false fame to the Augustinian contemplation of its quotation from the
Confessions (X.viii; 2.98–100):

And men go to wonder at the heights of mountains and the vast billows of the sea and broadest courses of rivers and the expanse of Ocean and the revolutions of the stars, and desert themselves [*relinquunt se ipsos*]. (F 1.159; 1.178)

The debate between contemplative and social, eternal and worldly—terms more exact than the now-familiar oppositions inner/outer, private/public—was Augustinian, with *The City of God* perhaps its exemplary text. We should recall, too, that the passage in the *Confessions* occurred in a long meditation on the force of memory—fundamental and essential link with the divine sphere (on Petrarch and Augustine, see especially, Courcelle, *Confessions*; Greene, *Light*; and Luciani).

This is no misreading, but surely partial (see Harries 152–60 and O'-Connell; for its ambiguity, Ascoli, "Petrarch's Middle," Billanovich, Durling, Martinelli, Robson). Petrarch continued with a set of letters to Dionigi, to Robert of Anjou, King of Sicily, to his secretary Barbato da Sulmona and others, fêting their author's close ties to the man he lauded as typifying the philosopher-prince, reveling in the unique difficulty and glory of being offered the laurel prize in both Rome and Paris and in the worldly pleasure of climbing another hill, the Capitoline, to be crowned prince of poets (F IV.2–9). These preceded four consolatory letters (F IV.10–13), one on the value of good domestic help (F IV.14), and four on moderation in display of learning, use of wealth and sexual relations (F IV.15–19). Worldly life was central, even at its most earthy: if the first of the two letters urging a friend to drop his sexual liaisons alleged a wish to lift a "malign weight from the soul" (F 1.198, 1.226), mild salaciousness and flaunting of Plautus belied this tone. Deliberately, then, Petrarch placed the "Ascent" in worldly context: as the letter itself insisted, a person's first tie was to the divine, but as long as the soul was incarnate, it endured mundane concerns and interests, its circles of personhood. Crucial as was the divine, it was just one circle—although Ascoli usefully observes Petrarch's "trinitarian" naming of Mont Ventoux—Spirit, with its main peak "Filiolum," Son, but "by antiphrasis," said Petrarch, since as the area's highest peak it was truly "Pater," Father, of all those around ("Petrarch's Middle" 21). As Petrarch surely knew, living most of his life there, Provençal *fiholo* (Filiolum) really meant source or stream. The metaphorical connotations of this, along with those of Ventosus, windy (or *spiritus, pneuma*), supplement the play on hills, mountains, cliffs, valleys, rocks, thorns, country paths that is the whole letter's exploration of exchange between the material, animate and divine. Further, opening the letter by comparing their climb to a Macedonian King Philip's ascent of Mount Haemus to reconnoiter the territory for his war against Rome, Petrarch made the civic and political spheres equally vital to the letter.

Indeed, one may not ungenerously read the first letter of the next book, addressed to Barbato on the death of Robert of Sicily, as less concerned with the King's ascent to heaven than Petrarch's loss of a superior patron: "For whom in future shall I stay awake at night? To whom shall I dedicate mental abilities and intellectual pursuits, however minor? Who will raise crushed hopes, who rouse mind benumbed? I have had two guiding inspirers for my abilities, this year has taken both from me" (F 2.3–4, 1.228). His worldly interest in Robert and his friend Giacomo Colonna (the second "*ingenii dux*" named) did not signal indifference to the contemplative and the soul's path to the divine. It did imply scales not easily weighted away from the earthly; a powerfully Augustinian sense of the world's pull. The many references to Cicero, the great public figure and political person of Latin antiquity, were no less vital than those to Augustine. Writing of his double loss, Petrarch made sure to name his "Lelius" (Lello di Pietro Stefano dei Tosetti, a Roman supporter of the Colonnas) as sharing his grief for Giacomo: "Lelius" named for Scipio's Laelius in Cicero, the *De amicitia*'s embodiment of friendship.

A person's surroundings, contemplative and public, divine and social, eschatological and political, animate and material, were not incompatible. They were different. Still, we have also seen that we cannot yet oppose surroundings and persons in this easy way. Growing experience of differences, distances, strains and tensions among the needs of these surroundings did not prevent their intertwining. Who-ness was still composed of and embedded in its multiple circles. To speak, I repeat, of anything suggesting "private" and "public" is deeply to mislead. What modern western readers treat as Petrarch's private being was no less made by public presentation, epistolary or poetic, than his person as courtier, political polemicist or scholar. Too, the imprisoned soul bent on reunion with the divine was no less public a selfe: its essence was forged (and experienced) by its place in a community of Trinity and angelic host, saint and sinner, God and all souls. This is not too far a stretch: the very idea of a self-contained individual, separate from and preceding communal bonds, was diabolic. The truly solitary life, separate from the divine, human, social and material could never be a good. Selfe was ever public, made and existing in "assemblies and gatherings." That was why the political and social ones "called states" were not inimical to selfe's ultimate union with the divine: *communitas* was the shared reality of all spheres of the person.

The quasi-sacred figure of Mont Ventoux must be read in a secular context of personal glory and political success as symbolized by the Capitoline of the succeeding letters. It was also the Capitoline that led Petrarch, in an astonishing passage, into something like a fusion of the singular, the political and the divine. Writing to Morando again of the moral and social disasters of the present age, the poet fulminated anew over Rome. Our ancestors, he said, managed to hold the Capitoline against the barbarians by unusual valor. Now, only recourse to God would suffice. "If by calling celestial aid to protect us we defend the fortress of our Capitoline from so great a surrounding army of barbaric vices, if we set an unyielding front against the strident errors of the rabble, we shall be stronger than Manlius, Marius and Caesar himself." In heathen times walls protected from the enemy, rest from night dangers, camp from winter:

For us there is no rest, no time-out of peril, no winter, no truces, no night. Nothing is ever secure and at peace, we constantly strive for our salvation, we stand always to battle, are tested, besieged, driven. Enemies are within the walls, already armed they approach the very fortress of reason, they advance shelters, direct battering rams, set fires, climb towers; nor are ladders raised against the walls otherwise than once at Troy, ladders of crimes against walls of souls [*animarum*]. What do you hope that I should say? They break in on our very tables and bedrooms and rush upon our throats, and what is nearly the end, the whole rabble, armed with errors, wields the sword for our enemies. In this uncertain and pitiless battle there is no hope of victory except from heaven; thence let us seek it, my friend. (F XX.1: 4.6, 3.125)

What began as another lament over the particular state of Rome and, by synecdoche, the state of Italy and the wider world, quickly became Christian grief over the world's fallen state. Rome—more exactly, the Capitoline—became the struggling individual soul, imprisoned in body and besieged by errors and vices consequent on that incarnation. Personal valor might suffice for pre-Christian heathens to ward off vice and the errors of the "left-hand path," but now Christ and divine grace were needed. More importantly, the soul, because it was "Rome," was *not* singular (Petrarch's form was the genitive plural, *animarum*). Here soul(s) were not those of single persons but identified with the very center of social and political being. Stability of the state itself, against the vices and errors of those who would throw it into doubt and decay, stood against the impossible fixity of solitary identity. Petrarch now glorified the active life because the very way for soul to return to its origin, to fight successfully against the flesh, lay through political community. The passage is remarkable in that it does not so much *say* this, as *do* it in the way its sentence structure collapses the one into the other: Capitoline into soul, actual warfare into spiritual struggle, tyranny of the crowd into assault of vice and errancy, social into eschatological strife.

The passage catches perfectly how the particular was always in community, and how community was not just background but essential source and abode of the singular, composed of singulars (*animarum*) and producing them. They depended on it, it depended on them, and both (all) were ultimately seated in the divine. This is the series of complex and distinctive relations I have been trying to capture. Some such idea of community or society always grounded who-ness. Petrarch's prose writings certainly revealed a strong sense of growing tensions and strains in the experience of person and its surroundings. The passage just quoted marks vehement struggle. At the same time, these writings implied a strong experience of their unity, whose statement Petrarch thought the essential purpose and ground of poetry.

CHAPTER TWELVE

"Sparsa anime fragmenta recolligam"

The subtlety and obscurity of this unity of personal being was what Petrarch thought the finest poets best grasped, who wrote to give pleasure, to placate and laud the divinity and so that "a certain artful, exquisite and new form be made" (F X.4: 2.302, 269). They treated all human affairs, he told his brother, but especially enabled one to grasp the civil or political, not with "excessive familiarity . . . but so that it be seen by the few and sought with hard attention." Still, poets did not separate human activities, endeavoring to utter "more obscurely" the three paths of pleasure, practice and contemplation (X.5: 2.313, 2.78). We saw in Chapter 9 that many thought these paths themselves threefold, Hugh of St. Victor stressing the practical as "divided into solitary, private, and public; or, put differently, into ethical, economic, and political; or, still differently, into moral, managerial, and civil. Solitary, ethical, and moral are one; as also are private, economic, and managerial; and public, political, and civil" (II.19: 74). Familiar circles of human, social and material, these were the poet's great subjects. Just as Virgil had paradigmatically taught the moral and singular in the *Eclogues*, the familial and economic in the *Georgics* and the political in the *Aeneid*, Petrarch said to Francesco Nelli, so "the supreme goal of (poetic) eloquence is to match great things with words and to show the beautiful outline of the hidden mind in words artfully woven [*verbis arte contextis*]" (XII.5: 3.24, 2.147). The poet was a weaver, added sonnet 40 of the *Rime sparse*, who "wove" or "glued" together "one truth with another" (l.4). (I call the *Rime* indifferently by its three names: this, from the first poem's first line; *Rerum vulgarium fragmenta*, Petrarch's title; *Canzoniere*, given by later editors.)

These many circles and objectives were why, he told the abbot of St.-Bénigne, poetry was sweet, but could be grasped only "by rare minds," exacting "a negligent and selective contempt for all things, with an elevated, abstract mind and appropriate nature" (XIII.7: 3.83, 2.201). These elevated difficulties were why poets worked at obscurity. The great poet, he said to Gherardo in the letter about the three paths, dwelt in shadows, avoided familiarity and was "to be seen by few and approached with difficulty" (X.5: 2.313, 2.78). *Canzone* 105 of the *Rime* humorously parodied this: its first two lines, "I never more want to sing as I used, / when no one understood me," preceding 88 deliberately obscure ones. He stressed the point in the *Praefatio* to the *Liber sine nomine*, explaining that the (first) *Bucolicum carmen* was purposely "ambiguous," "a kind of cryptic poem which, though understood only by a few, might possibly please many" (*Liber* 163; Zacour trans. 27). This was why the poet could rightly be saved from civic punishment for just being a poet and "dedicated to such sacred labors," as Cicero argued on behalf of Archias and some now hoped to do for Cola di Rienzo—a hope Petrarch sadly held vain: the reason was good, but Cola was no poet. The political arena owed the poet and the Muses such honor as would overcome even public condemnation because their service, *officium*, was civic (XIII.6: 3.76–77, 2.196–97). That was why poet and orator were usually taken together, rhetoric grounding their strength. But the poet also had "a certain inner and divinely given energy." For that reason, he reaffirmed in his *Collatio laureationis*, the oration delivered on receiving the laureateship on April 8, 1341, Cicero defended Archias (13–14; Hatch 301–2). Poetry, further, was tied to the divine. Boyle in fact finds Petrarch's view of poetry primarily theological and prophetic (*Petrarch's* 12–16).

Praising St.Jerome to Boccaccio, who had decided to give up letters, Petrarch asked how Jerome could have served church and state or "imbued his letters and books with so much oratorical light" had he ever so decided. "For as the true [*verum*] is to be sought from truth [*a veritate*], so, I ask, whence is an artistic and embellished way of speaking to be sought if not from eloquence? Jerome himself did not deny that this was proper for poets and orators, and it is too well known to need proof" (S I.5: 1.56, 1.23). One recalls the language of light Petrarch used of Birel to express the Carthusian Prior's divinely granted intermediary role between the human and the divine—not to speak of his using the *verum*/*veritas* relation to clarify the working of poetic diction. This does not equate the two cases or make the poet divine. It suggests that the poet's place was also a mediator's, not between the divine and worldly, but between person and society, between *animum* (even *anima*), *ingenium* and *officium*, the many levels and folds of civic community. This restriction is not tight, if we recall that the last *canzone* of the *Rerum vulgarium fragmenta* hymned the Virgin, appealing for her help in reaching God.

Still, the poet's (or orator's) *oratio artificiosa atque ornata* was source of *civic* rectitude and mirror of the finest and most appropriate aspirations chiefly because this language best expressed truths of familiar expectation and society's most exact understanding of its own nature and workings. Given the complexities poetry rendered, it was inevitably obscure. Its very lack of immediate and ready clarity was, Petrarch urged, the best guarantee of its precision. But it was not elitist, even if intelligence and education were needed to parse it. Poetry was obscure because the complex difficulties whose truths it spoke required an especially detailed and sweepingly capacious apprehension of language, and an ability to manipulate its hardest subtleties to match and express intricately knotted truths. The accuracy with which Petrarch took poetry to render the *norms* of human social community suggests that we look to this poetry for its rendition of personhood and selfe, against the broader context of its civic *officium*.

Petrarch ended the *Secretum* by telling Augustine: "Adero michi ipse quantum potero, et sparsa anime fragmenta recolligam, moraborque mecum sedulo" (214). He meant to: "be as present to my selfe as I can, and shall collect scattered fragments of soul, and attentively linger with me." Of course, he added, even as they spoke, "many great affairs awaited" him, "mortal" as they were: subjecting himself to their difficulties would prepare him to pass from the world's shadows into heavenly light. For the *Fragmenta* do not invoke endless changeability of a "self" in love or undermine a subject's "self identity," as many scholars, critics and translators say of Petrarch and other early Renaissance writers. Such turns of phrase presuppose existence of an individual (modern) self, one that the poetry dissolves. They beg the question. Petrarch's sense of who he is is inseparable from the great civic affairs which are part of him. One wonders whether the "scattered fragments of soul" are not the spheres of being we have so much seen. Their difficulties *have* to be confronted because they are what it is to be human at all. Struggling to bring them together prepared him to pass into heavenly light exactly because their joining was what made a person *humanior*, and to become more human was to reach toward the divine.

This movement was that of the *Canzoniere*: from the scattered fragments of the first poem to their recollection in Christ's "gathering in of [Petrarch's] last breath in peace" that ends the final poem (366), addressed to the Virgin, that she recommend him to her Son, true man and true God:

> raccomandami al tuo Figliuol, verace
> omo et verace Dio,
> ch'*accolga* 'l mio spirto ultimo in pace. (my italics)

This was that "lyrical drama" needing to be "read consecutively from beginning to end" of which Mark Musa writes in the Preface to his edition
and translation of the *Canzoniere* (ix). Certainly, Teodolinda Barolini is
right to remind us that this is no achieved conversion, that in the final
poem "the poet's will . . . is still commanding itself to be full," and that
Augustine saw this as signaling that conversion had yet to occur: "For if
the will were full, it would not command itself to be full, since it would
be so already" ("Making" 38 and note 63; Augustine, *Confessions*
VIII.9).

But saying, again like Augustine, that fusion with the divine was
wanted, not *achieved*, misses a point. From antiquity to Descartes, human
will was *always* imperfect, toiling to rule the opposing horses pulling reason's chariot. Reason, the spark of the divine in the soul, was sure. Hugh
of St. Victor typically said of it: "the third power of the soul [after the nutritional and sense-perceiving powers that it rules] . . . is rooted entirely in
reason, and it exercises itself either in the most unfaltering grasp of things
present, or in the understanding of things absent, or in the investigation of
things unknown" (I.3: 49–50). Aquinas said no other. Nor did Petrarch,
interpreting Virgil describing Aeolus holding the winds in their mountain
caves as depicting reason controlling the passions of the soul:

And I, examining each word, actually hear [*audivi*] the fury, hear the fierce struggle, hear the raging storms, hear the rumble and roaring. These can refer to anger.
On the other hand, I hear the king sitting on his throne, hear him holding his
scepter, hear him subduing with might and restraining with chains and prisons.
Who can doubt that this also refers to reason? (*Secretum* 124)

Petrarch's sevenfold repetition of the verb *audivi* underscored that he was
talking of analyzing (poetic) words, read and above all *heard*. The
rhythms and sounds of his words echo the point, underscoring both reason's ability to control the passions and poetry's ability to render "great
things with words." Human will, though, was scarred and lamed by being the actor between soul and body. This still caused Montaigne's ever-
uncertain and hesitant mental *branloire perenne*. It will be when Descartes inverts this relation, making will perfect and reason flawed, that
space is made for a different experience. Until then, imperfection of will
caught between body and soul meant that as long as one was living in the
world, only the effort *toward* the divine was possible—that was the difference in the final *canzone* between Laura as the Virgin, and the poet.
Even so, the poet came as near as secular life allowed.

For the *canzone*'s closing words recall Augustine's *Confessions* drawing to their end: "Domine deus, pacem da nobis . . . pacem quietis,
pacem sabbati, pacem sine vespera"—"Give us peace, lord God, . . .

peace of repose, peace of the sabbath, peace without evening" (XIII.35). They recall the course of that writing into the closure of its last three books' exegesis of Genesis: God's breath or spirit ordering creation so that his creature could be redeemed by reabsorbing *its* spirit (*spirto*) to all eternity. The divine "gathering" ending the *Canzoniere* closes the opening earthly "scattering": especially if we recall that the first poem, naming the scattering and lamenting his worldly past, is formally simultaneous with the last. Offered as a preface written after the collection's composition, it instructed the reader how to read it. These two poems told the reader that between the scattering and the gathering lay the world, the practice of person and all life. The *Canzoniere* was Petrarch's reaffirmation of a sense of embedded who-ness. Here, now, the divine sphere offered "rescue," however halting, from the fragmentation provoked by and suffered in some others. It was, again, Rome against Avignon, accepting Augustine's hierarchy of the spheres of being as sole way to resolve new fraught tensions. Just as Hugh of St. Victor had the soul's nutritive and sensitive powers absorbed by, and subordinated as "servants" to, the rational, so here earthly life's spheres were absorbed as subordinate experiences into that of the divine.

The structure and poetic forms of the *Canzoniere* grounded this reaffirmation. If Petrarch "redefined . . . the sonnet, canzone, and sestina forms" (Musa/Manfredi, "Introduction" xiii), in choosing them, he knew their recognized meanings. "The poems of the *Canzoniere*," Holmes remarks, "are highly conventional; nearly every metaphor, linguistic pattern, and metrical form employed in them already appears in early vernacular (Occitan or Italian) lyric." This does not deny his "consummate ability as a poet." It sets him in context (181). To explore this helps avoid seeing in him a priori the poet of oft-claimed new self-consciousness. What Petrarch "redefined" were known and experienced ways of making and expressing meaning. What were they? How did he change them? If he did.

Of the 366 poems of the *Canzoniere* of Petrarch, 29 are *canzoni*, nine are *sestine* [one of these a double], seven are *ballate*, four are *madrigali*, and 317 are sonnets. In the *Canzoniere* these forms are not kept separate, but are so mingled as to afford a pleasing variety. *In view of the consistent practice of the separation of canzoni and sonnets in MS collections of pre-Petrarchan lyrics, Petrarch's procedure in mingling canzoni and sonnets [was] clearly seen to constitute a notable poetic innovation.*

Ernest Hatch Wilkins adds that the earlier tradition was so strong that many copyists of his poems "in some sense separate the *canzoni* and the sonnets" (266). Wilkins' study of many Petrarch manuscripts further lets him assert that Petrarch took "special care" in transcribing *canzoni* and *sestine*, suggesting that he took these to be "of a type distinctly other and higher than the sonnet type" (111). Neither this nor the idea that the mixing of forms was "to afford a pleasing variety" goes without saying. But we need to examine these forms to get at what Petrarch was doing.

Scholars have long argued that the inventor of the sonnet form was the thirteenth-century Giacomo da Lentino ("Giacomo Notaro") at the Sicilian court of the emperor Frederick II. Opining that Giacomo, "if not the inventor of the sonnet, [is at least] the first sonneteer whose works have come down to us," Elias L. Rivers treats his sonnets as if they *did* set the form—with just one variant in his "twenty-four love sonnets" (42). The variant was a runover in one between octave and sestet (54–55). Spitzer saw even tighter formal conformity, showing that Rivers' "enjambement" resulted from misreading the manuscripts ("Una questione"). Such formal invariance in the creation of a new form makes one pause: first efforts are unlikely to be so assured. But claims about primacy matter little. What *does* are broader arguments drawn from them. These affect understanding of the *Canzoniere*.

Paul Oppenheimer argues that with the sonnet was born "the modern mind." Created—or at least "mastered" (Langley ed. xxv)—by Giacomo, it was "the first lyric of self-consciousness, or of the self in conflict." The sonnet did not just "express" or "perform" "emotional problems." It set them so that "they might now actually be resolved, through the logic of a form that turned expression inward, to a resolution in the abiding peace of the soul itself, or if one were not so certain of the existence of the soul, in reason. Reason, after all, was perceived as a manifestation of God's mind and divine love" (*Birth* 3–4). The end of Oppenheimer's penultimate sentence is rooted in the tradition that Frederick affirmed reason over faith in various scandalous ways. Many think the emperor's court and courtiers markedly secularized, basing their thinking partly on Frederick's political and military struggles with the papacy, partly on their thrice having led to his excommunication. The poet Giacomo would have reflected this secularizing tendency (Zagarella). But assertions of Frederick's faith in reason were propaganda in this ideological strife and cannot be taken to have reflected actual transformation in his and his society's thought and experience. And when Oppenheimer takes his argument in the direction of the last sentence quoted, concerning reason as God's mind and divine love in the human soul, he suggests the extent to which there is nothing "modern" in the personhood expressed.

He argues that the octet/sestet form fulfilled a specific numerological design, notably that they were held to "contain" a twelve-line whole, such that the final couplet could be divided off as an almost separate conclusion. The sonnet thus contained a harmonic proportion 6:8:12, reflecting the "fabric of the soul" and "cosmic order" as Giacomo could have found them in Plato's *Timaeus* (*Birth* 189). So he "constructed [the sonnet] according to the architecture of the soul and of heaven, and set it in the music of the spheres" (190). Giacomo probably knew the *Timaeus*, translated into Latin early in the thirteenth century either at the University of Naples or at the emperor's court, and the poet may well have been using its proposals to reproduce "the architecture of the soul, even the architecture of the meditative mind of God, in words on a sheet of paper" (22–23).

This suggests nothing "modern" in any new introspection the sonnet may have shown. Nor did the sonnet *originate* such a thing. It is better taken as symptom of tensions already observed. Like the contemporary phenomena of confession and Tempier's condemnation of Averroist theses mentioned in Chapter 10, the sonnet showed a resolving of tensions and a resetting of person disturbed. It did so by resituating them in the hierarchy of heaven and earth, divine and secular, that gave the post-Augustinian grounding of embedded selfe. However the sonnet developed later, whatever tense forebodings it contained and later facilitated, it did not at first reflect any conflicted *modern* self.

A fine instance of the difference is Giacomo's own "tenth" sonnet, whose play on love and glass recalls Chapter 1's glassy images. Oppenheimer writes of its complex "play on glass and mirrors, on the fragility of both, and on their ability—despite how easily they may be shattered—to allow sunlight to pass through them or reflect off them harmlessly." The poem has light and love "defacing," "reflecting," causing "pain" and perhaps eventually enabling the lovers to unite in them (in the sestet) under the new "combined" image of "fire." The poem treats the "intense emotional 'light'" of the experience of falling in love (29). Were the poem as Oppenheimer depicts and freely "translates," he might have a point. The poem does not support this analysis:

> Sì come il sol che manda la sua spera
> e passa per lo vetro e no lo parte,
> e l'altro vetro che le donne spera,
> che passa gli ochi e va da l'altra parte,
> così l'Amore fere là ove spera
> e mandavi lo dardo da sua parte:
> fere in tal loco che l'omo non spera,
> passa per gli ochi e lo core diparte.
>
> Lo dardo de l'Amore là ove giunge,
> da poi che dà feruta sì s'aprende
> di foco c'arde dentro e fuor non pare;

e due cori insemora li giunge,
de l'arte de l'amore sì gli aprende,
e face l'uno e l'altro d'amor pare.

(ed. Antonelli 286; slight variant in Langley 68)

If the first line *may* imply possibility of breakage, nothing implies Oppenheimer's "shattering," whose evocation is aleatory. A strong point of the sonnet is that the sun's—and love's—"spear" do *not* "part" the glass, that the body's, the eyes' and the soul's outer cover remains whole and unbroken. One of the poem's points would be lost were this not so: that the forms of body, senses and, ultimately, soul remain undamaged even while passion or sin may burn within in that anguished tension which Héloïse named. At the same time the suffering is brief and equilibrium quickly reestablished. This final sense of completeness agrees with Oppenheimer's interpretation of the sonnet form as marking jointure of soul and heavens' fabric, of universe and incarnate soul. It denies any showing of a new "modern mind."

The poem is not easy to translate because Giacomo plays on so many multiple senses: *spera* can be a ray, a small round mirror, a sphere, the third person singular of the verb "to hope," perhaps even a verb made from *spera* as a mirror. Similarly, he uses *parte* as a verb meaning to break, a noun meaning whatever is "behind" the eyes—presumably here the soul, but also the heart—the root of a verb meaning to sunder, divide or remove. Words like *giunge*, *aprende*, *pare*, even perhaps *passa* become unstable. The second tercet tames and unifies this connotational multiplicity, echoing the completeness just mentioned. Verbal ambiguities are reconciled as are the lovers. So I translate the sonnet as follows (with thanks to Daniel Javitch for his patient help):

> Just like the sun, which sends out its ray
> and passes through glass and does not break it,
> and [like] the other glass which mirrors women,
> which traverses the eyes and goes to the soul,
> just so does Love wound wherever it intends,
> and sends its dart into one's soul/heart:
> wounds in a place where a man does not expect,
> traverses the eyes and divides the heart.
>
> Love's dart, there where it reaches
> once it wounds, kindles
> a fire that burns within unseen without;
>
> and joins two hearts together,
> teaches them the art of love,
> so that each decks the other with love.

A main point is that the external wholeness and unharmed appearance of the medium through which pass sun's ray, women's image and love's dart, at first painful, at last brings beneficent warmth. The simile involves the burning and heat that the sun's ray *can* cause once it has gone through the glass, that a woman's image in a glass *can* cause once it has passed through a man's eyes and into his soul and that love's dart *does* cause. At the same time, none of these show any such effects *outside* the media through which they pass or off which they reflect. The sun's warmth is finally beneficial (indeed essential), women's image necessary to the welfare of men's soul and love's dart eventually requited in shared emotion. The sonnet shows a wholeness of body, the passibility of heart and soul (*l'altra parte, sua parte*—"soul" seems better than "heart," although in the second case the word is a bridge to "lo core")—and the final (Platonic?) union of two souls that is love's fulfillment. It is achieved via the mutual look characterizing earlier experiences of personal being. *Who* one was was inseparable from whom one was *with*—one was always two or more. It matters that the sonnet is in the third person. What it narrates is *im*personal. I do not say that Giacomo did not write personal love sonnets. He did. This is not one. But Oppenheimer makes his free translation of *Sì come il sol* his core case for Giacomo's modern sense and experience of self. Its imagery and motifs work directly *against* the notion of an introspective individual self (which one cannot find in other sonnets either, however "personal"), expressing themes of final security of being that contrast directly with the instances proposed at the beginning of Chapter 1. (I recall Petrarch's identical use of a stable and clear "glassy" selfe in poems 37, 95 and 147, cited in Chapter 1. Indeed, in the path of Giacomo's sonnet from verbal and spiritual instability to final reconciliation, is the same pattern as underlies Petrarch's *Rime sparse* as a whole.)

Too, if Oppenheimer's general numerological interpretation of the sonnet form makes sense—as Marianne Shapiro's analogous interpretation of the sestina, invented by the troubadour Arnaut Daniel more or less at the same time, suggests it does—this particular sonnet's closure serves to confirm the ultimate stability of the person's enlacement in the world. Shapiro's argument is that the sestina form—particularly in Petrarch's hands—articulated and "resolved" two traditionally asymmetric concepts of time, one linear, the other cyclical. The Petrarchan sestina, focusing on "an amorous event," joins the "story, as history imitated in the linearity of poetic process, and the myth, the primordial and primitive origin of an indefinitely recurring theme," through whose bond "the myth establishes its dominance." Functioning in this way, the poems, through history and myth, create "a literary symbol that, as such, constantly invites interpretive investigation. At the same time, the verbal recapitulations within sestinas call on the resources of memory, and the reader becomes involved in a spiraling extension of the words, without establishing for any one of them a simple, fixed meaning." This phenomenon reinforces Shapiro's thought that the sestina structure is also characterized by "the lack of a center" (*Hieroglyph* 4: for Petrarch's sestinas, see 63–90, 99–140, 210–13).

Others have noted a play of "myth" and "history." Nancy Vickers sees it as a tension characterizing the entire *Canzoniere*, and while she focuses on Petrarch's *personae* as caught between narrative and myth rather than on formal traits, her language is strikingly similar to Shapiro's. The *Canzoniere* is a "narrative—if one can call it that—"composed of "an instant of first appearance and a life-long attempt at recreating, at making represent, that instant." The desire to "depict a woman of indescribable beauty" was what first made Petrarch's speaker a poet, and still "permits his speech." Yet the very "indescribability . . . threatens that same speech" ("Body" 100; cf. "Diana" 105). Vickers thus writes of an absent center, of spiraling meanings, of the "paradox" of an "act of describing" that "questions the very possibility of description" ("Body" 100–101). These suggestions further emphasize the tensions we have seen characterizing the age in general and Petrarch's prose writings in particular, witnesses to a sense of a once securely embedded selfe under acute pressure. The "myth" would be his effort to counter them with a more solid surety. Actually, these apparent *in*securities themselves do more. They let Petrarch speak in the "many voices" (Musa/Manfredi xi) that *are* the multiple spheres of human being, even though, we shall see, they now need pulling together by the "higher," divine, sphere.

At the same time, his creation in the *Canzoniere* of a different potential "closure," even a different "myth," does finally offer reestablishment of some "security." The word *myth* is unfortunate, unless it just names a fictive and/or ideological resolution of contradictions and tensions, enabling what is at least *experienced* as secure and reliable praxis. That is what Petrarch achieved in the *Canzoniere*. Making a verbal whole from ostensibly and ostentatiously "fragmented" bits, the collection confirmed the security of the person doing the making. I suggest that it did so as well for the "person" being made as part of the collection and the role she plays in it. Vickers argues that the poet's "self"-making needed "repetition of his lady's dispersed image. We never see a totalizing description of Laura" ("Body" 102; cf. "Diana" 96). Actually the final hymn to the Virgin may be just that—not to speak of the collection as a whole (certainly such disempowering was not experienced by the great number of women poets who later wrote Petrarchan sequences, often "subversive" but usually explicitly enabled by the *Canzoniere*). As important, when

Vickers asks what any one poem does for the *speaker*, she finds that not only "the lady is corporeally scattered." So, too, is "the lover emotionally scattered; and the relation between the two is, by extension, one of mirroring" ("Body"104; "Diana" 104). Thomas Greene quotes just such mirroring in *canzone* 50: "Ahi crudo Amor, ma tu allor più m'informe / a seguir d'una fera che mi strugge / la voce e i passe e l'orme" (Ah, cruel Love, you then most shape me / to pursue the voice and steps and prints / of a wild beast who destroys me). "By a mysterious and inexplicable circularity," he remarks, "hunter becomes hunted" ("Petrarch" 37; *Rime* 50, ll.39–41).

The collection *is all* the poems together, a carefully collated whole. If we discard ideas of a modernizing self-making and recall experiences of personhood so far explored, these statements infer a quite different interpretation, one that Vickers immediately emphasizes in writing of how "Petrarch's figurations of the speaker/Laura relationship" take various mythical or divine figures and apply them alternately to both: "The space of that alternation is, of course, a median one—a space of looks, mirrors and texts" ("Body" 104; "Diana" 105). We recall the ancient Greek sense of who-ness, established in mutual gaze. We are reminded that it takes two or more to make a person; that a person exists *only* in "public" social relations, communal spheres of being—the point Cavarero makes in *Relating Narratives.*

The relation starts from the opening sonnet, the one giving the collection its popular name:

> Voi ch'ascoltate in rime sparse il suono
> di quei sospiri ond'io nudriva 'l core
> in sul mio primo giovenile errore
> quand'era in parte altr'uom da quel ch'i'sono (1.1–4)

> You who hear in scattered rhymes the sound
> of those sighs that I used to feed the heart
> in my first youthful error/errancy
> when (I) was in part another man from what I am

From the opening "You," the poet begs his listener/reader to listen to him, to look at him, to be his judge. In this poem, offered as a later judgment not only on a former selfe but on "scattered verses" now gathered into a different whole, he appeals to present readers to look at the elements of his youthful mistakes and wanderings and compare them to what this very collection says he is now:

> Ma ben veggio or si come al popol tutto
> favola fui gran tempo, onde sovente
> di me medesmo meco mi vergogno;

et del mio vaneggiar vergogna è 'l frutto,
e 'l pentersi, e 'l conoscer chairamente
che quanto piace al mondo è breve sogno. (9–14)

But now I well see how of everyone
I have for long been the talk, whence often
of my very selfe within I am ashamed;

and of my raving shame is the fruit,
and repentance, and knowledge clear
that whatever pleases in the world is fleeting dream.

He had always existed as part of a community, but in his youth, he implies, to be the talk of the crowd and garner fame was a matter of *personal* satisfaction, emphasized by the long drawn-out "me" of the first tercet's last line: "di me medesmo meco mi . . . ." This is the Augustinian worldly "I." It was, he stresses, in the past. Now he is ashamed of it. Now he sees clearly, "ben veggio": it was a delirium, *vanneggiar*, to regret. Now, "knowing clearly," he recognizes these pleasures as delusory. This is the present *persona* on whom he asks his reader to look, one which, by collecting the scattered rhymes, brings itself into existence *as* object of others' gaze. It is a *persona* rebuilt from and in all these poems; not of any one of them, but of their gathering. Rather, it *is* the *persona* of one inasmuch as that one sums up the *Canzoniere*'s "story," capping it with the memory of the end of Augustine's *Confessions*. I mean the final hymn to the Virgin, whose prayer confirms through and through the truth of the opening sonnet's final tercet. But the collection only bears this fruit if two kinds of others read it. The ones are the *Canzoniere*'s secular readers addressed by its first word, *Voi*, for whom he has necessarily been a *favola*: as we all are in life. The others are Laura and the Virgin, or Laura-become-Virgin: the *tu* that organizes the final *canzone* and appeals to a divine community. These communities from different spheres are asked now to look differently upon his soul. Both are necessary for his soul to *be* different. Both are necessary as an exchange of gazes, as an exchange of words, a creation of *favole*, a word derived, Mazzotta observes, from *fari*, to speak (144). Without them he has no being.

Chapter 1 began with the late sixteenth- to early seventeenth-century breakdown of this mirroring and mutual regard, which dramatically marked the sense that a familiar experience of identity had lost its ground. What is remarkable about the *Canzoniere* is that it succeeded, for the space of its text, in rebuilding that experience: because of the tensions already noted. For it was from the play of these tensions—absence against presence, scattering against gathering, story against myth, empty center against whole—that the speaker could make his mirrors, resituate a mutual looking.

Of poem 23, a *canzone* where among his several metamorphoses the speaker is also Actaeon changed into a stag for having seen Diana naked, Vickers observes how Petrarch changed Ovid's story so that instead of Diana having the last word, it is Actaeon who asserts finally that "I'll tell the truth [*Vero dirò*]" (l.156) ("Body" 108; "Diana" 108). The earlier story may relate his scattering. This one does not. Here, the "lonely stag" still flees "the rage of my own hounds" (l.160), relishes further loving transformations (ll.161–65), still enjoys the laurel whose "lovely shade / clears every lesser pleasure from my heart" (l.169). This Actaeon lives on to write the next 343 poems. Diana/Laura has seen and sees him, he has seen and sees Laura/Diana. As long as the poems keep going so does their mutual experience of being. They do more. This truth-telling Acteon is also the poet, we saw at the start of this chapter, who weaves "one truth with another" (sonnet 40). *canzone* 50, where we saw Greene note a "mysterious" reversal of hunter and hunted, dwells on the continuity of the very "canzon" the poet is now singing/writing (l.71), as it insists on eyes, their "fixing," their "seeing" and the singer's "showing." Indeed, like so many others, the "Acteon" *canzone* 23, echoes in little the movement of the whole *Canzoniere*. Its Ovidian first line appeals, like the opening sonnet, to early youth: "Nel dolce tempo de la prima etade," in the sweet season of first age, before love brought endless disturbance into the soul. But that disturbance is also loss of "memory" (l.15), indeed "forgetting of one's selfe" (l.19). Love's passion repeats the loss that is soul's when born into body. The "dolce tempo" and "prima etade" (not "*my*," as it is always translated) is *also* the impassible essence known to the soul before birth. The joy of the "dolce ombra," sweet shade, of laurel that gladdens the heart at the end of the poem (l.168), bringing closure to the disturbed beginning, thus prefigures the healing of the collection's final hymn. Many poems follow this trajectory. We should not exaggerate any "absent center."

For Freccero, too, finds such an absence vital to Petrarch's mythic establishment of self, the poet composing "lyric fragments" into a [self-]portrait with "no temporality . . . , immune from the ravages of time." "All traces of temporality and contingency" taken from the *Canzoniere*, "the lyrics themselves counterfeit a *durée* by their physical proximity" ("Fig Tree" 21, 29). Against such a view, Roland Greene perceives Petrarch's invention of the lyric sequence as a fictive "temporal process," referring to his "obsession with temporality as a cultural and epistemological problem" and noting the massive recurrence of time words in the *Canzoniere* (22, 62).

Barolini, too, studies time as central to the collection, arguing that the traditional naming of Petrarch's two Parts as "Laura's life" and "Laura's death" is as flawed as it has often been thought, and misdirects the meaning of the *Rerum vulgarium fragmenta*. For her, the division between the two—and the blank pages in the manuscripts that mark it—signals transition itself, not the transitoriness of any particular life. The first poem that begins the second part (264) is itself a *canzone* about transition. The second two (265 and 266), poems about Laura's life but out of chronological order, ironically call attention to time. The fourth poem (267) is the first mourning poem. Barolini argues that the move from Part 1 to Part 2 shows "a remarkable consonance between form and content," the very idea and fact of transition (10–11). "Part 1 is dominated by non-narrativity, by the refusal or inability to move forward" (11). It marks the poet's sealing in the world, the fleeting dream of the first sonnet's last line. Part 2 reintroduces time and narrativity, real movement ending in the repentance and clear knowledge also claimed in the opening sonnet. These differences are, Barolini insists, dominances, not absolutes: "the genius of the genre lies precisely in its balancing of both" (3). Too, she reminds us that not only Laura is celebrated and mourned in Part 2. Sonnet 266 is an anniversary poem for the poet's eighteen years' love for Laura and fifteen years' friendship with Cardinal Giovanni Colonna. 269 is a sonnet mourning them both. Part 2 explores time's return, human bonds, movement, the real possibility of a reconciliation out of this life.

This reading does not contradict the last two of the *Canzoniere* I want to mention as important for understanding the who-ness grounding the work. I refer to Thomas Roche's numerological reading, which recalls Oppenheimer's and Shapiro's concerns and stresses temporality, identity and the circles of humanity. He shows that the *Canzoniere* established a Christian cycle, "formally structured around four major events in the Christian year: Good Friday, Advent, Christmas, and Lent" (172). Petrarch's central sequence of April 6s structures the *Canzoniere*—the day of his first sight of Laura in 1327, of her death in 1348, of his arrival in Rome for his coronation as laureate in 1341—and recalls the Christian tradition's focus on that date: the day of humans' creation, their fall, Christ's crucifixion and, some thought, the second coming. Too, if one sets the 366 poems against their successive days, starting with the April 6, Good Friday, sonnet that opens Part 1, the transition *canzone* 264, opening Part 2, falls on Christmas Day: "Part I," writes Roche, "dealing with the inception and growth of his love, begins with the death of Christ; Part II, dealing with the death of his love, begins with the birth of Christ" (165). The mixed series of poems that follows 264 gives way to a series of 52 sonnets, forming a symbolic year of mourning, stopped by three non-sonnets (323–25). Poem 326 matches February 25, which, in 1327, fell on Ash Wednesday. It suggests that the following last forty poems symbolically render the forty days of Lent, "leading up to 366, that great hymn to the virgin, which is associated with April 5, which in 1327 was Palm Sunday, the day of Christ's triumphal entry into Jerusalem" (167). The *Rime* tell an Augustinian story of a worldly sinner for long misdirected by a human love of whose true force he was ignorant, at last seeing divine love actually *before* Laura's death (mourned in poem 267) and in the now dead Laura the possibility of a transformation from earthly desire to heavenly charity. Against the structuring morality of the annual Christian cycle, "Petrarch counterpoints the agony of his earthly love and his growing awareness of the disparity between it and the heavenly love he ultimately sought" (172). This fits well with Barolini's analysis: the death of Christ beginning Part 1 signals stasis and lack of growth, his birth, new awareness of life's meanings and movement to new understanding.

Holmes notes that the *Canzoniere*'s complexities underline the fact that Petrarch explicitly used "a typological structure typical of medieval poetry, the traditional Christian pattern of sin, repentance, and redemption, and was well aware of the exemplary dimension of his first-person speaker" (187–88n5). The number of poems matching the days in a year plus one, or a leap year, both the pages, the "foglie sparse," and the poems "become metaphors for the disjointed yet continuous days and nights of human existence." Nor are they just the days of a year. They are "the years of the speaker's life, [as is] made explicit in the anniversary poems." The "gran giornate" of poem 272 (l.2) may be the "strides" of Death (as Musa has it), and are certainly the "stages" of a human life (as Durling translates). They are also literally the "days" or "day's work" (172): "the formal structure of the work is imitative of both human existence and the cosmos conceived as a whole." Like many earlier poets,

Petrarch implies a multiplicity of levels: the individual poem can be read as a figure for the book, which can be read as a figure for a human lifetime, which can be read, in turn, as a figure for human history. Each narrative resembles the others in terms of its transience; on every level, things eventually reach a point at which all expectation has finished and the whole action has passed into memory, like a song, or, more to the point perhaps, like the breeze ("l'aura"). (175)

Such "levels" rejoin our now-familiar spheres of being.

For all these reasons, Freccero is surely wrong to assert that while Augustine's fig tree (in whose shade he experienced his conversion) joined a whole theological tradition, Petrarch's laurel was limited to himself. Nor, in this same individualist line, did Petrarch claim to be the *only* poet, rather just outstanding "among [his] contemporaries" (*Secretum* 43; "Fig" 26). These arguments miscast what the *Canzoniere* was about. It was embedded in both theological and secular traditions, the latter in-

cluding modern Dante and the troubadours and a Greco-Latin heritage
reaching back to laurels of mythical Orpheus and divine Apollo. On this
embedding, Musa and Barbara Manfredi are expansive:

The writings of Varro, Catullus, Horace, Virgil at his most parodic, Ovid at his
peak and in exile; of Cicero, Propertius, Juvenal, Seneca, Ausonius, Boethius, the
St. Augustine of the *Confessiones*, and numerous others find expression in the
Canzoniere, along with the lyrics of goliardic, the Sicilian, and Provençal poets,
of Cavalcanti, Dante and the *dolce stil nuovo* ("sweet new style"), which Petrarch
inherited by virtue of being born in 1304. The individuality of Catullus, the eminent rationalism and amused stoicism of Cicero, the cosmopolitanism and dra-
maticity of Seneca, the metaphoric fecundity of Ovid, the sharp-tongued literal-
ness of Juvenal, and literary playfulness of the Horace of *Ars poetica*, all inform
the styles Petrarch reveals to us in these poems. (Musa/Manfredi xiv)

That it also ties into a theological tradition is already manifest.
    His very love for Laura was established on the day of Christ's Passion
(sonnet 3), when "the sun's ray turned pale with pity" (ll.1–2), and
throughout the *Canzoniere* the poet is aware, as Holmes says, that "the
lover's adoration of the laurel . . . ought to lead rather to a contemplation
of Christ" (178), to a move toward and, ideally, into a sense of eternity.
Unlike Dante, Petrarch never achieves this. He never does so because of
his overwhelming sense, constantly repeated, of being materially caught,
in life, in a material body. The straining toward the divine and experience
of imprisonment away from it are endlessly figured. On one well-known
occasion it leads him to compare an old pilgrim coming to Rome to look
on the image of Christ, whom he hopes to join in heaven, to himself looking for Laura (16, ll.9–14). Ugo Foscolo thought this poem blasphemous
(he should have read Gaspara Stampa's matching poem in which her
lover becomes greater than god! we shall see). It marks, rather, just how
thoroughly the circles of being were imbricated. That is why the notion of
love's prison, unable to be escaped while on earth, was the prison of the
body (e.g., 76), the rock on which one founders in this life (80). Earthly
love is the very mark of the soul's bodily imprisonment (81, 86). The image is constant. It is why Laura is at once block to and hope of a passage
to things divine (204). Too, the sacrifice of his love for her, as a rejection
of earthly sin, can make Laura into a more powerful path to the divine
(214). Time is all-important. The pursuit of Laura itself marks earthly
time's flight, the fleetingness of its years toward death (30, ll.13–14), but
of the hope, as well, of reaching finer shores, as sestina 30 ends:

> L'auro e i topacii al sol sopra la neve
> vincon le bionde chiome presso a gli occhi
> che menan gli anni miei sì tosto a riva. (ll.37–39)

Gold and topaz in sun above the snow
are vanquished by the golden locks close by those eyes
that lead my years so quickly to the shore.

Petrarch had himself earlier explained just how the laurel was *not* limited to himself. In his "Coronation Oration," he explained the laurel's "properties" by drawing on illustrious predecessors, mostly Virgil, but also Horace, Ovid, Lucan, Persius, Suetonius. By its fragrance it signaled "the fragrance of good repute" and glory sought by poets and kings, by bodily action in the last case, spiritual contemplation in the first. Its shadiness signaled a place of rest from such labors. The incorruptibility of its leaves showed how poets "preserve from corruption both their own fame and the fame of others." It was, too, "a sacred tree, to be held in awe," appropriate to religious sacrifice, used in temples and, indeed, "for the Capitol itself." Reputedly, if sleepers were touched by the laurel their "dreams come true." Poets, "who are said to be wont to sleep on Parnassus," covertly showed truths understood by the instructed, mere dreams to the ignorant. In the same way, poets shared Apollo's laurel as those who foretold the future truthfully. Its being evergreen signaled immortality and why it was "said to be beloved by Apollo and sacred to him," for the god was said to have loved Daphne, and Greek *daphnē* had "the same meaning as Latin *laurus*. Both poets and kings loved the immortality of their repute won through war or genius." This joined the last "property": that the laurel was immune to lightning, as the poet's work made him secure from blighting by the "thunderbolt" of the ages (*Collatio*, Wilkins 309–12). All these and more became central to the *laura* of the *Rerum vulgarium fragmenta*. They speak equally to profane and sacred, secular and holy, to being in the material and physical world and in the divine, to being in social and in political circumstance, to the being of the soul.

Nowhere was all this captured better than in sestina 142 (although *canzone* 23 catches much of it). The "lovely leaves" of the laurel/Laura protect him from the burning love that Venus (third heaven) had burned down on him (1–3). They become, too, "l'aura amorosa," "the loving breeze" that melts the snow and "renews the season," so that flowers and branches bloom across the meadows (4–6). In these lines Laura/l'aura is the life that flows through the universe as *psuchē*, the *spiritus* that was material air, corporeal spirit and vivifying power of the soul. The poet's stress on the material world throughout this sestina is not, though, more than his emphasis on the thought that the laurel also ties him to the divine, it being the tree "most loved in heaven" (12). Thus the earthly love he feels for the "graceful branches," the "lovely branches" (7, 14), is transfigured by the "supernal light" (17) in which they are bathed. His earthly attachment mediates the call "from heaven" (20), guides him with its "gentle and clear light," via the laurel branches scattered on earth, through "woods, rocks, fields, rivers and hills" (23, 25), to higher achievement: "Altr'amor, altre frondi, et altro lume, / altro salir al ciel per altri poggi / cerco (che n'è ben tempo), et altri rami"—"Other love, other leaves, and other light, / other climb to heaven by other hills / I seek (the time's well right), and other branches" (37–39). The experienced intertwining of divine, personal (always at least *à deux*) and material could not be better expressed. The sestina hardly distinguishes them, its form holding them in a finely iterated whole.

The *Rerum vulgarium fragmenta*'s overall structure matches what we have seen of the sonnet and sestina forms in themselves. It and they again return us to the embedded person. Who the poet is is inseparable from the divine sphere which is a part of him. The same is ultimately the case for Laura as well—whether or not she was a real or an imaginary person, or whether, as Roche suggests, she was a real woman about whom Petrarch was making fictions. In any of these cases, the point remains that the divine was integral to what and who she was as well. The poet is also inseparable, I suggested, from the social, material and other spheres. That is why poems like sonnet 27 and *canzone* 28 make appeals to unite Italy by bringing the polity together on behalf of a new crusade. It is why the Babylon of Avignon finds its way into so many of the poems (e.g., 114, 136–39). It is why *canzone* 53, addressed either to Cola or to Stefano Colonna, is an appeal to bring together the *fragmenti sparsi* of Italy itself, making an equation between the material, personal and spiritual on one hand and the political on another. *Canzone* 128 thus has an Italy in fragments, whose agony requires that the "Rettor del cielo," Ruler of heaven (l.7), come down and cure it, putting the broken land together again. Here, its geography—carefully built by God to keep Italy whole against German encroachment (ll.33–35)—fragmented by internal strife, actually *is* a human body needing cure, just like his own in this vale of tears (ll.38ff.). The poet and the construction of the poem will enable these reconciliations (ll.113–22).

To understand who the people of these poems were, we needed to know that these structures of individual poems as well as that of the whole *Canzoniere* embedded a particular experience of the world and humans in it. This experience may have become fraught, but it is still within its stabilizing force that we have to read these tensions. Holmes is, I think, quite right to see the *Canzoniere*'s poems as going "a long way toward overcoming the oppositions between the speaker's different parts or different selves, and towards providing his readers with the illusion of temporal continuity." He offers a personal being "represented as permanently fixed and stable" yet also "a composite of disparate parts" as in poem 112, whose fourth line reads "l'aura mi volve, et son pur quel ch'i' m'era," "Laura [or the breeze, earthly existence] turns me about, and I am still just what I was." She observes that this can also read: "Laura turns me about, and I am still that chimera," the mythical beast combining lion in front, goat in the middle and snake behind (184). This tension with which the first part of the *Canzoniere* is thoroughly fraught is little by little surmounted in the second. This culminates in the final mighty hymn, conjoining earthly Laura and all the social relations she marks, material world: "*terra*," earth or "dust" (366, l.13); sociopolitical world needing "di giustizia il Sol che rasserena / il secol pien d'errori oscuri e folti"—"the Sun of justice who brightens an age filled with dark and thick errors" (l.45); the personal world that is the poet's own reconciliation; and the divine world, overcoming the run and flight of time ("sì corre il tempo et vola": l.132) and accepting the poet's "final breath in peace" (l.137). The great poetic sequence holds tension in stability and offers its readers the possibility of reconciliation with the divine as an act of becoming "more human."

This is very different from what some of his women "successors" were to do with his project just over a century and a half later. I think of Stampa starting her own sequence competitively against Petrarch: "Voi, ch'ascoltate in queste meste rime," "You who listen to these mournful verses," and who then goes on not in regret, but appealing to her women readers for praise of her "danno sì chiaro [so noble sorrow]." For her, life was not Petrarch's "breve sogno" but a place where "such great love, such high fortune" as have been created for the writer of *these* poems were above all to be envied (1, ll.10–14). Love, she wrote in sonnet 24, might be torment and raging passion, but no cause for regret, for they are blessed (*benedetti*). Petrarch fell in love on the day of the Passion under a bright sun, Stampa did so on Christmas Day. Her beloved, to whom alone now her "thoughts and hopes and glances turn" surpassed in nobility, gentility and bravery "all others whom the sun looks on," including, presumably, Christ himself, born on that day (2, ll.12–14). In a later sonnet (209), she observes that Christmas Day to her means less the coming of Christ than the "delightful" (*adorno*) day on which "Love spread its nets" for her (ll.5–6). She took the point even further in sonnet 17, where her beloved becomes as great as or greater than God to the angels, whom she does not envy because her own *diletti*, delights, "are such and so abundant / They cannot be contained in earthly heart." The eyes she praises in her poems are as glorious as the light in which they bask. They only surpass her joy in that theirs is everlasting, while hers must come to an end. Even this becomes a means, though, to subvert Petrarch's project.

First, the poetry itself contains that end in the poet's continual out-bursts of anger against her beloved for his infidelities, absences and cold-ness. In this last, her male lover actually becomes Laura, like "the pale moon" his heart is "colder" than her "warm desire" (4, ll.10–11). In sonnet 7, she builds a kind of blason of her beloved, "scattering" him as Petrarch had Laura. But this scattering matches, is perhaps revenge for, his infidelity (l.8). Second, then, her *canzoniere* itself marked love's end as her choice and affirmation: half way through, she changes the lover ad-dressed. She could hardly affirm her agency more dramatically. So she does in sonnet 104, another inversion of Petrarch's *canzoniere*, bursting into a paean on physical love: "O notte, a me più chiara e più beata / che i più beati giorni ed i più chiari": "O night, to me more glorious and more blessed than the most blessed and glorious days" (ll.1–2). Here, she may again recall the high days of the Christian calendar—especially Christmas. Above all she claims agency against her lover, social expecta-tions and Petrarch. Such moments authorize her chief claim. Not only will her beloved endure only through her poetry, he being an inferior poet who should not waste ink and paper (117, ll.1–2), but she, through it, will reach the infinite (98), making miracles and "alone defeating infin-ity" (91, l.14): "Lassa, ch'io sola vinco l'infinito." This repeated claim set her in (successful) competition with the greatest poets. Neither Petrarch nor Virgil nor Homer, she wrote in sonnet 114, would "be able to tell the truth" about her beloved and her love, so reason tells her she "should stay silent" (ll.5–8). On the contrary, she wrote her entire *canzoniere*, in-sisting on its grandeur and glory, and noting in her last sonnets ("last" only because her editors have changed her original ordering, undermin-ing her further originality), again contrary to Petrarch, that she cannot at-tain to the divine, there being a block between her and God (e.g., sonnets 307, 308).

In light of her opening sonnet and its praise of earthly love, of her con-stant appeals to the great poetry it has let her write and of her delight in the "sufferings" enabling the poetry and her fame, it is by no means clear that this inability to reach God was cause for sorrow. Indeed, where Pe-trarch sealed off earthly torments of love, ambition, political yearning and desire for glory between the opening sonnet and closing hymn, the last suggesting a sort of closure in the divine, the first a simultaneous look back at earthly sinning that he can call *past*, Stampa reveled in tor-ments, anguish and glory that are not only *now*, but ongoing. The Pe-trarch who "experienced" the "sinful" torments recounted in the *Can-zoniere*, as Sara Elena Díaz observes in echo of Mary Moore (36), "is not the same man who writes. From his removed vantage-point, the author can reformulate his existence into a fiction with a beginning, middle and end" (19), although it is not clear that this is a "fiction"—or in what sense it might be. Stampa's poetry, though, "contains no such retraction." She too, we saw, prefaced "her *Rime* with a retrospective sonnet," but it was one of celebration. And she writes her poems as one "still buffeted by passions" (19), rejoicing in them and raging at them, without apology or shame.

These "liberatory" gestures can be found in many contemporary women writers (Marcia Weston Brown has traced some of them with fine distinctions, as has, very recently and more briefly, Janet Levarrie Smarr). One thinks as well, for instance, not just of Stampa's compatriot, Vittoria Colonna, but of the celebrated Lyonnaise "belle cordière," Louise Labé, who similarly gloried in celebrating her love by responding directly to Petrarch (writing her first sonnet in Italian, imitating his sonnet 161 in her second) and on the back of an angry rejection of "the wrong men have been doing to us by depriving us of the good and honor that would come to us" from knowledge of arts and sciences. Women could and should, she added, outdo men in these affairs (*Oeuvres* 41). The "Débat de folie et d'amour" that opened her sole collection, has an angry goddess "Folie" (the same Folly as that of Erasmus' encomium) blinding Eros for insulting and threatening her: "What temerity has a child to address a woman, outrage and insult her with words; and then even try and kill her" (54). Like Stampa, Labé insisted on a woman's right to physical freedom in love and on the poet's right to express it, famously playing on an "etymology" of her own name (*Labé* = *labium* = "lip") in her eighteenth sonnet:

> Baise m'encor, rebaise moy et baise:
> Donne m'en un de tes plus savoureus,
> Donne m'en un de tes plus amoureux:
> Je t'en rendray quatre plus chaus que braise.
> Las, te pleins tu? ça que ce mal j'apaise,
> En t'en donnant dix autres doucereus.
> Ainsi meslans nos baisers tant heureus
> Jouissons nous l'un de l'autre à notre aise.

> Kiss me again, kiss me again and kiss:
> Give me one of your most tasty ones,
> Give me one of your most loving ones:
> I'll give you back four hotter than hot coals.
> Alas, do you complain? let me calm your hurt,
> By giving you ten more soft ones.
> So mingling our joyous kisses
> Let us delight in each other at our ease.

(131: XVIII.1–8)

These cases suggest openings toward a different sense of personal being, even as they make use of strains found in Petrarch. I look more
closely at another instance in Chapter 15. For these cases were nonetheless forged against a general experience of personal being still far closer
to that expressed by Petrarch, however fraught it may have become.

CHAPTER THIRTEEN

Surrounded Selves and Public Being

Sixteenth-Century Strains

Not for nothing, one must think, was Petrarch's *Canzoniere* so vital a work for people in the early sixteenth century. That "books of his poetry were used as fashion items" surely matters, however we explain the fact. It was then "common for Italian women to wear a miniature volume of his poems—a *Petrarchino*—dangling from their waists" (Emck 13). At one level they just showed acquaintance with popular styles. But they couldn't do so unless they agreed with accepted norms of experience. The *Canzoniere* signaled those norms.

Care is needed with remarks that we would like to construe in maybe more modern terms. So: "'Homines non nascuntur, sed finguntur,' Erasmus wrote—men are fashioned rather than born—a formula which might be taken as the motto of the Humanist revolution." The sentence is Thomas Greene's, and he adds that this "metaphor of fashioning implies that a man's nature is essentially formless, like wax, essentially neutral, and not, let us note in passing, tainted with original depravity," the sin inherent in all humans since the Fall ("Flexibility" 249).

I am not sure where Erasmus made the quoted remark, but by now we can see that almost everything is wrong with this reading of it. Many things can be "fashioned" (if that *is* the "right" translation of *fingere*). The deponent and passive verbs matter. From Hippocratics to Galen, Plato to Seneca, Augustine to Hildegard, the Arab doctors to Petrarch, people experienced themselves as being crafted, molded or fashioned into their humanity, working and being worked to become *humanior*, made so by and in their surroundings. This did not at all imply that human nature was formless, like wax or neutral—let alone "essentially" so. On the contrary, it fit with the universe in exact ways. This did not mean, either, any "radical stasis" of human nature, as we earlier saw the same critic urge. What it meant was finding the "best" fit, that one which most closely matched the "spheres" of being which were who *this* particular person was. Nor did this fashioning imply that humanity was no longer tainted with original depravity. In Christian experience, the divine sphere could and did readily accommodate original sin. To argue that the European Renaissance newly experienced a suppleness of personal being and that its educational manuals sought to use it to form new kinds of people from youth, as Greene then does, is to forget that *paideia* had *always* done this. How did an early fifteenth-century humanist urging parents to mold children while their minds were still flexible differ from Socrates in the *Republic* explaining how to mold the future guardians of the city, or Cicero in *De oratore* and Quintilian in the *Institutio* showing how to form "rhetoricians," future civic leaders and teachers? One had always had to inculcate *hexeis, habitus,* early because they were later "*difficile mobilis,* resistant to change" ("Flexibility" 249). Writing of implanting good education early, Erasmus specified these connections, reminding his reader that the clarity of a prince's education (like everyone's) was "why Plato wanted" to avoid complexities and "insecurities" before the young mind was well formed (*Education* 46). Nothing in such advice was particularly ancient, medieval or early modern (or modern: recall Simone de Beauvoir's celebrated "One is not born, but rather becomes, a woman" [301]).

The issue is not the molding or fashioning, but what is being molded. Certainly, tensions had grown in an older experience of who one was. There were growing feelings of definitive decay in identity and of an inability to sense the person in the world—or at least to analyze once familiar experiences of personhood. Many writers expressed a kind of defensiveness, as if needing to throw up uneasy barriers against increasing uncertainties. Hence the importance of figures like Hélisenne de Crenne, discussed in Chapter 15, who seem to begin to cross such barriers, affording glimpses of different possible experiences. Nonetheless at least through the sixteenth century the experiences we have been exploring remained essential ground. An older sense of who-ness predominated—as well as yearnings for it. In later chapters, I explore specific writers more closely. In this one, I take exemplary writers from across the century and from many parts of western Europe (two of whom, Loyola and Montaigne, will be principal matter of later chapters) to try and show this more or less constant background. For this reason, too, I deliberately take writers from all moments of the century (from earlier, in two or three cases). I mark this chronological *branloire* as often as seems useful but want the reader to feel this experience as life's background noise. The next chapters show gradual reshapings in and against that background.

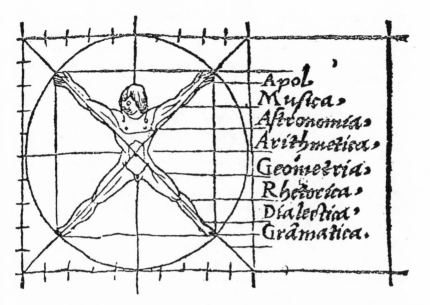

Figure 9. Geofroy Tory, the matrix of all letters, from *Champ Fleury* (1529).

Much of this may seem familiarly banal. This may be the point. Edwin Duval's showing that Rabelais' *Tiers* and *Quart Livres* are formally structured by concentric circular narratives is not foreign to this background (see *Design/*Tiers 233–34 for an overview). Grounding experience was still the familiar circles of being. I try to take these in turn, starting with the divine and going on to the animate, the sociopolitical, the physical—although such divisions are for the moment no less artificial than they have always been. Indeed, the continuing difficulty of separating them for analytical purposes is one evidence of their continuing strength. We shall see by the end of this book that the "divisions" became naturalized as the experience of embedding broke down.

But through the sixteenth century, being was mostly felt as inseparably woven in its total ecosystem, characterized, as it had been for countless predecessors, as a universe of "sympathies." A vital illustration from Geofroy Tory's 1529 *Champ fleury* shows a circle containing a human figure whose arms and legs are radii centered on its navel. It is the matrix of all letters, rational language and knowledge (Figure 9). Such typical images dramatize how the bond between the divine and the world, human constitution and character, nutrition, climate, geographic location, the planets, the zodiac—and so much else—remained axiomatic. A typical descriptive example is found a century before Tory, fifty years after Petrarch, in Alfonso Martínez de Toledo's 1438 *Arcipreste de Talavera*. Following the pseudo-Aristotelian *Secreta secretorum*, popular throughout the middle ages, Martínez defined relations of human body, planets, and zodiac:

Aries is masculine, and rules the creature's head; its planet is Mercury. Taurus, feminine, rules the neck; its planet is Venus. Gemini, masculine, rules the arms; its planet is Mercury. Cancer, feminine, rules the breast; its planet is the Moon. Leo is masculine, rules the heart; its planet is the Sun. Virgo is feminine, rules the stomach and womb; its planet is Mercury. Libra is masculine, rules the navel; its planet is Venus. Scorpio is feminine, rules the shameful parts; its planet is Mars; Sagittarius is masculine, rules the thighs and spine; its planet Jupiter. Capricorn is feminine, rules the knees; its planet is Saturn. Pisces is feminine, rules the feet; its planet is Jupiter. (III.vi: 210)

Martínez omitted masculine Aquarius here, but not in another major division, separating the signs by threes into sanguine (hot and wet: Gemini, Libra, Aquarius [III.ii]); choleric (hot and dry: Aries, Leo, Sagitarius [III.iii]); phlegmatic (cold and wet: Cancer, Scorpio, Pisces [III.iv]); melancholic (cold and dry: Taurus, Virgo, Capricorn [III.v]). Two centuries later, Walkington still echoed this list, albeit inverting the order of the last two (*Optick* 77, and recall Figure 2). These divisions showed that the planets and zodiac did not just "rule" specific body parts and organs but related generally to humors and temperaments, and so to regimen, health, behavior and all other aspects of human life, including the passions . . . and so the soul. Medical horoscopes, used to evaluate relations between the zodiac and parts of the body, like political and life (animate?) horoscopes and other forms of holistic prognostication, remained standard procedures far into the seventeenth century (consider Kepler's 1627 *Rodolphine Tables*, with its purpose of facilitating both astronomical and astrological calculations). Contemporary with Walkington, Fludd endlessly depicted such relations as those of microcosm to macrocosm (Figure 10) or zodiac to body organs and members (Figure 11).

Certainly Aquinas, and Vives later, denied astrological influence on mind and will, Vives equivocating over body (Aquinas, ST 1a.2ae.9.5; Vives, *Tratado* II.xi:100–101). Aquinas felt it made human affairs too materially determined. He did not query the fact of a sympathetic universe but a distancing of the divine from its direct role in human affairs. Martínez's book IV actually responded to his own description's seeming denial of human free will, and so to Aquinas' denial of all such determining influences (which worried Vives, too). Giovanni Pico's attack on

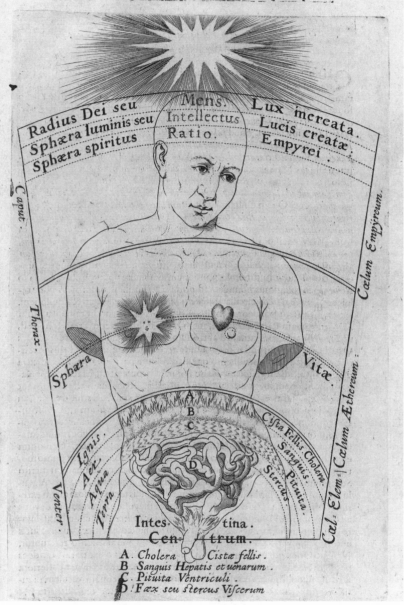

Figure 10. Robert Fludd, relations of microcosm and macrocosm, from *Utriusque cosmi*. Photo: Bancroft Library, University of California, Berkeley.

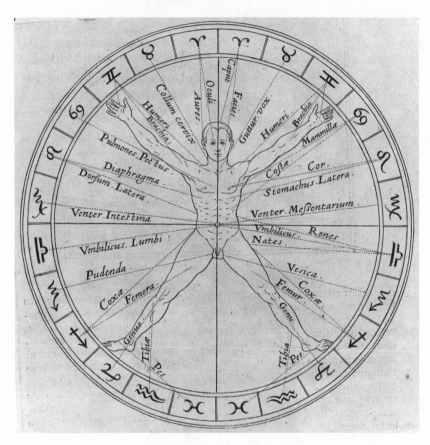

Figure 11. Robert Fludd, the zodiac and human organs and members, from *Utriusque cosmi*. Photo: Bancroft Library, University of California, Berkeley.

astrology chiefly targeted blasphemous material determinism (besides misreckoning, fraud and downright lies), though most "specialist astrologers," Anthony Grafton observes, were not determinist at all, admitting numerous modifying factors (*Cardano's* 85; cf. 94). Reasons for attack overlapped those for which others credited influences: as being actual and deeply emblematic of an integrated universe and divine authority. Like Fludd and myriad others, Girolamo Cardano set most of his work in this experience, as Grafton shows, although Ficino got into trouble with his passionate support for such views in his 1489 *Liber de vita*. How little one must esteem humans, Montaigne wrote in his "Apologie de Raimond Sebond," when thinking of the dominion and power these bodies have not only over our lives and circumstances of our fortune, . . . but over our very inclinations, our talk, our wills, how they rule, direct, and move us at the mercy of their influences, as reason tells us and finds it. . . . Then see how not just one man, nor one king, but monarchies, empires, and the whole lower world moves to the sway of the least celestial motion. (*Oeuvres* 2.12.428–29)

At midcentury, Melanchthon took for granted "coelestes causas" and change due to "diversas stellarum commixtiones" (*Liber* 84, 87), as did Montaigne's contemporary du Bartas, who saw God in their motions, enabling human freedom of prediction and reaction (Quatrieme jour ll.405–96). "Distribution of the heavens" marked His presence. Others, like Montaigne's fifteenth-century model, Ramón Sabunde (Martínez's contemporary), less emphatic on planetary influence, were equally vehement about the universe's integration. Sabunde saw it as the fundamental sign of divinity in the world. However created things varied, Montaigne translated in 1569, "yet there is a same order and like disposition. They are arranged and ordered together in one body and one society [*en un corps et une société*]." "Experience," he went on,

thus teaches us that all things aim for one another's benefit; that they sustain and help each other through mutual satisfactions [*s'entre-soutiennent et s'entre-aident par plaisirs mutuels*]; and that the lowest serve proportionately equally to those above them. Thus they compose an order, a polity, in short, a unity. We must therefore conclude that one alone orders, governs, binds up, and unites all in a single society [*en mesme société*]. (ch. iv: 9.12–13)

"The general clasp and common lock of this rich concatenation and union of the world is love" (ch. cxix: 9.207). Here again was a version of "ennobling love," coming down from Greek and Latin antiquity, and continuing, with adjustments, beyond the middle ages.

"Religious" ideas of soul, mind and body mattered as much to habitual grasp of the nature of human being as medical, legal or political ones. Addressing these issues in his "Apologie," Montaigne, so often taken to show a new secular cast, exalted Aquinas as "that mind, full with infinite erudition and wondrous subtlety, alone capable of such conceptions" as those distilled in Sabunde's *Theologia naturalis* (2.12.417). For Montaigne, too, the divine sphere was an essential part of being. It is no surprise that after translating the *Theologia*, he wrote his longest, perhaps central, essay on Sabunde, imbued with theological speculation.

Sabunde had died in 1436. The *Theologia* was first printed in 1487. Because it argued that knowledge of Christian mysteries could be wholly derived from nature, the Council of Trent put the work on the Index. Widely known through the end of the seventeenth century, it had editions across western Europe. A Latin abridgement of 1498 also had many editions, while Montaigne's translation (the second in French) had at least seven between 1569 and 1641. His beginnings with Sabunde matter. It was not only the "Apologie"'s assumptions about humanity, society, life and divinity that stayed rooted in the Catalan's work. The "holistic" understanding of human being, essential to Sabunde, remained Montaigne's.

Twenty years after Montaigne's translation, Sabuco thought solitude the worst possible state for humans, made as they were for society, and found "love of neighbor" as needful as "friendship and good social intercourse [*conversación*]": "el amigo es otro yo" (chs. xxvii–xxix: 344–46). Aristotle's *Magna moralia* had used the phrase: a friend "is such and of such kind" as to "be another I" (1213a11–13). So had Zeno, said Diogenes Laertius: "Who is a friend? . . . another I [*allos egō*]" (7.23). Sabuco, too, thought human society braided in a whole environment. She explained, echoing Hippocratic argument, that a change in familiar "airs, waters and places" could bring death (ch. xxxiv: 347–48). Overall, she echoed Ficino: "whenever two people are brought together in mutual affection, one lives in the other and the other in him. In this way they mutually exchange beings [*Vicissim huiusmodi homines se commutant*]" (*Commentary* 50, 144). "Lors double vie à chacun ensuivra," wrote Labé, "Chacun en soy et son ami vivra [Then a double life for each will follow. / Each will live in herself and in her beloved]" (XVIII. ll.9–10: 131). Love, urged her "Débat de Folie et d'Amour," harmonized the universe. Such duality, "distribution," unity, "commutation" and community—deeply reminiscent of ancient experience—showed how to be human was foremost to be indivisibly enveloped in community and a whole life world.

These broad postulates matter. They rooted Elyot's, Huarte's and Walkington's analyses of human faculties, to repeat a gamut of writers named in Chapter 1. Of these I especially consider Huarte, because his work was so important to Montaigne. These postulates underpinned Huarte's analysis of *ingenio*, whose different aptitudes in different humans he sought to explain. Indeed, he insisted: "Everything Galen wrote in his book is the foundation of this my work" (*Examen* cap.ii [1594 ed. reformada, cap.iv]: 88). Most interestingly, they explain why the Christian Huarte was at pains carefully to distinguish the human soul from *ingenio* and all other human faculties (as we saw Walkington do with "soule" and "minde"). The last were embedded in the world, dependent on primary physical qualities; soul was unaffected by them, one and the same in all humans. "The soul," Vives had written, "is one alone in each human, though within its being [*esencia*] are its diverse public or private activities, as are arts and sciences for humans" (*Tratado* II.xii: 103). The point had been made more formally by Aquinas, more or less directly from Aristotle, distinguishing soul as essence and act from soul as body's form.

The soul is indeed very distant from the body if we consider the condition of each separately, so that if each had a separate being [*esse*], many media would have to intervene. But since the soul is the form of the body, it has no being separately from the being of the body, but by its being is united to the body immediately. This is the case with every form which, if considered as an act, is very distant from matter, which is a being [*ens*] only in potency. (ST 1a.76.7)

Protestant Melanchthon later said little else: every human had one soul breathed into them like "divine light" (*Liber* 16–18). Du Bartas echoed the idea more or less verbatim (Sixieme jour ll.711–15). The soul's nature provoked Hydra-headed debates. They contained no prototype of the commonly shared good sense of Descartes' *Discours de la méthode* or of the *Meditations*' willful rational soul—at least according to their usual interpretation. (See Étienne Balibar for ones that overlap with mine.) The debates adhered to a long tradition which Pierre Courcelle summarizes: "The folding-in on oneself is not, most often, an egotism." Rather was it quite the contrary. In its divers philosophical versions (Platonic, Stoic or other), it was discovery of who one was as part of a whole, as in Epictetus' thought that human reason gave a "personal freedom" by which alone one was "a fragment of God, a carrier of God immanent within one" ("'Nosce'" 293, 267). To be of and in the divine sphere was still central to the experience of who-ness. The true egotism, as Augustine had observed, was to move away from divinity, to break its wholeness. Thus did Montaigne's Sabunde distinguish a path leading "to true joy" from one leading to "the misery of him who is abandoned to disordered love of himself." As Joseph Coppin paraphrased Sabunde, while the "man who loves God above all has no other fear than that of offending God, the egoist sees the causes of trouble and anxiety multiply infinitely: his life is wholly ruined by them" (*Montaigne* 104). But selfe-discovery was not just in God. It was also "self-actualization through an equal . . . other" (Logan 140): that "other I" named by so many.

Sabunde ceaselessly urged the point that egotistical concentration on isolated selfe broke all spheres apart, the bodily, the elemental, the social, the familial, the divine:

Imagining fevers, illness and death gives him constant worries. He fears thirst, hunger, water, earth, air, fire, animals and humans, since all these things can lessen his health or destroy his life. Further, because he loves his own honor, his own reputation, praise and fame, he consequently fears everything that can reduce or make him lose them. Because he loves corporal pleasures and joys, he also fears torture, cold, heat, bitterness, poverty and a million other things than can take them from him: especially as he loves all those who depend on him and can bring him aid and consolation. His friends, his children, his parents, his wife and his brothers, and things that serve him—like house, property and animals—he certainly fears everything that can in any way damage any of these things. That is how bad fear is ceaselessly multiplied. (*Théologie* ch. clxxviii: 9.321)

The chapters where Sabunde dwells on this topic are very Augustinian in their treatment of the egoist's exclusion from the heavenly city (the two cities being a constant theme). So the person who has only, in a repeated phrase, "amour à soy [selfe love]" "is against God and without God" (ch. cxli: 9.243). So, as the heading of chapter cxliii has it, "selfe love [*l'amour de soy*] produces all the world's vices" (9.246), and these vices are of removal from God and other people.

To Aquinas, soul had been an "intellectual principle" put in humans by God, whose end and "final happiness" was a "vision of the Divine Essence" equivalent to "union with God" (ST 1a.2ae.4.8; 5.1). For Sabunde, two centuries later, the reason always to keep close relations between one's soul and all other creatures was likewise to advance "in knowledge of one's selfe [*cognoissance de soy-mesme*]" (ch. lxiii: 9.104) and of "one's maker," to glorify His "goodness, excellence, nobility, dignity, and power" (ch. ciii: 174), and finally to recognize the soul as "the seat of the only creator. There must God have his place . . . his sacred majesty must alone rule, preside, and there exercise his sacrosanct authority . . . , humans' highest good is to be joined with God" (ch. cviii: 187). Ficino similarly argued in 1476 that intellect's aim was to reach "the infinite perfection which is God, through love, thought, and worship." Once back whence it "received the fire," it "will be entirely filled with the whole light" (*Five* 207–8). Ten years later, Pico in turn asserted the highest happiness of humans to be "made one with God" (*Dignity* 225).

Nearer Huarte was Vives, who early in the sixteenth century explained that soul's essence was mostly hidden from humans:

but as [it was] formed by God to unite itself with Him in eternal felicity, one cannot define it better than by affirming it to be of the divine substance itself, so able to share in the divinity and unite with it that its knowledge gives birth to love; and uniting itself so that it forever finds the highest happiness. (*Tratado* II.xii: 102)

Melanchthon, too, saw soul as "divine light" infused in the human body, presence of God's will, in whose *aeterna consuetudo* lay its end and final cause. God's "*Logos and Holy Spirit*" were in us "just as the Sun scatters its light and heat in the air," and through grace, belief, and prayer would finally unite the soul with Him (*Liber* 17, 67, 96, 154, 178). The thought was ever-present. This was how Sabuco understood human wisdom, leading soul, "that God alone holds," to knowledge of itself in God (ch. lx: 359). Du Bartas said the same, adding "that (God's) holy image / was imprinted in your soul, when his living Spirit, to animate your body, filled you with a sacred breath" (Sixieme jour ll.912–14). Contemporary with Sabuco and Montaigne, Timothy Bright, penning a medical *Treatise of Melancholie* in 1586, wrote of the body "as a most pretious tabernacle and temple, wherin the image of God should afterward be enshrined." The soul, thus enshrined as divine "inspiration," would "glorifie his name" (34–39). The experience and concept were ubiquitous.

In 1531, Vives urged "perfection of humans' nature" in God as its "highest good" to be the goal of education, which acted, he said in his 1524 school manual *Introductio ad sapientiam*, via the soul, by which one is "like God himself" and through which one could become "god-like" (*Education* I.ii: 18; I.iv: 30; *Introduction* 86). Again, Melanchthon echoed the view. But for neither philosopher, doctor, theologians, nor Platonic, Erasmian or Lutheran humanist could this tell how and why animals—especially humans—differed in acts and capacities, or the nature of such acts and capacities. This was a problem Aquinas had faced (e.g., in ST 1a.85.7), and of which Vives was later hugely conscious. It was what Huarte wished to explain, but through an analysis of whose consequences he could provide practical resolution. The issue would have set a smaller dilemma were it not for attendant problems of free will and divine authority, complicated by assumptions that humans were somehow deeply one and alike.

Huarte's "soul," like just about everyone's, was less a human than a divine perfection. Ringing changes on Aquinas, one could say not so much that soul was individuated as that humans somehow shared a divine vitality that "made his abode" in the human body, as the 1594 English version of Huarte had it (*Examen/Examination* 26). Richard Carew's 1594 translation of Camillo Camilli's 1582 Italian was in fact extremely close to the Spanish: often more so than his own English could comfortably allow. As to the point just made, he always translated Huarte's "*estar en*," used of the soul's presence in the body, by "making his abode in." "Nothing," Huarte humorously wrote, "so offends the rational soul as to dwell in a body burdened with bones, fat, and flesh"—even though the soul "chose its place" (cap. vii: 154). Such turns of phrase were Huarte's usual way to describe the body/soul relation. They were everyone else's as well.

Martínez de Toledo, fifteenth-century forerunner on disturbances of temperament caused by mad love, wrote of "the rational creature's soul" as a "supracelestial" entity set in an "inferior body" by God (IV.ii: 274; III.i: 206). Unlike body, "supracelestial [soul] is not subject to planets or signs, fate or fortune, nor does it suffer passions or miseries when in this world; for it is created clear and pure by God, and is subject to no other [*a otro ninguno es sojecta*]" (IV.ii: 274). Sabunde, in Montaigne's translation, considered the true being of humans to be

out of itself [*hors de soy*], removed a great distance, absent from its proper home that it never saw, ignorant of its value, not knowing itself, being exchanged for a thing of nought, a brief joy, an idle pleasure, a sin. So if it wants to rediscover itself, its original worth, nature, and first beauty, it must come back to itself and return home. To do so, since it has forgotten its home, other things are needed to bring it back and lead it back home. A ladder is required to help it climb back to itself and see itself again. (ch. i: 9.2)

The entire goal of human life, Montaigne's spiritual mentor held, was to return to the soul's original *domicile* from its earthy material banishment. Climbing Mont Ventoux, Petrarch had been arrested by Augustine's thought that pleasure in the world, however innocent, made humans "desert themselves." A little later, he wrote in the *Secretum* of the body as "a dark, dirty, plague-ridden prison," filled with "filth and horror." "Too long," Augustine ended their conversation, "have you been exiled from your country and from your selfe. It is time to go back" (80, 172). Yearning for the divine, the soul was caught in countless material spheres.

Two centuries on, Ignatius of Loyola wrote of the "soul being incarcerated in this corruptible body and the whole composite in this valley, as if exiled among brute beasts: the whole composite, I say, of soul and body" (*Ejercicios* §47: 221–22). The *Spiritual Exercises* aimed to recover soul's divine purity and likeness to God and make the prison into "a temple of my created being" (§235: 258). Vives echoed the view, even though incarnate mind faced huge obstacles: "shut up as it is in dark corporeal prison, encircled by shadows, it is deprived of knowledge of many things" (*Tratado* 42: I.xi). In the Sixth Day of his *Sepmaine*, Du Bartas agreed that the soul was captive in the body as in a tomb, waiting only to fly back to its original home (ll.789–91). Sabuco thought selfe banished to "este mundo de destierro" (ch. lxi: 360). Less hopeful believers, like Walkington, saw the soul "pent vp and fettred in these his corps as in a dungeon," whose misuse (as by the "fatnes" mocked by Huarte) damaged "the heavenly infused soul" in "thraldome." "Bodies were the prisons and bride-wels of our soules, wherein they lay as manacled and fettered in Giues." The physiologist Walkington often did not distinguish soul from "this minde of ours [which] hath his abode in this darkesome dungeon, this vile mansion of our bodies," able to act "his part well" only after "it step vpon the heavenly stage" (9–11, 20–21).

That was by this time an unusual confusion, although du Bartas shared it. What could it mean for the "*minde* [to] step vpon the heavenly stage"? Aquinas had certainly been less than clear on the distinction, but Loyola (like Sabunde), echoed him in assuming that mind, through its three powers of memory, understanding, and will, *helped* the soul on its path toward heaven. So he wrote that mind, *entendimiento*, should on occasion retreat from worldly things, the better to concentrate "on serving its Creator and benefiting its own soul" (*Ejercicios* §20: 213). This required meditative effort, for mind and its powers were forever tied to body. But the last aim was to become conscious of soul as the presence in body of "the Creator of all creatures" (§316: 279). Vives shared this view that will, intelligence and memory enabled humans to attain the "eternal felicity" for which they were made (*Tratado* 55). The finest meditation had to be "of the heavens, contemplation of God, the greatest and most excellent able to be thought, all cloud removed, and highest truth made manifest, not with probability, but with the best of certainties, seeing and knowing the causes of all things in their very author, our understandings being at the same time freed from this dark and gloomy prison" (II.x: 96). His *Introductio ad sapientiam* was itself a meditative exercise taking in all life's activities, working through Christ to God in whom, said its final prayer, "be all honor and glory." Melanchthon adopted analogous arguments and an identical trajectory in his *De anima*. So, again, did du Bartas in his best-selling *Sepmaine*.

Most often, legal, theological or medical concerns met. Writing of the heat that was with moisture essential to life, Vives equated it with "divine love," and made it coeval with the soul's incarnation: "By means of [heat] the soul is wholly maintained in the body; it is its most powerful instrument; and equally by heat, or as it were by divine love, is diffused the life of our souls" (*Tratado* 14). Thus was soul put in the body at Creation: "In the suitable and now readied matter, God infused soul on the faculties of matter itself and those of forming nature, according to His established law" (II.xix: 123). Melanchthon echoed such thoughts. Elite debate was not identical with ideas, arguments and experience of a less-educated public, but they more than overlapped. However different the terms, Ginzberg's sixteenth-century Friuli miller imagined and experienced personhood, description relates, as one of total embedding in a world whose nature recapitulated his own. Of such overlap, Chapter 14 shows more.

This view of soul in body as a kind of particularized infusion drawn from one divine spirit could not solve the problem Huarte undertook, of understanding humans' varied mental abilities: a problem that moves us from the divine (and sometimes material) to the animate sphere. "For the rational soul dwelling in the body," he began his original chapter 5 with usual phrase, "it is impossible to do contrary and different works if it does [not] have a particular instrument for each one" (cap. iii: 92; cap. v: 117). Everyone shared the idea that all souls had one identical nature and the consequent problem it posed with regard to differences in mental ability. Vives was clearest: "Truly the soul is one in each and every animal; as in each body there is a 'form' by which it lives, though differing in its faculties and functions, as there are many needs and functions in a single person, which are discharged in different places and times by various instruments and aids" (*Tratado* I.xii: 53). Variety of mental and other abilities was his constant theme, differences shading to inconstancy. Loyola, too, considered such different abilities (*Ejercicios* §18: 211–12). It surely echoed earlier understandings of multiple circles of being, and Bynum is quite right to speak of Galen's idea of a person as "an entity of multiples" (*Metamorphosis* 144).

Galen had tautologically begun the *Natural Faculties* by noting that all living things were moved by a vital principle, *phusis*. In Latin, this became *natura*. Huarte used the term *naturaleza*. Among animate beings, animals differed from plants in that "perception and motion by purposive choice [*kata prohairesin*: giving reasons to passible acts] are peculiar to" them and could be called effects of the soul (*psuchē*). Growth and nutrition were common to all and to be thought of as effects of "nature" (*Natural Faculties* I.i: 2–3). Soul, then (or more exactly, three animate powers, vegetative, sensitive and cognitive, with three forms of action, natural, vital and animal), sufficed to explain how animals differed from plants and how the first possessed perception and purposive choice. All shared *natura*. This was thoroughly Aristotelian and, by now, Thomist.

Natura still bound humans ineluctably to englobing material processes that included Elyot's "Thynges naturall . . . Elementes, Complexions, Humours, Members, Powers, Operations and Spirits": common to all and interdependent (*Castel* sig. 1r). Hence the importance for Loyola of using the five senses, along with the three powers of mind, to help the soul on its path to the divine and union with God: "el traer," the drawing, he called it, "de los cinco sentidos" (*Ejercicios* §§65–70, 121–66, 132–34, 204, 247–48). They were, Walkington agreed, "instruments which are the hand-maids of the soule" (*Optick* 24–25). Both echoed Aquinas, who had noted that mind and intellect knew only via the senses, aptly called, therefore, "instruments of the soul" (ST 1a.75.1; see 1a.78.3, 84.2–3). This Aristotelian argument was pursued through the later era by Vives and others, the Valencian writing that the senses and temperament were "instruments of the mind" (*Tratado* II.vi: 81; cf. II.xii: 49–54). Melanchthon, recalling the endlessly repeated old saw, "nihil esse in intellectu, quod non prius fuerit in sensu," nothing is in the mind that was not first in the senses (*Liber* 108), spent nearly two-thirds of this *De anima* on an exposition of the physical body, its humors and its senses, all serving mind and its powers, themselves subject to the soul's finality. Soul was embedded in the material no less immediately than in the divine.

Drawn directly from Galen and Aristotle, Huarte's explanation of the principles of all this needs citing in full if we are to grasp properly the continuing *embeddedness* of human being:

Aristotle and the other natural philosophers go more into detail, and call Nature [*naturaleza*: i.e., what gives *ingenio* its particular aptitudes] whatever the substantial form that gives being to a thing and is the source of all its acts. In this sense, our rational soul may reasonably be called nature [*naturaleza*], since from it we obtain the formal being that we have as humans, and the same is the source of whatever we do and act.

But since all rational souls are of equal perfection, that of the sage as well as that of the fool, one cannot say that nature in this sense is what makes a human able; for if this were true all humans would have equal wit and wisdom. So the same Aristotle sought out another sense of nature as the reason and cause of a person being able or unable, saying that the temperament of the four primary qualities—warmth, cold, moisture, and dryness—must be called *nature*, for from this are born all a person's abilities, all virtues and vices, and the great variety of minds [wits, intellects] that we see. (*Examen* cap. ii: 86–87)

Many, of course, made analogous distinctions between what was God's and what *natura*'s, what divine or substantial and what material or "natural" (not least Augustine in distinguishing men's and women's identical souls from material and social sex and gender differences).

So variety of *ingenios* had nothing to do with the never-changing "rational soul [*ánima racional*]," even if one could say, Huarte went on, that through the "varying temperament and contrary disposition" seen in each age of a person, "the soul did certain actions in childhood, others in youth, and others in old age" (cap. ii). The "agent intellect" within the soul had been for Aquinas the very presence of "God Himself" as creator of and in the soul, as such invariable (ST 1a.79.4). By divine grace, Martínez de Toledo had also noted, the human soul knew good and evil, had power of will to act on "natural judgment [*natural seso*]" with God's help, and so was capable of reflexive contemplation (IV.i: 236–38).

This reflection needed light from within. Ficino explained: "where intellect is present, intellect which is, as it were, a kind of eye turned toward the intelligible light, there also the intelligible light which is God shines and is honored and loved and worshiped" (*Five* 207). A sense of internal divine light, perhaps with, but far more than, the idea that "the eye of the artist is elevated to celestial heights and made godlike" (Connors 74; cf. Grafton, *Alberti* 102, 105–6), is surely the meaning of the

disembodied winged eye that Leon Battista Alberti placed below his pro-
filed head on a 1435 medal (Figure 12). A bit later, Pico and Charles de
Bovelles both echoed the Augustinian and Platonic thought, while sixty
years after, Vives agreed that, "as corporeal eyes need an exterior light to
see, the mental eye also needs an interior light to know and understand."
By "supernatural light, whose knowledge is named wisdom," one saw
things "immutable and perpetual" (*Tratado* II.ix: 93). Melanchthon said
the same: "As light helps the eyes, so passible intellect [*intellectus patiens*] is said to be helped by its maker" (*Liber* 148); this light was supplied through the soul by God as its sun (154, 169). Du Bartas repeated
them (Sixieme jour ll.735–42). Such were soul's divine or "supracelestial" powers, its "immaterial" qualities, unchanged, still wrote Walkington, by its "sympathetic" relation with its host body, and which it retained when at last "segregated and made a free denizen in the heavenly
citty" (24, 32).

Moving, then, from the divine to the animate sphere, humans could be
individuated only by the operations of their much varying "mindes," *ingenios*, and difference explained by the action of *naturaleza*. Aquinas had
explained that the intellectual principle could only be *actual*, as "mind"
or "intellect," after being moved by, and itself then reacting through will,
reason and memory on, phantasms drawn from the senses: "in the present state of life in which the soul is united to a passible body, it is impossible for an intellect to understand anything except by turning to the
phantasms" (ST 1a.84.7). Except for agent intellect itself, all these differed by varying abilities, external circumstances and dispositions of the
body. People could have, wrote Martínez a century and a half later, more
or less *seso*, mind/brain, more or less *juizio*, judgment (IV.i: 237). Vives
likewise thought varieties of mind and its instruments changed as temperament moved one way or another "by the power of nature [*por suges-
tión de la naturaleza*]" (*Tratado* II.iv: 69).

"Natura facit habilem," Huarte ended the analysis quoted earlier with
a mildly triumphant flourish: a nature whose qualities were everywhere
the same. He added that Galen had proved how "the habits of soul [*las
costumbres del ánima*] follow the temperament of the body where it
dwells," and how "because of the warmth, coldness, moisture and dryness of the region where people live, of the food they eat, of the liquids
they drink, and of the air they breathe, some are fools and others wise,
some brave and others cowards, some cruel others merciful, some secre-
tive others open." The mixture of qualities explained differences of temperament among nations, provinces, even localities "not more apart than
a short league," as well as single persons (*Examen* cap. ii: 87–88). The
view was a Hippocratic and Galenic maxim echoed by all. Sabuco, we

Figure 12. Leon Battista Alberti, medallion (*ca.* 1435). Photo: National Gallery of Art, Washington, D.C., Kress Collection: 1957.14.125.

saw, thought such differences deadly if one ignored them, and her compatriot treated them hardly less seriously. One recalls Marco Polo's tale of
the king of Kerman's experiment to show how humans were "good, even-
tempered, meek, and peaceable" or villainous, evil and warlike according
to difference of soil (*Travels* 63). It could only be in these varieties of
"*mind*" that one might look to find anything remotely approaching a
modern western notion of individualized identity.

Vives devoted a chapter of his *Treatise on the Soul* to mental varieties
(II.viii). In *De tradendis disciplinis*, he explained the differences and proposed how pupils of diverse abilities and constitutions should be taught
(*On Education* I.iv, II.ii–iv: especially II.iii, recalling the *De anima*).
More exactly than Vives, Huarte explained the causes of these varieties
and how different *ciencias* should be taught to diversely abled young people. Montaigne agreed that in "sufficiency of soul and interior qualities
. . . there is more distance between any human and another than between
any human and any animal." "There are as many degrees of mind as
fathoms from here to heaven, and just as numberless" ("De l'inégalité qui
est entre nous": 1.42.250–51). So the good tutor, he held in 1580, must
teach "according to the capacity of the soul he has in charge," adding in
1595 that teaching must be adjusted to "minds of such divers measures
and shapes." Only so would children profit ("De l'institution des enfans": 1.26.149). Minds varied in quality and ability, and were also subject always to every level of their surroundings; circles echoed, wrote
Guillaume Budé in the disciplines taught, connected "as if there were a
circular chain of knowledge [*quasi orbiculata disciplinarum series*]"
(quoted in Logan 132). Minds were placed under one divine rule, led by
the same natural laws, caught in the same material world and owed "subjection and obedience [*la subjection et l'obeissance*]" to the polity in
which they dwelt, as Montaigne wrote in "Nos affections s'emportent au
delà de nous" (1.3.19)—a title stressing the experience of passible *subjection*: "Our affections [passions] carry themselves [are carried/borne]
beyond us."

Partly because of this diversity, and partly because of wider inconstancy of mind, he insisted in "De la coustume et de ne changer aisément
une loy receüe":

Public society has no place for our thoughts; but the rest, such as our actions, our
labor, our wealth and our very life, one must lend and abandon to its service and
to common opinions. . . . For it is the rule of rules, and general law of laws, that
each observe those of the place one is. (1.23.117)

For Montaigne as for Vives, Melanchthon and Huarte, as soul shared in
the divine and mind was subject to one nature, education was a social-

ization echoing and buttressing temperamental varieties characterizing persons, communities, localities, nations, climates, geographies and every imaginable material nature. Education, for all four, also included the care and proper function of the primary qualities in body, nourishment, training and physical environment.

The emphasis on the universal presence and efficient operation of the primary material and elemental qualities was essential, and Huarte (like others) endlessly reiterated and belabored the point, finding it useful on one occasion to repeat it thrice over:

The variety of humans, as well in composition of body as in mind and conditions of the soul, comes from living in regions of different temperament [*temperatura*], of drinking diverse liquids, and of not all using the same foods. And so, as Plato said: "some through varying winds and motions differ among themselves in customs and kind; others through the waters; or through the particular food produced from the earth; as a result of which humankind is enabled to do all things better or worse not only in their bodies, but in their minds"; as if one were to say: "some humans differ from others either because they breathe diverse airs, or drink different waters, or do not all take the same food; and this difference is not only found in the comportment and composition of the body but also in the mind of the soul [*el ingenio del ánima*]." (*Examen* cap.xii: 239 [1594, cap.xiv])

"Todas las tierras del mundo" varied in moisture, dryness, cold, heat, sweetness and bitterness, produced different kinds of drink and food, and so different sorts of human bodies, minds, and souls. In this addition to the 1594 edition, Huarte gave three principles. The first was that among the four possible combinations of elemental qualities, hot and moist mattered most in the loss and corruption of all things. The second was again that

not all the lands of the earth are of a same quality. Some, says Hippocrates, are humid, others dry, some hot and others cold, some sweet and others bitter, some insipid and watery and others salty, some raw and others easy to cook [*unas crudas y otras fáciles de cocer*], some rough and others smooth. Nature did not do this by chance and without thinking, but with much forethought and care, attentive to the great variety of plants and seeds that have to sustain themselves from the earth, because they do not all use the same food.

The third principle, then, was that plants, like animals, nourished themselves in accordance with their natural qualities (old cap.xv, parte iii; new cap.xxi: 412–13). Huarte now added these three principles to his earlier discussion of proper feeding and raising of children (343–63). All these things had to receive proper attention in feeding and raising children to make them "*ingeniosos y sabios*" (413). For similar reasons, if less precisely, Montaigne, throughout "De l'institution des enfans," stressed the need for early acquaintance with the widest variety of nations, climates, languages and peoples. Like Melanchthon (*Liber* 79–87), Vives had urged the same Galenic points, emphasizing the unshakeable bond between elements, humors, temperaments, between senses and elements ("the eyes are fiery, hearing and smell airy, taste watery, and touch earthy": *Tratado* I.xii: 48), between the earth, humans and the universe. The "Deuxieme jour" of du Bartas's *Sepmaine* was almost entirely given over to exploration of the elements' play in heaven, earth and humans.

Many assert Huarte to have been unusual, even exceptional. But on the fundamental ideas we have been exploring and the universality of their causes and principles, he was typical. That is what makes so useful the clarity with which he expressed and tried to solve the problem that sixteenth-century thinkers perceived unanimously: the contradiction between universality of soul and its source and particularity of mind. Equally unanimous was the tendency of solutions seeking to maintain universality, society and community, and to deny particularity. Most, from Erasmus and Vives to Montaigne and Robert Burton, agreed that in a global environment of natural sympathies and universal temperaments, the community made its citizen-subjects, as Cervantes showed (see Chapter 1 above) and Montaigne told. Society imitated in respect of body and mind the role of the divine regarding soul. Indeed, divine authority had arranged matters to just this end, said Montaigne clearly in "De la coustume et de ne changer aisément une loy receüe":

Christian religion has all the marks of extreme justice and utility; but none clearer than the strict injunction of obedience to the Magistrate and maintenance of public order [*manutention des polices*]. What a marvelous example we have been given of divine wisdom, which, to establish the salvation of humankind and direct this its glorious victory over death and sin, has chosen to do so only by means of our civil order [*qu'à la mercy de nostre ordre politique*]. (1.23.119–20)

Moving from the divine sphere through that of the human mind to that of society, Montaigne insisted on their utter imbrication. Indeed, each echoed and maintained the other, no less than they did, we have amply seen, the material spheres. Here, surely recalling Cicero's equation of god and magistrate—god *as* divine magistrate (*Tusculans* I.xxx.74), Montaigne insisted on the same equation between the divine and the sociopolitical.

Melanchthon had identically remarked that God had "so ordered human life" as to equip mind with "laws or notions teaching right things, preventing harmful," and society with "magistrates who defend those doing right, and expel and remove those doing harm," so showing us wisdom and justice, and how we were to be his image and imitators. The heavens, the earth, plants and animals might not know God, but they obeyed him. Angels and humans did so by will and intellect subjected to the soul (*Liber* 124–25). All that was why, wrote Montaigne as he continued the discussion just cited, private imaginings, disorderedly separated from the wholeness of things and ever subject to affections, had no place in the public sphere:

seeming to me most iniquitous to want to submit public and fixed bodies and obligations to the instability of a private fantasy [*d'une privée fantasie*] (private reason has only private jurisdiction) and to undertake with divine laws what no policy would allow with the civil, of which, even though human reason has many more dealings with them, the former are still supremely judges of their judges. (1.23.120)

To claim originary subjective power muddled private and public, *priuatus* (particular, non-public) and *publicus*. It clothed glassy essence in communal authority, the mind's *branloire perenne* in the stability of civic being. It gave free rein to Sabunde's (or Augustine's) "amour à soy." It ignored that after the divine, material society alone made personhood in the well-tempered universe.

This was why Johann Weyer, in his *De praestigiis daemonum* (1563; sixth edition 1583), seeking to explain why even those who thought that some women could be witches could still not hold them responsible agents, turned not to "personal" or "psychological" argument, but the legal commentary of the *Digest*, on the basis and nature of *society*'s laws. Weyer's first book explained what devils and demons were and described their abilities and limits. His next four argued that the "stupid, worn out, unstable old women" usually prosecuted as witches were either suffering from delusions brought on by disturbed humors or/and being used as "instruments of the demon's will" (*Witches* III.v–vi: 180–81). In either case, they were innocent, because, as we saw earlier, society's law defined both instances as not being willed: "when a person is in error [as when deluded] there is no 'will' and when a person is in ignorance [as when used] there is no 'consent'." Such a one was equivalent either to an *unwilling* or a mad person (VI.xxvii: 570). Weyer's chapter on the matter was really a compilation from the *Digest* on will and consent (II.1.15: 1.47), unwilling (L.17.174: 1.925) and the insane (XII.1.12: I.192).

The view echoed Aquinas no less than legal opinion. He had been clear that coercion and ignorance "made acts involuntary" (ST 1a.2ae.6.5, 8). Both made the mind unable to use will and understanding properly. For Aquinas, along with memory, these composed the soul's power of mind or intellect which, through these faculties, knew and acted on bodies (1a.79.1, 6; 1a.84.1). Because, so long as they were in passible body, will was tied to passions and understanding to sensuous phantasms, the one was always subject to violence (including that of evil spirits), the other to errant information. They always depended on affects from without. Petrarch had likewise shown Augustine recalling how the wise, *sapientes*, held that if no consent was given, if "will lacked from an act, then no sin was involved" (*Secretum* 38). So Loyola warned against suffering violence and error in "acts of understanding in reasoning [*del entendimiento discurriendo*] and those of will in working with the affections [*de la voluntad affectando*]" in spiritual exercises (*Ejercicios* §3: 208). These views testify to experiences of passible and social who-ness quite different from a modern western practice of self and subject.

Weyer's views seemed to contradict the current norm expressed by such as Jean Bodin and later by Martin Antonio Delrio. They and most others held a witch's relation with demons and her (or occasionally, his) making of events against the natural order (so-called *lusus naturae*) to demand testing and proving by torture and punishment by death. The grounds of this belief did not touch individual guilt or subjective responsibility either, but a breach of divine institutions for which *no* human individual could possibly, Weyer observed, be responsible:

As for the women themselves, they are mortal and all their capabilities depend upon the relationship and harmony between body and spirit. By virtue of the latter, they can do nothing except to know and to will; by virtue of the former, they can do only so much as the limits of earthly senses allow. And so they cannot attain to things above their power or potential, nor can they do anything at all which contradicts the senses. (*Witches* VI.xxvii: 561–62)

Loyola used the concept to theological ends, of a kind of mortal sin involving giving "consent to evil thought, meaning then to act just as one has consented [*consentimiento al mal pensamiento, para obrar luego así como ha consentido*]" (*Ejercicios* §36: 218). Although not committed, the evil had already, as it were, subjected the will, which has *consented* to it. A later Jesuit writer, Robert Persons, would similarly write in his 1607 *A Treatise Tending to Mitigation towards Catholick Subjects* that "there may be mental Heresy, when a man in his mind doth affirme, or give consent to any Heresy in his hart, for the which he may be damned everlastingly . . . though he should never utter the same in word or writing to any" (325; quoted by Hanson, *Discovering* 6). Perhaps in this hesitation between affirmation and consent, willing and accepting, is the mark of a beginning change.

My point is that even in its disagreements the conversation was shared, and that it was still *this* conversation up to and beyond the end of the sixteenth century. Weyer defined subject, who-ness, as a place in community: rational will and purposive choice—"assent"—were matters of law. Loyola saw it as marking a place in divinely instituted order. "Subject" could be defined *only* as of a secular social, material or divine world order. Indeed, we saw in Melanchthon and Montaigne, these were scarcely distinguishable.

I will return right away to this understanding of subject as submission to divine order, material world and civic collectivity. But first a question does arise. If one could turn to social law for a decision on personal responsibility, did it not presuppose, as now, that a person could, in certain states and conditions of will and knowledge, be judged responsible? Yes, no doubt. The issue, though, we saw especially in Chapter 3, concerns the nature of the responsibility and agency involved. It was not that there was no way to establish "private" intention—or even know it: which might be the modern difficulty in law. Rather was it that action *meant* according to divine, human, social and material pattern. Everyone agreed that an animal had neither reason nor will in any sense that could make it purposefully responsible for particular acts. Yet the burghers of Basel burned a rooster at the stake in 1474 for the "heinous and unnatural crime" (against natural order) of laying an egg. The rooster "did not fit" (Edgerton, *Heritage* 14). This was said of witches by Jakob Sprenger and Heinrich Krämer in their 1486 *Malleus maleficarum,* by Bodin in his 1580 *De la démonomanie des sorciers* (replying to Weyer) and by Delrio in his influential 1599–1600 *Disquisitiones magicarum.* Their acts were *lusus naturae,* just as personally eccentric conduct was socially "monstrous" for Melanchthon and Montaigne, we saw earlier. (Needing explanation are cases of animals punished for things that did fit, treated as responsible in the same way as humans, as one deduces, says David Berreby, "from court records of caterpillars in Italy excommunicated for eating crops and a bear in the realm of James I of England executed for murdering a child.")

Surely, one may ask, though, to note lack of intention or personal responsibility, as Weyer did in his Book 6, at least hints at a possible "nonlack," even if no actual presence? As in other cases, we may see here a foretoken of future imperative change. A kind of "hole" in analysis was implied; one to be filled by some notion of a responsible agent, such as Hélisenne de Crenne seems close to forging. Maybe Cervantes, too, like Montaigne, was struggling toward something such. But for that was first needed a concept of stable mind. Soul incarnate could clearly not do, trapped in its dungeon of the body and passible by nature, either quiescently separate from the body (as in Martínez's earlier claim) or ever restless in it until at last it left (as more in Petrarch's):

Our souls [said Cervantes' Auristela to Periandro], as you well know, and as they have taught me here, are always in constant motion, and cannot stop except in God, as in their center. In this life, desires are infinite, and ones link up with others and extend themselves, and end up forming a chain that sometimes reaches to heaven and sometimes immerses itself in hell. . . . only knowing and seeing God is the highest glory. (Cervantes, *Trabajos* IV.x: 292)

"I could," lamented Hamlet in these same years, "be bounded in a nutshell and count myself a king of infinite space, were it not that I have bad dreams" (II.ii.251–53). The bad dreams of this restless soul in its bodily nutshell, caught by the sway of the infinite desires or passions to which is prey human mind in its body, consequently bound in a chain leading to heaven or hell, found its final surcease only in God, its "center," of whom its knowledge and sight were its greatest glory. Sabunde's *Theologia* had been founded on the idea (as had Augustine's thought earlier, and an entire Christian meditative tradition), while Ficino had argued how the restless mind would only achieve final rest after ascending to God's "universal truth and goodness" (*Five* 198–99). All agreed. "Our mind," said Michel de l'Hospital in 1560, "wanders in darkness and cannot, blind, discern the true"—lines Montaigne wrote on his library wall (*Oeuvres* 1423). The entire aim of Sabuco's *Conocimiento de sí mismo* was to control the passionate motions of mind. "I resemble," du Bartas echoed yet again, "uncertain, the inconstant blade, / That moves with the wind on the sharp peak of a lofty steeple: / Belonging not at all to itself, but changing place and master as often as the wind." Like Montaigne, du Bartas insisted that the very fact that human bodies united "water, air, fire and earth" meant that they were "ceaselessly agitated by intestine war" (Deuxieme jour ll.909–10).

Cervantes' image differed neither from Martínez's or Vives', nor from that of Aquinas or Augustine. For the latter, the idea of "selfe" somehow separate from God meant that the will had been turned from forging a path back to the divine and become subject to affections and desires: a turning Weyer held to exonerate "witches," but against which Aquinas and Loyola alike warned. Just so did Augustine accuse himself, after the gratuitous teenage theft of pears, of having let *affectus* fix his will, made an evil *habitus*, modeled his "free will" to more diabolical falls from Grace. "My will the enemy held, and thence had made a chain for me, and bound me," he wrote in a phrase echoed by Cervantes and others (*Confessions* VIII.v.10: 152; for the theft: II.iv.9ss).

The *Confessions* were, as Peter Brown says, "the story of Augustine's 'heart', or of his 'feelings'—his *affectus*." They were, the word *confessio* meant, "an accusation of oneself" aimed simultaneously at "praise of God." As—and because—they explored mind, will and passions, so they "were a prolonged exploration of the nature of God, written in the form of a prayer, to 'stir up towards Him the intellects and feelings of men'" (*Augustine* 169, 175, 166—quoting Augustine's *Retractationes* II.32). They recounted intellectual reflection as path to the divine, and the well-led life as prevision of the meaning of Creation: hence the concluding chapters on Genesis. Platonic as they were, the *Confessions* reflected an eclectic mixture of traditions, Stoic no less than Platonic. In the 1530s, Sir Thomas More's Tower writings exactly repeated the pattern. It was this, too, that Montaigne had found in Sabunde, who had grounded his quest for surety on reflexive selfe:

nothing is more familiar, more inward and more particular to each than oneself to selfe [*que soy-mesme à soy*]. . . . Since no created thing is nearer to man than the very man to selfe [*l'homme mesme à soy*], everything proved to him by himself [*de luy par luy-mesme*], by his nature and by what he knows certainly, of all that will he remain both very sure and very clear. . . . That is why man and his nature must be the means to prove everything about man, to prove everything about salvation, happiness, unhappiness, evil and good: otherwise never will he be certain. So let him begin by knowing himself [*à se cognoistre soy-mesme*] and his nature, if he wants to know anything true of himself [*de soy*]. (*Théologie naturelle* chap. i: 9.2)

This was Montaigne's starting point and continuing ground of the *Essays*. The *soy* in question, Sabunde immediately explained, was that *soy* endlessly far removed "from itself" and its "proper home" which incarnation, exactly, kept from being itself. It could be itself only "in the most perfect and last unity" with God. Reflexive being was subject *of* the divine world, able to be grasped only as such (*Théologie* 9.15). Vives shared the view. "In what are you human?" Flexibulus asked Grinferantes in the dialogue on education in the Valencian's 1539 school text, *Linguae latinae exercitatio*: "In all of me," replied the latter. "If you are so only through the body, are you different at all from the beasts?" "No, truly." "Then I do not believe this 'all of you,' for you have reason and understanding." Only by training mind and its faculties, by *habitus* and resulting *prohairesis*, teaching the soul to right habit and rational assent, did one become truly human. Thus one acquired humility and charity, becoming beloved of all and finally "pleasing to eternal God," the true end of life (*Diálogos* 133, 138). Petrarch, we saw, held the same view, ending his *Secretum* by asserting: "I shall be as present to myself as I can, and shall collect scattered fragments of soul, and diligently linger with me" (214). Even if he failed, Augustine had now taught him that soul achieved fulfillment only in God. True selfe was one with God: which is why he offered the *Secretum* as a meditation on death.

Only *after* the departure of this soul, perhaps, could a place be found such that the "hole" mentioned earlier could actually be filled. Only once that idea of the soul had gone could a new idea of mind and self replace it: one that did not take their substance to be "supracelestial."

For whatever the soul portrayed by Cervantes' Auristela hoped for "vpon the heavenly stage" or "in the heavenly citty," as Walkington put it, so long as it was incarnate it was only the *branloire perenne* of restless private fantasy described and followed by Montaigne in his book: until this, too, ceased its pain in death. This mind's "amour de soy," Sabunde had said, was font of all discord (ch. cxliv: 9.248–49). For Montaigne, mind—even soul—lived prey to bodily desire: "Nos affections s'emportent au delà de nous" (1.3). The third-person reflexive of this title depicts passions more urgently active than "us." He began: "We are never within us [*chez nous*], we are always beyond [*au delà*]" (*Oeuvres* 18): homely echo of Augustine and Petrarch, Sabunde and Vives. Personhood was a fleeting *moy mesme*, he wrote in his essay on education, "which will be other tomorrow as chance takes it," without "*authorité.*" One was always subject to external impressions, images creating affections: "A strong imagination generates the event," Montaigne quoted scholarly maxim. "I am," he went on, "of those who feel the imagination with great force. Its impression pierces me." His solution was not to resist it, but to remove occasion for its making such impression (1.21.95). In the world, this fleeting passible selfe contrasted with another way of being, one settling into quite different orders of subjection, avowing, for instance, he told Diane de Foix, "the enduring title you have to my service [*l'ancienne possession que vous avez sur ma servitude*]," the last word nearly synonymous, he later noted, with "subjection"; although the context of this last comment was Montaigne's stressing the need for the tutor to teach youth subtle differences like "what is courage, temperance and justice; what the difference between ambition and avarice, servitude and subjection, license and liberty" (147, 158).

Stability was to be found in being subject to those who ranked above one: "we owe subjection and obedience [*la subjection et l'obeissance*] equally to all Kings, because that concerns their office [*elle regarde leur office*]" (1.3.19). The good tutor must shape youth's will to be "a most loyal servant of his prince, most affectionate and most courageous" (1.26.154)—these were the virtues of a public subject, whose place as well in the divine sphere needs no further emphasis. Absent from all this was any self-sufficient interiority, whose instability, rather, of *vie privée* or of *privée fantasie*, had to be kept from the public realm of subjection (1.42.257–58):

Our usual way is to follow the inclinations of our appetite, left, right, up, down, as the wind of circumstances takes us. We think only what we want, only at the instant we want it, and change like that animal which adopts the color of the place where you set it. What we planned just now, we soon change, and just as soon retrace our steps; it is just motion and inconstancy.

Passible "we," he concluded, was subject to other forces: "We don't go; we are carried away, like things afloat, now gently, now violently, as the water is angry or calm" (2.1.316).

Sir Thomas Wyatt had earlier managed to use this very passibility, placing himself in the *Penitential Psalms* (32, ll.333–39) to be "plunged up" from despair by God's spurring the soul toward Him (Greenblatt, *Renaissance* 123). Such was one relief for du Bartas' or Montaigne's indecision: "Whoever studies himself very closely," added the latter, "finds in himself, and even in his very judgment, this spinning and discord. I have nothing to say of myself . . . without confusion and muddle" (2.1.319). This counterpoised the separated soul (when they were not conflated). Indeed, du Bartas was careful to say so when vowing that he preferred to remain in doubt of the nature of the heavens, until "Relieved of the vicious mantle / Of this rebel body, which with weighty counterpoise ever presses down and represses my soul, / I myself go to see the beauties of the place: / Then when I wish to see nothing but God's face" (Deuxieme jour ll.948–52).

That was why Loyola urged that the best condition "to follow whatever one felt to be more for the glory and praise of God our Lord and salvation of my soul" was to be "as a scale in balance [*come en medio de un peso*]": stability in irresolution (*Ejercicios* §179: 247). Soul incarnate could be disturbed or serene at different times, and one best chose one's life in "tranquil time, when the soul is not agitated by divers spirits and uses its natural powers freely and calmly" (§177: 246). Ficino had said the same: the mind makes "more progress at rest than in motion" (*Five* 198). Vives also likened calm judgment of processes of reason, memory, and imagination, to "something in the mind like a sure rule and norm, or like the pointer of a balance [*el fiel en la balanza*]" (*Tratado* II.v: 76). This would stop the ordinary differences and contradictions of mind from wandering into mere inconstancy (II.ix: 94–99). It kept mind balanced between subjection to the divine within and nature without (*On Education* I.iv: 30). For Loyola, this happy state of soul was distinguished as time of "spiritual consolation," most approaching its divine origins, from one of *desolación espiritual*: "darkness of the soul, turmoil within it, inclination toward things low and earthly, restlessness from many disturbances and temptations, leading to loss of faith, without hope, without love, being wholly slothful, tepid, sad, and as if separated from its Creator and Lord" (*Ejercicios* §317: 279: Fourth Rule, concerning "the various motions that are provoked in the soul"). Loyola's description recalls the terms Seneca used to describe the evil visited on the unwise person. Loyola knew little or nothing of Seneca when he wrote the *Ejercicios*. This, too, suggests long continuities in sensibility.

Montaigne's answer as to the place of this soul, its training and keeping in regard to the social and divine, was detailed by Marie de Gournay. In her 1635 Preface to the *Essays*, she defended her "father" against criticism on grounds that "we have no experience of portraying oneself [*on n'a pas accoustumé de se despeindre soy mesme*]." To improve public and private life, he thought "he could teach you nothing better," she wrote, "than the use of yourself [*que l'usage de toy mesme*]; and he teaches you it now by argument, now by demonstration" (xxx–xxxi). Vives agreed that education was training in "the use of your selfe," the better to act in the public sphere: a "passifying" of person, training in right *habitus* and in consequent "natural" rational assent. Further, said Gournay, not only did Montaigne correct the minutest errors of public behavior, but his disclosure of "his errors and faults in this description of himself" was means to "witness to them [*les confesser*]." He thus obeyed God's law to "love thy neighbor as thyself." Use of the selfe answered social *and* divine demand, banishing lies and hypocrisy (xxxij–xxxiij). Christ had set the same duty, and neither "St. Augustine nor St. Jerome neglected the same witnessing." Training this passible selfe, she ended, met wider needs of public justice and divine authority (xxxiij).

Gournay was in an earlier mainstream, notably represented, too, by Loyola. His *Ejercicios* are important not only for the specific experiences they record and their wide influence, but—in the present context—because those experiences so grounded Gournay's younger contemporary, Descartes. Trained by the Jesuits, imbued with their teachings on subject and community, he always strove, I argue in Chapters 17 and 18, to reestablish an older experience of community that his own analyses jeopardized. He, too, still lived passible experience.

CHAPTER FOURTEEN

Persons, Passions, Pictures

Loyola with Alberti

That experience may still seem odd to those not sharing it. Montaigne, one of Descartes' admired influences, continued his essay "On the Force of the Imagination" by explaining how its impressions made him *become* someone else: "The view of another's pains hurts me physically, and my feeling is often appropriated by that other's feeling. A constant cougher irritates my lungs and throat"; when with a sick person: "I seize the illness I watch and lodge it in me" (1.21.95). The essay studies how these affections, always externally caused, are strong enough to move one into something like another being. One recalls claims, usual in medical literature, about how things seen and experienced by a woman during conception and pregnancy changed a child's form and temperament. Just so did Thomas Hobbes assert that he owed his meek and fearful temperament to his mother's fear of the Armada while he was *in utero*. This sense of being altered in one's essential nature to the point of actually becoming another by force of material or other impression, of being *physically* one with a collective life-world, not as an unusual or one-off experience but as a general mark of being human, furnishes apparently more risible examples.

In *Conquest of Abundance*, Paul Feyerabend remarks that: "some aspects of Florentine public life during the Quattrocento implied rather unusual views about personal identity" (32n23). As an example he cites a joke played by Filippo Brunelleschi on an acquaintance. Following Decio Gioseffi, Feyerabend later explains how Brunelleschi

constructed a new identity for a woodcutter, Manetto di Jacopo Ammannatini, called the Fat One. Playing carefully rehearsed parts and rearranging Manetto's surrounding (apartment, furniture, etc.), Brunelleschi, together with a group of conspirators, all known to Manetto, treated him as if he were somebody else until Manetto started defending the new, illusory identity. Here was proof that things are seen or felt to be "what they are" only in appropriate circumstances and that there exist other circumstances, not at all difficult to arrange, which may dissolve one's sense of self: even the self is not "given," but depends on (unnoticed) projections. (99n9)

Feyerabend does not say that Manetto felt himself a specific somebody, "a common acquaintance called Matteo Mannini," and "no longer the Fat woodcutter" (Gioseffi 11). It was not that a "self" was "dissolved." It was that the sense of personal identity *depended* on a collective totality. The possibility of the "joke" depended on experiences like those we have been seeing.

This surely helps explain the celebrated mid-sixteenth-century case of an "identity" thief in southwestern France, familiar in English from Janet Lewis' 1941 novel, *The Wife of Martin Guerre*, based on a nineteenth-century account, now retold from research on sixteenth-century materials by Natalie Davis in *The Return of Martin Guerre*. The case's principal elements are told in a 1561 *Arrest memorable* published by Jean de Coras, presiding judge in the final trial.

In 1548, after a quarrel with his father over land and property, the twenty-four-year-old Martin Guerre abruptly left his wife of ten years, Bertrande de Rols, their son and their village of Artigat, and disappeared. Eight years later, in 1556, he apparently came back to resume his place in village life and his wife's bed. Three years and two more children later, he contested the use made of his land during his absence by his uncle, Pierre Guerre, who countered with the claim that this returned Martin was an impostor. By the time the case went to trial villagers and Guerre's extensive family were thoroughly divided. After an inconclusive local trial and with new evidence supposedly come to light, Pierre rearrested Martin immediately, the case being appealed to the high court in Toulouse. The new evidence included rumors that Martin had lost a limb fighting for Spain in the Low Countries and now wore a wooden leg, a cobbler's assertion that Martin's shoe size was a bit different from what he remembered and claims by a nearby village innkeeper and another that they had long since recognized him as one Arnaud du Tilh, who had even given the second man "two handkerchiefs to take to his brother, Jean du Tilh" (Davis, *Return* 58).

Some thought Pierre had made up much of this. He did now add that his suspicions went back years. By July 1560, it looked as if Martin would be acquitted. Then, late that month, a peglegged man claiming to be Martin Guerre turned up in Toulouse. The judge confronted him and Pierre impromptu, and the uncle right away recognized his nephew (*Return* 84). So did his sisters and so, wrote Coras, did Bertrande de Rols, judging by her involuntary reactions. These events effectively ended the trial, and du Tilh confessed just before he was hanged on September 16, 1560. Even so, enough doubts remained for Montaigne to remark later that Coras should have suspended judgment (*Essais* 3.11.1008: "Des Boyteux"). How could an impostor have convinced not only the villagers, but Guerre's family and even his wife that he was their companion, nephew, brother and husband? How could this other live with Martin's wife and fill his place and functions in village life under the name of and as Martin Guerre? At least, doubts there were for Montaigne, but perhaps, for him (Chapter 16 suggests), tensions were by then at a less bearable pitch. That they were already getting there may have been why it was so necessary for the community to resolve the issue in the case of Martin Guerre and Arnaud du Tilh.

Guerre and du Tilh seem not to have met before. Somehow du Tilh learned enough from various people to know "his relatives and neighbors, . . . to furnish precise details of domestic life, including items of dress packed away in a household chest" (Brooks 104), and to be able exactly to take Guerre's place in village and family life. While the two men apparently shared some bodily scars and marks (none hard to fake), it is not clear how alike they were. At the trial it was said that Pierre and Bertrande had both had doubts when du Tilh presented himself as Martin in 1556, but had shrugged them off on grounds of his harsh experiences and of his being now bearded and more mature (*Return* 42). Pierre added that he had wondered why his nephew was no longer the strong active man he had been and had forgotten the Basque words of his youth (for the Guerres had come from Hendaye when Martin was a child). He had ignored these doubts. The new Martin knew enough other fairly intimate things to satisfy memory. For, as Peter Brooks observes, his "claim to identity was based entirely on memory: the villagers' visual memory of what he looked like and his memory of who was who in Artigat and what they had done together in the past"—this in an age when peasants had "no painted portraits and indeed no mirrors" (*Troubling* 104).

But what of de Rols? Surely she must have known? Still, her marriage with Martin had been arranged when they were both unusually young. For the first eight years of their marriage, he had been impotent. They finally succeeded in having a child only after various magical ploys and exorcisms. How much of this time had Bertrande spent at her parents' home? How many daily hours Martin in the fields? At trial, Bertrande agreed that the new Martin had been a better lover. Given their earlier difficulties and a long silent absence, lack of recognition was surely possible. Perhaps Janet Lewis' novelist's imagination would not be far wrong:

When she thought of Martin as perhaps dead, his remembered features suddenly dissolved, and the more she strove to recollect his appearance, the vaguer grew her memory. When she was not trying to remember him, his face would sometimes reappear, suddenly distinct in color and outline. Then she would start and tremble inwardly and try to hold the vision. But the harder she tried, the dimmer grew the face. The same thing had happened to her, she now remembered, after her mother's death. The belovèd image had faded. An impression of warmth, of security, the tones of the voice, the pressure of the hand had remained, but she could not see her mother's face. (*Wife* 47)

For someone to fit into such faded memories, reworking their exact parameters, might not be so difficult; especially with identity experienced as relational, dependent on collective interactions. Coras certainly believed de Rols innocent of collusion in du Tilh's imposture.

Davis remarks that Martin "was wanted in Artigat" (*Return* 43). He was needed in many circles, as "not only a husband, but also an heir, a nephew, and an important peasant proprietor in Artigat" (51). Brooks adds that his disappearance "created a kind of structural gap in the familial economics of the village, as well as in the life of Bertrande" (*Troubling* 104). In this, he partly follows Davis' opinion and Stephen Greenblatt's, who still rather trips on anachronistic premise in arguing that Martin's "inner life" was simply ignored. Legal and social need required indifference to "the psychic experience of his infancy . . . and beneath infancy to his biological individuality" as things "irrelevant to the point of being unthinkable" ("Psychoanalysis" 135). Unthinkable, indeed, but Greenblatt has them more just sidestepped: "The crucial historical point is that for Montaigne, as for the judge in the trial, Jean de Coras, what is at stake in this case is not psychic experience but rather a communal judgment that must, in extraordinary cases, be clarified and secured by legal authority" (136). Montaigne, we saw, had in fact begun to fear a gap between communal judgment and personal identity. "At issue," Greenblatt says, "is not Martin Guerre as subject but Martin Guerre as object, the placeholder in a complex system of possessions, kinship bonds, contractual relationships, customary rights, and ethical obligations" (136–37). This subject/object distinction is not possible. At stake was "psychic experience," but no Freudian one. To use such terms is a bit like Cottingham's arguing that the Greeks needed a concept of psychoanalytic subconscious. Brooks rightly remarks on the importance of the fact that all the memories brought up at the trial were those "of adult life" (*Troubling* 105). The point is that one became *humanior* as one better integrated all the circles of one's being—those, for example, that Greenblatt lists as marks of "external" conditions, enabling Brooks to write of them as "roles assumed" (106). Such integration was an achievement of adulthood, accomplishment of a mature stage of moral life.

Du Tilh might be "assuming" such roles, just because they were not him. For Martin Guerre, though, they *were* him. The question facing Pierre, Bertrande, Martin's sisters, villagers and judge was who was assuming and who was being. Du Tilh *became* the person he stood for because he fit the "appropriate *circum*stances," became his adopted *persona* because he fit the village society (cf. Gurevich, *Origins* 245–48). The community had to know whether that *persona* was mask or person. It matters that Pierre's mistrust peaked when the new Martin's challenge threatened the very circumstances organizing family and village. Who he was as a person was not just an issue of mind or body (I think of A. J. Ayer's or Bernard Williams' arguments against other analytical philosophers over the vital import of body to personal identity: *Problems* 1–25). It was above all fit with and maintenance of the multiple surrounding actualities that involved other peoples' sense of who *they* were. These circumstances were essential.

Had Martin returned earlier, while du Tilh was still in entirely good repute, these circles still solid, he would have had more difficulty in being recognized: he would then no longer fit the community and its life-world. Indeed, in such an instance one may well wonder what it means to be "recognized." Like Odysseus in Chapter 2 (and in Cavarero's reading: *In Spite* 13–31), Guerre would have come as a stranger to the community. Because his exact role had been taken over, he *would not be able to be recognized*. Had Penelope's suitor Antinous become her husband and so king of Ithaca, perhaps Odysseus could not have been recognized either: although Antinous was not wanting to take Odysseus' place in the same way as du Tilh did Guerre's. Lewis intimated a connection early in her novel, describing Martin's father (whom Martin was being raised to replace): "He sat at ease in the stiff-backed, rush-bottomed chair, his dark jerkin laced to the throat, his right hand resting on the edge of the table, vigilantly surveying his household, like some Homeric king, some ruler of an island commonwealth who could both plough and fight, and the hand which rested on the table was scarred as from some defensive struggle in years long gone by" (*Wife* 26). The circles of being that Greenblatt names as a system of possessions, kinship bonds, contractual relationships, customary rights, ethical obligations, along with all those others we have seen before *were* Martin Guerre's "psychic experience."

These are different experiences of person from anything now felt in the modern west, but surely not incomprehensible. Du Tilh's identity theft was deeply serious—nowadays such theft depends on the *absence* of an actual physical body; his depended on its *presence*. "Just" a joke may have been played on Manetto. But like the theft, the joke could only work if being a person was understood and experienced in ways such as we have been exploring. The same, I take it, is the case of the "Induction" of

Shakespeare's *The Taming of the Shrew* (*ca.* 1593), making the drunken
sleeping Christopher Sly butt of the same joke. There, too, what mattered
was to create a new set of surroundings, to establish a new "fit":

> What think you, if he were conveyed to bed,
> Wrapped in sweet clothes, rings put upon his fingers,
> A most delicious banquet by his bed,
> And brave attendants near him when he wakes,
> Would not the beggar then forget himself? (Ind. i.35–39)

Elaborate instructions then make conspirators of all, and Sly recognizes
himself as the nobleman they pretend him to be. Of course, this is given
to us as the staged creation of a *persona* in what we know is a play.
The joke was not on a person (as in Manetto's case) but on an experience that was perhaps no longer quite believable—or quite understandable. Shakespeare repeated the game in having Oberon turn Bottom
into an ass in *A Midsummer Night's Dream* (*ca.* 1595) even more the-
atrically—although there, as in *Taming*, the victim was also given
wife/lover, servants, new surroundings with new denizens. In *Toward
Dramatic Illusion*, I many years ago explored, rather unawares, the
early seventeenth-century French theater as one whose idea and meaning depended on *all* characters being composed in terms of this sort of
"circumstantial" being.

Such cases argue that the experience of "embedded being" was indeed
general. It explains something about sixteenth-century French writers
that Lucien Febvre noticed critically: "One thing is striking in all cases:
with a few very rare exceptions, they don't know how to make a lifelike
sketch [*un croquis*], capture a likeness [*une ressemblance*], fix a character
[*camper un personnage*] in flesh and blood before the reader" (*Problème*
471). He spoke of an "inability" to *visualize* individual appearance. Having insisted that modern interpreters should try to understand sixteenth-
century people in terms of their own theories of soul and "psychology"
(197–206), it is slightly odd that Febvre chose to criticize this mode of
presentation rather than analyze it. For we need to ask: "lifelike" for
whom? what view of "human personality" was at issue? what reader? or
spectator? what does "visualize" mean here? or, indeed, "in flesh and
blood" (*en chair et en os*)? We may also bear in mind, and see in a moment, the importance here of Michael Baxandall's comment that painters
quite deliberately avoided painting particulars precisely because people
were used to particular kinds of visualization and sought to provide
forms furthering those kinds and the experience of which they were a
part.

Loyola's *Spiritual Exercises* connects these issues, and so is especially useful. When he wrote them, Loyola belonged to no learned elite. He had undergone conversion, but remained the ignorant soldier he had been, reader of romances and popular religious tales. Ignacio Iparraguirre writes of his "scholarly ignorance and exceedingly scanty [*escasísima*] intellectual formation at the time he composed this book" (*Ejercicios*, Introducción 182). Echoing his Society's tradition, Iparraguirre takes this as proof of God's hand in writing the *Exercises*. Loyola's early Jesuit biographer, Pedro de Ribadeneira, wrote that the founder began writing the *Exercises* while in retreat at Manresa and then at the monastery of Montserrat in 1522. He was then, his biography's early English translation had it, "so vnlearned, that he could only write and read":

in this very tyme he wrote the book which we call the *Spiritual Exercises*, which is so replenished with documents, and excellent instructions in spirituall matters, that it clearly appeareth, how the unction of the Holy Ghost taught him & supplied the want, which at that time he had of study & learning. (*Life* 25–26)

Ribadeneira repeated the remark about Loyola's eighty-page notebook on the Holy Trinity compiled while he was at Manresa in 1522: "knowing at that tyme no more than only to write, and read" (187). Loyola no more belonged to an intellectual elite than did Guerre or du Tilh, whatever his more elevated social rank.

Written mostly in 1522–23, before Loyola's training at Alcalá and Paris or even his pilgrimage to Jerusalem, the *Exercises* were refined until 1535. They echoed a devotional tradition in which he had read. They agreed with highest philosophical and theological opinion. They also echoed common belief. Their assumptions about personal being imbued not just a rare work like Montaigne's *Essays*, but popular manuals like those of Elyot, Huarte, Sir John Harington and Walkington. Not confined to higher faculties of theology, medicine and law, these assumptions dwelt in the nooks and crannies of everyday life. They were widely and commonly shared. The advice books show as much, filled with and delineating a now familiar experience of embedded personhood. The *Exercises* was well disseminated and known by the 1550s.

It spoke in the theological sphere to issues of reason and will, knowledge and consent. It stressed analogy of divine and secular subjection. It repeated Augustine's confessional trajectory, setting it in a wide *popular* tradition of *imitatio Christi*. It presupposed and depended on contrast of rest (ultimately in God) and confusion (in the world), of consolation and desolation. It was thus immersed in Stoic thinking (cf. §155: 241; §157: 242) and the matter of things indifferent:

Humanity [*el hombre*] is created to exalt, venerate, and serve God our Lord, and by this means to save its soul [*su ánima*]. . . . This is why it is necessary to hold us indifferent to all created things . . . only desiring and choosing what most leads us to the end for which we are created [*para el fin que somos criados*]. (§23: 214–15)

As one would expect, meant for use by anyone and everyone, the *Exercises* embody a usual idea and experience of soul and psychology. The experience they delineate was based more in an understanding of popular experience than in sophisticated reasoning from intellectual authority.

Still, Loyola was not as ignorant as his followers asserted, eager for evidence that the *Exercises* resulted from a visitation of the Holy Ghost. Ribadeneira wrote that while Loyola was recovering from the leg wounds that ended his military career, he read a *Life of Christ* (probably Ludolphus of Saxony's, but maybe Jean Gerson's or one attributed to St. Bonaventure, actually "by an Italian Franciscan of the late thirteenth or early fourteenth century": O'Malley 46), and the *Lives of the Saints* of Jacobus de Voragine (*Life* 7), a work of representative lives starting with Christ and then working from Adam and Moses down to and through saints, whose lives typified Christian existence. This typification was the usual way to understand human being. It grounded the *Spiritual Exercises* as it did other meditational works known to Loyola. The recently deceased abbot of Montserrat, García Jiménez de Cisneros, had himself written an important *Ejercitatorio de la vida espiritual* that Loyola read. Explaining that the "desired end [of human life was] union of [the human] soul with God" and noting Gerson's *Mount of Contemplation* as an exemplary *ascent* toward heaven, Jiménez explained that this ascent began in a fear whose ground was "the changefulness and instability of this world, wherein a man may never remain in one state, nor know if it be worthy of love or of hatred"(*Book* 18, 58). This was first in a long series of sinful things to fear in this life which the exercitant was to call to mind by reason and memory on the "Monday" of meditation on sin (58–76). The "next" day's meditation was to be on death, again depending on reason and memory (77–81). These "days" were symbolic days of the holy week: the first seven-day series of "purgative" exercises were actually to last a month (100). Loyola's *Exercises*, too, were intended to be monthlong.

On Wednesday, wrote Jiménez, one meditated on the hell that naturally followed contemplation of sin and death: "represent to thyself a terrible abyss" (82). This was done via the five senses in such a way as to provoke a "torment of each of the senses" (83). One had to try and experience hell's torments in one's very body. Thursday saw a meditation on the last judgment, Friday called up the story of the passion, which again one had to feel in the senses, leading this time to salvational prayer

(86–92). Through Saturday to Sunday, the week ended in contemplation of the glory of heaven, imagination now the principal power (97–99). This "purgative" series of exercises was to cleanse exercitants of attachment to sinful worldly life. They then moved on to an "Illuminative Way" and finally a "Unitive and Perfective Way" (104–73). The first corresponded to faith, the second to hope, the third to charity. Jiménez owed this tripartite division, he said, to Richard of St. Victor, one of several explicit sources: Gerson, Aquinas, Bonaventure, St. Bernard, Augustine, Jerome and more. But Richard was his most extensive and most constant reference.

In the *Benjamin Major (The Mystical Ark)*, Richard had written that you began meditation with contemplation of the ark "as it represents Christ" (*Twelve* 151). The life of Christ was the archetype of right life on earth; through its contemplation you understood the nature and meaning of earthly life. Such contemplation was hard and dangerous. It had to use human faculties which necessarily threatened to sink you back into the world. Reason, Richard wrote in the *Benjamin Minor (The Twelve Patriarchs)*, "never rises up to cognition of the invisible unless her handmaid, imagination, represents to her the form of visible things . . . without imagination she would not know corporeal things, and without knowledge of these things she would not ascend to contemplation of celestial things" (57). Imagination, however, a faculty of soul-in-body, depends on sensation. "But sensation nonetheless has her hands full. . . . It is sensation who is accustomed to season the foods of carnal delights, to serve them to affection. . . . Who is it other than sensation that influences the affection of the soul with longing for carnal pleasures and inebriates with their delight?" Nonetheless, since "the guidance of sensation" was needed to create passions, and so to awaken imagination, which in turn was to serve reason and so lead to higher contemplation, you had to use sensations, being always wary of "their vice" (58). The sequence gave Richard the six (or three) kinds of contemplation, levels of ascent toward heaven on which Jiménez later drew. In the *Benjamin Minor* Richard offered these as: (1) "in imagination and according to imagination only," (2) "in imagination and according to reason," (3) "in reason and according to imagination," (4) "in reason and according to reason," (5) "above but not beyond reason," and (6) "above reason and seems to be beyond reason." These give the three: "two in imagination, two in reason and two in understanding" (161). Imagination was directed "to sensible things only," reason "to intelligible things only," understanding "toward intellectible things only" (164).

Jiménez took these over in his purgative, illuminative and perfective ways, and generally in the path of all meditation from the worldly to the heavenly. Contemplation of worldly sin brought you to Christ as its redeemer. So the first contemplation of Christ dwelt on his physical presence in the world. Through the senses the exercitant was moved to know redemption's pain and glory: "affection and heartfelt desire . . . dwell ever on both [Christ's] life and death" (*Book* 223). This corresponded, said Jiménez, to Richard's *mentis dilatatio*: the first stage, in imagination. You next contemplated Christ as God and man, an exercise occurring in conception, picking up Richard's *mentis sublevatio*: the raising of mind to and by reason. Finally you reached knowledge and love of God, Richard's "*mentis alienatio*, or ecstacy of the spirit" (220–26). Contemplation of the life of Christ via the imagination involved several steps: imagining (as a picture) the last supper, for instance (248–50), experiencing an *imitatio* of the passion and telling it to yourself (255–63). Of this, Jiménez wrote: you "must consider it according to three ways or manners: namely, the fact thereof, the manner and the cause." You began by telling yourself the story (fact), continued by contemplating Christ's demeanor (manner) and ended by being moved "to devotion and to tears" when finally understanding that his suffering was to redeem your sins (264–66).

Bonaventure had provided an idea of the path to God at once similar and dissimilar. Martz has noted the huge importance of the *Meditations on the Life of Christ* attributed to him, seeing in it a "prototype of the imaginative meditation cultivated by the Jesuits, and at the same time an immense difference." It was the first in its insistence on picturing events, indeed on moving into them. It was the second in being purely affective. Unlike Loyola (or Jiménez and Richard), this work's author wanted not to make use of the intellect, but to distance it, keeping the "wise men and the commentators" away (*Poetry* 75). This may be the case for the *Meditations*; it certainly was not for Bonaventure's *Journey of the Mind to God*. Like Richard, Bonaventure envisaged six steps and "graduated powers of the soul, whereby we ascend from the lowest things to the highest things, from things outside us to those that are within, and from the temporal to the eternal. These six powers are the senses, imagination, reason, understanding, intelligence, and the summit of the mind or the spark of synderesis." These had to be "cleansed by justice, trained by knowledge, and perfected by wisdom" (*Journey* 6–7). Unlike the others, and especially Loyola, Bonaventure did not in any detail *use* these. They were aspects of being to which the soul directed its powers, with God's help, to cleanse, train and perfect. They made us aware of God's majesty in the world and did not themselves make the kind of affective appeal that the others called for. More importantly, perhaps, Bonaventure did not assert a contemplative path that *combined* senses and powers of reason. At least in *The Journey* the soul's functions of memory (retention and foresight), intellect (faculty of conception, understanding and intuition) and elective powers (faculty of "counsel, judgment, and desire") (18–21) were separate from the senses, affections and imagination—which were, indeed, mostly to be avoided as trammeled in the world.

The point is not whether Loyola was or was not "original." He would have found the idea incomprehensible—and anything approaching it a sign of something wrong. Truth lay in shared, familiar experience. Like all these, the *Exercises* assumed that all human souls, divinely created as they were, were the same. They differed by incarnation. Loyola aimed to give a "a way to prepare and dispose the soul to rid itself [*para quitar de sí*] of all disordered affections, and, them gone, to seek and find the divine will in the disposition of one's life [*de su vida*] for salvation of the soul" (§1: 207; I keep as close as I can to the Spanish). The mind [*entendimiento*] was to be detached from the variety of earthly things, and focus on "serving its Creator and helping its own soul [*su propia ánima*]." The soul would then be "more able to draw near and unite with its Creator and Lord" (§20: 213). Not only Jiménez and his predecessors held a like view, but Erasmian Vives, Protestant Melanchthon and heterodox Sabunde and Montaigne. Indeed, the first's *Introductio ad sapientiam*, the second's *De anima* and the others' *Théologie naturelle* offered identical projects: most of the second half of the last traced Christ as the path of *soy* to salvation and union with God (chs. cclii–cccxxi: 10.172–424). For Loyola, too, *imitatio Christi* was the ideal universal path. After a first week of broad meditation on sinfulness, the exercitant dwelt on Christ's life, passion, and resurrection (§4: 208). But from the start, the aim was to use the three powers of mind, memory, understanding and will, to make oneself Jesus-like.

Starting by *remembering* the first sin, that of the angels, one next *reasoned* on its act and meaning, finally using the *will* to identify with it via the affections ("moviendo más los afectos con la voluntad"). One did the same for the sin of Adam and Eve, for other single people's sins and for one's own, at last fully knowing the justice of eternal damnation. One took sin on oneself, face to face with Jesus on the cross (§§50–53: 222–23). The technique did not change. One meditated through the descent to hell, again echoing Christ's trajectory (indeed talking with him: §§65, 71: 226). One meditated oneself into the life of Christ, from Anunciation on (§91: 230–31). Imitation was explicit: "to imitate you in suffering [*pasar*] all injuries and all abuse and all poverty, actual and spiritual" (§98: 232). One sought "knowledge of the true life shown by the highest and true leader, and grace to imitate him" (§139: 239). The ideal was "to imitate and appear more really as Christ our Lord," take poverty not riches, insults not honors, reckoned "worthless and a fool for Christ

. . . rather than wise and prudent in this world" (§167: 244). So, too, Protestant du Bartas held "the Cross . . . the ladder leading humans to immortal glory" (Septieme jour ll.275–76) by way of their "divine spirit, sacred, pure, wondrous, / not finite, not mortal, not mixed, not palpable" (Sixieme jour ll.759–60). The sequence of *nons* emphasized the soul's difference from body and the transformation enabled by identification with Christ. The pattern mirrors Montaigne's and others' experience of actually *becoming* another, fitting oneself to other circumstance.

Imitatio in this sense was the *content* of the *Exercises*. The ordered "syntax" of meditation that Loyola elaborated echoed the process: from human senses, mind and passions, to union with the divine. First, one set out the *historia* on which to meditate. One next made a *composición* "with imagination's vision" (*con la vista imaginativa*) of the geographical place where it occurred (§§111–12: 234–35). Imagination's reception of the events thus *seen* provoked corresponding passions: one really *participated* affectively in the events (as Montaigne was to describe himself as doing). Affectively, one became Christ by opening oneself to *receive* through the senses those passions that would stir the imagination and make us *feel* Christ's experience as really ours. We may have seen sufficiently to what physiological and psychological experience this corresponded, but it is worth quoting Boyle's particularly clear exposition of it apropos of Loyola himself, not of the *Exercises* but of the *Acta*, his third-person so-called "autobiography":

Loyola habitually described affective states not as welling from within the self, as in modern psychology, but as invading it from without. During this convalescence desires to imitate the saints are "offered" to him. The more common verb is that various states "come" (*venir*) to him. Accusatory stirrings about failure of duty "come" to him; the temptation to sloth "comes" to him, its relief "comes" to him; even the assent of his own will to resume eating meat "comes" to him; a temptation concerning righteousness "comes" to him; a great impulse to protest an attempted rape "comes" to him. (*Loyola's* 40)

Far from strange, these descriptions were wholly typical. In the *Exercises*, one turned the will onto these affections, using both to internalize divine love, because actually experiencing the meaning of Christ's redemptive incarnation, *becoming* him through them. This made one "reflect in my selfe [*reflectir en mí mismo*]" on the divers instances and draw fruit from the reflection. One ended with a prayer to affirm nearness to the divine (§114–17: 235). The sequence was invariable: *historia* and composition, analysis, colloquy, prayer. The aim of content and syntax was to bring the soul to see and unite with the divinity, its place of origin. For that reason directors had not to impose themselves, but let the ex-

ercitant relate immediately to the divine (§15: 210) and typical images of
the divine that the exercitant narrated in imagination. They were *typical*
because they had to be common and readily available to all. They were,
Beaujour remarks, an artificial memory, "made up of a set of coded
topoi, foreign to the biography and place of origin of each individual."
Typicality was their purpose (*Miroirs* 55–56).

Roland Barthes' "criticism" of Loyola's poverty and banality of imagination in describing, for example, hell and the stages of Christ's life is
thus odd (*Sade* 55–56). Loyola's aim was not to propose "his" version of
these matters, but to give a template that the exercitant would fill out, adjusting universal faith to individual hope. He did this by providing a *felt*
event into which the exercitant could possibly *fit*. Not through Loyola
but through the soul, the exercitant was to work back to the divine by *becoming* the imagined actors. Barthes' remark is the odder in that he refers
to his much-admired Georges Bataille who said just this, writing of how
Loyola sought to let the exercitant *fit* into a dramatic staging: "Represent
to yourself, he says, the place, the characters of the drama, and be there
as one among them; get rid—stretch your will to the purpose—of hebe-
tude, the absence to which words tend" (*Expérience* 26). Loyola's technique for creating this fit was precise. It matched, too, two familiar sets
of practices that confirm how widespread were the experiences the *Exercises* relied on. One of these practices was distinctly popular, involving
means and goals of exhortatory sermons. The other might be reckoned to
belong to elite culture, save that since Loyola was entirely unlikely to
have had access to it by such channels, we must suppose its themes to
have been diffused in the cultural air he and everyone breathed. It involves arguments made especially by Alberti apropos of perspective art.

The importance of the second is seen through Loyola's *historia* and
composición, where theological, medical and legal assumptions carried
into a circle one might call "psycho-aesthetic": persons as subjects of
physiological bodies, passions and passibly reacting minds moved by images from without. Loyola's meditational technique was an *imitatio*, a
technique of identifying one's being with a *type* of divine act. The means,
we saw, were exact and repetitive.

The director began by "narrating faithfully the history of the particular contemplation or meditation [*narrar fielmente la historia de la tal con-
templación o meditación*]," by "summary or brief" emphasis on main
"points." The reason to stress these principal and simple lines was that

the contemplating person, taking the true foundation of the *historia*, deliberating
and reasoning for oneself [*por sí mismo*], and finding something that makes the
historia a little clearer or more felt [*que haga un poco más declarar o sentir la historia*], whether by reasoning itself or by how much the mind is illumined by di-

vine grace, [gains] more spiritual taste and fruit than if he giving the exercises had largely stated and amplified the *historia*'s meaning. Not vast knowledge fills and satisfies the soul, but the sense and taste of things. (§2: 207–8)

The *historia*'s plain lines were evoked by intellect using a technique Loyola called "traer la historia de la cosa" (drawing the history of the thing), a constantly recurring phrase (§§102, 111, 191, 201, 219, etc.). Called up as well by memory, the *historia*'s details were fixed by imagination using the five senses (severally or together) to make a *"composición"*—another point so endlessly reiterated as to make examples idle. Implicitly or explicitly, this sensuous composition always followed the drawing of the *historia* that was object of the contemplation. Will was then brought to bear on the passions roused by this *composición*, so that the sins and pains drawn were truly suffered and resolved. The aim was to move the *ánima* internally, establishing intimate knowledge of the divine. The process exactly followed the hierarchy set out by Aquinas, each instance *subject* to, moved by, the preceding. By using the senses, imagination, reason and will, the mind came to know divine truth through the soul.

This had a close analogue in perspective theory, where thirteenth- and fourteenth-century ideas had culminated in Alberti's *De pictura* (*ca.* 1435). Giving mathematical and geometrical rules of perspective, Alberti argued that not size but *"historia"* most "satisfied the intellect." What he meant by *historia* has spawned scholarly debate, though consensus is now wide on what the word meant when he took it up. In classical antiquity, *historia* was a subgenre of rhetoric, referring first to inquiry into "the facts of a disputed matter," then to the written account of the inquiry's results (Greenstein 275). This meaning changed as *historia* joined figural biblical interpretation, exploring "one event as harbinger of another." This event (or person) was material and visualization basic to its sense. Theologians eventually saw illustrations and *historia* as equally related "to higher truth" (Greenstein 276–79). By the thirteenth century, *historia* and its vernacular cognates had gained a "secondary denotation" of a "pictorial representation of a narrative scene" (281). Dante applied the term to sculpture (Toynbee 195–97, Greenstein 281–82). Boccaccio had his temple of Mars in *Palamon and Arcite* "tutto istoriato" (Wharton 2.305). Paget Toynbee adds other medieval Latin and vernacular instances of a usage that lasted at least into the seventeenth century (197–98).

Historia, then, named visualized and visualizable relations of persons or events. Seeing and being *affected* by seeing incorporated narration. In Alberti, *historia* particularly named a pleasing ordering of planes rendering bodies and their relations to express story and passions. This *historia* was the end of *compositio*. More precisely, as Baxandall describes it:

By *compositio* he means a four-level hierarchy of forms within the framework of which one assesses the role of each element in the total effect of a picture; planes go to make up members, members go to make up bodies, bodies go to make up the coherent scene of the narrative paintings:

> *Compositio* [Alberti wrote] is that method of painting which composes the parts into the work of art. . . . The parts of the *historia* are bodies, the parts of the body are members, the parts of the member are plane surfaces.

Baxandall shows that this echoed what "every schoolboy in a humanist school had been taught to apply to language, in which, by *compositio*, one built words [planes] into phrases [members] into clauses [bodies] and finally into a period [*historia*]" (*Giotto* 130–31). Alberti powerfully combined *historia* as narrative ordered by a strict rhetoric with *historia* as ordered *seeing*.

As both, the best *historia* "captivates the eye of learned or unlearned spectator with delight and motion of the soul [*cum voluptate et animi motu*]." It had abundance and variety, yet such simplicity and clarity as tragic and comic poets attained with their few characters. When those painted clearly showed "motion of the soul [*animi motum*], then will *historia* move spectators' souls [*animos . . . spectantium movebit*]. . . . These motions of soul are known from motions of body" (*On Painting* 72, 78, 80, translation adjusted and checked with Alberti's 1436 *Della pittura*). Geometrical perspective explicitly aimed at moving the soul's passions: those "motions of the soul [*motus . . . animorum*] that the learned call affections, like anger, grief, joy, fear, desire, and others of the sort." Painters would learn these by experience and association with "poets and orators" (82, 94). They expressed these passions in perspective painting whose *historia* conformed to rules of pleasing beauty noted elsewhere as: "a form of sympathy and consonance of the parts within a body, according to definite number, outline and position, as dictated by *concinnitas*, the absolute and fundamental rule of Nature" (*On the Art* IX.v: 303). These were the same assumptions as lay behind Loyola's techniques, intended specifically to provoke *mociones del ánima*.

So it is not surprising to find one of Loyola's English followers suggesting that exercitants prepare by looking at an image of the scene or action that they aim to share. Describing Loyola's *Exercises*, and especially the moment of the "composition of place," Martz quotes the Jesuit John Gibbons explaining how we must see

the places where the thinges we meditate on were wrought, by imagining our selves to be really present at those places; which we must endeavour to represent

so lively, as though we saw them indeed with our corporall eyes; which to performe well, it will help us much to behould before-hand some Image wherin that
mistery is well represented, and to have read or heard what good Authors write
of those places, and to have noted well the distance from one place to another, the
height of the hills, and the situation of the townes and villages. (Martz 27; Gibbons §2, ¶10)

Martz does not elaborate on this advice to prepare for meditation by
looking at a picture, but the proposal relates closely to the first set of
practices that I mentioned as useful for understanding the experience of
being basic to the *Exercises*: exhortatory sermons. Baxandall cites a 1491
sermon by the Dominican Fra Michele da Carcano, in which the preacher
explains that to make sermons persuasive one needs to use painted images. People had their feelings more easily moved by them, and would be
more swiftly and fully instructed and roused to devotion (*Painting* 41).

For the painter, says Baxandall, this meant that clarity, attraction and
memorability had to characterize paintings that provided stirring renderings of holy stories (43). For the images needed by preachers, "the painter
was a professional visualizer of" such stories. But "what we now easily
forget," Baxandall adds, "is that each of his pious public was liable to be
an amateur in the same line, practised in spiritual exercises that demanded a high level of visualization of, at least, the central episodes of the
lives of Christ and Mary. To adapt a theological distinction, the painter's
were exterior visualizations, the public's interior visualizations" (*Painting*
45). This is no ready distinction. Like Richard of St. Victor, Jiménez and
everyone, and following how the affections functioned, Loyola knew that
internal visualizations always began as external ones. It might have been
surprising if Loyola had *not* turned to painters' vocabulary. Baxandall
cites a 1454 *Zardino de oration*, written for young girls, explaining "the
need for internal representations and their place in the process of prayer."
Internal representations started as external ones, "impressed" on the
mind by "imagination." The author instructed his readers in the need
clearly to visualize actual places of the Passion, its people and their actions, *seeing* them in their physical reality. This done, the youth was to go
alone to her room and fully absorb what she has seen and felt: "Moving
slowly from episode to episode, meditate on each one, dwelling on each
single stage and step of the story. And if at any point you feel a sensation
of piety, stop: do not pass on as long as that sweet and devout sentiment
lasts" (46).

This solitary seeing was why painters did not particularize people, depicting them, rather, as "general, unparticularized, interchangeable types.
They provided a base . . . on which the pious beholder could impose his
personal detail" (48). This was not specific to the painter, but common

across the board, whether in Guerre and du Tilh, in Febvre's writers or Loyola himself. Mark Jarzombek has identically analyzed the quasi-"autobiographical" characters of certain of Alberti's other writings. They appear, he writes, "as tropes that articulate a type of private philosophical language. But it is not a language that can be interpreted simply as a psychological self-portrait. Alberti's autobiographical methodology stands nearer the medieval idea of *exempla*, of patterns that repeat themselves again and again, and thus aims beyond a description of individual reality." In fact, nothing is "private" here or unusual in giving seemingly personal experiences as "instantly typified, depersonalized, and transformed into generalizing postulates." They make the writer part of and constituted by a collectivity (Jarzombek 3–4). Grafton similarly shows Alberti forging a life by "a ready-made template" drawn from antiquity, buried in public "communities of hearers and readers," articulating "arenas" in which he and others were to fit, "realms" that were who he was (*Leon* 25, 27, 29). Grafton's biography shows how this "spherical" being was achieved.

This understanding of a person was as essential to the *Exercises* as it was to the sermons allied with them. This had long been so. Writing of sermons, saints' lives, *exempla* and the like, Gurevich notes that medieval authors used "plenty of *loci communes* and habitual, familiar *topoi*." It was not just that people "found satisfaction in familiar verities and formulas . . . in endless variations on themes that had been set once and for all" (*Medieval* 10). It was that they were who they were by virtue of these familiarities. All these stories *had* to repeat one another, had to be "already known" (20): they portrayed and exhorted exemplary versions of everyone's life.

"The best guide we now have to the public exercises" of this picture reading and of setting oneself to be affected by them in these ways, says Baxandall, "is the sermon." Preachers "drilled their congregations in a set of interpretive skills right at the core of the fifteenth-century response to paintings." "In the course of the church year . . . , the popular preacher moved over much of the painter's subject matter" explaining how to be affected, understand and meditate on their themes (did Petrarch's *Canzoniere* offer a like practice?). "Such sermons were a very thorough emotional categorization of the stories, closely tied to the physical, and thus also visual, embodiment of the mysteries. The preacher and painter were *repetiteur* to each other" (*Painting* 48–49). These were old practices in the fifteenth century, going back at least to popular medieval preaching. Gurevich offers a thirteenth-century compendium of popular moral tales used in sermons and other directive texts, miracles and such often set in contemporary context so that author and hearers "could have

been present at these occurrences and witnessed them" (*Medieval*
22–23). Jean-Thiébaut Welter writes of the *exemplum* used by preachers
in their sermons and others in equally popular sorts of writing as "a tale
or description" whose aim was to strike (3). It was, said Alain de Lille in
the twelfth century, a "*showing*" (Welter 67). "The themes of painter and
sculptor," says G. R. Owst, "are the themes of the pulpit." Preachers
made "word-pictures" whose vernacular "vivacity and directness" meant
to bring "the medieval audience . . . under their spell." The sermon's
"lively little descriptions" depended on the bond between "medieval art
and religious instruction" (*Literature* 2, 31, 40, 47). Carolly Erickson
talks of an "openness to visual sensation" (*Medieval* 33), creative of pas-
sional effects wholly foreign to modern western experience. Events, actions and situations related in pictures and word-pictures became their
auditors' and spectators' own.

In this context Petrarch's Augustine taught Francesco to imagine physically and spiritually the torments of hell. Venturing such meditation, he
had to experience death in the body, "stiffen, tremble and grow pale,"
feel death agony, undergo "a thousand punishments, a thousand tortures;
the wailing shrieks of hell, the sulfurous rivers, darkness and avenging Furies . . . ; if all these come before your eyes at once, not as fiction but as
truth, not as possibilities but as necessary and inevitable things close to
actuality even now, and if amid these anxieties you meditate on these
things not lightly nor desperately but with filled with hope" (*Secretum*
56). Only by the *becoming-other* enabled by this image-making and performed experience could soul be one with God, for its "exaltation and
glory" (*Exercises* §179–80: 247). So Loyola's fourth week ended with a
prayer offering back the soul: "Take, Lord, and receive all my liberty, my
memory, my understanding and all my will, all my wealth and possession; you gave it to me, Lord, to you I return it; all is yours, use it according to your will; give me your love and grace, for that suffices me"
(§234: 258). The divine could then return, making the body a "temple."
Such was the ideal path. But, before death, soul incarnate never rested at
its end, any more than it did in Petrarch. The *Exercises* required constant
repetition because the soul's distance from divine origin, its need to work
through the body, required constant vigilance.

Loyola set a final rule to that effect: "by its own reasoning from *habitus* and consequences of concepts and judgments, or by the good or evil
spirit, [the soul] forms divers propositions and purposes, which are not
given immediately by God our Lord, and so need to be very well examined before being given entire credit or put into action" (§336: 283). The
way to secular *sapientia, sabiduría, sapience* or wisdom, in Vives for example, adopted the same assumptions about the senses, passions, reason

and will, the last relying on reason as "master and preceptor" (not sovereign), not forced to any determined act, but deciding among or combining (we saw both Petrarch and Augustine say of God's multiple truths) several advanced by reason controlled by mind/soul, whose essence was divine (*Tratado* II.xi: 97). Anything like a self-contained subject or self was by definition as untrustworthy for Vives and Loyola as for Augustine—or du Bartas or Montaigne for that matter, who wrote that such a self could be fooled even when prayer was in question: "A true prayer and religious conciliation of us with God cannot fall into a soul impure and subject to Satan's dominion" (1.56.310: "Des prières").

When Loyola said that one drew near truth by "looking at my selfe [*mirando a mí mismo*]" (§53: 223), he did not assert any fullness of subjectivity. The reference in this instance is again to "me" as "the soul in me." Too, *sí, sí mismo* and the possessive adjectives attending these turns of phrase were simply reflexive. Impersonal, they were a *sí* that was to become the *same* (*mismo*) as the teacher and all souls: the aim being to know the "way back" from particular body to universal divinity-experiencing soul as the same divine presence in all (§§230–37; §316). Likewise, *reflection* in Vives "comes" (*viene*: the word and its implications recall Loyola) as a balanced gaze not on "self," but on the condition and content of mind and, eventually, the soul and its union with the divine. It "investigates the interior of the mind and reflects on it as on itself, so as to recognize its content, measuring its quality and quantity." Thence it used the internal light of reason seen earlier (*Tratado* II.ix: 93). By and large, Montaigne mirrored this pattern, heir to and imbued with Sabunde's thought—although the *Essays* do hug the precarious edge of Cervantes's Vidriera.

Just as the *Spiritual Exercises*' content and syntax expressed an absence of "personal self," so did its very grammar. Throughout it used a neutral reflexive voice, emphasizing that soul, mind and their powers were *not* particular, but typical in all humans. "The Ignatian *I*," writes Barthes, "has nothing to do with *being*, . . . its use is wholly transitive, imperative. . . . It is in fact the *shifter* ideally described by linguists, whose psychological vacuity, whose purely locutory being assure a sort of *errance* across indefinite [verbal] persons" (56). At the same time, the very need for reflection signaled human littleness: "consider what a thing is all creation compared to God: then I alone—what can I be? [*pues yo solo— ¿qué puedo ser?*]" (§58: 224). Sometimes the neutral reflexive yielded to "*hombre*" and the third person. Usually this was when human action in and affected by the world was being considered. *Yo* or the verbal first person indicated either littleness of human being or misguidance of will and understanding into sinfulness: as when humility was object of the exercise

(§165). This was exactly Vives' criticism of Grinferantes' "all of me," in the *Exercitatio*, whose fundamental educational axiom was also humility (*Diálogos* 140: "Los preceptos de la educación"). One may recall that Loyola's "autobiography" was written in the third person and properly titled *Acta*, as in the Acts of the Apostles.

The neutral reflexive voice, available in Romance languages or Greek, does not exist in English, and its sense, translators observe, is hard to catch. Loyola's contemporaries used "selfe," "selfesame" or even "same," but the usage is lost. Translations of the *Exercises* serve historians even less than those of other works: translators wanting to satisfy the original's meditational aim must adopt modern experiences of being. One of the most careful, Louis J. Puhl, acknowledges difficulties of accuracy but sees small harm in translating, for example, the impersonal "traer a la memoria" as "I will call to mind." Because impersonal construction, he says, often turned to "a personal one," he uses "I" throughout (174; and see his earlier remarks: vii). Another careful translator, George E. Ganss, claims "to add and subtract nothing" by adjusting Loyola's thought to how "a modern English-speaking writer would be likely to express it" (118). He, too, always has "I." This changes the meaning entirely. Loyola's neutral constructions produced a sense of common soul *becoming* personal and—precisely—being drawn back from it by meditation and prayer: back to the soul in divine truth and purity (Vives' point in the dialogue mentioned). This was the very purpose of the typifying sermons and paintings. The pattern of Loyola's language captured that movement; echoing a meditational syntax that ran from *composición* of visual image (incarnate, as it were) to memory, understanding and will, and on to divine colloquy and prayer.

Loyola's *yo*, Vives' *ego*, fixing Augustine's devil's brood, had much to do with Huarte's *ingenio*: it marked what was particular in humans. Loyola's education away from sin to fulfill the goal for which "*soy criado*" (§179: 247) was akin to Huarte's or Montaigne's training to develop diverse aptitudes. It was again a question of training *habitus* so that the will would know the right choice to make to satisfy legitimate collective expectation. Loyola stressed person's place in a divine scheme, the others in a social. Like Montaigne (or Cicero), Loyola marked the parity. A first week's exercise had one see oneself a "great sinner . . . bound in chains to face the supreme eternal judge, imagining as example [*trayendo en exemplo*] how chained prisoners meriting death face their temporal judge" (§74: 228). The next week, an exercise involved "applying the example of the temporal king named above to Christ our Lord," that one might grasp how, "if we consider such a call by an earthly king to his subjects [*sus súbditos*], how much more worthy [it is] of our consideration to behold Christ our Lord" (§95: 231–32). These subjections were identical to those holding or sought in other spheres, like mind/body itself—"such that sensuality may obey reason and all inferior parts be more subject [*más subiectas*] to the superior" (§87: 229). Du Bartas repeated these subjections in the "Sixieme Jour" of his later bestseller.

The purpose of the last was that "mis intenciones, acciones y operaciones" serve "divine majesty" (§46: 221). It was the same in its sacred realm as Montaigne's subjection of *vie privée* to *devoir public* in the social. For him, as for so many, to let personal instability enter the public realm was sure catastrophe. Shakespeare's Coriolanus determined his end in tragedy by choosing to reject ties of nature and civic duty, and "stand / As if a man were author of himself / And knew no other kin," authorizing glassy essence (V.iii.35–37). Wyatt's was a beneficent response in this familiar experience of who-ness (see Chapter 13). Coriolanus' was malevolent. Loyola's "good" *intención* reacted directly to the choice, taking the "simple" way of "regarding only the end for which I am created": "praise of God our Lord and salvation of my soul" (§169: 244). *Coriolanus* echoed the prevalent Elizabethan and Jacobean view that any "inner power" seen as self-sufficient "was more likely to represent a subversive or even demonic quality, the ability to operate secretly beyond the constraints of constituted [or divine] authority" (Hanson, *Discovering* 17–18).

For Vives, Montaigne and Huarte, the goal was the analogous one of social well-being and stability. De Gournay naturally analyzed Montaigne's "use of the selfe" as enabling subjection to the commonweal. One was *subject* to its ends just as, Aquinas had argued, intellect was "subject to knowledge, and [was] changed from ignorance to knowledge by reason of its being in potency with regard to the intelligible species" (ST 1a.75.5). Loyola's *intención* has a meaning close to its etymology: "a holding forth" of something in the mind; similar to Huarte's use of *intención* to indicate a particular strength of conception (see Chapter 13). Just so, Aquinas had written, "man understands through the soul." This "subject" was not a "prime mover" or agent, a "First Act" or an "active potency." It was a "receptive potency," Aristotle's passible soul. Its acts resulted from action *on it*. In that sense, precisely, Aquinas reminded his reader of Aristotle: that the soul was "a clean tablet on which nothing is written." It was a passible potency able to receive for good or evil (ST 1a.75.3 and 5; 1a.79.2). With this we come full circle.

Loyola and those viewed in the last chapter still experienced some personal being like this, one in which *passion* still meant what it etymologically said. "We may therefore say that the soul understands as the eye sees," Aquinas wrote, "but it is more correct to say that man understands through the soul" (ST 1a.75.1). Thence shone the internal light enabling reason and reflection to act that Vives, and Melanchthon after him, equated with the eye's need for external light. As mind was subject to soul (Loyola's hierarchy), so body was to mind. The phantasm produced by bodily sense was "to the intellect what color is to the sight": the event moving it. "The body is necessary for the action of the intellect not as its organ of action, but by reason of the object." So we should not say that Socrates understands, "but that he or his phantasms are understood" by intellectual soul. Vives told pupils: "in humans, the body is obedient to the soul; and the will to the mind; and the mind, to God. If anything deviates from this order or perverts it, it is in error": Augustine's devil's brood again, Montaigne's fear for civic order, or Coriolanus' choice to authorize himself (*Introduction* 100).

Soul and mind (imagination and memory, understanding and will) were subject on the one hand to divine essence, on the other to material nature: to the second as provider of objects of knowledge through the senses, on which the mind could then reflect and act by the light cast on it from the soul. Aquinas also called the soul the "agent intellect." For him, as for Loyola and Vives, it was so "by reason of its participation in intellectual power" or "a superior intellect," Aristotle's impassible soul, "by which the soul is helped to understand." This was not a wholly distinct being, but "in the soul some power derived from a higher intellect, whereby it is able [for instance] to light up the phantasms." "This separate intellect," Aquinas ended, "is God himself" (ST 1a.79.4). Two and a half centuries later, Vives, like Loyola, was briefer: "we say [the soul] inhabits [the body] because it is God in the body itself," the "active power" operating through mental faculties and agencies of sense (*Tratado* I. xi: 49). This was almost everyone's thought.

The view of person as in a hierarchy of *subjections* was clear to Montaigne and Cervantes, and grounded Vives', Loyola's, Melanchthon's and Huarte's work as it had Aquinas'. Montaigne saw the end of human autoreflection as leading the soul to God, a view echoing Sabunde's ladder of being serving human selfe-, and thence immediately divine, knowledge. Montaigne, too, saw human faculties and abilities as subject to the divine, rising to it only "if God lends extraordinary help." Then alone, "one will rise up, leaving and renouncing one's own means, letting oneself be lifted and drawn up by purely heavenly helps." No human act, but only "Christian faith . . . may hope for this divine and miraculous metamorphosis" (II.xii.589: "Apologie"). Inconstant private mind yielded not just to the social subject but to the divine, as Don Quijote's madness did to free and clear reason and heavenly consolation at the end of his novel, freeing him from "sins," "misty shadows of ignorance" and mortal life's "absurdities and deceits," and preparing him for heaven: "Blessed be almighty God, who has done me so much good! At the last, his mercies are without limit, humans' sins neither abridge nor block them!" (II.74: 2.587). Soul and mind were subject to the divine within as to the social and natural without. Person to society and nature, senses to mind, mind to soul, soul to God, were analogous forms of selfe and subjection. They were, though, increasingly fraught with tensions.

Much later, the many "versions" of Guerre's story on the Jacobean stage (Greenblatt, "Psychoanalysis" 139–40), of impostures, impersonations and mixed identities, suggest anxious, even anguished, fears apparently absent from Guerre's case. Doubt and discord there were, but *not* Hamlet's agonizing uncertainty, Lady Macbeth's perverted terror or Lear's tormented passage through loss of identity to death. These are not "versions." They signal breakdowns in experiences of who-ness culminating growing tensions, echoing experiences recorded in Chapter 1. Loyola's insistence that the *Exercises* required constant repetition may show hesitancies and doubts, as if keeping the relations of selfe and subjection, of person to society and nature, senses to mind, mind to soul and soul to God, needed endless battle. If so, we have seen, he was not alone. Too, seeing humans as having to "work through" their now-familiar spheres as *a series of "subjections,"* a word he uses a great deal, he implies a growing sense of agency, though doing so still in a familiar possible context. A directly contemporary woman writer like Hélisenne de Crenne offers a glimpse of possible future changes of context.

CHAPTER FIFTEEN

Hélisenne's Story

Collective Love, Singular Anger

In September 1538, Jean-Jacques de Mesmes, lieutenant civil au Châtelet de Paris, signed the privilege granted to the Parisian "bookseller and printer" Denys Janot to publish Hélisenne de Crenne's *Angoysses douloureuses qui procedent d'amours* (95: henceforth AD; for the English: *Torments* [TL] sometimes altered). The book, whose title page gave its author's name as "Dame Helisenne" and her purpose as that of "exhort[ing] all people not to follow mad Love," appeared later the same year. In Pierre Sergent's 1541 edition (and in four others that appeared by 1560), the privilege was replaced on the title page's verso by a poem addressed by the author to her "Lisantes," her women readers:

> Dames d'honneur et belles nymphes
> Pleines de vertu et doulceur,
> Qui contemplez les paranymphes,
> Du regard, des cueurs ravisseur:
> L'archier non voyant, et mal seur
> Vous picquera, prenez y garde.
> Soyez tousjours sur vostre garde,
> Car tel veult prendre, qui est pris.
> Je vous serviray d'avantgarde
> A mes despens, dommage et pris.

> Nobles ladies and fair maids
> Full of virtue and sweetness,
> Who contemplate the servitors
> Of the gaze that steals hearts,
> The unseeing and unsure archer
> Will strike you. Beware.
> Be always on your guard,

For the trapper may be trapped.
I shall serve you as vanguard,
At my expense, pain and woe. (AD95–96n; TL3)

This liminary poem, urging the book's women readers not to flirt with seductive looks (and books?) lest they be taken in their own snares and destroyed by uncontrollable love, partly reiterated the title. Doing so, it stressed the author's role as *exemplum*, figure of models to be followed or avoided. It stressed a *public* persona: "I shall serve you as vanguard, At my expense, pain and woe." At the same time, if she and her book are among the "paranymphes" her readers contemplated, her *exemplum* was equivocal: "paranymphe" meant a lady- or gentleman-in-waiting, but also a person who presented and praised a prospective doctor at the University of Paris, so any learned supporter or mediator (Buzon ed., *Angoysses* 96n). Teacher and mediator, the poem also made the paranymphe a seducer.

The poem's last phrase is notable for its monetary terms, *despens, dommage* and *pris*, all three of which can be translated as financial "expense." The terms were not accidental, given that the novel makes much of Hélisenne's and her husband's wealth, against her lover Guenelic's poverty, his being "of low estate" (AD110, 143; TL14, 32), and, further, that it was a financial dispute over land that put Hélisenne in the way of mad love by bringing her to this town (AD101; TL9). At the poem's end, she suggests that though she has put out her money wastefully, the book turns it to a credit that readers can make "useful and profitable" (synonyms frequent in *Angoysses*, here AD221; TL73). The association of wrongful love with wasteful economic exchange offers a powerful metaphor, and one that makes the equivocal *exemplum* positive.

It may remind us of a just later novel, Rabelais' *Tiers livre* (1546), whose third and fourth chapters gave Panurge's encomium to debit and credit as exchanges essential to well-ordered society. Hélisenne certainly knew popular works like Cicero's *De officiis* and Seneca's *De beneficiis* which Panurge took his reasoning about collective exchanges and society to copy. Michael Screech thinks that Rabelais made clear that Panurge's paean was comic, and corrected by Pantagruel's Plutarchan and humanistic rejection of usury in the next chapter of the *Tiers livre*, which forcefully adopted one of Erasmus' popular *Adages*: *Felix qui nihil debet* (II.7.98) (*Rabelais* 225–31). Too, Plutarch's *De vitando aere alieno*, a compilation of commonplaces urging "Thou shalt not borrow," was widely familiar in the Renaissance (and before) and Pantagruel *was* echoing it. But the issue is harder, and controversy over the tone and meaning of Panurge's argument unceasing. Critics agree that he is the figure of self-love (*"philautie"*) that Pantagruel accuses him of being. "Self-love" marks a person as unfit for society. Self-love, Labé held, "rejects true and full Love, which does not seek its own profit but that of the beloved," bonds beyond singularities (*Oeuvres* 63). Screech and those adopting his now-predominant view assert that the context of Panurge's encomium marks it as a comic debasement. It actually attacked a self-love that claimed a right to judge others as it refused to pass like judgment on itself, was blind to current mishaps and unable to foresee future ones—at least as they touched its own case. Since such self-love undid the humanist prudential social ideal, Panurge was a figure of comic mockery.

This is a two-edged sword. However unworthy Panurge's *philautie*, it offers a different take on the claims made for social constraints, and André Tournon rightly doubts the prevailing view that the *Tiers livre* attacks self-love (*"En sens,"* esp. 59–65). One can read Panurge as challenging a humanist ethic of prudence much as I shall suggest Hélisenne did. Panurge figures a critique of society and of a habitual view of what society should be. Taking his *laudatio* seriously is not one with taking it straight. Its linking of debit/credit relations with those of marriage is no less serious for its humor. *He* may abuse them for his own pleasure-loving improvidence, but to offer them as powerful patterns of one another is surely valid and, Duval observes, "would have appeared perfectly acceptable to any Renaissance reader" (*Design/*Tiers 44). Screech does not dissent, writing elsewhere: "the matter that Panurge misuses is not at all absurd. On the contrary, Panurge will correctly describe notions common among Platonist and other physicians. . . . The comic lies above all in Panurge's impertinence, which abuses this divine material" (*Tiers livre*, ed. 48n50; cf. his Introduction xiv–xvi and footnotes 37–53). Françoise Joukovsky agrees, asserting that Panurge "deforms the Neoplatonic theme of cosmic love, universal bond" (*Tiers livre*, ed. Preface 13). The "abuse" or "deformation" is by no means simply comic.

Seneca's widely known essay was not ironic or comic in associating bonds holding society and people together and those conjoining the world and the universe. He certainly put money among them. It is no contradiction that other writers by now as familiar, notably Plato and, just before Hélisenne's time, Ficino, in his renowned commentary on Plato's *Symposium*, made love the steel of these bonds. Ficino had finished the second version of his commentary in 1475, translating it right away into Italian and lecturing on it "in response to popular demand." It was published in his edition and translation of Plato's *Opera* in 1484 and 1490 (Jayne, Introduction to *Commentary* 18, 13–14). Another edition appeared at Lyon in 1533. Ficino urged that love was "the creator and preserver of all natural things." Because of the procreative instinct of creation and preservation,

the holy spirits move the heavens and bestow their gifts upon everything beneath them. Because of this, the stars spread their light among the elements. Because of this, fire attracts air through mutual participation in its own heat, so air attracts water; water earth; and vice versa, earth attarcts water to itslf; water the air; and air, the fire. In the same way, plants and trees, also desirous of propagating their own seed, bear offspring like themselves. Brute animals also, and men, carried away by the charms of the same passion, are aroused to the procreation of offspring.

Just so, "like things are preserved by like, and . . . Love attracts the like to the like. Every part of the earth, joined by mutual love, links itself with other parts of earth like itself" (*Commentary* 148–49). One recalls Sabunde or—just after Hélisenne—Labé's (or Apollo's) claims for Love in her "Débat de Folie et d'Amour."

Love, said Ficino, was "desire for beauty." Beauty marked "the harmony of several elements" set "in the soul," in the "several virtues," "in material objects," in "several colors" and "tones." Beauty being harmony, it followed that "love [sought] only what [was] temperate, moderate, and decorous." "Pleasures and sensations which [were] so impetuous and irrational that they jar[red] the mind from its stability and unbalance[d] a man, love [did] not only not desire, but hate[d] and shun[ned]" as the opposite of beauty. "A mad lasciviousness," he warned, dragged "a man down to intemperance and disharmony" (*Commentary* 130). Conversely, the beauty that fired true love shone from God "through the Angelic mind," the "World-Soul and the rest of the souls," "Nature" and "corporeal Matter," fitting "the Mind with a system of Ideas . . . the Soul with a series of Concepts," sowing "Nature with seeds" and providing "Matter with Forms." "In much the same way, in fact, that the single light of the sun lights up four bodies, fire, air, water, and earth, so the single light of God illumines the Mind, Soul, Nature, and Matter" (140). Small wonder if he likened this beauty and its conjoint love to a center and four circles, recalling earlier experiences: "The single center of everything is God. Around this continually revolve four circles: Mind, Soul, Nature, and Matter" (135). Thus did love—universal, virtuous, ennobling, public—hold everything in harmony and symmetry.

It was this symmetry that gave economic exchange such power to depict the wider bonds of society, world and universe, and of person within them. These years, indeed, saw a flood of burlesques of this depiction. Marie-Madeleine Fontaine sees them as part of the lively debates on usury. She shows Panurge's paean—even its symmetries—indebted to Sperone Speroni's dialogue on usury in *I Dialoghi* of 1542, with a precursor in Ruzzante's second prologue to *La vaccària* (staged in 1533), tying debts and marriage, liberality and marital freedom ("Rabelais"; Ruzzante, *Teatro* 1046–47). Lazare Sainéan (418–19) finds a minor source in the "Capitolo del debito" of Francesco Berni's 1538 *Rime burlesche*, but ignores its linking of debt and marriage (ll.46–48: *Rime* 204). John Lewis names François Habert's 1542 *Songe de Pantagruel*, with comic lines about a loan retrievable when all social ills are healed and the world restored (*Songe* ll.556–86). This may have decided Panurge's remark at the start of his eulogy about repaying his debts "es calendes grecques," and provoked his Land of Cocayne treatment. But how deeply serious was the tie between debit/credit relations and wider social bonds is underscored by the fact that in 1579, Hubert Languet and Philippe du Plessis Mornay, likely authors of the notorious and influential monarchomach polemic, *Vindiciae, contra tyrannos*, in explaining the triple contractual social relation between God, monarch and people, depicted people's relation to God via Roman law governing debtors and creditors (38–40, 166).

Besides Ruzzante and Berni, Hélisenne could perhaps have known none of these last at the time of her novel's appearance in 1538 or of its 1541 second edition with the liminary poem. Indeed, despite Ruzzante's wild popularity in the Veneto, could she really have known his *Vaccària*, not published until 1551? Speroni's *Dialoghi* appeared in 1542, and in French only in 1551, but an overlap is intriguing. There, a "Dialogo della discordia" directly followed the "Dialogo della usura" (*Opere* 1.97–165). In the one the goddess Usura explains the benefits of credit to human wellbeing, with the importance of gratitude and amity, in the other the goddess Discordia shows Jupiter the necessity of discord to all movement in human life, with Mercury intervening at the end to back her. Given how *Angoysses* starts, and that it ends in a divine dispute incited by Mercury, adjudicated by Jupiter and closed by Mercury's actions, it is hard not to see a tie with Speroni, although divine disputes, as between Pallas and Venus, like Hélisenne's, were literary commonplaces. A holograph note on Speroni's manuscript says that he finished the usury dialogue on May 29, 1537 (Fournel 73). Given the paradoxicality of these dialogues (alone in the collection), we may reasonably date them close together. Did they circulate? Abroad? To publishers? We do not know. Nor do we know whether Hélisenne or her publisher/patron knew Italian, although Janot published translations from that language (Hélisenne, *A Renaissance* 15–17). One would like to know more, because such influences help track general changes in sensibility and particular experiences of personhood. But the fact of similarities matters more than exact influences. The second show only an author's reading, the first an atmosphere breathed, a sensibility shared. These examples indicate that symmetric images of debit/credit and love relations were so familiar that a writer did not need to stress their wider import for bonds of community. Readers would recognize and connect them.

What Hélisenne suggested in her poem, as Ficino and Martínez de Toledo had said earlier, was that misguided love broke collective bonds, became pure waste, the triple *expense* of a person who has quit such bonds. Closer to Hélisenne than Ficino, Symphorien Champier had paraphrased the Italian on this point, asserting in the fourth book, "Livre de vraye amour," of his 1503 *Nef des dames vertueuses*:

The fury and madness of carnal and sensual desire leads to expense [*prodigalité*], intemperance, infamy and vile things. While love drives and desires beauty. And since infamy and ugliness are contrary to beauty, the motions of love and carnal appetite are contraries, which is why this carnal and sensual appetite cannot be called love. (*Livre* 52)

Hélisenne developed the point in her dedicatory epistle, writing of the "vain and unchaste love" that had caused her suffering and misfortune, and asking her lady readers for their compassionate tears, alone able to give her "quelque refrigeration medicamente [some healing coolness]." She was asking these readers to include her in a new community, her whose heart was still "disturbed by infinite desires and amorous spurrings [*aguillonnemens*]." Her lasting grief and pain were such that her "trembling hand remain[ed] motionless" (AD96–97; TL7). Thereby, of course, she would be unable to write the book begun soon after being shut away by her husband, in hope of eventually getting it to her beloved and so overcoming her misery (AD218; TL72); the book that Mercury would find at the end of the story and take to the realms of Parnassus, where Jupiter would solve the dispute between Venus and Pallas over its rightful possession by ordering its publication in Paris (AD500–503; TL198–99).

But, said Hélisenne in her dedicatory epistle, thinking of the compassion all women would join to give *her* and how her *exemplum* would help *them* avoid the snares into which she fell and the broken compacts and fractured society she has made, she began to: "find words again [*reverberer*] and regain my strength, praying to her who is mother and daughter of the high-thundering creator to be willing to help my sorry memory and sustain my feeble hand, so as to be able to write this well for you" (AD97; TL7). By this exchange of credit, her writing would rebuild the community broken by her "vaine et impudicque amour" (AD96; TL7). She returns to the point in closing the first part, justifying her *hardiesse*, audacity, to write of "unchaste loves," as a "useful and profitable" example of the "insane madness" induced by yielding to such passion. There she tells her "most dear and honored ladies" how she wishes them to be as continent, wise, faithful and chaste as Penelope, Thetis, Dido, Lucretia and others (AD221–22; TL73). The examples are not accidental: they are also Hélisenne.

So Hélisenne seemingly offered her novel as actual public reparation for fictional public harm, remaking communities to replace those broken by the fictive heroine's yielding to personal desires. The broken communities were not just the marital one—with all it held of divine, familial, social, financial and legal warrant—but wider ones involving, simply, acceptable relations between members of society: after all, one of the results of Hélisenne's and Guenelic's embrace of their love is their death and so the breaking of numberless other bonds, to say nothing of the disgraces and disturbances caused along the way. The book was to heal these losses, not just with the women's community called for at the outset, but at least two others into which this community would be set at the end: a divine one symbolized by Mercury and his fellow gods and by prayers uttered to a Christian God, and a sociopolitical one symbolized by Paris: city of wisdom (says Pallas), where "is found an infinite multitude of wonderfully studious people. And so one can rightly call this noble city a true fount and source of wisdom and knowledge," one filled with "noble orators, poets and historiographers" (AD503–4; TL199).

This mixing of the real and the fictive has led to contorted controversy over separating author, narrator(s) and protagonist—separations, writes Diane Wood, "difficult to resolve" because of "slippage between various levels of 'fiction'" (149). Hélisenne was most likely Marguerite Briet, married to Philippe Fournel, lord of Crenne, a small fief in today's Aisne. Born about 1510 in nearby Abbeville, she died probably toward the end of 1552 (Buzon ed., *Angoysses* 9–10). Debate is inexhaustible as to whether her three original works, *Angoysses*, the 1539 *Epistres familieres et invectives* and 1541 *Songe* related autobiographical truth or were fictional, *Angoysses* and *Epistres* then being respectively the first sentimental and first epistolary novel in France. Not long before, René d'Anjou had cast his *Livre du cuers d'amours espris* as quest romance, autobiographical letter and dream of a "love-smitten heart." To seek fact/fiction distinctions may be to ask anachronistically modernizing questions. Among other things, it is to want to discover person as a psychologically unique whole, a self that stays coherently the "same" over time and place, independently of its contexts and communities. No such experience or idea was available to Hélisenne (which is how the novel's second p art can change Guenelic to being not at all of "low estate"), and I propose that in *Angoysses* she and the rest are who they are precisely in the degree to which they *are* members of communities, to which they *do* therefore have to change with one another, to which they *are* inseparable parts of each other, inextricable "mutualities"—as Wilson Harris has it in a different context (*Womb* 13, 18). That is why Hélisenne had to rebuild broken communities. Wood's insistence that the protagonists of *Angoysses* were entirely "cut off from society" and that the novel as a whole was "totally lacking" in any "social context" (143–44) is only half true.

To show this, I consider Hélisenne's selfe-presentation as *exemplum*, look at the communities whose rupture and reconstruction the writings concern, analyze the who-ness they engage and explore the structure of the two works of special interest here, *Angoysses* and *Epistres*—the latter apparently creating space and need for something new. One matter is that their very writing, I repeat, is itself one communal aspect of a *persona* called Hélisenne who is, therefore, both fictive *and* actual: whose *person* is what it is *by* writing and what it is *in* the writing. Like Petrarch before and Montaigne after, Hélisenne and her book are one: not that she is her heroine, but that her heroine and her heroine's environment are "part" of who *she* is. The novel's tale is one arena of her person. So, too, is its telling. So in some way the destruction recounted in the novel *can* be healed by writing the novel. That is why the author's new *hardiesse* of the end of Part One matches the *hardiesse* to which the heroine accedes early in the story, the one harmful, the other profitable.

Too, the writing is communal not only in its call to (re)construct a collective. Like other works of its time and before, it was composed "communally." *Angoysses* wove many threads: Boccaccio's *Fiammetta* (with a first French translation in 1532 and one by Hélisenne's publisher in 1541), Antoine de La Sale's *Petit Jehan de Saintré* (early fifteenth century?), Jean Lemaire de Belges' *Illustrations de Gaule et singularitez de Troye* (1511–12), a version of Ovid's *Metamorphoses* printed at Lyon in 1532 titled *Grand Olympe des hystoires poetiques du prince de poesie Ovide Naso* (that also took from Lemaire), Jacopo Caviceo's 1508 *Il peregrino*, whose 1527 French translation was issued at least ten times by 1540 (Buzon ed., *Angoysses* 31–36) and Jean Bouchet's 1536 *Angoisses et remedes damours*. Besides works named earlier, I add the *Roman de la Rose*. Hélisenne's confinement in a lonely chateau echoes the Rose's. Both are to be rescued by the lover; both incorporate debates on the nature of love and other moral issues. Describing their first exchange after finding Hélisenne again, Guenelic writes of "her rose-like mouth" (AD438; TL174): a cliché, to be sure, but pointed here. Similarly, *Epistres* takes off from a long tradition of *artes dictaminis*. Both works were composed as elements in a community of texts, altogether usually. It is surely wrong to read this psychoanalytically, as showing how "the text's Self is to a large extent produced by the gaze and the voice that come from the Other," a woman having to "impersonate" "authoritative male authors"—male "super-ego" "punishing" the female "ego"—or, alternatively, as a "montage . . . criticizing culture" (Cottrell 13–14). Analysis shows, on the contrary, that all writers shared this communal making. Theorists endlessly advised it. Further, the role of the gaze in the constitution of who-ness cannot be put in terms of "self" and "other," still less in those of male and female. These are muddling anachronisms.

For I shall suggest that *Angoysses* is largely a conservative work that looks back to older genre and gender constructions and social and personal expectations even as it offers a lingering after-image of a community of women writers and readers (following, after all, the narrator's death—as if there were no place for a woman claiming such freedoms). Even this after-image was mediated by male figures: from Jupiter who settles the dispute between warrior reason (Pallas) and love (Venus) by ordering the book's publication, through Mercury who first takes the book to Parnassus and then returns it to earth, to Quezinstra who will oversee actual publication. *Angoysses* thus showed victimization and subjection of women of the sort that Christine de Pisan, in the dispute over the *Roman de la Rose*, had shown to follow inevitably from Jean de Meung's views. *Epistres* advanced a vision closer to the sort of assertion made in Christine's *Livre de la cité des dames*—not incidentally printed by Janot in 1536. *Epistres* built from the old *ars dictaminis* something like a new personal figure striving to occupy a room of her own.

We have seen the preliminary texts of *Angoysses*, from title page through dedicatory poem to epistle, establish the name Hélisenne as that of an *exemplum*. Here, one cannot separate an "author's" from a "narrator's name" as Jerry Nash does in *Epistres*, Crenne from Hélisenne (12–14: his edition henceforth EFI). (M. J. Baker separates author and protagonist even further, as "Marguerite" and "Hélisenne," flouting Hélisenne's own naming and compounding anachronisms; Wood divides author, narrator, letter-writer and protagonist into no fewer than eight.) The title page of *Epistres* may seem to divide the two parts of Hélisenne's name: *Les epistres familieres & invectives de ma dame Helisenne, composées par icelle dame, De Crenne* (Familiar and invective letters of my lady Helisenne, composed by that lady, De Crenne) (EFI57). But care is needed: three of the *Epistres familieres* are signed "de Crenne" (1, 2 and 4), and the book ends by saying that it is by "ma dame Helisenne" (120). Further, the title's *icelle* refers directly to the preceding "Helisenne" and so really joins the two.

The name de Crenne does close Parts 1 and 2 of *Angoysses*, but I submit that *Epistres*' opening "separation" signals what was at least *fictively* new in the second book: principally that in *Epistres* the *persona* named Hélisenne moves from *exemplum* to personal agent, and one who is eventually to act willfully *against* other such agents. In *Angoysses*, on the contrary, Hélisenne is always *acted on*, from the very title naming the "amorous torments, *endured* for her lover Guenelic" (AD98; TL7, my italics). Through her early years, her story is of "being born," "being deprived of her father," being married, finding her husband "very agreeable to [her] [*il m'estoit si tres agreable*]," becoming "his only pleasure, he giving [her] mutual and reciprocal love" (AD98-99; TL8). She receives, is afflicted, suffers; in short, is characterized by *passibility*, receptivity to impulses, effects and passions that impinge from without: the material world, but other circles of being as well, divine, social, interpersonal, biological and more.

At the start of her story, Hélisenne relates this passibility to her unwitting haste to put herself in love's snares, "not knowing the fate and misadventure to which I had soon to succumb," and to "the nature of the feminine sex (which is never settled from seeing and being seen)" (AD101; TL9). The first phrase cited here, "ignorant la fortune et maladventure, ou briefvement je debvoye succumber," compasses many of these aspects. Hélisenne's *ignorance* and the fate, *fortuna*, to which she is subject join with the sense of *succumbing* to them, being *set under* them, and with *having* to be (*devoir*). About the surrounding world, fortune, love, knowledge even, she can do little or nothing. All are passions and events that happen to her. At this stage, the figure she most wished to emulate, for she might then have seen the future, is "la Troyenne Cassandra," a seer known not only as never believed, but as a special victim of gods, people and events, sufferer not actor. Yet ignorance of the future was, says Hélisenne: "divine predestination, because I know I shall serve as example to others" (AD101-2; TL10). Her *exemplum* is precisely that of the passible, suffering human, who, right away and as if by lightning, is struck and captured (*pris*) by love for a figure seen across the alley between their house and another, before which she is helpless: "by force I was compelled [*par force estoye contraincte*] to turn my eyes toward him"; "I could not withdraw my eyes" (AD102-3; TL10). A monk later suggests that men differ in this: they "freely submit [*se soubmettent*] to love," and boast of "deceptions, ruses and adulations" (AD153; TL38). Hélisenne adopts this (supposedly male) stance, while Guenelic, as interested as she in "seeing and being seen," is no less disturbed by passion.

Love is caused wholly by external effect, looks exchanged through two windows and across a street, whose force lies in what they show of the lovers' outward appearance. Their force relates to no prior inward disposition. It supposes, rather, absence of any such disposition. Person is characterized by receptivity to affects from without. Love is a "venom" that enters and perturbs the soul unawares (AD148; TL35). Mind, spirit, soul (*esperit*) is "utterly transported by the intolerable vehemence of love which dominate[s] within [one] with such great force as to dissipate and annihilate all [one's] powers" (AD161; TL41). Love comes from the power of the other's look striking from without, piercing heart and soul and depriving one of personal surety. It is, though, misleading to speak of deprivation, since from the outset Hélisenne is presented strictly in terms of outward beauty, of honorable family and fine reputation. To be a person is still to be a person *for others*. This explains the form of her husband's dismay when Hélisenne makes to kill herself. Not only, he protests, would she be admitting to having "lost her good reputation," but would cause him to be held the rest of his life "in less esteem" (AD143; TL32). *All* human acts are public.

What love and other uncontrolled passions change, one might say, is the other or others for whom and in terms of whom one is a person. This of course also alters the sense one has of who one is. As Hélisenne laments to the monk later in the story:

Alas, the thoughts and infinite regrets by which I am excessively tormented and tortured are not for the just pain I ought to have for my wicked sins, but come to me [*me procedent*] on account of the countless desires and amorous spurrings by which I am oppressed, and which it is impossible for me to manage to resist. For I love so ardently that I would far prefer to be deprived of life than of the sight of my beloved. Thoughts like these about my unbearable woes should easily incline you to take pity on her whom, from her excessive love, you see in a langorous illness far worse than a violent death. (AD149; TL35)

Hélisenne makes clear that she is the *recipient* of this love and its effects. One could readily cite endless such passages. For matters were so from the start, when her lover: "cast a look on me that pierced right through me to the heart, and had such power that at that moment I remained bereft of my selfe [*de moy mesmes je demouray privée*], and lost all composure" (AD162; TL42). This look can clearly therefore be experienced as "curative": "happy look that has so much power that when I am in extremity it can revive and vivify me" (AD163; TL42–43). One recalls Giacomo da Lentino's sonnet.

Because, here, the "revival" painfully disrupts familiar communities, it is essentially harmful, an "evil coming from the passions of the soul [of which] excessive love is the cause" (AD161–62; TL42). More, "love is a passion in the soul which most often reduces us to distress and grief" (AD167; TL45). "Calamitous passions" like these (AD161; TL42)—love, distress, grief, pity, anger and others to which in *Angoysses* love gives rise—had had their science since the philosophy and medicine of antiquity. They were, one recalls, "things suffered" (Latin *patior*), motions of the soul caused by its being incarnate and so "affected" or "perturbed" by external effects. They were a main cause of the soul's derogation from its rational, natural and divine origins. Plato, Aristotle and their followers held that the rational intellect had to learn to control these passions. Most Stoics, we saw, thought them a disease of the rational soul whose only cure was total rejection, an *apatheia* or utter lack of passions (Greek *pathēmata*). Taking from both, Augustine thought excess passion the devil's work, drawing the soul from its true goal of rational union with God. Ficino argued that bad passion destroyed the bonds of the world, society, the human and the divine. If diagnoses differed, consequences of yielding to the passions were the same: descent into unreason and, at worst, inhumanity, for they contradicted essential human characteristics of reason, language and sociability.

Hélisenne exemplified such failures. At first, "reason still dominated" within her and struggled with passions, but could give only a series of disastrous *exempla*: Helen and Troy's destruction; Medea, her abuse at Jason's hands and her murder of her children, "poor woman in despair"; Eurial and his wife Lucretia, who died of grief over his forced departure; Lancelot, Guinevere and King Arthur's and his knights' loss of reputation; Tristan and Iseult, their grievous harms and "damnable loves." These examples that reason offers her anyway fail when she is again attacked by "the sensual appetite," which assures her that her love is all right provided it is hidden "in her heart" (AD103–5; TL11–12). Christine de Buzon notes that this chain of women's names, capitalized in the text, builds the narrator/author's name: the first, *HE-LENE*, and first syllable of the last, *YSEUL*, form Hélisenne; the second syllables of the series *MEDEE, LUCRESSE, GENEVRE* form de Crenne (Introduction, *Angoysses* 25). So it is no surprise if Hélisenne is proud later to equate herself with these *exempla* or similar ones, their mythic or legendary grandeur outweighing catastrophic unreason. She thus uses them in a letter sent to her lover ostensibly to dissuade his pursuit, in fact to urge him to desire her more: "If Leda's daughter," she says of Helen, "had led a chaste life," Troy would have been safe; if Dido had been faithful, her reputation would have (AD132–33; TL26). These cases mean what they did, but their aim is reversed: Hélisenne uses them to urge Guenelic that she become like them. Indeed, Buzon adds (Introduction 22), the name Hélisenne transposes others of these *exempla*: Helen and Elissa, Dido's other name (linked in the letter just mentioned), Iseult and Polixena (Polisenne), Pyrrhus' victim after the fall of

Troy, sacrificed as Hélisenne may be, she thinks, after conversation with her lover becomes too open (AD170; TL47).

Even when she seems to lean momentarily in an opposite direction, she imagines herself as a sequence of such *exempla*, becoming one of their company: begging the Furies to give her a sword such as Ovid's Aeolus gave his daughter Canache with which to kill herself for her criminal love (*Heroides* 11); enable her to jump to her death like Isiphile (*Heroides* 6; Boccaccio, *De mulieribus* ch.16), let her swallow poison like Socrates, hang herself like Phyllis from despair at her lover's absence (*Heroides* 2), or, failing her own active intervention, be bitten by a snake like Hesperia (*Metamorphoses* 11, ll.749–95; Lemaire, *Illustrations* II.9) or swallowed by the earth like Dathan and Abiram in Numbers 16.1–35 (AD140–41; TL30–31). But she soon reverts to her earlier proposals, that lovers with minds far more sublime than hers were unable to resist love's passions: David who murdered to "enjoy Bathsheba," wise Solomon who "was an idolater in love," Aristotle who madly loved his "Remya" (after a medieval tradition about one Hermia), Hercules who dressed as a woman for his beloved Iole (i.e., Omphale) and many more (AD150; TL36). The monk to whom she offers this list counters with another: Penelope's continence and fidelity in waiting for Ulysses; Oenone's fidelity to Paris after he had left her for Helen; Roman Lucretia's chastity in killing herself for honor after Tarquin's rape (AD154; TL38–39). The last two of these, at least, are curious *exempla* for him to offer, since Oenone let Paris die by refusing to heal his wounds, while Hélisenne has already failed in the suicide stakes—which is why she is talking to the monk in the first place. Indeed, Hélisenne later takes the cases of Penelope, Lucretia and Oenone to assert just how powerful is her love's effect on her (AD175, 198; TL49, 61).

All these *exempla*, in fact, emphasize the effects of passion on reason and the soul, in the single case of Penelope perhaps to be admired, but in every case as unresistingly received by the lover and as overwhelming of reason as it is in Hélisenne's. One becomes in the strongest etymological sense, as Hélisenne remarks, "pediseque et subjecte" (AD203; TL63), slave and subjected *to* the passions. The ancient cases and that of the story's narrator become parallel *exempla* of the same force of the passions and the same passible human nature. So she shows in the cases just mentioned and, near the end of the novel's Part 1, first by a series of ancients who managed to kill themselves, of whom she has therefore fallen short (AD207; TL65), then by four other cases from antiquity, three of them new: "Porcia for Brutus, Cornelia for Pompey, Laodamia for Protesilaus" and, again, Dido for Aeneas. This time, all their suffering together, she protests, falls short of hers (AD212–13; TL68).

For her, too, the passions are a disease. Thus her husband did not realize that: "my illness was incurable" (AD145; TL33). No medicines help: "because I was as much tortured by the passions of the soul as by corporeal illness" (AD196; TL60). They are a disease caused by affects acting virtually as external instruments imposed, or imposing themselves, on the person who suffers them. But whether overturning reason as an external imposition or destroying it as an internal canker, the passions are anyway ruinous of one's humanity:

Love is nothing but an oblivion of reason, and is unfitting for a prudent person since it disturbs the judgment and breaks elevated and generous souls [*esperitz*]; it weakens all strength; it makes the person sad, angry, prodigal, bold, proud, harmful, forgetful of God, of the world and of one's selfe [*soymesmes*]. And in the end it keeps them in misery, distress, languor, martyrdom and inhuman affliction, and most often leads them to a cruel death through despair worthy of damnation. (AD203; TL63)

In Part 2, Quezinstra repeats this assertion as warning to Guenelic: "this sensual appetite is an incurable infirmity from which arise forgetfulness of God and one's selfe [*soymesmes*], loss of time, diminution of honor, harsh conflicts, rivalries, jealousies, denigrations, exiles, murders, the body's destruction and the soul's damnation" (AD241; TL83).

Under passions' dominance, says an old woman to Hélisenne at the end of Part 1, "madness dominates reason" (AD215; TL70). Shaking reason's foundations causes other momentous harms and breaches the virtues. When Hélisenne's passion makes her tell Guenelic an obvious lie, he is amazed, believing: "that love's impetuousness had broken in me the bonds of temperance and moderation" (AD128; TL24), chief virtues, Cicero had held in the *De officiis*, of social life, without which society could not subsist, a point Ficino echoed and expanded in his *Symposium* commentary. But it was no less the case that outside society humans were, quite simply, not humans. That was why, in the longer passage just cited, Hélisenne wrote that the *prudent* person rejects passion, prudence being the supreme Ciceronian (and Aristotelian) virtue of human life in society. Their supporting reason gone, loss of such virtues was another mark of a breakdown of community—and of humanity.

The sufferer shows these losses in the very body, echoing physiologically the intemperance and disharmony that breaks social, human and, we shall see, divine bonds:

I rose like a madwoman, and without managing to say the first word to answer him [her husband], I began to tear my hair and rip and bloody my face with my nails, and with my piercing feminine cry pierced the hearers' ears. When I could speak, like a woman completely estranged from reason I said to him . . . (AD118; TL18)

Examples are many. Always this madness has external signs of loss of control and so of humanity—like Seneca's exploration of anger's effects.

In this instance, privation of reason and physical symptoms of the passions causing it come together. The case is constant, whether Hélisenne is overcome by her love or her husband's interruption: "And then just like the sea's waves agitated by a wind, I began again to move and tremble all over, and for a long time was speechless" (AD169; TL46).

Shaking, changing color, fainting, weeping, heart palpitations, collapses characterize Hélisenne. They are physiological symptoms of yielding to passions. A person's physical presence in the material world also changes in ways marking a loss in what one may call a strength of being human, in the stable security of physical relation with, in and of the material world. Her husband upbraids Hélisenne, and:

> my amorous heart was throbbing in my breast, changing color, I right away became pale and cold; then afterwards a vehement heat drove the pale color from me and I became hot and scarlet, and was compelled to withdraw because of the rush of sighs by which I was agitated, and showed it by clear signs, outward gestures and spasmodic movements. And when I wanted to say something by way of complaints and outcries, the extreme distress of my hurt interrupted my voice, I lost appetite for eating, and sleeping was impossible for me. (AD107; TL13)

As the description acutely indicates, symptoms of the singular instance are those of Hélisenne's life in general. Her misguided love has unlocked her from the world and set her amiss. The reason is clear, as Quezinstra explains later to Guenelic after upbraiding him as nearly blasphemous for believing that the stars rule humans' lives—a view rejected by quoting Augustine. But if, he adds:

> one means to say that humans' manners are dispositionally and contingently varied according to the disposition of the stars, that may be true and not at all opposed to faith or reason; for it is manifest that the diverse disposition of the body has much to do with the variation and mutation of the affections of morals and temperaments, as the author of the six principles says. Thus cholerics are naturally inclined and prompt to anger; the sanguine are kindly; melancholics are miserable; phegmatics lazy. But this is not at all inevitable, since the mind has control over the body, when it is helped by grace: so we see many cholerics who are sweet and amiable, and many melancholics who are kindly. Because the power of celestial bodies works on and has some causal role in the composition and quality of temperaments, it follows that it can have some small dispositional and contingent effect on human manners and conditions, however much more the power of inferior nature does for the quality of temperament than the power of the stars does. (AD479–80; TL190)

Just as passions disconnect the soul from reason and its proper relation with things spiritual, so they rupture the body's stable relation with the physical world of which it is a literal part, and so split it from its

proper relation with things material. One's own physical and personal being are not all that change. So inevitably do relations *between* people.
Loss of reason is also loss of public virtue. Others, from antiquity forward, had said this. So does Hélisenne: "O Guenelic, excessive passions
most often win out over virtue" (AD194; TL59). Of course, he had long
since been shocked by her demonstration of this in her intemperate lie
about her husband's ignorance of their relationship.

The overthrow of interpersonal relations and destruction of society
and virtuous human bonds are both caused and symbolized by Hélisenne's new readiness to lie to her husband: "I quickly invented a clever
lie" (AD106; TL12). Or she would try to calm him by "pretending to be
grievously affected by illness" (120; 19), or by "pretending to wish to be
reformed" (145; 33). This soon reaches a paroxysm when she admits, on
being made to go to confession, that she can do nothing but "pretend
and feign things" (145; 34). Finally it becomes constant habit when
woken in the night by amorous fears and terrors, for instance, quickly to
find a clever lie, "artificiele mensonge" (190; 57). She also now lies to
herself, convincing herself, for example (more than once), that: "my husband does not suspect me at all" (109; 14). She again tells Guenelic that
her husband "has neither doubt nor suspicion of me" (169; 46), although it had so surprised him earlier as to make him think love had destroyed her "temperance and moderation" (128; 24). She repeats the lie
to him even after being drastically beaten by her husband for the very
thing she still denies (174; 49). Continual lying, she allows, does change
her personality: "I had become bold and audacious [*hardye et auda-
cieuse*], and until that time had been shy" (114; 16). This *bad* audacity
matches her *in*temperance in passion, *in*justice toward her husband and
*im*prudence in social relations, the fourth virtue of *fortitudo* also made
dissolute.

One could call the ploy of using the *exempla* of Helen and Dido, ostensibly to put off Guenelic but in fact to heighten his desire, another way
of lying to her lover, sign of just how bold and audacious she has become.
This teasing ruse is one of which she does not tire, using it again after he
has a second time expressed his love, this time not in a letter but face to
face: "I did not wish to declare my heart's secret to him, not to banish or
drive him away but to inflame him to greater ardor" (AD167–68; TL45).
Her husband, too, notes the change in her character and its cause. Catching Hélisenne with a love letter and her reply, he tells her not to give him:
"a clever lie (such as you now know how to use)" (136; 28). Concerned,
too, as she has been for her "good reputation" (116; 17), she becomes
ever less so, more frustrated and impatient, bolder and willing to flout
conventions needed for the safeguard and welfare of social order. Héli-

senne's increasingly constant lying signals growing tension between a demand to act *on her own behalf* and the experience of being part of communities: a point which will return.

We have seen reputation and esteem as essential signs of a stable society, where a person's relation to other people defines at once who she and they are and the community as a whole. As Hélisenne's personality changes, therefore, so do those of people around her. The faithful servant who gives wise counsel to the household early in the novel's first part becomes the treacherous one who, by relaying Hélisenne's continuing amorous suffering to her husband, causes the final rupture. Through most of the first part, Hélisenne portrays her husband as loving and thoughtful despite one explosion of anger. Later, not only does he give her a beating so violent that the servants have to intervene (AD171; TL47), but gives way to sadistic fantasies reminiscent of Peter Greenaway:

I want to catch him in my woods, then I'd right away get cruel revenge by making him suffer great and innumerable torments. Then, after my appetite was sated with torturing him, I'd make you a present of his body all broken and lacerated; and right away shut you in a tower where by force and duress I'd make you lie with him, then after make him wear out his detestable and wretched life by the most cruel and ignominious death possible for me to think up. (AD179; TL51)

If her husband is unable to catch Guenelic in his woods, he does finally shut Hélisenne in a tower.

Guenelic undergoes analogous changes of personality, accusing Hélisenne of varied nastiness, so that she finds herself complaining of his "iniquity," causing her "extreme and anguished suffering." He now uses "harsh words," creates "fresh occasions for vexation" and commits "outrageous cruelty" (AD186; TL55). This is all the worse for being a passion she must suffer: "however wicked and bad I knew him, it was not in my power [*ma faculté*] to diminish my love, for it was so strongly imprinted in my heart that continually day and night his image [*son simulachre*] represented itself in my wretched memory" (AD188; TL56). This destruction of character is such that the second part of the novel begins by trying to rectify it. Indeed, one could say that Parts 2 and 3 exist to reestablish Guenelic's virtue so that he—or his memory—can be readmitted to a community: he was not really, Hélisenne protests, of lesser estate, simply less wealthy. He was of knightly rank and, the chivalric romance seeks to show, of knightly comportment (AD229–31; TL77–78). Doing this, the argument sets him and his lady in an older dispensation, one where who they are is legitimated and valorized by the stock community of courtly knight and ideal lady. Here, in that both die, this older community fails, and will be replaced by the finding and publishing of the book itself, whose writing and reading therefore stands in for lost and broken communities—and leads directly, as the later text tells us, to *Epistres.*

But these broken social and personal relations are not the whole of the story told in *Angoysses.* Even the community of the divine is rocked. Of this, the most astonishing signal is a moment where Hélisenne, in the very process of giving a sort of confession to a monk, insists that even God could not make her "desist from love." Nor does this suffice. She moves into something like a psalm, asserting that if God can do nothing for her, yet

A single glimpse of my beloved can give me color if I am pale; if I am sad, it can cheer me; if I am weak, it can fortify me; if I am ill, it can restore my health; and if I were about to die, it easily has power to revive me. (AD149–50; TL35–36)

I am reminded of Stampa's sonnet 17 favoring her lover over God, alluded to in Chapter 12: "Io non v'invidio punto, angeli santi"— "I don't at all envy you, holy angels . . . [that] you always stand before the face of God, / For my delights are such and so abundant / They cannot be contained in human heart, / While I stand before the divine and bright lights / Of him of whom I must ever write and sing" (ll.1–8).

Later, Hélisenne will pray to God as one who can save her—from her husband and herself (AD179; TL52). Although this is a passing moment replaced before the end of her own story by more pleas to the gods of love to help her, it corresponds to what comes in Parts 2 and 3, where the quest can readily symbolize that of a more holy grail, a search to repair souls incarnate placed in jeopardy. Just so had Hélisenne, confessing her love to her husband, cried to him to take his sword to her, to make: "my soul transmigrate from this unhappy corporeal prison" (118; 18). Similarly, when a bit later she has made as if to kill herself, her husband tells her how she should beware lest: "when your soul were separated from your wretched body, a dismal dwelling-place would be assigned to it on account of the enormous and execrable sin you would have committed" (143; 32). The monk to whom she is sent to confess not unaturally repeats the view: "Have you no regard or consideration for the fact that when we have died to the world and our soul is divested of this miserable corporeal clothing, if by cupidity or wickedness it is [*elle se treuve*] fetid and stained, in perpetuity and forever a doleful dwelling-place will be assigned to it" (148; 35).

These are not just metaphors. We must take this view of the nature of being human as seriously as the author did. Hélisenne and Guenelic are jeopardizing the immortal souls in them, risking eternal separation from the divine community. Loss of reason, of the soul's intellectual function, by yielding to passion, is the earthly mark of that risk. If one cannot describe such unreason as *willed*, it being always depicted as "irresistible," it is certainly *accepted*: the victim yields wittingly, *knowing* the consequences. To do so is to move away from humanity. It is also to move from God. It does so by pressing one's *singular* right to satisfy what one is tempted to call individual desire—in the authorial Hélisenne's view—antisocial in nature and effect: in nature because loss of reason literally dehumanizes, in effect because it really breaks all communal bonds. It is to yield to the selfe-love, *philautia*, that had been "since Plato the worst of vices" (Screech ed., *Tiers livre* xv). One may not be wrong to see these passionates as Augustinian figures singularized as "selves" marked *by* the devil (Quezinstra several times cites *The City of God*: AD477–82; TL189–91) and *for* the devil, derogations from the human graced by the possibility of salvation. Another reference of *Angoysses* Part 1 may well be Augustine's *Confessions*, which Guenelic recalls on his deathbed by comparing his grief at the death of Hélisenne to that of Augustine for his mother as the saint told it there. This recall directly follows Hélisenne's last prayer to God for salvation and just precedes his own (AD468–70, 484–85; TL185–86, 192).

Angoysses contains the tale of these shattered communities—divine, social, personal (soul, mind and body) and material (stable physical body in the world). It also figures this fragmentation by its three distinct parts, told in three different voices—Hélisenne as herself, Hélisenne as Guenelic, and finally Quezinstra (again of course by Hélisenne)—and in three distinct genres or styles: sentimental fiction, chivalric romance, fantastic history. Perhaps this was again a reminiscence of Ficino's *Commentary*, where he glossed Pythagorean belief "that a trinity was the measure of everything" by saying "that God governs things in threes, and also that things themselves are defined according to a triple classification": creation, attraction and finishing (133). Hélisenne's book, Guenelic's, and finally the two chapters where Quezinstra tells their deaths echo this classification. (It may further echo in another triple telling of the story: *Angoysses, Epistres* and *Songe*—although we saw that this had precedents.) For one can say that *Angoysses contains* this shattering in another sense: keeping it in bounds. The writing itself—the *fact* of writing, of addressing an audience and entering a dialogue with it—tries to *show* and *make* a reintegration of the person into spheres of community. The book (found next to Hélisenne's dead body) becomes the end of the tale, by its printing and circulation in and from the learned city of Paris. The community it will create is preceded by the reconstruction of other broken bonds: Mercury anoints Hélisenne's and Guenelic's "noble bodies so as to preserve them from corruption" (AD489; TL194); the two have already confessed their sins and prayed for salvation; both have reset their bodies, souls and minds. Their souls are sent together to the Elysian Fields, their bodies buried with due ceremony by Mercury and Quezinstra (494, 497; 196, 197). The social remains, whose repair Quezinstra starts by publishing this book, keeping his oath to the dead that their memory be preserved and his duty to the living to show them not to let passions dominate reason (506; 201).

Epistres is something like the opposite of this: leading toward the possibility of a different sense of personal being and so of a different community. It goes from *ars dictaminis* to willful self-expression and rejection of the other, or, at least, of an- and some others (via the letter written in her husband's name that lets Hélisenne later establish her *persona* as aggressive intellectual respondent, speaking in her own name and that of women more generally). Now, it is told in letters as a direct expression of the person who forges the space: "De Crenne" is a kind of editor of "Hélisenne"'s letters, though she also *is* Hélisenne (and signs three of the letters). Too, starting where *Angoysses* stops, appealing to Plato and praying to God, she stresses a nostalgic community bound in love and friendship whose reestablishment was proposed by the manner of Hélisenne's and Guenelic's deaths, burial and redemption and by the book's publication. In a passing adverbial phrase, "*à bonne raison*," which should be given full weight, de Crenne stresses, too, that this community accords with reason—at any rate with a certain reason:

[I] shall follow [*ymiteray*] divine Plato's advice. When he tells in his *Timaeus* that in all our works we must implore divine help, he says so with good reason [*à bonne raison*]. For without God's favor it would not be in human power [*faculté*] to finish any useful thing. So, calling on this divine clemency, I beseech him to make me worthy of his help. (EFI61–62; *A Renaissance* 37: henceforth PIL, with translations often changed)

Epistres as a whole moves away from the nostalgic communities this opening reflects, in a movement that picks up pace. It is noteworthy that the final invective letter assaults, precisely, a whole community, a "little town" that she accuses of having mistreated her lover and his friend. Further, this letter closes with Hélisenne's demand, addressed presumably to her (ex-?) husband, that he pass on to his "companions" and co-citizens her wish that "what befell Dathan and Abiram may befall them" (EFI161; PIL107), and they be swallowed in the earth. If we recall that in *Angoysses* Hélisenne hoped rather that their fate would befall her, and if we take full note that this is the final word of *Epistres*, we begin to measure the distance between *Angoysses* and *Epistres*, between the start and end of *Epistres* and above all between who Hélisenne is at the start and end of this transformation.

We have already seen who she is in respect of the nostalgic community—communities—recalled at the work's outset. The job now is to follow her toward something apparently quite different, perhaps new. This is not to set "community" against "individuality." It is not to forget that letter-writing itself implied a community of "correspondents" and a wide "social context" (Wood 143–44). It is the case that by their very nature, letters seem to forge a dialogue and make communities. But I say, "seem to," because I shall suggest that *Epistres invectives* seeks to make a quite other "dialogue" from that of the *familieres*. To note the difference is to foresee the possibility of a different kind of community: one where the person is not made by context, but claims the right to define and make herself as free woman and erudite and authoritative writer. Not for nothing, I shall emphasize, will her dominant passion no longer be that of love, but of anger.

Still, *Epistres* initially picks up on the rational communities indicated in Hélisenne's overall opening address to the reader. I suggested that *Epistres* begins more or less as an *ars dictaminis*, a work offering its letters as a collection showing its readers how to write the correct sort of epistle for diverse occasions. These showed how letter writing depended not only on matter and purpose, but on who the recipient was, who the writer, what their respective ranks, their relationship and so on. The aim was to provide a tool showing people how and enabling them to establish, function in and maintain firm and stable social relations. The *artes dictaminis* were also, that is to say, an education in civil association. I shall suggest that *Epistres* presupposes this. Implicitly, too (all critics observe), the *familieres* appeal to Cicero's *Epistolae ad familiares* and its many avatars, including Petrarch's *Rerum familiarum libri* and maybe the exchange between Abelard and Héloïse, whose first letter was offered as a consolation from Abelard to a friend, but which, in its entirety, was a renowned model for epistolary exchange between lovers, subversive of social norms. Further noteworthy, as Wood observes, is that the first eight familiar letters all dwelt on communities: convent, court and, most notably, family and friendship.

Hélisenne's first letter laments and apologizes for her inability to remain in a convent where she has recently stayed, writing in glowing terms of its virtuous life and recalling the divine sustenance whose loss and regaining was one of the themes of *Angoysses*, and to which she had appealed at the end of her address to the reader just preceding this first *Epistre familiere*. Thinking on the discretion and wise virtue of the nuns and abbess, she regrets her departure with particular bitterness:

in feeling myself deprived of the very great happiness that was given me by watching your holy way of life: the good examples, assiduous worship of God, frequent abstinences, virginal continence, sober words, averted look, constant solitary life, well-ordered hours, widespread charity, together with contempt for the world, rigorous penance, extreme diligence in devout prayers, and sovereign patience exhibited in all things. (EFI64; PIL39)

Here she names all the things that she will quit with a vengeance as the letters progress. Readers who already knew the *Angoysses* (as would all readers of editions from 1543 on, since *Angoysses, Epistres* and *Songe* were henceforth bound together) would readily see in this regret preparation for the counter story to come. Its opposition of a life in the world and a life in God, though, does not yet suggest loss of ideal community— since, as we know from Augustine and others, there could be a bad and a good life in the world, a Babylonian and a Roman. What we do see in the course of the *familieres*, I suggest, is a move from the divine (in this letter), to Rome and finally to Babylon. What follows in the *invectives* is a move to a quite other sense of the possibilities of worldly community.

At present, Hélisenne explains that she would have pledged herself to the convent and religious life: "had I not been pushed by filial obedience into my forced and involuntary return" (EFI64; PIL40). Given her later choices, I see this as refusal of one sort of traditional passible community. Electa Arenal holds the later, seventeenth-century, convent a site where women joined "utter humility and determined self-assertion" with "competitiveness" (traits ascribed to Teresa of Avila in the sixteenth century before Isabel de Jesús in the seventeenth) ("Convent" 152). But however one takes, with Arenal, the even later Sor Juana de la Cruz, it is far from clear that when Isabel claimed to equal Teresa she was doing other than inscribe herself in an *imitatio*, figuration of a collective institution—as Fernández observes for "the entire canon" of early modern Spanish writings of this sort (*Apology* 11). This seems clearer yet in the sixteenth- and even seventeenth-century Spanish, New Spanish and Peruvian lives and works Arenal and Stacey Schlau offer in *Untold Sisters*. Theresa Lamy has shown how such inscription is a good way to read the prodigious Juliana Morell's early seventeenth-century auto-presentation. Writing a *selfe* no doubt bore different weight for women than men (as it surely did for Hroswitha or Hildegard). It did not infer autonomy in any modern western sense. To quit the secular sphere (whether for a female or a male space) did not imply change in the experience of what it was to be a person. Hélisenne refused adherence to a convent whose passible order she describes with care. She and others will make a space for a potentially quite different experience.

Hélisenne's second letter thanks a relative for a letter and, apologizing for being unable to visit, explains her "forced" return and inability to leave as due to her old mother's dangerous illness (EFI68; PIL41). Filial duty binds her to care for her. She applauds her relative for having affianced her daughter to "a rich, young, wise, handsome and virtuous nobleman" (67; 41), and on the fact that her "son's faithful spouse is pregnant, and expects to be delivered of her desired offspring about the time of the wedding ceremony" (69; 42). These opening letters concern family life, good love, legitimate sexual relations and continuity of the familial communities they enable and represent. The third letter goes on in like vein, consoling a cousin whose chastity and integrity have been slandered, recalling "chaste Suzanna" whose purity and patience soon showed her innocence.

Such slander forecasts what will happen to Hélisenne herself, although the victim here indeed seems innocent. The move from legitimate to illegitimate sexual relations matters. Although in this case the accusations are false—at least, Hélisenne takes for granted that they are—they foretell a slide from good to bad love, even as they tie into the fourth letter's preoccupations, commiserating with a friend banished from court also because of slander. She again advises patience, urging that sureties of a good community will ultimately defeat calumny. By now, though, as we move into a world increasingly characterized by slander, potential disgrace, exile and the vicissitudes of sexual love, we are prepared for the fifth letter, addressed to a particularly close friend, Galasie, in which Hélisenne rails against the "illicit love" by which she is "overcome" (*atteincte*) (the published English translation, "she is having an illicit love affair," entirely loses the possible character: EFI 80; PIL48).

Hélisenne still forcefully backs the collective status quo. One must avoid "suffering a vehement passion in the soul, which comes from love." "Love is a dream full of error, madness, temerity and selfishness. It ultimately leads its followers to such extreme misery that their pains are found almost intolerable. Certainly anyone who feels herself intoxicated by this poisonous evil is deprived of rest" (EFI79; PIL48). But her vehemence on behalf of custom grows ambivalent. She goes on to list men who have betrayed their illicit lovers, as is usual, she says, for such "false, faithless and lecherous" men (80; 49). Thinking on such things, she writes, one should have little faith in this "deceitful and fraudulent male sex" (81; 50). So women must take the same control over themselves as men claim:

For a person does whatever she intends, our soul being nothing but a mere potentiality, with which we do as with a wax image that we can augment or diminish according to our free will, and with such ease that the soul grieves over what it can as well rejoice over: our life is nothing but a will; and where it leads, the soul will follow. (82; 50)

This willfulness appears to offer something unfamiliar. The aim, it seemed, as in the earlier letters, was to help the victim of passion, whether sorrow, fear or love, defeat and reject it. Now doubts enter.

Nonetheless, the sixth letter seems to maintain the more familiar condition, save only, perhaps, that here—as in the next letter—she aggressively consoles a male friend while criticizing his lapses. She consoles Meliadus on his loss of wealth, whose effect on him astounds her, for his upset has divided his virtuous soul: "in your person there no longer lives that virtue which I earlier thought was to make a perpetual home in you" (EFI83; PIL51). She writes that he has reached the age of which Plato said that as the eyes of the body grow dim, so those of the soul grow bright (86; 53). As the soul's ties with the body weaken so it should detach itself from the worldly things represented by his wealth, whose loss should therefore not only not bother his soul, but prepare it for higher things. The same point is made in the seventh letter, in which she consoles her friend Guisnor on the death of his wife, whose soul, she writes "is now in great joy . . . since it has left the prison of the human body and is unburdened of its frail mortal members" (90; 55). Her eighth letter closes this appeal to older communities by calling on her friend Clarice to reject a love that contradicts her father's wishes. This circles back to the familial concerns of the second and immediately subsequent letters.

These letters all suppose the desirability of an older familiarity of whoness, one fitted in divine (via appeals to God as well as Plato) and human (family, court, convent) communities, in relations of subordination that are often spelled out: daughter to mother, courtier to prince, daughter to father. At the same time, threats of slander, exile, disgrace and illicit love destabilize these communities. In the eighth letter, this is manifest in the very ambiguity of Hélisenne's advice that Clarice break off a love affair which her father reproves. She should follow "Helisa . . . subsequently called Dido, which from the Phoenician language is translated as meaning 'Virago, exercising manly deeds'." This is the Dido who, in the *Aeneid* and *Heroides*, built Carthage after her husband's death, as Hélisenne emphasizes (EFI95; PIL59). Nash sees in this passage an image central to what he calls Hélisenne's forceful self-image and strong feminism ("Renaissance" 393–94). But what she does not say here is that Dido was better known for her suicide after Aeneas' abandonment. In *Angoysses*, Hélisenne twice listed her among deserted women suicides, like those used again as examples in Hélisenne's fifth familiar letter dissuading Galasie from her illicit love. This ambiguity as to what exactly Dido figures prepares us directly for the last five letters of the *familieres* and the descent into Babylon: Hélisenne's own seizure by mad love.

For in the ninth letter, Hélisenne tells Clarice to pretend indifference to her lover so as to fool her father. She approves her friend's pretense that her love is not for a man but for Christ, and of her opposing her father's objections that she can take no vows without his permission by appealing to her right to seek her immortal soul's salvation. In this way, she agrees, Clarice can avoid a marriage she abhors and give her lover time to show her father the truth and depth of his affection. It may be, she adds, "that Fortune, tired of persecuting you, will now favor you; and if, despite your view, she smiles on you, beware lest through intemperate joy you give sign of this love, which you have so far hidden with sense, patience and discretion" (EFI98; PIL60–61). We shall see more of this Fortune. Suffice it to say, here, that the virtues of the holy life, advanced in the first letter, have become "virtues" of a quite different sort. Patience and discretion are now deceits easing illicit love, ways of manipulating socially and familially accepted behavior. This insistence on pretense and dissembling suggests that Hélisenne has already yielded to the illicit love that she announces to her old friend Galasie in the tenth familiar letter, expressing her determination to fulfil it.

But, she laments to Galasie in her next letter, Fortune opposes her love (EFI103; PIL64): "since the last letter which was sent from me to you, I have been so viciously attacked by false reports that, unable to tolerate such persecution, I have fallen into such extreme bodily infirmity that I was hoping for nothing but to visit the dark kingdom whose gate the triple-headed dog guards" (103–4; 65). The remark reverses all her earlier advice to others, both on mad love and on countering slander. Too, she writes, her lover's departure from the city and apparent betrayal add to her misery, although they do offer occasion to try out an aspect of her earlier advice by recalling that "by long tradition, mutability and fickleness are held natural attributes of men." Far from strengthening her will, the thought further confounds her (106; 66). She has truly left Rome for Babylon, although her miseries are not yet at an end: her twelfth letter, addressed to Quezinstra, tells that her husband has placed her in "captivity." All she can do is beg her friend to intercede: "not to discontinue remonstrating with my husband, so that by the elegant artifice of your honeyed words he begins to know how very wrong he is to find means to torture and afflict me" (111; 69). As Georgina Dopico Black observes, confinement in the husband's home was in fact "idealized in the conduct literature." Of her Spanish case, Dopico Black notes the common word-play to the effect that the perfect married woman, *La perfecta casada*, as Fray Luis de León titled his 1583 best-selling work, was so "by virtue of being perfectly housed or encased (*casa-da*)" (19). Hélisenne's imprisonment by her husband may be an extreme, but in tale and drama not unusual, case, as instances of such confinement attest from Cervantes' "El celoso extremeño" (to say nothing of the *Roman de la rose*) to Molière's *École des femmes*. But Hélisenne's reaction to it and to what she perceives as her lover's abuse is new and important.

The thirteenth and last familiar letter she now writes at the request of a friend who wants to give news of her to a companion of his. He has asked her to write in code, so that only his companion will be able to understand its meaning. The reader of *Angoysses* will recognize these two as Quezinstra and Guenelic, although except in the previous letter's heading neither of them is anywhere named in the *familieres*. Hélisenne writes a letter in which she adopts something like the *persona* of the Rose from the earlier *Roman*. She asserts that she is not at all "blinded by passion" into believing bad things about her beloved. On the contrary: "I am even more eager to yield up to you the castle besieged by you than you are to possess it" (EFI113; PIL70). She pursues this conceit of the besieged castle throughout the letter, telling its recipient at one point that he should pretend to raise his siege, but only so as to renew the assault with fresh vigor, and perhaps fresh success, having lulled its defenders by such dissimulation and deceit, just as Caesar did, showing "himself always desirous of peace and rest" while always "very carefully considering military affairs . . . : nothing deceives another more than dissimulation." Again she gives advice exactly opposite that she gave earlier. Here again, she rejoices in her ability to lie to her guardian "avec face hardie," with a bold face, explaining how she managed to convince him that no "theft of his castle" was intended (118; 73–74). As in *Angoysses*, she becomes expert in lies and deceit.

If we understand this as fundamentally undermining—besieging—established communities, then she is directly opposing the warnings that flowed from writers like Vives, Melanchthon and Montaigne, that one shun all things "monstrous," all things that oppose, precisely, familiar communities. Here a place, at least, is being made for demands of a different notion of agency, one *separating* itself from these *familiar* collectivities. Other things, as well, happen in this last letter. Adopting the *Roman de la rose* as an allegory of her condition, Hélisenne not only forecasts her own *Songe*, but takes a distance from her condition. She turns her own story into such an allegory, preparing us for the claim in her first *invective*, written to her husband, that *Angoysses*, which he had been persuaded by her detractors to believe was written "to immortalize an unchaste love" had been written "only to avoid idleness," that is to say, as a "fiction" (EFI126; PIL81). Saying this, she declares her husband to be a *bad* reader—unlike her and the women readers to whom she appeals. To assert the story as a fiction is to assert her status as woman of letters, imaginative writer and public intellectual. Too, composing this let-

ter as allegory, she distances herself from her love, justifying her remark
to its addressee that she is *not* blinded by it. Distance lets her rationalize
her love and make it *reasonable*. Certainly, she ends this last familiar letter by saying that she would write more were it not that "the passions of
the soul along with infirmity of body" forced her to close (120; 75). But
we immediately have to ask *what* passions.

For the dominant passion of the *invectives* is no longer love, which,
even debased, could yet potentially be a version of the supreme social passion. The dominant passion becomes anger, reversing Seneca's strictures.
He held, we saw, that anger destroyed your humanity, reduced you to
madness and cut you from the community. The view was general in antiquity, as Montaigne was to write in his essay on anger (2.31), forty
years after Hélisenne, agreeing with the tradition. Anger was one of the
deadly sins, shown in painting and sculpture through the middle ages as
a woman (*Ira*) "so full of her own wrath that she was doomed to turn it
against herself in suicide," literalizing Seneca's condemnation and often
picturing his description (Rosenwein 3–4; cf. Little 14–27). Bad love
could be equally destructive. The difference is that in Seneca anger could
do no other. Lester Little does record a Christian tradition of anger as "a
righteous zeal that could marshal passion and thus focus energy to fight
constructively against evil" (12), a tradition Richard Barton finds echoed
in feudal habit (155). Such zeal ultimately supported good (Christian)
love, itself unambiguous in opposing destructiveness and grounding good
collective relations. So, in *Angoysses*, Hélisenne constantly regrets the
personal, familial, social and religious destructiveness of bad love. In the
invectives bad love is abated. If not quite gone, it certainly fades in pas-
sional importance. Good love disappears altogether. Anger becomes a
way for the woman protagonist to assert herself *in* society, to forge a different social *persona*, one marked above all by aggressive assertiveness. In
this it differs from Seneca's, because Hélisenne's anger can be controlled
and turned to useful ends.

Fifty years on, Sabuco would write in the "coloquio de el conocimiento de si mismo," opening her *Nueva filosofía* by exploring "the affections, and passions of the soul," that "the affection of anger and grief"
was the first passion. At least it did most harm (*daño*), product of all passions. Did this also reflect a woman's frustration, validated by countless
claims that Sabuco's father must have written her work, a woman unable
to? The source of Sabuco's anger would be like that of Hélisenne's or
Stampa's: beyond social and personal subjection, experience of real disenfranchisement and alienation. No man of any rank suffered this to any
such degree as did all women. Maybe this is why in other treatises on the
passions (by men), the first two passions were always love and its oppo-

site, hate—although, studying the passions in the *Rhetoric*, Aristotle did discuss anger and calm before friendship (1378a31–1382a20: but he was treating the force of persuasive oratory rather than the passions *per se*). Nash says that *Epistres* used anger "actively for the purposes of 'feminist critique.'" Anger "is the first impulse of Hélisenne's art" ("Exerçant" 38, 40). It is not the first. Anger as such, the *passion* of anger, develops from the flow of *Epistres* as a whole in the book's last five invective letters. Their use of anger signals a move broader than, inclusive of, "feminist critique." Nash elides passionate anger with Hélisenne's "*fureur*," defined as "her divinely inspired *fury* or purpose" ("Fury" 211). That "fury" may be a first impulse of her art, but is quite different from her newly developed anger, whose power, especially in the last of the *invectives*, Nash rightly emphasizes (215–17).

The broader move is that this use of anger shows *the potential emergence of a new sense of identity, at the same time implying need for a new collectivity to accommodate it. Anger could replace love as the passion that best made sense of a changing experience of social identity, ultimately enabling a new conceptualization of the public sphere.* Perhaps the mystical horror, terror and fear evidenced in the writing of some religious women, as in that of Isabel de la Cruz explored by El Saffar in *Rapture Encaged*, was another face of this same coin: marking withdrawal from a social world into convent or hermitage and a sense of alienation at the very root of being.

Here, I am struck by Elizabeth Hanson's study of the effect of state inquisitions, using torture, set up in England from the early 1580s to the first years of James I's rule. The dates coincide with those of Sabuco's writing, an overlap hinting at emerging consensus, at Lezra's meaningful "events." Chiefly meant to block Catholic designs on English polity, trials victimized mostly priests and their defenders. Before detailing her argument, Hanson says in general: "The hostile discovery of another's innermost being, with its concomitant insistence on that other's secrecy, constitutes one of the most prevalent and historically specific versions of inter-subjectivity in Renaissance England" (*Discovery* 1). Hanson does not assert that a modern sense of self developed in these hostile conflicts (reflected in Hamlet's protest that the king's spy, Guildenstern, "would pluck out the heart of my mystery": III.ii.356–57). Rather did they contribute to making space for such an eventual emergence.

Of interest in this regard is the earlier state torture of Protestant Anne Askew. Hanson explains that in Askew's account of her racking, printed after she was burned for heresy in 1546, "what she calls attention to is simply her resistance to their force, not a conscience whose privacy she defends" (89). Forging herself as a New Testament *imitatio*, Gwynne

Kennedy suggests, "particulars of character or individual history largely" did not matter (*Just* 159). Elaine Beilin (29–47) sees much the same phenomenon. Did England's innovation look to enemy Spain? Dopico Black is eloquent on how inquisitional aims (with their literary echo) put hostile pressure on bodies, especially women's, Moors' and Jews'. Initially, it seemed not to engage who-ness, let alone involve anything potentially new.

Perhaps a hint of its starting to do so was why Montaigne vehemently rejected just this hostility, describing it at the end of his essay on anger as a conflict between two impassioned angers. He denied Aristotle's idea that anger could be a useful weapon: we control weapons, anger controls us (2.31.698). Montaigne may have been thinking, too, of Erasmus' constant pleas against anger: notably at the outset of *The Education of a Christian Prince* (1516), opposing it (with "ambition . . . greed, and flattery") to the wise love of the good prince for his people and country, as symbolized by "that virtuous and beautiful Shunamite, in whose embraces David, wise father of a wise son, took his sole delight" (2). Throughout the *Education*, Erasmus set anger against the good and virtuous love that should be a prince's ruling passion: mark of the "king bee" holding the swarm together, but having no sting: nature depriving him of fierce but counterproductive strength, "leaving his anger ineffective" should he feel it (29). As such he was "the heart . . . embedded in the body" (69). A prince "conquered by anger," rousing others to anger and anarchic revolt, was a tyrant (59; cf. 102, 105). Justus Lipsius, Montaigne's contemporary, trod the same line uneasily. His 1584 *De constantia* held angry violence natural to humans (e.g., *Two*, I.xv–xvi: 106–10), so in his 1589 *Politicorum libri sex*, he told princes and their counselors to avoid this passion, always "reckoned amongst the vniust causes of warre," (*Sixe*, III.vi: 49; V.iii: 129–30). Still, the angry prince would be "more honourable" in showing, than in hiding, anger (II.xvii: 39–40).

Further in the future, Descartes held anger a good passion, if properly controlled and directed. And does not a form of anger frame Hobbes' state of nature? of humans in constant mutual war? of competitive desire for "power after power"? These differed quite from the zealous anger that Little and Barton study. Stephen White, too, sees lordly feudal anger as a regular maneuver in specific power relations, part of a "stable, enduring discourse of disputing, feuding, and political competition" (142). Its effects had "normative force" and were "highly conventionalized and socially generated" moments in collective negotiation (145, 150). Barton says the same: it marked "negotiation and compromise" (162). Such anger was not grounding. All knew it as an intervention in a personal, social and political organization whose founding premises were quite other.

The anger I write of became sociopolitically and personally foundational. When the first thinkers of political contract, Michel Hurault de l'Hospital and Guillaume du Vair, called this a *lien de justice* in 1590–93, they were responding to angers of civil war in France that had reduced the land, they said, to a shambles of conflicting sovereignties. They turned not to the familiar idea of a sovereign prince but to this new one of a "judicial bond," an abstract and agreed legal union that would bring people to set aside differences and restore civil society (Reiss, *Meaning* 35, 47–51). Perhaps they were inspired by a work like the *Vindiciae*, whose authors argued that angry property disputes required recourse to one sovereign authority, while preservation of life and liberty "against all force and injustice" needed "bounds of piety and justice" to be set (93, 149, 183). In the *Philosophical Rudiments Concerning Government and Society*, Hobbes was to say that he got the idea of a founding "covenant" from that of legal "justice" (*English Works* 2.vi; Reiss, *Meaning* 86–87). Like Hanson's hostile discovery, these angry conflicts, specified as such by writers like Hurault and du Vair, were turned to the uses and formation of a new idea of society and concomitant identity.

In her "Preambule aux Invectives," Hélisenne attacks the goddess Fortune who she had hoped might help her friend Clarice, but who harmed all: "her intolerable cruelty so angers me [*me stimule*] that she forces me (despite my nature to the contrary) to undertake Invective Letters." Her remark on her (old) contrary nature matters, as she moves to newly aggressive verbal assault: "O wicked Fortune, made goddess of this blinded world, how is it that your wheel is always turning to the benefit and advantage of others? O cruel one, don't you see how loathsome it is to remember your ways? O odious one, why don't you consider how burdensome are your variability and inconsiderateness?" (EFI123; PIL78). She continues in this vein for four pages of the original edition, preparing us for the first invective letter addressed to her husband. Here, ignoring the sorts of accommodation offered earlier, Hélisenne attacks with unwaveringly hostile anger, even while urging that he is wrong to accuse her of illicit love, mistaking her novel for autobiography. Too, she asks, claiming unchanging identity, as she had been "modest and temperate" in her youth, how could he imagine her otherwise now (126; 81)?

Since the last familiar letters showed that this was hardly true, at least when they were written, we must assume that the lies and deceit are continuing. But now, contrary to *Angoysses* and most of *Epistres*, they are not regretted, but become *anger*'s instruments. I suggested that Hélisenne's ever more incessant lying marked growing tension between a demand to act on her own behalf and the experience of being part of a community. This is now actually established. She uses lies to assert her

independent agency. To analogous purpose, she echoes her husband's remark in *Angoysses* about her actions bringing infamy on him, by stating
that his are doing so on her (EFI128; PIL83). He, she insists, is using customary social demand to make her seem guilty and keep her in subjection. Maintaining her innocence, she asserts that *had* she wished to grat-
ify her desires, she could easily have done so, nothing he could do could
have stopped her (130; 85). This aggressive claim to dissociation from his
social norms, to free agency and the force of will to effect them is new. So
are her absence of guilt about lying and fear about being discovered. The
first is a corollary of her anger, the second of her husband's being a bad
reader. Because of this, he and other men are to be excluded from her
new community.

For she next writes a letter purporting to be from her husband to her.
In this second letter, he rages at her in even stronger terms, becoming little less sadistic in his threats than he had on occasion been in *Angoysses*.
But as all critics note, he exceeds personal invective to rage in the usual
abstract misogynist terms of all anti-women writers, asserting all women
to be dissipated, libidinous and evil, and finally threatening her with
damnation of her eternal soul (EFI139; PIL91). This enables Hélisenne to
respond in kind in the third letter, at the same time showing her erudition, scholarship and ability to sustain an ordered argument. Doing so,
she further accuses him and other misogynists of misreading and misus-
ing sources. While she maintains her aggressive anger, accusing him of
deadly hatred, of now ineffective slander and madness (141; 92–93), she
takes the intellectual high road in defense of herself and all women. Rejecting his generalized obloquy made from cases of a few bad women and
observing that by this token one could scorn all men, she adds that many
men have drawn opposite conclusions from associating with good
women. In almost all cases, she says, his bad women were actually good
women, victims of men (143; 94): which casts new light on Dido as Aeneas' victim. Listing many women from the Bible and ancient sources,
she displays her erudition and strong mind in turning each of her husband's arguments against him. Forcefully taking her place in debate on
the status of women, she stakes her claim as a *good* reader in one of the
burning public issues of her time.

She continues to do so in the fourth invective letter, addressed to
Elenot, a man she accuses of attacking her scholarly and intellectual
work, but of being mad even to think of participating in literary life.
Again she angrily attacks every facet of his assault on women intellectuals and writers and, further, his very capacity for doing so. She accuses
him of foolish presumption in engaging a person and a topic equally beyond his abilities, thus accusing him, too, of being a bad reader. After list-

ing the Muses, she again lists a long sequence of learned women from the
Bible and antiquity, adding now an encomium of Marguerite de Navarre,
equated with Plato, Cato, Cicero and Socrates. After these refutations of
his general point she returns to her anger over his slander of her own
writings. "Silence" he clearly "finds difficult," she says, but he must learn
to shut his mouth because only slander and idiocy come from it
(EFI152–53; PIL101). Proud to participate on her own terms in the
learned intellectual community of Paris, she fears he can still do her
harm. He needs punishing with the "monstrous ears" that Midas was
given for his similar beastliness (154–55; 102–3). It is now her opponent
who has become "monstrous."

She thus accuses Elenot, as she had her husband, of being a *bad
reader*. Neither knows how to read her writings, or, by implication, others'. She has stepped into a new (intellectual) community, and neither of
these men, nor others like them, merit a place in it. This community is
dependent, initially at least, on aggressively defending positions, on angry
competition. People need to learn to read in new ways. Neither her husband nor Elenot have done so. This is why she has had to unloose, she
says, "the fury of my pen" (EFI155–6; PIL104). The comment prepares
for the angriest letter: a fifth and final one addressed to a whole town, accused of lying, slander, treachery, depravity and perversion of all values.
This is the anger of Achilles, destructive of communities, tabooed, feared
(Muellner) and placed under curb throughout antiquity (William Harris),
now turned to new purpose. They, too, have slandered her behavior and
writing. Worst is their leader, doubtless her husband. He has even come
to Paris to continue his treacheries against her, her writings and intellectual activities. He has failed because here is now *her* community not his.
She wishes on him the sort of masochistic punishment he had earlier
wished on her (161; 107). The letters end on this climactic note of aggressive anger. Hélisenne has affirmed her right to her community and to
fix the terms of her place in it. Whatever conservatism the genre of the
Songe may represent, one might think her translation of the first four
books of the *Aeneid* (1541) a kind of confirmation of that place.

Hélisenne (along with contemporaries like Stampa, Labé and others
who equally aggressively claimed their own "glorious" poetic communities and right to the aggression) insisted on the need for a place for emergent conceptions—and perhaps experiences—of who-ness, and offers
emergent terms for its formation and that of communities in which it
might function. Ann Jones argues in *The Currency of Eros* that sixteenth-
century women writers in France, Italy and England staked their literary
claims on an often collective creation of new women's communities,
against men's aggressive efforts to dominate and exclude them, so refus-

ing an "impure combative realm that disguises masculine callousness as duty and permits injustice to continue unchecked" (125). A difficulty with such claims is that to experience being as "collective" was normal for everyone, regardless of gender. Perhaps by the mid-1500s this experience was increasingly fraught. It was still typical. Less so is the new anger, potentially altering person and its manifold contexts. Here, as the links proposed between Hélisenne, Hurault, du Vair and Hobbes make clear, I agree with Diane Purkiss, who argues that if we recall that marriage was a central metaphor for relations between monarch and subject, "used by political theorists to explore" questions of resistance, rebellion, tyrannicide and their justifications, we can see the many "unruly wives" of Renaissance writing less as "proto-feminist" than "proto-democratic." ("Introduction" xxii). Many now make analogous points (e.g., Davis ["Women"], Jordan, Matchinske, Parker).

Of the turn of the sixteenth–seventeenth century in England, Gwynne Kennedy agrees that "the language with which women's anger is described and represented carries with it attitudes about social class relations, racial identity, and other categories of experience" (22). Women's anger was a growing focus of debate from mid-sixteenth century, taken by men to show women's weakness and by women to "contest and rewrite stereotypes in order to legitimize their anger and arguments" (31) and assert that women could "be justifiably angry at texts and writers who attack women" (50). While a work like the 1589 *Jane Anger Her Protection for Women* seems to assert a new sense of self through anger, it is uncertain whether Jane Anger was a pseudonym and whether, if so, it concealed a man or a woman. More to my purpose might be Elizabeth Cary's 1613 *The Tragedy of Miriam*, where Kennedy shows anger the dominant passion among the women principals (60–74): except that Miriam and Doris both think self-control the woman's part, while Salome, using anger effectively, is presented as evil (and see Raber, but critical comment is legion). Overall, in texts Kennedy explores, women's anger was represented "as a legitimate response" to women's domination by men (162).

The many classicizing plays on Medea, Trojan women, Hecuba and Iphigeneia, suggest, says Purkiss, how Renaissance writers found it "necessary" to portray the threatening "individual" through violence done to women (xxvii). One such play offers a useful counter example to Hélisenne's case: the English version of Euripides' *Iphigeneia* done by Jane, Lady Lumley, around 1553, where (pretended) marriage was quite literally turned into a sacrifice—as Senex observes to Agamemnon: "Thou haste prepared grevouse thinges, O kinge, for thou haste determined to sacrafice thy owne childe, under the colour of mariage" (*Three Tragedies* 12, ll.111–13: all *sic*). It did so in terms of love versus anger.

Iphigeneia was presented as to be sacrificed to the welfare of a male community, the "over a thousande shippes" and their crews whose betrayal Menelaus accused Agamemnon of preparing (14–15, ll.215–19), destroying their loving community by sparing his daughter: "If you wolde have frindes, you weare best to love them, whom you desier to helpe" (16, ll.269–70). When Menelaus changed his mind and commiserated with his brother, suggesting that he save Iphigeneia, it was Agamemnon's turn to speak of the needs of Greek solidarity, as he later did of acting "by compulsion of the hooste" (18, ll.338–65; 28, l.720). From this "companye of men," Clytemnestra was excluded (21, l.466). On their behalf Iphigeneia was to be killed. Here, anger was not Iphigeneia's but Achilles', insulted that she was brought to the army under false pretenses of marriage with him, so that her sacrifice "wolde turne to no small dishonor to" him (24, ll.571–72). The anger was also, says Iphigeneia, Clytemnestra's (30, l.795). For Iphigeneia finally agreed to be sacrificed for what she and Achilles both called "the commodite of my countrie," an idea she embroidered at length (29, l.763; 30, ll.803–10; 34, ll.928–29).

Lumley's *Iphigeneia* is a confirming counter case. In it anger was futile, neither Achilles nor Clytemnestra could save Iphigeneia, slain for the "commodite" of the country and loving community of men. Can one argue that her choice to *will* her own sacrifice was a form of agency? It was presented not at all as such, but as submission to the community's demands and needs. The play is of interest here because it, too, depicts a conflict involving personal identity and social and political welfare as between love and anger. Lumley returned to an older dispensation, with a version of the purely destructive anger that made Achilles so equivocal a hero for the Renaissance. Hélisenne, Sabuco, the well-named Jane Anger (would this were a Mary Wroth pseudonym!—unfortunately then only two years old) . . . , these and others were bringing something new to emergence.

What women did *not* have was a recognized "authorizing" *place* in the community. Earlier writers had expressed that exclusion via anger: Christine de Pisan in some parts of her 1405 *Cité des dames* or Laura Cereta writing to a correspondent in 1487 that denigration of her abilities provoked angry words "born mostly from [her] visceral parts" and freed her mind to "exercise its own powers" (Ep 56: 130). But this did not seriously rattle *who* they were, and Christine, telling in the *Chemin de longue étude* how she was led to heavenly heights by the sacred "Sybille," expresses her own fears by remarking how her guide need have none: "Je sçay bien que vous n'avez garde / De perir ycy, car passible / Corps n'avez pas [I well know that you have no worry of dying here, because you have not a passible body]" (ll.1718–20; I thank Peter Haidu for this reference). The Sybil belonged to the impassible universe. Christine was very aware of death and being passibly subject to human fear, trembling and all other affections.

In Hélisenne's case, the particular place occupied by a woman in the French sixteenth century led further: to an at least provisional creation and sense of a different kind of identity. She shows how constraints on women led to changes in the experience of who-ness that, through anger, were able to be more or less firmly articulated in ways that the men treated in the last chapters were unable to approach—from, I would say, lack of the kind of fundamental pressures suffered by someone like Hélisenne. This chapter has suggested that it may be women's experience that at least glimpsed (for the moment) a new articulation of experience that men were unable or felt no pressing need to affirm. Descartes' later close philosophical association with women would also fit such an analysis. Hélisenne forged a new identity against men's oppression, from the "advantage" (a) of not having avowed public being, (b) of thus avoiding the sources of men's sense of identity loss and (c) of having to fight back against an oppressor very specifically seen and understood. Hélisenne was fighting for a recognized place in what would be a new "authorizing" system (hence the importance of right reading), understanding that to do so meant fighting also for new sorts of community and identity to accompany it. She was unusual in glimpsing anger as *constitutive* of such new identities.

At the same time, from the man's side, it may be, anger responded to the mystery and fear of such a possible constitution. Those against whom Hélisenne rails in the last two Invective Letters are presented as uncontrollably angry against her. She asserts that this is because they do not know how to *read* her, how to understand her. The inquisitional efforts mentioned were, precisely, efforts to read the Other's body aright. In most cases, like Askew's recounting, the goal seems to have been not so much to make people say *who* they were as what they had (or had not) *done*. But, at least by the end of the sixteenth century, the greatest fear was that relations of events, acts and persons were broken, unable to be analyzed for unequivocal meaning: a same deed might be real, apparent, guessed or invented—it gave no access to *who* a person was. Cervantes' "Novela del celoso extremeño" told the story of the wealthy elderly Carrizales who shut his beautiful young wife Leonora in a house built like a prison or convent. Even so the rake Loaysa managed to get into it and Leonora's bed. As long as "the will remains free," the tale ended, no prison or penalty affected deeds or revealed their real nature or meaning (*Novelas* 2.135). Dying of "anger" and "grief" (2.130), Carrizales never knew that Leonora was as innocent as he had once thought. She had successfully fought off Loaysa, her professions of love to Carrizales were sincere, her retreat to a convent after his death confirmed both. Hélisenne's and Sabuco's anger limned a new willful position. Elenot's, Hélisenne's husband's or Carrizales' anger denoted inability to control that position, even to "read" it. The Other's opacity was becoming an anxious and angering difficulty. In Cervantes, this was simultaneous with the new sense of humans' "glassy essence" from which his Rodaja suffered and of whose ignorance in the great Shakespeare's Isabella tartly complained.

Montaigne, often seen as most dramatically creating a new sense of identity, was as much a "transitional" figure as Hélisenne. He analyzed the gap between an actual public *subject* (one subjected to a sovereign polity) and a publicly illegitimate *fantasie privée*, the *branloire perenne* that was all right in the library but if let out brought only anarchy, counterpart to Hélisenne's anger. Anger (anarchy, civil war, destruction) came from bringing the latter into the former's sphere. This "duality" was embedded in an experience of subjected person whose presence in Montaigne we saw in Chapter 13. If Hélisenne is the "personal," he is the "political," asserting that the "personal" brought into the political sphere would be disastrous, but also that the personal—as intimated by Hélisenne—exists, *if* it does, only as endless movement, unable, therefore, to offer stable foundation for any being or its experience.

CHAPTER SIXTEEN

Public Subject, Personal Passion

Montaigne

No analysis of who-ness in these years can ignore Montaigne, widely thought a paragon of something like a modern western "self, inaugurat[ing] a kind of subjectivity that outruns his age's concept of the human being"—"first, perhaps sole, practitioner in his time . . . of a *philosophie de la conscience*" (Maclean, *Montaigne* 15, 122). Still, the topic may seem so worn as makes its return superfluous. But we see, especially after Chapter 13, that we need to read Montaigne anew. Many have shown his ambiguities and antinomies. Some hold him parent of a willful "Cartesian" subject, others, sign of a time when it had yet to be composed. Disputes go on between those stressing the sentence, "Each man bears the entire form of the human condition" (3.2.782), and those favoring the remark, "I do not make the common error of judging another by what I am," with its caution: "I desire only that one judge us each in ourself, and not gauge me according to common *exempla*" (1.37.225). But these work together: "form" is soul divinely breathed into body; person results from a "marriage" between soul and particular material body (2.17.622–23). I shall not dwell on ambiguity and paradox, which seem predicated anachronistically on the putative existence of a modern western self, nor summarize the library of writings on Montaigne. I shall try to set him in the history recorded in earlier chapters and in his own sociocultural environment.

Montaigne used "subject" in two ways. One named the "public" person, *subject* to a sovereign authority. The other named the matter of his book (not to be elided with himself as one of its "subjects") or the worldly matter that passibly *subjected* one's *fantasie*: "the senses do not understand the foreign subject but only their own passions; so that *fantasie* and appearance are not of the subject but only of the sense's passion and feeling [*souffrance*]" (2.12.585). He never used "subject" to mean the consciousness that appeared in efforts to seize thought in process: "I do not picture being [*l'estre*]. I picture becoming [*le passage*]" (3.2.782). Montaigne called this unstable subject-matter *fantasie privée*. The terms were exact. *Fantasie* transcribed into the vernacular Aristotelian *phantasia*, that part of the mind where *phantasmata* were constituted, bridge between world and mind, crossroads where sense impressions and reason met, *subjected* to the "passion et souffrance" impressed by matter. *Fantasie* named a movement of literally impassioned thinking, separate from the public sphere and, indeed, a danger to it. This moving *fantasie* no longer named exactly Aristotle's mental site of sense images but nor did it name modern imagination, cognition or judgment. Nearer the older meaning, it named the arena of Shakespeare's "shaping fantasies" of thought which "informed"—*gave form to*—reason's productions: giving reason's creations "a local habitation and a name" (*Midsummer Night's Dream* V.i.5–17). Ian Maclean observes that Montaigne typically used "form" in an Aristotelian or quasi-Aristotelian sense (*Montaigne* 37). It was *privée* because while the images were common, the informing and reason were in a person's mind and had nothing to do with the demands of the public sphere. As *privées*, they were form*less* as far as the public sphere was concerned.

For *privée* had no modern sense either. It meant "not public." Sixteenth- and early seventeenth-century dictionaries still defined *priuatus*, its cognates and vernacular transcriptions as meaning a person without public office and duty or a condition answering no public need or demand. This was pretty much Justinian's meaning. Even had Montaigne not been a trained lawyer, *parlementaire* and thrice mayor of Bordeaux (juridical posts), this was still the one sense he could give the word *privé*. It was defined in contradistinction to the formal public sphere, not in affirmation of any empowered "self-contained" subjectivity. That it could be defined only against the public sphere was why *fantasie privée* imperiled that sphere. Its "unpublic" nature made it liable to escape its rule. Just as activities identified as *priuata* in Justinian were *public*, or not private in any modern western sense, and *subject* to control by the public sphere—which is what any legal code is about—so motions of the *fantasie privée*, as they were subject to the senses and external provocation, had also to be subject to rule of public needs, duties and obligations. In practice this meant severing such motions from the public sphere. Anything else would lead, and had led historically, Montaigne reiterated, to anarchy.

What Manfred Koelsch calls a "gedoppelte Mensch" (*Recht* 91–97) was not unique to Montaigne. It was key in a work like the *Vindiciae, contra tyrannos*, drawing on Roman law to separate *universi*, public representatives of civil society (*universitas*), from *singuli*, those without public duties. Working this routine distinction, Montaigne attended specially to the nature of the abstract *singulus*. As *fantasie privée* gave potential place to Hélisenne's angry *singula*, so it gave a start of existential solidity to *singulus*. His division of public subject and *fantasie privée* turned the last onto emergent paths. James I's later claim of public "absolute Prerogatiue" in the untouchable "mystery of State" and "priuate Prerogatiue" of "my priuate right, betweene me and a Subiect" (ed. McIlwain xl; "Speech in Star Chamber, 1616," ed. Sommerville 212–14, 218), enlarged the novelty of the second even as it asserted mixed titles for kingship leading to later English strife.

In Montaigne this duality *in no way* marked, in itself, any sort of opposition. Subject and *fantasie privée* were essential aspects of who-ness. That their relation had become problematic resulted from tensions and transformations we have been following. The embedded person was living a changing experience, we saw in Chapter 13, but Montaigne expressed still essentially the same sense of being. If the political subject had a "being," an essence, one might find it in the constant movement of thought constituting its "non-public" space; if this last had an "existence," it was due to its "projection" into the concrete world of the social. Montaigne was clear that any such projection required training of *habitus*. Only so could inchoate being become something else and something more. Such training was in familiar ancient terms of the mutually exchanged gaze: "Having trained myself since childhood to look at/reflect my life in others' [*à mirer ma vie dans celle d'autruy*], I have gained a studied ability at it, and, when I think of it, I let few things around me escape that serve the purpose: looks, humors, speeches" (3.13.1053). Only by such means, if at all, could *fantasie privée* be made, if not publicly serviceable, at least "unpublicly" controllable.

The terms "being"—essence—and "existence" are anachronistic in the sense I have just used them, partly because neither refers to the kind of stable entity they now name, partly because the bond between *fantasie* and subject was still informed by a sense of person constituted mutually and of many spheres of being. The dilemma Montaigne conveyed was that their glue of the soul's "consciousness" of these bonds was crumbling, its assured stability sapped by a sense of itself as a *branloire perenne*, a seesaw subject to endless motion, an *yvresse naturelle*, natural inebriation (3.2.782), barely expressible: "I picture chiefly my cogitations, a formless subject that cannot get material embodiment. I can hardly even couch it in this airy body of words" (2.6.359). Like the later James I, "René, king of Sicily" might be able to do a portrait of himself, ordinary Montaigne had no paintbrush and words failed (2.17.637; cf.

Maclean, *Montaigne* 69–70). To set unformed *fantasie privée* "against" public subject, but hold it at least subject to training in *habitus*, did offer some stability. Too, so far were they from being contradictory or in opposition that they offered a schema wholly analogous to that characterizing public sovereignty and civil society.

For Montaigne's (and others') "duality" echoed the form of "the King's double body" imaged in the phrase of succession, "The King is dead, long live the King," and elucidated by Ernst Kantorowicz. A prince's "mystical" and immortal body, guaranteeing a state's stability and permanence, contrasted with the present, particular, mortal body, subject to the laws and punctual relations of the given society and historical moment. The "mystical body" guaranteed the stability of the state's "body" and was identified with it, as the English poet Thomas Carew captured well about 1624 during James I's last illness: "Entring his royal limbs that is our head, / Through us his mystic limbs the paine is spread, / That man that doth not feel his part, hath none / In any part of his dominion" (*Poems* 35). Montaigne took the concept for granted:

We owe subjection and obedience equally to all kings, for that concerns their office; but esteem, and affection, we owe only to their virtue. Let us serve political order by suffering them patiently when they are unworthy, hiding their vices, aiding their indifferent actions with our approbation when their authority needs our support. (1.3.19)

The duality of the prince's mystical and material bodies was a long-pedigreed idea basic to a certain order of sovereignty. One could already find something like it in Seneca's *De clementia*, where Nero, as emperor, was depicted as the soul of the state, the state as his body: "tu animus reipublicae tuae es, illa corpus tuum" (I.v.1). Strengthened through the middle ages and affirmed especially in ideas of divine right at the end of the sixteenth century, the theory of the double body guaranteed the stability of one kind of social and political order—although one should speak less of theory than "mentality," for Kantorowicz finds it more in juridical, legal and polemical practice than in theoretical documents. The mystical body warranted the continuity of the *res publica*. In Montaigne, as in the *Vindiciae* and elsewhere, the idea matched that of the public subject, the *universus*, servant and guarantor of established political order, maintained by legitimate authority and guaranteed by God through the prince's mystical body. But the prince, a living being, had a physical body that moved, changed, died. Here was the "perennial seesaw" (3.2.782) describing everything in this lower world and, above all, the private, singular person: "seeing that the merest pinprick and passion of the soul is enough to take away the pleasure of being monarch of the world. At the gout's first agony, in vain is one Sire and Majesty" (1.42.254). Montaigne agreed with Xenophon, whose *Hieron* had its king say that "even in the enjoyment of pleasures kings are in worse condition than private citizens [*les privés*]" (1.42.255). Kings, highest magistrates and living embodiments of the order of state, could never shed their public role.

Other magistrates could be both *singuli* and *universi*; if not at the same time. Montaigne depicted himself as having experienced this. Just as the *Vindiciae* distinguished between person as *singulus* and person as representative of the people, magistrate or *universus*—or even the *fidelis* we saw in Chapters 10 and 11—so Montaigne explained that in his role as mayor of Bordeaux he was able to free himself of the perennial movement suffered by the singular person. Elected mayor *in absentia*, he wrote:

On my arrival, I analyzed myself faithfully [*fidelement*] and conscientiously, just such as I feel myself to be: without memory, without vigilance, without experience, and without vigor; without hate as well, without ambition, without greed, and without violence; so that they should be informed and instructed as to what they were to expect of my service. (3.10.982)

Montaigne offered himself, *qua* magistrate, as a man without qualities, a person without passions, whose singularity had no role in public duties—the result of being trained to a particular *habitus*. "Messieurs de Bordeaux," the city's *jurats*, had elected him because of his *descent*, because of his father before him (3.10.982–83). He had been elected not for personal qualities but for genealogy and rank.

As an officer of state and public representative he was no more a singular person than the prince. The passions to which a *singulus* was subject had to be purged. The *universus* had to have "knowledge of causes" to "conduct [those public] affairs" of which the *singulus* had "only the suffering [*souffrance*]" (3.11.1003). Unlike the prince, though, others could withdraw from public service to become *singuli* again: "For whoever is happy to settle himself by his hearth, and can govern his household without strife and lawsuits, is as free as the Doge of Venice" (1.42.257). Like Diocletian, a prince might *want* "to retire to the pleasure of a private life" (258), but could not avoid being always present as a public person. The prince's "private" being, Montaigne wrote constantly, was secondary and had to be suppressed. It was why every advice book written for princes always had a section, often of great length, about the need for princes to control—indeed extinguish—their passions. All other members of society had a certain choice:

In truth, our laws are free enough, and the weight of sovereignty touches a French nobleman hardly twice in his life. Essential and actual subjection [*la subjection essentielle et effectuelle*] affects only those among us who agree to it [*qui s'y convient*] and who like to gain honor and wealth by such service. (257)

This idea of freedom returns us to the double subject. For here was the *social* equivalent of thought as free ongoing *process*: "Things in themselves perhaps have their own weights and measures and qualities; but inside, within us, it [the soul] allots them their qualities as it sees fit" (1.1.290). But the freedom to *withdraw* from the public sphere was only that. For if singular "freedom" intruded in the public domain, it brought confusion. A celebrated passage situates Montaigne in a whole itinerary of his age's political thought:

I have seen in Germany that Luther has left as many divisions and quarrels over the uncertainty of his opinions, and more, as he raised over holy scriptures. Our dispute is verbal. I ask what is nature, pleasure, circle, substitution. The question is over words and is paid in the same: "A stone is a body." But if you pressed: "And what is body?"—"Substance"—"And what is substance?" and so on, you would finally drive your respondent to the end of his lexicon. We swap one word for another word, often more unknown. I know better what man is than I know what is animal or mortal or rational. To satisfy one doubt, they give me three: it is the Hydra's head. (3.13.1046)

This follows a long discussion of the many interpretations of laws by jurists, and precedes an appeal to simplify these laws and eliminate learned glosses that increase "doubts and ignorance" (1044) and lead to "an irregular, perpetual motion, without model and without target" (1045). For these reasons, the very "authority" of the laws was "confused and inconstant" (1050).

Montaigne assembled here a whole set of questions: about right and law; religious opinion and so the civil wars; language and its relation to things and concepts; inconstancy; the person and what it was capable of knowing. It is useful to link these passages to another from the same 1588 edition, addressing these questions. Like the longer one above, it helps tie Montaigne to a certain theoretical "development" concerning the state and power, subject and sovereignty and my main question of the experience of the person. Here, he wrote explicitly of the civil wars, considering those who sought to "upset the state":

All sorts of new depravity joyfully draw from this first fertile source images and models to trouble our polity. People read into our very laws, made for the remedy of this first evil, apprenticeship and excuse for every kind of wicked enterprises; and what Thucydides says about the civil wars of his time is happening to us: that in favor of public vices people baptized them with new milder words, bastardizing and softening their true names. (1.23.119)

Thucydides' remarks became a cliché of political thought at the civil wars' close, notably among several writers who played major roles in public life and in what Pierre Mesnard calls "the rise of political philoso-

phy." These let us situate more easily Montaigne's considerations on subject, sovereignty, political power relations and changing experiences of
the person.

In August 1570, Louis Le Roy signed at Saint-Germain-en-Laye the
dedication to his *Exhortation aux François pour vivre en concorde, et
iouir du bien de la Paix*. He addressed it to Charles IX who, at the same
place and time, signed the pact called "The Peace of Saint Germain,"
"ending" the second war of religion. Le Roy's work stressed that single
sovereignty, concretized in the king's person, was essential to the continued existence of "all the kingdom" (2r). He set the stability inherent in
such sovereignty (an idea possibly culled from Jean Bodin's 1556 *Methodus*, but the issue was burning) against the disaster ensuing from political
sedition, chief result of the nobles' discontent (10r). This upheaval's major sign was utter disarray in the sense of language, as he showed by quoting Thucydides at length (44v–46v). The reference became a routine way
to emphasize the relation between furious political sedition, angry over-
turn of state sovereignty, inconstancy of the person and linguistic confusion.

Le Roy, in 1570, opposed unique kingly sovereignty to the reality of
sovereignty scattered by aristocratic pretensions. It was clear that the so-
called wars of religion masked a different struggle: between an old "feudal" concept of power relations and a new concept yet to be found. In the
meantime, angry confusion reigned, which all found disquieting but
which deceived few exponents: the issue, they accused, was less religion
than political and dynastic interests, whose diversity sowed confusion
over public obligation and sovereignty. It stemmed, Montaigne insisted,
from granting unwonted identity and privilege to the private person:

> Public society has no place for our thoughts; but the rest, our actions, our work,
> our wealth and our very life, must be lent and abandoned to its service and com-
> mon opinions. . . . For it is the rule of rules, and general law of laws, that each
> obey those of the place where he is. (1.23.117)

Or again, he adds, "it takes a lot of self-love and presumption to have
such esteem for one's opinions that one must overthrow public peace to
establish them and introduce so many inevitable evils" (1.23.118). To
make public acts from private thought was to "usurp the authority to
judge" (1.23.120), to usurp sovereignty. No one could *choose*, by his
own act, to convert his being as *singulus* into existence as *universus*.

The last chapter already named Hurault, whose *Second discours sur
l'Estat de France* of 1593 denounced the ambition and self-interest of the
house of Lorraine. These had, he charged, led to thirty years of war: "For
religion was not yet at stake; they took it only for want of a better pretext" (116). After a short history of the civil wars, he gave a specific ex-

ample of struggles between various interest groups to show how these angry wars played out concretely, stressing that at stake was indeed sovereignty:

Just man, if at this moment you wanted to see the image of confusion and disorder, you would find it clearly painted in that party [the *Ligue*]. To begin with the
duke of Mayenne calls himself *Lieutenant general of the Royal State and Crown
of France*. This is a great illusion: can there be a *Lieutenant*, if there is no head?
And who is head if not the king? Yet the majority of their party wants no king. *As
to the State*: formerly one heard talk of the States [*Estats*] of France, but never of
the State: or if one heard it named it was when one said, "the King and his State."
In that case the state was named in terms of obedience and not of command: and
these madmen place it at the head. (146)

Montaigne, also concerned with legitimate kingship and the subject's
relation to it and the state it embodied, voiced analogous views in a passage added after 1588, referring to Huguenot denial of obedience to the
prince after the Saint Bartholomew massacre and to League rejection of
it after Henri III's assassination and Henri IV's succession:

See the horrible impudence with which we toss divine reasons about, and how ir-
religiously we have both rejected and retaken them, according as fortune has
changed our place in these public storms. This proposition, so solemn: whether it
be permitted for a subject to rebel and take arms against his prince in defense of
religion . . . remember in whose mouths, this past year, the affirmative of this was
the buttress of one faction, the negative the buttress of which other; and now hear
from what quarter comes the voice and directive of both sides, and whether the
weapons make less din for this cause than for that. (2.12.420)

The question in debate was of rebellion and sovereignty. It was manifestly
changing the very idea of the state. This is no new finding, but it matters
that the change did not draw first on theoretical abstraction but on the
experience of actual conditions, and applied immediately to concrete life.
Doing so, it inevitably engaged the experience of who and what one was
as a person *in* that life.

According to Hurault, the Catholic League insisted that the head of
state was no more than the guardian ("lieutenant general") of *a state that
was itself sovereign*. Hurault argued that the phrase, "State of France,"
had always before signified the king's domain over which he was sovereign: an inalienable domain and "proper" characteristic of the king's immortal body. This was the meaning of the doctrine of the king's two bodies. If sovereignty became characteristic of the state itself (and so an
abstract concept, not personified by the king, which would eventually
need the doctrine of contract to explain and fix the relation of the sovereign state to its individual members), what counted was the state's immortality, not that of the king's mystical body. The consequence, wrote

Hurault, was utter confusion of a state that had no language. Since there was no sovereign prince, the officers of the ex-king no longer knew "how to pronounce, they dare not speak in the name of the King [Henri IV], they do not want to speak in the name of the people and even less in that of Monsieur de Mayenne, for by the statutes of the Kingdom they can recognize no one but he who has absolute command" (147).

One faced ultimate disorder in a "divided multitude of authorities" (147). It was the birth of anarchy, literally: loss of a single head generated limitless proliferation. Hurault complained of the creation of communes in the cities ("councils of certain persons of low degree in whose hands all authority has been placed"). This "new democracy ha[d] undermined" the principal "Royal column," which was "justice": "Following the example of the capital city of Paris, all the other cities are doing the same thing; we have a Republic in every town" (148). If events so continued, all other cities, big and small, would do the same: "And thus by degrees there will eventually be no village in France that has not made itself into a sovereign state" (149). In 1588, Montaigne saw this "novelty" as disastrous: "The bond and weave [*contexture*] of this monarchy and great ship [*bastiment*] having been disjointed and dissolved, especially in its old age, by [such novelty] gives unlimited opening and access to such harm" (1.23.118).

Hurault accused the League of hopeless contradiction. On one hand it assumed state sovereignty, on another it favored splintering this very state, making the country's local units into an angry fighting heap of tiny sovereignties. His argument turned on the essential thought that state and prince were inextricably linked. Royal sovereignty (inherent in the mystical body) was the keystone of the state: this stone removed (by denying the king's unique sovereignty) the state fell. Each part separated and chaos ensued—whence Montaigne's constant call for "natural and simple obedience," an obedience that had to be by "subjection" and not by "discretion," personal choice (1.17.73). If the abstract state were sovereign, the concrete singular subject was adrift. To what actuality could it be subjected? Worse, the limitless proliferation of sovereign authorities of which Hurault complained could logically end only in that singular subject, potentially in conflict with all others. Such was the ultimate anarchy these writers feared. The experience of *being* as belonging in encircling communities (still stressed by Descartes) was feared sapped and destroyed.

It was why subjected obedience was essential: "The ordinary discipline of a State that is in health does not provide for these extraordinary happenings; it presupposes a body that coheres in its principal members and *offices*, and common consent to its observance and obedience." Later,

perhaps recalling the traditional image of the soul's rational powers rein-
ing in its unstable sensitive and runaway appetitive ones, Montaigne
added: "The law-abiding pace is a cold, deliberate and disciplined one,
and is no good for resisting a lawless and unbridled pace" (1.23.121).
One of the Christian religion's principal merits was its "precise injunction
of obedience to the Magistrate and maintenance of government"
(1.23.119). To this 1588 statement, he later added that it seemed

very iniquitous to want to submit public and immutable constitutions and obser-
vances to the instability of *privée fantasie* (private reason has only private jurisdiction), and to undertake against divine laws what no polity would endure
against civil laws, which, although human reason deals much more with them,
are still sovereign judges of their judges; and the utmost skill serves to expound
and extend their accepted use, not to deflect it and innovate. (1.23.120)

For Montaigne, divine laws, civil laws and magisterial sovereignty were
still imbricated spheres, a "coherent body" that would be fractured by
usurpation of "mastery" (1.17.73), of "authority to judge" (1.23.120).
The concrete results of these usurpations were everywhere visible: "the
bond and weave of this monarchy and great ship having been disjointed
and dissolved" (1.23.118).

Bodin's doctrine of sovereignty in his 1576 *Six livres de la république*
did not basically differ from such arguments. It grounded every reply to
the question posed most clearly by Étienne de La Boétie regarding "la
servitude volontaire": how to explain that millions of people obey one?
Huguenots after the Saint Bartholomew massacre and the League after
Henri III's death, we saw Montaigne lament, took the question to justify
sedition (2.12.420). Hobbes' final reply would be the same as Montaigne's: to give free rein to "private fantasy" already supposed that the
state did not exist, that there was no legitimate order and hence no society, since, as Hobbes wrote in his *Behemoth*, the latter required the former. Both writers replied by accentuating the *volontaire* rather than the
servitude. Sovereignty would lie for Hobbes not in the prince as Magistrate but in the state as a collective enterprise *represented* by princely authority (Montaigne had no such idea, since for him voluntary obedience
involved not at all people's "rights" but their "duties"). It was to be John
Locke, in his 1689 *Treatise of Civil Government*, who would confirm the
idea that sovereignty inhered in the state, whatever forms of representation it might now take. Such views were already not unusual by late in
the English civil wars, and Samuel Hartlib, probable author of a 1648
pamphlet titled *Rectifying Principles*, expressed the army's views as: "The
State at large is King, and the King so-called is but its steward or Highest
Officer" (in Wedgwood, *Trial* 88).

Even in England, such views were probably minority until the 1688 Glorious Revolution. At the close of the French civil wars, such a solution was far off, even if debates leading to it were well under way (the links between these wars and later English political thought are long familiar: see, e.g., Gooch, Figgis and Salmon; and for a punctual case, Reiss, "Utopie"). As we saw toward the end of the last chapter, Hurault conceived such a solution, although it deeply dismayed him:

Ce n'est pas tout, car bien que les villes capitales des Provinces auroient chassé le Roy, auroient tué tous les nobles, conquis chacune son ressort & son baillage, il faut encores qu'entre elles, apres elles prenent quelque forme de gouuernement & qu'il se trouue vn lien de iustice qui les tienne ensemble.

This is not all, for even when the capital cities of the provinces have chased out the King, killed all the nobles, conquered each their own province and bailiwick, they will still together have to take some form of government afterwards and some judiciary link will have to be found to hold them together. (149)

This "judiciary link" (*lien de justice*) was a new idea. What was it if not a contract? Hurault described it as an abstraction. Describing it as grounded in a concept of "justice," he did not write an expected, "they will have to find" (the natural syntax after "elle prennent"), but "will have to be found." The phrase *qu'il se trouve* said that the link would, more exactly, have to "find itself"; the subjunctive *tienne* implied doubt that it could work.

The formula suggests that for Hurault the question was not one of concrete alliance or of persons but of abstract doctrine allowing return to ordered civil polity. The phrase, *lien de justice*, was echoed by du Vair in his 1592–93 "Exhortation à la paix," calling on the League for "so solid a bond of goodwill and close a judiciary link" (66). Not much later, in 1603, the Calvinist thinker Johannes Althusius also saw society as bound by an abstract judicial *pactum*. Like the *Vindiciae*'s authors, he envisaged a society of corporate associations in which *singuli* had no political role but were protected by what he called the social "symbiosis." In this, he echoed Montaigne and others who denied the *singulus* any public role, but Althusius accepted no traditional monarchic idea and explicitly rejected Bodin's arguments. Whatever its variants, this abstract idea of state constitution implied a different idea and experience of being its subject. "Hobbesian," too, was Hurault's idea that lack of such a link led necessarily to evil, since, he agreed with Lipsius, that was the principal trait of men *en masse*: "I do not believe that they could ever agree on anything except doing evil; for good action is not to be found amid such confusion." He added that anyway "man's nature is evil [*meschant*]" (150). Confusion, disorder, harm and finally death—"you won't last long this way"—would necessarily follow destruction of the "ruling lord's" sovereignty (151). One cannot but recall Hobbes' famous remark that in the state of nature "the life of man is solitary, poore, nasty, brutish, and short" (*Leviathan* 1.13).

That was why, Hobbes was to say, voluntary cession of the individual's power to a central authority was essential. Hurault said nothing else, but, rejecting his own abstract link, he retained a very different idea of central authority. According to Hobbes, the fundamental natural right was protection and conservation of one's life. It followed, for a rational being, that the fundamental natural law was the law of peace (*Leviathan* 1.14). For Hobbes the "natural" consequence was the contract founding civil society, emerging from a rational accord among individuals possessed each of the same free will and full power, until relinquishing it freely and willingly. For Hurault this safe condition depended on a prince's act and subject's recognition of the advantage of obedience: this is the difference I noted between will linked to right and will linked to duty. Hurault transformed a call for peace directed at all combatants in the present civil wars into affirmation of the king's sovereignty in his state. Let the king think of peace, he said,

for perhaps this is one of the great secrets of his state. Peace offers the advantage that subjects necessarily bring their will and assent into obedience of the Prince, otherwise there would be no peace. War and force cannot achieve this end. For true obedience relies on free will and not force. When a king commands peoples who are voluntarily obedient, he possesses in himself alone the force of his scepter and needs no one else but himself. (192–93)

He underscored that this king would have no need of the officers, captains, princes and nobles to whom he then owed his crown's security, and so would avoid such elements as had led to present chaos and loss of sovereignty. On his subjects' part, will corresponded to duty and duty marked a fixed place in a social hierarchy. Difference in rank in no way affected subjects' equality with regard to royal sovereignty, provided the sovereignty was absolute. This mutual dependence was not "proto-contractual" in any Hobbesian sense of contract, although it was not foreign to a contractual theory that *was* common in Hurault's day, naming a constitutive accord between two separate entities, people and prince, ratified by a third, God, to whom the others owed separate and mutual allegiance, *fides*. Hurault's notion of peaceful mutual allegiance between prince and people (ratified by divine authority and allegiance) seems closely tied to earlier ideas of mutual affection and love as the glue of social bonds. He opposed it exactly to the abstract *lien de justice* which a deeply conflicted and angrily divided polity would, contrariwise, require.

For both Hurault and Montaigne it was duty that cemented the mutual relation of utility, dependence and affection. Speaking of a teacher's need to train his pupil to his social obligations, Montaigne insisted: "If his tutor is of my humor, he will form his will to be a very loyal, very affectionate and very courageous servant of his prince; but he will cool in him the desire to attach himself to him other than by public duty" (1.26.154). This thought was no theoretical abstraction. It answered a need for mediation between conflicted extremes: the Huguenot party of Henri de Navarre and the League, Protestantism and Catholicism (however much viewed as a hypocritical pretext), old high feudal nobility and new high (often ennobled) bourgeoisie, increasingly divided centers of power—be they Protestant cities or great old fiefs—and ever-stronger tendency toward centralization of power and consolidation of state into nation. The perfect symbolic mediation of this last would be Henri de Navarre's transformation into Henri IV, his conversion for political reasons from Protestant to Catholic (perfectly matching Montaigne's oft-repeated idea that public duty required suppression of "private fantasy") and his passage from the Béarn and Pau, his native city, to the Île de France and Paris, capital of the future nation-state.

Theoretical duty had its practical counterpart in the activities of the thinkers, statesmen, highly placed functionaries and lawyers known as the *Politiques*. They functioned as mediators, practically between opposing parties, theoretically between old and new conceptions of the state. Hurault's case is exemplary. Grandson of the famous chancellor of France, Michel de l'Hospital, he was Henri de Navarre's chancellor. Among many tasks were diplomatic missions on the king's behalf. His duties were such that he was inevitably suspected of Protestantism, although no one discovered his actual beliefs. When Henri became king of France, Hurault was named governor of Guillebeuf. He died in 1592. Montaigne's ties to Henri, his court, diplomacy and political affairs are today well known (if not in all details). On missions for Henri, he was harassed on the same grounds as Hurault. We have the essayist's and others' testimony on his acquaintance with the great chancellor (La Boétie's friend before Montaigne was). Circumstances suggest his familiarity with Hurault. It is no surprise that many coincidences exist in their thought.

The interest is beyond anecdote. At issue are debate and strife leading directly to the idea of the liberal state. In this light, consider the case that Hurault and Montaigne (less explicitly) both took up, that of the duke of Mayenne. He was second son of François de Lorraine, duke of Guise, and brother of Henri I de Guise and Cardinal Louis de Guise. After his brothers' assassination on December 23–24, 1588 (on Henri III's orders), Mayenne raised Burgundy and Champagne, and took Paris on February

15, 1589. There he organized as local authority a *Conseil général d'union*, template for the disintegration of sovereignty Montaigne and Hurault deplored. Throughout this period, or anyway for the term of the November–December 1588 Estates of Blois which ended in the Guise assassinations, Montaigne was present in the north, along with Étienne Pasquier, who named him in this context:

We were, [Montaigne] and I, familiars and friends, thanks to a meeting of minds and a common culture. We were together in the city of Blois at the time of that famous assembly of the Three Estates in 1588, whose end brought about so many of France's misfortunes. (*Lettres* 2.379)

These personal connections matter. One may describe all these people, Pasquier, Hurault, Montaigne, Henri IV himself, as Max Horkheimer does Bodin:

The inclination to remain personally neutral in religious questions, to subordinate religion to reasons of state, to turn to the strong state as the guarantor of secure trade and commerce corresponds to the conditions of existence of a moneyed bourgeoisie and its alliance with the absolute monarchy. ("Montaigne" 277)

The issue was first of all one of stability and certitude. Although care is needed as to what was going on. It was not that they thought religion *subordinate* to the state but that they increasingly separated the two spheres. Too, if a strong state guaranteed security of commerce and exchange, it also guaranteed a familiar experience of personal identity. That was why, when Le Roy spoke of sedition, splintering sovereignty and confusion of language—and so of reason—he cited Thucydides at length on misuse of language as symptom and cause of the social upheaval of civil war. Upset of *logos* was also upset of identity. For Le Roy, as later for Hurault and Montaigne, single royal sovereignty was opposed to the sociopolitical disintegration provoked by nobles and city councils and to the uncertainty of a language and reason that false usage was destroying simultaneously.

I earlier called this a cliché. Le Roy's work anyway enjoyed international renown. In the 1580s, the Englishman Gabriel Harvey opined that it would be hard to find a scholar who was not reading "Le Roy on Aristotle or the *Six Books* of Bodin" (Skinner 2.300). But the idea of a tie between language, reason and society was ubiquitous. To destroy them was to destroy the three traditional elements of what it was to be human at all, or those that most clearly distinguished humans from other animals. Seneca had argued that anger destroyed exactly these qualities of the human. War, especially civil war, was anger expanded over society at large. In 1587, a year before the edition of the *Essais* containing the first appearances of Montaigne's reference to Thucydides and the famous passage comparing the multiplicity of linguistic interpretations to "the Hydra's head," François de la Noüe published his *Discours politiques et militaires*:

The wise historian Thucydides describes summarily how the Greeks governed themselves during civil discord. . . . As soon as an insolent remark was made somewhere, he says, everyone else found the nerve to say something worse, either in order to do something new or to show that they were more assiduous than the others, or more insolent and eager to avenge themselves: and all the evils which they committed they disguised with praiseworthy titles, calling temerity magnanimity; modesty pusillanimity; precipitate indignation virility and boldness; consultation and prudent deliberation pale tergiversation. In this way, whoever showed himself always furious was reputed a loyal friend; and whoever contradicted him was held suspect. . . . Today I ask if in similar actions we have not equaled the Greeks. (55–56)

La Noüe was a considerable personage, a famous soldier (known as "Iron Arm," *Bras de fer*) and chief lieutenant of Gaspard de Coligny. Yet he merits a place beside other "mediators." Although he was a Huguenot leader, it was to him that Charles IX turned in order to attempt a reconciliation with his party after the Saint Bartholomew massacre. Like Montaigne and Hurault, he was seen as participant in the potential rise of a different future. Like them, he understood the confusion of language, social relations and political life as one and the same problem.

The same can be said of the duke of Alençon, Henri III's youngest brother, who, blaming foreign (i.e., Italian) influence at court, joined Protestant forces at Dreux on September 15, 1575. He, too, was pictured as a mediator, to whom Innocent Gentillet addressed his "souhait pour la France" at the end of his 1576 *Anti-Machiavel*: "That he will extinguish the fires of our civil wars in the countryside and cities, and like a French Hercules cut off the heads of this monster who still today shows itself a sworn enemy to our laws" (635). Twenty years earlier, in his *Arraisonnement* of 1569, François de Belleforest had called these confusions "the tortuous Hydra of rebellion" (68r: mispaginated for 60r). In 1593, Hurault applied the same metaphor to the League itself:

It is thus that we must consider generally the Party of the League today, this monster having been formed of many members which, for having been ill-proportioned from the outset, have rendered it so terrifying that it is no wonder if it has been seen to have several heads, like a serpent engendered from the earth's putrescence. (153)

"I sent your Grace," said the archbishop in Shakespeare's *2 Henry IV* (1597–98):

The parcels and particulars of our grief,
The which hath been with scorn shoved from the court,
Whereon this Hydra son of war is born,
Whose dangerous eyes may well be charmed asleep
With grant of our most just and right desires,
And true obedience, of this madness cured,
Stoop tamely to the foot of majesty. (IV.ii.35–42)

This was especially close to Hurault's thought. Recall that the arch-bishop's plea, concerned with a rebellion (although he pretends other-wise), precedes a series of deceptions, traps and apparent betrayals: that of John of Lancaster toward the rebels and of Hal toward Falstaff and then his father, Henry IV, when he "removes" his crown. At much the same moment, Pasquier was angrily assailing the Jesuits, saying that they chiefly acted to destroy kingdoms, justifying regicide in book and ser-mon, legitimating transfer of sovereignty (from French Bourbons to Spanish Hapsburgs), menacing papal authority and church stability, fo-menting rebellion and civil war by act and word. At the end of the third book of his *Iesuites Catechisme*, published in both French and English in 1602, the anti-Jesuit "Advocate" of this long dialogue exclaims to his Jesuit interlocutor: "your Companie is not the Senate you speake of, but a Monster, which hath farre more heads than a Hydra, against the which I will be another French *Hercules*, to maule and massacre them" (237v).

All applied the metaphor at once to disintegration of political and lin-guistic orders, and of reason, collective relations and personal identity. Pasquier earlier applied it to Guisard political maneuverings: again tying Montaigne and himself, Guise, Mayenne and the actual situation of France to this metaphor concerning state, language and identity, and so to particular political, theoretical and experiential moves. In a letter writ-ten to "Monsieur Airault Lieutenant Criminel d'Angers," Pasquier spoke of the assassination of the duke and cardinal of Guise during the meeting of the Estates General at Blois:

You should know that the King was enraged by several matters which occurred to his disadvantage during our assembly, and which he thought were only due to the bidding of these two Princes. He felt that the more flexible he showed himself to-ward our members, the more intractable they became toward him (such that it was truly a Hydra, one of whose heads cut off gave birth to seven others; so much so that three or four days before Monsieur de Guise had quarreled with him both about his status as Lieutenant General and about the town of Orléans [which was *ligueur*]). He thus decided [*il se delibere*] to have the two Princes done to death, thinking that their death would also be that of all these new councils. (*Lettres* 2.21)

The Hydra metaphor was not new but had new meaning (for older, see Reiss, "Montaigne" 147–48n19). Pasquier's use is notable not just because of the complexity of the familiar elements that it conjoined, but because it tied in detail the birth of angry political factionalism to the birth of too many words (*nouueaux Conseils, une dispute, il se delibere*), the Estates themselves being a long series of talks. The meaning of the metaphor meshed with that of the Thucydides passage: subject, sovereignty, power, language, right, law, war, peace, personal and national identity were all concepts, experiences and practices semi-hidden in these texts of Montaigne. One could not separate language from reason or both from issues of stable identity, all sharing the inconstancy proper to things human: "'We reason rashly and unthinkingly,' says Timaeus in Plato, 'because, like us, our reasonings [*discours*] have a large share of chance'" (1.47.276). Montaigne urged that human reason, "ridiculous" and "risible," could not guarantee language (*discours = logos*), on which the social order and one's own identity nonetheless depended. Nor could language be a guarantor, for it, too, shared constant motion. Only the *law* (itself prey to multiple interpretations) could resist: "Commonwealths that kept themselves in a regulated and well-governed state, like the Cretan or Lacedaemonian, made no great account of orators" (1.51.292).

In opposition to the law, speech—the use made of language—served to "manipulate and agitate a mob and a disordered populace." It persuaded "the herd" and "the ignorant" in a state where "things were in perpetual turmoil." In such cases, speech *could* offer itself as "a medicine," if a perilous one: for it appealed to the constant oscillation of private being, not to the loyalty of the public one. Either it provoked anarchy (Mayenne in Paris) or was of use only where anarchy already reigned: like Rome at the end of the Republic, "when affairs were in the worst state and when the storm of civil wars shook them." This returns us to the Thucydidean commonplace. The best way to prevent the pernicious developments it illustrated was to secure one man's power: it "is easier to safeguard him, by good education and good counsel, from the impress of that poison" (1.51.293). This *habitus*-trained power "of a monarch" in turn guaranteed "good government" of the state. Law and the state's order thus rested on the prince's unique sovereignty, situated in the mystical body, whose guarantor was God and His reason. His stability directly opposed human reason: "Now our human reasons and *discours* are like heavy and barren matter; God's grace is their form; it is that which gives them shape and worth" (2.12.424–25). The plenitude of divine reason stood in opposition to "the inanity, the vanity and nothingness of man." "Divine majesty" stood as the only true reason against the nothingness and instability of human reason: "It is to this alone that knowledge and wisdom belong; this alone that can have some self-esteem, and from which we steal what we account and prize ourselves for" (2.12.426). This is not to be dismissed as Montaigne's notorious skepticism. Rather does it record a complex schema of the human situation in the natural, social and divine spheres. Here, human reason, largely useless, let reasoning persons experience their own universal weakness. There, not infinitely distant, God's reason and grace imparted form to actualize potential reason, "engraving" on human reason's "carte blanche . . . whatever form He likes" (2.12.486). Between the two was the space of ordered civil society, best guaranteed by a prince who shared divine permanence and reason (in the mystical body) and the human (the material body): a kind of Christ in little, pastor of his subjects. The prince's participation in both realms assured the functioning of the law: the divine secured the role of duty, the human left a space for "will." Lacking in this schema so far is the placement of the singular person, characterized by inconstancy and incertitude. *Not* lacking is the constant sense of seething angry conflict, in which weak, divided, yet complacent "human reason is a double-edged and dangerous sword" (2.17.638).

We may be too familiar with Montaigne's remark that "each man bears the entire form of the human condition." Difficulties arise when we try to understand it; more still if we look for one meaning. Three and a half centuries of western thinking have built belief that human being, at least in essentials, is ever and everywhere the same. It sees this sameness and essence as a subjectivity firmly grounded, if not always easily located. This is so even when we hold it unable to be grasped ontologically "in itself" (like Sartre in *Being and Nothingness*) or psychologically in process (by psychoanalysis). This subjectivity nonetheless stands as human being in itself, *fons et origo* of all human activity. No doubt Marxism thought it escaped this idea and experience. Yet until events caught Soviet Marxism, maybe the main crisis of western Marxism, at least, came from perception of a need to make room for it. Even allowing for Lacanian notions of the constructed subject and others' efforts to make it just an "effect" of a particular sociopolitical organization or apparatus, western concepts of the subject still fall in a line stemming directly from "Cartesianism." And if one seems bound to name Descartes here it is because he has been taken to mark a moment when western philosophy and experience acquired a quite new inflection. The last chapters try seriously to adjust such claims as far as Descartes himself is concerned, but it is undeniable that subsequent thinking and experience *did* take what they called "Cartesianism" to embody their inflection.

Montaigne, like Hélisenne and others, may be precursor of such an inflection. He was not of it. A "Cartesian" idea and experience of the subject are not in him—or Descartes. The context of this "universal being," this "entire form," which Montaigne could easily "dislike" (3.2.782, 791), leaves little doubt regarding its significations. The essential characteristic of the universal "human condition" was its "perennial seesaw," in which "stability itself" was "nothing but a more languid motion." Montaigne could never picture this universal "being" because it existed nowhere as such. He could only picture a "passage." "We go harmoniously and at the same pace, my book and I" (3.2.782–83), he added after the 1588 edition; as he did: "I have no more made my book than my book has made me, a book consubstantial with its author" (2.18.648). This is old hat. But one can only conclude from it that the "universal being" is universal by its divine form and mortal motion and inconstancy, thanks to which no stable "subject" is to be grasped. But the divine form cannot be finally known in this life, where "there is no end to our inquiries: our end is in the other world" (3.13.1045). While like earthly being, the universal character of the world, of "all things," was eternal instability. The movement of being, the passage thus pictured, was the essential form of the human: whence followed, exactly, the fact that one could "attach all moral philosophy to a common and private life just as well as to a life of richer stuff" (3.2.782).

The sentence, then, that "each man bears the entire form of the human condition," so often used to show Montaigne's "discovery" of a modern western concept of subjectivity (of the willful and self-possessive subject, no doubt, but above all of a self always and everywhere the same and constant in itself), was caught in contradiction in the very passage that introduced it. Certainly, validation for later glosses seems offered soon after: "There is no one, if he listens to himself, who does not discover in him [_en soy_] a form his own [_une forme sienne_], a master-form [_une forme maistresse_], which struggles against education and against the tempest of passions that oppose it" (3.2.789). So here could be _une forme maistresse_, a deep self fighting against customary habits, against those learned by training—social expectation—and against the irrational passions stemming from the very humanity of the individual of which this subjectivity composes the "still, quiet center of being." To the modern western mind this is admirable: a Cartesian subject. It describes, though, a more traditional soul.

Otherwise we are again in contradiction. The very next paragraph insists on "corruption and filth," disease, guilt, sin, vice and ugliness, the constant companions of humankind (3.2.789). It insists, that is, on the fact that humans in their social (and other) relations never escaped the rule of the passions or everything vicious in those relations. In practice, if anything in this "master-form" was other than the soul whose full satisfaction could only be in the divine, then it stayed hidden, fitfully glim-mering, perhaps, as a kind of *desire*, but a desire forever unsatisfied. Far from some innate structure of mind, this would signal the *absence* of such a subject, not its presence. In Montaigne's text such an idea was explored only through contradiction and opposition.

In the *Essais*, this "subject" is glimpsed, retroactively, only by these signs of its absence. In Descartes, the subject begins to be there—at least potentially—by the (incidental) start of its agent presence. When Mon-taigne stated that even "conscience" itself was "born of custom" (1.23.114), trained into *habitus*, he denied one of the elements vital to the modern concept of self: the innate moral sentiment central in Mon-tesquieu and Rousseau, as in Adam Smith and Kant. Nor was it really questioned by Freud, since he lodged the moral sense in the superego as the presence of a socialization fully assumed *by* the psyche. This assump-tion presupposed the psyche's self-identity, its presence to itself. Mon-taigne denied any experience of a subject reflective on its self. This, says Maurice Merleau-Ponty, was just what Montaigne could *not* experience. Thinking could never be stabilized so as to reflect on its own being and action (which was why it could end only in God):

He never tired of experiencing the paradox of a *conscious being*. At each instant, in love, in political life, in perception's silent life, we adhere to something, make it our own, and yet withdraw from it and hold it at a distance. Descartes will overcome the paradox and make consciousness mind. . . . Montaigne's con-sciousness is not mind from the outset; it is tied down at the same time it is free, and in one sole ambiguous act it opens to external objects and experiences itself as alien to them. Montaigne does not know that resting place, that self-posses-sion, which Cartesian understanding is to be. The world is not for him a system of objects the idea of which he has in his possession; the self is not for him the pu-rity of an intellectual consciousness. ("Reading" 199)

Actually, rather than "overcome the paradox," Descartes *enabled* its overcoming. Nor was "self-possession" at all clear. But that is for my last chapters. Merleau-Ponty catches Montaigne's sense of thinking's division from the real, yet its temptation to make itself its measure. That is why he insisted that it be kept utterly apart from the public sphere. Elsewhere, Merleau-Ponty suggests why so many have sought a modern subject in Montaigne: it became hard for modern westerners to grasp the idea—far less the experience—of some "non-reflective" being once experience of being had built in that of its self-thought, once "the 'I think' had been pronounced." All we can manage is the proposal of a *pre-reflective cogi-to*. But this is just a projection of the *cogito*, like the notion dear to mythographers (and theologians like Augustine) of some no-time, *illud tempus*, projected as the *other* of history. For, Merleau-Ponty adds, "subjectivity was not waiting for philosophers as an unknown America waited for its explorers." They constructed, invented, it. No self of this sort exists prior to the *cogito*—or a certain understanding of it ("Everywhere" 152–53). There is no depth of "nothingness" at the core of being, no negation which thence enables the limit and possession of all positivities. For Montaigne there *was* no way to put a stop to movement; no wish to, either.

Two motions ruled "the earth, the rocks of the Caucasus, the pyramids of Egypt" and humans. All moved "with the public motion and with their own" (3.2.782). The phrase is obscure. Does he mean external and internal motions? a social motion and the universal one characterizing all things? For present concerns, the difference does not matter. In human beings, the exterior *was* the social; the interior *was* the private—and thereby also universal. The private (non-public) *was* motion, thought in process that was not yet reason, since by definition disordered. The freedom of the singular person lay in keeping that private space while sharing in the social order, which was anyway condition *sine qua non* for maintaining this private "freedom." One had to learn not to confuse the two. The training of *habitus* by the mutual gaze we saw earlier was one way to avoid doing so. What Montaigne wrote about inheritances in this respect could equally well be applied generally: our goods "are not ours personally, since, by civil law and without us, they are destined to particular heirs." They were of the public sphere and so, while singulars had some discretion, it was "abusing this liberty unreasonably to have them serve our frivolous and private fantasies [*nos fantasies frivoles et privées*]." One had to follow "the common and legitimate arrangement" which followed public law and custom (2.8.377–78). Only so could one avoid "the natural instability of our behavior and opinions" (2.1.315).

On this question, Montaigne never hesitated. In the social sphere the private (and universal) moving being (or *patient*, perhaps) had no function. Nor did the self-justifying, unpublic language that it used:

I think the same way about these political arguments: whatever part they give you, you have as good a chance as your opponent, provided you do not contravene the most obvious and plain principles. And therefore, for my humor, in public affairs there is no way so bad, provided it be old and stable, that is not better than change and commotion.

This was so whatever might be the present corruption:

The worst that I find in our state is instability, and the fact that our laws, any more than our clothes, can take no settled form. [In the false freedom given to the private, it] is very easy to accuse a polity of imperfection, since all mortal things are full of it; it is very easy to generate in a people contempt for their ancient customs: never did a man undertake it who did not succeed. As for reestablishing a better state in place of the one they have ruined, many have come to grief of those who have undertaken it. (2.17.639)

The sole means whereby things became a bit more stable (or continued so, if one had the luck to live in a stable state) were custom, public polity and recognition that in the realm of public affairs "frivolous and private fantasy" had to be replaced by public subject: "I give small allowance to the prudence of my conduct; I readily let myself be led by the public order of the world" (2.17.639). Only the authority and customary acceptance of lawful political order under a sovereign *universus* could guarantee constancy. Its interest was the public subject, and its law had no concern with the inconstant, private person.

This law of state assumed acceptance by the subject, as sociopolitical function, of a certain order, out of ("voluntary") duty and interest. It guaranteed not just the material well-being of the subject but its ruled use of reason, which, without law, was mere directionless wandering, unable to help anyone except "by accident" (2.6.358). This was why Montaigne insisted on the *Essais*' movement and the fact that they did not concern his public being: "It is not my acts [*gestes*] that I write down, it is me, it is my essence." But that is indiscernible, for actions, like passions, come to it from outside: "they bear witness to their own role, not mine, except by uncertain conjecture: samples displayed by a particular" (2.6.359). They mark the gap between mutable *fantasie* and social and political being dependent on customary acts visible to all.

So, like all *Politiques*, Montaigne found obedience to custom, law and known authority essential: "In this quarrel by which France is presently tossed by civil wars, the best and soundest party is certainly that which upholds the old religion and polity of the country" (2.19.650–51). For him, Frieda Brown notes, the concept of a local, particular society mattered above all (*Religious* 82–83). A society corresponding to any idea of universal justice was impossible: the universal was either human and worldly mutability or a divine constancy to which humans acceded only after death: "Justice in itself, natural and universal, is regulated otherwise and more nobly than is that other, special, national justice, confined to the need of our polities" (3.1.773). The worst evil was not failure to reach universal justice, which was God's alone. The worst evil was disorder. Natural human reason was disordered drift useless to the social sphere (though "God's grace" might give it a form moving it toward His universality): whence Montaigne's "Machiavellianism," leading him to say, for instance, that in some conditions a ruler might be forced to yield "his [private, and so universal] reason to a more universal and powerful reason," that of the state (3.1.777).

Here, the comparative "more" signals three spheres: (1) universal nature, private person, errant reason; (2) ordered customary society, public subject, reason of state, sovereignty visible in the prince's human body; (3) God, divine reason, sovereign secured by the mystical body. The private person was related to the second sphere by will, the public subject to the third sphere by duty, with the prince as mediator. The rule of law was essential to this order of things: "To keep oneself wavering and mongrel, to keep one's affection unmoved and without preference in one's country's troubles and in public division is, I find, neither beautiful nor honorable" (3.1.770). The *singulus* no less than the *universus* had an obligation to sustain this order. For years, this order stayed central to the idea of divine right and the (official) theory of the relation between the social sphere and the person, king and divinity. The English royalist poet Abraham Cowley still voiced it plainly in a 1639 poem addressed to Charles I after the Pacification of Berwick and ensuing peace between England and Scotland: "Welcome, great Sir, with all the joy that's due / To the return of *Peace* and *You*, / Two greatest *Blessings* which this age can know: / For *that* to *Thee*, for *Thee* to Heav'n we ow" (*Poems* 22, cited in Wedgwood, *Poetry* 55).

The state, coherence, law and ordered reason were a whole. Corrupted reason or, rather, unbridled "natural" reason, visible in false use of language, led to the state's ruin, in fact signaled it. Since only right use of words establishes mutual understanding, Montaigne wrote, whoever misuses them, with broken promises, for example, betrays human society. Speech is the one tool through which wills and thought communicate. It interprets our soul. When it fails, we have no more hold on each other, no more mutual knowledge. If it deceives us, it breaches all relations and social bonds (2.18.650). A good linguistic order guarantees a reasonable subject, and this subject is therefore inseparable from its sociohistorical circumstance (the *Essais*' errant language, like the private natural reason it expresses, must be well separated from the sociopolitical sphere, even when it speaks of it). That is why Montaigne insisted on participation in government and "public society": "our very life, must be lent and abandoned to its service and common opinions" (1.23.117). To accept "treachery, debauchery, avarice, and . . . every sort of inhumanity and cruelty" (3.6.889), as the French did during the wars of religion and as the natives of America were forced to do by European conquerors, was to accept a condition of disordered reason, hand in hand with destruction of discourse and acceptance of anarchy. Something else was needed to heal angry and competitive strife. Montaigne altogether resisted the kind of subject it was projecting—visible in Hélisenne, Sabuco or Hurault. His own reaction looks back, rather, to an older dispensation.

The social subject became guarantor of a well-ordered society and historical process to the precise extent that it denied its own "universality." This subject was not "Cartesian." It could not take itself from the here and now, politically, socially or temporally. It was unavailable to share in any such abstract *lien de justice* as Hurault and du Vair envisaged. Reason, social equity and the king's "paternal" authority conformed strictly to each other: so says a remonstrance addressed to Henri III in 1583, signed by Montaigne and the Bordeaux *jurats* (1373–78). Montaigne had no concept of anything like a "self" that could grow into self-realization. There were two "selves." One was but an errant passage, subject to the slings and arrows to which flesh and soul were heir. The other was publicly reasonable, inserted in and subject to the sociopolitical sphere. Montaigne said this quite clearly in a passage added for the 1595 edition:

This variation and contradiction that is seen in us, so flexible, has made some imagine two souls, and others two powers, that accompany and trouble us, each in its way, one toward good, the other toward evil, such sudden diversity not being easy to reconcile with a simple subject. (2.1.318)

If by the word "good" we understand *order* and by "evil" *disorder*, an interpretation authorized by the essay, we again find my argument. For order in Montaigne was always what conformed to the "well-governed" state, the society *bien policé*; whereas evil, disorder, was always anarchy, the release of human passions and desires drawing us toward necessarily vicious extremes. We have amply seen the terms into which this opposition was translated no less at the personal than at the state level. As Shakespeare's Henry V says in reference to just this political context in 1598–99: "Every subject's duty is the king's, but every subject's soul is his own" (*Henry V*, IV.i.166–68).

Writing of the normative grammars of the second half of the seventeenth century, Foucault writes: "it is in the very nature of grammar to be prescriptive, not because it would like to impose the norms of language, beautiful and faithful to rules of taste, but because it ascribes the radical possibility of speaking to the ordering of representation" (*Mots* 101). I have argued that the near "metaphysical" need of such grammars then (echoing demand for a new kind of order found in all realms of knowledge) responded to an earlier loss of order in the world, loss of an order taken to owe nothing to humans, its guarantor "divine will" or "world soul." As long as people and their world were subsumed under an order transcending and containing them, human classifications not only could be, but were best, disregarded. This was Montaigne's constant point: "I distrust our mind's inventions." Such is the infinity of circumstances that in seeking order, "human wit wastes its efforts [*y perd son latin*]"

(2.37.744, 762). The disappearance of transcendent order, however, imposed the need for a will to order that was properly human. Writers and thinkers like Hélisenne, Stampa, Sabuco, Hurault, du Vair, were beginning to make new places and persons to fit them.

The sixteenth century lived progressive loss of that all-surrounding external order, echoed in growing tensions in the sense of personal identity. That loss was felt first in those very spheres where it had been most closely experienced, social, political, theological and moral. Machiavelli's analysis of political practices had obviated any need for divine intervention, as Cardinal Reginald Pole warned the emperor Charles V as early as 1539. The French religious wars raised the same problem acutely: reading commentators and polemicists of the age fast convinces one of the vast influence of Machiavelli's analysis—however often they assert the contrary. In the sphere of the *res publica*, civil war, revolts, famines, disease, inflation, rampant unemployment, collapse of feudal bonds and uncertainty of mutual obligation between prince and subject were all strikingly patent signs, lived in the very flesh, of the recognized order's instability and dissolution.

One response offered in the next century would be hypostasis of the subject into a willful possessive individual, with rights forged in a crucible of angry conflict and parallel debate about social, political and moral legitimacies. This subject would legitimate its sociopolitical relations by claiming to solve the fury of otherwise endless war and succeed in imposing *its* order as legitimate polity and legitimation of its identity. The new knowledge attending on these would be the parallel imposition of the individual's own will on nature. All the powers necessary to civil order would be invoked by a new centralized state, eventually legitimized by the contract and its presupposition: the cession of the power of each individual in favor of one sovereign authority which, representing all, would warrant society's peace and good order. This solution was still unavailable to sixteenth-century thinkers. Although Bodin elaborated theoretical bases for absolute sovereignty in 1576, followed by others who began to focus the grounds of such sovereignty in an abstract agreement, it would be years before any actual state apparatus matched their formulation. In France it came with Louis XIV, once the crown had bested its opponents in the Frondes, built on terrain readied by Richelieu. In England it came with Oliver Cromwell's protectorate in the mid-1650s and James II's three years' reign that ended with his exile in 1588. These were radical forms of a model built on a sense of the subject-self as the stable originator of desire, will, action, knowledge and power.

Without constitution of such a self, disorder could not be undone in this way: "I paint the passing"; "stability itself is nothing but a more languid motion." Montaigne's private person could never be a firm, stable unit—let alone actively impose itself. Hence a reply to his friend La Boétie's question: Why do millions let themselves be crushed by one man's power, when they need but abstain to break it? Even abstention, Montaigne implied, supposed that these voluntary slaves (as La Boétie called them) could fix themselves as self-selected agent-subjects. If they could so act, they were a prince's equals, not his subjects: a status implicit in Machiavelli. If they could so act, they were equal parties to angry conflict. For Montaigne, the public subject got its being from its bond to a sovereignty incarnate in the prince's person. This subject might somehow keep free and "for itself" its errant *fantasie*, but *as subject* it had duty to society and its welfare. In the private sphere, a singular person was no subject at all, save in the sense of "being subjected to" passions over which its sole "control" was assent: "those passions which touch us only on the crust cannot call themselves ours. To make them ours, the whole man must be involved," mindful thought was needed (2.6.356). The true subject was a function of prince and polity. In a letter to Henri IV of January 18, 1589, advising the new king on his right bearing toward his new subjects, Montaigne spelled this out. He need only show care: "popular inclinations are moved in waves; if the trend is once established in your favor, it will be carried by its own motion to the end." It sufficed for the king to show his people "a paternal and truly royal protection" (1398).

If private being were to constitute itself as a fixed agent/subject, it would necessarily act conflictually against civil order and polity: hence the many analyses of the seething ambitions of the House of Lorraine and self-proclaimed sovereign cities; hence also, if the tradition is founded, Montaigne's advice to Henri de Navarre after his victory at Coutras not to pursue Henri III's forces and so take rebel status. The king need not abuse his subjects. He had but to show himself. Montaigne's parent metaphor was exact: hence, too, the added horror of the Saint Bartholomew massacre. The king had vitiated his relation to the people. Until then one could hold that violence was being committed only by those seeking to oppose the king's legitimate power, establish a new religion or subvert feudal obligations. The massacre risked total confusion, severance of all points of stability. Bodin's new concept of sovereignty, Hurault's and du Vair's proposals to found it on an abstract accord between fragmented authorities (not just cities, towns, villages, hamlets, but, at the limit, individual people) were signs of emergent political solutions. Montaigne's solution was more retrospective. He constantly extolled the experience of a familiar dispensation, recovery of ancient stability and old union of church and state, confirmation of paternalist royal sovereignty and older experiences of identity.

Montaigne's experience of *fantasie privée* and of the selfe's inconstancy did not contradict his desire for a stable political order. Nor was it just that the latter guaranteed the possibility and containment of the former. No less did the singular person's lack of fixity and stability guarantee the state's stability and the public subject's place in it: that was the *only* place where something like an "individual" with a more or less secure status could be situated. In the face of social and political crisis, Montaigne kept from losing his footing by using elements placed at his disposal by the political theory and practice of his age which seemed pertinent to the stabilization of civil life *and* personal experience. He and his contemporaries were living through a violent storm that was tearing up the foundations of old securities, by no means in France alone: Spain knew war, revolt and demographic calamity; the Low Countries were in revolt; the German lands were roiled by post-Reformation dissension; Italy suffered constant conflict among cities; England faced potent threats from continental powers, deep uncertainty about the succession and fast-changing social and economic conditions. The fraught sociopolitical, moral and theological conflicts of the time posed anguishing dilemmas for the experience of what it was to be a person. Its anchors in now-conflicted spheres, spheres whose ultimate stability had still enabled Petrarch to defeat the sense of personal fragmentation, and return, in some way, to older stabilities of identity, those anchors were being torn from their embedding.

Montaigne asserted the need for obedience to the laws and customs of one's local society, a need that Descartes reiterated as an interim measure in the *Discours de la méthode*'s *morale par provision*. At the same time, Montaigne was sure that what guaranteed the working of voluntary duty and the subject's loyalty to the sovereign prince was the conformity of sociopolitical reason and equity. In settled times constant reaffirmation of the person's public role and private reticence and of the sovereign's maintenance of reason and equity to assure the person's obedience would not have been needed. That they now were signals a moment of passage. Synchronically, it was a matter of wending a path between political extremes. Diachronically (seen retrospectively), the need was to move between two different concepts of universal order: one that was "external" to the human, to which the latter submitted, to which it was subject; another that would be somehow "due" to humanity. An evidence of the last was new weight given to the passion of anger. Another evidence, also able to be seen as a response to the threats created by that passion, was the quest for universal grammar, conceived as exactly matching human reason's structure, universal but at once individual and particular: the "good sense" of Descartes' opening sentence of the *Discours*.

In this, there was at least one intermediary theoretical step, widespread, leading toward a new idea of order. For the essayist, a subject's only solid anchorage was fixed public order. In the last decades of the sixteenth century jurists and historians believed they had found, or could find, the certainty of universal reason in that sociopolitical order rather than in either divine system or individual reason. Exploring François Hotman's 1567 *Anti-Tribonian*, J. G. A. Pocock notes that the jurist "proposes a plan of legal training in which the pupils undertake a comparative study of all known and valuable systems of law with the aim of distilling the essential principles of juristic reason which are common to all." This was "the principle known as neo-Bartolism, which came to dominate French juristic thought towards the end of the century, its central concept being that of discovering the fundamental principles of all systems of law" (*Ancient* 23). Bodin's *Methodus* sought the same principles. Montaigne, sure of the primacy of local polity, thought this merely multiplied "agitation," "contradiction," "doubt" and "diversity" (2.12.566; 3.13.1044).

But one can easily see the conceptual resemblance between this project and the effort that would develop three-quarters of a century later to find a universal grammar able to provide the constants of human reason and discourse, defining both the human *per se* and *qua* individual. The difference between them is no less essential. Neobartolists envisaged a sociopolitical and juridical universal, as Descartes would still do in dedicating his 1616 law theses. Universal grammar assumed instead *the universality of the structure of individual reason*, as Descartes would in the ideas of *mathesis universalis* and Method in 1619 and 1637. Montaigne could never find nor even conceive such structures. He thought local sociopolitical order the best "reason" available, one in whose terms the prince, *universi* and subjects had to act. Abstract "universal" human reason was unsure. Ordered reason stemming from and characterizing a stable agent self did not exist.

For Hobbes and Locke, rational law and polity became a function of individual reason, which could be characterized according to the laws furnished by a universal grammar. Those were indeed the very terms with which Hobbes prefaced his *Philosophical Rudiments Concerning Government and Society*: "not to point which are the laws of any country, but to declare what the laws of all countries are" ("Preface to the Reader," *English Works* 2.23). Here, though, these general and universal laws were possible because they stemmed from a single reason, a human mind whose act of creating civil society was exactly equivalent to the divine *Fiat* of the Creation in Genesis, as Hobbes was to write in the Introduction to *Leviathan*. Montaigne's thought then generates a reading vital to an emergent future. The "passage," constant motion, that was *fantasie privée* would modulate into cognitive reason. It would become reason conscious of the continuity and surety of its own working: in short, the reason of a later interpretation of Descartes' *cogito*. The (public) subject would be abstracted as a Cartesian or Baconian *morale par provision*, enabling the social being's action while protecting the being of "method" and reason's "new instauration," until such time as the subject of that last could oversee change in political and social order, when they would coincide. For the time being the separation seemed essential. As Horkheimer observed of Montaigne and contemporary Protestant thinkers, both rejected human thought "insofar as it comes into contradiction with the given legal order" ("Montaigne" 276).

The concept of universal laws in the sociopolitical and juridical spheres, necessary, given permanent inconstancy of private reason on one hand and gradual disappearance of belief in divine intervention in human affairs on another, would itself be replaced by a concept of universal laws governing individual reason and *producing and creating* civil society and the state. Such reason would be deemed *originative* (the reason of a *fiat*). The Neobartolist idea was unsatisfactory, hard as it was to perceive any fundamental unity in social systems, far less any structural identity, given diversities more striking than any similarities, as Montaigne tirelessly repeated. With individual reason given originative status, it was easier to set things right (for they were, Giambattista Vico would say after Bacon, "made by us"), and after Locke the way was open for *De l'esprit des lois* and analysis of diversities subject to human thinking structurally everywhere and always identical to itself. For Montesquieu, the relation between this thought and sociopolitical structures would, in an ideal system, be immediate—the very immediacy making the system ideal.

For Montaigne, there were still two kinds, even domains, of reason. One signaled motion of the private sphere. Moved to the social, it was the sand on which La Boétie fancied founding a utopian society of amicable "mutual recognition," *entrecognoissance* (Reiss, "Utopie"); a fancy Montaigne refused: for him, in an atypical anti-Ciceronian (and anti-Aristotelian) move, friendship was a strictly *private* affair. But moved to the social sphere in another way, this reason gave the angry conflictual exchanges in which Hélisenne glimpsed the possibility of a very different agent subject. The other kind of reason became a path to Descartes' provisional morality. An issue for the future was to articulate them on one another. Again, it was theories of contract that succeeded in doing so. The thought-in-process of Descartes' *Meditationes* would become a voluntary subject beyond the *Passions de l'âme*. In turn, this would become the fixed subject able to establish divers versions of social contract. These later developments were, though, deeply *un*-Cartesian.

CHAPTER SEVENTEEN

Descartes, Collective Tradition and Personal Agency

That the modern, western, self-possessive, centered and willful subject has its philosophical foundation in Descartes' *cogito* is a commonplace of our culture. People in the western street take subjective individualism for granted. Philosophers deploy as much energy against this Cartesian "error" as they do against its counterpart that divided subjective mind from objective body. They defend it with equal fervor. That the same thinker put the new subject to its earliest psychological analysis in his *Passions de l'âme* is probably less a commonplace only because that analysis has seemed more closely tied to now-unfamiliar seventeenth-century doctrine and discussion. I query these commonplaces, agreeing with Susan James that the idea that Descartes upheld "an absolute distinction between states of the body and states of the soul . . . will not stand up once the Cartesian account of the passions is taken into account" (*Passion* 17). Descartes' earlier writings already forbid any such absolute distinction. The idea and experience of subject in Descartes was always deeply fraught. A close analysis of the development of the *Meditations* shows us how.

I shall not make the foolish claim that the highly intelligent people who have seen such a foundation in Descartes' work have been wrong for three and a half centuries, though some plainly are. Drawn from Kant's blunt assertion that the *cogito* expressed "a transcendental syllogism" holding the assurance of "existence in general" (Brown, "Kant's" 171), Friedrich Nietzsche's claim, that "the upshot of Descartes' argumentation" is that "[t]here is thinking, therefore there is something that thinks" and that this *precedes* the problematizing of thinking (*Will* 268, fr.484), has no more foundation than has Hassan Melehy's exegesis of it to the effect that *cogito* always already includes the "I" of a self (129; cf. Harries

297, 305). Still, the *Discours de la méthode, Meditations* and *Principia philosophiae* did elaborate grounds of a subject defining itself in terms, as many put it at the time, of *savoir, vouloir, pouvoir* and *faire*: reason, will, power, action. The establishment of this subject required that it be source of knowledge and action and site of a "new beginning." Descartes sometimes said so, even as he fought the hard need to set aside history and memory that such a beginning implied (Reiss, *Against*, chap. 5), and faced the problem of the multiplicity of subjects: what I am calling *community*. In this chapter, that term has two meanings, echoing the emergent argument and experience the chapter explores. The one is of a society grounding subjects, the other of a society grounded *in* subjects. To establish subjects as such a source and site was to suppose their particular developmental history unimportant, since they composed a universal by definition out of history. One could not fully adopt the idea, far less *be* such a subject, without assuming such isolation. There lies much of the dilemma: blindness was presupposed; the subject so defined had to be its own universal origin.

But if one starts by seeing that Descartes and others, facing a vastly troubled sociopolitical context and a tense experience of personhood within it, *argued* themselves to such a claim about the "subject," then the importance of the idea's own history becomes evident. At the same time, it displaces the subject from its axiomatically central position. Too, we better understand Descartes' difficulties with issues of history and memory just signaled, and those of individual and community to which he alludes when writing of a scientific community in the *Discours* and exploring political relations in correspondence with Elisabeth, as we shall see in the next chapter. The grounds of his difficulties with these issues are clearer once reset in the context of his developing arguments and in that of his education and the debates in which he shared. We begin then to see that this potent "subject" is best characterized as what I call a "passage technique": a philosophical—or other—means to get from one way of thinking about things to another, using, reordering elements present in that earlier way to respond to new exigencies of context and practice; a means, not an end.

A passage technique is not a "working theory." Acting as a *bridge* to get from a to b, it offers no hypothesis about b. Rather does it offer a liberating context in which it is eventually possible to formulate such hypotheses. These can only come from a theoretical base taken to be reliable. Passage techniques assume not only an *unreliable* theoretical base but the need to create a new base that *will be* reliable. One may say that working theories become possible in science (for example) once passage techniques have served their cultural purpose. Perhaps this thought later underlay Hegel's idea of philosophical effort and duty, of which Jonathan Rée has recently said: "In the world of the *Phenomenology*, a truth is nothing but a corrected error, and the edifice of knowledge is built not of sublime transcendent facts but of ordinary mistakes, duly exposed and chastised, named and shamed. Consciousness wins through to absolute truth entirely by its own deluded efforts" (5). What if this process had always been a technique of thinking?

We are in fact familiar with such techniques in Descartes. The most immediately obvious is the celebrated "morale par provision" offered in part 3 of the 1637 *Discours*. These techniques were actually a constant device of his thinking, crucial to its development. He found them just where we would most expect him to have done so: in that neoscholastic training which he so often praised. In the 1616 dedication to his law theses, although he said he was now quitting it to focus on the single science of the law, he first noted how that training had allowed him to travel across "the vast waters of the sciences and all the rivers that flow from them so plentifully" ("Licence" 126–27). More familiar is the similar praise of his Jesuit education's breadth in part 1 of the *Discours*, again regretting its final inadequacy (AT 6.4–10).

How seriously Descartes took his Jesuit education is shown by his plans in the early 1640s to make the *Principia* a textbook reply to scholastic theses. Indeed, while he agreed that he held many views opposed to those of his Jesuit teachers, he held theirs the best education available. "Philosophy," he wrote on September 18, 1638 to a close friend, the mathematician Florimond Debeaune, who had sought advice on his son's schooling, "is the key to the other sciences" and a good course in the subject should be taken. "There is nowhere in the world," he added, "where I judge it better taught than at La Flèche" (AT 2.378). We should start, then, with some idea of that education, its assumptions, its style and content.

The preceding chapters have shown that the idea that a private, self-reflexive subject could think, act and exist in isolation had no tradition behind it. Quite to the contrary, one would have to look hard to find anything of the sort before the European seventeenth century, although we glimpsed emergent beginnings. Certainly Descartes' teachers held no such view. Their experience of theological debate and political dispute, pedagogical practice founded on oral exchange, and an intellectual style grounded in commentary, controversy and public intercourse made all their work intensely communal.

Such notions as authorial sovereignty, individual primacy or pure inquiry held neither for them nor for those whose work they took as the necessary ground of learning. In Aristotle's practice, for example, meaning arose from a dialogue with predecessors and contemporaries. Inquiry itself was the principal element in a life of *eudemia* whose ground and necessary context was social intercourse. The subject was a social not a private one. The concept of *zōion politikon* made community the ground of being. Aristotle's *Rhetoric*, central to Jesuit pedagogy, was held by its author and his followers to teach techniques foundational of the *polis*. Its vital object was to enable "rational discourse about the intelligible reality of politics" (Arnhart 3). His *Ethics* spoke wholly to communal life (Bodéüs convincingly analyzes his ethical thought in this light). Reading Cicero's letters, dialogues and speeches, as the Jesuits' pupils did from earliest schooling, shows how that Athenian ideal lived on in Roman form.

Ideas of subjective authority and individual inquiry did not hold for Augustine either, for whom meaningful concepts were a recapturing of seeds put in the mind by God and inquiry a path to the Divine. They did not hold for Aquinas, who sought to join these powerful traditions and whose concerns were furthered by Descartes' own Jesuit teachers at the college of La Flèche. They did so via the extensive Aristotle exegeses of the thinkers of Coimbra, Salamanca, Alcalá and the Collegio Romano, as they also made exhaustive use of all those just named and of the lay commentaries issuing from Padua, Florence, Rome and elsewhere. Knowledge and meaning were sought in past agreement and present debate. The first conditions of inquiry were dialogue and exchange. Such was the age's general style of learning, from conversation to altercation and polemic (at its least edifying, to theft and calumny). In the Jesuits' case these conditions of inquiry and style of learning reinforced the communal ideals that were the basis of their Society and the teaching emanating from it. As John O'Malley puts it: "social, national, and racial egalitarianism and harmony were the ideals they held up for themselves, for that was what they read about the first Christian communities of the New Testament" (*First* 59).

We must take this pedagogy, *scientia* and *sapientia* as seriously as Descartes did. He made them his measure partly because he held Jesuit thought, embodied in the Coimbran commentators, in Pedro Fonseca, Francisco Toleto, Antonio Rubio and above all Francisco Suárez, the strongest philosophy of his day, partly because an initial vesting of conceptual authority in the individual *cogito* was a main novelty of his own thought. (I stress "initial": it was a passage technique.) To this last, Jesuit pedagogy afforded a sharp contrast of method, form and content. After Aristotle, Cicero, Augustine, Aquinas and medieval thinkers, neoscholastics grounded argument in ongoing debate with previous authorities and with earlier and current opponents. Prelection, repetition, disputation, explanation, defense of opinions and the *concertatio* were the basic pedagogical exercises. The 1599 *Ratio studiorum*'s first explanation of *concertatio* is revealing:

The concertatio, which is usually conducted by the questions of the master or the corrections of rivals, or by the rivals questioning each other in turn, must be held in high esteem and used whenever time permits, so that honorable rivalry, which is a great incentive to studies, be fostered. Some may be sent individually or in groups from each side especially from the officers; or one may attack several; let a private seek a private, an officer seek an officer; or even let a private attack an officer, and, if he conquers, let him secure his honor or some other award or sign of victory, as the dignity of the class and the custom of the place demand. (*Ratio* 203: "Rules Common to the Professors of the Lower Classes," rule 31)

The military metaphors are particularly interesting. The "officers" and "privates" were pupils who had been separated into two sides for purposes of debate. *Concertatio* was not used just in rhetoric, the highest of the five "lower classes," but from the very earliest grammar class (*Ratio* 234: "Rules of the Professor of Lower Grammar Classes," rule 9). Exchange and fierce debate grounded knowledge of authority and the opinion essential to all understanding. That was why and how such contemporaries of Descartes as Jean Duvergier, François Garasse, Marin Mersenne, Gabriel Naudé, François Ogier and his good friend Jean de Silhon put exhaustive effort into refuting deists and arguing about Stoics, Rosicrucians, skeptics and others in the 1620s. And with respect to Descartes himself, we may wonder why he should wish to refute neoscholastics, if the full meaning of his work lay only, as so many have asserted, in the work itself and in the lone questing mind. The refutation would be unneeded and confusing.

What, more importantly, could we then make of his determined collecting of "Replies" and "Objections" to the *Meditations*? Of earlier efforts to do the same for the *Discours* and its *Essais*? How could we understand his 1640–42 "Responses" to them? Their mere existence belies notions of self-sufficiency. Their aim was to create the *Discours*' community of thinkers and doers. It was also to enable elaboration of thought itself. How else can we fathom the widely accepted idea that Descartes' career resulted largely from an impromptu interjected disquisition at a late 1628 Paris gathering, provoking Pierre de Bérulle to urge him to dedicate himself to philosophical research and put his talents in service "to humankind"? This event was at the home of the papal nuncio, Cardinal Francesco Bagno, gathering many scholars (including Mersenne) to hear the "sieur de Chandoux" offer a new philosophy rejecting the scholastic. All approved save Descartes, who soundly took it apart and gave examples of his own new method's power (Baillet 1.160–66: here 165). In the same light we better grasp the five-year-long (1641–45) dispute with Ghisbert Voet and Martin Schoock—however bitter it was (see Descartes and Schoock)—and many briefer ones, like his efforts, reacting to critical theses on the *Essais* and the final Objections to the *Meditations* by the Jesuit Pierre Bourdin in 1640 and 1642, to engage the entire Society (Baillet 2.70–85, 162–65). Even more in this light should we view the making of the *Passions de l'âme* in dialogue with the Princess Elisabeth from 1645–47. Lastly, of course, Descartes elaborated much of his thinking via the vast correspondence pursued with so many important intellectual and political figures in the Low Countries, England, Sweden and France.

Descartes did not conclude these procedures from his own work. They were the air people breathed. In his case, they were honed by eight years of Jesuit schooling. When Isaac Beeckman first met him in Holland in 1618, he noted in his *Journal* that this "Poitevin" was deeply versed in the work of many Jesuits and other learned and scholarly men: "cum multis Jesuitis alijsque studiosis virisque doctis versatus est" (Beeckman 1.244, also excerpted in AT 10.52). Descartes himself said as much in the *Discours*, as he often did elsewhere.

At stake was not just a style of thought and its content. The air breathed also lay over action and event. The Jesuits were deeply alive to their role in these. Participation in worldly life was an essential goal of their thinking and teaching.

So it was for Descartes. In the 1647 preface to the translated *Principes*, he insisted that the final goal of any philosophy was "the highest and most perfect moral system, which, supposing a complete knowledge of the other sciences, is the ultimate level of wisdom" (AT 9B.14). Adrien Baillet only echoed Descartes in saying that he had been working toward this all his life (1.115). This ethics would enable "not just prudence in worldly matters but a perfect knowledge of everything humans can know, as much for the conduct of life as for the conservation of health and discovery of all the arts" (AT 9B.2). Two years earlier he had expounded to the Princess Elisabeth the human condition such a *morale* addressed: "one is really one of the parts of the universe, and yet more particularly one of the parts of this earth, one of the parts of this State, of this society, of this family, to which one is joined by one's home, one's oath, one's birth. And the interests of the whole of which one is a part must always be preferred to those of one's own particular person" (AT 4.293: September 15, 1645). At one level, Descartes was perhaps just recalling the Cicero of his college days: "But since, as Plato has admirably written, we are not born for ourselves alone, but our country claims a share of our being and our friends a share; and since, as the Stoics hold, everything that the earth produces is created for human use; and as humans, too, are born for the sake of humans, that they may be able mutually to help each other, in this we must follow nature as guide, serve the general good by exchange of duties, giving and receiving, and so by skills, deeds and talents bind together the society of humans with humans" (*De officiis* I.vii.22). This elaborated on Plato's letter to Archytas of Tarentum (358a). Descartes was imbued with the first, he probably knew the second. Montaigne had echoed the idea. In this light we better understand the end of philosophy as public "gentleness and harmony [*douceur et concorde*]" (AT 9B.14).

This posed a dilemma. By sixteenth century's end, the European world was everywhere seen in a state of unsolvable disarray. The very inadequacy of the finest of educations evidenced that something was wrong in the grounds and techniques of understanding, if they could no longer provide analysis of and consequent action in world and society. The problem was how to achieve a new instauration, as Bacon put it. Descartes' new grounding of thought in the *cogito* led to an individual subject. A dilemma, then, was the meeting of that subject and the multitude of subjects that "community" inevitably became. To define subject as a lone self-centered thinking essence seemed to mean that community was inconceivable save as ubiquitous conflict: Hobbes' state of nature. That is indeed how later thinkers took it. Hobbes' "covenant" became its settled solution.

Some other solution might have been possible had Descartes' subject been held the means it was, rather than the end it became. Then community could still have been considered the origin and end of political thinking. As it was, claim based on community yielded to claim based on the individual. Duties and obligations yielded to freedoms and rights. These are but two of the drastic changes that later thinkers have taken to characterize the period and found most clearly embodied in Descartes' thinking, when they do not make it the actual source of such transformations. *That* is wrong simply because anxieties and debates grounding such changes long predated him. But it *is* assuredly the case that *cogito* and Cartesian subject could be taken to give them particularly solid foundations. I am suggesting that Descartes himself had something else in mind.

Just as the idea and practice of community were basic in assumption, style and content to Jesuit education, so was the use of pedagogical or philosophical bridges to get from one level of thinking and training to another. Let me give examples.

The first step in education was to learn to speak and write Latin. For three years, pupils in *Grammar* worked from basic parsing to complex versifying and prose dispute. They read ever harder texts by Cicero and some others, having started with the former's *Familiar Letters*. By the third year, they got to his *Paradoxa Stoicorum, De senectute, De amicitia, Somnium Scipionis*, and in the fourth, *Humanities*, to speeches like *Pro lege Manilia* and *Pro Archia*. Students would eventually read most or all Cicero. His writings deeply concerned issues of community, society and politics. One could not possibly escape them; certainly not in the oral expository and debating techniques used by the Jesuits. Grammar itself was tendered not just as a means to language use, but as essential to concordant social community. Emmanuel Alvarez's standard grammar made the point at its outset, and major Jesuit educators like Ribadeneira, Suárez and Juan de Mariana insisted on it elsewhere. Grammar did not just ground later learning. It was the *bridge* to a clearer idea of living in community *concordissime*, as Alvarez had it (6). This, too, was an ancient echo. In the *De oratore*, Cicero had observed that a person who did not know proper grammar would be incapable of rational thought and its expression. People would rightly "think him not just not an orator but not human" (III.xiv.52).

In the second term of the second year of *Grammar*, pupils studied a hugely popular work, one used everywhere in schools through the Renaissance (and into the nineteenth century). Cebes' *Tabula* offered an allegory of the road to the true and the good, a reply to the question Descartes later drew from Ausonius: "Quod vitae sectabor iter?"—"What path in life shall I follow?" Stoic in emphasis (although its philosophical sympathies are disputed), it described a painting depicting three, maybe four, enclosures through which humans passed on their way to wisdom. Two things are specially relevant here. The first is a character standing just outside the first gate serving a cup of varied amounts of error and ignorance to humans as they enter life: *Suadela* (Deceit)—opposed to *Genius*, who offered right guidance. *Suadela* was a figure of mischief whose malign influence the successful sage would at last transcend. The second thing is the work's gloss on *doctrina*, the divers disciplines composing familiar knowledge. These were actually *falsa disciplina* that, even so, provided a *lingua*, a language the sage could use to reach true wisdom and the good.

My first example, grammar, was a routine pedagogical device. These second two seem to have given Descartes and others actual models for thinking from the false to the true. *Suadela* had several dramatic counterparts, ranging from the *deus maleficus* of Book 2 of Plato's *Republic*, on which Jean de Serres embroidered at length in the margin of the great 1578 Stephanus edition of Plato, asserting that before the city's magistrate could achieve rectitude, justice and wisdom, the mere idea of such a *deus maleficus* had to be expelled (*Platonis opera* 2.379). A similar idea could be found in a work by a member of Descartes' family's social circle at Poitiers: Duvergier's 1609 *Question royalle*, which asked whether in peacetime any conditions obliged a subject to save a sovereign's life knowing it would mean loss of one's own. Duvergier wrote of the need of a "sens clair & net," without impediment from change of medium or "Devil's illusion" (*Question* f.17r–v). This fear of illusion clearly ties into the cases recalled at the start of Chapter 1. And did Descartes know *Don Quijote*, where a similar deceitful figure occurs in relation to madness (Nadler)? Too, one might consider Tirso de Molina's devil a deceiving figure in *El burlador de Sevilla*, although *Don Quijote* may be more apposite for present purposes. These cases show Michael Williams wrong to say that "the materials of the First Meditation [were] all traditional" except for "the evil deceiver" (29). Still, I cite them not to raise irrelevant issues of "originality," but as versions of a familiar road to knowledge, an *iter* or *hodos*—as in *met(a)hod(os)*—from uncertainty to certainty: passages to wisdom. Not for nothing did Leibniz later praise the moral allegory offered by Cebes' *Tablet* for being inconclusive, serving instead "to waken the mind": a remark recalling Descartes' *morale par provision* (*Nouveaux* 6.385).

The idea of drawing a rational *lingua* even from false doctrine is still more striking. Here, Cebes' allegory named a stable device of Jesuit education, one that Descartes explicitly reiterated as early as the *Regulae*. Each stage of education was carefully presented as a way to use what had preceded even while surpassing it. Each gave a "language" paving a way to its own supersession (I almost said *Aufhebung*). A clear rapid example may be taken from a student's fifth year, that of *Rhetoric*. For many this was their last. Those like Descartes it prepared for the next three years of philosophy, in his time divided into logic and ethics, physics and metaphysics, and mathematics (Ariew 9). The *Rhetoric* year turned on Cyprian Soarez's *De arte rhetorica*, on which pupils had actually begun work in the second semester of *Humanities*: another bridge. In the second semester of *Rhetoric*, similarly, quite new questions were broached. Along with rhetoric proper, students were to explore such things as "hieroglyphics, Pythagorean symbols, apothegms, adages, emblems and enigmas" (*Ratio* 214: "Rules for Professors of Rhetoric," rule 13).

The rule sent teachers and students to widely popular and significant areas of study. One, rooted in the humanist past, involved chronology, calendars and world history, thinking to find there an ark holding a single unified knowledge of humanity. Its techniques were computation of astronomical and astrological data, examination and comparison of calendars and temporal cycles from all known cultures and theologies, exegesis of historical and chronological works of equally wide spread, and interpretation to this end of, precisely, "hieroglyphics, Pythagorean symbols, apothegms, adages, emblems and enigmas." This history was not to be found only in written documents. Its elements were held subject to exact calculation, dependent on the physical world.

This tied into another area of study, with shoots pushing toward a different kind of future: that of the "magical" and "scientific" aspects of symbols and enigmas. Aspects of their treatment questioned the very rhetoric being learned, querying relations between the true and the probable, fact and opinion. Modern scholars have begun to show that much that was written on "natural" magic adumbrated what is now called science. This is not only because natural magic "aimed . . . at producing changes in the physical environment desired by the operator," by mechanical or other device; nor even because such effects could be "experimentally" tested against expectations (Shumaker, *Natural* 3). No less importantly, writers questioned claims made for the occult effects of words, tokens, symbols, incantations, spells, charms and such.

Lacking natural or rhetorical explanation, an effect should be held a superstitious figment. Such was the Jesuit Delrio's aim in the first book of his influential *Disquisitionum magicarum libri sex* of 1599–1600: to apply rational analysis to worldly effect. Study of symbols led the student from the poetry, essays and history of *Humanities* to issues in rational logic. It also bridged rhetorical analysis and the mathematical and scientific studies introduced in the second semester of the logic year, even though natural philosophy did not formally begin until the next. Similarly, too, questions of free will and necessity arose in the final year, but were not debated until the theology years, open only to those who were to enter the Society. Descartes would of course raise them constantly in later writings.

All this was not unlike the *lingua* of the false doctrine offered in Cebes' *Tabula*. Each stage of education, while not actually falsifying preceding ones, showed that they had to be superseded. So when Descartes urged the deficiency of poetry, history, rhetoric or familiar mathematics, he was repeating his schooling. False doctrine, said the *Tabula*, lay in the letters and mathematics of trivium and quadrivium, not to speak of medicine, law and the rest. They were needed to bridle the young. They did not themselves improve one. They gave a *lingua* to guide toward the true. As Descartes wrote in the second Regula (late 1619), the Schools' method of learning, erroneous as it was, sharpened "the minds of the young":

Yet I certainly do not condemn the way of philosophizing that others have hitherto devised, nor those war machines that are scholastic probable syllogisms, excellent for (oratorical) battles. For they exercise the minds of the young, pushing them to rivalry. It is far better their minds be formed by opinions of this sort—

even if they are evidently uncertain since they are disputed among the learned—than they be left free and to their own devices. Without guidance they might run upon precipices, but so long as they stay in their master's footsteps, they may occasionally stray from the truth, but will take a path safer at least in that it has already been tested out by more expert heads. (AT 10.363–64)

Echoing the Jesuit handbooks, Descartes drew from his education this idea of a *raison par provision*. It would let one think even as one worked for an accurate and right rational method. It would avoid but learn from errors of those "exceptional minds" who had, he said in the *Recherche de la vérité*, "almost all copied those travelers who, having left the high road to take a short cut, remain lost among thorns and precipices" (AT 10.497). Passage techniques responded to tensions and shocks of an age obscurely aware of being in transition. They let familiar tools be forged into new ones. In the Jesuit *Rhetoric* class, symbols, hieroglyphs and enigmas were introduced to let a reformed Aristotelian logic reply to them, just as, in a next step on a student's path, masters used mathematics to reply to the logic. Each step was a *provisional reason* on a way to full wisdom and that *summum bonum* which still preoccupied Descartes and his correspondents at mid-century. Indeed, the approach to God in the third Meditation was itself carried out as a series of bridging movements in which thought's awareness of its imperfection was a mark of its improvableness, of God's perfection and of thought's ability to move from the first toward the second (AT 7.47).

Method, too, was a bridge to right reason, full knowledge and always revisable praxis, a corrective to reason's imperfection. That is why its presentation gave way to three *"Essais,"* not applications but trials providing explorative patterns. They were forging a new *language* from an old, moving toward a goal whose shape was not wholly foreseeable. So Daniel Garber is right to argue that a 1637 Method differed from what Descartes would apply later: adequate to cope with separate but interconnected problems, it was insufficient to treat the interconnections themselves ("Descartes"). From his Reply to Mersenne's second Objections to the *Meditations*, we can trace how Descartes actually got from neo-Aristotelian resolutive and compositive, analysis and synthesis, to Method—itself always a *raison par provision*, a *becoming* (Reiss, "Neo-Aristotle").

It has taken time to get from showing how basic were assumptions about idea and practice of community to showing the ubiquity of passage techniques, especially the importance of *raison par provision*. But we are already into enigmas of *cogito* and subject. For rational Method implied such stability of thought as Montaigne denied. The leaning, stumbling, windblown, sinister subject of Descartes' November 1619 dreams sought provisional security in reliance on the rational *iter* of neoscholastic masters: the text cited from the second Regula seems to date from the same time. But the *Regulae* as a whole proposed a more precise *mathesis*, based on decomposing elements of a physical dilemma to find a first intuition (or more than one) from which a mathematical analysis could then rebuild the complex dilemma—a version of familiar resolutive/compositive techniques. What such a *mathesis* could not explain was how to trust the first intuition. The *Discours* likewise simply took for granted the power of the historical "I" with which the first parts began, and drew from it the "we" of the scientific community with which the last two parts ended. Such a passage from "subject" to community needed a more substantial grounding. The *Meditations* gave it.

They gave it on the back of a move from an epistemological query to an ontological reply. Descartes' invention of an idea of subjective agency in the *Meditations* arose in an effort to solve questions vital to neoscholastic, skeptic and natural philosophical debates of the age, about what one could know and how one could know anything not already in the mind. In part 4 of the *Discours*, the idea of "a substance whose whole essence or nature is simply to think" (AT 6.33) led directly to an idea of God. The epistemological problem became ontological. It did so, first, because imperfect thinking both implied the possibility of a perfect thinking that was not human and seemed to need such extra-human—divine— agency to guarantee the reliability of human reason, assurance of secure knowledge. It did so, second, because the subsequently secure action of that reason seemed to need the transferral of divine will to the nature of being human. This raised basic difficulties in ethics and politics because that idea of agency seemed to break with an ethics of community with which Descartes was not only imbued from his training but which he thought the ground of any sustainable human society. In the "Lettre-Préface" to the 1647 translation of the *Principes de la philosophie*, this was philosophy's final goal: "I mean the highest and most perfect moral system, which, presupposing a complete knowledge of the other sciences, is the ultimate level of wisdom" (AT 9B.13–14). This system would produce public "gentleness and harmony [*douceur et concorde*]," permit discovery of ever "higher" truths and establish "perfection of life" in private and public "concord" (18, 20). This community was not founded on cohabitation of individual willful agents. It was grounded in a personhood conceived as itself "communal."

It then became a matter of trying to "get back" to an older sense of who-ness now sapped by an idea of agency that had been only a passage technique toward solving quite different sorts of problems. This older sense of who-ness was both that of experience and necessary: without it the ethical community seemed in boundless jeopardy. Descartes was clear about keeping elements of this older dispensation: "Just as in knocking down an old house," he wrote in part 3 of the *Discours*, "we ordinarily keep the remnants to use in building a new one, so, in destroying all those of my opinions which I found to be ill-founded, I made various observations and acquired many experiences which have since been of use to me in establishing more certain ones" (AT 6.29). To follow that movement and its implications we need to turn from part 4 of the *Discours* to the full treatment of the issue in the third and fourth *Meditations*.

As we know, the first worked a retreat from the outside world, from the senses and their risk of madness—or a different *ratio* (we saw in Chapter 1)—in a new search for the right road to security of reason, culminating in the now-familiar *genium . . . malignum*. The second Meditation concluded that even were there such a "malign deceiver," the very ability to suppose so proved, "ego sum, ego existo; certum est." "I" must at least be *res cogitans* (AT 7.27). This something thinking could as yet rely on nothing but awareness of itself as thinking process. This stays close to Montaigne's *fantasie privée*, whose thinker could take no part in the public arena of the citizen subject fixed in public hierarchies, just because of thought's *branloire perenne*. Indeed, Descartes began this second Meditation by paraphrasing Montaigne:

For what did I formerly think me to be? A man. But what is man? Shall I say a rational animal? No, for then one would have to ask what animal is, what rational, and so from one question I would fall into more and harder ones. (AT 7.25).

This was Montaigne protesting that such inquiry exhausted the lexicon (3.13.1046). *Res cogitans* was the formula ending what Descartes also saw as bootless spawning of "subtleties." So we must scrutinize this *res cogitans*. It is a concept no modern vernacular can really echo.

Descartes reached it by means of a process remarkable (to a modern western exegete) in how it objectified expression of anything like personal being—remembering that Latin could and did express the site of thinking and saying by a first-person verb needing no separate (pronominal) expression of "selfness." Having dismissed possible attributes of personal being as unreliably knowable, he asked whether, nonetheless, these things could in fact differ "ab eo me quem novi," from this "me" that [I] know. For the moment he could say nothing of that. He could only assert that something, the present thinking process, existed: "Novi me existere," (I) know "me" to exist. But he had to ask: "what may be that 'I' that I know" (quaero quis sim ego ille quem novi) (AT 7.27). This led to *res cogitans*, an expression much misunderstood because largely untranslatable. In medieval and renaissance Latin, *res* could mean "thing" in pretty much all its modern senses. Equally typically it just meant the referent of a word or concept, without regard to ontological status (cf. Maclean,

Montaigne 62). Descartes used the latter sense when querying the referent or "thought-thing" that this "I" is: "sed qualis res? Dixi, cogitans," "but what sort of thing/referent? I have said: a thinking" (AT 7.27). To render the phrase joining the two terms as "thinking thing" or "chose pensante" is inevitable. It also entirely misleads, as Descartes' separation of them in the just-cited passage suggests: "But what am (I) therefore? A thinking something [*Sed quid igitur sum? Res cogitans*]. What is this? Certainly doubting, conceiving, affirming, denying, willing, not willing, imagining, as well, and feeling" (AT 7.28).

What, he asked, of all these acts could be separated from this present act of thinking—of being conscious? ("Quid est quod a mea cogitatione distinguatur?") Could any be separated from what may be called "me ipso," source of this thinking? Acts of doubting, conceiving, willing and others clearly came from this "source." But clarity was undermined by the dubitative subjunctives "affirming" it: "Nam quod ego sim qui dubitem, qui intelligam, qui velim, tam manifestum est, ut nihil occurrat per quod evidentius explicetur," "for what the 'I' may be who may doubt, conceive, will, is so evident that nothing may be found to explain it more clearly" (AT 7.29). An obvious problem existed: how to establish something like the place from which thinking happened. It was natural that Descartes should have recourse, precisely here, to the image of thinking as Plato's errant horse which, for time being, was to be given free rein before eventually being bridled, and to the equally long-lineaged wax block, whose recognition depended not on its matter but on the thought of it (AT 7.29–30; cf. Lezra 102–16). These offered approaches to the third Meditation's effort to establish thinking's place. There he began by ascertaining that the process of thinking was not agent, but passible subject, reactive to "something": "ut, cum volo, cum timeo, cum affirmo, cum nego, semper quidem aliquam rem ut subjectum meae cogitationis apprehendo [as, when (I) wish, fear, assert, deny, (I) always understand something like the subject (the lying under) of my thinking]" (AT 7.37).

The last phrase can perhaps better be translated: "something like (whatever is) subjected to my thinking." Neither *ego* and its cognates nor *res cogitans* were at this stage any sort of agent. They were names given to the "place" where thinking (as any form of mental activity) went on or, better yet, they were simply the referents *subjected to* that thinking process. This was why the third Meditation went on to seek a sure God, and the fourth to distinguish the true and the false: they had to provide grounding. But in this exercise something had already changed in this thinking process: it had become an internal agency.

Before we examine how Descartes worked this out, we need to glance at how the process of thinking could itself be offered as necessitating a thought of a perfect thinking process or, as Descartes put it, of "God." He addressed the question in the third Meditation, teasing out of *this* present thinking process a reliable one to transcend it. At this point Descartes was trying to draw the potentially greater certainties of this "higher" process from the very act of thinking. Evidently, he wrote, if this present thinking could have an idea of a thinking process more perfect than this one now going on then that idea must come from somewhere "prior" to this thinking, for a lesser cannot precede a greater, just as "non potest calor in subjectum quod prius non calebat induci [heat cannot be induced in a subject(ed) that was not previously heated]" (AT 7.41). Here again, Descartes emphasized the *subjected* nature of the thinking process. The continuing arguments of the third Meditation depended on this assertion: one had to find an *ideam . . . primam*, a first idea, that was like an "archetype" making lesser ideas (AT 7.42).

This idea was one of a thinking that was "more perfect" than this thinking going on, right now, in "me," an idea that was in itself "clear and distinct." Indeed, as the idea of absolute clarity and distinctness it was necessarily the clearest and most distinct idea that "my" present thinking could have (AT 7.46). "God" was first of all the idea of a thinking process whose perfection could not derive from a here-and-now process whose imperfection was clear: *cogitans* had to be aware of its ability (and concern/interest/desire/capacity) gradually to increase in knowledge (AT 7.47). By definition, perfect thinking would not be subject to such growth: it would always already have full knowledge. Behind this reasoning hovers the "impassible" universal soul of Aristotle's *De anima* set against "passible" soul incorporated in the human body. For Descartes, when this "I" process of thinking thought perfection, it could only think a perfect *rem cogitantem* (AT 7.49). "God" was first the idea generated from this thinking of a perfect thinking process (AT 7.52). Descartes was always to hold this view of the soul as a thinking *subjected* to passions coming to it either through the senses, or innately, or "by prior dispositions in the soul" or "by movements of its will," as he wrote to the Jesuit priest Denis Mesland in 1644:

I put no difference between the soul and its ideas, other than that between a piece of wax and the various shapes it can receive. And just as it is not properly an action, but a passion in the wax to receive various shapes [*figures*], it seems to me that it is also a passion in the soul to receive such and such an idea, and that only its volitions [*ses volontés*] are actions; and that its ideas are put [*sont mises*] in it partly by objects that touch the senses, partly by impressions that are in the brain, and partly, too, by the dispositions which preceded [a given idea] in the soul itself, and by the movements of its will. (AT 4.113–14; May 2, 1644)

The force of the active verbs in Descartes' last clauses is important and needs careful notice. They name active events *received by* the passible soul. Anthony Kenny's now standard translation in *Philosophical Writings III* replaces *sont mises* by "it receives" and all the following active verbs by noun phrases. As in usual translations of *res cogitans*, this loses the older tradition in whose terms Descartes conducted his arguments and alters them to something modern readers recognize as "Cartesian." Here, we have needed to see how, in his arguments about thinking and about God, Descartes himself made something approaching subjective willful agency *out of* older habits of mind and experiences of being.

To transform this ever-moving passible thinking into an agent, *cogito* or *ego cogito*, exemplified a trope with which Descartes' studies in rhetoric familiarized him: "personification, the pre-eminent rhetorical figure of agency," as Victoria Kahn says (554). For Descartes, as for his teachers, rhetoric was always a road to something else, a bridge. Here, it enabled a particular sort of passage. As the thinking process became an agent, not only reasoning (including doubting, imagining, denying, affirming) but also *willing* had to characterize it. As an agent, the *cogito*'s own contents were converted into its ground. As an agent (after the arguments for God had been made), it held the idea of agency fuller than its own, capable, indeed, of everything. This idea of something perfect and greater than itself cannot have been made by the *cogito*, Descartes argued, since a lesser cannot make a greater, and these current dilemmas of thinking show "me" to be not perfect and so not self-made. Perfection by definition includes existence (of perfect *res cogitans*; Greek *ousia*): we call that perfection God.

Agency's willfulness became abstract absolute will. But *cogito*'s security was grounded above all in a *recta ratio*, a right reason, whose foundations, *per se*, could not deceive. It could reach wrong conclusions from wrong information, but that was distinct from the rectitude of the rightly organized process itself. So it is not surprising that after personifying supreme agency, as Descartes returned in the fourth Meditation to further explore its foundations (in issues of reason, freedom, matters indifferent, truth and falsehood), he made this a definition of the human's secure relation with God: "I recognize it to be impossible that he should ever deceive me; for in every fraud or deception is to be found some imperfection" (AT 7.53). The same was so for the faculty of judgment that such a God placed in one, since a perfect being could not *set out* to falsify.

Truth was the identified ground and end not only of Method, but also of the subject, as well as of reason, morality and a communal ethics — what we more usually choose to call politics. And truth was being approached, here, by means of arguments no longer familiar, but which were once common in both theology and rhetoric: arguments about "things indifferent." For Christians these were matter of worldly knowledge or action irrelevant to salvation or damnation. Their idea came primarily from Stoic debate, where *adiaphora* referred to a class of morally neutral things to be preferred or rejected according to one's purpose and one's situation (Saunders 104–10). For Stoics, the material world was wholly composed of such *adiaphora*. Descartes certainly knew the work of Neostoic thinkers like Lipsius (himself trained by Jesuits, who used his writings in their schools), Pierre Charron, du Vair, Erycius Puteanus and others. Students of the Jesuits were anyway introduced early in their education to *indifferentia* through Cicero's *Paradoxa*.

Things concerning God were clearly not indifferent—hence the need to ground truth there. About everything else not only was there room for debate, but perhaps, too, no way to determine a decision. To personify the *cogito* as willful agency and find its *exemplum* in God explains why Descartes insisted that it was "only the will, or freedom of choice, that I experience within me to be so great that I can grasp the idea of none greater; so much so that it is above all through the will that I understand myself to bear some image and likeness of God" (AT 7.57). It also explains why God, will and the ground of truth were virtually equated. Otherwise truth itself would fall into the realm of the indifferent and of mere rhetorical advantage: as Kahn puts it, some absolute truth was needed "as a check on the weakness of individual judgment and the indeterminacy of the rhetorical 'wars of Truth'" (555). But how could mere assertion of such truth distinguish it from falsehood? In *Areopagitica* (1644), John Milton approached Descartes' "solution": "For who knows not that Truth is strong, next to the Almighty; she needs no policies, nor stratagems, nor licensings to make her victorious; Those are the shifts and the defences that error uses against her power." But here, truth fast became as slippery as falsehood, changeable as Proteus, turning "herself into all shapes" (*Areopagitica* 328; Kahn 555–57).

Truth of this sort would indeed be protean. Made from rhetoric as the site where things indifferent were debated, it was at once its supreme figure and personification of rhetoric's own inventiveness. Such truth would necessarily be conflated "with the realm of things indifferent" (Kahn 557). That is exactly what Descartes would avoid. There had to be certainty and security of truth able to ground the willful self *for right action in the world*. That was why Descartes explored *indifferentia* in just this context, continuing the passage I earlier quoted:

for [the will, *or free will*] consists simply in that we can do or not do (that is, affirm or deny, pursue or flee), or rather, simply in that we are brought [*feriamur*] to an affirming or denying, a pursuing or fleeing what is proposed to us by the intellect [*nobis ab intellectu proponitur*] in such a way that we sense we have been determined to it [*ad id determinari*] by no external force. For me to be free, I do not need to be able to be moved two ways, but on the contrary, the more (I) lean in one direction, whether because (I) understand evidently that truth and goodness lie in it or because God so disposes my inmost thoughts, the more (I) choose more freely. Neither divine grace nor natural knowledge ever diminishes freedom, but rather increases and confirms it. (AT. 7.57–58)

To hesitate between possibilities, he added, to hold a choice "indifferent," was "the lowest level of freedom." To lack constraint was but anarchic license: "not at all perfection of will, but defect of knowledge, or some negation: for if I always saw clearly what is true and good, I should never deliberate over what is to be chosen or judged; and so although I would evidently be free, I could never be indifferent" (AT 7.59). I am reminded of an incandescent phrase in Vincent Yu-chung Shih's translation of Liu Hsieh's (465–522 A.D.) celebrated critical work, *The Literary Mind and the Carving of Dragons*. Writing of the Chinese classic *Book of Poetry*, Liu remarked that "the single idea that runs through [its] three hundred poems . . . is freedom from undisciplined thought" (43). "Freedom from undisciplined thought" exactly catches Descartes' thought here, freedom from Montaigne's *branloire perenne*. The will can be "indifferent," Descartes continued the passage just cited, only where its knowledge is insufficient. There it should make no choice at all: "if I abstain from making a judgment, it is clear I am acting rightly and not erring" (AT 7.59). Free will and things indifferent were not of transitory concern, and Descartes returned to them in two letters to Mesland in 1644 and 1645 (AT 4.115–16, 173–75). They set conditions for passages *par provision*—a withholding of decision until certainty was possible. That was as much the reason for not publishing the *Monde* in 1633, as for giving the *morale par provision* in 1637. We start to see how subject itself needs to be seen as the provisional instrument it was: a rhetorical tool to ground new formations of truth and society. Not incidentally, in this light, did Descartes try to forge a rational community from the *Meditations* themselves, in the *Objections* and *Replies*.

Even more, to apply once-theological argument to a citizen's life in community would not be overly hard: or at least to know what was needed for it. A moral measure was needed to direct clear-sighted grasp of the true and good, that "highest and most perfect moral system" proposed in the "Lettre-Préface" to the *Principes*. This measure would give the same bounds of control and sureties of truth in the sphere of ethics and politics as God did in those of ontology and theology. Once found, it could rule the fine concord of public and private life which Descartes also named there. So when he took up the fourth Meditation's argument in the *Passions de l'âme* to apply it to relations between desire and truth, passion and goodness, freedom and order (§§144–48), he phrased it so as to join theological, psychological and political connotations: "I see in us only one thing able to give us legitimate reason to value us [*de nous estimer*], namely the use of our free will [*libre arbitre*] and the empire we have over our volitions [*volontés*]." This, he said, as he had nine years before, "makes us in some way like God, by making us masters of ourselves" (§152: AT 11.445). The 1644 *Principia* had echoed such assertions (Pt. 1, §§6, 35: AT 8A.6, 18). The *Passions de l'âme* began to offer the needed moral measure. The two paragraphs after the one just cited defined "generosity" as mutual selfe-knowledge and sharing among subjects.

The *Passions* were trying to generalize thoughts Descartes first advanced in a September 1646 letter to the Princess Elisabeth about Machiavelli's *Prince*. Through them *cogito* and subject, whatever its initial self-possessive agency, might be reinserted in community. To have made even an *idea* of personal agency foundational of a thinking subject set huge difficulties for continuance of traditional forms of community. This agent/subject was always potentially clashing with other subjects whose active goals competed. That was no doubt why Descartes, writing to his friend Hector-Pierre Chanut in November 1646, said that all passions were good except one: anger (AT 4.538). Anger bred offending exchanges: Hélisenne's opening, Montaigne's worry, Hurault's and du Vair's polemic. Descartes had lived with the sociopolitical context of the dilemma from long before the *Meditations*. Drawing this discussion about personhood toward western modernity, I want to suggest that he used that context in trying to resolve the dilemma. We shall see him torn on a cusp between traditional experiences of identity and community and later ones. We shall also see that he could *only* work them out in a conjuncture of the public and the private or, as many now prefer to say, the political and the personal.

CHAPTER EIGHTEEN

Selfehood, Political Community and a "Cartesian" Future?

Descartes aimed to compose a complete systematic philosophy. After Aristotle, this meant *organon*/method, analyses of the material world and its grounding (metaphysics), and analyses of the human, its world, actions and establishments. Its culmination would be that most perfect moral system that Descartes said was the goal of his scientific studies. "Politics" was the final element in such a moral system, so it is no surprise that in the *Discours* and the 1640s correspondence with Elisabeth political questions often took center stage. This chapter is interested not in putative future political applications of his philosophy (Guenancia, Leroy, Negri), but in actual politico-theoretical aspects of his thinking and their connection with the passage-technique establishment of subjective agency. Descartes' relations with the Royal House Palatine and firsthand knowledge of European political and military conditions, particularly events of the Thirty Years' War and associated polemics emanating mostly from the exiled Palatine court and Sweden, were of crucial importance both to his efforts to respond to the problem that arose from setting subjective agency against community and to his development of a different idea of personal agency, identity and the political association that (necessarily) accompanied them.

Descartes' first published work was the 1637 *Discours*. He chose to frame its supposedly only epistemological arguments in reflections instantly reminding its readers of the current wars and their origins. In the so-called *Observations* of 1619, Descartes recorded a dream "involving the Seventh Ode of Ausonius, which begins *Quod vitae sectabor iter?*" "What road in life shall I follow?" In the *Olympica*, he put the exact date as November 10: "full of enthusiasm, convinced [I] had discovered the foundations of a marvelous science" (AT 10.216–17). The *Discours* told that this revelation occurred while he was "returning to the army from the emperor's coronation," in the celebrated *poêle* "in Germany, where I had been called by the wars that are not yet ended there" (AT 6.11): or "here," he might have added, since in 1635 Richelieu had taken France into what would later be known as the Thirty Years' War. David Lachterman humorously termed this "a retreat from the *polis* to the *poêle*" ("Descartes"). The deliberate tie Descartes made between the personal and the political was important.

The new emperor Ferdinand's accession and Catholic fervor were what had provoked the Bohemians to revolt and elect a Protestant monarch to their throne. The duke of Bavaria's army, to which Descartes was "returning," he said, was the force that would defeat Frederick V, elector Palatine and newly created king of Bohemia, outside Prague on November 8, 1620, and which would eventually occupy and despoil the Palatinate itself. Frederick was the father of Descartes' later correspondent, the princess Elisabeth. Descartes would not meet the princess until 1642, but the wars were still ongoing, as he noted, while he was writing the *Discours* probably during 1627–37. The conflicts were not over until October 1648, with the signing of the Treaty of Westphalia, although France and Spain continued hostilities until the signing of the Treaty of the Pyrenees in 1659: a continuation affecting the French revolts of the Frondes. Descartes' choice of frame for the Method indicated a sphere of principal concern, one too long underemphasized.

Historians argue that the Treaty of Westphalia made the political map of modern Europe. I suggest that its general context also made conditions for a sea-change in the experience and understanding of personal and political identity. Descartes' writing was embedded in that context. The Treaty was not an isolated event. In England, in 1648, Parliament voted to bring Charles I to trial. In France, the parliamentary Fronde began at the end of August with insurrection in Paris, justifying Anne of Austria's and Jules Mazarin's fear that their country might follow England's path to civil war and subversion of monarchy (Knachel 18–49). For Descartes, who wrote of all these affairs, the moment was personally uncertain. He was in Paris from May 1648 when events began which ended in the eruption of the first Fronde. He wrote of them anxiously in a letter to Elisabeth. He had been wanting to leave Holland for what had been a more peaceful Paris. He was now disappointed (AT 5.198). Too, while the Lower Palatinate had been restored to Elisabeth's older brother by one of the clauses of Westphalia and Descartes invited to go there, he wrote to her on February 22, 1649, that it was presently too war-torn and would be truly "agreeable" only "after two or three years of peace" (AT 5.285). So it was that Queen Christina's invitation to Sweden seemed to come just at the right time—even though he wrote ambivalently about it to Chanut on March 31, 1649 (AT V.326–27).

Descartes' epistolary remarks on the political events of the last years of the Thirty Years' War suggest that if he did "retreat" from the public arena in 1619, he returned to the fray less than twenty-five years later. The retreat was anyway more symbolic than real. It is virtually sure that he fought at Prague in 1620. He roamed Europe for the next few years, "withdrawing" to Holland only in 1628. Even then he was by no means aloof from public events, corresponding constantly with some of those most closely involved. His civil "retreat" was analogous to the project of the *Discours* "to undertake studies within myself too," the thinking that led to the "discovery" of Method (AT 6.10). This was a process always accompanied by material experiment: in medicine, anatomy and biology, in optics (including manufacturing instruments), in meteorology, astronomy and other physical sciences.

Once the Method was finished in 1637, Descartes was sure of having found a tool able to yield all knowledge, although, said the Preface to the French *Principes*, practical difficulties meant that "several centuries may pass before people actually deduce from these principles all the truths that can be deduced from them" (AT 9B.20). This Method, I argue, was less that of part 2 of the *Discours* than that set out in part 6, the *Géométrie, Dioptrique* and Replies to the Objections to the *Meditations*. It meant constructing hypotheses, observing and experimentally testing worldly events, verifying the hypotheses and setting new ones. It led "to knowledge of true events in the world insofar as 'truth' was just their predictability and reproducibility" (Reiss, "Neo-Aristotle" 217–22: here 221). By the end of the 1640s, Descartes had gone far toward deducing fruits of Method applied to sociopolitical dilemmas and had shown, in his correspondence with Elisabeth and in the *Passions* that derived from their exchanges, how this involved changes in the experience of both personal and social identities, changes demanded by the construction of subjective agency in the *Meditations*. Method, here, showed how to order authority in the state, as well as relations between sovereign and subjects and among subjects. Descartes himself seems to have hoped to reconstruct a community based on love and friendship. Others drew from the terms of his thought elements for a contractual, conflictual civil society (not so much *his*, as representative of thinking and practices which his thought exemplified). While Descartes clarified his views on these matters only in the second half of the 1640s, he seems to have thought Method capable of being applied to them even as he wrote the *Discours* a decade earlier. It matters, then, to show how deeply he set this writing in the actualities of a specific history.

Descartes finished the *Discours* between late 1635 and June 1637, when Jean Maire issued it at Leiden. Years earlier, in a letter of March 30, 1628, Descartes' friend Jean-Louis Guez de Balzac had asked to know how his "project on the story [*histoire*] of [his] Mind" was advancing (AT 1.570–71). Was this the first part of the *Discours*? Since the find of a broadsheet announcing Descartes' defense of his law theses in 1616, we know that aspects of this part went back to this time: dedicating the theses to his uncle he observed the merely preparative nature of his education and hoped for a single guiding reason for all areas of knowledge ("Licence"). If the writing of the *Discours* did occupy, on and off, the ten years from 1627 to 1637, as shown by evidence offered by Gilbert Gadoffre in an important series of essays, we are speaking precisely of the middle years between the time of the dreams, when Descartes first turned seriously to epistemological and metaphysical questions, and the year of his "flight" to Sweden from the tumult of France in revolt, a war-torn Palatinate and a Holland he no longer found congenial. These years were exactly those of the Thirty Years' War. In letters to Elisabeth he frequently advised on events and her family's political situation. The timing of the *Discours* may be anecdotal. It is not trivial.

To clarify its full significance I review other facts of the military and political events which Descartes recalled at the start of part 2 of the *Discours* and assumed familiar to his readers. These actualities matter because this writing is as crucial to understanding Descartes' further thoughts on identity and polity as later letters, especially the one written to Elisabeth in September 1646 in answer to her request that he say what he thought of Machiavelli's *Prince*.

Frederick had been Ferdinand's rival for the Empire. After the election and coronation of the new emperor (witnessed by Descartes, he told his readers), whose anti-Protestant repression during the years since he had been king of Bohemia (1617) had already alienated his subjects, the Bohemians offered their crown to the young elector. Over much opposition he unwisely accepted, provoking the most serious political struggles of his age, in the wars whose resolution thirty years later determined European order for the next three centuries. He entered Prague in late summer 1619 with his queen, Elizabeth, daughter of England's James I, from whom Frederick expected military aid in vain (a failure for which James was popularly castigated at home, though Frederick could be seen as usurping a legitimate throne, making it hard for a sitting monarch to support him, especially one whose own Protestantism kept him prey to Catholic European enmity). Known as the Winter King because of his reign's length, Frederick was defeated at the Battle of the White Mountain in early November 1620. The duke of Bavaria soon expropriating his Palatinate, he and his family went into exile, finally finding asylum at The Hague. The loss of the Palatinate was the engine that kept the wars going. To Descartes, that loss made the Palatinate into a base of "zero power" analogous to the mind in a state of radical doubt, from which a new order could be made by methodical ordering of foundations of society as Method ordered common sense.

Frederick's winter was the same whose "onset detained" Descartes "alone in a stove-heated room" at Ulm in Germany (AT 6.11). The future philosopher of Method had gone to Holland in early 1618 or late 1617 to do his military apprenticeship, like so many others of his age and class, in Maurice of Nassau's model army. Five weeks after the emperor Matthias' death on March 20, 1619, Descartes set out from Breda, where he had been barracked, and set sail on April 29, first for Denmark, he told Beeckman (AT 10.165–66), eventually for Germany and the August coronation of the emperor Ferdinand. He was, he had written a few days before to the same friend, on his way to sign up with the Duke Maximilian of Bavaria although he "suspected there would be a lot of men under arms, but no fighting" (AT 10.162). His few extant letters to Beeckman from this time are a mixture of mathematical and other discoveries, tales of his travels, expressions of ambition concerning his new science and remarks on the political and military troubles (AT 10.151–66). The mix continued, and Frederick's defeat corresponded to another date given by Descartes: "In the year 1620, I began to understand the fundamental principles of a wonderful discovery" (AT 10.216), presumably that foretold by the 1619 dream. Since Descartes stressed political and military events in the *Discours* (yet more, we shall see), we can safely think that he meant to link them with his other interests. And if, in 1637, Descartes knew few, if any, of the chief personages involved in these events, he certainly knew some of their associates. In later years, he was to know some of them personally, sustaining practical political concerns.

Frederick's queen was James I's daughter. The (ex-)elector died in 1632. Two of his sons, Rupert and Maurice, were to fight for their uncle Charles I in the English civil wars (Rupert went on to head the English navy for his cousin Charles II in the Dutch wars after the Restoration). Frederick's and Elizabeth's daughter Sophia was to become the mother of the elector of Hanover, future George I of England. During the 1640s, teen-age Sophia became go-between for Descartes and her sister Elisabeth when the latter thought their exchange of letters was getting too risky, as they were now writing directly on political matters, Machiavelli, reason of state, the behavior of princes (especially her brothers'). Descartes had already raised such issues in the *Discours*. His remarks on Machiavelli and princely behavior recalled aspects of the *morale par provision*, whose context Descartes had explicitly politicized.

It was Elisabeth to whom Descartes dedicated his 1644 *Principia* and at whose behest he elaborated and then published the *Passions* in 1649. To her he wrote in January 1646 praising the "prudence" of another brother, Edward, who had married Anne de Gonzague, princess of Mantua and the king of Poland's sister-in-law in April 1645, and soon converted to Catholicism. Elisabeth was outraged, but Descartes argued that, lacking might, such behavior was a way to help rebuild their House. His conversion showed that God used all means to bring humans back to Him (said to the piously Protestant Elisabeth!), but especially that her brother was capable of the "worldly prudence [*la prudence du siècle*]" needed to restore "fortune" (AT 4.352).

These remarks could be taken to smack of Machiavelli: religion in service to the state or princely prudence as knowing how to attract and tame fortune by *virtù*. Pierre Mesnard speaks of Descartes' "so-called Machiavellism" (*Essai* 190); most other commentators on this aspect of his thought agree. French civil war polemics had made such ideas commonplace. To Cardin Le Bret and Richelieu, Balzac and Naudé, they were clichés. Analysis of Mazarin's diplomatic correspondence of the 1640s shows that he, his ambassadors and spies were all sure that English parliamentarians were using religion as a pretext to seize power. Mazarin thought Charles wrong not to take the puritans' religion and then crush them after consolidating his power (Knachel 26–32). This would have been rational prudence and political virtue. But Descartes' worldly prudence was also Cicero's *prudentia*, integral virtue of all who lived well in the world. For Pierre Charron, Montaigne's "disciple," it was "the knowledge and choice of things to be desired or avoided; the just estimate and selection of things; the eye that sees, directs and orders all. It consists of three things of equal importance: consulting and deliberating well, judging and resolving well, directing and effecting well" (3.1.545). This definition tied the public counsel whose virtue Montaigne had stressed to a lucid rationality that could be collective or personal. In Charron it was the first, and he grounded his discussion wholly on the four ancient virtues. But his definition clearly held other possibilities of agency.

Writing to Elisabeth about her family three years after his letter about Edward, Descartes showed similar flexibilities. On February 22, 1649, he wrote to console her after her uncle's execution, which marked "the grievous conclusion of England's tragedies." At least, this death was "more glorious, happier and sweeter" than that suffered by "common men" (AT 5.281–82). Was this to signal the greatness of the princess' royal house? Were admiration for Charles' courtly self-control and sympathy for his death (as he said) to be turned to prudential advantage? There was, anyway, no little ambivalence in Descartes' passing directly from thus consoling Elisabeth to a brief discussion of Queen Christina's interest in his work, but of her silence on matters pertaining to the Palatinate and Westphalia, in which Sweden had been a principal player.

Descartes offered a reason for this silence: "since the conditions of the peace are not as favorable to your House as they could have been, those who contributed to it are in doubt as to whether you think ill of them, and for this reason hold back from showing you friendship" (AT 5.283–84). This led straight to discussion of those conditions and what her older brother Charles-Louis (Karl-Ludwig) ought to be doing to rebuild and consolidate their power. Charles I died on February 9 (New Style: January 30, Old), but since the signing of the Treaty of Westphalia the previous October, Descartes remarked *en peine*, he had yet to hear whether her brother had accepted it, let alone made the necessary responsive moves. While peace had not restored all their father's territories, he agreed, the Treaty had restored the Lower Palatinate and established a new Electorate (the original staying with Bavaria, whose 1620 seizure of the Upper Palatinate was confirmed). Descartes was distressed that nothing could come of nothing. Charles-Louis had to begin building somewhere.

As before, what concerned him was how to establish—re-establish— a legitimate and good society. That the Palatinate lacked force might well make for a more legitimate state:

When what is a matter of the restitution of a state occupied or disputed by others who have the upper hand in force, it seems to me that those who only have justice and the rights of people on their side should never insist on satisfying all their claims. They have far greater cause for gratitude to those who get some of them redressed, however small a part it be, than for hatred of those who retain the rest. (AT 5.284)

Additionally, the "prudence" that encouraged one to stay friends with all might go further toward "maintaining one's position." For all this prince knew, the greater powers might have restored his lands to avoid the danger of any one of them becoming too powerful, since they would obviously prefer no Palatinate to another potential rival. This need for balance might eventually provoke the mutual destruction it was designed to prevent, and so the Palatinate's forceful resurgence. The prince must know how to bide his time (AT 5.284–85). Descartes did not spell out this last, but it would agree fully with the advice he had given Elisabeth about her brother Edward.

These efforts to adjust reason and force, prudence and utility, communal experience and personal interest, marked all Descartes' thinking about politics and the identities and persons it supposed. These cases show that his seemingly "abstract" thinking cannot be separated from concrete historical event and actual experience. That was why I mentioned his dependence on experiment and observation in scientific study. Basic to the scientific reason that would lead to the highest and most perfect moral system, they related to that reason as observation of political actuality related to the sociopolitical sphere actualizing the same moral system. It is in this sense that the Palatinate stood as the rational "zero point" mentioned earlier.

Its present impotent position was equivalent to the isolation "in a stove-heated room" of 1619: a point from which to think and make the new. Lack of power was a moment of suspension identical to that of radical doubt. From it, social reason and *right* public ethics could be rebuilt. In both cases, there was a "dialectic" between conceptual withdrawal and material experience. In its part 1, the *Discours* gave the *histoire*, the "*fable*," of a mind. That story had to be suspended to allow rediscovery of humans' shared good sense and the methodical reason able to actualize it. Similarly, Descartes initially suspended the history of his time: not just in the *poêle* of 1619, but in Holland from 1628, whence he wrote to Balzac on May 5, 1631, praising the United Provinces' tranquility against the turbulence everywhere else (AT 1.203–4). He repeated this commentary at the end of part 3 of the *Discours*, making it an aspect of his "desire" to merit the esteem in which he was held, part of which meant fulfilling his duty to public welfare:

Exactly eight years ago . . . this desire made me resolve to move away from all places where I might have acquaintances and move here, to a country [Holland] where the long duration of war [the Eighty Years' revolt against Spain] has established such orders that the armies maintained here seem to serve only to make people enjoy the fruits of peace with all the more security, and where, among the mass of a very busy people more concerned with its own business than curious of others', I have been able to live as solitary and retired as in the most remote deserts without lacking any of the comforts found in the most populous cities. (AT 6.30–31)

As a conceptual starting point, this was a constant refrain; repeated as late as a letter to Hector-Pierre Chanut on February 26, 1649, when he regretted having been in Paris at the outbreak of the first Fronde (AT 5.293), and often to Elisabeth. At the start, as in the first Meditation, world events, historic tumult, concrete experiences, were conceptually incidental. Only of this initial stage of thought as a kind of Husserlian *epochē* is Henri Gouhier right to speak of Descartes' separation of reason and experience (271–80). The separation marked a particular moment of thought, not a whole system's logic. Descartes emphasized interplay of thought and experience in a May 1646 letter to Elisabeth:

I have no doubt that [the maxim on "civil life"] Your Highness proposes is the best of all: that it is better in such matters to follow experience than reason, for one rarely has to deal with reasonable people, as all should be, so that one could judge what they will do from mere consideration of what they should do. And often the best advice is not the most successful. That is why one is obliged to take risks [*de hasarder*], and put oneself in the power of fortune. (AT 4.412)

Risk taking or guesswork (*hasarder*), inconstant experience, unreason . . . This seems much *à la Montaigne*, as Léon Brunschvicg observes (*Descartes*)—although we have begun to see what Descartes did with these reminiscences. Too, we have seen him proposing reasonable political means for getting fortune on one's side. Experience in civil affairs and personal and/or general reason were not inevitably opposed. Humans could be trained into habitual use of their common good sense: Method as *habitus*. And as methodical use of right reason could be trained, so could methodically ordered social experience, and, eventually, "generous" application of the passions. Descartes was always clear on the need for rational experience (as opposed to a "raw experience" that both Bacon and Galileo dismissed as not just unusable but strictly *meaningless*).

Good sense was to Method as human history to methodical civil society. Descartes hoped that such an equation would enable an agent subject to be re-articulated on a civil community of traditional values. In part 6 of the *Discours*, he proposed this equation, comparing progressive linear acquisition of methodical scientific knowledge to that of economic or military power:

For the case is much alike for those who gradually discover truth in the sciences and those who, starting to become rich, have less trouble making large acquisitions than they had before, when they were poorer, making much smaller ones. Or they may be compared to army commanders, whose forces tend to grow in proportion to their victories, and who need more skill to maintain their position after losing a battle than they do to capture towns and provinces after winning it. For to try and defeat all the difficulties and errors that prevent us from reaching knowledge of the truth is truly to fight battles, and we lose one whenever we accept some false opinion concerning an important question of general import, and need much more skill afterwards to regain the state we were in before than to make great progress when we already have principles that are firmly grounded. (AT 6.66–67)

The military metaphor harks back to Descartes' Jesuit training. We shall soon see how important to relations between individual and society were habit and knowledge of truth discussed here. Now, I want to highlight three ideas: the creation of a foundation, the linear process of growth (see, too, Matheron 90) and the relation between the search for truth and civil and military power, between Method as an order of reason and Method as an order of society.

For all this implied that one removed oneself from the tumult of political and social history for the same reason that one removed oneself from the prior history of one's mind. Montaigne had separated the two because *fantasie privée* brought into the public sphere would destroy it. Descartes thought, rather, that eventual right practice required one first to find right rule, and this was that "marvelous science" sought from the *Regulae* through the *Discours* to the *Meditationes*. A utopian solution to Montaigne's problem? Perhaps. But Descartes, writing to Mersenne on November 20, 1629, about a possible universal language, ended by saying that Method itself presupposed "great changes in the order of things, and the whole world would have to be a terrestrial paradise; something to be proposed only in the realm of fiction" (AT 1.82). Just eight years later, he made public this utopian Method, remarking a further ten years on, in the preface to the *Principes*, that the Method would ultimately permit everyone to accede to knowledge of all truths. Surely the state, society and subject among them.

Until this enlightened time, humans would have to live by experience, not reason, since they did not act like "reasonable people." Once rational "prudence" ruled events, a true sovereign would have no difficulty, but "all humans would have to be perfectly sensible, so that knowing what they must do, one [would] be sure of what they will do." Even that might not suffice, for all humans had their "free will" and only God knew its motion. The gap between perfection of will and imperfection of reason made for these difficulties. Too, due to differences between peoples' reason and temperament, two "inferiors" could often better judge each other's future actions than a superior could either's. To judge what a person would do required sharing the same intellectual capacity. All this meant, wrote Descartes to Elisabeth in the November 3, 1645, letter that I have been quoting, was that methodical reason was essential if anarchy was to be avoided (AT 4.334). *Pace* James Schall and others, Descartes did indeed assert "that agreement in civil affairs [would] result from his philosophical method" (263–64).

On one side were actual society, common sense, experience and history, on another the rational communal state, Method, reason and invention of a new instauration—or adjustment of an old. The will of the thinking subject was to create fresh knowledge to replace former age-old authority and new relations within the social and political. Montaigne's old public subject would be that of the *morale par provision*, of concrete history to be purified and changed. Old private being could now be established as willful agent subject, in the lucid stability of the *cogito*. Reason, virtue, habit and the good conduct to follow would let the new subject be concretized in history: a history where force and reason, virtue and power, community and subject drew each to the other. Parts 2 and 3 of the *Discours* already gave the needed bridge, necessary passage techniques; as they also affirmed, via the *poêle*, we shall see, that a general new foundation was indeed at issue.

Descartes presented the work as a history of a thinking subject, first recounting rejection of an authoritative past and abrogation of a particular history. But I dwelt on his relations with the Palatine court and knowledge of general European crisis because, second, he immediately gave political meaning to his search for a philosophical Method based in this rejection and abrogation. Besides framing it with the ongoing war, he emphasized an architectural metaphor long applied in political theory and, at least since Bacon, to the idea of a new conceptual instauration. Descartes undertook a new construction, even as he disingenuously claimed to set bounds on it:

> It is true that we do not see all the houses of a city pulled down for the sole purpose of rebuilding them in a different way and to make the streets more beautiful; but we do indeed see many having theirs pulled down in order to rebuild them, sometimes even being forced to do so when the houses are in danger of falling down on their own and when the foundations are not well secure. By this example I was persuaded that it would not be reasonable for an individual [*un particulier*] to plan to reform a State, by changing everything from the foundation up and overturning it in order to set it up again; nor, again, to reform the body of the sciences or the order established in the schools for teaching them. (AT 6.13)

He said that he wished only to correct his own thinking, lead his life on principles firmer than the "old foundations," and not reform "even minor matters affecting public institution" (AT 6.14). While these did show some "imperfections," any stable situation was preferable to change. Nonetheless, he had just asserted, the best-ordered states were certainly those that from the outset "observed the basic constitutions established by some prudent law-giver. Just as it is certain that the state of the true religion, whose basic ordinances God alone has made, must be incomparably better ruled than all the others" (AT 6.12). He then instances Sparta, long-lived because properly ordered by the single legislator Lycurgus. This whole passage leads one to conclude again that Descartes actually saw state, scientific and educational reforms in tandem. The *Discours* already contained and was immediately followed by first steps in the scientific reform that he denied undertaking (the *Dioptrique*, the *Météores* and the *Géométrie*). It was further followed by the *Meditations* as concerned foundations and then by the psychology of the *Pas-*

sions. Educational reform continued in the *Principia*, written explicitly to replace older school manuals.

Should we not see Descartes' analyses in his correspondence with Elisabeth (and his direct relations with political players) as no less concrete an effort, if not directly to reform the state, at least to have his ideas filter into the political sphere? A sphere, he always said, more intractable than those of science and education—and more dangerous. That Descartes saw it in this light is shown in precautions taken to hide that part of their correspondence. On October 10, 1646, he even proposed to Elisabeth that they write in cipher (AT 4.524). The worry is only explained as a fear that other readers would think them aiming toward new political establishment. Concealment applied to Elisabeth and him the rule of prudence applauded in Edward and desired in humankind at large. The *Discours* itself applied such prudence in denying that its new foundations applied to all spheres of human action. A more celebrated moment is to be similarly understood.

We have already seen that Montaigne gave Descartes some important points. Brunschvicg recalls others: the idea of ubiquitous good sense and the importance of military apprenticeship in youth's development (*Descartes* 115–16, 126–27). For Montaigne such apprenticeship could not but be bound up with his era's civil wars. Good sense and armies bring us inevitably to Descartes' German *poêle* and revelation explicitly set in wars that began as one between Protestant Bohemia and Catholic Empire, upstart Palatine and settled Hapsburg. By 1637, Descartes and his readers knew that the wars in whose onset he had participated were remaking the face of Europe as earlier Protestant-Catholic war had remade France's. His celebrated *poêle* was as much literary reminiscence as real memory. It was familiar as a metaphor for revolt and renewal.

At the start of the earlier French wars, Pierre de Ronsard had written in praise of Lorraine, opposed to Germany, in strikingly similar terms. In his "repetition" Descartes chose to put himself in the position of those whom the poet saw in 1560 as the originators of rebellion:

> O bien-heureux Lorrains, que la secte Calvine,
> Et l'erreur de la terre à la vostre voisine
> Ne deprava jamais! D'où serait animé
> Un habitant du Rhin en un poësle enfermé,
> A bien interpreter les Saintes Escritures,
> Entre les gobelets, les vins et les injures?

> O happy Lorrainers, whom the Calvinist sect and the wrong of the land bordering on yours never perverted! How could a Rhine dweller closed up in a stove-heated room manage to interpret Holy Scriptures well, between cups, wine and abuse?

("Discours à Loys des Masures" ll.49–54: *Oeuvres* 2.571)

This elegy was dedicated in 1560 to the poet Louis des Masures, who had converted to Protestantism two years before. Descartes knew Ronsard's work well. Given the talk of city and concept building with which Descartes followed his own repetition of the *poêle*, it is relevant that the poem's next two lines directly referred to the same things, recalling a statue owned by des Masures: "Let whoever will believe it, Friend, I vow / By your beautiful Amphion never to believe it." Amphion was the poet-builder of Thebes. Descartes would not lose the irony that Ronsard addressed his disbelief in the legitimacy of Protestant revolt to a friend who had converted, was thus already a rebel, and yet who owned the statue of the city-making poet. Ronsard went on that "The other day while sleeping," he saw Joachim du Bellay's skeletal presence. How not to recall Descartes' dream in his *poêle*? In Ronsard's, du Bellay counseled his friend not to accept change. Since Descartes was later adopting the place of the Germans in their *poêle*, it is hardly surprising that he was also promoting change and the new. His now fully demonstrated Augustinian leanings (Janowski, Menn) may count, as well, in this Protestant "identification."

The literary model's importance, whether from Ronsard or Montaigne, is not that it saps in any way the reality of Descartes' experience. It simply associated it, in this case, with political and religious rebellion. Much earlier, in his *Petit Jehan de Saintré*, Antoine de la Sale had used the German *poêle* to debase the chivalric ideal and turn from an older cultural tradition. When the evil abbot derided Saintré to his Lady (the two interlocutors being guilty of sexual betrayal), reversing the chivalric ideal in a text nonetheless sympathetic to it, he chose this same metaphor: "further, my lady, I tell you more. When these knights or squires go off to do their knightly deeds and have bid farewell to the king, if it is cold they go off to those German stove-heated rooms [*pales*] and play around with girls all winter" (277). Again, the *poêle* depicted a reversal of norms: chivalric ideal, poetic romance and cultural tradition. In Torquato Tasso's *Gerusalemme liberata* (1.41–42), Guelpho and his German soldiers spent nights drinking in these rooms. In Ludovico Ariosto's earlier first Satire (which Descartes probably knew), the poet gave "il caldo de le stuffe," the heat of the stoves, as reason for his not going to Hungary in 1517, breaking with his patron Ippolito d'Este and changing his life (*Satires* 8). Contemporaneously, in the colloquy *Diversoria* ("Inns"), Erasmus pilloried German inns, drinking and overheated stove rooms ("*alemmanica hypocausta*") (*Colloquies* 147–52). One wonders if Descartes' closer predecessor, Cervantes, did not refer to the same image at the start of the second book of *Don Quijote*, when speaking, precisely, to the right organization of civil society:

In the course of their conversations they happened to discuss the principles of statecraft—as they are called—and methods of government, correcting this abuse and condemning that, reforming one custom and abolishing another, each one of the three setting up as a fresh legislator, a modern Lycurgus or a brand-new Solon. To such a degree did they fashion the commonwealth that it was as if they had taken it to the forge [*fragua*] and brought away a different one. (2.1)

Again, I do not propose that Descartes was referring to these predecessors, however well he may have known some among them. The point is simply that the *poêle* metaphor was familiar to his readers as marking a break with the past and an assertion of revolt and renewal. So, in the next century, Jean Le Rond d'Alembert was not mistaken when he wrote that Descartes could "be thought of as a leader of conspirators who, before anyone else, had the courage to rise against a despotic and arbitrary power and who, in preparing a resounding revolution, laid the foundations of a more just and happier government, which he himself was not able to see established" (80). To adopt Descartes' image of the state and science as houses to be raised on new foundations, adding the philosopher's sense of secret political revolt, was perspicuous. In Descartes these background memories lay hidden: more evidence of "prudence" and confirmation that his early motto, *larvatus prodeo*, "I go forward masked" (AT 10.213), was to be taken seriously. Yet the spirit underlying the prudence was there for all to see: the prudence would otherwise have been unnecessary.

This was not the only time that Descartes used such references, switching their apparent value to vital effect. Many have noted that the *Discours'* first sentence "began" in Montaigne's essay, *De la praesumption* (2.17), although Étienne Gilson showed its general shape as proverbial at least from Plato (*Discours*, commentary 85–88). But Brunschvicg, for one, arguing unoriginality, altogether ignored Montaigne's context (*Descartes* 115–16). He might have taken warning from what Descartes did with earlier remarks in the same essay: "It is a cowardly and servile humor to go and disguise and hide oneself under a mask, and not dare to have oneself seen as one is. That is how men stand ready for perfidy" (630). Descartes adopted this mask as his motto. Montaigne's aim was to show that we all fool ourselves about the truth and our own worth: "People commonly say that the fairest division nature has made of its gifts is that of sense: for there is no one who is not happy with what it has given them" (641). The closing irony queried the thought, stressing human reason's inconsistency and unreliability. Not so Descartes, who added, rather, that people were not wrong: they just did not use good sense properly. *That* was the issue. It mattered that in these familiar references Descartes was *showing* a switch in values: that relations between singular persons and society did not have to involve the former's inconstancy and unreason or depend on fortune and guesswork. The thinking subject could act rationally in and on history. This would be the real revolution. Descartes' use of literary reference was subtly significant. Textual precedents clarified a revolutionary meaning, helping the reader see the full implications of the *Discours*, as well as his relations with other thinkers of political instauration and reordering of identity.

Between words of prudence about the state, urged in the "reform" passage in part 2 of the *Discours* cited earlier, and the tale of the *poêle* and his German adventure, Descartes set a series of significant similes. First, "works composed of several parts and made by the hand of diverse craftsmen" usually had "not as much perfection" as "those on which one person has worked." Second, "buildings that a single architect has undertaken and completed are usually more beautiful and better ordered than those that several have tried to patch up by adapting old walls that had been built for other purposes." Third, he applied these dicta without delay to the construction of entire cities, "the state of the true religion, whose basic rules God alone has made" and to the excellence of the laws enacting Sparta's constitution, which, "devised by one person, all tended to one end" (AT 6.11–12). That these were clichés of political theory matters in grasping Descartes' purpose. It is useful to quote a passage from Machiavelli's *Discourses*, even though Descartes told Elisabeth in October or November 1646 that he had only read them very recently (AT 4.531):

Happy indeed should we call that state which produces a man so prudent that men can live securely under the laws which he prescribes without having to emend them. Sparta, for instance, observed its laws for more than eight hundred years without corrupting them and without any dangerous disturbance. Unhappy, on the other hand, in some degree is that city to be deemed which, not having chanced to meet with a prudent organizer, has to reorganize itself. And, of such, that is the more unhappy which is the more remote from order; and that is the more remote from order whose institutions have missed altogether the straight road which leads to its perfect and true destiny. For it is almost impossible that states of this type should by any eventuality be set on the right road again; whereas those which, if their order is not perfect, have made a good beginning and are capable of improvement, may become perfect should something happen which provides the opportunity. (*Discourses* 1.ii: 105)

Where did Descartes set himself in this accounting? In his well-known letter of September 1646 to Elisabeth about *The Prince*, he adopted several aspects of this more generous concept of state and sovereign authority and of those who live in and under them, adjusting it to his own ideas of prudence and right, virtue and interest, reason and utility.

To give this letter its full weight, since it leads into the "conclusion" of this analysis of persons and communities between Greek antiquity and the inception of European modernity, I recall another element of the passage just cited from part 2 of the *Discours*, of prime import when we speak of an *instauration* in the context of the European seventeenth century. It lies in the order true religion/methodical constitution of state; the move taking us from God to Sparta. The move already reveals the human *Fiat* with which Hobbes ushered in the "Pacts and Covenants" founding Leviathan. The *Fiat*'s premises were already in Bacon, whose Great Instauration and "Novus Atlas" were praised by the anonymous author of the preface to the *Passions* (perhaps Descartes, perhaps the abbé Claude Picot) as the only attempts before Descartes at a systematic construction of something really new (AT 11.320). In this treatise on the passions, Descartes again emphasized just which aspect of mind permitted the analogy between divine and human *Fiat*, and so not only the move from God to the City, but also one from agent subject to civil society:

I see only one thing in us that could give us just reason to esteem ourselves, namely, the use of our free will and the empire we have over our volitions. For it is only for actions that depend on this free will that we can with reason be praised or blamed, and it makes us in some way like God by making us masters of ourselves, provided we do not lose through cowardice [*lâcheté*] the rights it gives us. (§152: AT 11.445)

Empire, will, reason, actions, godlike humans, mastery and rights . . . Descartes might well have been thinking of his chiding the elector Charles-Louis in his February 1649 letter to Elisabeth for his failure in all these respects, by not returning to the Palatinate: this in the year in which the *Passions* were published. The word *lâcheté* was the word Montaigne used to qualify the contrary view when speaking of masks in his essay on presumption. It was free will that Descartes related to needs of worldly prudence in his November 1645 letter to Elisabeth, earlier cited at some length. In an "Author's Epistle to the Reader," Hobbes was to write that like the Spirit of God moving over the deep in the second verse of Genesis, the true philosopher had to let his "reason move upon the deep of his [own] cogitations and experience." The "method must resemble that of the creation." A direct analogy existed between "the order of the creation" and the "order of contemplation." As Descartes in the *Meditations* had hypostatized thinking into an agent subject with its requirements of action, so here Hobbes hypostatized these processes of reason into the state and civil society with *its* forms of action, here derived from, found in, one's "cogitations and experience" (*English Works* 1.1). The very organization of mind meant that God, the philosopher and the legislator,

like architect, city builder, person of wealth and army commander, acted
alike. True rational order applied in all spheres of action. Free will was
not just any old element of mind. It was directed to action. Whatever
"rights" we had lay in taking full and prudent responsibility for such action. This relation of will to ordered action matched that of reason to human "freedom" as the fourth Meditation's "freedom from undisciplined
thought."

This resulted from the power of our free will and its relation to a reason incommensurable with it. This was the moment in the Meditation
when Descartes stated for the first time the power of human will, its
equivalence with God's and its ability to act well when reason is clear and
not to do so when it is not. It was a thought on which he never failed to
insist:

But even if he who created us may be all-powerful, and even if he took pleasure
in deceiving us, we do not fail to experience in us a liberty such that whenever we
please we can abstain from believing things we do not know well, and so avoid
ever being mistaken. (*Principes* 1.§6: AT 9B.27)

This 1647 French version differs slightly from the 1644 Latin, which is
ambiguous as to whether the "mistake" is of reason or of consequent action (AT 8A.6). It is both, because freedom of will directs both thought
and action, or, to be precise, directs the thought that leads to action,
there being a pure thought that "consists in perceiving by the understanding" (1.§32: AT 9B.39). This thought is that passible kind we saw
in the last chapter as *receiving* ideas, in the same way as the senses receive
impressions or the soul receives passions: it "extends only to the few objects that present themselves to it, and its knowledge is always very limited." It was incommensurable with will, which "can in a sense seem infinite, because we perceive nothing able to be the object of some other
will, even of that immense [will] that is in God, which our own may not
also reach." Because of this we often act on it beyond our knowledge, and
so mistakenly (1.§35: AT 9B.40).

In the same year as the French *Principes*, he repeated humans' and
God's "sharing" of this supreme free will. Writing to Christina on December 20, 1647, he exaggerated the point, perhaps because he was writing to a ruler:

besides that free will is in itself the noblest thing in us, insofar as it makes us
somehow like God and seems to exempt us from being subject to him, so that its
good use is thus our greatest benefit, it is also the one most properly ours and
most important to us. It follows that it can also beget our greatest satisfactions.
(AT 5.85)

The volitions of which he would speak in the *Passions* were tied to the passions. They were those reactions, urges and desires whose excesses will and "generosity" had to control, most especially anger's case (§§202–3: AT 11.480–81). *Libre arbitre* was higher will, freedom to order life's actions. It was the will that "used reason" to create and institute any ordered system. As Benedict de Spinoza would say: where experienced action was concerned, "Voluntas et intellectus unum et idem sunt [Will and intellect are one and the same]" (*Ethics* 76.2: 49).

The thought of free self-directing human will was of a different order from what could have been thought before—especially as a good. Absent from Montaigne and others, slightly closer to Descartes a representative sample can be seen in that supposed apostle of new reason, the poet François de Malherbe. He ended his "Consolation à Monsieur du Périer": "To will what God wills is the only wisdom / That gives us rest" (*Oeuvres* 43). Written in 1598, this expressed the typical, even banal, sentiment of human subordination to the divine. Yet just because the consolation was a set piece, often reflecting a kind of stoical reliance on human reason, the thought of the human will's absorption into the divine is the more significant in its difference from what would later be found in Descartes. It was still Wyatt's sentiment. To see how far it differed from Descartes' view, one need but recall his consolation to Elisabeth on her uncle's execution, no less than his manner of "turning" Ronsard or Montaigne.

But mounting this free human agency gave Descartes a dilemma. Its agent, with its rights and freedom, seemed directed against the community whose maintenance was essential for human happiness. Such happiness, for all, had seemed possible only in a society not of rights and freedom but duties and subordination. I have also been urging that despite what most commentators have held, Descartes *was* in fact deeply concerned with this aspect of a person: to have divided the subject from community was to have made it less, not more, human (in the correspondence with Elisabeth, Descartes took Seneca as the ground of his discussions about morality).

Comparisons to Machiavelli, Bacon and Hobbes, and Descartes' use in the *Discours* and elsewhere of metaphors pertaining to political community are the tip of an iceberg. Just showing the elements of the *Discours* makes one doubt the limits Descartes affected to set on the use of Method. The more so, when he returns to the architectural metaphor at the start of the work's part 3. Here, it compared his provisional morality to a comfortable temporary dwelling, useful while building a new home, letting him meanwhile follow habitual laws, although their sole virtue was that of habit. For there was no reason to suppose there were not people "as sensible [*bien sensés*] among the Persians or Chinese as among us," although they obeyed different opinions and laws (AT 6.23)—another Montaigne reference. Descartes wrote that humans became different because they had been "raised from infancy among the French or Germans," "among the Chinese or cannibals" (AT 6.16). They differed not in common good sense but in custom and training. The thought hinted that under different laws, habits and opinions of all human societies lay one set of rational rules. These could be found and used to order societies just as Method ordered the "bon sens" that everyone shared.

This was Hobbes' goal in his 1642 *De cive*: not "to point what are the laws of any country but to declare what the laws of all countries are." Descartes read the bit more prescriptive Latin: "ne quicquam dissererem de cujuscunque civitatis legibus speciatim, id est, ne quae sint, sed quid sint leges, dicerem" (*English Works* 2.xxiii: *Opera* 2.152). Hobbes had read the *Discours* in 1637, when Sir Kenelm Digby lent him a copy (Mintz 10). In Paris from 1640, he stayed in close touch with its philosophical circles. He and Descartes fell out over his Objections to the *Meditations*. But Descartes wrote to an unknown correspondent, probably in 1643, that he had read the *De cive*, thought "its author the same as he who wrote the third objections against my *Meditations*" and could only say that he found "him much more astute in moral philosophy [*la morale*] than in metaphysics or physics" (AT 4.67). Descartes studied the *De cive* closely enough to have made notes and comments. Pierre Gisony, a physician and natural philosopher in Pierre Gassendi's circle, wrote to Hobbes from Paris on May 15, 1659, that he had read "some objections that M. Descartes once made against the excellent treatise on Politics [*De cive*]: they consist of ten or twelve lines" (Hobbes, *Correspondence* 1.502).

This is not to assert that the two philosophers shared views. They did not, as we know from Hobbes' writings on the *Meditations* and as Gisony's "objections" implies. I indeed argue that Descartes was trying to return to some older sense of community, one founded on love and friendship (included in the connotations of his *générosité*) against a conflictual contractual one referring, rather, to "anger." These connections show, though, that Descartes and Hobbes were thinking about the same sets of questions. The *Discours* was not the only place where the former stated the need to accept common experience while awaiting discovery of the one true ethical rule (in morality and politics) or one Method (in epistemology, metaphysics or science). Later, Method in hand, he would still warn readers of the *Principia*, that patience was needed: "it is certain that in regard to the conduct of our life we are obliged often to follow opinions that are only probable, because opportunities for action in our business would almost always be gone before we could free ourselves of all our doubts" (AT 9B.26). Provisional morality was to let the thinking agent's will act on the basis of *doxa*, until it could do so on a method found to underlie currently different moral or political activities of different societies (it is useful to note that Descartes called a *morale* what Gisony called a *Politique*: Hobbes' *De cive*).

While insisting on the universality of good sense and need of methodical reason from the first sentence of the *Discours*, Descartes stressed in part 2 that a city, society or state guided only by fortune would be no more effective than good sense failing to follow the right path of Method. This established an analogy showing that experience and habit guiding the *morale par provision* were to be eliminated as soon as a rule equivalent to Method was found. Too, while "the will of some men using reason" was far better than mere hazard (AT 6.12), better still was that of one: to have many trying to lead risked making a pattern as fantastic and disordered as that resulting from chance. In morality and politics as in mind and knowledge what was needed, at least initially, was one person using reason, guided by a free will that guaranteed the rights of the thinking subject in action. This was close to Machiavelli's claim in the *Discourses*, a work in which, contrary to *The Prince*, Descartes saw "no harm" (AT 4.531), that:

One should take it as a general rule that rarely, if ever, does it happen that a state, whether it be a republic or a kingdom, is either well-ordered at the outset or radically transformed *vis-à-vis* its old institutions unless this be done by one person. It is likewise essential that there should be but one person upon whose mind and method depends any similar process or organization. (1.xi: 132)

Again, this was why Descartes upbraided Charles-Louis.

Solution of his questions about relations between the individual and society, subject and state, and the seeming opposition between historical experience and methodical reason as regards those relations, had to await constitution of knowing and being. Achieving this in the *Meditations*, Descartes created the new problem of the agent subject. Still, just as the old history of mind was to be superseded by a new order of thought, so the civil morality of common habit and opinion, provisionally accepted, was to be superseded by a new rational society. Descartes' determination to advance "slowly," "like a man walking alone and in the dark," did not alter the goal of "seeking the true method of attaining knowledge of everything of which my mind might be capable" (AT 6.16–17). This included science, education and society, and he again stressed the connection in explaining the four rules of Method, comparing their reduced number to laws whose rarity meant "that a State is much better ruled" (AT 6.18). Just so, he wrote, reaching the end of part 3, he had managed to pull down the "old house" and build "more certain opinions" (AT 6.29). These could not be separated from their author's social obligations, his activities inseparable from his place in a civil community. As Descartes began part 2 by setting the discovery of the idea of Method in a particular history of angry conflict, so in the last part 6, he quickly set the results of Method in the context of a different social ideal. His discoveries, he said, required that he communicate them to the public sphere, for this was the law of good society:

As soon as I had acquired some general notions about physics and, as I began to test them on various particular problems, had noticed just where they could lead and how much they differ from the principles used up to now, I thought I could not keep them hidden, without sinning gravely against the law that obliges us to procure, to the extent of our abilities, the general good of all humanity [*le bien général de tous les hommes*]. (AT 6.61)

The view of society against whose background he was writing the *Discours* bore tangible obligations. Life's brevity, and one person's inability to do everything needed to complete these discoveries, entailed other communities within the larger one: hence the duty "to communicate faithfully to the public all the little I had discovered," giving others the possibility to extend it, and the need to create a scientific community, enabling

the best minds to try and go further, contributing, each according to inclination and ability, to the experiments that have to be done and also communicating to the public all they will have learned. Successors would thus begin where predecessors end, and in this way, linking the lives and works of many, we would all go together far further than anyone alone could do. (AT 6.63)

To be sure, perilous situations might exist where communication would be undesirable and some discoveries best kept secret. Even so, while only the knower would be situated to decide, the decision depended on a still wider understanding of community:

For although it is true that everyone is obliged to procure, to the extent of his ability, the good of others, and that to be useful to no one is to be strictly worthless, it is nonetheless true as well that our concerns must extend further than the present day, and that it is good to omit things which may perhaps be of some profit to the living when the intention is to do other things which bring greater profit to our posterity. (AT 6.66)

Here, Descartes was possessor of new knowledge and its key, alone able to decide its implications on behalf of the greater public good. One begins to see the complications of the relation between agent subject and community. What assured the decision's rectitude? Descartes' reply was simple: right reason, good sense ordered by Method.

This task also fell to the good prince, likewise identified with the *cogito*'s subject: willful self acting through Method. In his September 1646 letter to Elisabeth, on *The Prince*, Descartes agreed that in the public sphere princes, too, must stay silent on certain things for the wider good: "the chief motives for the actions of princes are often such special circumstances that unless one is oneself a prince or has long participated in their secrets one could not imagine them" (AT 4.592). Bacon and Hobbes expressed this view (Reiss, *Discourse* 190–93, 203–4). But where they thought these secrets part of the sway of sovereign power, Descartes thought them part of a prince's duty to do all possible for a general welfare of which, in a yet-imperfect society, others were ignorant.

Only the thinking agent subject could as yet make such decisions. It alone knew the truths at issue. It alone could properly use free will to guide its actions. It grounded the first two maxims of the *morale par provision*, where Descartes determined not to be shaken from this ethic (until replacing it with a higher morality). The same determination marked the good prince who, said Descartes in this letter, must be "inflexible with respect to such things as he has been seen to have decided even if they are harmful to him": To be deemed irresolute would be worse (AT 4.490). The will, he added in article 153 of the *Passions*, was tied to a "firm and constant resolution to use it well": thus one pursued knowledge of truth and the path of virtue (AT 11.446). Charron also gave this dual ground of truth and virtue, opening his political chapters by saying, "the first thing needed before any action is knowledge of state: for the first rule of prudence is knowledge," and adding, "after this knowledge of state, which is a sort or preparatory matter, the first thing needed is virtue" (*Sagesse* 3.2.551). Descartes gave them the same order.

The relation between the historical community and the subject of rational knowledge and willful action always involved power, duty and interests. The state had to be ordered to recognize these aspects of the social sphere: the necessity tying the subject to all, yet need not to undo the rights of each. Descartes made this point in the same 1646 letter, urging that "everyone's felicity depends on oneself," and explaining that that was why one "must keep oneself firmly beyond the sway of fortune" (AT 4.492). The year before, in a September 15 letter to Elisabeth, he had linked this last condition to the same idea of community as in the *Discours*:

Once we have thus recognized God's benevolence, our soul's immortality and the immensity of the universe, a truth yet remains whose knowledge I think most useful. This is that although each of us is a person separate from others, whose interests are therefore somehow distinct from everyone else's, yet one must be aware one cannot survive alone, that one is indeed one of the parts of the universe, and more especially one of the parts of this earth, one of the parts of this State, this society, this family, bound to it by one's abode, one's oath, one's birth. And one must always prefer the interests of the whole, of which one is a part, to those of one's particular person; yet with restraint and caution, for one would be wrong to expose oneself to great evil to procure only a small good for one's kin or country; and if a man is alone worth more than all the rest of his town, he would not be right to want to ruin himself [il n'aurait pas raison de se vouloir perdre] to save it. But if one referred everything to oneself, one would not fear to harm others greatly if one thought to gain thereby some small convenience, and one would have no true friendship, no fidelity, no virtue of any sort; whereas considering oneself part of the community [le public], one takes pleasure in doing good to everyone, and is not even afraid to risk one's life to help others when occasion offers; indeed one would lose one's soul, if one could, to save others. (AT 4.293)

Much of this could come from Cicero, Seneca, Plutarch—or Montaigne. Again we see the hard play of subject and community: of the subject whose reason and will came first and the community which nonetheless required the subject's duties and service as *integral* and essential part of its whole. Decisions might be the rational subject's; they were constrained by obligation within the community. Still, to will against one's own interest, at least when the issue was disproportionate, ran counter to reason and freedom: "il n'aurait pas *raison* de se *vouloir* perdre." Yet subject and community were not wholly at odds. Not just ethics or ontology gave reasons to be part of the community. So did self-interest. "For if we think of ourselves alone," he wrote to Elisabeth three weeks later (October 6), "we can enjoy only our own particular goods. Whereas if we think of ourselves as part of some other body, we share its common goods, yet without thereby being deprived of any of our own" (AT 4.308). Self-interest was reason adjusted to concrete historical experience and actual event. One should be ready to do good to others, he had written to Elisabeth in January 1645, because of the likelihood of receiving "numerous good services" in return (AT 4.356). While Descartes finally drew different conclusions, such remarks gave hostages to an idea and experience of civil society other than what he sought. They echoed the idea of accumulation hinted in the *Discours*, expressed as an increase of financial, military and scientific possession, power and knowledge. Participation was also a way to augment one's power, possessions and pleasure. The thinking individual should participate in community to serve its own interests (the advice to Elisabeth about her two brothers proposed as much).

Momentarily, Descartes approached the argument Bernard Mandeville deployed a century later in the *Fable of the Bees*, imagining a society that lasted by reinforcing each's interests and increasing their goods. He ended his October 6, 1645, letter to Elisabeth:

I confess it hard to tell how far reason commands us to be interested in public affairs. But anyway the issue needs no great nicety: it suffices to satisfy one's conscience, and to that end we may largely follow our fancy. For God has so ordered things, and joined humans in such close community, that even if each tied everything to himself and had no care for others, he would not fail to work for them usually on everything in his power, provided he did so with prudence. Especially if he lived in an age when manners were uncorrupted. Besides, just as doing good to others is better and more glorious than obtaining it for oneself, so it is the greatest souls who are most inclined to it, and make least fuss of the wealth they possess. (AT 4.316–17)

This was close to private vice as public virtue and laissez-faire; except that Descartes had in mind obligation and duty more social than individual. That is why he immediately added that only "base souls [*ces âmes basses*]" acted solely from such interest.

His own behavior offered an *exemplum* of serving one's interest while seeming not to, and staying open to community. Feigning to be at leisure, he succeeded in "pursuing [his] project" to make "progress in the knowledge of truth" (AT 6.30) and benefit present and future community. It was his technique, he had said to Balzac in 1631 and repeated in the *Discours*, to make his own space even in the busiest public sphere. *Larvatus prodeo*. He said to Elisabeth in the September 1646 letter that the good prince must likewise retain the "honors" and "respect the people believe due to him," letting "appear publicly only his most solemn actions, or those that all can approve, keeping his pleasures for his private life" (AT 4.489–90). At issue was always to balance social obligation and interests of the personal agent. The longer passage just quoted from the letter of the year before shows a sort of break. The first two sentences seem to argue how to serve one's interests in face of present society, advancing masked to gain one's own end. The last sentence envisaged a society of good custom and great souls, where all interests converged (God being the reassuring mediator, as in the *Meditations*). Three weeks before (September 15, 1645), we saw, he had been forceful about balancing public and self-interest, asserting that the latter should *never* dominate the former. It did so, he now remarked, only in the case of those "base souls."

This society would be possible only when truth was known and then only when it became *habit*. As Descartes said in the last-mentioned letter, "only two things are required, it seems to me, for one to be prepared always to make good judgment. One is knowledge of truth, the other the habit of recalling that knowledge whenever occasion requires" (AT 4.291). He stressed the point: "I have said above that apart from knowledge of truth, habit is also needed to be prepared always to judge well." Otherwise real events, actual experience in the world, might divert us: "which is why the School is right to speak of virtues as habits" (AT 4.295). He summarized the argument in the *Passions*, insisting that will's "weapons" rule conduct: "its proper weapons are firm and determined judgments about the knowledge of good and evil." Only "knowledge of the truth" grounded judgments allowing will to act (§§48–49: AT 11.367–68). Passions producing action did so only from desire. That the will know how to regulate desire was thus morally essential. Only methodical knowledge let will achieve that regulation (§144: AT 11.436–37).

Before such knowledge became general, before this community of great souls and good judgment was created, a way had to be traced through society as it was, even while sheltering the person. To that end, maybe for a last time, Descartes pursued the idea of the single subject agent, establishing a relation between it and society showing the laissez-faire of a century later. In the January 1646 letter cited briefly earlier, he elaborated to Elisabeth;

What [*la raison qui*] makes me think that those who do nothing but to their own utility must as well as others be working for others and trying to please all, as much as is in their power, provided they [*s'ils veulent*] use prudence, is that it usually happens that those thought serviceable [*officieux*: a Ciceronian word] and quick to please, also receive many good services [*offices*] from others, even those they have never helped, which they would not receive if they were thought of another humor; and that the work they do to give pleasure is not as great as the advantages gained from the amity of those who know them. . . . As for me, the rule I have most obeyed in my life's entire conduct has been to follow only the high road and believe the best part of cunning is not to want to use cunning at all. The common laws of society, all tending toward our doing good to one another, or at least doing no harm, are, I think, so well established that whoever follows them honestly, without deceit or fraud, leads a far happier and safer life than those who seek their utility by other paths; who, in truth, sometimes succeed, through others' ignorance and fortune's favor; but much more often they fail, and, thinking to make their fortune, are ruined. (AT 4.356–57)

But society seemed dysfunctional and in crisis: religious wars, Thirty Years' War, revolts against Spain in the Low Countries, Portugal, Sicily, Naples and Catalonia, emergencies in Russia, Poland, Sweden and Switzerland, civil war and revolution in England, universal questioning of forms and ways of knowing, crises in education, economic and commercial dislocation, stutterings of rising technology. How were people to cope? Provisionally, said Descartes, one had to live as if nothing were upset; adopting custom and opinion but working for a new instauration. Beyond the social sphere, was one stable, trustworthy thing: thinking itself, good sense ruled by Method. Method enabled knowledge of truth, truth enabled good judgment, good judgment enabled habit of virtue, virtue enabled right action. This series was right use of the free will in which we equaled God. Will's action, by "officious" prudence and interest, and collective and personal advantage and utility, was to create the society of great souls benefiting all. But how to get from individual action, serving private interest in an imperfect society, by means of mask and provisional morality, to this new society where all acted to everyone's benefit?

This was the prince's role. Even fixed habit was soon replaced: "this habit can be acquired by a single action and needs no long practice" (*Passions* §50: AT 11.369). This vastly affected the civic sphere. The wise prince, having true knowledge, judgment, methodical reason and ability to direct will to shared interest, could fast effect change and new establishment (Descartes' reason to fault Charles-Louis). Absent Method, the ideal was Erasmus': "A good prince has the obligation of looking to the welfare of his people even at the cost of his own life if need be"; or, in a passage presaging the ground of Descartes' letter: "He is supreme in goodness, and all his goodness flows from him to other men as from a spring. Therefore it would obviously be quite absurd for the greatest proportion of all the state's misfortunes to arise from him who is supposed to be the source of goodness" (*Education* 14, 23). A prince's "subiects," Lipsius echoed, quoting Cicero, "are wont to be" like him: "every one fashioneth himselfe after the example of the king" (*Sixe* 26). In antiquity, the thought had been Aristotle's (*Nicomachean Ethics* 1103b3, *Politics* 1260a15–33), in the middle ages Aquinas' (ST 1a.2ae.92.1), most recently in the same tradition Francisco de Vitoria's (164–65, 219–21). Descartes thus opposed his methodical prince to Machiavelli's in his September 1646 letter replying to Elisabeth's request that he give his opinion of *The Prince*.

He began by returning to the *Discours'* architectural metaphor. It no longer referred, even supposedly, only to mind. Civil society was explicitly the issue. Too, a constructive Method now existed. Descartes could go beyond the merely possible arguments of the *Discours* to offer a civic science equivalent to those of the *Essais*. Assuming one could acquire "a State by just means," he deplored Machiavelli's contrary assumption: "just as when you build a house whose foundations are so bad as to be unable to support high and thick walls you are forced to make them weak and low, so those who have begun their establishment by crimes are usually obliged to continue committing crimes, and could not stay in power if they tried to be virtuous" (AT 4.486). The state *had* to be founded and maintained on the ground of Method, knowledge of truth and that habit of generous virtue which meant you supported others' interests because you attended your own. In a state based on crimes everyone could become prince; the first to succeed, Descartes agreed with Machiavelli, would usurp the usurper. But this first angry "avenger" would logically be followed by a succession of others, producing endless conflict (AT 4.487). He had earlier remarked to Elisabeth that "anger can often provoke in us such violent desires for vengeance that it makes us imagine more pleasure in punishing our enemy than in saving our honor or life" (AT 4.285: September 1, 1645). Anger was the worst passion, he wrote in his treatise, because as Seneca had said, it "troubled the judgment" and turned us against others (§§202–3: AT 11.481). It was the fundamentally antisocial passion (§§199–203). Machiavelli's state was based on it.

One of the good prince's tasks was to stop this tendency. For while he criticized Hobbes for believing "all humans evil" (AT 4.67), Descartes did not really think that many were anything else (Baillet, 2.173–74). Because many souls *were* base, the good prince would prudently distrust people, he wrote about *The Prince*: "For whatever loyalty you plan to use, you must not expect the same in return. You must assume others will deceive you whenever it is to their advantage. And the stronger may indeed succeed when they wish, but not the weaker" (AT 4.489). This was the counsel he practiced with Charles-Louis. Charron had just said that "the principal reason for this necessity [of prudence in political matters] is the wicked nature of man, most savage and hard to tame of all animals" (3.1.547), but it was a cliché of the contemporary wartime polemics that Descartes knew, as it had been in argument from Machiavelli through Hurault. Thus, disapproving of *The Prince*'s Chapter 15, where Machiavelli stated that the good man would always be ruined, Descartes replied that that would be so only if "by good man, he means a superstitious and simple one" (AT 4.490), if, that is to say, he was opposing the prudent prince, knowing evil and general corruption, to the prince who was just naive. That was what Machiavelli *was* talking about.

So was Descartes, instantly adding another view of the good person and prince: "he who does everything right reason dictates." The rational prince was one who, knowing "the wicked nature of man," could tame and guide him toward new habit, just as the philosopher of Method would teach all to use right reason. In the *Principia*, again echoing Charron (3.2) and others, Descartes was explicit: "the power men have over each other was given them so that they might employ it in discouraging others from evil" (1§38: AT 8A.19). The French translation, authorized by Descartes but with changes that were both his and Picot's, turns "others" into "their inferiors" (AT 9B.41). The sovereign's will was the counterpart of the rational individual's. Will to good action necessarily accompanied true knowledge and virtuous judgment. These characteristics created a present division between those who were wicked, irrational and ignorant of reason's methodical use of good sense, and the others: philosophers and good princes. He thus wrote to Chanut in 1647: "It is true that I usually refuse to write down my thoughts about morality. I do so for two reasons. One is that nothing provides the ill-disposed with an easier pretext for calumny. The other is my belief that it is only for sovereigns, or those delegated by them, to be concerned to regulate others' behavior" (AT 5.87). The division between the good and the evil needed not last. The good prince, sovereign mind, changed others' habit.

Above the merely self-interested strife of other agents, the new prince had to establish the new. Relying on right Method, this prince was not bound by the same (provisional) rules as others and *could not* go wrong:

in the instruction of a good prince, though new to a State, I think quite contrary maxims [from Machiavelli's] must be proposed, and we must suppose that the means used to establish himself were just; as indeed I believe they almost always are when the prince using them believes they are. For justice among sovereigns has other limits than among ordinary people [*des particuliers*], and I think that in these affairs God gives right to those to whom he gives might. (AT 4.487)

The methodical prince's might was legitimate. Might did not make right, but the prince's justice in the sphere of its sovereign power was legitimate by definition, as Bodin, Charron and Hobbes had argued. Descartes held that the prince's *will*, ruled by Method and knowledge of truth, necessarily led to good judgment. This sovereign knew good and evil as well as justice and legitimacy. Habit, Descartes wrote to Elisabeth on October 6, 1645, agreeing with "conscience" and "inclination," would inevitably make this prince act to protect others' interests with his own (AT 4.316).

Elisabeth found these notes on Machiavelli equivocal and, in practice, dangerous. Replying critically on October 10, she said that the actions Machiavelli proposed, and that her respondent criticized insufficiently, certainly led "to the establishment of a state," but of one where "at least in popular opinion the prince is a usurper" (AT 4.520). Her own House would legally return to the Palatinate, but the phrase, "au moins en l'opinion du peuple," refers to its generation-long exile from its throne, emphasizing that they were addressing actuality. In June 1643, Elisabeth fretted that she lacked time for thought, due to "the interests of my House, which I cannot neglect" (AT 3.684). Descartes' advice about her brothers and remarks on her uncle targeted real political conditions. Elisabeth's mention of her brother Philip's "treaty with the Republic of Venice" in an April 1646 letter on quite other matters shows that she thought Descartes concerned with political reality, though in that instance he did not react—or not in writing.

Replying to her October letter, Descartes agreed about legality, but said that Machiavelli would have argued differently if real Italian conditions had been otherwise (a point again showing that neither of them thought their exchange only theoretical). When one had "no reason to fear," institution of authority could be "more generous" (AT 4.531). That is how he wrote of a prince's friendship. One should never abuse this "sacred" social bond by feigning it (AT 4.488). Amity marked the obligation a person owed others: "obligation" signaling, we saw, enlightened play of everyone's interests, allowing proper working of the society based on method, will and reason. To fail friendship was to fail social renewal. The individual's interest, protected by amity, was that of the thinking subject whose will allowed the institution of Method. So to fail friendship was to fail knowledge of truth, prudence, good judgment and the subject agent itself. It was to oppose the *cogito* and what it was to be human at all. Descartes explored this grounding friendship in the *Passions* as "generosity."

This was the full self-respect that came from knowing that one was human only through "free disposition of one's volitions," that one was due "praise or blame only as one used them for good or bad," that one had "a firm and constant resolution to use them for good" and that one was therefore completely "virtuous" (§153: AT 11.445–46). Those with such knowledge were the "great souls" of whom he wrote: "Those who are generous in this fashion are naturally led to do great things, and yet to undertake nothing of which they do not feel themselves capable. And because they think nothing greater than to do good to other people and to scorn their own interest, they are always perfectly courteous, affable and serviceable [*officieux*] to everyone. At the same time they are entirely masters of their passions" (§156: AT 11.447–48). These great souls were not necessarily born so. Generosity was a virtue like others, and "what are commonly called virtues are habits of the soul which dispose it to certain thoughts." With the ancients, Descartes firmly believed that one could be trained and educated into such habits. One could learn the "advantages that come from a firm resolution to use well" one's free will and "excite in oneself the passion" leading to the desire so to use it, thereby "acquiring the virtue of generosity, which [is], as it were, the key to all the other virtues and a general remedy against all the disorders of the passions" (§161: AT 11.453–54). The worst of the passions whose excess and disorder it cured was anger, against which "generosity is the best remedy" (§203: AT 11.481). The philosopher and the good prince, then, could *train* people into generosity and reestablish a society based on everyone's sense of mutual duties, *offices*.

Descartes did not think this utopian. We have amply seen that his and the princess Elisabeth's exchanges were as rooted in concrete history as in political theory. The person who was to act in this generous society was not a figment of theory either. The passions of the soul were anchored in human physiology. Indeed, as he often repeated, they were exactly what showed "the intimate union between" soul and body, the fact that "our soul is joined to the whole body" (*Principes* 1§48, 4§189: AT 9B.45, 310). Two different "substances" though they were, it was still "impossible to unite them further" (1§60: AT 9B.51). There was no doubt, he reiterated early in the *Passions*, that "the soul is truly joined to all the body, and one cannot properly say that it is in one of its parts to the exclusion of others, because it is one and somehow indivisible" (§30: AT 11.351). Most of the first part of the *Passions* concerned the body's physiology. The passions marked material being.

The point is that Descartes sought to unite real, physical people into real society. He had superseded need for a *morale par provision*, using known opinion, custom and habit. He stressed change. To achieve this, the good prince had to direct gently and almost secretly. It was no easier to "persuade" people of what was "just" than to offend them with what "they imagine unjust" (AT 4.491). Care depended on the prince's prudence and *savoir faire*: "you must not attempt to draw people abruptly to reason, when they are not accustomed to understand it; but you must try little by little, whether by public writings, through the speech of preachers, or any other means, to have them comprehend it" (AT 4.491). So wrote Descartes on Machiavelli. Since generosity not only established friendship but countered anger, such a society would work actively *against* the vision of persons and conflicts that necessitated the society of contract.

Clearly, here, the good prince was the generous, rational being of the *Passions*. With huge changes in ideas (and experiences?) of community and identity, this prince's goal nonetheless stayed that of safeguarding— or reestablishing—an "Erasmian" loving community. *This* reason of State *was* Reason, "generous" reason. Community could now consist of individual selves, each embodying a reason common to all, shared by all, worked by all. One wonders whether *trained* "generosity" was not an answer to Stoic *oikeiōsis*, the innate reason that naturally drew humans into rational community. Descartes replaced that innate urge by a trained one, functioning, however, in much the same way and to the same end, for more independent selves. (I hope to take up this issue at greater length elsewhere.) These selves also embodied the play of will and necessity, reason and passion, consent and coercion, intention and effect, freedom and necessity that became the terms of civil association. The self/subject embodying these terms was, to use a metaphor that after the previous chapter we can now readily understand and expand, personification of a particular locus of turmoil, conjuncture of dismay. By this personification, an agency was formulated that enabled resolution of those conflicts. It eventually absorbed them. But putting their elements into a solution, to change the metaphor, produced a new precipitate, a new compounded formation. Its thinkers had little truck with Descartes' vision of community or, for that matter, of personal and communal identities.

Conclusion

Metaphors are one thing—decorative or banal. Facts on historical ground are another. Still, metaphors and facts are never separate. If a vital contrast rose unexpectedly between the passions of love and anger in this analysis' later stages, it did not do so from lingering memory of nostalgic opposition between *Gemeinschaft* and *Gesellschaft*, a now century-old idea describing a supposed passage from holistic community to competitive societies of capitalist exchange. It did so because people experienced who-ness, relations with others and texture of common surroundings in ways that they most readily named via those passions. Hélisenne, Stampa, Sabuco, even Hurault, were not looking to establish anything new and different. They named real experience, and the naming became an element of what emerged, of what *could* emerge. The locus of turmoil that was the ever-more tensed, fractured and inconstant selfe was part of a similarly fraught social sphere, itself image of a material and spiritual world "crumbled out againe to his Anatomies . . . / all in peeces, all cohaerence gone" (Donne, "First Anniversary" ll.212–13: *Poetical* 214). Selfe experienced that actuality and increasingly analyzed it so. In that sense, it needed no personifying. It was, after all, as much experienced being as Descartes' passionately physical agent subject. What was eventually personified was the passage to a specific *kind* of agency. Person was no longer nexus of multiple communal circles, exemplary figure or divine instrument, nor fraught erratic mover. Person was becoming universal actor and knower in a rational universe, whose agency could intervene in and resolve the very sources of conflict.

The last chapters used Descartes' work to explore this agency's evolution, experience and understanding. To say that he *made* that agency is to get things backwards. His work typified and exemplified changing understanding. As we have seen, debate and experience were everyone's. In any case, much of the work explored in the last chapter was also the princess Elisabeth's. Efforts to understand moral and political identities followed the course of dialogue between the two. That makes it the more valuable: not the thought of a solitary thinker isolated in his *poêle*, it was a hard debate between two people deeply aware of the actual world, personal and sociopolitical. When Descartes reacted to Elisabeth's queries about her or others' depression or illness, solaced her in grief or weighed the efficacy of taking the waters of Spa, dialogue bore as much on what it was to be human as did exchanges about the good life, the best State or the Palatinate. For Descartes and Elisabeth, to be human was still to be webbed in concrete situations: physical world, human body, political society, divine actuality . . . Fludd's 1617 depiction of the world's woven circles was not yet alien (Figure 13), even if Bacon now saw them as a fraud of human desire for "order and regularity in the world," devising "conjugates and relatives which do not exist": "hence the fiction that all celestial bodies move in perfect circles" (*Novum organum* I.xlv).

In Elisabeth's and Descartes' exchanges, after the agency "established" in the *Meditations*, arose the idea of persons as self-dependent subjects, who should be free citizens of a non-coercive community. That vastly complicated any sense of society as a community whose nature and being were essential and *prior* aspects of who one was. Thence came the analysis of a society bound by "generosity," not contract. This very analysis shows that it is hard to talk of "typicality." People disagreed in these ongoing debates. Besides other appeals to generous community, in the shape of the paternalist pastoral monarchy defended by Robert Filmer, Locke's opponent (implicit in facets of the Descartes/Elisabeth exchanges), or in divers republicanisms, arguments for contractualism (also of different kinds, republicanism among them) increasingly predominated.

Fifty years on, Mary Astell did echo Descartes and Elisabeth, calling her subjects "Rational and Free Agents," who should be free of any government ruling by "Arbitrary Power"—perceived as "evil in itself" (*Reflections* 17). She analyzed these agents in ways drawn nearly verbatim from the *Passions* and elsewhere (she often named and cited Descartes in her writing):

Because as Irrational Creatures act only by the Will of him who made them, and according to the Power of the Mechanisme by which they are form'd, so every one who pretends to Reason, who is a Voluntary Agent and therefore Worthy of Praise or Blame, Reward or Punishment, must *Chuse* his Actions and determine his Will to that Choice by some Reasonings or Principles either true or false, and in proportion to his Principles and the Consequences he deduces from them he is to be accounted, if they are Right and Conclusive a Wise Man, if Evil, Rash and Injudicious a Fool. If then it be the property of Rational Creatures, and Essential to their very Natures to Chuse their Actions, and to determine their Wills to that Choice by such Principles and Reasonings as their Understandings are furnish'd with, they who are desirous to be rank'd in that Order of Beings must conduct their Lives by these Measures, begin with their Intellectuals, inform themselves what are the plain and first Principles of Action and Act accordingly. (*Serious* 62)

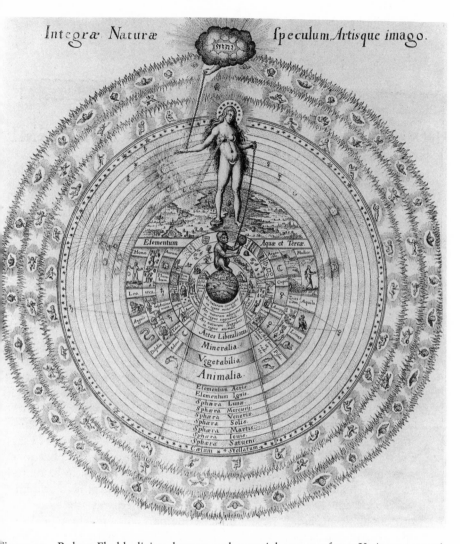

Figure 13. Robert Fludd, divine, human and material cosmos, from *Utriusque cosmi*. Photo: Bancroft Library, University of California, Berkeley.

They, too, were to compose a virtuous community linked by

Generosity, which (so long as we keep it from degenerating into Pride) is of admirable advantage to us in this matter. It was not fit that Creatures capable of and made for Society, shou'd be wholly Independent, or Indifferent to each others Esteeem and Commendation; nor was it convenient considering how seldom these are justly distributed, that they shou'd too much regard and depend on them. It was requisite therefore that a desire of our Neighbours Good Opinion shou'd be implanted in our Natures to the end we might be excited to do such things as deserve it, and yet withall a Generous neglect of it, if they unjustly withheld it where it was due. (*Serious* 74)

This community worked not in anger and contest but in shared search for "Truth": "If then instead of Jostling and Disputing with our Fellow Travellers, of bending all the force of our Wit to Contradict and Oppose those advances [in truth] which they make, we wou'd well understand, duly Employ and kindly Communicate our Peculiar Talent, how much more Service might we do our Lord, how much more useful might we be to one another? What vast Discoveries wou'd be made in the wide Ocean of Truth? How many Moral Irregularities wou'd be observ'd and rectify'd?" (*Serious* 89). Like Descartes, she thought society could be ruled to mold "reason" and "prudence." Her analysis of the "wise man" and "rash and injudicious fool" posited understanding of the passions also drawn from Descartes. That they imperiled reason only confirmed "the mutual Relation between the Understanding and the Will, and shews how necessary it is to take care of both, if we wou'd improve and advance either" (*Serious* 64). That they remained part of a worldly whole was why they could be organized to establish the generous community.

Christopher Allen thinks Descartes' contemporary, Nicolas Poussin, depicted this in his painting (in contrast to Charles Le Brun and other "post-Cartesian" artists and art theorists). He did "not represent the passions as existing separately." They were physically, psychologically and spiritually tied to body, soul and circumstance. "Everything starts with the particularity of the situation, the unique human conjunction. More importantly still, it begins with the *significance* of the event, that is to say the totality of the social, political, metaphysical or religious implications and consequences—depending on the subject—of the event to be represented." The meaning of the image, "in the fullest sense of its moral import for all concerned," what Poussin titled its *pensée*, was "the epicentre of Poussin's painting." It conditioned "the particular psychological response of each protagonist, and thus *endows the experience from the first with a collective character*. The figures in a Poussin painting are 'taking part' in an event, not aggregatively constituting it: *the collective aspect is a priori*"—again, in contrast to Le Brun (Allen 87, my italics).

Debates about human identity long continued. They were not just about person as Astell's "rational and free agent" but, too, the social identity and political society it implied. For this universal actor in a rational world, intervening in the very sources of conflict, seemed prior to and apart from the world and society on which it acted; doing so, indeed, in a strictly calculative way. People fast espoused numerative aspects of Method or Hobbes' "Euclidean" and "Galilean" civil science. In the 1680s, Pierre Corneille's nephew, Bernard de Fontenelle, gave a choice instance in historiography: "Someone of considerable wit, just taking account of human nature, could deduce all past and future history, though never having heard tell of any event" ("Sur l'histoire," *Textes* 216–17). He was not ironic. Most held analogous views. They grounded ideas of progress and the optimism of Enlightenment. In his *Cours de philosophie*, Descartes' disciple, Pierre-Sylvain Régis, tied Hobbes' to his master's voice in treating political formation of societies, cession of individual rights, duties of sovereign and subject, mixing them with Le Bret and Nicholas Malebranche, and urging a Cartesian society because "in the state of nature, passions rule, war is perpetual, poverty inescapable, fear never leaves, &c." (*Cours* III.493). That "&c." signaled the debt to Hobbes. The personified *cogito* united in civil society because in nature human life was "solitary, poore, nasty, brutish and short," and person the "unaccommodated . . . poor, bare, forked animal" of Lear's vision on a desolate moor under a pelting sky (III.iv.109–10)—jointure of angry conflict.

Rejected into a state of nature before civil society as beasts or even monsters, recalled in times of new constitutions and internal peace (more or less) as suffering victims of violent civil or religious wars, these unnecessary zeds were to be replaced by the rational consenting subjects of a new establishment that would subdue angry strife, real (the French wars of Hurault, the English of Hobbes' *Behemoth*) or abstract (in Hobbes' *Leviathan* or Régis' *Cours*). This notion of consent, grounded in the legalism of contractual debate, further strengthened the personification of rational thinking: it gave the subject a title of judgment, justification of will, claim to decision. In Hobbes, writing in exile in 1640–42, the moment of consent was hardly separate from ongoing conflict or the civil association it was held to permit. Things were clearer ten years on, but never so clear as for Locke, who made reason precede conflict, and contract be the latter's foreseeable resolution. Contract, resulting from reason, was not just civil society's originating instance, but condition of its continuance, now requiring ongoing consent of rational subjects. For Locke, unlike Descartes, not all such subjects were even potentially equal. That assumption was basic for Montesquieu and Rousseau, who invented increasing numbers of stages to separate an original rational subject from eventual needs of association; especially for Rousseau, seeking to deny inequalities of contractual society by articulating a "general" will on the particular.

These several terms—subject and society, individual and public interests, freedom and power, will and equality, state and society, contract and community, nature and training—and efforts to reconcile them satisfactorily, became the themes of the future thinking of western "liberalism" about the political arena, moral action and the self. Like Descartes, not to mention Richelieu or his own slightly younger contemporary Astell, Leibniz asserted that *any* action resulted from the self's combining of knowledge and will. The elements were so embraced, however, that you could equally say that will and power were founded on knowledge. Knowledge and will, properly used, amounted to the wisdom and goodness able to establish the generous community, In that respect, Leibniz's idea of power and its potential could have come straight from Descartes:

Justice is nothing else than that which conforms to wisdom and goodness joined together: the end of goodness is the greatest good, but to recognize it wisdom is needed, which is nothing else but knowledge of the good. . . . Thus wisdom is in the understanding and goodness in the will. And justice, as a consequence, is in both. Power is a different matter, but if it is used it makes right become fact, and makes what ought to be really exist, in so far as the nature of things permits. (*Political* 50)

This notion of justice had become central to considerations about social constitution at least since the 1650 exchanges between William Davenant and Hobbes (Reiss, *Meaning* 86–87, 91–93 and *passim*). Leibniz may have been drawn toward Descartes', but it was Lockean efforts to reconcile contradictions that furnished major terms for the future, especially in the ideas of contract being between human beings who were not only rational agents but property owners, and being a process enduring throughout the life of society.

Locke, too, added the idea of "concept" as the rational tool establishing the move from individual perception to communal meaning. A concept put *my* (now clearly "my") perception in a context of sense that was publicly comprehensible. *Concept* was the epistemological equivalent of the sociopolitical *contract*, articulating the individual on the public. But Locke was pulled toward older forms of thought. Apropos, precisely, of the problem of personal identity, he thought that "Reflection," which grounded it (*Essay* 2.27.§9), though not "Sense" because it did not concern "external Objects," was "very like it, and might properly enough be call'd internal Sense," acting on internal "Objects" in like manner (2.1.§§4, 7). John Perry calls the view controversial (13): as indeed it was for the later western thinkers whom Perry collected to discuss the matter. The view was surely a residue of kinds of thought and experience still found in Descartes. It proposed that reflection was, like the senses, a *possible reaction* to given "objects," enabling the understanding called "identity" (Descartes' writing of res cogitans as subjecta to the process conceiving it). This passible reaction functioned by present awareness and memories of past awarenesses to which reflection could also possibly react (2.11; 2.27.§10). This nostalgic trace did not deter a new secure sense of self that let Locke replace the body's brittle glass vase or constraining earthen prison with an altogether more homely and contented "Clay Cottage" (Some §2: 84).

Late seventeenth-century debate in aesthetics did with the idea of "taste" what "concept" did in epistemology, and "contract" in politics: taste, "good taste," signaled how my perception of the beautiful, the fine and the good, was adjusted to the norms agreed by the community. Taste, it may be, later played the same role in ethics: in the guise of Kant's categorical imperative, as my reference to the "good" means to suggest. But Descartes had already proposed an equivalent idea in his use of the terms "virtue" and, more precisely, "generosity." They signaled how one's own powerful self-esteem was to establish and be articulated on right relations with all others.

All these terms, responses to and enabled by "Cartesian" passages and becomings, marked resolutions of conflicts in distinct areas of action and thought. Freedom and coercion, consent and control, reason and passion were now seen as modes of relation between individual and society, one and many, self and others. They premised a disjunction whose most startling early expression may be Blaise Pascal's reaction to Descartes' comment in the second Meditation about looking through his window and seeing not "men walking in the street," but "hats and coats which could hide ghosts" or automata. "Sed judico homines esse," "I judge them to be men," he wrote in Latin, making them subjects of the verb "to be," in the form of his "ego sum" (AT 7.32). "Mais je juge que ce sont de vrais hommes," "I judge that they are true men," his translator rectified, making them objects of this thought (AT 9.25), truer to later Cartesianism than to Descartes. "What is the moi?" asked Pascal in response:

A man who goes to the window to see the passersby, if I pass by, can I say that he put himself there to see me? No, for he is not thinking of me in particular. But someone who loves someone because of her beauty, does he love her? No, for smallpox, that will destroy the beauty without destroying the person, will make him no longer love her.

And if someone loves me for my judgment, for my memory, do they love me, myself? No, for I can lose these qualities without losing my self. So where is this self, if it is neither in the body nor in the soul? and how to love the body or the soul, except for these qualities, which are not what makes the self, since they are perishable. . . . So one never loves anyone [on n'aime donc jamais personne], but only qualities. (Pensées, ed. Sellier, no. 567; ed. Lafuma, no. 688)

Pascal assumed a *moi*, a self, dependent not at all on another, indeed, radically different and unknowable by that other. Cave suggests that dialogue still mattered (*Pré-histoires* 116n15), but true internal dialogue was incommunicable, by Pascal's own assertion (the true "person" that Locke distinguished from the "man": *Essay* 2.27.§15; Cave 118). External dialogue was of the deaf: the other could not see *me*, love *me*. Descartes protested a distance to be overcome. Pascal insisted on its intransigence as an ontological and social fact of being (and turned from society to a transcendent God). Descartes sought something more tenuous, less *resolved-resolute*: give and take in a community whose *priority* still made duty and obligation primary for a willfully rational subject. Maybe that was no more socially practicable than Pascal's radical loner. He did not go to the Palatinate in 1649 because things were still shifting and would be "agreeable" only after "two or three years of peace" (AT 5.283). That was a different sort of shifting, and choosing to go to stable Stockholm was not wiser. The later sureties of possessive individualism and authoritarian liberalism (Reiss, *Meaning* 93–96, 275–77) have proven hardly less drastic in their outcomes.

Still, it may have been a century, as Peter Miller argues, before primacy of community in political theory, even if as an ever more nostalgic ideal, yielded to that of the individual. Anthony Pagden shows two eighteenth-century Italian thinkers, Paolo Mattia Doria and Antonio Genovesi, arguing for a state and society based on *fede*, trust: the *fides* of my Chapters 9–11, which Genovesi called "reciprocal friendship" (Pagden 70–71). Étienne Balibar makes a not dissimilar point about the late seventeenth century, specifically of Spinoza and Leibniz, of whom he remarks that they elaborated "a new concept of individuality . . . on theoretical bases which, by our standards, would appear 'holistic' or profoundly anti-individualistic" ("What?" 226). Perhaps we may see all this, too, as a historically necessary but perilous passage technique.

The new terms constructed from the debates of the 1630s–50s stayed inevitable terms of reference: right conceived in terms of interest and property, society imagined in those of the willful rational subject, the individual made the basic "building block" and taken, *qua* subject, as equal to all others: having for that reason an equal right to own and use *his* prudent but aggressive talents in some degree of assured "freedom." Main difficulties were then those of deciding who got how much and what was shared. What was the relation between the individual and an authority whose existence maintained the order necessary to society? What power did the individual possess and what was its nature in regard to that authority? Did their powers differ in any basic way? Where should one situate sovereign power? What rights did the individual have in relation to it? What was shared? How? Then, too: what relation held between the individual and others? What were the individual's rights against or with those of others? What free will could the individual retain, however reasonable and prudent, when battling others? What were the relations of force, rights, duties and obligations between discrete monadic individuals in an ordered society, if it was to avoid anarchic chaos? How much was common? The ground of these questions was new.

Experience of person as subject to some mediating and mediated act, event or being, civic order and law, material world and divine system, held on far into the seventeenth century (still, we saw, in Locke) and no doubt later. Peter Brown sees remains of Platonism in the opening lines of *Paradise Lost* (*Augustine* 166). He may be right. But they shared a wider comprehension of being:

> So much the rather, Thou Celestial Light,
> Shine inward and the mind through all her powers
> Irradiate, there plant eyes, all mist from thence
> Purge and disperse, that we may see and tell
> Of things invisible to mortal sight!

Published in 1667 (probably written between 1655 and 1665), this echoed many of those we have seen, early and late. At about the same time, two plays by a renowned dramatist, still immersed in what was nonetheless for most western Europeans a conservative and nostalgic past, inhabited the same field of understanding and experience, confronting it with now clearly emergent experience.

At the end of Pedro Calderón de la Barca's *Las armas de la hermosura* (1652: Ali Zaid brought this to my attention), Coriolano celebrates Rome's restoration to balance and grant of education and public participatory freedoms to its women by saying: "siendo las mujeres / el espajo cristalino / del honor del hombre, ¿como / puede, estando a un tiempo mismo / en nosotros empañado? [Women being the crystalline mirror of men's honor, how can it be at the same time tarnished in us?]" (*Obras* 1285). Much could be said of these passible (or is it now just passive?) women reflecting men's honor. *This* mirror image is older than those which opened Chapter 1, save only that it wants, here, to affirm a new stability—one contrasting utterly with the mirror that, at the end of Shakespeare's 1607 *Coriolanus*, reflected a monster. Then, in *Eco y Narciso*, played in 1661 and published in 1672, Calderón told the story of Eco's unrequited love for Narciso and her resulting death or, rather, metamorphosis into air. But we would do wrong to think Narciso turned only inward to self-love. In the end, he could love only his image, any deeper soul was out of reach: "Y yo solo el crístal toco, / Y no el alma del crístal [And I touch only the glass, / And not the soul of the glass]." He internalized Pascal's abyss between self and other. But he and Eco, with their tragic inabilities and consequent deaths, left more contained selves behind in Narciso's mother, Liríope, and Eco's suitors, Febo and Sylvio. *Their* tragedy was to live in a past able to be known, in Liríope's description, only as "aire y flor" (292b: Jornada III, ll.453–54). In a sturdy new present, the peasant Bato, urging that only "fools would believe" what they had just seen, ended by setting the tale of Narciso's obsession with the glassy mirage of his self(e) in Bacon's picture of past experience as fiction: "whether true or not, that's what the fable is" (297).

And this has been mine.

Bibliography

PRIMARY SOURCES

CCCM = Corpus christianorum: Continuatio medievalis
PL = Patrologiae cursus completus: Series latina

Abelard, Peter. *Ethical Writings: His* Ethics *or "Know Yourself" and His* Dialogue between a Philosopher, a Jew and a Christian. Translated by Paul Vincent Spade. Introduction by Marilyn McCord Adams. Indianapolis: Hackett, 1995.
———. *Ethics.* Edited, with introduction and translation by D. E. Luscombe. Oxford: Clarendon, 1971.
———. *Historia calamitatum.* Edited and introduction by Jacques Monfrin. Paris: Vrin, 1959.
———. *Opera.* Edited by Victor Cousin, with Charles Jourdain and Eugène Despois. 2 vols. Paris: Auguste Durand, 1849–1859.
———. *See also:* Héloïse; McLaughlin; Muckle; *and* Radice (all in Primary).
Aetios of Amida. *The Gynaecology and Obstetrics of the VIth Century, A.D.* Translated and edited by James V. Ricci. Philadelphia: Blakiston, 1950.
Alberti, Leon Battista. *Della pittura.* Edited by Luigi Mallè. Florence: Sansoni, 1950.
———. *On Painting and Sculpture: The Latin Texts of "De pictura" and "De statua".* Edited and translated by Cecil Grayson. London: Phaidon, 1972.
———. *On the Art of Building in Ten Books.* Translated by J. Rykwert, N. Leach and R. Tavernor. Cambridge, MA: MIT Press, 1988.
Alembert, Jean Le Rond d'. *Preliminary Discourse to the Encyclopedia of Diderot.* Translated by Richard N. Schwab, with Walter E. Rex. Introduction and notes by Richard N. Schwab. Indianapolis: Bobbs-Merrill, 1963.
Alexander of Aphrodisias. *On Fate.* Text, translation and commentary by Robert W. Sharples. London: Duckworth, 1983.
———. *Traité du destin.* Edited and translated by Pierre Thillet. Paris: Belles Lettres, 1984.
Althusius, Johannes. *The Politics.* An Abridged Translation of the Third Edition of *Politica methodice digesta, atque exemplis sacris et profanis illustrata.* And including the Prefaces to the First and Third Editions. Translated and intro-

duction by Frederick S. Carney. Preface by Carl J. Friedrich. Boston: Beacon, 1964.

Alvarez, Emmanuel. *De institutione grammatica libri tres*. Rome: Gulielmus Facciottus, 1595.

Anselm, St. *Basic Writings: Proslogium, Monologium, Gaunilon's In Behalf of the Fool*. Translated by S. N. Deane. Introduction by Charles Hartshorne. 2nd ed. La Salle, IL: Open Court, 1962.

———. *The "De grammatico" of St. Anselm: The Theory of Paronymy*. Notre Dame, IN: University of Notre Dame Press, 1964.

Aquinas, St. Thomas. *Summa contra Gentiles*. Translated and edited by Anton C. Pegis, James F. Anderson, Vernon J. Bourke and Charles J. O'Neil. 5 vols. 1955–1957. Reprint, Notre Dame, IN: University of Notre Dame Press, 1975.

———. *Summa theologiae*. Latin text and English translation, introductions, notes, appendices, and glossaries. [Translated by Fathers of the English Dominican Province.] 60 vols. [Cambridge:] Blackfriars; New York: McGraw-Hill; London: Eyre & Spottiswood, 1964–1976.

———. *See also*: Aristotle, *On Interpretation*.

Arcipreste de Talavera. *See*: Martínez de Toledo.

Aretaeus of Cappadocia. *The Extant Works*. Edited and translated by Francis Adams. London: Sydenham Society, 1856.

Ariosto, Ludovico. *The Satires of Ludovico Ariosto: A Renaissance Autobiography*. Translated by Peter Desa Wiggins. Athens, OH: Ohio University Press, 1976.

Aristophanes. *The Complete Plays*. Edited by Moses Hadas. 1962. Reprint, New York: Bantam, 1971.

Aristotle. *The Complete Works*. Revised Oxford Translation. Edited by Jonathan Barnes. 2 vols. Princeton: Princeton University Press, 1984.

———. *De anima (On the Soul)*. Translation, introduction, and notes by Hugh Lawson-Tancred. Harmondsworth: Penguin, 1986.

———. *De motu animalium*. *See*: Nussbaum, ed. (in Secondary).

———. *Nicomachean Ethics*. Edited and translated by H. Rackham. 2nd ed. 1934. Reprint, Cambridge, MA: Harvard University Press, 1990.

———. *On Interpretation: Commentary by St. Thomas and Cajetan (Peri hermēneias)*. Translated by Jean T. Oesterle. Milwaukee, WI: Marquette University Press, 1964.

———. *On the Soul; Parva naturalia; On Breath*. Edited and translated by W. S. Hett. 1936. Reprint, Cambridge, MA: Harvard University Press; London: Heinemann, 1975.

———. *Parts of Animals*. Edited and translated by A. L. Peck; *Movement of Animals; Progression of Animals*. Edited and translated by E. S. Forster. 1937. Reprint, Cambridge, MA: Harvard University Press; London: Heinemann, 1955.

———. *Posterior Analytics*. Edited and translated by Hugh Tredennick. *Topica*. Edited and translated by E. S. Forster. 1960. Reprint, Cambridge, MA: Harvard University Press; London: Heinemann, 1976.

Arnim, Hans Friedrich August von, ed. *Stoicorum veterum fragmenta [Svf]*. 4 vols. Leipzig: Teubner, 1903–1905, 1924.

————, [with] W. Schubart. *Hierokles, Ethische Elementarlehre (Papyrus 9780)*. Berliner Klassikertexte 4. Berlin: Weidmann, 1906.

Askew, Anne. *The Examinations*. Edited by Elaine V. Beilin. New York: Oxford University Press, 1996.

Astell, Mary. *Reflections upon Marriage*. In *Political Writings*, 1–80. Edited by Patricia Springborg. Cambridge: Cambridge University Press, 1996.

————. *A Serious Proposal to the Ladies*. New York: Source Book Press, 1970. [Containing reprint of *A Serious Proposal to the Ladies for the Advancement of their True and Greatest Interest*. Part I: *By a Lover of her Sex*. The Fourth Edition. London: Printed by J. R. for R. Wilkin . . . , MDCCI. (1st ed. 1694); and *A Serious Proposal to the Ladies*. Part II: *Wherein a Method is offer'd for the Improvement of their Minds*. London: Printed for Richard Wilkin . . . , 1697.]

Augustine, St. *The City of God Against the Pagans*. 7 vols. Edited and translated by George E. McCracken [1]; William M. Green [2, 7]; David S. Wiesen [3]; Philip Levine [4]; Eva Matthews Sanford and W. M. Green [5]; William Chase Greene [6]. London: Heinemann; Cambridge, MA: Harvard University Press, 1957–1972.

————. *Confessions*. Translated by William Watts, 1631. Edited by W. H. D. Rouse. 1912. Reprint, Cambridge, MA: Harvard University Press; London: Heinemann, 1988–9.

————. *De magistro*. In *The Greatness of the Soul; The Teacher*, translated and edited by Joseph M. Colleran. 1950. Reprint, Westminster, MD: Newman Press, 1964.

————. *De trinitate*. Translated by A. W. Haddan. In Augustine, *On the Holy Trinity*, 1–228.

————. *On Christian Doctrine*. Translated and edited by D. W. Robertson, Jr. Indianapolis: Bobbs-Merrill, 1958.

————. *On Lying*. Translated by H. Browne. In Augustine, *On the Holy Trinity*, 455–77.

————. *On the Holy Trinity, Doctrinal Treatises, Moral Treatises*. Vol. 3 of *A Select Library of the Nicene and Post-Nicene Fathers of the Christian Church*. Edited by Philip Schaff. 1956. Reprint, Grand Rapids, MI: Eerdmans, 1978.

————. *La trinité*. Vols. 15 and 16 of *Oeuvres de Saint-Augustin*. Text of the Benedictine edition, translated and edited by M. Mellet, OP, and Th. Camelot, OP [vol. 16 by P. Agaësse, SJ, with J. Moingt, SJ]. Introduction by E. Hendrikx, OESA. Paris: Desclée de Brower, 1955.

Avicenna (Husain ibn Abdullāh ibn 'Alī ibn Sīnā). *Liber canonis Auicenne reuisus & abomni errore mendaque purgatus summaque cum diligentia impressus*. Venice, 1507. Facsimile reprint, Hildesheim: Olms, 1964.

————. *Livre des directives et remarques (Kitāb al-'išārāt wa l-tanbīhāt)*. Translated and edited by A.-M. Goichon. Beirut: Commission Internationale pour la Traduction des Chefs d'Oeuvre; Paris: Vrin, 1951.

————. *Poème de la médecine; 'Urğūza fī't-Tibb; Cantica Avicennae*. Texte arabe, trad. fr., trad. lat. du XIIIe siècle. Edited by Jahier and Abdelkadar Noureddine. Paris: Belles Lettres, 1956.

————. "Poem on the Soul." In Browne, *Literary History*, 2.110–11.

──── . *A Treatise on the Canon of Medicine of Avicenna, Incorporating a Translation of the First Book.* Translated, edited, and commentary by O. Cameron Gruner. 1930. Reprint, New York: Augustus M. Kelley, 1970.

Bacon, Francis, Lord Verulam. *The Advancement of Learning and The New Atlantis.* Edited by Arthur Johnston. Oxford: Clarendon, 1974.

──── . *The Works.* Edited by James Spedding, Robert Leslie Ellis and Douglas Denon Heath. 15 vols. Boston: Taggard & Thompson, 1861–1864.

Baillet, Adrien. *La vie de Monsieur Des-Cartes.* 2 vols. Paris: Hortemels, 1691. Facsimile reprint, Hildesheim: Olms, 1972.

Barker, Andrew D., ed. *Greek Musical Writings.* 2 vols. Cambridge: Cambridge University Press, 1984–1989.

Beeckman, Isaac. *Journal . . . de 1604 à 1634.* Edited by Cornélis de Waard. 4 vols. The Hague: Martinus Nijhoff, 1939–1953.

Belleforest, François de. *Arraisonnement fort gentil et proffitable sur l'infelicité qui suyt ordinairement le bonheur des grans: Avec un beau Discours sur l'excellence des Princes du sang de France.* . . . Paris: Iean Hulpeau, 1569.

Berni, Francesco. "Capitolo del debito." In *Rime burlesche,* 202–11. Edited by Giorgio Bàrberi Squarotti. Milan: Biblioteca Universale Rizzoli, 1991.

Boccaccio, Giovanni. *Boccaccio on Poetry: Being the Preface and the Fourteenth and Fifteenth Books of Boccaccio's "Genealogia deorum gentilium".* Translated and edited by Charles G. Osgood. Indianapolis: Bobbs-Merrill, 1930.

──── . *Boccace "Des cleres et nobles femmes": Ms. Bibl. Nat. 12420 (Chap. I–LII).* Edited by Jeanne Baroin and Josiane Haffen. Annales Littéraires de l'Université de Besançon 498. Paris: Belles Lettres, 1993.

──── . *Famous Women [De mulieribus claris].* Edited and translated by Virginia Brown. Cambridge, MA: Harvard University Press, 2001.

Bodin, Jean. *Methodus ad facilem historiarum cognitionem.* In *Oeuvres philosophiques,* 99–269. Edited by Pierre Mesnard. Paris: Presses Universitaires de France, 1951.

──── . *Les six livres de la république.* Edited by Christiane Frémont, Marie-Dominique Couzinet, and Henri Rochais. 6 vols. Paris: Fayard, 1986.

Boethius, Anicius Manlius Severinus. *Fundamentals of Music [De institutione musica].* Translated and introduction by Calvin M. Bower. Edited by Claude Palisca. New Haven: Yale University Press, 1989.

──── . *Liber de persona et duabus naturis.* In *Opera omnia,* 2. 1337–54. Edited by Jacques-Paul Migne. *PL* 64. Paris: J.-P. Migne, 1860.

Bonaventure, St. *The Journey of the Mind to God.* Translated by Philotheus Boehner, OFM. Edited by Stephen F. Brown. Indianapolis: Hackett, 1993.

──── . *Meditations on the Life of Christ, attributed to St. Bonaventure.* Translated by Sister M. Emmanuel. St. Louis: B. Herder, 1934.

Brandolini, Raffaele. *On Music and Poetry (De musica et poetica, 1513).* Translated and edited by Ann E. Moyer, with Marc Laureys. Tempe: Arizona Center for Medieval and Renaissance Studies, 2001.

Bright, Timothy. *A Treatise of Melancholie.* London: Thomas Vautrollier, 1586. Facsimile Reprint, introduced by Hardin Craig. New York: Columbia University Press, for Facsimile Text Society, 1940.

Brutus, Stephanus Junius, the Celt. *See:* Languet and Mornay.

Calderón de la Barca, Pedro. *Eco y Narciso.* In *Las comedias,* 2.273–97. Edited by Juan Jorge Kell. 4 vols. Leipzig: Ernest Fleischer, 1827–1830.

———. *Obras completas.* Vol 1. Edited by Angel Valbuena Briones. Madrid: Aguilar, 1959.

Campbell, David A., ed. *Greek Lyric.* 5 vols. Cambridge, MA: Harvard University Press; London: Heinemann, 1982–1993.

Carew, Thomas. *The Poems of Thomas Carew, with his masque Coclum Britannicum* [sic]. Edited by Rhodes Dunlap. Oxford: Clarendon, 1949.

Cary, Elizabeth, Lady Falkland. *See: Three Tragedies.*

Cassirer, Ernst, Paul Oskar Kristeller, and John Herman Randall, Jr., eds. *The Renaissance Philosophy of Man.* 1948; rpt. Chicago: University of Chicago Press, 1948.

Cavalcanti, Guido. *The Complete Poems.* [Text edited,] translated, introduction and notes by Marc A. Cirigliano. New York: Italica, 1992.

Cebes. *Cebetis Thebani Tabula,* e Græco in Latinam conversa per Ludovicum Odaxium Patavinum. In Censorinus, *Index librorum* [etc., incl. *Epicteti Encheiridion*]. Bononiae [Bologna]: Benedictus Hectoris Bononiensis, 1497.

———. *The Tabula of Cebes.* Edited and translated by John J. Fitzgerald and L. Michael White. Society of Biblical Literature, Texts and Translations 24, Graeco-Roman Religion Series 7. Chico, CA: Scholars Press, 1983.

Celsus, Aulus Cornelius. *De medicina.* Edited and translated W. G. Spencer. 3 vols. Cambridge, MA: Harvard University Press; London: Heinemann, 1935–1938.

Cereta, Laura. *Laurae Ceretae Brixiensis feminae clarissimae epistolae iam primum e MS in lucem productae.* Edited by Jacopo Filippo Tomasini. Padua: Sebastiano Sardi, 1640.

Cervantes Saavedra, Miguel de. *El ingenioso hidalgo Don Quijote de la Mancha.* Edited by Luis Andrés Murillo. 2 vols. 1978. Reprint, Madrid: Castalia, 1991.

———. *Novelas ejemplares.* Edited by Harry Sieber, 2 vols. Madrid: Cátedra, 1992.

———. *Los trabajos de Persiles y Sigismunda.* 1952. Reprint, Madrid: Espasa-Calpe, 1980.

———. *The Trials of Persiles and Sigismunda, A Northern Story.* Translated by Celia Richmond Weller and Clark A. Colahan. Berkeley: University of California Press, 1989.

Champier, Symphorien. *Le livre de vraye amour.* Edited by James B. Wadsworth. The Hague: Mouton, 1962.

Chanson de Roland, La. See: Whitehead, ed. (in Primary).

Charron, Pierre. *De la sagesse.* Edited by Barbara de Negroni. Paris: Fayard, 1986.

Christina of Markyate. *The Life of Christina of Markyate: A Twelfth-Century Recluse.* Edited and translated by Charles H. Talbot. Oxford: Clarendon, 1959.

Christine de Pisan. *Le chemin de longue étude.* Édition critique du ms. Harley 4431. Translated by Andrea Tarnowski. Paris: Livre de Poche, 2000.

————. *The Livre de la cité des dames of Christine de Pisan: A Critical Edition.* Edited by Maureen Cheney Curnow. 2 vols. Ph.D. diss., Vanderbilt University, 1975. Ann Arbor, MI: University Microfilms International, 1985.

Cicero, Marcus Tullius. *De fato.* In *De oratore, Book III; De Fato; Paradoxa Stoicorum; Partitiones oratoriae,* Edited and translated by H. Rackham. 1942. Reprint, Cambridge, MA: Harvard University Press; London: Heinemann, 1968.

————. *De finibus bonorum et malorum.* Edited and translated by H. Rackham. 2nd ed. 1931. Reprint, Cambridge, MA: Harvard University Press; London: Heinemann, 1951.

————. *De inventione; De optimo genere oratorum; Topica.* Edited and translated by H. M. Hubbell. 1949. Reprint, Cambridge, MA: Harvard University Press; London: Heinemann, 1968.

————. *De natura deorum; Academica.* Edited and translated by H. Rackham. 1933. Reprint, London: Heinemann; Cambridge, MA: Harvard University Press, 1961.

————. *De officiis.* Edited and translated by Walter Miller. London: Heinemann; New York: Macmillan, 1921.

————. *De oratore, Books I–II.* Edited and translated by E. W. Sutton. Completed and introduced by H. Rackham. 1942. Reprint, Cambridge, MA: Harvard University Press; London: Heinemann, 1967. [For Book III, *see*: Cicero, *De fato.*]

————. *De senectute; De amicitia; De divinatione.* Edited and translated by William Armistead Falconer. 1923. Reprint, Cambridge, MA: Harvard University Press; London: Heinemann, 1971.

————. *On Duties.* Edited and translated by M. T. Griffin and E. M. Atkins. Cambridge: Cambridge University Press, 1991.

————. *Paradoxa Stoicorum. See*: Cicero, *De fato.*

————. *Tusculan Disputations.* Edited and translated by J. E. King. Rev. ed. 1945. Reprint, Cambridge, MA: Harvard University Press; London: Heinemann, 1950.

Constantinus Afer. "Constantinus Africanus' *De coitu*: A Translation." Translated by Paul Delany. *Chaucer Review* 4.1 (Summer 1969): 56–65.

Coras, Jean de. *Arrest memorable, du Parlement de Tolose: contenant vne histoire prodigieuse d'vn suppose mary, aduenue de nostre temps.* . . . Lyon: Barthelemy Vincent, 1618. (1st ed. Lyon: Antoine Vincent, 1561.)

Corpus iuris canonici. Edited by Aemilius Friedburg. 2 vols. Leipzig: Bernardus Tauchnitz, 1879–1881.

Corpus iuris civilis. Institutiones [Justiniani]. Edited by Paul Krueger; *Digesta [Justiniani].* Edited by Theodor Mommsen, revised by Paul Krueger. 3 vols. 16th ed. Berlin: Weidmann, 1954.

————. *See also*: Justinian.

Cowley, Abraham. *Poems.* Edited by A. R. Waller. Cambridge: University Press, 1905.

Dante Alighieri. *Literary Criticism of Dante Alighieri.* Translated and edited by Robert S. Haller. Lincoln: University of Nebraska Press, 1973.

Delrio, Martin Antonio, SJ. *Disquisitionum magicarum libri sex. Quibus continetur accurata curiosarum artium, & vanarum superstitionum confutatio, vtilis Theologis, Iurisconsultis, Medicis, Philologis.* . . . Moguntiae [Mainz]: Apud Johannem Albinum, 1612. (1st ed. 1599–1600.)

―――. *Les controverses et recherches magiques* . . . *divisées en six livres, ausquels sont exactement & doctement confutées les Sciences Curieuses, les Vanitez, & Superstitions de toute la Magie.* . . . Translated and abridged from the Latin by André du Chesne. Paris: Iean Petit-pas, 1611.

Demosthenes. "In Neaeram." In *Demosthenes VI*, 347–451. Edited and translated by A. T. Murray. 1939. Reprint, Cambridge, MA: Harvard University Press; London: Heinemann, 1956.

―――. *Plaidoyers civils, tome IV (Discours LVII-LIX)*, edited and translated by Louis Gernet. Index by J. A. de Foucault and R. Weil. Paris: Belles Lettres, 1960.

Descartes, René. [AT] *Oeuvres*. Edited by Charles Adam and Paul Tannery. New ed. 11 vols. Paris: Vrin/C.N.R.S., 1964–1976.

―――. *Discours de la méthode*. Edited by Étienne Gilson. Paris: Vrin, 1925.

―――. *Discours de la méthode*. Edited by Gilbert Gadoffre. 2nd ed. Manchester: Manchester University Press, 1961.

―――. "La licence en droit de Descartes: Un placard inédit de 1616." Edited by Jean-Robert Armogathe, Vincent Carraud and Robert Feenstra, *Nouvelles de la République des Lettres* (1988–II): 123–45.

―――. *The Philosophical Writings*. Edited and translated by John Cottingham, Robert Stoothoff, Dugald Murdoch [with Anthony Kenny for vol. 3]. 3 vols. Cambridge: Cambridge University Press, 1985–1991.

―――, and Martin Schoock. *La querelle d'Utrecht*. Edited and translated by Theo Verbeek. Paris, 1988.

Diels, Hermann, ed. *Die Fragmente der Vorsokratiker: Griechisch und deutsch*. 9th ed. revised by Walter Kranz. 3 vols. Berlin: Weidmann, 1959–1960.

Dio Chrysostom. [*Discourses.*] Edited and translated by J. W. Cohoon and H. Lamar Crosby. 5 vols. Cambridge, MA: Harvard University Press; London: Heinemann, 1932–1951.

Diogenes Laertius. *Lives of Eminent Philosophers*. Edited and translated by R. D. Hicks. 2 vols. Revised ed. 1972. Reprint, Cambridge, MA: Harvard University Press; London: Heinemann, 1991.

Dionysius of Halicarnassus. *On Literary Composition*. In *Critical Essays*, 2.14–243. Edited and translated by Stephen Usher. 2 vols. Cambridge, MA: Harvard University Press; London: Heinemann, 1974–1985.

Donne, John. *Poetical Works*. Edited by Herbert Grierson. 1933; rpt. London: Oxford University Press, 1966.

Du Bartas, Guillaume de Saluste. *La sepmaine (texte de 1581)*. Edited by Yvonne Bellenger. 2 vols. Paris: Nizet, 1981.

Duvergier de Hauranne, Jean. *Question royalle et sa decision*. Paris: Toussainct du Bray, 1609.

Elyot, Sir Thomas. *The Castel of Helth 1541*. Facsimile reprint, New York: Scholars' Facsimiles & Reprints, n.d.

Epictetus. *The Discourses as Reported by Arrian, The Manual, and Fragments.* Edited and translated by W. A. Oldfather. 2 vols. 1925–1928; rpt. Cambridge, MA: Harvard University Press, 1989.

Erasmus, Desiderius. *Adages.* Translated by Margaret Mann Phillips. Annotated by R. A. B. Mynors. 4 vols. *Collected Works of Erasmus* 31–34. Toronto: University of Toronto Press, 1982–1992.

———. *Ciceronianus or a Dialogue on the Best Style of Speaking.* Translated by Izora Scott. In her *Controversies over the Imitation of Cicero in the Renaissance,* 17–130. Davis, CA: Hermagoras, 1991.

———. *The Colloquies.* Translated by Craig R. Thompson. Chicago: University of Chicago Press, 1965.

———. *The Education of a Christian Prince.* Translated by Neil M. Cheshire and Michael J. Heath. With the *Panegyric for Archduke Philip of Austria.* Translated by Lisa Jardine. Edited by Lisa Jardine. Cambridge: Cambridge University Press, 1997.

Euripides. *Andromache.* In *Euripides II: Children of Heracles, Hippolytus, Andromache, Hecuba,* 265–389. Edited and translated by David Kovacs. Cambridge, MA: Harvard University Press, 1995.

———. *Andromache.* Translated by John Frederick Nims. In *Euripides III,* 69–119. Edited by David Grene and Richmond Lattimore. Chicago: University of Chicago Press, 1958.

———. *Helen.* Translated by Richmond Lattimore. In *Euripides II,* 189–260. Edited by David Grene and Richmond Lattimore. Chicago: University of Chicago Press, 1956.

———. *Hippolytus.* In *Euripides II* [ed. Kovacs: see *Andromache*], 115–263.

———. *Ion.* Translated by Ronald Frederick Willetts. In *Euripides III* [ed. Grene and Lattimore: see *Andromache*].

———. *Iphigenia in Aulis.* Translated by Charles R. Walker. In *Euripides IV,* 216–307. Edited by David Grene and Richmond Lattimore. Chicago: University of Chicago Press, 1958.

Evelyn, John. *Elysium Britannicum, or The Royal Gardens.* Edited by John E. Ingram. Philadelphia: University of Pennsylvania Press, 2001.

Ficino, Marsilio. *Five Questions Concerning the Mind.* Translated by Josephine L. Burroughs. In Cassirer, [et al.], eds., 193–212.

———. *Marsilio Ficino's Commentary on Plato's Symposium.* Text, translation and introduction by Sears Reynolds Jayne. University of Missouri Studies 19.1. Columbia: University of Missouri, 1944.

Fitzpatrick, Edward Augustus, ed. *Saint Ignatius and the Ratio Studiorum.* New York: McGraw-Hill, 1933.

Fludd, Robert. *Utriusque cosmi maioris scilicet et minoris metaphysica, physica atqve technica historia . . .* 2 vols. Oppenheim: Hieronymus Gallerus for Johan-Theodorus de Bry, 1617–1620.

Fontenelle, Bernard le Bovier de. *Textes choisis (1683–1701).* Edited by Maurice Roelens. Paris: Éditions Sociales, 1966.

Fragmente der Vorsokratiker. See: Diels, ed.

Gaius. *The Institutes*. Part I: Text with Critical Notes and translation by Francis de Zulueta. Oxford: Clarendon, 1946.

Galen[us, Claudius]. *Opera omnia*. Edited by Carolus Gottlob Kühn. 22 vols. Leipzig: Carolus Cnoblochius, 1821–1833.

———. *Compendium Timaei Platonis, aliorumque dialogorum synopsis quae extant fragmenta*. Edited by Paulus Kraus and Richardus Walzer. *Plato Arabus*, 1. London: Warburg Institute, 1951.

———. *De elementis ex Hippocratis sententia / On the Elements According to Hippocrates*. Edited, translated and commentary Phillip De Lacy. Berlin: Akademie, 1996.

———. *De partibus artis medicativae: eine verschollene griechische Schrift in Übersetzung des 14. Jahrhunderts*. Edited by Hermann Schöne. Greifswald: Julius Abel, 1911.

———. *De placitis Hippocratis et Platonis / On the Doctrines of Hippocrates and Plato*. Edited, translated and commentary Phillip De Lacy. 3 vols. Berlin: Akademie, 1978–1984.

———. *De semine / On Semen*. Edited, translated and commentary Phillip De Lacy. Berlin: Akademie, 1992.

———. *In Platonis Timaeum commentarii fragmenta*. Edited by Henricus Otto Schröder, with Paulus Kahle. Leipzig: Teubner, 1934.

———. *On the Natural Faculties*. Edited and translated by Arthur John Brock. 1916. Reprint, London: Heinemann; Cambridge, MA: Harvard University Press, 1963.

———. *On the Passions and Errors of the Soul*. Translated by Paul W. Harkins. Introduction and Interpretation by Walter Riese. Athens, OH: Ohio State University Press, 1963.

———. *On the Therapeutic Method, Books I and II*. Translated, introduction and commentary by R. J. Hankinson. Oxford: Clarendon, 1991.

———. *Selected Works*. Translated and edited by P. N. Singer. Oxford: Oxford University Press, 1997.

———. *See also*: Brain (in Secondary).

Garzoni, Tomaso. *Il teatro de' vari e diversi cervelli mondani*. . . . Venice: Paulo Zanfretti, 1583.

Gellius, Aulus. *The Attic Nights*. Edited and translated by John C. Rolfe. 3 vols. 1927. Reprint, Cambridge, MA: Harvard University Press; London: Heinemann, 1960–1961.

Gentillet, Innocent. *Anti-Machiavel. Édition de 1576*. Edited by C. Edward Rathé. Geneva: Droz, 1968.

Giacomo da Lentini. *Poesie*. Edited by Roberto Antonelli. Rome: Bulzoni, 1979.

———. *See also*: Langley, ed. (in Primary).

Gibbons, John. "The Practical Method of Meditation." [Prefaced to] *An Abridgment of Meditations of the Life, Passion, Death, and Resurrection of Our Lord and Saviour Iesus Christ. Written in Italian by the R. Father Vincentius Bruno of the Society of Iesus*. Translated by John Gibbons. [St. Omer]: n.p., 1614.

Goulart, Simon. *Thresor d'histoires admirables et memorables de nostre temps*. . . . 2 vols. Cologne: P. Marceau, 1610. (1st ed. 1600.)

Gournay, Marie Le Jars de. "Preface sur les Essais de Michel, seigneur de Montaigne." In *Essais de Michel de Montaigne*, 1.ix–xlix. New ed. 5 vols. Paris: chez Lefèvre, 1818.

Guibert of Nogent. *Self and Society in Medieval France: The Memoirs of Abbot Guibert of Nogent (1064?–c. 1125)*. Edited, introduction, and notes by John F. Benton. Translated by C. C. Swinton Bland, revised by the editor. New York: Harper Torchbooks, 1970.

Habert, François. *Le songe de Pantagruel*. Introduction by John Lewis. *Études Rabelaisiennes* 18, 108–62. Preface by M. A. Screech. Geneva: Droz, 1984.

[Harington, Sir John.] *The School of Salernum; Regimen sanitatis Salernitatem.* The English Version by Sir John Harington. [With] "History of the School of Salernum" by Francis R. Packard; "A Note on the Prehistory of the Regimen Salernitatis" by Fielding H. Garrison. New York: Augustus M. Kelley, 1970.

Hélisenne de Crenne. *Les angoysses douloureuses qui procedent d'amours*. Edited by Christine de Buzon. Paris: Champion, 1997.

———. *Les angoysses douloureuses qui procedent d'amours, première partie*. Edited by Paule Demats. Paris: Belles Lettres, 1968.

———. *Les epistres familieres et invectives*. Edited by Jerry C. Nash. Paris: Champion, 1996.

———. *Les epistres familieres et invectives de ma dame Helisenne*. Edited by Jean-Philippe Beaulieu with Hannah Fournier. Montreal: Presses de l'Université de Montréal, 1995.

———. *A Renaissance Woman: Helisenne's Personal and Invective Letters*. Translated and edited by Marianna M. Mustacchi and Paul J. Archambault. Syracuse, NY: Syracuse University Press, 1986.

———. *Le songe de madame Hélisenne de Crenne: 1541*. Preface and notes by Jean-Philippe Beaulieu. Paris: Indigo & Côté-Femmes, 1995.

———. *The Torments of Love*. Edited by Lisa Neal. Translated by Lisa Neal and Steven Rendall. Minneapolis: University of Minnesota Press, 1996.

Héloïse. *From the Letters of Two Lovers*. Edited by Ewald Könsgen. Translated by Neville Chaivaroli and Constant J. Mews. In Mews, 179–289 (in Secondary).

———. *See also*: Abelard; McLaughlin; Muckle; *and* Radice (all in Primary).

Herbert, George. *The Complete English Poems*. Edited by John Tobin. London: Penguin, 1991.

Herodotus. *The Persian Wars*. Translated by George Rawlinson. Introduction by Francis R. B. Godolphin. New York: Modern Library, 1942.

Hierocles. [*Elements of Ethics*.] Text ed., Italian translation, and commentary by Guido Bastianini and A. A. Long. In *Corpus dei papiri filosofici greci e latini* [*CPF*]: *Testi e lessico nei papiri di cultura greca e latina*, Pt. 1, vol. 1.2, 268–451. Florence: L. S. Olschki, 1992.

———. *See also*: Arnim, with Schubart.

Hildegard of Bingen, St. *The Book of the Rewards of Life (Liber vitae meritorum)*. Translated by Bruce W. Hozeski. 1994; rpt. New York: Oxford University Press, 1997.

———. *Causae et curae*. Edited by Paulus Kaiser. Leipzig: Teubner, 1903.

———. *Epistolarium.* Edited by Lieven Van Acker. 2 vols. CCCM 91–91A. Turnhout: Brepols, 1991–1993.

———. *Liber divinorum operum.* Edited by Albert Derolez and Peter Dronke. CCCM 92. Turnhout: Brepols, 1996.

———. *Liber vite meritorum.* Edited by Angela Carlevaris, OSB. CCCM 90. Turnhout: Brepols, 1995.

———. *Opera omnia.* Edited by Jacques-Paul Migne. *PL* 197. Paris: Garnier & J.-P. Migne successores, 1882.

———. *[Physica] Liber . . . subtilitatum diversarum naturarum creaturarum.* Edited by Charles-Victor Daremberg and Friedrich Anton Reuss. In Hildegard, *Opera omnia,* 1125–1352.

———. *Scivias.* Edited by Adelgundis Führkötter, OSB, with Angela Carlevaris, OSB. 2 vols. CCCM 43–43a. Turnhout: Brepols, 1978.

———. *Scivias.* Translated by Mother Columba Hart and Jane Bishop. Introduction by Barbara J. Newman. Preface Caroline Walker Bynum. New York: Paulist Press, 1990.

———. *Symphonia.* A Critical Edition of the *Symphonia armonie celestium revelationum [Symphony of the Harmony of Celestial Revelations].* Introduction, translation and commentary Barbara J. Newman. Ithaca, NY: Cornell University Press, 1988.

Hippocrates. *De l'ancienne médecine.* Edited and translated by Jacques Jouanna. Paris: Belles Lettres, 1990.

———. *Hippocratic Writings.* Edited by G. E. R. Lloyd. Translated by J. Chadwick, W. N. Mann, I. M. Lonie and E. T. Withington. 1978. Reprint, Harmondsworth: Penguin, 1983.

———. *Oeuvres complètes.* Edited and translated by Emile Littré. 10 vols. Paris: J. B. Baillière, 1839–1861.

———. *[Works.]* 8 vols. Edited and translated by W. H. S. Jones [1–2, 4]; E. T. Withington [3]; Paul Potter [5–6, 8]; Wesley Smith [7]. London: Heinemann; New York: Putnam; Cambridge, MA: Harvard University Press, 1923–1995.

Hobbes, Thomas. *The Correspondence.* Edited by Noel Malcolm. 2 vols. Oxford: Clarendon, 1994.

———. *Les éléments de droit natural et politique.* Translated and edited by Louis Roux. Lyon: Hermès, 1977.

———. *The English Works.* Edited by Sir William Molesworth. 11 vols. London: John Bohn, 1839–1845.

———. *Opera philosophica.* Edited by Sir William Molesworth. 5 vols. London: John Bohn, 1839–1845.

Hroswitha of Gandersheim. *The Non-Dramatic Works of Hrosvitha.* Text, translation and commentary by Sister M. Gonsalva Wiegand, OSF. Saint Louis, MO: n. p., 1936.

———. *The Plays.* Translated by Larissa Bonfante, with Alexandra Bonfante-Warren. Oak Park, IL: Bolchazy-Carducci, 1986.

Huarte de San Juan, Juan. *Examen de ingenios para las ciencias.* Edited by Esteban Torres. [Ed. de 1575.] Barcelona: Promociones y Publicaciones Universitarias, 1988.

————. *Examen de ingenios: The Examination of Mens Wits (1594).* Translated Out of the Spanish by M. Camillo Camilli. Englished Out of the Italian by Richard Carew. Facsimile reprint, introduced by Carmen Rogers. Gainesville, FL: Scholars' Facsimiles & Reprints, 1959.

Hugh of Folieto. *De medicina animae.* In *Hugo de S. Victore, 1183–1202.* Edited by Jacques-Paul Migne. *PL* 176. Paris: Garnier & J.-P. Migne successores, 1880.

Hugh of St. Victor. *The Didascalicon: A Medieval Guide to the Arts.* Translated and edited by Jerome Naylor. 1961. Reprint, New York: Columbia University Press, 1991.

————. *See also*: Hugh of Folieto.

Hume, David. *A Treatise of Human Nature.* Edited by Ernest C. Mossner. Harmondsworth: Penguin, 1969.

Hurault de l'Hospital, Michel. *Second discours sur l'estat de France.* In *Quatre excellens discovrs sur l'estat present de la France . . .* , 99–243. [Paris]: n.p., 1593.

Isidore of Seville. *Traité de la nature / [De natura rerum].* Edited by Jacques Fontaine. Bordeaux: Féret & fils, 1960.

Jacobus de Voragine. *The Golden Legend or Lives of the Saints as Englished by William Caxton.* Edited by F. S. Ellis. 7 vols. London: Dent, 1900.

Jiménez de Cisneros, García. *Book of Exercises for the Spiritual Life, written in the year 1500 by García Jiménez de Cisneros. [Ejercitatorio de la vida espiritual.]* Translated by E. Allison Peers. [Montserrat]: Monastery of Montserrat, 1929.

John of Salisbury (Ioannes Saresberiensis). *Metalogicon.* Edited by J. B. Hall, with K. S. B. Keats-Rohan. *CCCM* 98. Turnhout: Brepols, 1991.

Justinian. *The Digest.* Latin Text edited by Theodor Mommsen, with Paul Krueger. English translation [by many] and edited by Alan Watson. 4 vols. Philadelphia: University of Pennsylvania Press, 1985.

————. *The Institutes.* Translated and edited by J. B. Moyle. 5th ed. Oxford: Clarendon, 1913.

————. *See also*: *Corpus iuris civilis.*

Kempe, Margery. *The Book of Margery Kempe.* Translated by B. A. Windeatt. Harmondsworth: Penguin, 1985.

ibn Khaldūn, 'Abd-ar-Rahmān Abū Zayd ibn Muhammad ibn Muhammad. *The Muqaddimah: An Introduction to History.* Translated by Franz Rosenthal. 3 vols. New York: Pantheon Books, for the Bollingen Foundation, 1958.

King James VI and I. *The Political Writings of James I.* Edited by Charles Howard McIlwain. Cambridge, MA: Harvard University Press; London: Humphrey Milford, Oxford University Press, 1918.

————. *Political Writings.* Edited by Johann P. Sommerville. Cambridge: Cambridge University Press, 1994.

Labé, Louise. *Oeuvres complètes: Sonnets-Élégies; Débat de folie et d'amour; Poésies.* Edited by François Rigolot. Paris: Garnier-Flammarion, 1986.

Langley, Ernest F[elix], ed. *The Poetry of Giacomo da Lentino: Sicilian Poet of the Thirteenth Century.* Cambridge, MA: Harvard University Press; London: Humphrey Milford, Oxford University Press, 1915.

Languet, Hubert, and Philippe du Plessis Mornay. *Vindiciae, contra tyrannos: or, Concerning the Legitimate Power of a Prince over the People, and of the People over a Prince*. Edited and translated by George Garnett. Cambridge: Cambridge University Press, 1994.

La Noüe, François de. *Discours politiques et militaires de Seigneur de la Noüe. Nouvellement recueillis & mis en lumiere*. Basel: François Forest, 1587.

Lanyer, Aemilia. *The Poems of Aemilia Lanyer: Salve Deus Rex Judæorum*. Edited by Susanne Woods. New York: Oxford University Press, 1993.

La Sale, Antoine de. *Jehan de Saintré*. Edited by Jean Misrahi and Charles A. Knudson. Geneva: Droz, 1965.

Lawn, Brian, ed. *The Salernitan Questions: An Introduction to the History of Medieval and Renaissance Problem Literature*. Oxford: Clarendon, 1963.

Lefkowitz, Mary R., and Maureen B. Fant, eds. *Women in Greece and Rome*. Toronto: Samuel-Stevens, 1977.

Leibniz, Gottfried Wilhelm von. *Nouveaux essais sur l'entendement humain* [1703–5]. In *Philosophische Schriften*, edited by Leibniz-Forschungstelle der Universität Münster. Vol. 6. Berlin: Akademie-Verlag, 1962.

———. *The Political Writings*. Translated and edited by Patrick Riley. Cambridge: Cambridge University Press, 1972.

Lemaire de Belges, Jean. *Illustrations de Gaule et singularitez de Troye* [1511–12]. In *Oeuvres*, vols. 1–2. Edited by Auguste Jean Stecher. 4 vols. 1882–1885. Reprint, Geneva: Slatkine Reprints, 1969.

Lemnius, Levinius. *De habitu et constitutione corporis, quam Graeci κρασιν, triviales complexionem vocant libri duo*. Antwerp: G. Simon, 1561.

Le Roy, Louis. *Exhortation aux François pour vivre en concorde, et iouir du bien de la Paix* [with: *Proiect ou dessein du Royaume de France.* . . . , and: *Les Monarchiques . . . ou de la Monarchie et des choses requises à son establissement . . .*]. Paris: Federic Morel, 1570.

Lipsius, Justus. *Six Bookes of Politickes or Civil Doctrine, Written in Latine.* . . . Translated by William Jones. London, 1594. Facsimile reprint, The English Experience 287. Amsterdam: Theatrum Orbis Terrarum; New York: Da Capo Press, 1970.

———. *Two Bookes of Constancie. Written in Latine.* . . . Translated by Sir John Stradling. Edited by Rudolf Kirk, with Clayton Morris Hall. New Brunswick, NJ: Rutgers University Press, 1939.

Locke, John. *An Essay concerning Human Understanding*. Edited by Peter H. Nidditch. 1975. Reprint, Oxford: Clarendon, 1982.

———. *Some Thoughts Concerning Education*. Edited by John W. and Jean S. Yolton. Oxford: Clarendon, 1989.

———. *Two Treatises of Government*. Edited by Peter Laslett. Cambridge: Cambridge University Press, 1960.

Lodge, Thomas. *The Workes of Lucius Annaeus Seneca: Both Morall and Naturall*. London: William Stansby, 1614.

Long, Anthony A., and David Sedley, eds. *The Hellenistic Philosophers*. 2 vols. Cambridge: Cambridge University Press, 1987.

Loyola, St. Ignatius. *Ejercicios espirituales*. In *Obras completas*, 207–90. Edited by Ignacio Iparraguirre, SJ, and Candido de Dalmases, SJ. 3rd ed. rev. Madrid: Biblioteca de Autores Cristianos, 1977.

——. *The Spiritual Exercises and Selected Works*. Edited by George E. Ganss, SJ [et al.]. New York: Paulist Press, 1991.

——. *The Spiritual Exercises of St. Ignatius: Based on Studies in the Language of the Autograph*. Translated and edited by Louis J. Puhl, SJ. Chicago: Loyola University Press, 1951.

Lucretius Carus, Titus. *[De rerum naturae] / De la nature*. [Text, translation,] introduction and notes by Henri Clouard. Revised and corrected ed. Paris: Garnier, 1954.

Lukács, Ladislaus, SJ, ed. *Monumenta Paedagogica Societatis Jesu*. New ed. 7 vols. Rome: Monumenta Historica Soc. Iesu, 1965–1992.

Lysias. *[Orations.]* Edited and translated by W. R. M. Lamb. 1930. Reprint, Cambridge, MA: Harvard University Press; London: Heinemann, 1976.

Machiavelli, Niccolò. *The Discourses*. Edited by Bernard Crick. Translated by Leslie J. Walker, SJ. Revised by Brian Richardson. 1970. Reprint, Harmondsworth: Penguin, 1978.

Macrobius, Ambrosius Theodosius. *Commentary on the Dream of Scipio*. Translated and edited by William Harris Stahl. New York: Columbia University Press, 1952.

Maimonides, Moses. *The Guide for the Perplexed*. Translated by M. Friedländer. 2nd ed. 1904; rpt. New York: Dover, 1956.

——. *The Medical Aphorisms*. Translated and edited by Fred Rosner and Suessman Muntner. 2 vols. in 1. 1970–1971. Reprint, New York: Bloch Publishing for Yeshiva University Press, 1973.

Malherbe, François de. *Oeuvres*. Edited by Antoine Adam. Paris: Gallimard, 1971.

Martianus Minneius Felix Capella. *The Marriage of Philology and Mercury*. Translated by William Harris Stahl and Richard Johnson with E. L. Burge. Vol. 2 of *Martianus Capella and the Seven Liberal Arts*. 2 vols. New York: Columbia University Press, 1971–1979.

Martin of Braga, St. *Martini episcopi Bracarensis Opera omnia*. Edited by Claude W. Barlow. Published for the American Academy in Rome. New Haven: Yale University Press; London: Geoffrey Cumberlege, Oxford University Press, 1950.

——. *See also*: Haselbach (in Secondary).

Martínez de Toledo, Alfonso. *Arcipreste de Talavera o Corbacho [o Reprobación del amor mundano, 1438]*. Edited by Michael Gerli. Madrid: Cátedra, 1979.

McLaughlin, T. P. [ed.] "Abelard's Rule for Religious Women" [personal letter VII]. *Mediaeval Studies* XVIII (Toronto: Pontifical Institute of Mediaeval Studies, 1956): 241–92. (Concludes edition of letters begun by J. T. Muckle.)

Melanchthon, Philip. *Liber de anima*. In *Opera quae supersunt omnia*, 13.5–178. Edited by Carolus Gottlieb Bretschneider. 28 vols. Halle: Schwetschke, 1834–1860.

Menander. *[Plays and Fragments.]* Edited and translated by W. Geoffrey Arnott.

3 vols. Cambridge, MA: Harvard University Press; London: Heinemann, 1979–2000.

Milton, John. *Areopagitica; A Speech of Mr. John Milton for the Liberty of Unlicenc'd Printing. To the Parliament of England.* In *The Prose of John Milton,* 266–334. Edited by J. Max Patrick. Garden City, NY: Doubleday Anchor, 1967.

Montaigne, Michel Eyquem de. *Oeuvres complètes.* Edited by Albert Thibaudet and Maurice Rat. Paris: Gallimard, 1962.

————. *See also:* Gournay, *and* Sabunde.

Muckle, J. T. "Abelard's Letter of Consolation to a Friend (*Historia calamitatum*)." *Mediaeval Studies* XII (Toronto: Pontifical Institute of Mediaeval Studies, 1950): 163–213. (Edition of letters completed in next two entries and by McLaughlin, T. P.)

————. "The Personal Letters between Abelard and Heloise [letters I–IV]." *Mediaeval Studies* XV (Toronto: PIMS, 1953): 47–94.

————. "The Letter of Heloise on Religious Life and Abelard's First Reply [letters V and VI]." *Mediaeval Studies* XVII (Toronto: PIMS, 1955): 240–81.

Nauck, Augustus, ed. *Tragicorum graecorum fragmenta.* 2nd ed. Leipzig: Teubner, 1889.

Nemesius of Emesa. *De natura hominis, Graece et Latine.* Edited by Christian Friedrich Matthei. Magdeburg: Gebauer, 1802. Facsimile reprint, Hildesheim: Olms, 1967.

————. *De natura hominis.* Translated by Burgundio of Pisa. Edited and introduction by Gérard Verbeke and J. R. Moncho. Leiden: E. J. Brill, 1975.

————. *A Treatise on the Nature of Man.* Edited by William Telfer. In *The Library of Christian Classics 4: Cyril of Jerusalem and Nemesius of Emesa.* Philadelphia: Westminster Press, 1955.

O'Faolain, Julia, and Lauro Martines, eds. *Not in God's Image: Women in History from the Greeks to the Victorians.* New York: Harper & Row, 1973.

Pachtler, G. M., SJ, ed. *Ratio studiorum et institutiones scholasticae Societatis Jesu per Germaniam olim vigentes collectae concinnatae dilucidatae.* . . . 4 vols. [2, 5, 9, 16.] In *Monumenta Germaniae Pedagogica.* . . . General editor Karl Kehrbach. Berlin: A. Hoffmann, 1887–1894.

Paré, Ambroise. *Oeuvres complètes.* . . . [Edited by] J.-F. Malgaigne. 3 vols. Paris: J.-B. Baillière, 1840–1841.

Pascal, Blaise. *Oeuvres complètes.* Edited by Louis Lafuma. Paris: Seuil, "l'Intégrale," 1963.

————. *Pensées.* Edited by Philippe Sellier. Paris: Mercure de France, 1976.

Pasquier, Étienne. *Écrits politiques.* Edited by D. Thickett. Geneva: Droz, 1966.

————. *The Iesuites Catechisme. Or Examination of their doctrine.* Published in French this present year 1602. And now translated into English. . . . Printed Anno Domini 1602. Facsimile reprint, English Recusant Literature 1558–1640, edited by D. M. Rogers, vol. 264. Ilkley, UK: Scolar Press, 1975.

————. *Les lettres d'Estienne Pasqvier Conseiller & Advocat general du Roy à Paris. Contenans plusieurs belles matieres & discours sur les affaires d'Estat de*

France, & touchant les guerres ciuiles. 2 vols. Paris: Iean Petit-Pas [and Laurent
Sonius for vol. 2], 1619.

Paulus Aegineta. The Seven Books. Translated and edited by Francis Adams. 3
vols. London: Sydenham Society, 1844–1847.

Petrarch (Francesco Petrarca). The Ascent of Mont Ventoux. Translated by Hans
Nachod. In Cassirer [et al.], eds., 36–46.

———. [Collatio laureationis.] "La 'Collatio laureationis' nel Petrarca." Edited
by Carlo Godi. Italia medioevale e umanistica 13 (1970): 13–27.

———. [Collatio laureationis.] "Petrarch's Coronation Oration." Translated by
Ernest Hatch Wilkins. In Studies in the Life and Works of Petrarch, 300–313.
Cambridge, MA: The Mediaeval Academy of America, 1955.

———. De vita solitaria. Edited by Guido Martellotti. Translated by Antonietta
Bufano. In Prose, 285–591.

———. De vita solitaria, Buch I. Kritische Textausgabe und Ideengeschichtlicher
Kommentar von K. A. E. Enenkel. Leiden, New York, Copenhagen, Cologne:
E. J. Brill & Universitaire Pers Leiden, 1990. [See also: The Life of Solitude.]

———. Epistolae de rebus familiaribus et variae. Edited by Giuseppe Fracassetti.
3 vols. Florence: Le Monnier, 1859–1863.

———. Epistole rerum senilium cxxviii diuise in libris xviii. In [Opera]. 2 vols. in
1. Venice: Simonis de Luere, for Andrea Torresano de Asula, 1501. 2. [7–198].
(No title-page, but matter listed: [1] Librorum Francisci Petrarche impressorum
annotatio, [2] Annotatio nonnullorum librorum seu epistolarum Francisci Petrarche. Unlike later editions [see Opera below], all letters are numbered, but
unpaginated. Each volume of the copy I have used [UC Berkeley, Bancroft Library fPQ4489.A1 1501] is paginated in an old hand, excluding front matter.)

———. Le familiari. Edited by Vittorio Rossi (Umberto Bosco for vol. 4). 4 vols.
Florence: G. C. Sansoni, 1933–1942. (Edizione nazionale delle opere di
Francesco Petrarca X–XIII.)

———. Le familiari [libri I–XI]. Introduction, translation and notes by Ugo
Dotti. 2 vols. Urbino: Argalìa, 1974.

———. Lettere senili. Translated and edited by Giuseppe Fracassetti. 2 vols. Florence: Successori Le Monnier, 1892.

———. Letters of Old Age/Rerum senilium libri I–XVIII. Translated by Aldo S.
Bernardo, Saul Levin and Reta A. Bernardo. 2 vols. Baltimore: Johns Hopkins
University Press, 1992.

———. Letters on Familiar Matters/Rerum familiarium libri, I–XXIV. Translated by Aldo S. Bernardo. 3 vols. Albany: State University of New York Press;
Baltimore: Johns Hopkins University Press, 1975–85.

———. Liber sine nomine. Edited by Paul Piur. In Petrarcas 'Buch ohne Namen'
und die päpstliche Kurie: Ein Beitrag zur Geistesgeschichte der Frührenais-
sance, 161–407: Latin text, 163–238. Deutsche Vierteljahrsschrift für Litera-
turwissenschaft und Geistesgeschichte 6. Halle and Saale: Max Niemeyer,
1925.

———. [Liber sine nomine.] Petrarch's Book Without a Name. Translated by
Norman P. Zacour. Toronto: Pontifical Institute of Mediaeval Studies, 1973.

———. The Life of Solitude. Translated and edited by Jacob Zeitlin. [Urbana]:
University of Illinois Press, 1924.

———. [*Opera*]. *See above: Epistole.*

———. *Opera quae extant omnia. . . .* 4t. in 2v. Basel: Henricus Petrus, 1554.

———. *Opera quae extant omnia. . . .* 4t. in 2v. in 1. Basel: Sebastianus Henricpetrus, 1581.

———. *Petrarch's Secretum.* Edited, introduction, notes, and critical anthology by Davy A. Carozza and H. James Shey. New York: Peter Lang, 1989.

———. *Prose.* Edited by Guido Martellotti, Pier Giorgio Ricci, Enrico Carrara, Enrico Bianchi. Milan: Riccardo Ricciardi, 1955.

———. *The Revolution of Cola di Rienzo.* Edited by Mario Emilio Cosenza. 2nd ed., with new introduction and bibliography by Ronald G. Musto. New York: Italica, 1986.

———. [*Rime sparse.*] *The Canzoniere or Rerum vulgarium fragmenta.* Translated into verse with notes and commentary by Mark Musa. Introduction by Mark Musa, with Barbara Manfredi. 1996. Reprint, Bloomington: Indiana University Press, 1999.

———. [*Rime sparse.*] *Petrarch's Lyric Poems: The "Rime sparse" and Other Lyrics.* Translated and edited by Robert M. Durling. Cambridge, MA: Harvard University Press, 1976.

———[*Rime sparse.*] *Petrarch's Songbook: Rerum vulgarium fragmenta.* Translated by James Wyatt Cook. Introduction by Germaine Warkentin. Binghamton, NY: Medieval & Renaissance Texts & Studies, 1996.

———. *Secretum / Il mio segreto.* Edited and translated by E. Carrera. In *Prose*, 22–215. [*See also: Petrarch's Secretum.*]

———. *Le senili.* Edited by Elvira Nota. Introduction, translation, and notes by Ugo Dotti. Vol. 1. Rome: Archivio Guido Izzi, 1993.

Phaedrus. [*Fables*]. In *Babrius and Phaedrus.* Edited and translated by Ben Edwin Perry. Cambridge, MA: Harvard University Press; London: Heinemann, 1965.

Philostratus, Flavius. *The Life of Apollonius of Tyana; The Epistles of Apollonius; and the Treatise of Eusebius.* Edited and translated by F. C. Conybeare. 2 vols. London: Heinemann; New York: Putnam's, 1912.

Pico della Mirandola. *Disputationes adversus astrologiam divinatricem.* Edited by Eugenio Garin. 2 vols. Florence: Vallecchi, 1946–1952.

———. *Oration on the Dignity of Man.* Translated by Elizabeth Livermore Forbes. In Cassirer [et al.], eds., 223–54.

Plato. *Collected Dialogues.* Including the Letters. Edited by Edith Hamilton and Huntington Cairns. 1961. Reprint, Princeton: Princeton University Press, 1963.

———. *Euthyphro, Apology, Crito, Phaedo, Phaedrus.* Edited and translated by Harold North Fowler. Introduction by R. W. M. Lamb. 1914. Reprint, Cambridge, MA: Harvard University Press; London: Heinemann, 1977.

———. *Platonis opera quae extant omnia.* Translated and edited by Jean de Serres, notes and emendations by Henri Estienne. 4 vols. [Paris]: Henr. Stephanvs, 1578.

———. *The Republic.* Edited and translated by Paul Shorey. 2 vols. 1930. Reprint, Cambridge, MA: Harvard University Press; London: Heinemann, 1982.

———. *The Statesman, Philebus.* Edited and translated by Harold N. Fowler;

Ion. Edited and translated by W. R. M. Lamb. 1925. Reprint, Cambridge, MA: Harvard University Press; London: Heinemann, 1952.

———. *Timaeus and Critias.* Translated and edited by Desmond Lee. 1971. Reprint, Harmondsworth: Penguin, 1977.

———. *Timaeus, Critias, Cleitophon, Menexenus, Epistles.* Edited and translated by R. G. Bury. 1929. Reprint, Cambridge, MA: Harvard University Press; London: Heinemann, 1975.

Pliny. *Natural History.* Edited and translated by H. Rackham [et al.]. 10 vols. Cambridge, MA: Harvard University Press; London: Heinemann, 1938–63.

Plutarch. *Moralia.* Edited by Frank Cole Babbitt [et al.]. 16 vols. 1927–1976. Reprint, Cambridge, MA: Harvard University Press; London: Heinemann, 1949–1976.

———. "That We Ought Not to Borrow." *Moralia X: 771E-854D,* 316–39. Edited and translated by Harold North Fowler. Cambridge, MA: Harvard University Press; London: Heinemann, 1936.

Polo, Marco. *The Travels.* Translated and introduction by Ronald Latham. Harmondsworth: Penguin, 1958.

Pomponazzi, Pietro. *Tractatus de immortalitate animae.* Translated by William Henry Hay II. With a Facsimile of the *editio princeps* [1516]. Haverford, PA: Haverford College, 1938.

———. *On the Immortality of the Soul.* Translated by William Henry Hay II. In Cassirer [et al.], eds., 280–381.

Porete, Marguerite. *Le mirouer des simples ames.* Edited by Romana Guarnieri. *Speculum simplicium animarum.* Edited by Paul Verdeyen, SJ. CCCM 69. Turnhout: Brepols, 1986.

———. *The Mirror of Simple Souls.* Translated and introduction by Ellen L. Babinsky. Preface by Robert E. Lerner. New York: Paulist Press, 1993.

Quintilianus, Marcus Fabius. *Institutio oratoria.* Edited and translated by H. E. Butler. 4 vols. 1920. Reprint, London: Heinemann; Cambridge, MA: Harvard University Press, 1963.

Qustā ibn Lūqā. *De differentia animae et spiritus.* In *Excerpta e libro Alfredi Anglici De motu cordis; item Costa-ben-Lucae De differentia animae et spiritus liber,* 115–39. Translated by Johannes Hispalensis. . . . Edited by Carl Sigmund Barach. Innsbrück: Verlag der Wagner'schen Universitaets-Buchhandlung, 1878.

Rabelais, François. *Le tiers livre.* Edited by M. A. Screech. Geneva: Droz, 1964.

———. *Le tiers livre.* Edited by Françoise Joukovsky. Paris: GF-Flammarion, 1993.

Radice, Betty, trans. and ed. *The Letters of Abelard and Heloise.* Harmondsworth: Penguin, 1974.

The Ratio Studiorum of 1599. Translated by A. R. Ball. In Fitzpatrick, ed., 119–254.

Régis, Pierre-Sylvain. *Cours entier de philosophie, ou systeme general selon les principes de M. de Descartes, contenant la logique, la métaphysique, la physique, et la morale.* 3 vols. Amsterdam: Huguetan, 1691.

Remains of Old Latin 1: Ennius and Caecilius. Edited and translated by E. H.

Warmington. 1935. Revised reprint, Cambridge, MA: Harvard University Press; London: Heinemann, 1988.

Ribadeneira, Pedro de. *The Life of B. Father Ignatius of Loyola, Authour, and Founder of the Society of Iesus.* Translated by W. M. N.p.: n.p., 1616. Facsimile reprint, English Recusant Literature 1558–1640, edited by D. M. Rogers, vol. 300. Ilkley, UK: Scolar Press, 1976.

Richard of St. Victor. *The Twelve Patriarchs [Benjamin Minor]; The Mystical Ark [Benjamin Major]; Book Three of the Trinity.* Translated and introduction by Grover A. Zinn. Preface by Jean Châtillon. New York: Paulist Press, 1979.

Ronsard, Pierre de. *Oeuvres complètes.* Edited by Gustave Cohen. 2 vols. Paris: Gallimard, 1950.

Rousseau, Jean-Jacques. *Discours sur l'origine de l'inégalité.* In *Du contrat social ou principes du droit politique* [and other political works], 25–122. Paris: Garnier, 1962.

———. *Essai sur l'origine des langues où il est parlé de la mélodie et de l'imitation musicale.* Edited by Charles Porset. Bordeaux: Ducros, 1970.

Rufus of Ephesus. *Oeuvres.* Text edited and translated by Charles Daremberg and Charles Emile Ruelle. 1879. Facsimile reprint, Amsterdam: Hakkert, 1963.

Rupert of Deutz (Rupertus Tuitiensis). *In Genesim.* In *De Sancta trinitate et operibus eius,* edited by Hrabanus Haacke. CCCM 21. Turnhout: Brepols, 1971.

Ruzzante [Angelo Beolco]. *La vaccària.* In *Teatro,* 1039–1179. Prima edizione completa. Text, translation and notes by Ludovico Zorzi. Turin: Einaudi, 1967.

Sabuco de Nántes y Barrera, Luisa Oliva. *Coloquio del conocimiento de sí mismo.* In *Obras escogidas de filósofos,* 325–72. Edited by Adolfo de Castro. Biblioteca de Autores Españoles 65. Madrid: Rivadeneyra, 1873.

Sabunde, Ramón. *La théologie naturelle de Raymond Sebon.* Translated by Messire Michel, Seigneur de Montaigne. . . . Preface by A. Armaingaud. 2 vols. In *Oeuvres complètes de Michel de Montaigne,* vols. 9–10. Edited by Arthur Armaingaud. 12 vols. Paris: Louis Conard, 1924–1941.

Selva, Lorenzo. *Della metamorfosi cioè trasformazione del virtuoso.* . . . Florence: Filippo Giunti, 1598. (1st ed. 1582.)

———. *La métamorphose du vertueux livre plein de moralité.* . . . Translated by I. Baudoin. Paris: D. Gilles, 1611.

Seneca, Lucius Annaeus. *Ad Lucilium epistulae morales.* Edited and translated by Richard M. Gummere. 3 vols. 1917–1925. Reprint, Cambridge, MA: Harvard University Press; London: Heinemann, 1979.

———. *Moral Essays.* Edited and translated by John W. Basore. 3 vols. 1928–1935. Reprint, Cambridge, MA: Harvard University Press; London: Heinemann, 1979.

———. *Naturales quaestiones.* Edited and translated by Thomas H. Corcoran. 2 vols. Cambridge, MA: Harvard University Press; London: Heinemann, 1971–1972.

———. *See also*: Lodge.

Shakespeare, William. *Complete Works.* General editor Alfred Harbage. Pelican Text Revised. 1969; rpt. New York: Viking, 1975.

Soarez, Cyprianus, SJ. *De arte rhetorica libri tres ex Aristotele, Cicerone et Quinctiliano praecipuè deprompti.* Paris: Thomas Brumen, 1573.
———. "The *De arte rhetorica* (1586) by Cyprian Soarez, SJ." Translated, introduction, and notes by Lawrence J. Flynn, SJ. Ph.D. diss., University of Florida, 1955.

Sophocles. *The Three Theban Plays: Antigone, Oedipus the King, Oedipus at Colonus.* Translated by Robert Fagles. Introduction and notes by Bernard Knox. 1982. Reprint, Harmondsworth: Penguin, 1984.
———. [*Works.*] Edited and translated by Hugh Lloyd-Jones. 3 vols. Cambridge, MA: Harvard University Press, 1994–1996.

Soranus of Ephesus. *Soranus' Gynecology.* Translated and introduction by Owsei Temkin, with Nicholson J. Eastman, Ludwig Edelstein and Alan Guttmacher. Baltimore: Johns Hopkins University Press, 1956.

Speroni degli Alvarotti, Sperone. *I dialoghi.* In *Opere*, vol. 1. Introduction by Mario Pozzi. 5 vols. [1740. Facsimile reprint,] Manziana (Rome): Vecchiarelli, 1989.

Spinoza, Benedict de. *Ethics.* In *Ethics and De intellectus emendatione*, translated by A. Boyle. Introduction by George Santayana. London: Dent; New York: Dutton, 1910.

Stampa, Gaspara. *Selected Poems.* Edited and translated by Laura Anna Stortoni and Mary Prentice Lillie. New York: Italica Press, 1994.

[*Svf*]. *Stoicorum veterum fragmenta. See*: Arnim, ed.

Tasso, Torquato. *Jerusalem Delivered.* Translated by Edward Fairfax [1600]. Introduction by John Charles Nelson. New York: Capricorn, 1963.

Three Tragedies by Renaissance Women: The Tragedie of Iphigeneia in a Version by Jane, Lady Lumley; *The Tragedie of Antonie* translated by Mary, Countess of Pembroke; *The Tragedie of Mariam* by Elizabeth Cary. Edited and introduction by Diane Purkiss. London: Penguin, 1998.

Tory, Geofroy. *Champ flevry. Au quel est contenu Lart & Science de la deue & vraye Proportiõ des Lettres Attiques, . . . proportionnees selon le Corps & Visage humain* [sic]. Paris: Geofroy Tory & Giles Gourmont, 1529.

Trotula de Ruggiero. *The Diseases of Women. A Translation of Passionibus mulierum curandorum* by Elizabeth Mason-Hohl. [N. p. (Los Angeles?):] Ward Ritchie, 1940.
———. *Sulle malattie della donne.* Edited by Pina Boggi Cavallo. Critical text, trans. and glossary by Piero Cantalupo. Palermo: La Luna, 1994.

Vair, Guillaume du. "Exhortation à la paix, adressée à ceux de la Ligue [1592–93]." In *Actions et traictez oratoires*, 63–109. Edited by René Radouant. Paris: Édouard Cornély, 1911.

Valerius Maximus. *Opera.* Edited by Salvini de Lennemas. 2 vols. Paris: Plon, 1845.

Varro, Marcus Terentius. *On the Latin Language.* Edited and translated by Roland G. Kent. 2 vols. 1938. Reprint, Cambridge, MA: Harvard University Press, 1993.

Vindiciae, contra tyrannos. See: Languet and Mornay.

Vitoria, Francisco de. *Political Writings*. Edited by Anthony Pagden and Jeremy Lawrance. Cambridge: Cambridge University Press, 1991.

Vives, Juan Luis. *Diálogos*. Translated by Cristóbal Coret y Peris. 1940. Reprint, Madrid: Espasa-Calpe, 1959.

———. *On Education: A Translation of the De tradendis disciplinis*. Translated and edited by Foster Watson. Cambridge: University Press, 1913.

———. *Tratado del alma*. 1942. Reprint, Madrid: Espasa-Calpe, 1957.

———. *Vives' Introduction to Wisdom [Introductio ad sapientem (Leuven, 1524)]: A Renaissance Textbook*. Edited and introduction by Marian Leona Tobriner, SNJM. New York: Teachers College Press, 1968.

Walkington, Thomas. *The Optick Glasse of Hvmors*. Introduction by John A. Popplestone and Marion White Mcpherson. 1631. Facsimile reprint, Delmar, NY: Scholars' Facsimiles & Reprints, 1981.

[Weyer, Johann.] *Witches, Devils, and Doctors in the Renaissance: Johann Weyer, "De praestigiis demonum."* Edited George Mora [et al.]. Translated by John Shea. Binghamton, NY: Medieval & Renaissance Texts & Studies, 1991.

Whitehead, Frederick, ed. *La chanson de Roland*. 2nd ed. 1946. Reprint, Oxford: Blackwell, 1962.

Wiedemann, Thomas E. J., ed. *Greek and Roman Slavery*. London: Croom Helm, 1981.

Xenophon. *See*: Pomeroy (in Secondary).

SECONDARY SOURCES

Aall, Anathon. *Der Logos: Geschichte seiner Entwicklung in der griechischen Philosophie und der christlichen Litteratur*. 2 vols. Leipzig: Reisland, 1896–1899.

Abboushi, Jenine. "French Cultural Imperialism and the Esthetics of Distinction." *The Yale Journal of Criticism* 13, no. 2 (2000): 229–65.

Abiodun, Rowland. *See*: Drewal, Pemberton and Abiodun.

Achebe, Chinua. *Conversations with Chinua Achebe*. Edited by Bernth Lindfors. Jackson: University Press of Mississippi, 1997.

Adams, Marilyn McCord. "Introduction." In Abelard, *Ethical Writings*, vii–xxvi.

Adkins, A. W. H. *From the Many to the One: A Study of Personality and Views of Human Nature in the Context of Ancient Greek Society, Values and Beliefs*. London: Constable, 1970.

Aers, David. "A Whisper in the Ear of Early Modernists; or, Reflections on Literary Critics Writing the 'History of the Subject'." In *Culture and History, 1350–1600: Essays on English Communities, Identities and Writing*, 177–202. Edited by David Aers. Detroit: Wayne State University Press, 1992.

Aertsen, Jan A., and Andreas Speer, eds. *Individuum und Individualität im Mittelalter*. Miscellania Mediaevalia. Veröffentlichungen des Thomas-Instituts der Universität Köln 24. Berlin: Walter de Gruyter, 1996.

African Charter on Human and People's Rights. *See*: Organization of African Unity.

Alic, Margaret. *Hypatia's Heritage: A History of Women in Science from Antiquity through the Nineteenth Century*. Boston: Beacon, 1986.

Allen, Christopher. "Painting the Passions: The *Passions de l'âme* as a Basis for Pictorial Expression." In Gaukroger, ed., 79–111.

Anderson, Perry. *Passages from Antiquity to Feudalism*. 1974; rpt. London: Verso, 1978.

Andrewes, Antony. *The Greeks*. 1967; rpt. New York: Norton, 1978.

An-Naim, Abdullah Ahmed, and Francis Deng, eds. *Human Rights in Africa: Cross-Cultural Perspectives*. Washington, DC: Brookings Institute, 1990.

Annas, Julia. "Epicurus on Agency." In Brunschwig and Nussbaum, eds., 53–71.

———. *Hellenistic Philosophy of Mind*. Berkeley: University of California Press, 1992.

———. *The Morality of Happiness*. New York: Oxford University Press, 1993.

Anscombe, G. E. M. "The First Person." In *The Collected Philosophical Papers of G. E. M. Anscombe 2: Metaphysics and the Philosophy of Mind*, 21–36. Oxford: Blackwell, 1981.

———. "Thought and Action in Aristotle: What Is Practical Truth?" In *New Essays on Plato and Aristotle*, 143–58. Edited by Renford Bambrough. London: Routledge & Kegan Paul, 1965.

Archer, Léonie J., ed. *Slavery and Other Forms of Unfree Labour*. London: Routledge, 1988.

———, Susan Fischler and Maria Wyke, eds. *Women in Ancient Societies: An Illusion of the Night*. New York: Routledge, 1994.

Arenal, Electa. "The Convent as Catalyst for Autonomy: Two Hispanic Nuns of the Seventeenth Century." In *Women in Hispanic Literature: Icons and Fallen Idols*, 147–83. Edited by Beth Kurti Miller. Berkeley: University of California Press, 1983.

———, and Stacey Schlau. *Untold Sisters: Hispanic Nuns in Their Own Works*. Translated by Amanda Powell. Albuquerque: University of New Mexico Press, 1989.

Ariew, Roger. *Descartes and the Last Scholastics*. Ithaca, NY: Cornell University Press, 1999.

Arnhart, Larry. *Aristotle on Political Reasoning: A Commentary on the "Rhetoric"*. De Kalb, IL: Northern Illinois University Press, 1981.

Arnold, Edward Vernon. *Roman Stoicism*. 1911. Reprint, New York: Books for Libraries Press, 1971.

Ascoli, Albert Russell. "Petrarch's Middle Age: Memory, Imagination, History, and the 'Ascent of Mount Ventoux'." *Stanford Italian Review* 10, no. 1 (1991): 5–43.

———. "Petrarch's Private Politics: *Rerum familiarum libri XIX*." Unpublished lecture, 1997.

Ayer, A. J. "The Concept of a Person." In *The Concept of a Person and Other Essays*, 82–128. London: Macmillan, 1963.

Babb, Lawrence. *The Elizabethan Malady: A Study of Melancholia in English Literature from 1580 to 1642*. East Lansing: Michigan State College Press, 1951.

Baker, M. J. "*Fiammetta* and the *Angoysses douloureuses qui procèdent d'amours.*" *Symposium* 27, no. 4 (Winter 1973): 303–8.

Bakhtin, Mikhail Mikhailovich. *See*: Vološinov.

Balibar, Étienne. "Citizen Subject." In Cadava [et al.], eds., 33–57.

———. "What Is 'Man' in Seventeenth-Century Philosophy? Subject, Individual, Citizen." In Coleman, ed., 215–41.

Barker, Sir Ernest. *Essays on Government.* 2nd ed. 1951. Reprint, Oxford: Clarendon, 1965.

Barker, Francis. *The Tremulous Private Body: Essays on Subjection.* London: Methuen, 1984.

Barolini, Teodolinda. "The Making of a Lyric Sequence: Time and Narrative in Petrarch's *Rerum vulgarium fragmenta.*" *Modern Language Notes* 104 (1989): 1–38.

Barresi, John. *See*: Martin and Barresi.

Barthes, Roland. *Sade, Fourier, Loyola.* Paris: Seuil, 1971.

Barton, Richard E. "'Zealous Anger' and the Renegotiation of Aristocratic Relationships in Eleventh- and Twelfth-Century France." In Rosenwein, ed., 153–70.

Bataille, Georges. *L'expérience intérieure.* Revised and corrected ed. Paris: Gallimard, 1954.

Bauman, Richard A. *Women and Politics in Ancient Rome.* London: Routledge, 1992.

Baxandall, Michael. *Giotto and the Orators: Humanist Observers of Painting in Italy and the Discovery of Pictorial Composition 1350–1450.* Oxford: Clarendon, 1971.

———. *Painting and Experience in Fifteenth-Century Italy: A Primer in the Social History of Pictorial Style.* 2nd ed. 1988. Reprint, Oxford: Oxford University Press, 1992.

Bayle, Pierre. *Dictionnaire historique et critique.* 2 vols. Rotterdam: Reinier Leers, 1697.

Bayon, H. P. "Trotula and the Ladies of Salerno: A Contribution to the Knowledge of the Transition between Ancient and Mediaeval Physick." *Proceedings of the Royal Society of Medicine* 33, no. 8 (June 1940): 471–75.

Beauchesne, Line. "D'une impossible démonstration à une paradoxale positivité: Le dialogue juridico-politique en matière de droits de l'homme." Ph.D. diss., Université Laval, 1984.

Beaujour, Michel. *Miroirs d'encre: Rhétorique de l'autoportrait.* Paris: Seuil, 1980.

Beauvoir, Simone de. *The Second Sex.* Translated and edited by H. M. Parshley. 1952. Reprint, New York: Vintage, 1974.

Beilin, Elaine V. *Redeeming Eve: Women Writers of the English Renaissance.* Princeton: Princeton University Press, 1987.

———. *See also*: Askew (in Primary).

Benhabib, Seyla. *Situating the Self: Gender, Community and Postmodernism in Contemporary Ethics.* New York: Routledge, 1992.

Benton, John F. "Trotula, Women's Problems, and the Professionalization of

Medicine in the Middle Ages." *Bulletin of the History of Medicine* 59, no. 1 (Spring 1985): 30–53.

———. *See also*: Guibert (in Primary).

Bergmann, Marianne. *Die Strahlen der Herrscher: Theomorphes Herrscherbild und politische Symbolik im Hellenismus und in der römischen Kaiserzeit.* Mainz: Philipp von Zabern, 1998.

Bernardo, Aldo S. "Letter-Splitting in Petrarch's *Familiares.*" *Speculum* 33, no. 2 (April 1958): 236–41.

———. *See also*: Petrarch, *Letters of Old Age* and *Letters on Familiar Matters.*

Berreby, David. "The 'Wise Apes' and Their Friends." *New York Times*, February 9, 1997, WK3.

Billanovich, Guiseppe. "Petrarca e il Ventoso." *Italia Medioevale e Umanistica* 9 (1966): 389–401.

Bloch, R. Howard. *Medieval French Literature and Law.* Berkeley: University of California Press, 1977.

Bloom, Harold. *Shakespeare: The Invention of the Human.* New York: Riverhead Books, 1998.

Blundell, Sue. *Women in Ancient Greece.* Cambridge, MA: Harvard University Press, 1995.

Bodéüs, Richard. *The Political Dimensions of Aristotle's "Ethics."* Translated by Jan Edward Garrett. Albany: State University of New York Press, 1993.

Bonfante, Larissa. "Etruscan Couples and Their Aristocratic Society." In Foley, ed., 323–42.

———. "Excursus. Etruscan Women." In Fantham [et al.], 243–59.

———. "The Women of Etruria." In Peradotto and Sullivan, eds., 229–39.

———. *See also*: Hroswitha, *The Plays* (in Primary).

Boxer, Charles Ralph. *The Portuguese Seaborne Empire, 1415–1825.* New York: Knopf, 1969.

Boyle, Marjorie O'Rourke. *Loyola's Acts: The Rhetoric of the Self.* Berkeley: University of California Press, 1997.

———. *Petrarch's Genius: Pentimento and Prophecy.* Berkeley: University of California Press, 1991.

Brain, Peter. *Galen on Bloodletting: A Study of the Origins, Development and Validity of His Opinions, with a Translation of the Three Works.* Cambridge: Cambridge University Press, 1986.

Brathwaite, [Edward] Kamau. *Contradictory Omens: Cultural Diversity and Integration in the Caribbean.* 1974. Reprint, Mona: Savacou, 1985.

Braund, Susanna Morton, and Christopher Gill, eds. *The Passions in Roman Thought and Literature.* Cambridge: Cambridge University Press, 1997.

Bremen, Riet van. *See*: Van Bremen, Riet.

Brind'amour, Lucie, and Eugene Vance, eds. *L'archéologie du signe.* Toronto: Pontifical Institute of Mediaeval Studies, 1983.

Brooks, Peter. *Troubling Confessions: Speaking Guilt in Law and Literature.* Chicago: University of Chicago Press, 2000.

Brown, Frieda S. *Religious and Political Conservatism in the "Essais" of Montaigne.* Geneva: Droz, 1963.

Brown, Jonathan. *Velázquez, Painter and Courtier.* New Haven: Yale University Press, 1986.

Brown, Marcia Weston. "Vittoria Colonna, Gaspara Stampa and Louise Labé: Their Contribution to the Development of the Renaissance Sonnet." Ph.D. diss., New York University, 1991.

Brown, Marshall. "Kant's Misreading of Descartes." In *Turning Points: Essays in the History of Cultural Expressions,* 156–72. Stanford: Stanford University Press, 1997.

Brown, Peter R. L. *Antiquité tardive.* [Translated by Claude Bonnafont.] In Veyne, ed., 225–99.

———. *Augustine of Hippo: A Biography.* 1967. Reprint, Berkeley: University of California Press, 1969.

———. *The Making of Late Antiquity.* Cambridge, MA: Harvard University Press, 1978.

Browne, Edward Granville. *Arabian Medicine.* Cambridge: At the University Press, 1921.

———. *A Literary History of Persia.* 4 vols. 1902–1924. Reprint, Cambridge: University Press, 1956–1959.

Bruns, Ivo. *Das literarische Porträt der Griechen im fünften und vierten Jahrhundert vor Christi Geburt* [1896]; *Die Persönlichkeit in der Geschichtsschreibung der Alten: Untersuchungen zur Technik der antiken Historiographie* [1898]. Facsimile reprint, Hildesheim: Olms, 1961.

Brunschvicg, Léon. *Descartes et Pascal, lecteurs de Montaigne.* New York: Brentano's, 1944.

———. *Le progrès de la conscience dans la philosophie occidentale.* 2nd ed. Paris: Presses Universitaires de France, 1953.

Brunschwig, Jacques. "The Cradle Argument in Epicureanism and Stoicism." In Schofield and Striker, eds., 113–45.

———, ed. *Les stoïciens et leur logique: Actes du colloque de Chantilly, 18–22 septembre 1976.* Paris: Vrin, 1978.

———, and Martha C. Nussbaum, eds. *Passions and Perceptions: Studies in Hellenistic Philosophy of Mind. Proceedings of the Fifth Symposium Hellenisticum.* Cambridge: Cambridge University Press, 1993.

Bulloch, Anthony W., Erich S. Gruen, A. A. Long, and Andrew Stewart, eds. *Images and Ideologies: Self-Definition in the Hellenistic World.* Berkeley: University of California Press, 1993.

Burckhardt, Jacob. *The Civilization of the Renaissance in Italy.* Translated by S. G. C. Middlemore. 2 vols. New York: Harper, 1958.

Burnyeat, Myles. "Ancient Freedoms." First of three unpublished lectures, "Freedom, Anger, Tranquillity: An Archeology of Feeling." Howison Lectures in Philosophy, University of California, Berkeley. 24–26 September 1996.

———, ed. *The Skeptical Tradition.* Berkeley: University of California Press, 1983.

———. *See also:* Schofield, Burnyeat and Barnes, eds.

Bynum, Caroline Walker. "Did the Twelfth Century Discover the Individual?" In

Jesus as Mother: Studies in the Spirituality of the High Middle Ages, 82–109. Berkeley: University of California Press, 1982.

———. _Metamorphosis and Identity_. New York: Zone, 2001.

———. _The Resurrection of the Body in Western Christianity, 200–1336_. New York: Columbia University Press, 1995.

———. _See also_: Hildegard, _Scivias_ (in Primary).

Cadava, Eduardo, Peter Connor and Jean-Luc Nancy, eds. _Who Comes After the Subject?_ New York: Routledge, 1991.

Calame, Claude. _Les choeurs de jeunes filles en Grèce archaïque_. 2 vols. Rome: Ateneo & Bizzarri, 1977.

Cantarella, Eva. _Pandora's Daughters: The Role and Status of Women in Greek and Roman Antiquity_. Translated by Maureen B. Fant. Foreword by Mary R. Lefkowitz. Baltimore: Johns Hopkins University Press, 1987.

———. _Passato prossimo: Donne romane da Tacita a Sulpicia_. Milan: Feltrinelli, 1996.

Carrithers, Michael, Steven Collins and Steven Lukes, eds. _The Category of the Person: Anthropology, Philosophy, History_. Cambridge: Cambridge University Press, 1985.

Carruthers, Mary. _The Book of Memory: A Study of Memory in Medieval Culture_. Cambridge: Cambridge University Press, 1990.

Carson, Anne. "Putting Her in Her Place: Women, Dirt, and Desire." In Halperin, Winkler and Zeitlin, eds., 135–69.

Cartledge, Paul A. "Serfdom in Classical Greece." In Archer, ed., 33–41.

Cavarero, Adriana. _In Spite of Plato: A Feminist Rewriting of Ancient Philosophy_. Foreword by Rosi Braidotti. Translated by Serena Anderlini-D'Onofrio and Áine O'Healy. New York: Routledge, 1995.

———. "Oedipus and the Self." Unpublished lecture. New York University, September 29, 2000.

———. _Relating Narratives: Storytelling and Selfhood_. Translated and introduction by Paul A. Kottman. London: Routledge, 2000.

———. _Tu che mi guardi, tu che mi racconti_. Milan: Feltrinelli, 1997.

Cave, Terence. _The Cornucopian Text: Problems of Writing in the French Renaissance_. Oxford: Clarendon, 1979.

———. _Pré-histoires: Textes troublés au seuil de la modernité_. Geneva: Droz, 1999.

———. _Recognitions: A Study in Poetics_. Oxford: Clarendon, 1988.

Clark, Gillian. _Women in Late Antiquity: Pagan and Christian Life-Styles_. Oxford: Clarendon, 1993.

Claus, David B. _Toward the Soul: An Inquiry into the Meaning of_ Ψυχέ: _Before Plato_. New Haven: Yale University Press, 1981.

Coleman, Janet. "The Individual and the Medieval State." In Coleman, ed., 1–34.

———, ed. _The Individual in Political Theory and Practice_. Oxford: European Science Foundation, Clarendon Press, 1996.

Colish, Marcia L. _The Mirror of Language: A Study in the Medieval Theory of Knowledge_. New Haven: Yale University Press, 1968.

————. "The Stoic Theory of Verbal Signification and the Problem of Lies and False Statements from Antiquity to St. Anselm." In Brind'amour and Vance, eds., 17–43.

————. *The Stoic Tradition from Antiquity to the Early Middle Ages.* 2 vols. Leiden: Brill, 1985.

Collinet-Guérin, Marthe. *Histoire du nimbe des origines aux temps modernes.* Paris: Nouvelles Éditions Latines, 1961.

Connors, Joseph. "The Lion of Florence." *New York Review of Books,* September 20, 2001, 73–78.

Cooper, Kate. *The Virgin and the Bride: Idealized Womanhood in Late Antiquity.* Cambridge, MA: Harvard University Press, 1996.

Coppin, Joseph. *Montaigne, traducteur de Raymond Sebon.* Mémoires et Travaux Publiés par des Professeurs des Facultés Catholiques de Lille, fasc. 31. Lille: H. Morel, 1925.

Costa Lima, Luiz. "The Joys and Sorrows of the Self." In *The Dark Side of Reason: Fictionality and Power,* 65–109. Translated by Paulo Henriques Britto. Stanford: Stanford University Press, 1992.

Cottingham, John. *Philosophy and the Good Life: Reason and the Passions in Greek, Cartesian and Psychoanalytic Ethics.* Cambridge: Cambridge University Press, 1998.

————. *See also:* Descartes, *Philosophical Writings* (in Primary).

Cottrell, Robert D. "Female Subjectivity and Libidinal Infractions: Hélisenne de Crenne's *Angoisses douloureuses qui procèdent d'amours.*" *French Forum* 16, no. 1 (Jan. 1991): 5–19.

Courcelle, Pierre Paul. *Les Confessions de St. Augustin dans la tradition littéraire.* Paris: Études Augustiniennes, 1963.

————. *Connais-toi toi-même de Socrate à saint Bernard.* 3 vols. Paris: Études Augustiniennes, 1974–1975.

————. "'Nosce te ipsum' du Bas-Empire au Haut Moyen Age." In *Il passagio dell'antichità al medioevo in occidente: Settimane di studio del Centro Italiano di Studi sull'Alto Medievo,* 265–95. Spoleto: Pressa la Sede del Centro, 1962.

————. "Tradition platonicienne et traditions chrétiennes du corps-prison (*Phedon,* 62b; *Cratyle,* 400c)." *Revue des Études Latines* 43 (1965): 406–43.

Cranz, F. Edward. "The Renaissance Reading of the *De anima.*" In *Platon et Aristote à la Renaissance: XVIe colloque international de Tours,* 359–76. Edited by J.-C. Margolin. Paris: Vrin, 1976.

Cultural Charter for Africa. See: Organization of African Unity.

Davis, Nathalie Zemon. "Boundaries and the Sense of Self in Sixteenth-Century France." In Heller, Sosna and Wellbery, eds., 53–63.

————. *The Return of Martin Guerre.* Cambridge, MA: Harvard University Press, 1983.

————. "Women on Top." In *Society and Culture in Early Modern France,* 124–51. Stanford: Stanford University Press, 1975.

Dean-Jones, Lesley. "Excursus. Medicine: The 'Proof' of Anatomy." In Fantham [et al.], 183–203.

————. *Women's Bodies in Classical Greek Science.* Oxford: Clarendon, 1994.

De Lacy, P. "The Four Stoic *personae*." *Illinois Classical Studies* 2 (1977): 163–72.

————. "Stoic Views of Poetry." *American Journal of Philology* 69, no. 3 (no. 275, July 1948): 241–71.

————. *See also*: Galen, *De elementis, De placitis, De semine* (in Primary).

Delatte, Louis, Suzanne Govaerts and Joseph Denooz. "Note sur *Spiritus*." In Fattori and Bianchi, eds., 55–62.

Deng, Francis Mading. *Africans of Two Worlds: The Dinka of Afro-Arab Sudan.* New Haven: Yale University Press, 1978.

————. *See also*: An-Naim and Deng, eds.

Denooz, Joseph. *See*: Delatte, Govaerts and Denooz.

Detienne, Marcel. "Ébauches de la personne dans la Grèce archaïque." In Meyerson, ed., 45–54.

Díaz, Sara Elena. "Pride and Palinode: Nautical Metaphors in Dante, Petrarch and Stampa." Unpublished seminar paper. Department of Comparative Literature, New York University, December 2000.

Dieterlen, Germaine, ed. *La notion de personne en Afrique noire.* Paris: Éditions du Centre National de la Recherche Scientifique, 1973.

Dihle, Albrecht. *The Theory of Will in Classical Antiquity.* Berkeley: University of California Press, 1982.

Dillon, John M., and Anthony A. Long, eds. *The Question of "Eclecticism": Studies in Later Greek Philosophy.* Berkeley: University of California Press, 1988.

Di Napoli, Giovanni. *L'immortalità dell'anima nel Renascimento.* Turin: Società Editrice Internazionale, 1963.

Dissanayake, Wimal. "Introduction. Agency and Cultural Understanding: Some Preliminary Remarks." In Dissanayake, ed., ix–xxi.

————, ed. *Narratives of Agency: Self-Making in China, India, and Japan.* Minneapolis: University of Minnesota Press, 1996.

Dizionario biografico degli Italiani. 56 vols. to date. Rome: Istituto della Enciclopedia Italiana, 1960–present.

Dodds, Eric Robertson. *The Greeks and the Irrational.* 1951; rpt. Berkeley: University of California Press, 1961.

Dopico Black, Georgina. *Perfect Wives, Other Women: Adultery and Inquisition in Early Modern Spain.* Durham, NC: Duke University Press, 2001.

Dover, Kenneth J. *Greek Homosexuality.* London: Duckworth, 1978.

————. *Greek Popular Morality in the Time of Plato and Aristotle.* Berkeley: University of California Press, 1974.

Drewal, Henry John, and John Pemberton III, with Rowland Abiodun. Edited by Allen Wardwell. *Yoruba: Nine Centuries of African Art and Thought.* New York: Center for African Art, with Harry N. Abrams, 1989.

Dronke, Peter. "As cidades simbólicas de Hildegard de Bingen." In *A simbólica do espaço: Cidades, ilhas, jardins,* 29–42. Edited by Yvette Kace Centeno and Lima De Freitas. Lisbon: Editorial Estampa, 1991.

————. *Poetic Individuality in the Middle Ages: New Departures in Poetry,*

1000–1150. 2nd ed. London: Westfield College, University of London Committee on Medieval Studies, 1986.

———. *Women Writers of the Middle Ages: A Critical Study of Texts from Perpetua (†203) to Marguerite Porete (†1310).* 1984. Reprint, Cambridge: Cambridge University Press, 1988.

———. *See also:* Hildegard, *Liber divinorum operum* (in Primary).

duBois, Page. *Centaurs and Amazons: Women and the Prehistory of the Great Chain of Being.* Ann Arbor: University of Michigan Press, 1982.

———. *Sappho Is Burning.* Chicago: University of Chicago Press, 1995.

———. *Sowing the Body: Psychoanalysis and Ancient Representations of Women.* Chicago: University of Chicago Press, 1988.

———. *Torture and Truth.* New York: Routledge, 1991.

Duby, Georges. *The Early Growth of the European Economy: Warriors and Peasants from the Seventh to the Twelfth Century.* Translated by Howard B. Clarke. London: Weidenfeld & Nicolson, 1974.

———. *See also:* Veyne, ed., Klapisch-Zuber, ed., *and* Pantel, ed.

Dumont, Jean Christian. *Servus: Rome et l'esclavage sous la république.* Rome: École Française de Rome, 1987.

Dumont, Louis. *Homo aequalis: Genèse et épanouissement de l'idéologie économique.* Paris: Gallimard, 1977.

———. *Homo hierarchicus: Essai sur le système des castes.* Paris: Gallimard, 1966.

———. "A Modified View of our Origins: The Christian Beginnings of Modern Individualism." In Carrithers, Collins and Lukes, eds., 93–122.

Durling, Robert M. "The Ascent of Mt. Ventoux and the Crisis of Allegory." *Italian Quarterly* 18 (1974): 7–28.

———. *See also:* Petrarch, *Petrarch's Lyric Poems* (in Primary).

Duval, Edwin M. *The Design of Rabelais's Quart Livre de Pantagruel. Travaux d'Humanisme et Renaissance* 324, *Études Rabelaisiennes* 36. Geneva: Droz, 1998.

———. *The Design of Rabelais's Tiers livre de Pantagruel. Travaux d'Humanisme et Renaissance* 316, *Études Rabelaisiennes* 34. Geneva: Droz, 1997.

Dzielska, Maria. *Hypatia of Alexandria.* Translated by F. Lyra. Cambridge, MA: Harvard University Press, 1995.

Edgerton, Samuel Y., Jr. *The Heritage of Giotto's Geometry: Art and Science on the Eve of the Scientific Revolution.* Ithaca, NY: Cornell University Press, 1991.

Ehrenberg, Victor. *The People of Aristophanes: A Sociology of Old Attic Comedy.* [2nd ed., revised and enlarged.] Oxford: Blackwell, 1951.

Elbaz, Robert. *The Changing Nature of the Self: A Critical Study of the Autobiographic Discourse.* London: Croom Helm, 1988.

El Saffar, Ruth S. *Novel to Romance: A Study of Cervantes's Novelas ejemplares.* Baltimore: Johns Hopkins University Press, 1974.

———. *Rapture Encaged: The Suppression of the Feminine in Western Culture.* London: Routledge, 1994.

Else, Gerald F. *Aristotle's Poetics: The Argument.* Cambridge, MA: Harvard University Press, 1963.

Emck, Katy. "Laura Answers Back." *Times Literary Supplement,* May 16, 1997, 13–14.

Engberg-Pedersen, Troels. "Discovering the Good: *Oikeiōsis* and *kathēkonta* in Stoic Ethics." In Schofield and Striker, eds., 145–83.

———. "Stoic Philosophy and the Concept of the Person." In Gill, ed., 109–35.

———. *The Stoic Theory of Oikeiōsis: Moral Development and Social Interaction in Early Stoic Philosophy.* Aarhus: Aarhus University Press, 1990.

Engbring, Gertrude M. "Saint Hildegard, Twelfth-Century Physician." *Bulletin of the History of Medicine* 8, no. 6 (June 1940): 770–84.

Erickson, Carolly. *The Medieval Vision: Essays in History and Perception.* New York: Oxford University Press, 1976.

Evans, John K. *War, Women and Children in Ancient Rome.* London: Routledge, 1991.

Fantham, Elaine, Helene Peet Foley, Natalie Boymel Kampen, Sarah B. Pomeroy and H. Alan Shapiro. *Women in the Classical World: Image and Text.* New York: Oxford University Press, 1994.

Fattori, Marta, and Massimo Bianchi, eds. *Spiritus: IVo Colloquio Internazionale del Lessico Intellettuale Europeo. Roma, 7–9 gennaio 1983.* Rome: Ateneo, 1984.

Febvre, Lucien. *Le problème de l'incroyance au XVIe siècle: La religion de Rabelais.* Rev. ed. Paris: Albin Michel, 1962.

Fernández, James D. *Apology to Apostrophe: Autobiography and the Rhetoric of Self-Representation in Spain.* Durham, NC: Duke University Press, 1992.

———. "The Bonds of Patrimony: Cervantes and the New World." *PMLA* 109, no. 5 (October 1994): 969–81.

Feyerabend, Paul. *Conquest of Abundance: A Tale of Abstraction versus the Richness of Being.* Edited by Bert Terpstra. Chicago: University of Chicago Press, 1999.

Ficara, Giorgio. *Solitudini: Studi sulla letteratura italiana dal Duecento al Novecento.* Milan: Garzanti, 1993.

Figgis, John Neville. *The Divine Right of Kings.* 2nd ed. Cambridge: Cambridge University Press, 1914.

Fillion-Lahille, Janine. *Le De ira de Sénèque et la philosophie stoïcienne des passions.* Paris: Klincksieck, 1984.

Fineman, Joel. *Shakespeare's Perjured Eye: The Invention of Poetic Subjectivity in the Sonnets.* 1986. Reprint, Berkeley: University of California Press, 1988.

———. *The Subjectivity Effect in Western Literary Tradition: Essays Toward the Release of Shakespeare's Will.* Cambridge, MA: MIT Press, 1991.

Finley, John Huston. *Homer's Odysssey.* Cambridge, MA: Harvard University Press, 1978.

Finley, Moses I. *The Ancient Economy.* Berkeley: University of California Press, 1973.

———. *Ancient Slavery and Modern Ideology.* 1980. Reprint, Harmondsworth: Penguin, 1983.

———. "Was Greek Civilization Based on Slave Labour?" In Finley, ed., 53–72.

————, ed. *Slavery in Classical Antiquity: Views and Controversies.* 1960. Reprint, with bibliographical supplement, Cambridge: Heffer; New York: Barnes & Noble, 1968.

Fiorentino, Francesco. *Pietro Pomponazzi. Studi storici su la scuola Bolognese e Padovana del secolo XVI con molti documenti inediti.* Florence: Successori Le Monnier, 1868.

Fitzmaurice-Kelly, James. "Phantasio-Cratuminos sive Homo Vitreus." *Revue Hispanique* 4 (1897): 45–70.

Five Hundred Self-Portraits. Introduction by Julian Bell. London: Phaidon, 2000.

Flaherty, Julie. "Music to a Retailer's Ears." *New York Times,* July 4, 2001, C1, 11.

Flanagan, Sabina. *Hildegard of Bingen, 1098–1179: A Visionary Life.* London: Routledge, 1989.

Flaubert, Gustave. *Oeuvres complètes.* 16 vols. Paris: Club de l'Honnête Homme, 1971–1975.

Foley, Helene Peet. *Female Acts in Greek Tragedy.* Princeton: Princeton University Press, 2001.

————, ed. *Reflections of Women in Antiquity.* New York: Gordon & Breach, 1981.

————. *See also*: Fantham [et al.].

Folkenflik, Robert. "Introduction: The Institutions of Autobiography." In Folkenflik, ed., 1–20.

————, ed. *The Culture of Autobiography: Constructions of Self-Representation.* Stanford: Stanford University Press, 1993.

Fontaine, Marie-Madeleine. "Rabelais et Speroni." *Études Rabelaisiennes* 17: *François Rabelais 1483(?)–1983*, 1–8. [Edited by Guy Demerson.] Geneva: Droz, 1983.

Forcione, Alban K. *Cervantes and the Humanist Vision: A Study of Four Exemplary Novels.* Princeton: Princeton University Press, 1982.

Foucault, Michel. "L'écriture de soi." In *Corps écrit 5: L'autoportrait*, 3–23. Paris: Presses Universitaires de France, 1983.

————. *Folie et déraison: Histoire de la folie à l'âge classique.* Paris: Plon, 1961.

————. *Histoire de la sexualité, 2: L'usage des plaisirs.* Paris: Gallimard, 1984.

————. *Histoire de la sexualité, 3: Le souci de soi.* Paris: Gallimard, 1984.

————. *Les mots et les choses: Une archéologie des sciences humaines.* Paris: Gallimard, 1966.

————. *See also*: Martin, Gutman and Hutton, eds.

Fournel, Jean-Louis. *Les dialogues de Sperone Speroni: Libertés de la parole et règles de l'écriture.* Marburg: Hitzeroth, 1990.

Frame, Donald M. *Montaigne: A Biography.* New York: Harcourt, Brace & World, 1965.

————. *Montaigne's Discovery of Man: The Humanization of a Humanist.* New York: Columbia University Press, 1955.

Freccero, John. "Autobiography and Narrative." In Heller, Sosna and Wellbery, eds., 16–29, 329.

————. "The Fig Tree and the Laurel: Petrarch's Poetics." In Parker and Quint, eds., 20–32.

Frede, Michael. *Essays in Ancient Philosophy.* Minneapolis: University of Minnesota Press, 1987.

————. "On Galen's Epistemology." In Frede, *Essays,* 279–98.

————. *The Origins of the Notion of a Free Will.* Berkeley: University of California Press, forthcoming.

————. "Philosophy and Medicine in Antiquity." In Frede, *Essays,* 225–42.

————. "Principles of Stoic Grammar." In Frede, *Essays,* 301–37.

————. "The Stoic Doctrine of the Affections of the Soul." In Schofield and Striker, eds., 93–110.

Friedrich, Hugo. *Montaigne.* Translated by Robert Rovini. Paris: Gallimard, 1965.

Frontisi-Ducroux, Françoise. *Le dieu masqué.* Paris: La Découverte, 1991.

————. *Du masque au visage: Aspects de l'identité en Grèce ancienne.* Paris: Flammarion, 1995.

Gadoffre, Gilbert F. A. "La chronologie des six parties." In *Le Discours et sa méthode: Colloque pour le 350e anniversaire du "Discours de la méthode,"* 19–40. Edited by Nicolas Grimaldi and Jean-Luc Marion. Paris: Presses Universitaires de France, 1987.

————. "Le *Discours de la méthode* et la querelle des anciens." In *Modern Miscellany, presented to Eugène Vinaver,* 79–84. Edited by T. E. Lawrenson, F. E. Sutcliffe, and G. F. A. Gadoffre. Manchester: Manchester University Press, 1969.

————. "Le *Discours de la méthode* et l'histoire littéraire." *French Studies* 2, no. 4 (October 1948): 301–14.

————. "Réflexions sur la genèse du *Discours de la méthode.*" *Revue de Synthèse* 63, ns.22 (January-June 1948): 11–27.

————. "Sur la chronologie du *Discours de la méthode.*" *Revue d'Histoire de la Philosophie et d'Histoire Générale de la Civilisation* ns. année 11, fasc. 33 (January–March 1943): 45–70.

————. *See also*: Descartes, *Discours* (in Primary).

Gadol, Joan [Kelly]. *Leon Battista Alberti: Universal Man of the Early Renaissance.* Chicago: University of Chicago Press, 1969.

Ganshof, F. L. *Feudalism.* Translated by Philip Grierson. Foreword by F. M. Stenton. 3rd English ed. New York: Harper Torchbooks, 1964.

Garber, Daniel. "Descartes and Method in 1637." In *PSA 1988: Proceedings of the 1988 Biennial Meeting of the Philosophy of Science Association,* vol. 2: *Symposia and Invited Papers,* 2256–36. Edited by Arthur Fine and Jarrett Leplin. East Lansing, MI: Philosophy of Science Association, 1989.

Gardner, Jane F. *Women in Roman Law and Society.* London: Croom Helm, 1986.

Garlan, Yvon. *Les esclaves en Grèce ancienne.* Paris: Maspero, 1982.

Garnsey, Peter. *Ideas of Slavery from Aristotle to Augustine.* Cambridge: Cambridge University Press, 1996.

Gauchet, Marcel. *Le désenchantement du monde: Une histoire politique de la religion.* Paris: Gallimard, 1985.

Gaukroger, Stephen, ed. *The Soft Underbelly of Reason: The Passions in the Seventeenth Century*. London: Routledge, 1998.

Gbadegesin, Segun. *African Philosophy: Traditional Yoruba Philosophy and Contemporary African Realities*. New York: Peter Lang, 1991.

Gill, Christopher. "Did Chrysippus Understand Medea?" *Phronesis* 28 (1983): 136–49.

———. "The Human Being as an Ethical Norm." In Gill, ed., 137–61.

———. "Panaetius on the Virtue of Being Yourself." In Bulloch, Gruen, Long and Stewart, eds., 330–53.

———. "Passion as Madness in Roman Poetry." In Braund and Gill, eds., 213–41.

———. *Personality in Greek Epic, Tragedy, and Philosophy: The Self in Dialogue*. Oxford: Clarendon, 1996.

———. "Personhood and Personality: The Four-*Personae* Theory in Cicero *De officiis* I." *Oxford Studies in Ancient Philosophy* 6 (1988): 169–99.

———, ed. *The Person and the Human Mind: Issues in Ancient and Modern Philosophy*. Oxford: Clarendon, 1990.

———. *See also*: Braund and Gill, eds.

Ginzberg, Carlo. *The Cheese and the Worms: The Cosmos of a Sixteenth-Century Miller*. Translated by John and Anne Tedeschi. Baltimore: Johns Hopkins University Press, 1982.

Gioseffi, Decio. "Realtà e conoscenza nel Brunelleschi." *La Critica dell'Arte* 85 (March 1967): 8–18.

Goldhill, Simon. *Foucault's Virginity: Ancient Erotic Fiction and the History of Sexuality*. Cambridge: Cambridge University Press, 1995.

Goldschmidt, Victor. "Logique et rhétorique chez les Stoïciens." *Logique et analyses* ns. 6 (1963): 450–56.

———. *Le système stoïcien et l'idée du temps*. 2nd ed. Paris: Vrin, 1969.

Gomme, Arnold Wycombe. *The Population of Athens in the Fifth and Fourth Centuries B.C.* Oxford: Blackwell, 1933.

———. "The Position of Women in Athens in the Fifth and Fourth Centuries." *Classical Philology* 20, no. 1 (January 1925): 1–25.

Gooch, George Peabody. *The History of English Democratic Ideas in the Seventeenth Century*. Cambridge: Cambridge University Press, 1898.

Gouhier, Henri. *Essai sur Descartes*. 2nd ed. Paris: Vrin, 1949.

Gould, John P. "Law, Custom and Myth: Aspects of the Social Position of Women in Classical Athens." *Journal of Hellenic Studies* 100 (1980): 38–59.

Gould, Josiah B. "The Stoic Conception of Fate." *Journal of the History of Ideas* 35 (1974): 17–32.

Gourevitch, Danielle. *Le mal d'être femme: La femme et la médecine dans la Rome antique*. Paris: Belles Lettres, 1984.

Govaerts, Suzanne. *See*: Delatte, Govaerts and Denooz.

Goyard-Fabre, Simone. "Descartes et Machiavel." *Revue de Métaphysique et Morale* 78, no. 3 (July–September 1973): 312–34.

Grabes, Herbert. *The Mutable Glass: Mirror-Imagery in Titles and Texts of the*

Middle Ages and English Renaissance. Translated by Gordon Collier. Cambridge: Cambridge University Press, 1982.

Grafton, Anthony. *Cardano's Cosmos: The Worlds and Works of a Renaissance Astrologer.* Cambridge, MA: Harvard University Press, 1999.

———. *Leon Battista Alberti: Master Builder of the Renaissance.* New York: Hill & Wang, 2000.

Gramsci, Antonio. *Selections from Cultural Writings.* Edited by David Forgacs and Geoffrey Nowell-Smith. Translated by William Boelhower. London: Lawrence & Wishart, 1985.

———. *Selections from the Prison Notebooks.* Edited and translated by Quintin Hoare and Geoffrey Nowell-Smith. New York: International Publishers, 1971.

Grass, Günter. *Die Blechtrommel: Roman.* Darmstadt: Luchterhand, 1959.

———. *The Tin Drum.* Translated by Ralph Manheim. 1961. Reprint, New York: Vintage, 1990.

Gravel, Pierre. *Pour une logique du sujet tragique: Sophocle.* Montreal: Presses de l'Université de Montréal, 1980.

Green, Otis Howard. *"El licenciado Vidriera*: Its Relation to the *Viaje del Parnaso* and the *Examen de ingenios* of Huarte." In *The Literary Mind of Medieval and Renaissance Spain: Essays,* 185–92. Introduction by John E. Keller. Lexington: University Press of Kentucky, 1970.

Greenblatt, Stephen Jay. "Psychoanalysis and Renaissance Culture." In *Learning to Curse: Essays in Early Modern Culture,* 131–45. New York: Routledge, 1990.

———. *Renaissance Self-Fashioning: From More to Shakespeare.* Chicago: University of Chicago Press, 1980.

Greene, Roland. *Post-Petrarchism: Origins and Innovations of the Western Lyric Sequence.* Princeton: Princeton University Press, 1991.

Greene, Thomas M. "The Flexibility of the Self in Renaissance Literature." In *The Disciplines of Criticism,* 241–64. Edited by Peter Demetz, Thomas Greene, and Lowry Nelson. New Haven: Yale University Press, 1968.

———. *The Light in Troy: Imitation and Discovery in Renaissance Poetry.* New Haven: Yale University Press, 1982.

———. "Petrarch *Viator*: The Displacements of Heroism." *The Yearbook of English Studies* 12 (1982). Special Number: *Heroes and the Heroic,* 35–57. Edited by G. K. Hunter and C. J. Rawson, with Jenny Mezciems. London: Modern Humanities Research Association, 1981.

Greenstein, Jack M. "Alberti on Historia: A Renaissance View of the Structure of Significance in Narrative Painting." *Viator* 21 (1990): 273–99.

Griffin, Miriam T. *Seneca: A Philosopher in Politics.* Oxford: Clarendon, 1976.

———. *See also:* Cicero, *On Duties* (in Primary).

Gruner, O. Cameron. *See:* Avicenna, *Treatise on the Canon* (in Primary).

Guenancia, Pierre. *Descartes et l'ordre politique: Critique cartésienne des fondements de la politique.* Paris: Presses Universitaires de France, 1983.

Gurevich, Aron Iakovlevich. *Categories of Medieval Culture.* Translated by G. L. Campbell. London: Routledge & Kegan Paul, 1985.

————. *Medieval Popular Culture: Problems of Belief and Perception.* Translated by János M. Bak and Paul A. Hollingsworth. Cambridge: Cambridge University Press, 1988.

————. *The Origins of European Individualism.* Translated by Katharine Judelson. Oxford: Blackwell, 1995.

Gyekye, Kwame. *An Essay on African Philosophical Thought: The Akan Conceptual Scheme.* Cambridge: Cambridge University Press, 1987.

Haidu, Peter. *Aesthetic Distance in Chrétien de Troyes: Irony and Comedy in* Cligès *and* Perceval. Geneva: Droz, 1968.

————. "Althusser Anonymous in the Middle Ages." *Exemplaria* 7, no. 1 (Spring 1995): 55–74.

————. *Lion-queue-coupée: L'écart symbolique chez Chrétien de Troyes.* Geneva: Droz, 1972.

————. "Semiotics and History." *Semiotica* 40 (1982): 187–222.

————. *The Subject: Medieval/Modern.* Forthcoming.

————. *The Subject of Violence: The* Song of Roland *and the Birth of the State.* Bloomington: Indiana University Press, 1993.

Hainsworth, George. "La source du 'Licenciado Vidriera'." *Bulletin Hispanique* 32 (1930): 70–72.

Halperin, David M. "Why Is Diotima a Woman? Platonic *Erōs* and the Figuration of Gender." In Halperin, Winkler and Zeitlin, eds., 257–308.

————, John J. Winkler and Froma I. Zeitlin, eds. *Before Sexuality: The Construction of Erotic Experience in the Ancient Greek World.* Princeton: Princeton University Press, 1990.

Hamesse, Jacqueline. "*Spiritus* chez les auteurs philosophiques des 12e et 13e siècles." In Fattori and Bianchi, eds., 157–90.

Hanning, Robert W. *The Individual in Twelfth-Century Romance.* New Haven: Yale University Press, 1977.

Hanson, Ann Ellis. "The Medical Writers' Woman." In Halperin, Winkler and Zeitlin, eds., 309–37.

Hanson, Elizabeth. *Discovering the Subject in Renaissance England.* Cambridge: Cambridge University Press, 1998.

Harding, Sandra G., and Merrill B. Hintikka, eds. *Discovering Reality: Feminist Perspectives on Epistemology, Metaphysics, Methodology, and Philosophy of Science.* Dordrecht: Reidel, 1983.

Harré, Rom. *Personal Being.* Oxford: Blackwell, 1983.

Harries, Karsten. *Infinity and Perspective.* Cambridge, MA: Harvard University Press, 2001.

Harris, William V. *Restraining Rage: The Ideology of Anger Control in Classical Antiquity.* Cambridge, MA: Harvard University Press, 2001.

Harris, Wilson. *The Womb of Space: The Cross-Cultural Imagination.* Westport, CT: Greenwood Press, 1983.

Harvey, E. Ruth. *The Inward Wits: Psychological Theory in the Middle Ages and the Renaissance.* London: Warburg Institute, 1975.

Haselbach, Hans. *Sénèque des IIII vertus: La Formula honestae vitae de Martin de Braga (pseudo-Sénèque), traduite et glosé par Jean Courtecuisse (1403).* Étude et édition critique. Berne: Herbert Lang; Frankfort a/M: Peter Lang, 1975.

Havelock, Eric A. *The Literate Revolution in Greece and Its Cultural Consequences.* Princeton: Princeton University Press, 1982.

———. *The Muse Learns to Write: Reflections on Orality and Literacy from Antiquity to the Present.* New Haven: Yale University Press, 1986.

———. *Preface to Plato.* Cambridge, MA: Harvard University Press, 1963.

Heckscher, William Sebastian. *Rembrandt's Anatomy of Dr. Nicolaas Tulp: An Iconological Study.* New York: New York University Press, 1958.

Hegel, Georg Wilhelm Friedrich. *Aesthetics: Lectures on Fine Art.* Translated by T. M. Knox. 2 vols. Oxford: Clarendon, 1974–1975.

Heinze, Max. *Die Lehre vom Logos in der griechischen Philosophie.* Oldenberg: Schmidt, 1872.

Heller, Thomas C., Morton Sosna, David E. Wellbery [et al.], eds. *Reconstructing Individualism: Autonomy, Individuality, and the Self in Western Thought.* Stanford: Stanford University Press, 1986.

Hendricks, Margo, and Patricia Parker, eds. *Women, "Race," and Writing in the Early Modern Period.* London and New York: Routledge, 1994.

Hersey, George L. *Architecture and Geometry in the Age of the Baroque.* Chicago: University of Chicago Press, 2000.

Higgins, William Edward. *Xenophon the Athenian: The Problem of the Individual and the Society of the Polis.* Albany: State University of New York Press, 1977.

Hollis, Martin. *Models of Man.* Cambridge: Cambridge University Press, 1977.

———, and Steven Lukes, eds. *Rationality and Relativism.* Oxford: Blackwell, 1982.

Holmes, Olivia. *Assembling the Lyric Self: Authorship from Troubadour Song to Italian Poetry Book.* Minneapolis: University of Minnesota Press, 2000.

Holt, J. C. *Magna Carta.* Cambridge: Cambridge University Press, 1965.

Horkheimer, Max. "Montaigne and the Function of Skepticism." In *Between Philosophy and Social Science: Selected Early Writings,* 265–311. Translated by G. Frederick Hunter, Matthew S. Kramer, and John Torpey. Introduction by G. Frederick Hunter. 1993; rpt. Cambridge, MA: MIT Press, 1995.

Horton, Robin, and Ruth Finnigan, eds. *Modes of Thought: Essays on Thinking in Western and Non-Western Societies.* London: Faber & Faber, 1973.

Hurd-Mead, Kate Campbell. *A History of Women in Medicine, from the Earliest Times to the Beginning of the Nineteenth Century.* Haddam, CT: Haddam Press, 1938.

———. "An Introduction to the History of Women in Medicine." *Annals of Medical History* ns. 5 (1933): 1–27, 171–96, 281–305, 390–405, 484–504, 584–600.

———. "Trotula." *Isis* 14, no. 2 (1930): 349–67.

Icaza, Francisco A. de. *Las "Novelas ejemplares" de Cervantes, sus críticos, sus modelos literarios, y su influencia en el arte.* 2nd ed. Madrid: Clásica Española, 1915.

Imbert, Claude. "Pour une structure de la croyance: L'argument d'Anselme." *Nouvelle Revue de Psychanalyse* 18 (Autumn 1978): 43–53.

———. "Stoic Logic and Alexandrian Poetics." In Schofield, Burnyeat and Barnes, eds., 181–216.

———. "Théorie de la représentation et doctrine logique dans le stoïcisme ancien." In Brunschwig, ed., 223–49.

Inwood, Brad. *Ethics and Human Action in Early Stoicism.* 1985. Reprint, Oxford: Clarendon, 1987.

Irigaray, Luce. *Sexes and Genealogies.* Translated by Gillian C. Gill. New York: Columbia University Press, 1993.

Irvine, Martin. *The Making of Textual Culture: "Grammatica" and Literary Theory, 350–1100.* Cambridge: Cambridge University Press, 1994.

Jaeger, C. Stephen. *Ennobling Love: In Search of a Lost Sensibility.* Philadelphia: University of Pennsylvania Press, 1999.

Jager, Eric. *The Book of the Heart.* Chicago: University of Chicago Press, 2000.

James, Adeola, ed. *In Their Own Voices: African Women Writers Talk.* London: James Currey; Portsmouth, NH: Heinemann, 1990.

James, Susan. *Passion and Action: The Emotions in Seventeenth-Century Philosophy.* Oxford: Clarendon, 1997.

Janowski, Zbigniew. *Index augustino-cartésien: Textes et commentaires.* Paris: Vrin, 2000.

Jarzombek, Mark. *On Leon Battista Alberti: His Literary and Aesthetic Theories.* Cambridge, MA: MIT Press, 1989.

Jolivet, Jean. *Arts du langage et théologie chez Abélard.* Paris: Vrin, 1969.

Jones, A. H. M. "Slavery in the Ancient World." In Finley, ed., 1–15.

Jones, Ann Rosalind. *The Currency of Eros: Women's Love Lyric in Europe, 1540–1620.* Bloomington: Indiana University Press, 1990.

Jordan, Constance. *Renaissance Feminism: Literary Texts and Political Models.* Ithaca, NY: Cornell University Press, 1990.

Just, Roger. *Women in Athenian Law and Life.* London: Routledge, 1989.

Kahn, Charles M. "Discovering the Will: From Aristotle to Augustine." In Dillon and Long, eds., 234–59.

Kahn, Victoria. "Revising the History of Machiavellism: English Machiavellism and the Doctrine of Things Indifferent." *Renaissance Quarterly* 46, no. 3 (Autumn 1993): 526–61.

Kambouchner, Denis. *L'homme des passions: Commentaires sur Descartes.* 2 vols. Paris: Albin Michel, 1995.

Kampen, Natalie Boymel. *See:* Fantham [et al.].

Kandinsky, Wassily. *See:* Schoenberg and Kandinsky.

Kantorowicz, Ernst H. *The King's Two Bodies: A Study in Medieval Political Theology.* Princeton: Princeton University Press, 1957.

Kay, Sarah. *Subjectivity in Troubadour Poetry.* Cambridge: Cambridge University Press, 1990.

Kelber, Wilhelm. *Die Logoslehre von Heraklit bis Origenes.* Stuttgart: Urachhaus, 1958.

Kennedy, Gwynne. *Just Anger: Representing Women's Anger in Early Modern England*. Carbondale: Southern Illinois University Press, 2000.

Kennedy, William John. *Authorizing Petrarch*. Ithaca, NY: Cornell University Press, 1994.

Kenny, Anthony. *Aristotle's Theory of the Will*. New Haven: Yale University Press, 1979.

———. *Will, Freedom and Power*. Oxford: Blackwell, 1975.

———. *See also*: Descartes, *Philosophical Writings* (in Primary).

Kenyatta, Jomo. *Facing Mount Kenya: The Traditional Life of the Gikuyu*. Introduction by B. Malinowski. 1938. Reprint, London: Heinemann, 1979.

Kerferd, George B. "The Search for Personal Identity in Stoic Thought." *Bulletin of the John Rylands University Library* 55 (1972–73): 177–96.

Kermode, Frank. *The Classic*. London: Faber & Faber, 1975.

Keuls, Eva C. *The Reign of the Phallus: Sexual Politics in Ancient Athens*. New York: Harper & Row, 1985.

King, Helen. *Hippocrates' Woman: Reading the Female Body in Ancient Greece*. London: Routledge, 1998.

Klapisch-Zuber, Christine, ed. *Silences of the Middle Ages*. [Translated by Arthur Goldhammer et al.] Volume 2 of *A History of Women in the West*. General editors Georges Duby and Michelle Perrot. Cambridge, MA: Harvard University Press (Belknap), 1992.

Klibansky, Raymond. "Peter Abailard and Bernard of Clairvaux: A Letter by Abailard." *Mediaeval and Renaissance Studies* 5 (1961): 1–27.

———, Erwin Panofsky and Fritz Saxl. *Saturn and Melancholy: Studies in the History of Natural Philosophy, Religion and Art*. London: Nelson, 1964.

Knachel, Philip A. *England and the Fronde: The Impact of the English Civil War and Revolution on France*. Ithaca, NY: Cornell University Press, 1967.

Knowles, David. *The Evolution of Medieval Thought*. 1962. Reprint, New York: Vintage, 1964.

Koelsch, Manfred. *Recht und Macht bei Montaigne: Ein Beitrag zur Erforschung der Grundlagen von Staat und Recht*. Berlin: Duncker & Humblot, 1974.

Kristeller, Paul Oskar. *Aristotelismo e sincretismo nel pensiero di Pietro Pomponazzi*. Padua: Antenore, 1983.

———. *Die italienischen Universitäten der Renaissance*. Schriften und Vorträge des Petrarca-Instituts Köln 1. Krefeld: Scherpe, [1953].

———. *Medieval Aspects of Renaissance Learning*. Edited and translated by Edward P. Mahoney. Durham, NC: Duke University Press, 1974.

———. "Philosophy and Medicine in Medieval and Renaissance Italy." In *Organism, Medicine, and Metaphysics*, 29–40. Edited by Stuart F. Spicker. Dordrecht and Boston: D. Reidel, 1978.

———. *The Philosophy of Marsilio Ficino*. Translated by Virginia Conant. 1943. Reprint, Gloucester, MA: Peter Smith, 1964.

———. *Renaissance Concepts of Man and Other Essays*. New York: Harper & Row, 1972.

————. "The School of Salerno: Its Development and its Contribution to the History of Learning." *Bulletin of the History of Medicine* 17, no. 2 (February 1945): 138–94.

————. *Le thomisme et la pensée italienne de la Renaissance.* Montreal: Institut d'Études Médiévales; Paris: Vrin, 1967.

————. *See also:* Cassirer [et al.], eds. (in Primary).

Krücke, Adolf Otto Hermann. *Der Nimbus und verwandte Attribute in der frühchristlichen Kunst.* Strasbourg: Heitz, 1905.

Kuriyama, Shigehisa. *The Expressiveness of the Body and the Divergence of Greek and Chinese Medicine.* New York: Zone, 1999.

Lacey, W. K. *The Family in Classical Greece.* London: Thames & Hudson, 1968.

Lachterman, David R. "Descartes and the Philosophy of History." *Independent Journal of Philosophy* 4 (1983): 31–46.

La Fontaine, J. S. "Person and Individual: Some Anthropological Reflections." In Carrithers, Collins and Lukes, eds., 123–40.

Lamy, Theresa M. "Juliana Morell: Child Prodigy, Religious Reformer, Spiritual Writer." Ph.D. diss., New York University, 1992.

Lange, Lynda. "Woman Is Not a Rational Animal: On Aristotle's Biology of Reproduction." In Harding and Hintikka, eds., 1–15.

Larrain, Carlos G. *Galens Kommentar zu Platons Timaios.* Stuttgart: Teubner, 1992.

Lea, Henry Charles. *A History of Auricular Confession and Indulgences in the Latin Church.* 3 vols. Philadelphia: Lea Brothers,1896.

Leff, Gordon. *William of Ockham: The Metamorphosis of Scholastic Discourse.* Manchester: Manchester University Press, 1975.

Lefkowitz, Mary R. *Heroines and Hysterics.* London: Duckworth, 1981.

————. *See also:* Lefkowitz and Fant, eds. (in Primary), *and* Cantarella, *Pandora's.*

Lejeune, Philippe. *L'autobiographie en France.* Paris: Colin, 1971.

————. *Le pacte autobiographique.* Paris: Seuil, 1975.

Leo, Friedrich. *Die griechisch-römische Biographie nach ihrer litterarischen Form.* Leipzig: Teubner, 1901.

Leroy, Maxime. *Descartes social.* Paris: Vrin, 1931.

Levi, Anthony. *French Moralists: The Theory of the Passions, 1585–1649.* Oxford: Clarendon, 1964.

Lewis, Janet. *The Wife of Martin Guerre.* San Francisco: Colt Press, 1941.

Lewis, John. *See:* Habert (in Primary).

Lezra, Jacques. *Unspeakable Subjects: The Genealogy of the Event in Early Modern Europe.* Stanford: Stanford University Press, 1997.

Lienhardt, R. Godfrey. *Divinity and Experience.* Oxford: Clarendon, 1961.

————. "Self: Public, Private. Some African Representations." In Carrithers, Collins and Lukes, eds., 141–55.

Little, Lester K. "Anger in Monastic Curses." In Rosenwein, ed., 9–35.

Liu Hsieh. *The Literary Mind and the Carving of Dragons.* Translated and edited by Vincent Yu-chung Shih. [Bilingual ed.] Taipei: Chung Hwa, 1970.

568   Bibliography: Secondary Sources

Lloyd, Antony C. "Nosce teipsum and conscientia." *Archiv für Geschichte der Philosophie* 46 (1964): 188–200.
Lloyd, Geoffrey E. R. *Demystifying Mentalities.* Cambridge: Cambridge University Press, 1990.
———. "The Invention of Nature." In *Methods,* 417–34.
———. *Methods and Problems in Greek Science.* Cambridge: Cambridge University Press, 1991.
———. *The Revolutions of Wisdom: Studies in the Claims and Practice of Ancient Greek Science.* Berkeley: University of California Press, 1987.
———. *Science, Folklore and Ideology: Studies in the Life Sciences in Ancient Greece.* Cambridge: Cambridge University Press, 1983.
———. "Who Is Attacked in *On Ancient Medicine?*" In *Methods,* 49–69.
———. *See also:* Hippocrates, *Hippocratic Writings* (in Primary), *and* Sassi.
Logan, Marie-Rose. "Writing the Self: Guillaume Budé's Poetics of Scholarship." In *Contending Kingdoms: Historical, Psychological, and Feminist Approaches to the Literature of Sixteenth-Century England and France,* 131–48. Edited by Marie-Rose Logan and Peter L. Rudnytsky. Detroit: Wayne State University Press, 1991.
Long, Anthony A. "Ancient Philosophy's Hardest Question: What to Make of Oneself?" *Representations* 74 (Spring 2001): 19–36.
———. "Freedom and Determinism in the Stoic Theory of Human Action." In Long, ed., 173–99.
———. "Greek Ethics after MacIntyre and the Stoic Community of Reason." In Long, *Stoic Studies,* 156–78.
———. *Hellenistic Philosophy: Stoics, Epicureans, Sceptics.* London: Duckworth, 1974.
———. "Hierocles on *oikeiōsis* and Self-Perception." In Long, *Stoic Studies,* 250–63.
———. "Language and Thought in Stoicism." In Long, ed., 75–113.
———. "The Logical Basis of Stoic Ethics." *Proceedings of the Aristotelian Society* 71 (1970–71): 85–104. Reprinted with a "Postscript" in Long, *Stoic Studies,* 134–55.
———. "Representation and the Self in Stoicism." In Long, *Stoic Studies,* 264–85.
———. "The Stoic Concept of Evil." *Philosophical Quarterly* 18 (1968): 329–43.
———. "Stoic Determinism and Alexander of Aphrodisias's *De fato* (i–xiv)." *Archiv für die Geschichte der Philosophie* 52 (1970): 247–65.
———. "Stoic Philosophers on Persons, Property-Ownership and Community." In *Aristotle and After.* Edited by Richard Sorabji. *Bulletin of the Institute of Classical Studies* suppl. 68 (1997): 13–31.
———. *Stoic Studies.* Cambridge: Cambridge University Press, 1996.
———, ed. *Problems in Stoicism.* London: Athlone Press, 1971.
———. *See also:* Bulloch [et al.], eds., *and* Dillon and Long, eds. (in Secondary); Hierocles, *and* Long and Sedley, eds. (in Primary).
Loraux, Nicole. *The Children of Athena: Athenian Ideas about Citizenship and*

the Division of the Sexes. Translated by Caroline Levine. Foreword by Froma I. Zeitlin. Princeton: Princeton University Press, 1993.

———. *Les enfants d'Athéna: Idées athéniennes sur la citoyenneté et la division des sexes*. Paris: Maspero, 1981.

———. *Les expériences de Tirésias: Le féminin et l'homme grec*. Paris: Gallimard, 1989.

———. *Façons tragiques de tuer une femme*. Paris: Hachette, 1985.

Luciani, Evelyn. *Les Confessions de St. Augustin dans les lettres de Pétrarque*. Paris: Études Augustiniennes, 1982.

Lukes, Steven. *Individualism*. Oxford: Blackwell, 1973.

———. *See also*: Carrithers, Collins and Lukes, eds.; *and* Hollis and Lukes, eds.

Lyons, John O. *The Invention of the Self: The Hinge of Consciousness in the Eighteenth Century*. Carbondale: Southern Illinois University Press, 1978.

MacIntyre, Alasdair C. *After Virtue: A Study in Moral Theory*. 2nd ed. Notre Dame, IN: University of Notre Dame Press, 1984.

MacLean, Ian. *Montaigne philosophe*. Paris: Presses Universitaires de France, 1996.

———. *The Renaissance Notion of Woman: A Study in the Fortunes of Scholasticism and Medical Science in European Intellectual Life*. Cambridge: Cambridge University Press, 1980.

MacMullen, Ramsay. "Women in Public in the Roman Empire." *Historia* [Wiesbaden] 29 (1980): 208–18.

Mactoux, Marie Madeleine. *Douleia: Esclavage et pratiques discursives dans l'Athènes classique*. Annales Littéraires de l'Université de Besançon 250. Paris: Belles Lettres, 1980.

Martin, Luther H., Huck Gutman and Patrick H. Hutton, eds. *Technologies of the Self: A Seminar with Michel Foucault*. Amherst: University of Massachusetts Press, 1988.

Martin, Raymond, and John Barresi. *The Naturalization of the Soul: Self and Personal Identity in the Eighteenth Century*. London: Routledge, 2000.

Martinelli, Bortolo. "Petrarca e il Ventoso." In *Petrarca e il Ventoso*, 149–215. Bergamo: Minerva Italiana, 1977.

Martz, Louis L. *The Poetry of Meditation: A Study in English Religious Literature of the Seventeenth Century*. [Revised ed.] New Haven: Yale University Press, 1962.

Mascuch, Michael. *Origins of the Individualist Self: Autobiography and Self-Identity in England, 1591–1791*. Stanford: Stanford University Press, 1996.

Matchinske, Megan. *Writing, Gender and State in Early Modern England: Identity Formation and the Female Subject*. Cambridge: Cambridge University Press, 1998.

Matheron, Alexandre. "Psychologie et politique: Descartes. La noblesse du chatouillement." *Dialectiques* 6 (1974): 79–98.

Mauss, Marcel. "A Category of the Human Mind: The Notion of Person; the Notion of Self." Translated by W. D. Halls. In Carrithers, Collins and Lukes, eds., 1–25.

Mazzotta, Giuseppe. *The Worlds of Petrarch*. Durham, NC: Duke University Press, 1993.

McLaughlin, Mary M. "Abelard as Autobiographer: The Motives and Meaning of His 'Story of Calamities'." *Speculum* 42, no. 3 (July 1967): 463–88.

Melehy, Hassan. *Writing Cogito: Montaigne, Descartes, and the Institution of the Modern Subject*. Albany: State University of New York Press, 1997.

Menn, Stephen Philip. *Descartes and Augustine*. Cambridge: Cambridge University Press, 1998.

Merleau-Ponty, Maurice. "Everywhere and Nowhere." In *Signs*, 126–58.

———. "Reading Montaigne." In *Signs*, 198–210.

———. *Signs*. Edited and introduction by Richard C. McCleary. Evanston, IL: Northwestern University Press, 1964.

Mesnard, Pierre. *Essai sur la morale de Descartes*. Paris: Boivin, 1936.

———. *L'essor de la philosophie politique au XVIe siècle*. 3rd ed. Paris: Vrin, 1969.

———. *See also*: Bodin, *Methodus* (in Primary).

Mews, Constant J. *The Lost Love Letters of Heloise and Abelard: Perceptions of Dialogue in Twelfth-Century France*. With [an Edition by Ewald Könsgen and] a Translation by Neville Chiavaroli and Constant J. Mews. New York: St. Martin's Press, 1999.

Meyer, Michel. *Le philosophe et les passions: Esquisse d'une histoire de la nature humaine*. Paris: LGF/Livre de Poche, "Biblio essais," 1991.

Meyerson, Ignace, ed. *Problèmes de la personne: Exposés et discussions*. The Hague: Mouton, 1973.

Michell, Humfrey. *The Economics of Ancient Greece*. New York: Macmillan; Cambridge: Cambridge University Press, 1940.

Miller, Peter N. *Defining the Common Good: Empire, Religion and Philosophy in Eighteenth-Century Britain*. Cambridge: Cambridge University Press, 1994.

Mintz, Samuel I. *The Hunting of Leviathan: Seventeenth-Century Reactions to the Materialism and Moral Philosophy of Thomas Hobbes*. Cambridge: Cambridge University Press, 1970.

Misch, Georg. *Geschichte der Autobiographie*. 4 vols. in 8. Frankfurt a/M: G. Schulte-Bulmke, 1949–1969.

———. *A History of Autobiography in Antiquity*. Translated by E. W. Dickes with the author. 2 vols. London: Routledge & Kegan Paul, 1950.

Momigliano, Arnaldo. *Lo sviluppo della biografia Greca*. Turin: Einaudi, 1974.

Moore, Charles A., with Aldyth V. Morris, eds. *The Status of the Individual in East and West*. Honolulu: University of Hawaii Press, 1968.

Moore, Mary B. *Desiring Voices: Women Sonneteers and Petrarchism*. Carbondale: Southern Illinois University Press, 2000.

Morris, Colin. *The Discovery of the Individual, 1050–1200*. New York: Harper & Row, 1972.

Morris, John N. *Versions of the Self: Studies in English Autobiography from John Bunyan to John Stuart Mill*. New York: Basic Books, 1966.

Morrison, Karl F. *"I Am You": The Hermeneutics of Empathy in Western Literature, Theology, and Art*. Princeton: Princeton University Press, 1988.

Mossé, Claude. *La femme dans la Grèce antique*. Paris: Albin Michel, 1983.

Most, Glenn W. "'A Cock for Asclepius'." *Classical Quarterly* ns. 43, no. 1 (1993): 96–111.

Moulinier, Laurence. *Le manuscrit perdu à Strasbourg: Enquête sur l'oeuvre scientifique de Hildegarde*. Paris: Publications de la Sorbonne; Saint-Denis: Presses Universitaires de Vincennes, 1995.

Muellner, Leonard. *The Anger of Achilles: Mēnis in Greek Epic*. Ithaca, NY: Cornell University Press, 1996.

Mugo, Micere Githae. *African Orature and Human Rights*. Human and Peoples' Rights Monograph Series 13. Roma, Lesotho: Institute of Southern African Studies, National University of Lesotho, 1991.

Musa, Mark, with Barbara Manfredi. "Introduction." In Petrarch, *Canzoniere*, xi–xxxvi (in Primary).

Nadler, Steven. "Descartes' Demon and the Madness of Don Quixote." *Journal of the History of Ideas* 58, no. 1 (January 1997): 41–55

Nardi, Bruno. *Saggi sull'aristotelismo padovano dal secolo XIV al XVI*. Florence: Sansoni, 1958.

———. *Soggetto e oggetto del conoscere nella filosofia antica e medievale*. 2nd ed. Rome: Ateneo, 1952.

Nash, Jerry C. "'Exerçant oeuvres viriles': Feminine Anger and Feminist (Re)Writing in Hélisenne de Crenne." *L'Esprit Créateur* 30, no. 4 (Winter 1990): 38–48.

———. "The Fury of the Pen: Crenne, the Bible, and Letter Writing." In Winn and Kuizenga, eds., 207–25.

———. "Renaissance Misogyny, Biblical Feminism, and Hélisenne de Crenne's *Epistres familieres et invectives*." *Renaissance Quarterly* 50, no. 2 (Summer 1997): 379–410.

———. *See also*: Hélisenne, *Les epistres* (in Primary).

Neaman, Judith Silverman. *Suggestion of the Devil: The Origins of Madness*. Garden City, NY: Doubleday Anchor, 1975.

Negri, Antonio. *Descartes politico, o della ragionevole ideologia*. Milan: Feltrinelli, 1970.

Newman, Barbara J. *Sister of Wisdom: St. Hildegard's Theology of the Feminine*. Berkeley: University of California Press, 1987.

———. *See also*: Hildegard, *Scivias* and *Symphonia* (in Primary).

Ngũgĩ wa Thiong'o. *Matigari*. Translated by Wangũi wa Goro. 1987; rpt. Oxford: Heinemann, 1990.

———. *Penpoints, Gunpoints and Dreams: Towards a Critical Theory of the Arts and the State in Africa*. Oxford: Clarendon, 1998.

———. *The Wizard of the Crow*. Translated by the author. Unpublished manuscript. Forthcoming.

———. *See also*: Okot.

Ní Dhomhnaill, Nuala. "Why I Choose to Write in Irish, The Corpse That Sits Up and Talks Back." *New York Times Book Review*, January 8, 1995, 3, 27–28.

Nietzsche, Friedrich. *The Will to Power.* Translated by Walter Kaufmann and R. J. Hollingdale. New York: Vintage, 1968.

Nolhac, Pierre de. *Pétrarque et l'humanisme.* New ed. 2 vols. Paris: Champion, 1907.

Norton, Glyn P. *Montaigne and the Introspective Mind.* The Hague: Mouton, 1975.

Nussbaum, Felicity A. *The Autobiographical Subject: Gender and Ideology in Eighteenth-Century England.* Baltimore: Johns Hopkins University Press, 1989.

Nussbaum, Martha Craven. *The Fragility of Goodness: Luck and Ethics in Greek Tragedy and Philosophy.* Cambridge: Cambridge University Press, 1986.

———. *The Therapy of Desire: Theory and Practice in Hellenistic Ethics.* Princeton: Princeton University Press, 1994.

———, ed. *Aristotle's* De motu animalium: *Text with Translation, Commentary and Interpretive Essays.* 1978. Reprint, Princeton: Princeton University Press, 1985.

———. *See also*: Brunschwig and Nussbaum, eds.

Nutton, Vivian, ed. *Galen: Problems and Prospects.* London: Wellcome Institute for the History of Medicine, 1981.

O'Connell, Michael. "Authority and the Truth of Experience in Petrarch's 'Ascent of Mt. Ventoux'." *Philological Quarterly* 62 (1983): 507–20.

Okot p'Bitek. *Africa's Cultural Revolution.* Introduction by Ngũgĩ wa Thiong'o. Nairobi: Macmillan, 1973.

———. *Artist the Ruler: Essays on Art, Culture and Values.* Foreword and Biographical Sketch by Lubwa p'Chong. Nairobi: Heinemann Kenya, 1986.

———. *Song of Lawino and Song of Ocol.* Introduction by G. A. Heron. 1972. Reprint, Oxford: Heinemann, 1984.

O'Malley, John W. *The First Jesuits.* Cambridge: Cambridge University Press, 1993.

O'Neill, John. *Essaying Montaigne: A Study of the Renaissance Institution of Writing and Reading.* London: Routledge & Kegan Paul, 1982.

Oppenheimer, Paul. *The Birth of the Modern Mind: Self, Consciousness, and the Invention of the Sonnet.* New York: Oxford University Press, 1989.

Organization of African Unity. *African Charter on Human and People's Rights.* In *Documents of the Organization of African Unity,* 109–23. Ed. Gino J. Naldi. London: Mansell, 1992.

———. *Cultural Charter for Africa.* [Document published by the OAU]. Port Louis [Mauritius: OAU], 1976.

———. *Panafrican Cultural Manifesto.* First All-African Cultural Festival, Algiers July 21–August 1, 1989. New York: Executive Secretariat of the OAU, 1969.

Ortega y Gasset, José. "Las dos grandes metáforas." In *El espectador, Tomo III y IV,* 241–62. 1923, 1925. Reprint, Madrid: Revista de Occidente, 1961.

Ottosson, Per-Gunnar. *Scholastic Medicine and Philosophy: A Study of Commentaries on Galen's Tegni (ca. 1300–1450).* Naples: Bibliopolis, 1984.

Owst, Gerald Robert. *Literature and Pulpit in Medieval England: A Neglected Chapter in the History of English Letters and of the English People.* [2nd ed.] Oxford: Blackwell, 1961.

———. *Preaching in Medieval England: An Introduction to Sermon Manuscripts of the Period c. 1350–1450.* 1926. Reprint, New York: Russell & Russell, 1965.

Ozment, Steven E. *The Age of Reform, 1250–1550: An Intellectual and Religious History of Late Medieval and Reformation Europe.* New Haven: Yale University Press, 1980.

Padel, Ruth. *Whom Gods Destroy: Elements of Greek and Tragic Madness.* Princeton: Princeton University Press, 1994.

Pagden, Anthony. *The Fall of Natural Man: The American Indian and the Origins of Comparative Ethnology.* 1982. Reprint, Cambridge: Cambridge University Press, 1986.

———. *Spanish Imperialism and the Political Imagination: Studies in European and Spanish-American Social and Political Theory, 1513–1830.* New Haven: Yale University Press, 1990.

Pagel, Walter. "Medieval and Renaissance Contributions to Knowledge of the Brain and Its Functions." In *The History and Philosophy of Knowledge of the Brain and Its Functions,* 95–114. Edited by F. N. L. Poynter. Springfield, IL: Charles C. Thomas, 1958.

Paige, Nicholas. *Being Interior: Autobiography and the Contradictions of Modernity in Seventeenth-Century France.* Philadelphia: University of Pennsylvania Press, 2000.

Panaccio, Claude. "La métaphysique et les noms." In *Culture et langage,* 249–81. Edited by J. P. Brodeur. Montreal: Hurtubise HMH, 1973.

Panafrican Cultural Manifesto. See: Organization of African Unity.

Pantel, Pauline Schmitt, ed. *From Ancient Goddesses to Christian Saints.* Translated by Arthur Goldhammer. Volume 1 of *A History of Women in the West.* General editors Georges Duby and Michelle Perrot. Cambridge, MA: Harvard University Press (Belknap), 1992.

Parel, Anthony J. *The Machiavellian Cosmos.* New Haven: Yale University Press, 1992.

Parker, Patricia A. *Literary Fat Ladies: Rhetoric, Gender, Property.* London: Methuen, 1987.

———, and David Quint, eds. *Literary Theory/Renaissance Texts.* Baltimore: Johns Hopkins University Press, 1986.

———. *See also:* Hendricks and Parker, eds.

Pascal, Roy. *Design and Truth in Autobiography.* Cambridge, MA: Harvard University Press, 1960.

Patterson, Cynthia B. *The Family in Greek History.* Cambridge, MA: Harvard University Press, 1998.

———. "*Hai Attikai:* The Other Athenians." *Helios* 13 (1986): 49–67.

Patterson, Lee. *Chaucer and the Subject of History.* Madison: University of Wisconsin Press, 1991.

———. "On the Margin: Postmodernism, Ironic History, and Medieval Studies." *Speculum* 65 (1990): 87–108.

Peerlkamp, P. Hofmann. *Liber de vita doctrina et facultate Nederlandorum qui carmina latina composuerunt.* Editio altera emendata et aucta. Lugduni-Batavorum: H. W. Hazenberg, 1843.

574   Bibliography: Secondary Sources

Pemberton, John, III. *See:* Drewal, Pemberton and Abiodun.
Pembroke, S. G. "*Oikeiōsis.*" In Long, ed., 114–49.
Peradotto, John, and J. P. Sullivan, eds. *Women in the Ancient World: The Arethusa Papers.* Albany: State University of New York Press, 1984.
Perry, John, ed. *Personal Identity.* Berkeley: University of California Press, 1975.
Petteys, Chris, with Hazel Gustow, Ferris Olin and Verna Ritchie. *Dictionary of Women Artists: An International Dictionary of Women Artists Born Before 1900.* Boston: G. K. Hall, 1985.
Pfeiffer, Rudolf. *History of Classical Scholarship: From the Beginnings to the End of the Hellenistic Age.* Oxford: Clarendon, 1968.
Pigeaud, Jackie. *La maladie de l'âme: Étude sur la relation de l'âme et du corps dans la tradition médico-philosophique antique.* Paris: Belles Lettres, 1981.
Pine, Martin L. *Pietro Pomponazzi: Radical Philosopher of the Renaissance.* Padua: Antenore, 1986.
Pocock, J. G. A. *The Ancient Constitution and the Feudal Law: A Study of English Historical Thought in the Seventeenth Century.* A Reissue with a Retrospect. Cambridge: Cambridge University Press, 1987.
Pomeroy, Sarah B. *Goddesses, Whores, Wives, and Slaves: Women in Classical Antiquity.* 1975. Reprint, New York: Schocken, 1976.
———. *Women in Hellenistic Egypt: From Alexander to Cleopatra.* New York: Schocken, 1984.
———. *Xenophon, Oeconomicus: A Social and Historical Commentary.* With a New English Translation. 1994. Reprint, Oxford: Clarendon, 1995.
———, ed. *Women's History and Ancient History.* Chapel Hill: University of North Carolina Press, 1991.
———. *See also:* Fantham [et al.].
Poovey, Mary. "'Scenes of an Indelicate Character': The Medical 'Treatment' of Victorian Women." In *The Making of the Modern Body: Sexuality and Society in the Nineteenth Century,* 137–68. Edited by Catherine Gallagher and Thomas Laqueur. Berkeley: University of California Press, 1987.
Porter, Roy, ed. *Rewriting the Self: Histories from the Renaissance to the Present.* London: Routledge, 1997.
Praechter, Karl. *Hierokles der Stoiker.* Leipzig: Dieterich, 1901.
Purkiss, Diane. "Introduction" to *Three Tragedies,* xi–xliii (in Primary).
Quint, David. *See:* Parker and Quint, eds.
Raber, Karen. "Gender and the Political Subject in *The Tragedy of Mariam.*" *Studies in English Literature, 1500–1900* 35, no. 2 (Spring 1995): 321–43.
Randall, John Herman, Jr. *See:* Cassirer [et al.], eds. (in Primary).
Ravenhill, Philip L. *The Self and the Other: Personhood and Images among the Baule, Côte d'Ivoire.* Monograph Series 28. Los Angeles: Fowler Museum of Cultural History, 1994.
Rée, Jonathan. "Baffled Traveller." *London Review of Books,* November 30, 2000, 3–7
Reesor, Margaret E. "Fate and Possibility in Early Stoic Philosophy." *Phoenix* 19 (1965): 285–97.

———. *The Nature of Man in Early Stoic Philosophy.* London: Duckworth, 1989.

———. "Necessity and Fate in Stoic Philosophy." In Rist, ed., 187–202.

———. *The Political Theory of the Old and Middle Stoa.* New York: Augustin, 1951.

Reiss, Timothy J. *Against Autonomy: Global Dialectics of Cultural Exchange.* Stanford: Stanford University Press, 2002.

———. *The Discourse of Modernism.* Ithaca, NY: Cornell University Press, 1982.

———. *Knowledge, Discovery and Imagination in Early Modern Europe: The Rise of Aesthetic Rationalism.* Cambridge: Cambridge University Press, 1997.

———. *The Meaning of Literature.* Ithaca, NY: Cornell University Press, 1992.

———. "Montaigne and the Subject of Polity." In *Literary Theory/Renaissance Texts,* 115–49. Edited by Patricia A. Parker and David Quint. Baltimore: Johns Hopkins University Press, 1986.

———. "Neo-Aristotle and Method: Between Zabarella and Descartes." In *Descartes' Natural Philosophy,* 195–227. Edited by Stephen Gaukroger, John Schuster and John Sutton. London: Routledge, 2000.

———. "Perioddity: Considerations on the Geography of Histories." *Modern Language Quarterly* 62, no. 4 (December 2001): 425–52.

———. "Significs: The Analysis of Meaning as Critique of Modernist Discourse." In *Essays in Significs,* 63–82. Edited by H. Walter Schmitz. Amsterdam: John Benjamins, 1990.

———. *Toward Dramatic Illusion: Theatrical Technique and Meaning from Hardy to "Horace."* New Haven: Yale University Press, 1971.

———. *Tragedy and Truth: Studies in the Development of a Renaissance and Neoclassical Discourse.* New Haven: Yale University Press, 1980.

———. *The Uncertainty of Analysis: Problems in Truth, Meaning, and Culture.* Ithaca, NY: Cornell University Press, 1988.

———. "Utopie versus état de pouvoir, ou prétexte du discours politique de la modernité: Hobbes, lecteur de La Boétie?" In *EMF: Studies in Early Modern France,* vol. IV, *Utopia 1: Sixteenth and Seventeenth Centuries,* 31–83. Edited by David Lee Rubin, with Alice Stroup. Charlottesville: Rookwood Press, 1998.

Renaut, Alain. *L'ère de l'individu: Contribution à une histoire de la subjectivité.* Paris: Gallimard, 1989.

Reynolds, Leighton Durham. *The Medieval Tradition of Seneca's Letters.* Oxford: Oxford University Press, 1965.

Riché, Pierre. *Education and Culture in the Barbarian West: From the Sixth through the Eighth Century.* Translated by John J. Contreni. Foreword by Richard E. Sullivan. 1976. Reprint, Columbia: University of South Carolina Press, 1978.

Riding, Alan. "Correcting Her Idea of Politically Correct." *New York Times,* July 14, 2001, A17, 19.

Rist, John M. *Augustine: Ancient Thought Baptized.* Cambridge: Cambridge University Press, 1994.
———. *Stoic Philosophy.* 1969. Reprint, Cambridge: Cambridge University Press, 1980.
———, ed. *The Stoics.* Berkeley: University of California Press, 1978.
Rivers, Elias L. "Certain Formal Characteristics of the Primitive Love Sonnet." *Speculum* 33, no. 1 (January 1958): 42–55.
Robins, Gay. *Women in Ancient Egypt.* Cambridge, MA: Harvard University Press, 1993.
Robinson, T. M. *Plato's Psychology.* 2nd ed. Toronto: University of Toronto Press, 1995.
Robson, Jill. "Petrarch Reading Augustine: The Ascent of Mont Ventoux." *Philological Quarterly* 64 (1985): 533–53.
Roche, Thomas P., Jr. "The Calendrical Structure of Petrarch's *Canzoniere*." *Studies in Philology* 71, no. 2 (April 1974): 152–72.
Romanowski, Sylvie. *L'illusion chez Descartes: La structure du discours cartésien.* Paris: Klincksieck, 1974.
Rorty, Amélie Oksenberg, ed. *The Identities of Persons.* Berkeley: University of California Press, 1976.
Rose, Mary Beth. "Gender, Genre, and History: Seventeenth-Century English Women and the Art of Autobiography." In *Women in the Middle Ages and the Renaissance: Literary and Historical Perspectives,* 245–78. Edited by Mary Beth Rose. Syracuse, NY: Syracuse University Press, 1986.
Rosenwein, Barbara H. "Introduction." In Rosenwein, ed., 1–6.
———, ed. *Anger's Past: The Social Uses of an Emotion in the Middle Ages.* Ithaca, NY: Cornell University Press, 1998.
Rossi, Paolo. *Clavis universalis: Arti della memoria e logica combinatoria da Lullo a Leibniz.* [2nd ed.] Bologna: Mulino, 1983.
Rowe, Christopher. "Philosophy, Love, and Madness." In Gill, ed., 227–46.
Rump, Johann. *Melanchthons Psychologie, (seine Schrift de anima) in ihrer Abhängigkeit von Aristoteles und Galenos.* Inaugural-Dissertation der philosophischen Fakultät der Universität Jena. Kiel: Marquardsen, 1897.
Ryle, Gilbert. *The Concept of Mind.* 1949. Reprint, Harmondsworth: Penguin, 1973.
Sainéan, Lazare. "Les sources modernes du roman de Rabelais." *Revue des Études Rabelaisiennes* 10 (1912): 375–420.
Salmon, J. H. M. *The French Religious Wars in English Political Thought.* Oxford: Clarendon, 1959.
———. *Society in Crisis: France in the Sixteenth Century.* New York: St. Martin's Press, 1975.
Sampayo Rodríguez, José Ramón. *Rasgos erasmistas de la locura del Licenciado Vidriera de Miguel de Cervantes.* Kassel: Reichenberger, 1986.
Sandbach, F. H. *The Stoics.* London: Chatto & Windus, 1975.
Santagata, Marco. *I frammenti dell'anima: Storia e racconto del Canzoniere di Petrarca.* Bologna: Mulino, 1992.
Sassi, Maria Michela. *The Science of Man in Ancient Greece.* Translated by Paul

Tucker. Foreword by Sir Geoffrey Lloyd. Chicago: University of Chicago Press, 2001.

Saunders, Jason Lewis. *Justus Lipsius: The Philosophy of Renaissance Stoicism.* New York: Liberal Arts Press, 1955.

Savalli, Ivana. *La donna nella società della Grecia antica.* Bologna: Pàtron, 1983.

Schall, James V. "Cartesianism and Political Theory." *The Review of Politics* 24, no. 2 (April 1962): 260–82.

Schaps, David M. *Economic Rights of Women in Ancient Greece.* Edinburgh: Edinburgh University Press, 1979.

Schiaffini, Alfredo. *Momenti di storia della lingua italiana: Le origini e il Duecento.* Rome: Studium, 1965.

Schlaifer, Robert. "Greek Theories of Slavery from Homer to Aristotle." In Finley, ed., 93–132.

Schlossmann, Siegmund. *Persona und prosopon im Recht und im christlichen Dogma.* Kiel: Lipsius & Tischner, 1906.

Schmitt, Charles Bernard. "Aristotle among the Physicians." In Wear, French and Lonie, eds., 1–15, 271–79.

Schoenfeldt, Michael Carl. *Bodies and Selves in Early Modern England: Physiology and Inwardness in Spenser, Shakespeare, Herbert, and Milton.* Cambridge: Cambridge University Press, 1999.

Schnorr von Carolsfeld, Ludwig. *Geschichte der juristischen Person.* Vol. 1. Munich: Beck, 1933.

Schoenberg, Arnold, and Wassily Kandinsky. *Letters, Pictures and Documents.* Edited by Jelena Hahl-Koch. Translated by John C. Crawford. London: Faber & Faber, 1984.

Schofield, Malcolm, Myles Burnyeat and Jonathan Barnes, eds. *Doubt and Dogmatism: Studies in Hellenistic Epistemology.* Oxford: Clarendon, 1980.

Schofield, Malcolm, and Gisela Striker, eds. *The Norms of Nature: Studies in Hellenistic Ethics.* Cambridge: Cambridge University Press; Paris: Maison des Sciences de l'Homme, 1986.

Screech, Michael Andrew. *Montaigne and Melancholy: The Wisdom of the Essays.* 1983. Reprint, Selinsgrove, PA: Susquehanna University Press, 1984.

———. *Rabelais.* Ithaca, NY: Cornell University Press, 1979.

———. *See also*: Habert, *Le songe*; Rabelais, *Le tiers livre* (in Primary).

Sealey, Raphael. *Women and Law in Classical Greece.* Chapel Hill: University of North Carolina Press, 1990.

Shapiro, H. Alan. *See*: Fantham [et al.].

Shapiro, Marianne. *Hieroglyph of Time: The Petrarchan Sestina.* Minneapolis: University of Minnesota Press, 1980.

Shumaker, Wayne. *English Autobiography: Its Emergence, Materials, and Form.* English Studies 8. Berkeley: University of California Press, 1954.

———. *Natural Magic and Modern Science: Four Treatises, 1590–1657.* Binghamton, NY: Medieval & Renaissance Texts & Studies, 1989.

Simon, Gérard. *Kepler astronome astrologue.* Paris: Gallimard, 1979.

Singer, Charles. "The Visions of Hildegard of Bingen." In *From Magic to Science: Essays on the Scientific Twilight,* 199–239. New York: Boni & Liveright, 1928.

Singh, Jyotsna. "Othello's Identity, Postcolonial Theory, and Contemporary Rewritings of *Othello.*" In Hendricks and Parker, eds. 287–99, 365–68.

Siraisi, Nancy G. *Avicenna in Renaissance Italy: The Canon and Medical Teaching in Italian Universities after 1500.* Princeton: Princeton University Press, 1987.

———. "The Changing Fortunes of a Traditional Text: Goals and Strategies in Sixteenth-Century Latin Editions of the *Canon* of Avicenna." In Wear, French and Lonie, eds., 16–41, 279–96.

———. *Medieval and Early Renaissance Medicine: An Introduction to Knowledge and Practice.* Chicago: University of Chicago Press, 1990.

———. *Taddeo Alderotti and His Pupils: Two Generations of Italian Medical Learning.* Princeton: Princeton University Press, 1981.

Skinner, Quentin. *The Foundations of Modern Political Thought.* 2 vols. Cambridge: Cambridge University Press, 1978.

Smarr, Janet Levarie. "Substituting for Laura: Objects of Desire for Renaissance Women Poets." *Comparative Literature Studies* 38, no. 1 (2001): 1–30.

Smith, Paul. *Discerning the Subject.* Foreword by John Mowitt. Minneapolis: University of Minnesota Press, 1988.

Smith, Roger. "Self-Reflection and the Self." In Porter, ed., 49–57.

Smith, Sidonie. *A Poetics of Women's Autobiography: Marginality and the Fictions of Self-Representation.* Bloomington: Indiana University Press, 1987.

Snell, Bruno. *The Discovery of the Mind: The Greek Origins of European Thought.* Trans. T. G. Rosenmeyer. 1953. Reprint, New York: Harper & Row, 1960.

Snyder, Jane McIntosh. *The Woman and the Lyre: Women Writers in Classical Greece and Rome.* Carbondale: Southern Illinois University Press, 1989.

Ṣofọla, 'Zulu. *Wedlock of the Gods.* London: Evans, 1972.

Solomon, Robert C. *Continental Philosophy since 1750: The Rise and Fall of the Self.* Oxford: Oxford University Press, 1988.

Sorabji, Richard. "Causation, Laws, and Necessity." In Schofield, Burnyeat and Barnes, eds., 250–82.

———. *Necessity, Cause, and Blame: Perspectives on Aristotle's Theory.* Ithaca, NY: Cornell University Press, 1980.

———. *See also*: Long, "Stoic Philosophers."

Soubiran, André. *Avicenne, prince des médecins: Sa vie et sa doctrine.* Paris: Lipschutz, 1935.

Soyinka, Wole. *Art, Dialogue, and Outrage: Essays on Literature and Culture.* [Edited by Biodun Jeyifo.] [2nd ed.] New York: Pantheon, 1993.

———. *Death and the King's Horseman.* 1975. Reprint, New York: Hill & Wang, 1987.

Spacks, Patricia Meyer. *Imagining a Self: Autobiography and the Novel in Eighteenth-Century England.* Cambridge, MA: Harvard University Press, 1976.

Spadaccini, Nicholas, and Jenaro Taléns, eds. *Autobiography in Early Modern Spain.* Minneapolis: Prisma Institute, 1988.

Spanneut, Michel. *Le stoïcisme des pères de l'Église de Clément de Rome à Clément d'Alexandrie.* 2nd ed. Paris: Seuil, 1969.

———. "Le stoïcisme et saint Augustin." In *Forma futuri: Studi in onore del Cardinale Michele Pelegrino*, 896–914. Turin: Bottega d'Erasmo, 1975.

Sparshott, F. E. "Zeno on Art: Anatomy of a Definition." In Rist, ed., 273–90.

Spelman, Elizabeth V. "Aristotle and the Politicization of the Soul." In Harding and Hintikka, eds., 17–30.

Spence, Sarah. *Texts and the Self in the Twelfth Century.* Cambridge: Cambridge University Press, 1996.

Spitzer, Leo. "Note on the Poetic and Empirical 'I' in Medieval Authors." *Traditio* 4 (1946): 414–22.

———. "Una questione di punteggiatura in un sonetto di Giacomo da Lentino (e un piccolo contributo alla storia del sonetto)." *Cultura Neolatina* 18 (1958): 61–70.

Ste. Croix, Geoffrey Ernest Maurice de. *The Class Struggle in the Ancient Greek World from the Archaic Age to the Arab Conquests.* Ithaca, NY: Cornell University Press, 1981.

———. "Slavery and Other Forms of Unfree Labour." In Archer, ed., 19–32.

Stein, Ludwig. *Die Psychologie der Stoa.* 2 vols. Berliner Studien für Classische Philologie und Archeologie 2 and 7. Berlin: S. Calvary, 1886–1888.

Stock, Brian. *After Augustine: The Meditative Reader and the Text.* Philadelphia: University of Pennsylvania Press, 2001.

———. *Augustine the Reader: Meditation, Self-Knowledge, and the Ethics of Interpretation.* Cambridge, MA: Harvard University Press, 1996.

Stolcke, Verena. "Invaded Women: Gender, Race, and Class in the Formation of Colonial Society." In Hendricks and Parker, eds., 272–86, 364–65.

Stough, Charlotte. "Stoic Determinism and Moral Responsibility." In Rist, ed., 203–31.

Strawson, Peter F. *Individuals.* London: Methuen, 1959.

Striker, Gisela. *Essays on Hellenistic Epistemology and Ethics.* Cambridge: Cambridge University Press, 1996.

———. "Following Nature: A Study in Stoic Ethics." In Striker, *Essays*, 221–80.

———. "Origins of the Concept of Natural Law." In Striker, *Essays*, 209–20.

———. "The Role of *Oikeiosis* in Stoic Ethics." *Oxford Studies in Ancient Philosophy* 1 (1983): 145–67. Reprinted in Striker, *Essays*, 281–97.

———. *See also*: Schofield and Striker, eds.

Sullivan, J. P. *See*: Peradotto and Sullivan, eds.

Sutton, John. *Philosophy and Memory Traces: Descartes to Connectionism.* Cambridge: Cambridge University Press, 1998.

Suvin, Darko, and Karatani Kôjin, eds. *The Non-Cartesian Subjects, East and West / Les sujets non-cartésiens, orient/occident. Discours Social/Social Discourse* 6, nos. 1–2 (Winter–Spring 1994).

Tambling, Jeremy. *Confession: Sexuality, Sin, the Subject.* Manchester: Manchester University Press, 1990.

Tatham, Edward Henry Ralph. *Francesco Petrarca, the First Modern Man of Let-*

ters: His Life and Correspondence. A Study of the Early Fourteenth Century (1304–1347). 2 vols. London: Sheldon Press; New York: Macmillan, 1925–1926.

Taylor, Charles. *Sources of the Self: The Making of the Modern Identity*. Cambridge, MA: Harvard University Press, 1989.

Taylor, Edward W. "*Measure for Measure*: Its Glassy Essence." *Cithara* 37, no. 1 (November 1997): 3–21.

Temkin, Owsei. *Galenism: Rise and Decline of a Medical Philosophy*. Ithaca, NY: Cornell University Press, 1973.

———. *See also*: Soranus (in Primary).

Tentler, Thomas. *Sin and Confession on the Eve of the Reformation*. Princeton: Princeton University Press, 1977.

Thomson, George. *Island Home: The Blasket Heritage*. And Tim Enright, *George Thomson: A Memoir*. Dingle: Brandon, 1988.

Tieleman, Teun. Review of Engberg-Pedersen, *Stoic Theory*. *Mnemosyne* 48, no. 2 (April 1995): 226–33.

Tournon, André. *"En sens agile": Les acrobaties de l'esprit selon Rabelais*. Paris: Champion, 1995.

Toynbee, Paget. "A Note on *storia, storiato*, and the Corresponding Terms in French and English, in Illustration of *Purgatorio*, X, 52, 71, 73." In *Mélanges offerts à M. Émile Picot*, 1.195–208. 2 vols. Paris: Édouard Rahir, 1913.

Trinkaus, Charles Edward. *In Our Image and Likeness: Humanity and Divinity in Italian Humanist Thought*. 2 vols. Chicago: University of Chicago Press, 1970.

———. *The Poet as Philosopher: Petrarch and the Formation of Renaissance Consciousness*. New Haven: Yale University Press, 1979.

Tripet, Arnaud. *Pétrarque, ou la connaissance de soi*. Geneva: Droz, 1967.

Tuck, Richard. *Natural Rights Theories: Their Origin and Development*. Cambridge: Cambridge University Press, 1979.

Ullmann, Walter. *The Individual and Society in the Middle Ages*. Baltimore: Johns Hopkins University Press, 1966.

———. *Medieval Political Thought*. 1965. Reprint, Harmondsworth: Penguin, 1979.

Universal Declaration of Human Rights [and additional Covenants and Protocols]. In *The International Law of Human Rights in Africa: Basic Documents and Annotated Bibliography*, 163–89. Edited by M. Hamalengwa, C. Flinterman and E. V. O. Dankwa. Dordrecht: Nijhoff, 1988.

Van Bremen, Riet. *The Limits of Participation: Women and Civic Life in the Greek East in the Hellenistic and Roman Periods*. Amsterdam: J. C. Gieben, 1996.

Vance, Eugene. *From Topic to Tale: Logic and Narrativity in the Middle Ages*. Foreword by Wlad Godzich. Minneapolis: University of Minnesota Press, 1987.

———. "Love's Concordance: The Poetics of Desire and the Joy of the Text." *Diacritics* 5, no. 1 (Spring 1975): 40–52.

———. *Mervelous Signals: Poetics and Sign Theory in the Middle Ages*. Lincoln: University of Nebraska Press, 1986.

———. *Reading the Song of Roland*. Englewood Cliffs, NJ: Prentice-Hall, 1970.

———. "Roland and the Poetics of Memory." In *Textual Strategies: Perspectives in Post-Structural Criticism*, 374–403. Edited by Josué Harari. Ithaca, NY: Cornell University Press, 1979.

———. "Roland, Charlemagne, and the Poetics of Illumination." *Oliphant* 6 (1979): 213–25.

———. *See also*: Brind'amour and Vance, eds.

Verbeke, Gérard. *L'évolution de la doctrine du pneuma du stoïcisme à S. Augustin: Étude philosophique*. Paris: Desclée de Brower; Louvain: Institut Supérieur de Philosophie, 1945.

———. *The Presence of Stoicism in Medieval Thought*. Washington, DC: Catholic University of America Press, 1983.

Vercruysse, Jérôme. "Hélisenne de Crenne: Notes biographiques." *Studi Francesi* 31 (1967): 77–81.

Vernant, Jean-Pierre. "Aspects de la personne dans la religion grecque." In *Mythe et pensée chez les Grecs: Études de psychologie historique*, 2.79–94. 2 vols. Paris: Maspero, 1971.

———. "Catégories de l'agent et de l'action en Grèce ancienne." In *Religions, histoires, raisons*, 85–95. Paris: Maspero, 1975.

———. "Ébauches de la volonté dans la tragédie grecque." In Jean-Pierre Vernant and Pierre Vidal-Nacquet, *Mythe et tragédie en Grèce ancienne*, 43–74. Paris: Maspero, 1972.

———. *Entre mythe et politique*. Paris: Seuil, 1996.

———. *Figures, idoles, masques*. Paris: Julliard, 1990.

———. "L'individu dans la cité." In *Sur l'individu*, 20–37. Contributions de Paul Veyne [et al.] au Colloque de Royaumont [22, 23, 24 octobre 1985]. Paris: Seuil, 1987.

———. *L'individu, la mort, l'amour: Soi-même et l'autre en Grèce ancienne*. Paris: Gallimard, 1989.

———. *Mortals and Immortals: Collected Essays*. Edited by Froma I. Zeitlin. Princeton: Princeton University Press, 1991.

———. *La mort dans les yeux. Figures de l'Autre en Grèce ancienne*. Paris: Hachette, 1985.

———. *Mythe et société en Grèce ancienne*. Paris: Maspero, 1974.

———. *Passé et présent: Contributions à une psychologie historique*. Edited by Riccardo di Donato. 2 vols. Storia e Letteratura: Raccolta di Studi e Testi 188–189. Rome: Storia e Letteratura, 1995.

———. "Preface to 'The Greek Man'." Translated by Pamela Lipson. In Suvin and Karatani, eds., 33–46.

———, ed. *The Greeks*. Translated by Charles Lambert and Teresa Lavender Fagan. Chicago: University of Chicago Press, 1995.

———, and Marcel Detienne. *Les ruses de l'intelligence: La mètis des Grecs*. Paris: Flammarion, 1974.

Veyne, Paul. "L'empire romain." In Veyne, ed., 19–223.
———. "Introduction." In Veyne, ed., 13–15.
———, ed. De l'empire romain à l'an mil. Volume 1 of Histoire de la vie privée. General editors Philippe Ariès and Georges Duby. Paris: Seuil, 1985.
———. See also: Vernant, "L'individu."
Vickers, Nancy J. "The Body Re-membered: Petrarchan Lyric and the Strategies of Description." In Mimesis: From Mirror to Method, Augustine to Descartes, 100–109. Edited by John D. Lyons and Stephen G. Nichols. Hanover, NH: University Press of New England, 1982.
———. "Diana Described: Scattered Women and Scattered Rhyme." In Writing and Sexual Difference, 95–109. Edited by Elizabeth Abel. Chicago: University of Chicago Press, 1982.
Vinogradoff, Paul. Roman Law in Medieval Europe. 3rd ed. Preface by F. de Zulueta. 1929. Reprint, Hildesheim: Olms, 1961.
Vlastos, Gregory. "Slavery in Plato's Thought." In Finley, ed., 133–49.
Voelke, André-Jean. L'idée de la volonté dans le stoïcisme. Paris: Presses Universitaires de France, 1973.
Vogt, Joseph. Ancient Slavery and the Ideal of Man. Translated by Thomas Wiedemann. Cambridge, MA: Harvard University Press, 1975.
Vološinov, Valentin Nikolaevich. Freudianism: A Marxist Critique. Translated by I. R. Titunik. Edited by I. R. Titunik, with Neal R. Bruss. New York: Academic Press, 1976.
———. Marxism and the Philosophy of Language [1929]. Translated by Ladislav Matejka and I. R. Titunik. New York: Seminar Press, 1973.
Waithe, Mary Ellen, ed. A History of Women Philosophers. 4 vols. Dordrecht: Nijhoff (for vol 1), Kluwer, 1987–1995.
Walker, Daniel Pickering. "Medical Spirits and God and the Soul." In Fattori and Bianchi, eds., 223–44.
Wallace, David. Chaucerian Polity: Absolutist Lineages and Associational Forms in England and Italy. Stanford: Stanford University Press, 1997.
Waller, Marguerite. Petrarch's Poetics and Literary History. Amherst, MA: University of Massachusetts Press, 1980.
Ward, John O., and Neville Chiavaroli. "The Young Heloise and Latin Rhetoric: Some Preliminary Comments on the 'Lost' Love Letters and Their Significance." In Wheeler, ed., 53–119.
Watson, Gerard. "Discovering the Imagination: Platonists and Stoics on phantasia." In Dillon and Long, eds., 208–33.
———. "The Natural Law and Stoicism." In Long, ed., 216–38.
Wear, Andrew, Roger K. French and Iain Lonie, eds. The Medical Renaissance of the Sixteenth Century. Cambridge: Cambridge University Press, 1985.
Weber, Walter. Symbolik in der abendländischen und byzantinischen Kunst: Von Sinn und Gestalt der Aureole. 2 vols. Basel: Zbinden, 1981.
Wedgwood, Cecily Veronica. Poetry and Politics under the Stuarts. 1960. Reprint, Ann Arbor: University of Michigan Press, 1964.
———. The Trial of Charles I. London: Collins, 1964.

Welter, Jean-Thiébaut. *L'exemplum dans la littérature religieuse et didactique du moyen âge.* 1927. Reprint, Geneva: Slatkine Reprints, 1973.

Wender, Dorothea. "Plato: Misogynist, Paedophile, and Feminist." In Peradotto and Sullivan, eds., 213–28.

Westermann, William Lynn. "Athenaeus and the Slaves of Athens." In Finley, ed., 73–92.

Wharton, Thomas. *History of English Poetry from the Twelfth to the Close of the Sixteenth Century.* 4 vols. Edited by W. Carew Hazlitt. 1871. Facsimile reprint, Hildesheim: Olms, 1968.

Wheeler, Bonnie, ed. *Listening to Heloise: The Voice of a Twelfth-Century Woman.* New York: St. Martin's Press, 2000.

White, N. P. "The Basis of Stoic Ethics." *Harvard Studies in Classical Philology* 83 (1979): 143–78.

White, Stephen D. "The Politics of Anger." In Rosenwein, ed., 127–52.

Wider, Kathleen. "Women Philosophers in the Ancient Greek World." *Hypatia* 1, no. 1 (Spring 1986): 21–62.

Wiedemann, Thomas E. J. *Slavery.* Greece & Rome, New Surveys in the Classics 19. Oxford: Clarendon, 1987.

———. *See also:* Vogt; *and* Wiedemann, ed. (in Primary).

Wiles, David. "Greek Theatre and the Legitimation of Slavery." In Archer, ed., 53–67.

Wilkins, Ernest Hatch. *The Making of the "Canzoniere" and Other Petrarchan Studies.* Rome: Edizioni di Storia e Letteratura, 1951.

———. *See also:* Petrarch, *Collatio laureationis* (in Primary).

Williams, Bernard A. O. *Problems of the Self.* Cambridge: Cambridge University Press, 1973.

———. *Shame and Necessity.* 1993. Reprint, Berkeley: University of California Press, 1994.

———. "What Was Wrong with Minos? Thucydides and Historical Time." *Representations* 74 (Spring 2001): 1–18.

Williams, Michael. "Descartes and the Metaphysics of Doubt." In *Descartes,* 28–49. Edited by John Cottingham. Oxford: Oxford University Press, 1998.

Wilson, Bryan R. *Rationality.* Oxford: Blackwell, 1970.

Wilson, Marcus. "Subjugation of Grief in Seneca's *Epistles.*" In Braund and Gill, eds., 48–67.

Winkler, John J. *The Constraints of Desire: The Anthropology of Sex and Gender in Ancient Greece.* New York: Routledge, 1990.

———. *See also:* Halperin, Winkler and Zeitlin, eds.

Winn, Colette H., and Donna Kuizenga, eds. *Women Writers in Pre-Revolutionary France: Strategies of Emancipation.* New York: Garland, 1997.

Wiredu, Kwasi. *Cultural Universals and Particulars: An African Perspective.* Bloomington: Indiana University Press, 1996.

———. *Philosophy and an African Culture.* Cambridge: Cambridge University Press, 1980.

Wood, Diane Sylvia. "The Evolution of Hélisenne de Crenne's Persona." *Symposium* 45, no. 2 (Summer 1991): 140–51.

Woods-Marsden, Joanna. *Renaissance Self-Portraiture: The Visual Construction of Identity and the Social Status of the Artist.* New Haven: Yale University Press, 1998.

Worp, J. A. "Caspar van Baerle." *Oud Holland* 3 (1885): 241–65; 4 (1886): 24–40, 172–89; 5 (1887): 93–125; 6 (1888): 87–102, 241–76; 7 (1889): 89–128.

Wright, M. R. "Presocratic Minds." In Gill, ed., 207–25.

Zagarella, Maria Nivea. *Jacopo Notaro e il laicismo fridericiano.* Catania: Giuseppe Maimone, 1994.

Zea, Leopoldo. *The Role of the Americas in History [América en la historia].* Edited by Amy A. Oliver. Translated by Sonja Karsen. Savage, MD: Rowman & Littlefield, 1992.

Zeitlin, Froma I. *Playing the Other: Gender and Society in Classical Greek Civilization.* Chicago: University of Chicago Press, 1996.

———. "Playing the Other: Theater, Theatricality, and the Feminine in Greek Drama." *Representations* 11 (Summer 1985): 63–94.

———. "The Power of Aphrodite: Eros and the Boundaries of the Self in the *Hippolytus.*" In *Directions in Euripidean Criticism,* 52–111, 189–208. Edited by Peter Burian. Durham, NC: Duke University Press, 1985.

———. "Thebes: Theater of Self and Society in Athenian Drama." In *Greek Tragedy and Political Theory,* 101–41. Edited by J. Peter Euben. Berkeley: University of California Press, 1986.

———. "Travesties of Gender and Genre in Aristophanes' *Thesmophoriazousae.*" In Foley, ed., 169–217.

———. *See also*: Loraux, *Children,* Vernant, *Mortals, and* Halperin, Winkler and Zeitlin, eds.

Zink, Michel. *La subjectivité littéraire: Autour du siècle de saint Louis.* Paris: Presses Universitaires de France, 1985.

Zumthor, Paul. "Autobiography in the Middle Ages?" *Genre* 6, no. 3 (March 1973): 29–48.

———. *Essai de poétique médiévale.* Paris: Seuil, 1972.

———. *Langue, texte, énigme.* Paris: Seuil, 1975.

Index

In this index, "f" after a number indicates a separate reference on the next page; "ff" indicates separate references on the next two pages. A continuous discussion over two or more pages is indicated by a span of page numbers, e.g., "41–48." An "f" or "ff" after a span indicates subsequent separate reference or references, e.g., "74–75f(f)." *Passim* is used for a cluster of references in close but not consecutive sequence. "Personhood" and "who-ness," "community" and "society," occurring everywhere, are not separately indexed. Some defining cases of "selfe," "self" and such are: they mark different experiences of who-ness. The several ancient elements, humors and qualities have entries only for discrete treatments. Greek cities are indexed, "Rome," when it means the Roman world (compared to "Greece"), is usually not. Contemporary writers are indexed only when named other than in a bibliographical parenthesis. People named in an enumeration or in another's quotation are not usually indexed unless also named elsewhere. Dates are given for people born before 1800.